THE CULTS OF URUK AND BABYLON

CUNEIFORM MONOGRAPHS 25

Managing Editor Geerd Haayer

Edited by

T. Abusch, M.J. Geller, M.P. Maidman
S.M. Maul and F.A.M. Wiggermann

BRILL • STYX
LEIDEN • BOSTON
2004

CUNEIFORM MONOGRAPHS 25

THE CULTS OF URUK AND BABYLON

The Temple Ritual Texts as Evidence for Hellenistic Cult Practises

Marc J.H. Linssen

BRILL • STYX
LEIDEN • BOSTON
2004

This book is printed on acid-free paper.

Library of Congress Cataloging-in-Publication Data

Linssen, Marc J.H.
The cults of Uruk and Babylon : the temple ritual as evidence for Hellenistic cult practices / Marc J.H. Linssen
p. cm. — (Cuneiform Monographs; ISSN 0929-0052 ; 25)
Originally presented as the author's thesis (doctoral–Vrije Universiteit Amsterdam), 2002.
Includes bibliographical references (p.) and index.
ISBN 90-04-12402-0 (alk. paper)
1. Cults–Iraq–Babylon (Extinct city) 2. Cults–Iraq–Erech (Extinct city) 3. Babylon (Extinct city)–Religion. 4. Erech (Extinct city)–Religion. 5. Akkadian language–Texts. 6. Assyro-Babylonian religion. I. Title. II. Series.

BL1620.L56 2003
299′.21–dc22

2003055865

ISSN 0929–0052
ISBN 90 04 12402 0

PRINTED IN THE NETHERLANDS

parentibus
uxori
liberisque

PREFACE

The text of this book was submitted as a dissertation, written under the supervision of Prof. dr. M. Stol and Prof. dr. R.J. van der Spek, in November 2002 to the Faculty of Arts of the Vrije Universiteit Amsterdam.

I would like to thank Marten Stol and Bert van der Spek for showing a genuine interest in my dissertation. Their comments and corrections on the different versions of the text saved me from numerous errors. I am grateful for their continuous support and patience, including during the years after I had left the university.

The Trustees of the British Museum are thanked for permitting me to collate and publish texts from the collection. During my visits to the British Museum W.G. Lambert kindly offered me much needed advise with the reading of some of the unpublished tablets.

I am also indebted to several scholars at the University of Leiden. Th.J.H. Krispijn helped me with many of the lamentation incipits. A.C.V.M. Bongenaar made some valuable comments on the manuscript. Special tribute is due to G. van Driel for his help and advice.

A.R. George kindly allowed me to use his article on temple ritual texts from Babylon before it was published. St. M. Maul suggested to me how useful A. Poebel's *Grundzüge der sumerischen Grammatik* still is, when struggling with the difficult Sumerian passages in Hellenistic texts.

I also wish to express my gratitude to D. Brown for correcting the English text.

Research for this study, carried out at the Vrije Universiteit Amsterdam, was financed by the Netherlands Organization for Scientific Research (N.W.O.) from February 1992 until February 1997.

A special word of thanks I owe to the editor, G. Haayer, for accepting this study for publication.

Edam, December 2002 M.J.H. Linssen

CONTENTS

SELECTIVE BIBLIOGRAPHY AND ABBREVIATIONS

The abbreviations used follow The Assyrian Dictionary of the Oriental Institute of the University of Chicago (*CAD*), and the Akkadisches Handwörterbuch (*AHw*).

A.E. — Arsacid Era

AUWE — *Ausgrabungen Uruk-Warka Endberichte.*

P.- A. Beaulieu — Antiquarian Theology in Seleucid Uruk, *ASJ* 14 (1992), 47–75.

P. - R. Berger — Das Neujahrsfest nach den Königsinschriften des ausgehenden Babylonischen Reiches, *CRRA* 17 (1970), 155–159.

J. A. Black — The New Year Ceremonies in Ancient Babylon: ⟩Taking Bel by the Hand⟨ and a Cultic Picnic, *Religion* 11 (1981), 39–59.

J.A. Black, *Eme-sal Cult Songs and Prayers* — *Eme-sal Cult Songs and Prayers*, *AuOr* 9 (1991), 23–36 (Fs. M. Civil).

F. Blome, *Opfermaterie* — *Die Opfermaterie in Babylonien und Israel.* Teil I, Romae, 1934.

A.C.V.M. Bongenaar — *The Neo-Babylonian Ebabbar Temple at Sippar. Its administration and its prosopography*, Leiden, 1997.

D. Brown, M.J.H. Linssen — BM 134701=1965–10–14,1 and the Hellenistic period eclipse ritual from Uruk, *RA* 91 (1997), 147–166.

G. Çağirgan, *Festivals* — *The Babylonian Festivals*, Birmingham, 1976 (unpublished diss.).

M.E. Cohen — *Balag* -compositions: Sumerian lamentation liturgies of the second and first millennium b.c., *SANE* 1/2, Malibu, 1974.

M.E. Cohen, *Eršemma* — *Sumerian Hymnology: The Eršemma*, Cincinnati, 1981 (Hebrew Union College Annual Supplements No. 2).

M.E. Cohen, *Lamentations* — *The Canonical Lamentations of Ancient Mesopotamia*, 2 volumes, Potomac, Maryland, 1988.

M.E. Cohen, *Cultic Calendars* — *The Cultic Calendars of the Ancient Near East*, Bethesda, 1993.

L.T. Doty, *CAHU* — *Cuneiform Archives from Hellenistic Uruk*, diss. Yale, 1977 (University Micro Films International, Michigan).

S.B. Downey — *Mesopotamian Religious Architecture. Alexander through the Parthians*, Princeton, 1988.

G. van Driel — *The cult of Aššur*, Assen, 1969.

A. Falkenstein — *Topographie von Uruk, I.Teil: Uruk zur Seleukidenzeit.* Ausgrabungen der Deutschen Forschungsgemeinschaft in Uruk-Warka, Band 3, Leipzig, 1941.

W. Farber, *TUAT II/2* — Rituale und Beschwörungen in akkadischer Sprache, in: *TUAT II/2*, Gütersloh, 1987, 212 ff.

U. Finkbeiner	*Uruk-Warka. Fundstellen der Keramik der Seleukiden- und Partherzeit*, in: U. Finkbeiner (ed.), *Materialien zur Archäologie der Seleukiden- und Partherzeit im südlichen Babylonien und im Golfgebiet. Ergebnisse der Symposien 1987 und 1989 in Blaubeuren*, Tübingen, 1993, 3–16.
B. Funck	*Uruk zur Seleukidenzeit*, Berlin, 1984.
G. Furlani, *Sacrificio*	*Il sacrificio nella religione dei Semiti di Babilonia e Assiria*, Roma, 1932.
G. Furlani, *Riti*	*Riti babilonesi e assiri*, Udine, 1940.
A.R. George, *BTT*	*Babylonian Topographical Texts*, Leuven, 1992.
A.R. George, *House Most High*	*House Most High. The Temples of Ancient Mesopotamia*, Winona Lake, Indiana, 1993.
A.R. George	Studies in Cultic Topography and Ideology. Review article on: B. Pongratz-Leisten, *ina šulmi īrub*, *BiOr* 53 (1996), 363–395.
A.R. George, *Studies W.G. Lambert*	*Four Temple Rituals from Babylon*, in: A.R. George, I.L. Finkel (eds.), *Wisdom, Gods and Literature. Studies in Assyriology in Honour of W.G. Lambert*, Winona Lake, Indiana, 2000, 259–299.
J.D. Grainger	*A Seleucid Prosopography and Gazetteer*, Leiden, New York, Köln, 1997.
A.K. Grayson	*Assyrian and Babylonian Chronicles* (TCL 5), New York, 1975
R.A. Henshaw	*Female and Male. The Cultic Personnel. The Bible and the Rest of the Ancient Near East*, Pennsylvania, 1994.
K. Kessler, *Festschrift J. Oelsner*	Hellenistische Tempelverwaltungstexte. Eine Nachlese zu *CT 49*, in: J. Marzahn, H. Neumann (eds.), *Festschrift J. Oelsner*, AOAT, Bd. 252, Münster, 2000, 213–241.
J. Krecher, *Kultlyrik*	*Sumerische Kultlyrik*, Wiesbaden, 1966.
A. Kuhrt	Berossus' *Babyloniaka* and Seleucid Rule in Babylonia, in: A. Kuhrt, S. Sherwin-White (eds.), *Hellenism in the East*, Berkeley and Los Angeles, 1987, 32–56.
A. Kuhrt and S. Sherwin-White	Xerxes' destruction of Babylonian temples, in: H.W.A.M. Sancisi-Weerdenburg, A. Kuhrt (eds.), *Achaemenid History II: the Greek sources*, Leiden, 1987, 69–78.
A. Kuhrt and S. Sherwin-White	The transition from Achaemenid to Seleucid Rule in Babylonia: Revolution or Evolution?, in: H.W.A.M. Sancisi-Weerdenburg, A. Kuhrt (eds.), *Achaemenid History VIII: Continuity and Change*, Leiden, 1994, 311–327.
W.G. Lambert	Donations of food and drink to the gods in ancient Mesopotamia, in: J. Quaegebeur (ed.), *OLA* 55 (1993), 191–201.
W.G. Lambert	Processions to the Akītu house. Review article on: B. Pongratz-Leisten, *ina šulmi īrub*, *RA* 91 (1997), 49–80.

B. Landsberger, *Kult. Kalender* — *Der kultische Kalender der Babylonier und Assyrer*, Leipzig, 1915.

A. Livingstone, *Mystical* — *Mystical and mythological explanatory works of Assyrian and Babylonian scholars*, Oxford, 1986.

E. Matsushima — Quelques textes relatifs à l'*elippu ša kusīti* (bateau du vêtement), in: H.I.H. Prince Takahito Mikasa (ed.), *Cult and Ritual in the Ancient Near East. Bulletin of the Middle Eastern Culture Center in Japan*, vol.VI, Wiesbaden, 1992, 7–21.

E. Matsushima — Divine Statues in Ancient Mesopotamia: their fashioning and Clothing and their Interaction with the Society, in: E. Matsushima (ed.), *Official cult and popular religion in the ancient near east.* Papers of the First Colloquium on the Ancient Near East - The City and its Life, held at the Middle Eastern Culture Center in Japan (Mitaka, Tokyo), March 20–22, 1992. Heidelberg, 1993.

St. M. Maul, *Herzberuhigungsklagen* — *'Herzberuhigungsklagen'. Die sumerisch-akkadischen Eršaḫunga-Gebete*, Wiesbaden, 1988.

St. M. Maul — *Zukunftsbewältigung*, Mainz am Rhein, 1994.

St. M. Maul — Gottesdienst im Sonnenheiligtum zu Sippar, in: *Munuscula Mesopotamica. Festschrift für Johannes Renger*, Münster, 1999.

St. M. Maul — Die Frühjahrsfeierlichkeiten in Aššur, in A.R. George, I.L. Finkel (eds.), *Wisdom, Gods and Literature. Studies in Assyriology in Honour of W.G. Lambert*, Winona Lake, Indiana, 2000.

G.J.P. McEwan, *FAOS* 4 — Priest and Temple in Hellenistic Babylonia, *FAOS* 4, Wiesbaden, 1981.

G.J.P. McEwan — Arsacid Temple Records, *Iraq* 43 (1981), 131–143.

J. Oelsner — Gesellschaft und Wirtschaft des seleukidischen Babylonien, *Klio* 63 (1981), 39–44.

J. Oelsner, *Materialien* — *Materialien zur babylonischen Gesellschaft und Kultur in hellenistischer Zeit* (revised version of: J. Oelsner, *Studien zur babylonischen Kultur und Gesellschaft in hellenistischer Zeit*, diss. Jena, 1970), Budapest, 1986.

J. Oelsner — Aus dem Leben babylonischer 'Priester' in der 2. Hälfte des 1. Jahrtausends v. Chr. (am Beispiel der Funde aus Uruk), in: J. Zablocka, St. Zawadzki (eds.), *Šulmu* IV. Papers Presented at the International Conference Poznan, 19–22 September, 1989, 235–42.

S.A. Pallis — *The Babylonian Akîtu Festival*, København, 1926.

B. Pongratz-Leisten, *ina šulmi īrub* — *ina šulmi īrub. Die kulttopographische und ideologische Programmatik der akītu -Prozession in Babylonien und Assyrien im I. Jahrtausend v. Chr.*, Mainz am Rhein, 1994 (Baghdader Forschungen Band 16).

J. Quaegebeur, (ed.)	Ritual and Sacrifice in the Ancient Near East. Proceedings of the International Conference by the Katholieke Universiteit Leuven from the 17th to the 20th of April 1991. *OLA* 55, Leuven, 1993.
M. Rutten	*Contrats de l'époque Séleucide conservés au musée du Louvre*, Paris, 1935 (Babyloniaca 15).
A.J. Sachs - H. Hunger, *Diaries*	*Astronomical Diaries and Related Texts from Babylonia. Volume I. Diaries from 652 B.C. to 262 B.C.*, Wien, 1988. *Volume II. Diaries from 261 B.C. to 165 B.C.*, Wien 1989. *Volume III, Diaries from 164 B.C. to 61 B.C.*, Wien, 1996. *Volume V, Lunar and Planetary Texts*, Wien 2001.
O. Schroeder	Das Pantheon der Stadt Uruk in der Seleukidenzeit auf Grund von Götterlisten und theophoren Personennamen in Kontrakten dieser Zeit. *SPAW* XLI (1916), 1180–1196.
S.E.	Seleucid Era
S. Sherwin-White	Seleucid Babylonia: a case-study for the installation and development of Greek rule, in: A. Kuhrt, S. Sherwin-White (ed.), *Hellenism in the East*, Berkeley and Los Angeles, 1987, 1–31.
S. Sherwin-White, A. Kuhrt	*From Samarkhand to Sardis. A new approach to the Seleucid empire*, London, 1993.
R.J. van der Spek	The Babylonian Temple during the Macedonian and Parthian Domination, *BiOr* 52 (1985), 541–562.
R.J. van der Spek	*Grondbezit in het Seleucidische rijk*, Amsterdam, 1986.
R.J. van der Spek	The Babylonian city, in: A. Kuhrt, S. Sherwin-White (ed.), *Hellenism in the East*, Berkeley and Los Angeles, 1987, 57–74.
R.J. van der Spek	Nippur, Sippar and Larsa in the Hellenistic period, in: Maria de Jong-Ellis (ed.), *Nippur at the Centennial. Papers read at the 35e Rencontre Assyriologique Internationale, Philadelphia 1988*, Philadelphia, 1992, 235–260.
R.J. van der Spek	New Evidence on Seleucid Land Policy, in: H. Sancisi-Weerdenburg e.a. (eds.), *De Agricultura. In Memoriam P.W. de Neeve (1945–1990)*, Amsterdam, 1993, 61–77.
R.J. van der Spek	The Astronomical Diaries as a Source for Achaemenid and Seleucid History, *BiOr* 50 (1993), 91–101.
R.J. van der Spek	" *… en hun machthebbers worden weldoeners genoemd." Religieuze en economische politiek in het Seleucidische Rijk*, Amsterdam, 1994.
R.J. van der Spek	Review article on: S. Sherwin-White, A. Kuhrt, *From Samarkhand to Sardis, BSOAS 57* (1994), 367–8.
R.J. van der Spek	Landownership in Babylonian Cuneiform Documents, in: M.J. Geller, A.D.E. Lewis, H. Maehler (eds.), *Legal Documents of the Hellenistic Period*, London, 1995, 173–245.

R.J. van der Spek	Cuneiform documents on Parthian history: the Raḫimesu archive, in: J. Wiesehöfer (ed.), *Das Partherreich und seine Zeugnisse. Beiträge des internationalen Colloquiums, Eutin (27.–30. Juni 1996)*, Stuttgart, 1998, 205–258.
R.J. van der Spek	New Evidence from the Babylonian Astronomical Diaries Concerning Seleucid and Arsacid History, *AfO* 44/45 (1997/98), 167–175.
SpTU	*Spätbabylonische Texte aus Uruk.*
K. van der Toorn	The Babylonian New Year Festival: New Insights from the Cuneiform Texts and their Bearing on Old Testament Study, *Suppl. VT* 43 (1991), 331–44.
TU	F. Thureau-Dangin, *Tablettes D'Uruk à l'usage des prêtres du Temple d'Anu au temps des Séleucides*, Paris, 1922 (Musée du Louvre. Textes cunéiformes Tome VI).
R. Wallenfels, *Seleucid Archival Texts*	R. Wallenfels, *Seleucid Archival Texts in the Harvard Semitic Museum. Text editions and Catalogue raisonné of the seal impressions*. Cuneiform Monographs 12, Groningen, 1998.

MONTHS

I	^{iti}BÁRA	nisannu	March/April
II	^{iti}GU$_4$	ajjaru	April/May
III	^{iti}SIG$_4$	simānu	May/June
IV	^{iti}ŠU	duʾūzu	June/July
V	^{iti}NE	abu	July/August
VI	^{iti}KIN	ulūlu	August/September
VII	^{iti}DU$_6$	tašrītu	September/Oktober
VIII	^{iti}APIN	araḫsamna	October/November
IX	^{iti}GAN	kislīmu	November/December
X	^{iti}AB	ṭebētu	December/January
XI	^{iti}ZÍZ	šabaṭu	January/Februari
XII	^{iti}ŠE	addaru	February/March

I. INTRODUCTION

I.1. Hellenistic Babylonia

The continuation of Babylonian culture in the Hellenistic period[1] is well established today. Work done by scholars like L.T. Doty, G.J.P. McEwan, A. Kuhrt, S. Sherwin-White, J. Oelsner and R.J. van der Spek[2] has shown that not only Uruk and Babylon, but also other Babylonian cities (Nippur, Larsa, Ur, Borsippa, Cutha and Kiš/Ḫursagkalamma)[3] flourished after the coming of the Greeks. Both archaeology and textual sources indicate that in these cities the Babylonian inhabitants stuck to their ancient traditions, which included the use of cuneiform. Whether Akkadian was still used as a *living language* in the Hellenistic period is uncertain,[4] but on the basis of the so-called Graeco-Babyloniaca tablets and Classical sources it has been argued that cuneiform could well have been read up to the third century A.D.[5]

The cuneiform sources also contain a wealth of information on the Babylonian cults and the temples in the Hellenistic period. It is the purpose of this study to examine these cults more closely and present an inventory of all attested cultic activities. The key question will be: can we use the temple ritual texts as evidence for Hellenistic cult practices? To answer this question we cannot restrict our research to the temple ritual texts alone; because these texts are literary compositions copied from older originals, we cannot be sure that what they depict about the public cult was actually taking place in the temples during the Hellenistic period. For this reason we will not only analyse the ritual texts in detail, but also compare the evidence with information gleaned from texts which are (unlike the temple ritual texts) unquestionably Hellenistic compositions, such as building inscriptions, legal documents (including prebend texts), chronicles and the so-called astronomical diaries. Which rituals, ceremonies and offerings are attested in these texts? Which deities and temples are mentioned, and does the pantheon attested in these texts correspond with the names of gods mentioned in the temple ritual texts? This comparison will hopefully tell us whether the cults of Bēl, Anu, Ištar and the other

---

[1] Because one of the most important characteristics of the Babylonian culture, the cuneiform script, survives not only during the Seleucid period, but also well into the Arsacid period, we will use in this book the more general term 'Hellenistic', which begins with the conquest of Babylonia by Alexander in 331 B.C. and continues up to the end of the Arsacid period (224/226 A.D.). Cf. J. Oelsner, *Materialien*, 51–57. On occasion we will also refer to texts as being 'Late Babylonian', which in this study means: written after Babylonia lost its independence (539 B.C.), i.e. during the Achaemenid or Hellenistic periods.

[2] See the Selective Bibliography.

[3] Perhaps also Marad, Der, Tell al-ʿAqar, Udannu, Telloh and Sippar, see R.J. van der Spek, in: Maria de Jong-Ellis (ed.), *Nippur at the Centennial*, 235 ff.; id., *Religieuze en economische politiek in het Seleucidische Rijk*, 11 ff.

[4] According to M.P. Streck (*Zahl und Zeit,* Groningen, 1995, xxiv), the possibility that (together with Aramaic) the Akkadian language was still spoken in small city regions in the Hellenistic period cannot be excluded.

[5] M.J. Geller, *ZA* 87 (1997), 43–95.

deities were alive and flourishing in the Hellenistic period, or whether, perhaps under the influence of the new Macedonian rulership, a process of change and decay had set in.

Because the textual evidence relating to the cults in the Hellenistic period concerns for the most part the main sanctuaries of Uruk (Rēš and Ešgal) and Babylon (Esagila), in this study we will confine ourselves to the cults of these two cities, although it should be noted that this undoubtedly results in a slightly distorted picture of Hellenistic Babylonia as a whole.

In I.2 the text material relevant for this study is discussed. In I.3 we will make some general observations about the cult, the priests and temple personnel and the cult-terminology. In chapter II all the ceremonies, rituals and festivals attested in the Hellenistic corpus will be described. In chapter III we will analyse the offerings, libations, fumigations, and purifications which were performed during the divine meal.

Much has been written on religion and cults in Mesopotamia, but only a few studies concentrated on the Hellenistic period. Exceptions are Furlani's studies on offerings and ceremonies,[6] and Blome's analysis of the offering materials,[7] which to a large extent are based on texts from the Hellenistic period. Since the publication of these books in the 1930's, much new evidence has been discovered and published. This was used in a limited way much later by McEwan in his dissertation on the temple organization and the temple personnel of Hellenistic Babylonia, with one short chapter on the cult.[8] As the author indicated himself, however this was only a 'limited outline of the main aspects of the cult during this period'.[9]

Other scholars took an interest in the cults of Hellenistic Babylonia. A short description of the gods and cult of Uruk was written by Rutten.[10] Furthermore Schroeder published an article on the pantheon of Uruk.[11] Falkenstein wrote an important study on the topography of Uruk, which concentrates to a large extent on the cultic buildings, and contains much important information on the cult;[12] this work has now partly been updated by George[13] and Pongratz-Leisten.[14] Beaulieu's article on the origin of the Anu-pantheon in Late Babylonian Uruk is important.[15] Finally, Konstanze Szelenyi-Graziotto published an article on the cult in Babylon in the Seleucid period.[16] Nevertheless, an extensive analysis of the Hellenistic cults of Babylonia, based on the latest evidence, is still missing. A new discussion is necessary.

---

6 *Sacrificio; Riti.*
7 *Opfermaterie.*
8 *FAOS* 4, 159–182.
9 159.
10 *Contrats de l'époque séleucide conservés au Musée du Louvre*, 36–63.
11 *SPAW* 41 (1916), 1180–1196.
12 *Topographie.*
13 *BTT.*
14 *ina šulmi īrub*. But see also the review articles of A.R. George, *BiOr* 53 (1996), 363–395 and W.G. Lambert, *RA* 91 (1997), 49–80.
15 *ASJ* 14 (1992), 47–75.
16 In: B. Funck, *Hellenismus. Beitraege zur Erforschung von Akkulturation und politischer Ordnung in den Staaten des hellenistischen Zeitalters. Akten des Internationalen Hellenismus-Kolloquiums 9.-14. Maerz 1994 in Berlin*, Tuebingen 1996, 171–194.

I.2. The texts[17]

The temple ritual texts are especially relevant for studying the Babylonian cults, since they give us the most detailed information on public cult activities in the sanctuaries of the cities.[18] These texts contain prescriptive rituals, recording what happened in the temple before the events in question, as a manual of ritual procedure.[19] Fortunately for the Hellenistic period a large corpus of these often very elaborate ritual texts is available.[20] They deal with instructions for all sorts of cultic proceedings, such as offerings and libations for the gods, and also prescribe prayers and cult songs which have to be recited; sometimes these recitations are not only referred to by their incipits, but are cited in full. The rituals deal with various subjects of the public cult, such as the New Year festival, the night vigil, the preparation of the kettledrum, building rituals for temples, and the evil consequences of an eclipse of the moon. This group of temple ritual texts will serve as the main source material for this study. Other relevant text groups, already collected by J. Oelsner,[21] are the explanatory and commentary texts,[22] cult songs,[23] calendar texts,[24] but also building inscriptions, chronicles, administrative documents,[25]

---

[17] For the bibliographic information on the texts mentioned here see the Text Index.

[18] For Akkadian ritual texts in general, see J.J.A. van Dijk, in: *Studien Falkenstein*, 233 ff.; R. Borger, *HKL* 3, 83–84, § 85; W. Farber, *TUAT* II/2, 212 ff.

[19] Rather than descriptive rituals, which are written after the events, and describe cultic events in the temple mainly for the purpose of recording cultic expenditures, cf. B.A. Levine, W.W. Hallo, *HUCA* 38 (1967), 17–20.

[20] Some of which have been published only recently, while for others older editions are available, in particular Thureau-Dangin's excellent study of temple ritual texts in *RAcc*. In the Appendix, some of these texts will be discussed anew. Also a few new fragments will be published in this book, for which see the Plates I–IV. When passages from these texts are quoted in this study, we confine ourselves to translations, and refer back to the Appendix for the transliterations and discussions.

[21] *Materialien*, 137 ff.

[22] Not listed as a separate group by Oelsner, but see p. 188 where some commentary texts from Uruk are mentioned. For explanatory texts and cultic commentaries in general see A. Livingstone, *Mystical*, 2 (for the distinction between the two) and especially 115 ff., chapters 4–6. Cf. also W. von Soden, *ZA* 51 (1955), 157, and R. Borger, *HKL* 3, 65–66, § 67.

Uruk: the explanatory text *TU* 47, containing important information on the mythical background of the kettledrum ritual (*lilissu*); commentaries are *SpTU* 1, nos. 140–143; see also no. 136. Babylon: BM 54312 (unpublished). In this explanatory text days 5 to 11 of the first month Nisannu are discussed, and therefore it possibly refers to the New Year festival. Unfortunately the tablet is badly damaged and the interpretation is difficult. The small script indicates that the text is Late Babylonian, possibly Hellenistic. Because of the invocational formula [*ina* INIM ^{d}EN] *u* ^{d}GAŠAN-*iá liš-lim* (U.E.), only attested in Late Babylonian colophons (see the literature mentioned in my comments on *TU* 39 U.E., in the Appendix), the text may be from Babylon. We will return to this text in a separate study. Another explanatory text, perhaps from Borsippa but found in Babylon, is BM 34035 (Sp I 131). The text partly explains rituals in terms of myths, by making use of symbolism. A large explanatory text, IM 44150 (+ //), was published by George (*BTT*, no. 18, 145 ff.). Of the five manuscripts, two or possibly three are Late Babylonian, and, because of the very small script, perhaps Hellenistic (cf. *TIM* 9, p. xii.). Col. III, 12'ff. deals with festivals, one of which is the *akītu*-festival.

[23] I.e. hymns and lamentations. In addition to Oelsner, we can add: hymns, Uruk: *SpTU* 2 no. 27 (to Ištar), and *BiMes* 24, 51 (to Adad). See also the hymn on Šamaš in the ritual text W 18828.

Lamentations (*taqribtu* and *eršemakku*), Uruk: *SpTU* 3, nos. 61–63; *SpTU* 4, no. 125, contains part of the lamentation IMMAL GUDEDE.

[24] In addition to Oelsner, we can add: Uruk: *SpTU* 3, no. 104, written by the well-known scribe Iqīša, is a calendar text for the 4th month Du'ūzu; it lists body parts of animals for every day, probably to be used in ritual activities. For the latest on Iqīša see J. Oelsner, in: J. Zablocka, St. Zawadzki (eds.), *Šulmu IV*, 236–7, with literature.

[25] In addition to Oelsner, we can add: apart from isolated publications, especially important is *BiMes* 24. A new group of texts was published by R. Wallenfells, *Seleucid archival texts in the Harvard Semitic Museum*. Not yet published by L.T. Doty is *YOS* 20.

and astronomical diaries.[26] Classical authors like Diodurus Siculus, Strabo, Josephus or Berossus (to name just a few) are important for reconstructing the political history, but are less informative so far as the Babylonian cult practices are concerned.

When studying the cults we are faced with several problems. While some of the ceremonies and rituals are well attested, about others we know only very little, and undoubtedly many more must have existed about which we know nothing at all. Because the Neo-Assyrian period has left us with many ritual texts, on occasion we will refer to some of these texts for parallels, because we may safely assume a common background for both Assyrian and Babylonian cult practices. However, a comparison between the two is not without difficulties, and it is clear that we are far from explaining the gaps in our knowledge of one period by looking at the other. Nevertheless, although many texts contain rituals for a special occasion, it must be expected that many of the offerings, libations, fumigations, purifications and recitations referred to in these texts reflect the common practice of the ordinary temple cult.[27] As far as the Neo-Babylonian period is concerned, we must keep in mind that relevant Neo-Babylonian references to the cults are often not from ritual texts, but from administrative and private documents.

Another problem is that many of the texts do not give us the information that we need: the texts often only record the ceremony, without explaining how and when it was performed, and what its function was. This makes it often very difficult to distinguish cyclical ceremonies from occasional ceremonies. It also leaves us insufficient data to compare and combine Assyrian and Babylonian cultic calendars.

In this section we will first list the temple ritual texts from Uruk and Babylon. Then the date of the texts is discussed.

Uruk

We can distinguish three groups of literary texts, distinct according to provenance, and dated to the Hellenistic period[28]:

1) the *Bagh. Mitt. Beih.* 2-texts. Most of these texts were found in the Rēš-temple area Le XVI 3.[29]
2) Hellenistic texts in *TU*. They were illicitly excavated and have become available via the antiquities market, but were probably found either at the same location in the

[26] Up to now four volumes of the astronomical diaries have appeared, cf. A.J. Sachs–H. Hunger, *Diaries*.

[27] Cf. G. van Driel, *Cult of Aššur*, 151–4. The most relevant texts for the Neo-Assyrian cult are briefly discussed in ib., 51 ff. Important for the monthly ceremonies is also the hemerological series *inbu bēl arḫim* 'Fruit (=epithet of the moon god Sîn), Lord of the month'; unfortunately only the description by B. Landsberger, *Kult. Kalender*, 100–45 is available, since most of the texts are not published. See also the comments on this series by G. van Driel, *Cult of Aššur*, 154–59, R. Labat, in *RLA* 4 (1972–1975), 319 f., and A. Livingstone, in E. Matsushima (ed.), *Official cult and popular religion in the ancient near east*, Heidelberg, 1993, 97–113.

[28] The material was brought together by J. Oelsner, *Materialien*, 139 ff.; see also id., in: J. Zablocka, St. Zawadzki (eds.), *Šulmu* IV, 235 ff., without taking into account the new texts published in *SpTU* 4.

[29] But not all tablets were found here, see J. Oelsner, *Materialien*, 143–44.

Rēš-temple area as the *Bagh. Mitt. Beih.* 2-texts,[30] or they came from other locations within the Rēš-temple.[31]

3) Hellenistic texts in the *SpTU* 1–5-collection. They were almost all excavated from the living quarters Ue XVIII 1, and are part of private archives.

Other illicitly excavated tablets may also have come from one of these places, as is indicated by the fact that Uruk scribes, attested for example in the colophons of *BRM* 4-texts, also turn up in the *TU*- and *SpTU*-texts (see below).

These texts can be attributed to four Uruk families, named after their ancestors Ekur-zakir, Sîn-lēqe-unnīni, Ḫunzû and Aḫûtu. These families were all connected with the temple and every family specialized in one profession, e.g. the Ekur-zakir members made their living as exorcists (*āšipu*); well-known are the exorcists Anu-ikṣur, Iqīša and Nidintu-Anu. The Sîn-lēqe-unnīni family specialized as lamentation priests (*kalû*); well-known is especially Anu-bēlšunu, son of Nidintu-Anu.[32] Rarely, also members of other families are attested as *kalû* or *āšipu*, e.g. the exorcist Anu-bēlšunu of the Ḫunzû-family.

The archives which can be reconstructed on the basis of prosopographical evidence contain a wide variety of text genres, but also show the scribe's particular professional interest: the exorcist is mainly concerned with incantations and incantation rituals, medical texts, omina and lexical lists, while the lamentation priest concentrates especially on cult song and ritual texts. The libraries of these scribes also contain other literary texts, referred to by Oelsner as 'Bildungsgut',[33] i.e. texts which were copied for educational purposes, e.g. omina, historical texts, but also, for example, parts from *Enūma eliš*. We may safely assume that the archives contain not only what the scribe needed for his profession, but also everything he had collected from the start of his career on. This also included legal documents, which are not only known from the *SpTU*-corpus, but also among the *Bagh. Mitt. Beih.* 2-texts found in Le XVI 3. This may indicate that not only the texts which are found in the living quarters Ue XVIII 1 were part of private archives, but also those which were stored in the Rēs-temple.[34]

There appears, then, to be no real difference between the archives kept in the temple and at home. The scribes appear to have stored their tablets both in the Rēš-temple libraries (*TU*, *Bagh. Mitt. Beih.* 2) and in the libraries in their private houses (*SpTU*). E.g. texts which belong to the archives of the exorcist Iqīša, son of Ištar-šuma-ēreš, descendant of Ekur-zakir, or to those of the exorcist Nidintu-Anu, son of Anu-bēlšunu, descendant of Ekur-zakir, have turned up from both the Rēš-temple area and the living quarters Ue XVIII.[35] This strongly suggests that the Hellenistic temple ritual texts were

---

[30] J. van Dijk, *UVB* 18 (1962), 43, id., *AfO* 20 (1963), 217.

[31] G.J.P. McEwan, *BiOr* 38 (1981), 639, n. 3, and J. Oelsner, *Materialien*, 144, n. 598.

[32] On the Sîn-lēqe-unnīni family see P.-A. Beaulieu, in *Festschrift J. Oelsner*, AOAT, Bd. 252, Münster, 2000, 1–16. For Anu-bēlšunu see L. E. Pearce–L. T. Doty, in ib., 331–341.

[33] *Šulmu* IV, 238.

[34] Perhaps kept in the *bīt qāti*, a storage room within the temple area owned by members of the priesthood, as suggested by G.J.P. McEwan, *BiOr* 38 (1981), 639. The archives which consist of legal documents have been examined by L.T. Doty, *CAHU*, 150 ff. Among the legal documents are many sales of prebend shares, indicating the connection between these archives and the temple. For some of these prebend texts see II.3.1. and II.4.1.

[35] *Šulmu* IV, 236–7.

not copied for personal interest alone, but also served a purpose in the temple cult (we will further illustrate this below). With this in mind we must now turn our attention to the temple ritual texts.

For the Hellenistic period we are fortunate to have some large fragments of a series of temple rituals from Uruk, which inform us about the public cult practices in the temples. The original series must have covered the whole year.[36] These temple ritual texts contain information about what went on from day to day, or describe rituals and festivals which were celebrated on special days of the year. Most of the temple ritual texts of the Hellenistic period deal with the cult of Anu in the Rēš-temple, and only one text is related to the cult of Ištar in the Ešgal-temple. Texts which belong to these series all have in common the fact that the priests who perform the ritual are addressed in the third person only, unlike rituals which are performed for a special occassion, where the leading priest is addressed in the second person (the 'you'-figure).

Very important for our understanding of daily practice in the temple is *TU* 38, a text with ritual instructions for daily offerings in the temples of Anu, Ištar, Nanāja and the other gods in Uruk.

Furthermore we have several texts which concern the New Year festival (*akītu*). *TU* 39–40 describes the New Year festival of the seventh month Tašrītu in Uruk. *BRM* 4, 7 describes a programme for the procession of the statue of Anu during the New Year festival, from his cella to the center of the Rēš-temple, and then going outside to the *akītu*-temple. It lists incantations and prayers to be recited during the procession.

We also have texts dealing with the New Year festivals of the first month Nisannu. *KAR* 132 describes the ritual for the procession of Anu to the *akītu*-temple, concentrating on the movements of the gods and the objects which accompany them during the procession. *Bagh. Mitt. Beih.* 2, no. 13 is a fragment describing a procession of the gods similar to *KAR* 132. *TU* 43, a fragment of a ritual for the New Year festival of the month Nisannu, contains a hand-raising prayer (*šuillakku*) for Anu; this text gives us more information on day 10 and 11 of this festival.

Another important text is *TU* 42 +: the text describes a festival for Ištar, and must have belonged to a larger series of temple ritual texts dealing with the cult of Ištar of Uruk. In which month this festival was celebrated is not clear. The obverse records the same ceremonies, which for days 8 and 9 of the New Year festival of Anu are also preserved (see *TU* 39–40). The last part of the obverse and the reverse describe the procession of Ištar from the Ešgal-temple to the *akītu*-temple, and resembles the Anu-procession described in *KAR* 132.

TU 41 contains a ritual for days 16 and 17 of an unknown month, describing the good-functioning of the temple ceremony (*šalām bīti*) and the vigil (*bajjātu*) held during

[36] Which is indicated, for example, by *TU* 38, where a list of offerings and ceremonies is given which are 'written down in (the tablets of) the rites for the whole year' (rev. 38). See also *TU* 39–40, which contains the rites for the seventh month Tašrītu, after which the colophon refers to the next tablet containing the rites of the eighth month Araḫsamna (*TU* 39, rev. 25 f.). Texts which describe ritual proceedings for the whole year on one single tablet are unknown as far as the Hellenistic period is concerned, but we do have *LKU*, no. 51, dated to the late Neo-Babylonian or early Achaemenid period, listing ceremonies for Bēlet-ša-Uruk, Uṣur-amassu and Aška'itu for all twelve months of the year. For the date see A. Falkenstein, *LKU*, 1.

the night in the Rēš-temple. Pongratz-Leisten[37] has suggested that this ritual perhaps was performed during the tenth month Ṭebētu, because *TU* 38 records offerings to the planets which have to be performed on top of the temple tower on the sixteenth of Ṭebētu,[38] which can be connected with *TU* 41, since there offerings are brought to the planets on the sixteenth day.[39] Because part of the ritual is performed by a priest addressed in the second person, *TU* 41 probably does not belong to the large series of temple rituals covering the whole year.[40]

The temple ritual text W 18728, published by Falkenstein,[41] was probably written in the Hellenistic period and deals with clothing instructions for different persons, including several priests and the king.[42] The Hellenistic text W 18828, also published by Falkenstein,[43] contains ritual instructions for work in the temple workshop (*bīt mummi*) with a hymn to Šamaš. Unfortunately only three lines of the ritual are partly preserved. The fragment *Bagh. Mitt. Beih.* 2, no. 14 is perhaps also a ritual.

The *Bagh. Mitt. Beih.* 2-texts and probably also *TU* 38–43 come from one or more locations within the Rēš-temple and appear to belong to the corpus of at least one exorcist (*āšipu*): *TU* 38 and *TU* 39–40 were written by the exorcist Šamaš-ēṭir, son of Ina-qibīt-Anu, son of Šibqat-Anu, decendant of the *āšipu*-family Ekur-zakir. The colophon of *TU* 38 states that the exorcist Kidin-Anu, descendant of Ekur-zakir, copied the text in Elam and brought it back with him to Uruk. The owner of *TU* 39–40 is also an exorcist, although not from the Ekur-zakir family: Anu-uballiṭ, son of Nidintu-Anu, son of Ina-qibīt-Anu, descendant of Ḫunzû. For *TU* 41–43 no colophons are preserved.

The colophon of *BRM* 4, 7 indicates that the text was written by Anu-balāssu-iqbi, son of the owner of the tablet, the exorcist Anu-aḫa-ušabši, son of Kidin-Anu, descendant of Ekur-zakir. It also informs us that the scribe 'has written (the tablet) for his (own) instruction, his long days, his well-being and the permanence of his position and set (it) up in Uruk *and* in the Rēš-temple, the temple of his lordship' (rev. 45–47), indicating perhaps that he made two copies, one for his private library at home and one which was kept in the temple, where it was available to the public cult. Furthermore, he wrote the text for himself, which shows that the text was part of his private archive. We have no other prosopographical information on Anu-balāssu-iqbi, but his father, Anu-aḫa-ušabši, is also attested as the owner of the chronicle text *SpTU* 1, no. 2 (dated 61 S.E.), found in the living quarters Ue XVIII,[44] which indicates that Anu-aḫa-ušabši had a private archive in his home in the Ue XVIII area, like the better known exorcists Anu-ikṣur, Iqīša, and Nidintu-Anu. *BRM* 4, 7 and the other texts which name Anu-aḫa-ušabši as the owner or scribe[45] may have come from this library as well, but it is equally possible that some

37 *ina šulmi īrub*, 45.
38 Rev. 32–34.
39 Obv. 22–28.
40 See II.8.6.
41 *UVB* 15 (1959), 40–44.
42 A ritual text of the late Neo-Babylonian or early Achaemenid period is *LKU*, no. 48, containing a ritual for the king. For the date see A. Falkenstein, *LKU*, 1.
43 *UVB* 15 (1959), 36–40.
44 Although not on the location where some of the the *Bagh. Mitt. Beih.* 2-texts were found (Ue XVIII 1), see J. Oelsner, *Materialien*, 143. See also n. 13 above.
45 See my introduction to *BRM* 4, 7, in the Appendix.

of these texts were kept in the Rēš-temple. Note that two of the Anu-aḫa-ušabši-tablets, *TU* 19 and W 18828 both probably come from the Rēš-area, although the exact location remains uncertain.

W 18728 was found together with W 18828 in the Rēš-temple. The contents of *KAR* 132 suggests that it belongs to the temple ritual series similar to *TU* 38–43, but the tablet comes from illicit digging and the colophon is lost.

A few texts which deal with the eclipse of the moon ritual perhaps also belong to this group. In *BRM* 4, 6 and BM 134701[46] the eclipse of the moon ritual is described extensively. Thompson, *CLBT*, pl. 1, contains some kind of (lunar eclipse?) ritual, and furthermore a lunar eclipse myth; col. B is partly duplicated by the Uruk text *BRM* 4, 6,[47] which makes it likely that the former was also written in Uruk.[48] This is confirmed by col. A, 27 where the Rēš-temple, and the Enamenna, the cella of Anu in the Rēš-temple, are mentioned. Although no colophons have been preserved which attribute these texts to the corpus of the *āšipu*,[49] we know that the exorcist plays an important role in the eclipse ritual.

A second group of temple rituals belongs to the corpus of the lamentation priest (*kalû*). They do not belong to the large series of temple ritual texts, but are rituals for special occasions. Several texts deal with the kettledrum (*lilissu*), most important of which is *TU* 44.[50] Partial duplicates are *Bagh. Mitt. Beih.* 2, no. 5, no. 7, and perhaps also the fragment no. 9. Here we should also mention *Bagh. Mitt. Beih.* 2, no. 6, a bilingual hand-raising prayer (*šuillakku*) for the consecration of the bull, whose hide is used to cover the kettledrum.[51]

The building rituals also belong to the corpus of the lamentation priest. *TU* 45 and *TU* 46 are in many ways very similar, but there are also important differences between them.[52] Other duplicates are *Bagh. Mitt. Beih.* 2, no. 10, and no. 11.

The texts belonging to this second group probably all come from the Rēš-temple area Le XVI 3. The colophons indicate that most of the texts belong to the archive of

---

46 The latter was published by D. Brown and the present author in: BM 134701 = 1965–10–14,1 and the Hellenistic period eclipse ritual from Uruk, *RA* 91 (1997), 147–166.

47 *CLBT*, pl. 1, col. B, 1–14 // *BRM* 4, 6, obv. 5–11.

48 Cf. W.G. Lambert, *JCS* 16 (1962), 74b. The fact that the tablet was written in Uruk, does not necessarily mean that J. Oelsner, *Materialien*, 207–8, was wrong in assuming that the tablet was probably found in Babylon.

49 Note however that Thompson, *CLBT*, pl. 1, col. B, 29 perhaps refers to 'the office of the exorcist' (*a-ši-[pu-ti*(?)]). See the Appendix.

50 The text is partly a duplicate of the Neo-Assyrian text *KAR* 60.

51 Important for our understanding of the kettledrum ritual is the Neo-Assyrian text *KAR* 50, which is apparently a shortened version of the ritual. On the obverse we find a bilingual incantation for 'the choice bull, the creation of the great gods'. The reverse describes the actual ritual. Part of the text is duplicated by K 6060 (*BBR* 2, no. 56) + K 10820 (see Plate II). Also relevant is the Neo-Assyrian text *IV R*[2], 23, no. 1 + K 9421 (for the latter see Plate III); here several recitations, known from other kettledrum ritual texts, are presented in full.

52 *TU* 46 is also partially duplicated by the Late Babylonian Uruk text *SpTU* 4, no. 141. The Late Babylonian text F.H. Weissbach, *Misc.*, no. 12 from Babylon is partially a duplicate of these texts. As *SpTU* 4, no. 141 it contains the beginning of the recitation *Enūma Anu ibnû šamê*, only referred to by its incipit is the Uruk version *TU* 46. Another part of this recitation is attested in the unpublished Rm 101 (see Plate IV and my comments on l. 24 ff. of F.H. Weissbach, *Misc.*, no.12, in the Appendix).

the lamentation priest Anu-bēlšunu, son of Nidintu-Anu, descendant of the *kalû*-family Sîn-lēqe-unnīni.[53] The owner of the tablet *TU* 44 is the chief singer of dirges (*galamāḫu*) Anu-aḫa-ittannu, son of Riḫat-Anu; we know from a private contract that he was also a descendant of Sîn-lēqe-unnīni.[54]

Babylon

Unfortunately, because most of the texts from Babylon come from illicit excavations, we are unable to establish where the texts discussed here were originally kept. Although it is quite possible that many of the Hellenistic temple ritual texts, and also administrative documents e.g. *CT* 49, constitute remnants of the (not yet found) Esagila archive, we must for now take as our starting point that for the origin of the texts both temple archives as private archives are possible.[55]

Originally, as in Uruk also in Babylon a series of temple ritual texts which covered the whole year must have existed, but only fragments of this have survived.[56] Important evidence for such a series is the ritual text DT 15 +, published by Thureau-Dangin in *RAcc.*, 127 ff. The surviving fragments belong to two tablets which are identified as tablet 22 and 23 of the ritual series, as is specifically stated.[57] The text refers to the public cult of Marduk, here called Bēl. It describes part of the New Year festival of the first month Nisannu, and concentrates especially on the prayers which accompanied the cultic activity. Unfortunately the fragments cover only day 2 to 5, and even these are not complete. In his unpublished dissertation Çağirgan discussed a short fragment from his private collection, referring to the first day of the New Year festival,[58] and furthermore, he used the unpublished text BM 32654 + 38193 ('extract from a mythological text') for the restoration of l. 69–79 of the New Year ritual.[59] Finally, the unpublished text BM 32485 (published here, see Plate I) is a fragment belonging to DT 109; the reverse contains part of the last lines of the ritual of day 5. The text on the obverse is almost entirely lost.

More information on (perhaps) the first month Nisannu comes from BM 41577, a ritual text from the Hellenistic period, which is published by A.R. George.[60] The text deals with a visit of Marduk to the cella of Bēl and Bēltīja in Esagila, probably during day 6 or 7 of the New Year festival, as George suggests.[61] Another possibly Hellenistic fragment, BM 47902 +, deals with events taking place in the *akītu*-temple *Bīt ikribi* during the New Year festival of Nisannu.[62]

---

53 See the introductions of these texts, in the Appendix.
54 See my introduction of *TU* 44, in the Appendix.
55 Cf. J. Oelsner, *Materialien*, 191–94.
56 Cf. W.G. Lambert, in: *OECT* 11, p. 23 f.; G. Çağirgan, W.G. Lambert, *JCS* 43–45 (1991–93), 89. For more information we have to look elsewhere, for example in the calender text *SBH* VIII, which is concerned with the rites of Nabû for the whole year.
57 See lines 216aff. and 472 ff.
58 *Festivals*, 1.
59 *Festivals*, 7–9. This text will be published by W.G. Lambert.
60 *Studies W.G. Lambert*, no. 1, 260 ff.
61 ib., 263.
62 W.G. Lambert, *RA* 91 (1997), 52–56.

For the month Simānu we are almost solely dependant on BM 32656, a temple ritual fragment probably from the Hellenistic period, which is published by A.R. George.[63] The rituals in this texts do not deal with the cult of Marduk or his son Nabû, but with the cult of Ištar of Babylon in the temple Eturkalamma, which must have had its own ritual series.

Until recently our most important source for the month Kislīmu was the calendar text *SBH* VII // *BRM* 4, 25. Important new evidence for the month Kislīmu is now available from a large Esagila-ritual text dealing specifically with this month, BM 32206 +.[64] The text, part of the ritual series of Babylon, describes city ceremonies in Babylon on days 3 and 4 of the month Kislīmu and gives us new evidence for cultic activities in this month. The procession to the *akītu*-temple outside Babylon is esspecially important.[65] The text also contains references to the so-called palm festival.[66]

The date of the texts

In many cases the text contains a colophon with the name of the writer and/or the owner, the place where the tablet was written, and a date.[67] Sometimes, when the date is lost or missing, prosopographical information can also help us in dating the text.[68] Other texts have to be dated on palaeographical, grammatical and linguistic grounds, e.g. the signs *lu* and *ku* written without the top horizontal wedge, the use of the aleph-sign ʾ on the end of words, or the prefix *ta-* and *tu-* for the third p. fem. sing. verb (an example of Aramaic influence).[69] A very small script is also an important indication for a late date. Sometimes the archaeological history of a tablet i.e. the place where, and stratum in which, it was found can help us. Nevertheless, we are not always able to date a text more specifically then 'Late Babylonian' (i.e. from the Achaemenid or Hellenistic period).

---

[63] *Studies W.G. Lambert*, no. 2, 270 ff., demonstrating a close affinity with the so-called Divine Love Lyrics, see II.8.5.

[64] Originally edited by G. Çağirgan, *Festivals*, 86 ff., it is now published by G. Çağirgan and W.G. Lambert, *JCS* 43–45 (1991–1993), 89 ff.

[65] See II.4.3.

[66] See II.8.2. More evidence for the month Kislīmu comes from the unpublished text BM 78076, a tablet dated to Darius, which describes days 2–15 in Esabad, the Gula temple in Babylon. This text, which contains important information on the palm festival, is published by A.R. George, *Studies W.G. Lambert*, no. 3, 280 ff. The unpublished temple ritual fragment BM 54901 (see II.8.2) probably also refers to this festival.

For the month Šabāṭu we do not have temple rituals which can be dated to the Hellenistic period. We do have a fragment which was published by W.G. Lambert in *OECT* 11, no. 47, and more information on this month is now available from BM 32516 // 41239 (the latter was published by A.R. George, *BTT*, no. 57). This text is published by A.R. George, *Studies W.G. Lambert*, no. 4, 289 ff.

Other fragments relating to temple rituals in Babylon are *VS* 24, 108 (+) 109 // 110 (B. Pongratz-Leisten, *ina šulmi īrub*, nos. 10–11, 236–39) and K 3446 + (see now W.G. Lambert, *RA* 91 [1997], 56–62), possibly referring to the New Year festival in Nisannu; see also the smaller fragments *CT* 51, 94–97, 99–102, 104, and A.R. George, *BTT*, nos. 40–45.

[67] See for example the rituals *BRM* 4, 7, which is dated 61 S.E. (251/0 B.C.), W 18828, dated 62 S.E. (250/49 B.C.), *TU* 46, dated 81 S.E. (231/0 B.C.), *Bagh. Mitt. Beih.* 2, no. 12, dated 112 S.E. (200/199 B.C.), *Bagh. Mitt. Beih.* 2, no. 6, dated 136 S.E. (176/5 B.C.), and *Bagh. Mitt. Beih.* 2, no. 5, dated 150 S.E. (162/1 B.C.). See also the explanatory text BM 34035 (Sp I 131), dated 111 A.E i.e. 175(!) S.E. i.e. 137/6 B.C. (see J. Oelsner, *Materialien*, 227).

[68] See for example the introductions of the ritual texts *TU* 38, *TU* 39–40, *TU* 44, and *TU* 45 and 46, in the Appendix.

[69] See W. von Soden, *GAG*, § 193.

We know that at least in some cases the texts are copied in the Hellenistic period from older originals, as is specifically stated for example in the colophons of *TU* 38, *TU* 39–40, *BRM* 4, 7, *TU* 44, and W 18828. For this reason we must assume that many if not all of our texts describe older rituals, going back several centuries. When were these older rituals written? For Uruk it is clear that the texts appear to have been adjusted to the Late Babylonian situation: the gods mentioned in the texts belong to the Anu-pantheon of the Late Babylonian period, and not to the Ištar-pantheon of the Neo-Babylonian period.

Also the topography of Uruk as manifested in the texts is clearly Late Babylonian: in the texts, the Rēš- and Ešgal-temples, and not the Eanna-temple complex, are the dominating sanctuaries of the city. Consequently most of our texts are probably copies of older rituals written at the latest during the fifth century.[70] However, it is possible that these texts are adaptations of even older rituals going back to the Neo-Babylonian period. We do not know much about these older rituals, but one example of such a document has been preserved which gives us some inside information on the cult in Uruk before the Anu-pantheon was introduced. This text, *LKU* no. 51, was probably written during the Late Neo-Babylonian or early Achaemenid period.[71] It appears to be a list of offerings, ceremonies and processions for the whole year, but also of the days, on which the lamentation priest (*kalû*) had to perform his cultic duties. The twelve months of the year are discussed, but the first two months, and part of the third are lost. The goddesses Bēlet-ša-Uruk (= Ištar), Uṣur-amassu and Aška'itu in the Eanna-temple are the main protagonists. The text is in many ways similar to the temple ritual texts from Hellenistic Uruk, especially *TU* 42 +, in which Ištar also plays an important part.[72]

The Babylon ritual DT 15 + (*RAcc.*, 127 ff.) may also be an adaptation of an older ritual going back to the Neo-Babylonian period. Thureau-Dangin assumed that the text was written during the Hellenistic period.[73] Zimmern concluded that 'dieses Neujahrsfestritual, wenigstens in seinem jetzigen Wortlaut, nicht etwa, wie mancher sonstige späte Text, eine sklavische Kopie aus älterer Zeit ist, sondern vielmehr auf der Grundlage älterer Vorlagen eine freie Konzeption des Neujahrsfestrituals für die Priesterschaft des Esagil-Tempels in Babylon aus der spätesten, seleukidisch-parthischen, Periode darstellt'.[74]

Finally, the important Late Babylonian Esagila-ritual concerned with the month Kislīmu, BM 32206 +, is possibly also of Hellenistic date, but refers back to older originals, as Lambert suggested.[75]

---

[70] See also I.3.
[71] See above.
[72] See A. Falkenstein, *LKU*, 2. For *TU* 42 +, see II.8.5.
[73] *RAcc.*, I.
[74] *ZA* 34 (1922), 192.
[75] *JCS* 43–45 (1991–93), 89–90.

I.3. The cult

Some general observations

According to Mesopotamian theology the gods are the creators of the world and of humans; the latter had to serve the gods in return for individual and communal prosperity and well-being. This service involved providing everything the gods needed to lead a comfortable existence, and was formalized in order to avoid any mistakes or negligence, which would have had disastrous consequences for the people and their cities. This formalized service for the gods is the cult.

In general, one could define a cult as a form, a practice in which the worshipping of a divinity takes place. In a cult communication with the divine is expressed in certain words, formulas, gestures and actions. One usually distinguishes between, first, a more individual worshipping, and secondly, a common worshipping, the official cult, which was performed by a community; the cult is then expressed in feasts and gatherings. Cultic acts such as offerings, purifications, cultic meals, prayers, incantations and processions, are often performed in or near sacred places like temples.

The Mesopotamians envisaged the cult in an anthropomorphic way: although the gods were thought to reside in heaven and the underworld, in every Mesopotamian city many gods also lived in their own temples. Furthermore, each city also had its own main god, a city patron, who resided in the major temple, where he or she was represented by an anthropomorphic statue. The statues were considered to be manifestations of the gods on earth; rather than being mere images they were regarded as extensions of the personality of the gods. The statues were identified with the gods in question and were considered to be like living beings, who, just like humans, had to eat, sleep, wake and be dressed, and were therefore in the center of ceremonies and presented with regular and special offerings. The statue 'served as the focal point for sacrificial activities'.[76]

The cultic proceedings were probably based on Babylonian court practices. Like a king living with his family and servants in the palace, in the temple the main god of the city lived with other gods who acted as his family and servants. Under the guidance of priests the inhabitants of the city were responsible for the worship and feeding of the gods throughout the year. However, the temple was not a place were everyone came together to worship the god. Only certain priests and other temple personnel, who were able to perform the often elaborate ceremonies and rituals, and on occasion, for example during the New Year festival, the king or a high official of the city, had access to the temple. There is much written evidence concerning the official temple cult, especially in the ritual texts. Of the private popular religion not much is known.[77]

---

[76] A.L. Oppenheim, *Ancient Mesopotamia*, 185. For the latest on the divine statues see P.-A. Beaulieu, *JNES* 52 (1993), 241, and A. Berlejung, *Die Theologie der Bilder*, Orbis Biblicus et Orientalis 162, Freiburg Schweitz, 1998, 20 ff. with earlier literature. See also Th. Jacobsen, in: P.D. Miller Jr., P.D. Hanson, S. Dean McBride (eds.), *Ancient Israelite Religion*, Philadelphia, 1987, 15 ff.

[77] For the latest on this subject see M. Dandamayev, in: A. Berlin (ed.), *Religion and Politics in the Ancient Near East. Studies and Texts in Jewish History and Culture*, Maryland, 1996, 35–45, especially 39 ff.; K. van der Toorn, *Family religion in Babylonia, Syria and Israel. Continuity and Change in the forms of Religious Life*, SHCANE VII, Leiden, New York, Köln, 1996; id., in: K.R. Veenhof (ed.), *Houses and Households in*

The temple was not only a religious centre. Although it was considered to be the house of the god (and as such all the temple property was the property of the main god of the temple) it was also an economic center, raising taxes (tithes), owning land, slaves and livestock, and taking part in trade and money-lending. In return the temple provided a large part of the income of citizens who performed certain duties in connection with the temple, either by distributing part of the temple income or by paying wages. Also leasing temple land to tenants was important. The temple was, together with the palace, to a large extent in charge of the land and the economic activities.[78]

A clear definition of the cult is never presented in texts from Mesopotamia. However, the colophon of the ritual text *TU* 38 gives us an idea of how the priesthood of Hellenistic Uruk envisaged the cult to be (rev. 44–50):

> '[44]Wax-table (containing) the rites for the Anu-worship, the pure *šuluḫḫu*-purification rites, the ritual regulations of kingship, including(?) the divine *šuluḫḫu*-purification rites of the Rēš-temple, the Ešgal-temple, [45]the Eanna-temple and the (other) temples of Tiranna, the ritual activities of the exorcists, the lamentation priests, the singers and the craftsmen, [46]all of them, who are subservient to the ..., not to mention all that concerns the apprentices, in accordance with the contents of the tablets, [47]which Nabopolassar, king of the Sealand, carried off (*šalālu*) from Uruk. And at that time(?) Kidin-Anu from Uruk, [48]the exorcist of Anu and Antu, descendant of Ekur-zakir, the high priest of the Rēš-temple, [49]saw [48]these tablets in the land of Elam and during the reign of Seleucus and Antiochus, the kings, [50]he copied and brought (them) to Uruk'.

Here, clearly, an attempt is being made to give a complete description of the cult in Uruk. The text first mentions the rites for the main deity Anu, followed by the purification rites. Then it refers to the duties of the king in the cult. The purification rites of all the temples of Uruk are recorded, after which those who are responsible for performing the cult in these temples are enumerated. Finally, it gives an explanation for the origin of the cult instructions.

The main temples and their gods

Where was the official cult practised?[79] In Babylon the ancient Esagila-temple complex was still the most important cultic building of the city in the Hellenistic period, constituting the centre of the Bēl-Marduk-cult.[80] The pantheon of Babylon remained

---

Ancient Mesopotamia, 40e RAI Leiden 1993, Leiden, Istanbul, 1996, 69–78.

78 See R.J. van der Spek, Landownership in Babylonian Cuneiform Documents, in: M.J. Geller, A.D.E. Lewis, H. Maehler (edd.), *Legal Documents of the Hellenistic Period*, London, 1995, 173–245.

79 For an up to date survey of the cult buildings of Hellenistic Uruk and Babylon, see J. Oelsner, *Materialien*, 78–97 and 112–126, with further literature. All relevant temple names for this study are collected in A.R. George, *House Most High*, with further literature. For the location of many of the temples and temple-parts see A.R. George, *BTT*, chapters 1–3, 1 ff. (Babylon) and chapter 6, 198 ff. (Uruk), and B. Pongratz-Leisten, *ina šulmi īrub*, especially chapter III, but note the review article of A.R. George, *BiOr* 53 (1996), 363 ff.

80 Scholars have argued that Esagila and other Babylonian temples were destroyed by Xerxes in 482 B.C., but this theory is without support, as has been demonstrated by A. Kuhrt and S. Sherwin-White, in: H.W.A.M. Sancisi-Weerdenburg, A. Kuhrt (eds.), *Achaemenid History II: the Greek sources*, 69–78;

unchanged in the Hellenistic period, as becomes clear not only from the ritual texts and other non-cultic sources, but also from a large group of cult songs;[81] although most of these texts are probably not Hellenistic compositions but copies of older originals, we know that these texts were still used for the cult of the old gods, because not only were many of these texts copied in Hellenistic Babylon, but their colophons indicate that these copies were used 'for singing' (*ana zamāri*), which can only mean that they were used in the cult.[82]

The Esagila-temple remained in use at least until the first century A.D. as we know from astronomical texts, the latest of which is dated to 75 A.D.[83] The astronomical diaries mention the assembly (*kiništu*) and administrator (*šatammu*) of Esagila in 78 B.C.[84] Other temples are attested in the archive of a temple official called Raḫimesu (94–92 B.C.)[85]: Eturkalamma, the temple of Ištar of Babylon,[86] Esabad, the temple of Gula in Babylon,[87] and furthermore the temples of Zababa and Ninlil,[88] Nabû-ša-ḫarê,[89] Madānu and the *akītu*-temple.[90]

In Uruk an important change came about during the Late Babylonian period. In the Neo-Babylonian period Inanna/Ištar was the most important god of the city of Uruk, living in the Eanna-complex, but in the Hellenistic period Anu was the most prominent deity, residing in the Rēš-temple, at that time the most important sanctuary of the city. Building inscriptions inform us about extensive building activities and reconstructions not only of the Rēš-temple of Anu, but also of the Ešgal-temple of Ištar during the Hellenistic period.[91] Several *akītu*-temples are known from Hellenistic Uruk.[92] The temple tower of Uruk, the largest ever constructed in Mesopotamia, was also built in the Hellenistic period.[93]

Evidence for the new pantheon in Uruk comes not only from ritual texts but also from cult songs, which like those of Babylon, were probably still used for the cult in the Hellenistic period.[94] Furthermore in the Uruk prebend texts and in proper names (as the divine name-element) also the same gods appear: Anu together with his spouse Antu was at the head of the new pantheon, consisting of Enlil, Ea, Sîn, Šamaš, Adad, Marduk,

---

M. Jursa, *AfO Beiheft* 25 (1995), 2 with n. 8; A.C.V.M. Bongenaar, *The Neo-Babylonian Ebabbar temple at Sippar*, 4.

81 G.A. Reisner, *SBH*. See now M.E. Cohen, *Lamentations*.

82 Cf. J. Oelsner, *Materialien*, 208.

83 A.J. Sachs, in: *Kramer AV*, 379–98. Cf. J. Oelsner, *Materialien*, 278, n. z.

84 A.J. Sachs–H. Hunger, *Diaries*, no. -77, A, obv. 8′, 10′; 27′–28′, rev. 30, B, rev. 15′.

85 See R.J. van der Spek, in: J. Wiesehöfer (ed.), *Das Partherreich und seine Zeugnisse*, 205–58 (cf. 253), with the latest collations, translations and comments on all texts belonging to this archive.

86 See II.8.5.

87 See II.8.1.

88 Apart from the Raḫimesu texts *CT* 49, 156, obv. 3 and *BRM* 1, 99, 2 also in A.J. Sachs–H. Hunger, *Diaries* no. -254, obv. 13′.

89 See II.8.3.

90 See II.4.5.2.

91 See II.6.4 and II.8.5.

92 See II.4.5.1.

93 S.B. Downey, *Mesopotamian Religious Architecture*, 18. L. Hannestad, D. Potts, in: P. Bilde (ed.), *Religion and Religious Practice in the Seleucid Kingdom. Studies in Hellenistic Civilization I*.Aarhus, 1990, 107.

94 J. Oelsner, *Materialien*, 170.

Papsukkal, Amasagnudi, Ištar, Bēlet-ṣēri, Nanāja, Bēlet-ša-Rēš, and Šarraḫītu.[95] How and when did this change come about?

According to the colophon of *TU* 38 the entire cult of the Hellenistic period in Uruk must have originated in the Neo-Babylonian period. Falkenstein interpreted this colophon as propaganda from the Urukaean priesthood designed to legitimate the Late Babylonian Anu-cult.[96] We know that this process of change from Ištar- to Anu-predominance took place over a longer period of time, and was not an invention of the priests of Hellenistic Uruk. Evidence from the Late Babylonian period has confirmed this: based on onomastic evidence Beaulieu concluded that probably between 521, the first regnal year of Darius I, and 424, the first regnal year of Darius II, Anu took over from Ištar.[97] After the conquest of the Neo-Babylonian empire by Cyrus in 539 the hegemony of the national god and the god of the capital, Marduk, came to an end. Provincial centers like Uruk were now free to promote their own version of the national pantheon, and placed Anu (not only the old deity of Uruk, but also, before Marduk's rise at the end of the second millennium, the god who presided (together with Enlil) over the national pantheon) at the head of this new pantheon. This was done in part by using the Middle Babylonian god list An = Anum, which was a source of inspiration for Urukaean 'antiquarian' theologians. Furthermore it is quite possible, as Pongratz-Leisten has suggested,[98] that tolerant Persian rulers allowed local cults to go their own way, since they were more concerned with political and economical matters in Babylonia. For Anu and his consort Antu a new temple complex was built, the Rēš-temple,[99] while Ištar and Nanāja, previously residing in the Eanna-temple, moved to the Ešgal-complex. In texts from the Hellenistic period the Eanna-temple is referred to only rarely, and apparently had lost much of its cultic function in favour of the Rēš- and Ešgal-temples.[100] We know that both of these temples still existed and functioned normally in the early Arsacid period.[101]

---

[95] See P.- A. Beaulieu, *ASJ* 14 (1992), 53–60. Cf. also B. Pongratz-Leisten, *ina šulmi īrub*, 136–143. Older discussions of the Uruk pantheon are O. Schroeder, in *SPAW* 41 (1916), 1180–1196; M. Rutten, *Contrats de l'époque Séleucide conservés au musée du Louvre*, 36–63.

[96] *Topographie*, 8–9. See also G. van Driel, *Cult of Aššur*, thesis 3: 'Het colophon van de tekst *TU* 38 wekt de indruk dat men bij deze tekst te doen heeft met een vervalsing ten bate van de heiligdommen van Uruk'. Similar view in P.A. Beaulieu, *Studies W.W. Hallo*, Bethesda, 1993, 47. For the colophon see also III.2.2.

[97] P.- A. Beaulieu, *ASJ* 14 (1992), 54–69. See also J. Oelsner, *Klio* 60 (1978), 103; id., *Klio* 63 (1981), 39–44; P.- A. Beaulieu, *OrNS* 64 (1995), 187 ff. (discussing Antu).

[98] *ina šulmi īrub*, 143.

[99] A. Falkenstein (*Topographie*, 8) already noted that a temple called Rēš is indirectly attested in texts from the Neo-Babylonian period: texts belonging to the Eanna-archive mention the goddess Bēlet-ša-Rēš. Note, however, that this goddess also appears in the annals of Sennacherib, cf. D.D. Luckenbill, *OIP* 2, p. 87, 31–33, where several deities dwelling in Uruk are mentioned, among which (in 31) is Bēlet-ša-Rēš (*šá re*ʾ*-e-ši*).

[100] Texts from Eanna become rare after the second regnal year of Darius I (520/19 B.C.), which has led some scholars to assume that Eanna was destroyed by Darius I. However, as M. Dandamayev has shown (*AMI* 25 [1992], 169–72), documentary evidence from the Late Achaemenid period clearly undermines this hypothesis.

[101] A quitclaim written during the reign of Mithridates II (K. Kessler, *Bagh. Mitt.* 15 [1984], 273–81, dated 108 B.C.) refers to the Rēš-temple, the Ešgal-temple and the other temples of Uruk and relates to the sale of prebend shares, which shows that temple service was still taking place. Cf. S. Sherwin-White, A. Kuhrt, *From Samarkhand to Sardis*, 155. In the astronomical diaries from Babylon Uruk is mentioned as late as 83 B.C., cf. A.J. Sachs–H. Hunger, *Diaries*, no. -82, A, obv. 20.

The officials

Who were responsible for the rituals and ceremonies in the temples?[102] In the Babylonian language there is no general word for 'priest'. There are officials whose duties are strictly confined to (religious) tasks in the temple, and who are considered to be initiates, i.e. who belong to a group of persons possessing secret knowledge, which may not be shared with outsiders. See for example the following warning in the Uruk kettledrum ritual *TU* 44, III, 29–30:

> '[29]This ritual procedure, which you perform, only the novice (*tarbûtu*) [30]may see (it); an outsider, someone who is not responsible for the rites (*la mār bēl parṣi*), may not see (it)'.[103]

McEwan has discussed all the 'priests' known from the Hellenistic period.[104] Most often mentioned in texts from Hellenistic Babylonia is the exorcist (*āšipu*).[105] We know that he played a major part in the temple rituals from Uruk[106] and Babylon.[107] It is this magical expert who takes charge of most ritual activities, because in many official rituals it was important to avert evil and obtain ritual purity by means of all sorts of magical activities. Many of our texts can be attributed to the corpus of the exorcist (*āšipūtu*).[108]

Furthermore there are special priests, who were responsible for performing the recitations, such as the singer (*nāru*), the lamentation priests (*kalû*) and the chief singer

---

102 In contrast to Egypt and Israel the administration of the temples in Babylonia was performed by civil servants who had no priestly duties. These civil servants were discussed by G.J.P. McEwan, *FAOS* 4, 25 ff. and R.J. van der Spek, *Grondbezit in het Seleucidische rijk*, 57 ff. (Babylon) and 79 ff. (Uruk) (an English summary in: A. Kuhrt, S. Sherwin-White (ed.), *Hellenism in the East*, Berkeley and Los Angeles, 1987, 57–74). Many references to Babylonian cultic personnel are also to be found in R.A. Henshaw, *Female and Male*.

103 Cf. G.J.P. McEwan, *FAOS* 4, 10. For this secret knowledge see P.- A. Beaulieu, *ZA* 82 (1992), 98 ff.

104 *FAOS* 4, 7 ff. (chapter I), with text references (see however the review articles). Among the texts published after McEwan's study, the Kislīmu ritual BM 32206 + is especially important for its additional information on priests and other temple personnel. Not attested elsewhere are the DUMU.NÍG.LA.LA, possibly to be read as *mār šalāti* (see G. Çağirgan, W.G. Lambert, *JCS* 43–45 [1991–93], 90–1), and, although very uncertain, the *ḫaṭṭaru* (ib., 101).

105 For the occasional reading [lú]MAŠ.MAŠ = *mašmaššu* instead of *ašipu* in the Late Babylonian period see my comment on *TU* 38, rev. 45, in the Appendix.

106 He is mentioned together with the lamentation priest, the singer and the craftsmen (in the colophon of *TU* 38, rev. 45). He is also mentioned together with the lamentation priest and the singer in the Uruk New Year festival (*TU* 39, obv. 35; rev. 19) and he takes part in procession during this festival (*TU* 39, obv. 27, with a temple enterer, *TU* 40, rev 6, 9, with the king; *BRM* 4, 7, passim, with the high priest, the temple enterer and the brewers), and recites incantations (*BRM* 4, 7, passim). He also takes part in the festival of Ištar (*TU* 42 +, rev. 30′). During the night vigil festivities he consecrates the Scepter, takes part in a procession with the torch together with the head temple enterer, the lamentation priests and the singers, and extinguishes the torch (*TU* 41, obv. 4, 33, rev. 19). He recites incantations during the eclipse of the moon ritual (*BRM* 4, 6, obv. 35 f.). Finally, he has a minor role in the kettledrum ritual and the building ritual, see II.5.3 and II.6.3.

107 The exorcist consecrates the temple (*RAcc.*, 140, 340 ff.) and recites incantations (*RAcc.*, 141, 355).

108 See I.2.

of dirges (*galamāḫu / kalamaḫḫu*).[109] The kettledrum ritual and the building ritual[110] belong to the text corpus of the lamentation priest (*kalûtu*).[111]

The leading priest in the temple is the *aḫu rabû* 'high priest';[112] he is especially well-known from ritual texts. Not mentioned by McEwan is the *ēnu*-priest.[113] Referred to only rarely in texts from Hellenistic Uruk and Babylon are the *šangû*, *lumaḫḫu* and *šuluḫḫû*.[114] The same is true for the cultic performers *assinnu*, *kurgarrû* and *urmaḫlullû*.[115] The diviner performing extispicy (*barû*) is not well attested in the Hellenistic period, which however is not a result of Greek influence, but must be explained by the fact that in the Hellenistic period divination was to a large extent replaced by astrology, as McEwan suggested.[116] This is confirmed by the fact that most of the texts in which the diviner is mentioned are in all probability Hellenistic copies of older originals.

Finally, the texts often mention the *ērib bīti* 'temple enterer', i.e. a person who is allowed to enter the restricted areas of the temple.[117] As Bongenaar convincingly argued, '*ērib bīti* is not a general word, class, position or honorific title, but has just one meaning: "the owner of an *ērib bītūtu* prebend"'.[118] Anyone who held certain offices or had to perform certain duties in the temple owned an *ērib bītūtu* prebend. It is therefore no surprise to find that 'priests', and also those experts and craftsmen who were needed inside the temple to perform their duties, such as the goldsmith (*kutimmu*), the carpenter (*naggāru*), the jeweller (*kabšarru*), the seal-cutter (*purkullu*), and the craftsman (*gurgurru*), were called *ērib bīti*.

The fact that a person designated as cook/baker (*nuḫatimmu*), brewer (*sirāšû*), oil processor (*ṣāḫitu*), butcher (*ṭābiḫu*), or miller (*ararru*) is sometimes also called *ērib bīti*, does not contradict Bongenaar's theory. Obviously a cook or butcher only delivered his goods and his work did not require admission into the restricted parts of the temple, but this does not mean that he did not hold other offices or perform other tasks which did make it necessary for him to enter the temple.[119] The fact that the *ērib bīti* is sometimes

---

[109] *kalû* was usually written [lú]GALA, but in the astronomical diaries [lú]LAGAR, cf. W. Horowitz, *RA* 85 (1991), 75, n. 4 with literature. For the lamentation priest see (apart from G.J.P. McEwan, *FAOS* 4, 11 ff.) M.K. Schretter, *Emesal-Studien*, Innsbruck, 1990, 135, J.A. Black, *Eme-sal Cult Songs and Prayers*, and R.A. Henshaw, *Female and Male,* 88–96. McEwan collected most of the textual references, but see also the Uruk text W 18728, obv. 10′ and 12′, which mentions the consecrated ('shaven') lamentation priest ([lú]GALA *gul-lu-bu*), probably belonging to the regular personnel of the temple, and the unconsecrated lamentation priest ([lú]GALA *la gul-lu-bu*). See II.5.1

[110] See II.5 and II.6.

[111] See I.2.

[112] For the reading *aḫu rabû* instead of *šešgallu* in texts from the Hellenistic period, see my comments on *TU* 38, rev. 48, in the Appendix.

[113] *TU* 42 +, obv. 16 (but see my comments on this line in the Appendix); *KAR* 132, III, 15.

[114] There is no evidence that the *gerseqqû*, usually translated 'attendant', or the [lú]ŠU.BAR.RA (cf. G.J.P. McEwan, *FAOS* 4, 8 and 11) had any priestly duties. Cf. J.A. Brinkman, *JCS* 35 (1983), 233.

[115] For the *assinnu* and *kurgarrû* and their participation in the so-called Divine Love Lyrics during the Arsacid period, as suggested by Ph.M. Hibbert, *WdO* 15 (1984), 93–95, see II.8.5.

[116] *FAOS* 4, 15.

[117] See G. Frame, *ZA* 81 (1991), 42 and A.C.V.M. Bongenaar, *The Neo-Babylonian Ebabbar temple at Sippar*, 146 f., with more references.

[118] Ib., 149.

[119] A good example is Marduk-šuma-iddin, called an *ērib bīti* of Esabad in *CT* 49, 161, obv. 6–7 (18-VI-93 B.C.), and referred to as a baker in AB 245 (G.J.P. McEwan, *Iraq* 43 [1981], 136 ff.), obv. 6 (18-VI-93 B.C.); cf. R.J. van der Spek, *BiOr* 52 (1985), 547–8. These texts belong to the archive of the official Raḫimesu. Another text from this archive (*CT* 49, 156, dated 10-II-93 B.C.) refers to the *ērib bītūtu*, a prebendary office

mentioned together with other priests or craftsmen is not surprising either, because in these cases the *ērib bīti*s are always mentioned as being the last in line, and should be interpreted as 'the (other) *ērib bīti*s'. This is confirmed by the ritual text *BRM* 4, 7, which describes a procession of Anu from the Rēš-temple to the *akītu*-temple. After Anu has left the cella Enamenna and has arrived at the Grand Gate, the high priest (*aḫu rabû*), the exorcists, the (other) *ērib bīti*s, and the brewers recite a prayer. This is repeated during the different stages of the procession until they reach the *akītu*-temple.[120] Because Anu has left the restricted temple area, the brewers, mentioned after the *ērib bīti*s because they are not allowed to enter the temple, can join in as bearers of the carrying pole (gišt*allu*).

As we saw, the colophon of *TU* 38 presents us with a list of priests and craftsmen who perform cultic proceedings in the temples: it mentions the ritual activities of the exorcists, the lamentation priests, the singers and the craftsmen (DUMU.MEŠ *um-man-nu*).[121] Together with the high priest (not mentioned in the colophon), these are the persons who are most often mentioned in the temple ritual texts, and who are responsible for performing the ceremonies and rituals. However, there is one other person, who also takes part in cultic activities on certain occasions: the king.

The king

We have many references to the king in the temple ritual texts. His tasks in the public cult (called the *sakkê šarrūtu* the 'ritual regulations of kingship') are referred to in the description of the Uruk cult in the colophon of *TU* 38.[122] The additional offerings of the king (*tardīt šarri*), mentioned in a list of offerings and ceremonies in *TU* 38 form part of these ritual regulations.[123] Furthermore the king takes part in the New Year festivals in Uruk and Babylon,[124] participates in the special festival for Ištar of Uruk,[125] recites *eršemšaḫungû*-prayers in the Uruk building ritual,[126] and appears in the last part of the lunar eclipse ritual in Uruk.[127]

The question is whether in the Hellenistic period the Macedonian kings participated in the cult activities in the same manner as did the Babylonian and Achaemenid kings in the previous periods. The temple ritual texts do not give us any information on this, but non-cultic sources, especially chronicles, building inscriptions and the astronomical diaries suggest that this is the case, and for a good reason too. As Sherwin-White and Kuhrt stated: 'in Babylonia (…) the Seleucid kings present a coherent picture of rulers who are no foreign enemy but constitute a legitimate and just dynasty, attuned to local gods and actively participating in cults. Here, the tradition of Babylonian kingship gave

of the temple enterer in the Day One temple i.e. the *akītu*-temple in Arsacid Babylon, which shows that the cult was still practiced in the first century B.C. The temple enterer is also mentioned in the Raḫimesu-text K. Kessler, in *Festschrift J. Oelsner*, no. 9 (94/3 B.C.).

120 Cf. obv. 3–4, 7, 10–11, 14–15, 18–19, 22–23, 26, rev. 39–40.
121 Rev. 45.
122 Rev. 44.
123 Obv. 38, rev. 38. See III.1 and III.7. 2.
124 *TU* 39–40, *KAR* 132; *RAcc.*, 127 ff. See II.4.5.
125 *TU* 42 +. See II.8.5.
126 *TU* 45. See II.6.
127 BM 134701. See II.7.4.

king and subject a framework to operate in. (...) The Seleucid kings seem effectively to have taken on, and could be felt to have fulfilled, some aspects of their Achaemenid and Babylonian inheritance'.[128]

The involvement of the Macedonian kings with the Babylonian temples has been described by Van der Spek[129]: Alexander started to restore Esagila in Babylon and his successors also undertook building renovations on the temples of Uruk and Babylon.[130] As will be illustrated in the following chapters, many references in the astronomical diaries indicate the active participation of the Macedonian king, or of high officials acting as his representatives, in the official cult in the temples, performing offerings and ceremonies or taking part in the New Year festival. The reason for this participation is religious (the king is representative of the people, honoring the gods and seeking support, advice and protection from danger from the gods for himself and his subjects), political (legitimation of his position, seeking support and goodwill from his people), and economic (using the wealth of the temples to provide an income for himself and to subsidize military campaigns).

Van der Spek describes the role of the king as the benefactor of the temples, who hopes to find moral and financial support for his political and military plans, but also as the robber of temple funds in times of crisis. On religious matters however the temples were usually left in peace. We do find in the astronomical diaries many references to special rituals which were held for one or more gods and 'for the life of' the king and his royal family. These were not necessarily imposed on the temples by the king, but may have developed spontaneously in the cities of the Seleucid empire, including Babylonia. The rituals for the king are usually referred to as ruler cults and are discussed elsewhere.[131]

Cult terminology

In the texts from Mesopotamia we find a wide range of general terms referring to the cult and to its different elements, e.g. 'ceremony (rite), ritual, ritual procedure/activity, festival' etc. Unfortunately most of these terms apparently have a general meaning: clear definitions are not given and the context often does not give us enough clues to distinguish one term from another.[132] We will list these terms here and discuss their relevance for the Hellenistic period.

A general word, attested from the Old Babylonian period on, is *parṣu* 'rite, cult', written syllabically but also with the Sumerograms GARZA and ME. The former originally stood for 'cult practice, rite', and ME for 'divine power, divine order', two different meanings which, according to Landsberger, assimilated into the Akkadian *parṣu*.[133] We

128 *From Samarkhand to Sardis*, 38–9.
129 *Religieuze en economische politiek in het Seleucidische Rijk*, 19 ff.
130 See II.6.4.
131 See II.8.7.
132 The translations of these terms used in this book usually follow the dictionaries *CAD* and *AHw*.
133 *AfK* 2 (1924–25), 64 ff.; see also E. Ebeling, *MAOG* V/3 (1931), 45 f.and K. Focke, *ZA* 88 (1998), 203, n. 20. For the Late Babylonian period see for example the Babylon building ritual F.H. Weissbach, *Misc*., no. 12, obv. 36.

have many examples from Hellenistic ritual texts. *Parṣu*, used as a more general reference to the entire cult, is attested in a passage from *TU* 38, where after the enumeration of several offerings and ceremonies the text states that these are 'written down in (the tablets of) the rites for the whole year' (*šá ina* GARZA *šá kal* MU.AN.NA *šaṭ-ri*).[134] Here the rites of the divine marriage (GARZA.GARZA *ḫa-šá-du*) are also mentioned,[135] and the colophon of this text begins with the rites for the Anu-worship (GARZA ᵈLX-*ú-tú*).[136] The term *parṣu* is also used in texts describing the New Year festivals from Uruk[137] and Babylon,[138] and in a kettledrum ritual text from Uruk, referring to someone who is not responsible for the rites.[139] In this ritual we also find *parṣu* used in combination with *kidudû* 'ritual'[140]: the bull is taken to be used for the rites and rituals (*a-na par-ṣi u* KI.DU.DU-*de-e*).[141] We also have one reference in an eclipse of the moon(?) ritual, but the context is difficult.[142] Finally *parṣu* is (rarely) recorded in the astronomical diaries from Babylon.[143]

nēpešu 'ritual, ritual procedure', often used in the plural (*nēpešū*), is especially well-known from the Neo-Assyrian period on, and is usually written syllabically. It is also mentioned in Hellenistic ritual texts.[144] Many times it is attested in the phrase *né-pe-ši šá* ŠU^{II} ˡᵘGALA '(This is) the ritual procedure of the lamentation priest', used to identify the ritual or a recitation, performed during a ritual, as belonging to the text corpus of the lamentation priest (*kalûtu*).[145] Furthermore, *nēpešu* is known from the kettledrum ritual (here with the exceptional writing DÍM.DÍM.MA),[146] the building ritual,[147] and the eclipse of the moon ritual.[148] In a Hellenistic temple ritual fragment dealing with

---

134 *TU* 38, rev. 38.

135 *TU* 38, obv. 37; rev. 37; see also *TU* 39, obv. 4 (*par-ṣi šá ḫa-šá-du*). See II.4.4.

136 *TU* 38, rev. 44.

137 *TU* 40, obv. 10–11: the rites of the sheep on the ninth day have to be performed as on the previous eighth day. *TU* 39, rev. 25 contains a reference to the rites of the seventh month Tašrītu.

138 *RAcc.*, 130, 38; 132, [185]; 136, 277 and 140, 336: the text refers to the rites of the *ērib bītis* which have to be performed 'as usual' (GIM *šá gi-na-a*). This text also mentions (131, 72) the rites of the destroyed temples of Uruk and Nippur: 'their rites are forgotten [since distant days ...]', and one reference is made (144, 425) to the rites of Esagila: '[I have not] made Esagila tremble, I have not forgotten its rites'.

139 *TU* 44, III, 30, cited above.

140 Written syllabically and KI.DU.DU.

141 *TU* 44, I, 4; 6. See the duplicate *Bagh. Mitt. Beih.* 2, no. 5, obv. 4; 6. See also the Neo-Assyrian ritual text *IV R*^{2}, 23, no. 1, I, 20 (*a-na par-ṣi ki-du-de-e na-šu-ka*).

142 *CLBT*, pl. 1, col. A, 10.

143 A (damaged) passage in A.J. Sachs–H. Hunger, *Diaries*, no. 155, A, rev. 8–17 mentions the performing of rites (*ana* DÙ-*eš par-ṣi*) on day 5-IV-156 S.E. (context not clear).

144 But also in other sources, as for example in the astronomical diaries; see A.J. Sachs–H. Hunger, *Diaries*, no. -256, obv. 20′; no. 229, B, obv. 6′; 11′; rev. 1[3′].

145 The Uruk *mīs pî* (washing of the mouth)-ritual: *Bagh. Mitt. Beih.* 2, no. 1 (+ //), 61. The Uruk kettledrum ritual: *TU* 44, IV, 36 (cf. Neo-Assyrian ritual text *IV R*^{2}, 23, no. 1, IV, 26: *né-pe-ši* NAM.GALA.KAM '(This is) the ritual procedure for the lamentation priesthood'). The Uruk building ritual: *TU* 45, obv. 15; rev. 2; *TU* 46, obv. 20; rev. 14; *Bagh. Mitt. Beih.* 2, no. 10, obv. 21; *Bagh. Mitt. Beih.* 2, no. 12, rev. 3′. See also the Neo-Babylonian ritual text *LKU*, no. 48, rev. 8 (*né-pe-ši* [*šá* ŠU^{II} ˡᵘGALA]; cf. rev. 6.

146 In the already mentioned warning formula *TU* 44, III, 29.

147 *TU* 46 is identified as belonging to the text corpus of the lamentation priest (obv. 20). In the following supplement(?) another reference is made to repeatedly performing(?) of the ritual procedure, obv. 21: *né-pe-ši i-te-né-ep-pu-š*[*ú*]; cf. the Late Babylonian parallel *SpTU* 4, no. 141, rev. 14.

148 *BRM* 4, 6, obv. 17 (see also obv. 2) the lamentation priest is said to sit down and perform the ritual procedure of the lamentation priest, until the moon has cleared up the eclipse.

the month Simānu, a ritual procedure of the afternoon (*né-pe-eš-š[ú šá mu-uṣ-ṣú-lal-lu*),[149] and a ritual procedure of the morning (*né-pe-eš-šú šá še-e-ri*)[150] is attested. A ritual procedure of 'Whe[n Anu created Heaven]' (*né-pe-šú šá e-nu-m[a* ^d^*A-nu ib-nu-ú* AN-*e*]), performed by the exorcists and the lamentation priests of Esagila, is recorded in an astronomical diary.[151]

epištu 'ritual act', rarely attested and almost always in the plural (*epšētu*) in Neo-Assyrian texts, is written syllabically, but also DÙ.DÙ and NÍG.DÍM.DÍM.MA. In the Hellenistic ritual texts we have a few examples from the kettledrum ritual.[152] In an astronomical diary it is mentioned together with a Greek festival called *puppē*.[153] The cognate *epuštu*, written DÙ.DÙ.BI, 'the pertinent (lit. its) ritual', i.e the ritual which accompanies the recited incantation or prayer, is not attested in Hellenistic ritual texts.[154]

Several other terms for cult, rite, service, festival etc. are known, which are, however, seldom attested or not at all in Hellenistic ritual texts. One of these terms is *sakkû* 'ritual regulations' (plur. tantum),[155] known from the Old Babylonian period, but also attested in texts from the first millennium B.C. In the Hellenistic ritual texts it is attested only once, in the colophon of *TU* 38 together with several other rites, referring to the ritual regulations of kingship.[156] Another rarely used word is *alaktu* (*alkatu*) '(ritual) activities', attested from the Old Akkadian period on. Like *sakkû* it is only known in the Hellenistic ritual texts from the colophon of *TU* 38, referring to the ritual activities of the exorcists, the lamentation priests, the singers and the craftsmen.[157]

Although the very common term *dullu* 'ritual, divine service, cult' is well-known from the Hellenistic period, for example in legal documents,[158] it is not attested in rituals.[159] Similar in meaning is *šipru* 'work, service'; only two examples from the Hellenistic ritual corpus are attested.[160] *Pelludû* 'cult' is not known from Hellenistic ritual texts, but it is attested in a calendar text from Babylon.[161]

Other terms like *mēsū* (plur. tantum), 'cults, cultic rites, rituals', and *kikkiṭṭû* 'ritual act' are not known from Hellenistic ritual texts. *nāṭu* is only attested in Neo-Assyrian rituals.[162]

---

149 BM 32656 (A.R. George, *Studies W.G. Lambert*, no. 2, 270 ff.), col. IV, 3′, see also 18′, col. V, 6.
150 BM 32656, col. IV, 8′.
151 A.J. Sachs–H. Hunger, *Diaries*, no. 270, B, rev. 16′. It probably belongs to the building ritual, see II.6.2. A 'ritual procedure of the gods' (*né-peš šá* DINGIR.MEŠ) is attested in A.J. Sachs–H. Hunger, *Diaries*, no. 229, B, obv. 6′; cf. also obv. 11′ and rev. 13′.
152 *Bagh. Mitt. Beih.* 2, no. 5, rev. 25 (broken contexts); 31. See perhaps also the parallel *Bagh. Mitt. Beih.* 2, no. 7, l. obv. 5′, written NÍG.DÍM.DÍM.MA, but restored; cf. *KAR* 60, rev. 13; see also rev. 3.
153 A.J. Sachs–H. Hunger, *Diaries*, no. -168, A, obv. 14–15. See II.8.4.
154 See the Neo-Assyrian kettledrum ritual *KAR* 50, rev. 1.
155 Cf. F. Thureau-Dangin, *RA* 11 (1914), 142, n. 5; W. von Soden, *ZA* 45 (1939), 78, n. 3.
156 *TU* 38, rev. 44.
157 Rev. 45–6.
158 See also II.8.7.
159 Cf. G. van Driel, *Cult of Aššur*, 158.
160 W 18828, rev. 3: *ši-pir* DINGIR-*ú-tu* 'service for the gods'; see also rev. 4; the eclipse of the moon ritual BM 134701, rev. 16: *šip-ri šá* ^d^*A-nù* 'the service for Anu'.
161 *SBH* VIII, III, 17.
162 See G. van Driel, *Cult of Aššur*, 158 f. with references.

A general term for 'festival' is *isinnu*, a word which goes back to the Old Babylonian period, and can refer both to a religious and a secular festival. Although a general use of *isinnu* is also known, more often it concerns a special festival identified by the name of a god, a temple or a month.[163] A special case is the festival of the New Year (*isinnu akītu*).[164] In the Hellenistic period *isinnu* is not attested in ritual texts. However, we have two occurrences in other texts, both referring to special festivals. First, in the ritual calendar *SBH* VIII, II, 7; here *isinnu* probably refers to the *akītu*-festival of the first month Nisannu in Babylon.[165] The second reference is recorded in an Arsacid administrative text from Babylon, AB 248,[166] which refers to day 25 of Simānu on which a temple festival of Esabad is celebrated.[167]

Finally we should mention *nigûtu* 'music, festival', not known from Hellenistic ritual texts, but attested in the chronicle texts.[168] From the astronomical diaries we know that it was still used in the Arsacid period.[169]

---

163 Cf. *CAD*, I, 195–7, 1; *AHw*, 388a, with many references.

164 Cf. *CAD*, I, 196, 1, d, 1′; *AHw*, 29a, 4, b and 388a,1, d; B. Landsberger, *Kult. Kalender*, 6 ff.; J. Renger, in: *CRRA* 17 (1970), 75–80; G.J.P. McEwan, *FAOS* 4, 163.

165 See II.4.5.2.

166 Cf. G.J.P. McEwan, *Iraq* 43 (1981), 141 ff.

167 See II.8.1.

168 Chronicle 13b, A.K. Grayson, *Chronicles*, 284, 15. The text will be discussed in II.4.5.2 and II.8.7.

169 A.J. Sachs–H. Hunger, *Diaries*, no. -105, obv. B 16′, 206 S.E. i.e. 142 A.E.; earlier examples are no. -245, B, 5′: for the third month a festival (*nigûtu*) was celebrated in a building whose name is lost (perhaps the palace of Laodike?); no. -158, B, rev. 18′.

II. CEREMONIES, RITUALS AND FESTIVALS

II.1. Introduction

Important elements of the cult are the ceremony, the ritual and the religious festival. A ceremony is a religious custom or rite for the opening or continuation of contact between man and the divine. The ceremony, together with the seasons (with which it was originally closely connected), was the basis for the chronology of the cultic year: the fixed days of the months, on which the ceremonies had to be performed, resulted in a calendar which was based on the cult.

Rituals and festivals consist of a complex of ceremonies, each of which have their own function, combined together to serve a different purpose. In general this purpose consists in averting evil which may threaten an individual or the community, by following a fixed set of rules which describe how humans must serve the gods and in return enjoy a secure and pleasant life.

The Mesopotamians offered mythological explanations for the cultic activities in the ritual texts. According to the Mesopotamians a ritual is often a re-enactment of a myth, because, as Lambert noted, they considered myths not to have happened once in a remote past, but were regarded to occur at regular intervals.[1] It is often difficult for us to assess how the Mesopotamians conceived a ritual to be connected with a particular myth. Sometimes the ritual itself contains an explanation. We also have explanatory texts which 'explain' some of these connections.[2] As Livingstone concluded, because for the Mesopotamians there is no fundamental difference between myth and ritual, the statues and symbols which are used in the temple rituals are in fact the deities which they represent, and the rituals in which they take part are therefore myths. These myths usually deal with struggles between major deities, which are derived from mythological events described in the epics *Enūma eliš* and *Anzû*. People mentioned in the rituals correspond to victorious deities in the myths, while animals or objects correspond to defeated deities or demons.[3]

In texts from Mesopotamia we find no clear definition of a ceremony. We do have an interesting enumeration of several ceremonies from Uruk in *TU* 38, which describes the amount of foodstuffs and drinks which have to be brought into the temples daily.[4]

---

[1] See W.G. Lambert, *JSS* 13 (1968), 104 ff., especially 112. A good example of a ritual explained by a myth is the kettledrum ritual, see II.5.2. For a survey of the history and development of the myth and ritual debate i.e. what came first, the myth or the ritual, see H.S. Versnel, *Transition and reversal in myth and ritual*, Leiden, New York, Köln, 1994[2] (Inconsistencies in Greek and Roman religion II. Studies in Greek and Roman religion, vol. 6, II), chapter I, 15–88.

[2] The explanatory texts explaining temple rituals by equating them with myths are discussed by A. Livingstone, *Mystical*, 115 ff. (chapters 4–6). See also I.2.

[3] *Mystical*, 115 and 169 f.

[4] The text is discussed in III.2.2.

Obv. 35–38 mentions loaves and date cakes which are used for several offerings and ceremonies:

> '35 ... Not included are (also) the large(?) loaves and the date cakes 36which are for the travel provisions of the gods, the *guqqû*-offerings, the *eššēšu*-ceremonies, the opening of the gate ceremonies, the clothing ceremonies, 37the holy water (basin) ceremonies, the night vigil ceremonies, the brazier ceremonies, the rites of the divine marriage, (the offerings of) the *kāribu*s 38and the additional offerings of the king'.

Apart from four groups of general offering gifts,[5] the loaves and date cakes are also intended for several ceremonies listed here: the monthly-celebrated *eššēšu*-ceremonies,[6] the daily-celebrated opening of the gate ceremonies (*pīt bābi*),[7] the monthly-celebrated clothing ceremonies (*lubuštu*),[8] the holy water (basin) ceremonies (*egubbû*), performed during purifications,[9] the monthly-celebrated night vigil ceremonies (*bajjātu*),[10] the brazier ceremonies (*kinūnu*),[11] and the rites of the divine marriage (*ḫašādu*), performed during the New Year festival, but also on other occasions.[12]

The reverse (35–38) mentions oxen and sheep for the same list of offerings and ceremonies (but without the travel provisions of the gods), and then adds (38–39):

> 'which are written down in (the tablets of) the rites (*parṣu*) for the whole year, in the Rēš-temple, the Ešgal-temple, the Eanna-temple and the (other) temples of Tiranna (= Uruk) for Anu, Antu and all the (other) gods'.

The list in these two passages is apparently an attempt to present a complete description of the regularly recurring offerings and ceremonies during the cultic year in Uruk. This is confirmed by the fact that the text refers to the marriage-rites, but not to the New Year festival (*akītu*),[13] nor to any other ritual or festival, which was celebrated only once a year or on special occasions, e.g. the kettledrum ritual or the building ritual.[14] The text mentions the opening of the gate ceremonies, but not the awakening of the temple ceremonies (*dīk bīti*),[15] which may be explained by the close connection between these ceremonies. Note that the night vigil ceremonies are mentioned, but not the closely connected good-functioning of the temple ceremonies (*šalām bīti*).[16] Because the list on the obverse is identical with the one on the reverse (with the exception of the travel

---

[5] The travel provisions of the gods (*ṣidītu ilāni*, see III.2), the monthly *guqqû*-offerings (see III.7.2), the offerings of the *kāribu*s (see III.7.2), and the additional offerings of the king (*tardītu šarri*, see III.2.2 and III.7.2). This part of the list will be discussed in III.1.

[6] See II.3.2.

[7] See II.2.2.

[8] See II.3.3.

[9] See III.6.2.

[10] See II.3.4.

[11] See II.4.6.

[12] See II.4.4.

[13] See II.4.5.

[14] See II.5 and 6.

[15] See II.2.1.

[16] See II.3.6.

provisions of the gods, only mentioned in the former), the possibility of the slovenliness of the writer can be excluded.

Because it is difficult to ascertain any logical schedule in the nature or sequence of the ceremonies in this list,[17] in this chapter another order has been chosen: first we will analyse the group which has a cyclical basis, i.e. which are performed on a daily, monthly or yearly basis,[18] although, as we will see, it is often difficult to determine whether we are dealing with monthly or yearly ceremonies and rituals, or whether they occur only occasionally. Then a few special rituals are discussed: the kettledrum ritual, the building ritual and the eclipse of the moon ritual. Finally we will analyse some festivals about which we know only little: a temple festival celebrated in Esabad, the temple of Gula in Babylon, a so-called palm festival in Esagila, a *ḫarû*-ritual in Esagila, a Greek festival, two special festivals for Ištar of Babylon and Ištar of Uruk respectively, and a nocturnal festival celebrated in the Rēš-temple complex. We will also discuss the so-called Ruler cults.

II.2. Daily ceremonies

The god was represented in the temple by an anthropomorphic statue, and therefore his daily life was taken care of by humans in an anthropomorphic way: ceremonies and rituals concentrated on the daily life in the temple and the meals which were served to the gods. An important element of this daily practice was the divine meal, which will be discussed in chapter III. Furthermore two ceremonies are known which were performed every cultic day in the temples: the *dīk bīti*- and the *pīt bābi*-ceremonies. They will be discussed in this section. But first we must briefly analyse the cultic day.

II.2.1. *The cultic day*

The Babylonian day (*ūmu*) was divided into seasonally varying watches (*maṣṣartu*), three during the day and three during the night, and into twelve unchanging 'double hours' (*bēru*).[19] A normal day began and ended with sunset,[20] between the first and last

[17] According to G.J.P. McEwan, *FAOS* 4, 163, the fact that *kinūnu* follows *bajjātu* in the list indicates that the former took place during the night vigils. However, this could be accidental. Furthermore, it is not likely that the list in *TU* 38 follows a chronological order, since in *TU* 39, obv. 13 it is stated that the *guqqû*-offerings follow the clothing ceremonies (*lubuštu*), whereas in *TU* 38, obv. 36 and rev. 36–37 they are mentioned before the clothing ceremonies.

[18] B. Landsberger, *Kult. Kalender*, 2 ff. for the first time suggested a separate discussion of ceremonies which were celebrated monthly and those which were celebrated yearly.

[19] Cf. R. Borger, *JEOL* 18 (1964), 326–7; D. Pingree, E. Reiner, *AfO* 25 (1974–77), 54 f.; C.B.F. Walker, H. Hunger, *MDOG* 109 (1977), 33–4; M.A. Powell, in: *RlA* 7 (1989), 467 f.; F. N.H. Al Rawi, A.R. George, *AfO* 38–39 (1991–1992), 55, n. 13.

[20] Cf. F. Thureau-Dangin, *Esquisse d'une histoire du système sexagésimal*, Paris, 1932, 43; E.C. Kingsbury, *HUCA* 34 (1963), 18; B.A. Levine, W.W. Hallo, *HUCA* 38 (1967), 47; S. Smith, *Iraq* 31 (1969), 74 ff.

double hour of the day (*bēr ūmi*),[21] when 'the sun (god) stands' (*Šamaš izzaz*) on the horizon.[22] The cultic day however had a different schedule[23]:

- the *dīk bīti* (awakening of the temple)-ceremony
- the *pīt bābi* (opening of the gate)-ceremony
- the serving and clearing of the two meals (*naptanu/tardennu*)[24] in the morning
- the serving and clearing of two meals in the evening
- the closing of the gate

It started at sunrise (*napāḫu ša šamši*),[25] or more precise shortly before sunrise, during the (last) double hour of the night (*bēr mūši*), before the gates of the temple were opened, with the *dīk bīti*-ceremony. The cultic day ended, after the two evening meals were served and cleared, with the closing of the gates. However, the beginning of the second cultic day of the New Year festival, held in the month Nisannu in Babylon, began two hours before dawn, i.e. the last double hour of the night and then began progressively earlier on each succeeding day, the third probably (the text is damaged) 1/3 double hours earlier, the fourth on 2/3 double hours earlier, until finally it began four hours before dawn, i.e. two double hours of the night,[26] either during the middle or during the last night watch (*šāt urri*).[27]

Cultic days, which included a night vigil (*bajjātu*),[28] had a different schedule[29]:

- the *dīk bīti*-ceremony
- the *pīt bābi*-ceremony
- the serving and clearing of the two meals of the morning
- the serving (and clearing)[30] of two meals of the evening

---

[21] See *LKU*, no. 51, obv. 7, 21, 26, rev. 36; *TU* 39, rev. 23 (the time of the main and second meal), see my comments on this line in the Appendix.

[22] See C. Wilcke, in: M. Mindlin, M.J. Geller, J.E. Wansbrough (eds.), *Figurative language in the Ancient Near East*, London, 1987, 91.

[23] See *TU* 39, rev. 15 ff., describing the normal proceedings of day 11 of the New Year festival of Tašrītu in Uruk; at the end of the cultic day there is no mention of the closing of the gate but the text states (rev. 23–4): 'The main and second (meal) of the (last) double hour of the day in the usual manner ditto', referring to the end of day 10 (rev. 14).

[24] See also III.2.1.

[25] Cf. *TU* 38, rev. 31; also in the Uruk night vigil ritual *TU* 41, rev. 28 and the Uruk eclipse of the moon ritual *BRM* 4, 6, rev. 31; see also the kettledrum ritual *KAR* 50, rev. 2 (Neo-Assyrian).

[26] *RAcc.*, 129, 1; 132, 157; 133, 217; 136, 285. Cf. G.J.P. McEwan, *FAOS* 4, 171. See now also the Hellenistic Temple ritual fragment BM 41577 (A.R. George, *Studies W.G. Lambert*, no. 1, 260 ff.), col. III, 23, and perhaps col. II, 14 (also dealing with the month Nisannu).

[27] In Babylon for half the year the night lasts less than 12 hours. This night was still divided into 3 watches, each of less than 4 hours (= 2 *bēru*). If something occurred 2 *bēru* before sunrise then during this half of the year it could not have occurred during the last watch, but during the middle watch. At the equinoxes (when day and night were realy equal to 6 *bēru* each) 2 *bēru* before sunrise is (ideally) at the beginning of the last watch of the night (*šāt urri*). For the *šāt urri*, the third and last watch of the night i.e. the morning watch, see also *TU* 48 (discussed in II.2.2), obv. 18.

[28] See also II.3.4 and II.8.6.

[29] See *TU* 39, rev. 3 ff., describing days 9 and 10 of the New Year festival of Tašrītu in Uruk; the beginning of day 9, with the *dīk bīti-* and the *pīt bābi*-ceremonies and the serving of the first morning meal, is lost.

[30] *TU* 41, obv. 13 informs us that the meal is not cleared, the vigil continues the entire night, and the gate is not closed (that is: not *yet* closed at the beginning of the evening, as on a normal cultic day).

– the night vigil
– the closing of the gate

On the following day:

– the *dīk bīti*-ceremony
– the *pīt bābi*-ceremony
– the end of the night vigil

The vigil (which was the last cultic event of the cultic day) started after the serving and clearing of the two meals of the evening, and ended not when the gate was closed at the end of the night, but on the next day, after the *dīk bīti*- and *pīt bābi*-ceremonies were performed.

In the ritual texts we also find other references to the time of day or night when a certain part of a ritual had to be performed. The New Year text from Babylon mentions cultic activities taking place after 1, 1 1/2, and 1 2/3 double hours of daytime have past (*bēr ūmu išqâ*).[31] In two cases the texts refer to the evening watch i.e. the first watch of the night (*barārītu*).[32] More often, however, the texts are less specific, referring to dawn (*namāru*),[33] to the late afternoon (*ša kīṣ ūmi*, lit. 'that of the cool of the day'),[34] to the evening (*līlâtu*),[35] or to the night (*mūšu*).[36]

II.2.2. *dīk bīti*

The first cultic ceremony of the day was the *dīk bīti* 'awakening of the temple'-ceremony.[37] It was performed during the last night watch, just before the end of the night vigil, before dawn, and before the gates were opened. The ceremony is attested in texts from the Neo-Assyrian and the Hellenistic periods. The function of the ceremony is never explicitly described, but probably the 'awakening' or 'arousing' of the temple refers to both the residents of the temple, the gods, and the priests, who have to wake up the gods to start a new day. The *dīk bīti*-ceremony was probably performed at the beginning of every cultic day, and was not a ceremony for special occasions. Although

---

[31] *RAcc.*, 132, 190 (1 1/2 double hours) for the third day; 140, 338 (1 double hour) and 141, 366 (1 2/3 double hours) for the fifth day.; see my comments on line 190 in the Appendix. For references to the morning (*šēr(t)u*) see the Kislīmu ritual from Babylon, BM 32206 +, II, 55 and the building ritual *TU* 45, obv. 6; 20; rev. 8; 20; *TU* 46, obv. 7; *Bagh. Mitt. Beih.* 2, no. 10, obv. 8; F.H. Weissbach, *Misc.* no. 12, obv. 5.

[32] *TU* 39, obv. 6; *TU* 41, obv. 14.

[33] *TU* 39, rev. 11; 16; *TU* 41, rev. 14; 27.

[34] *RAcc.*, 136, 280.

[35] *TU* 39, rev. 5. For *nubattu* 'vigil, evening', but also 'evening ceremony, evening meal' see II.3.5.

[36] *TU* 39, rev. 10; 15; *TU* 45, obv. 2; rev. 17; *TU* 46, obv. 2; rev. 3; *Bagh. Mitt. Beih.* 2, no. 10, obv. 2; F.H. Weissbach, *Misc.* no. 12, obv. 3.

[37] Usually connected with the verb *šakānu* 'to perform the awakening of the temple ceremony'. Cf. *CAD*, D, 140b, 2; *AHw*, 170a, 3; S. Langdon, *AJSL* 42 (1926–26), 123–4; G. Furlani, *Riti*, 168; G.J.P. McEwan, *FAOS* 4, 161; 169 ff.; B. Pongratz-Leisten, *ina šulmi īrub*, 65, n. 139, which however requires some corrections: *TU* 48 = AO 6467 (not 6457); there are mentioned not two *dīk bīti*-ceremonies but only one on the 24th day of Šabaṭu (K 2724 +, obv. 16–19); the time indication in *TU* 48, obv. 18 does not read *ina uddazallî*, but *ina šāt urri* (EN.NUN.UD.ZAL.LA) 'in the morning watch'; in *TU* 39 the *dīk bīti*-ceremony is attested for days 7 (not 6), 10 and 11 of Tašrītu.

it is not clear how exactly the ceremony was performed, we know that an important element of the ceremony was the reciting of lamentations (*taqribtu* and *eršemakku*) for the most important gods of the pantheon.

Important evidence for the *dīk bīti*-ceremony comes from three texts, which indicate that there was a fixed liturgy involving the *taqribtu*-lamentations for certain days of each month; the purpose of reciting the lamentations was to ensure that any offence (unknowingly) commited against the gods would be neutralized.[38] One text is *TU* 48, a calendar text from Hellenistic Uruk. Very similar to this text are K 2724 +, a calendar text from the Neo-Assyrian period, found in Aššur, and BM 50503, a calendar text from Neo-/Late Babylonian Sippar. All texts concentrate on the lamentation priests only, leaving the activities of other priests aside.[39] We will start with the text from Aššur.

K 2724 +

The Neo-Assyrian text K 2724 + lists lamentations recited to Aššur in the city Assur in the temple of Dagan and in Ešarra (but also lamentations recited to Ninlil (Mullissu), Marduk and Ištar).[40] The lamentations were recited by the lamentation priest. The text apparently began with the month Tašrītu.[41] The preserved portion of the text describes the liturgy from Šabaṭu up to the eleventh day of Nisannu. The relevant passage in K 2724 + reads[42]:

Obv.

7′ … EGIR ^{udu}SÍSKUR
8′ [DIŠ UD.22].KAM UMUN.ŠE.ER.MA.AL.⸢LA AN⸣.KI.A ÉR DILMUN$^{ki!}$ NIGIN.NA
9′ [ÉR].ŠÈM.MA *ana* AN.ŠÁR *ina* É.ŠÁR.RA EGIR-*šú* AN.ŠÁR ZI-*bi*
10′ $^{[d]}$UTU.GIN$_7$ È.TA ÉR Ù.LI.LI EN.ZU SÁ.MAR.MAR
11′ ÉR.ŠÈM.MA *ana* AN.ŠÁR *ina* É ^{d}DA.GAN *di-ik* É
12′ DIŠ UD.23.KAM UR.SAG.GAL ME.NI ŠE.ER.MA.AL.LA ÍL.LA ÉR
13′ AN.NA ZA.E MAḪ.ME.EN ÉR.ŠÈM.MA *ana* AN.ŠÁR *ina* É ^{d}DA.GAN EGIR ^{udu}SISKUR.MEŠ
14′ UD.DAM KI ÀM.MU.ÚS ÉR UMUN.BÁRA.KÙ.GA ÉR.ŠÈM.MA
15′ *a-na* AN.ŠÁR *ina* É ^{d}DA.GAN *di-ik* É
16′ DIŠ UD.24.KAM E.LUM BAR.RA ME.A ÉR NAM.MU.UN.ŠUB.BÉ.EN
17′ ÉR.ŠÈM.MA *ana* AN.ŠÁR *ina* É ^{d}DA.GAN EGIR ^{udu}SÍSKUR
18′ AM.E AMAŠ.A.NA ÉR UR.SAG ABZU.TA ÉR.ŠÈM.MA
19′ *a-na* [A]N.ŠÁR *ina* É ^{d}DA.GAN ⸢*di-ik*⸣ É
20′ [DIŠ UD.25.KAM S]IPA ⸢ZI.DA EDIN.NA.RA⸣ ÉR ALIM.MA UMUN.GÌR.[RA]
21′ [ÉR].ŠÈM.MA *ana* AN.ŠÁR *ina* É ^{d}DA.GAN EGIR ^{udu}SÍS[KUR]

---

[38] Cf. M.E. Cohen, *Eršemma*, 49.

[39] As in the kettledrum ritual and building ritual texts, see II.5.3 and II.6.3.

[40] Probably the ceremony was also performed for the other great gods, since A 485 + (E. Ebeling, *OrNS* 21 (1952), 135–141. Cf. B. Menzel, *Tempel*, no. 28), rev. 19–24 lists the gods who followed Aššur in the temple of Dagan, but without the recitation of lamentations. See also *TU* 48 below.

[41] Cf. M.E. Cohen, *Lamentations*, 22.

[42] The latest edition by St. M. Maul, in: A.R. George, I.L. Finkel, *Studies W.G. Lambert*, Winona Lake, Indiana, 2000, 402 ff.

22′ [A.AB.BA] ḪU.LUḪ.ḪA *šá* dAMAR.UTU ÉR ŠÀ.BA.NI GA.AN.ḪUN ÉR.ŠÈM.-MA *ana* AN.ŠÁR *ina* É dDA.G[AN *di-ik* É][43]

> '7′ ... After the sheep offering 8′[on day 22] "Lord, respected one of Heaven and Earth", the *taqribtu* (and) "Important one, who wanders abound" 9′the *eršemakku* to Aššur in Ešarra. Then Aššur will rise. 10′ "Come out like the sun", the *taqribtu* (and) "O, wise En, designer", 11′the *eršemakku* to Aššur in the temple of Dagan (during) the awakening of the temple ceremony. 12′On day 23 "Great hero, his ME is respected, elavated" the *taqribtu* (and) 13′"In heaven you are exalted", the *eršemakku* to Aššur in the temple of Dagan. After the sheep offerings 14′"It touches the Earth like a storm", the *taqribtu* (and) "Lord of the pure Dais", the *eršemakku* 15′to Aššur in the temple of Dagan (during) the awakening of the temple ceremony. 16′On day 24 "O, honored one, you have become angry", the *taqribtu* (and) "You should not desert me", 17′the *eršemakku* to Aššur in the temple of Dagan. After the sheep offering 18′ "The bull in his fold", the *taqribtu* (and) "The hero from the Apsu", the *eršemakku* 19′to Aššur in the temple of Dagan (during) the awakening of the temple ceremony. 20′[On] day 25 "For the faithful shepherd the Steppe", the *taqribtu* (and) "O, lofty one, migh[ty] lord" 21′[the *erše*]*makku* to Aššur in the temple of Dagan. After the sheep offering 22′"[The] raging [sea]" of Marduk, the *taqribtu* (and) "May it appease his heart", the *eršemakku* to Aššur in the temple of Dagan ⟨(during) the awakening of the temple ceremony⟩'.

Thus, a *dīk bīti*-ceremony is attested for days 22, 23, 24 and ⟨25⟩ of Šabaṭu for Aššur in the the temple of Dagan:

- on day [22] of Šabaṭu: the *taqribtu* UMUN.ŠE.ER.MA.AL.LA AN.KI.A and the *eršemakku* DILMUN NIGIN.NA are recited in Ešarra, and then, after the procession of Aššur from Ešarra to the temple of Dagan, the *taqribtu* [d]UTU.GIN È.TA and the *eršemakku* Ù.LI.LI EN.ZU SÁ.MAR.MAR are recited during the awakening of the temple ceremony;
- on day 23 of Šabaṭu: the *taqribtu* UR.SAG.GAL ME.NI ŠE.ER.MA.AL.LA ÍL.LA and the *eršemakku* AN.NA ZA.E MAḪ.ME.EN are recited. After the sheep offerings the *taqribtu* UD.DAM KI ÀM.MU.ÚS and the *eršemakku* UMUN.BÁRA.KÙ.GA are recited during the awakening of the temple ceremony;
- on day 24 of Šabaṭu: the *taqribtu* E.LUM BAR.RA ME.A and the *eršemakku* NAM.MU.UN.ŠUB.BÉ.EN are recited. After the sheep offering the *taqribtu* AM.E AMAŠ.A.NA and the *eršemakku* UR.SAG ABZU.TA are recited during the awakening of the temple ceremony;
- on day 25 of Šabaṭu: the *taqribtu* S]IPA ZI.DA EDIN.NA.RA and the *eršemakku* ALIM.MA UMUN.GÌR.[RA] are recited. After the sheep offering the *taqribtu* [A.AB.BA] ḪU.LUḪ.ḪA of Marduk and the *eršemakku* ŠÀ.BA.NI GA.AN.ḪUN are recited during the awakening of the temple ceremony.

These *taqribtu*s and *eršemakku*s are recited 'after the sheep offering(s)', as the text states. However, it is nor clear whether the lamentations recited before these offerings,

[43] See the parallels in obv. 11′, 15′, and 19′.

also belong to the *dīk bīti*-ceremony, or form a separate ceremony. The latter is suggested by day 22, where lamentations are recited in two different temples.

BM 50503

This text from Sippar, which was only recently published by Stefan Maul,[44] was according to the latter probably written during the late 8th and late 6th century B.C. It consists of a cultic calendar for Šamas, Aja and Bunene in Ebabbar, with lamentations and ritual instructions for four days: the first day is not indicated, but must be one of the first seven days of the month, since the second day indicated is the 8th, followed by the 15th and the 20th. The first day on which the lamentations were recited is probably day 1, as Stefan Maul convincingly argued.[45] The month during which these cultic activities are performed is the first month of the year (Nisannu), but the last lines of the text make it clear that the instructions also had to be used for the rest of the year.[46]

During these four days *taqribtu*s and *eršemakku*s are to be recited for Šamaš before sunrise, during the *dīk bīti*-ceremony, and before sunset (*lām līlâti*). Here we will concentrate on the lamentations recited during the *dīk bīti*-ceremony[47]:

- on day 1(?!) of every month: the *taqribtu* ABZU PE.EL.LÁ.ÀM, and the *eršemakku* DILMUN NÍGIN.NA;
- on day 8 of every month: the *taqribtu* U_4.DAM KI ÀM.MU.ÚS, and the *eršemakku* UMUN BÁRA KÙ.GA;
- on day 15 of every month: the *taqribtu* AM.E AMAŠ.A.NA, and the *eršemakku* UR.SAG ABZU.TA;
- on day 20 of every month: the *taqribtu* U_4.DÈ U_4.DÈ, and the *eršemakku* UR.SAG UT.U_{18}.LU.

The text presents us with clear evidence that the *dīk bīti*-ceremony was performed before dawn (*ina šēri*).[48]

TU 48

In a liturgical calendar text from Hellenistic Uruk,[49] *TU* 48, we also find a schedule of hymns to be recited with various offerings associated with the *dīk bīti*-ceremony for various days, performed by lamentation priests in the Ubšukkinaku, the central courtyard in the Rēš-complex, in front of the Anu-Antu-temple.[50]

---

[44] In: *Munuscula Mesopotamica. Festschrift für Johannes Renger*, Münster, 1999, 285 ff.

[45] Ib., 302–3.

[46] Ib., 289.

[47] For a discussion of the entire text see Stefan Maul's article.

[48] Obv. 1′–3′, 5′f., 10′f.

[49] The owner of the tablet, Mannu-iqāpu, son of Anu-iqīšanni of the family Sîn-lēqe-unninni is, as far as I know, not attested elsewhere. The colophon refers to him as 'apprentice lamentation priest', indicating that the text belongs to the corpus of the Lamentation priest. The text was probably found in the Rēš-temple area, along with other *TU*-texts, see I.2.

[50] Note that the activities of the lamentation priest in Uruk, as described in *TU* 48, are referred to in another Uruk text from an earlier date, *LKU*, no. 51 (see I.2), which not only describes offerings and ceremonies

II.2. Daily ceremonies

Several *taqribtu*s are listed on the obverse. The accompanying *eršemakku*s are not mentioned, but they were probably also recited together with their *taqribtus*.[51] In obv. 18 ff. the text lists lamentations recited during the *dīk bīti*-ceremony:

Obv.

1 UD.1.KAM *šá* ITI.TA.ÀM ABZU PE.É.LÁ.ÀM[52]
2 *a-na* ^{d}*A-nu* UD.2.KAM *šá* ITI.TA.ÀM
3 ÚRU ÀM.ME.ER.RA.BI[53] *ina še-rì ina* UGU *šu-uḫ-ḫu*
4 *a-na* ^{d}INNIN UD.7.KAM ÚRU A.ŠE.ER.RA[54] *rid*(?)*-da-ti*(?)
5 *ma-al-ṭi-ti sa-ra-qu a-na* ^{d}*A-nu*
6 IM.MA.AL GÙ.DÉ.DÉ[55] *a-na* ^{d}INNIN UNUG^{ki}
7 A.ŠE.ER.GIN$_7$ È.TA *a-na* ^{d}*Na-na-a*
8 UD.1.KAM *šá* ^{iti}BÁRA *ina* UGU *rak-su* E.LUM GU$_4$.SÚN[56]
9 *a-na* ^{d}*A-nu* UD.2.KAM UD.15.KAM *šá* ^{iti}BÁRA
10 A.AB.BA ḪU.LUḪ.ḪA[57] *ina še-rì ma-al-ṭi-ti*
11 *sa-ra-qa a-na* ^{d}*A-nu* UD.15.KAM *šá bi-ru-u*
12 *ina muḫ-ḫi šu-uḫ-ḫu* É.TÚR(?).GIN$_7$ NIGIN.NA.A[58] *a-na* ^{d}*A-nu*
13 UD.20.KAM *ina* UGU *šu-uḫ-ḫu* AM.ME AMAŠ.A.NA[59]
14 AL.GÙ *a-na* ^{d}*A-nu it-ti* ^{túg}*lu-bu-šú*.MEŠ
15 ABZU PE.É.LÁ.ÀM *a-na* ^{d}*A-nu*
16 ÚRU A.ŠE.ER.RA ME.NA KÚŠ.Ù
17 *a-na* ^{d}GAŠAN *šá* UNUG^{ki}
18 UD.1.KAM *šá* ITI.TA.ÀM *ina* EN.NUN.UD.ZAL.LA
19 *ina* UGU *ana*(?) *šub*(?)*-lam-mi*(?) ^{d}UTU.GIN$_7$ È.TA[60]

Rev.

1 *di-ki* É *a-na* ^{d}*A-nu u* E.LUM DI.DI.RA[61]
2 *a-na* DINGIR.DIDLI GE$_6$ GAR *šá* UD.7.KAM
3 UD.DAM KI ÀM.MU.ÚS$^{!}$ (copy: KU)[62] *di-ki* É *ana* ^{d}*A-nu*

---

for every month of the year, but on one occasion also points out that the lamentation priests and the singers have to perform 'like in every month' (obv. 21, cf. St. M. Maul, in: *Munuscula Mesopotamica. Festschrift für Johannes Renger*, Münster, 1999, 291, n. 29). See also II.5.3.

51 Cf. M.E. Cohen, *Eršemma*, 50.

52 Also in obv. 15. See M.E. Cohen, *Lamentations*, 47 ff.

53 See M.E. Cohen, *Lamentations*, 536 ff.

54 See M.E. Cohen, *Lamentations*, 65 ff.

55 See also M.E. Cohen, *Lamentations*, 604 ff. A Late Babylonian duplicate is *SpTU* 4, no. 125.

56 Also in the Uruk description of the night vigil, *TU* 41, rev. 31, and the Babylon Kislīmu ritual BM 32206 +, IV, 162. See M.E. Cohen, *Lamentations*, 272 ff.

57 Also in rev. 9. See M.E. Cohen, *Lamentations*, 374 ff.

58 Also in the eclipse of the moon ritual *BRM* 4, 6, rev. [53] and the duplicate BM 134701, obv. 14. See M.E. Cohen, *Lamentations*, 73 ff.

59 Also in rev. 5, and in the Uruk New Year text *TU* 39, rev. 15, the Uruk eclipse text *BRM* 4, 6, rev. 48, 49, 51, 52, and the duplicate BM 134701, obv. 7, 9, 11, 13. See M.E. Cohen, *Lamentations*, 152 ff.

60 Also in the Uruk building ritual text *TU* 45, obv. 5, and parallels *TU* 46, obv. 6; *Bagh. Mitt. Beih.* 2, no. 10, obv. 7. See M.E. Cohen, *Lamentations*, 95 ff. (cf. also 519 ff., *aḫû*).

61 Also in the Uruk New Year text *TU* 39, rev. 15. See M.E. Cohen, *Lamentations*, 175 ff.

62 Also in the Uruk building ritual *TU* 46, rev. 5, the *mīs pî*-ritual text *Bagh. Mitt. Beih.* 2, no. 1 (+ //), 9, and in the Kislīmu ritual from Babylon, BM 32206 +, IV, 158. See M.E. Cohen, *Lamentations*, 120 ff.

4 E.NE.ÈM.A.NI I.LU[63] UD ME LU(?) *ana* DINGIR.DIDLI
5 MI.GAR UD.15.KAM AM.ME AMAŠ.A.NA *di-ki* É
6 *a-na* ^{d}*A-nu u* AN E.LUM.MA[64] *ana* DINGIR.DIDLI
7 UD.14.KAM ⟨*šá* ^{iti}APIN⟩ AB.GIN$_7$ GÙ.DÉ.DÉ[65] ⟨*di-ki* É⟩ *ana* ^{d}GAŠAN *šá* UNUG^{ki}
8 ÚRU.ḪUL.ÀM.KE$_4$[66] *a-na* ^{d}*Na-na-a*
9 UD.18.KAM *šá* ^{iti}APIN A.AB.BA ḪU.LUḪ.ḪA
10 *a-na* ^{d}*A-nu si-it-ti* NU SAR

> 'Obv. ^{1}On day 1 of each month "The defiled Apsu" ^{2}to Anu. On day 2 of each month ^{3}"That city which has been pillaged!" in the morning over the *šuḫḫu*-stand ^{4}to Ištar. On day 7 "The city in sighing" … ^{5}the sprinkling of a *malṭītu* for Anu. ^{6}"The lowing cow" to Ištar of Uruk. ^{7}"Come out like a wail" to Nanāja. ^{8}On day 1 of Nisannu, over the offering accoutrements "Honored one, wild ox" ^{9}to Anu. On day 2 (and) 15 of Nisannu ^{10}"The raging sea". In the morning the sprinkling of a *malṭītu* ^{11}for Anu. On day 15 during the (first) double hour, ^{12}over the *šuḫḫu*-stand "The house is encircled like a cattle pen" to Anu. ^{13}On day 20 over the *šuḫḫu*-stand ^{14}they will recite ^{13}"The bull in his fold" ^{14}to Anu with the clothing ceremonies, ^{15}"The defiled Apsu" to Anu, ^{16}"The city in sighing, when will there be peace?" ^{17}to Bēlet-ša-Uruk. ^{18}On day 1 of each month, in the morning watch, ^{19}over the … "Come out like the sun" rev.^{1}(during) the awakening of the temple ceremony for Anu, and "The honored one who wanders about" ^{2}to the gods of the night will be performed. On day 7 ^{3}"It touches the Earth like a storm" (during) the awakening of the temple ceremony to Anu. ^{4}"His word is a wail!" … to the gods (of the night?) ^{5}will be performed. On day 15 "The bull in his fold" (during) the awakening of the temple ceremony ^{6}for Anu, and "The honored one of heaven" to the gods (of the night?). ^{7}On day 14 ⟨of Araḫsamna⟩ "Lowing like a cow" (during) ⟨the awakening of the temple ceremony⟩ to Bēlet-ša-Uruk, ^{8}"She of the ruined city" to Nanāja. ^{9}On day 18 of Araḫsamna "The raging sea" ^{10}to Anu. The rest is not written'.

The text lists *taqribtu*-lamentations for the 1st/2nd, 7th, 14th/15th and 20th days of every month, as well as special yearly lamentations during the months Nisannu and Araḫsamna. The text describes two cycles.

First, in cycle A, *taqribtu*-lamentations are listed for the 1st, 2nd, 7th, 15th and 20th days of every month, and also for the 1st, 2nd and 15th of Nisannu:

cycle A (obv. 1–17):

- every month on the 1st day: ABZU PE.É.LÁ.ÀM to Anu.
- every month on the 2nd day: ÚRU ÀM.ME.ER.RA.BI to Ištar
- every month on the 7th day: ÚRU A.ŠE.ER.RA to Anu
- every month on the 7th day: IM.MA.AL GÙ.DÉ.DÉ to Ištar-Uruk
- every month on the 7th day: A.ŠE.ER.GIN$_7$ È.TA to Nanāja

---

[63] After the incipit UD.ME.LU directly follows, while IV R^{2}, 53, I, 43 reads E.NE.ÈM.MÀ.A.NI I.LU I.LU; probably UD.ME.LU does not belong to the incipit (perhaps Akkadian 'the day of ME.LU'?). See M.E. Cohen, *Lamentations*, 186 ff.

[64] Also in *TU* 39, rev. 10, in *BRM* 4, 6, rev.[51] and [53] and the duplicate BM 134701, obv. 11 and 13. See M.E. Cohen, *Lamentations*, 208 ff. (see also ib., p. 25, n. 62).

[65] See M.E. Cohen, *Lamentations*, 533 ff.

[66] Also in K 2724 +, obv. 29; cf. M.E. Cohen, *Lamentations*, 650 ff.

3 special recitations:

- on the 1st of Nisannu: E.LUM GU$_4$.SÚN to Anu
- on the 2nd of Nisannu: A.AB.BA ḪU.LUḪ.ḪA to Anu
- on the 15th of Nisannu: A.AB.BA ḪU.LUḪ.ḪA to Anu
- every month on the 15th day: É.TÚR(?).GIN$_7$ NIGIN.NA.A to Anu
- every month on the 20th day: AM.ME AMAŠ.A.NA to Anu
- every month on the 20th day: ABZU PE.É.LÁ.ÀM to Anu
- every month on the 20th day: ÚRU A.ŠE.ER.RA ME.NA KÚŠ.Ù to Bēlet-ša-Uruk (= Ištar)

Furthermore, in cycle B, the lamentation priests had to perform, during the *dīk bīti*-ceremony, *taqribtu*-lamentations for the 1st, 7th, 15th and (20th) of every month, as well as special yearly recitations on the 14th and 18th of the month Araḫsamna; this was done 'in the morning watch' (*ina šāt urri*), as the text specifically states for day 1 (obv. 18), but most likely this also applies to days 7, 15 and (20):

cycle B (obv. 18-rev. 10):

- every month on the 1st day: ^{d}UTU.GIN$_7$ È.TA to Anu
- every month on the 1st day: E.LUM DI.DI.RA to the gods (of the night?)
- every month on the 7th day: UD.DAM KI ÀM.MU.ÚS to Anu
- every month on the 7th day: E.NE.ÈM.A.NI I.LU to the gods (of the night?)
- every month on the 15th day: AM.ME AMAŠ.A.NA to Anu
- every month on the 15th day: AN E.LUM.MA to the gods (of the night?)

3 special recitations:

- on the 14th day (of Araḫsamna): AB.GIN$_7$ GÙ.DÉ.DÉ to Bēlet-ša-Uruk (= Ištar)
- on the 14th day (of Araḫsamna): ÚRU.ḪUL.ÀM.KE$_4$ to Nanāja
- on the 18th day of Araḫsamna: A.AB.BA ḪU.LUḪ.ḪA to Anu.
- (every month on the 20th day).[67]

After day 1, 7 and 15, we go back to day 14, apparently of Araḫsamna, as in rev. 9. Rev. 7–8 refers neither to the *dīk bīti*-ceremony nor to the month Araḫsamna, but the text is not without mistakes. The text gives in chronological order the days on which the *taqribtu*-lamentations had to be recited every month, interrupted by lamentations on special days: first, in obv. 1–17, day 1, 2 and 7 of every month, followed by day 1, 2 and 15 of Nisannu; then picking up the chronological order with day 15 and 20 of every month. Secondly, in obv. 18-rev. 10 (during the *dīk bīti*-ceremony), day 1, 7 and 15 of every month, followed by day 14 and 18 of Araḫsamna; then picking up the chronological order with day 20, which however is not written since the text is

[67] G.J.P. McEwan (*FAOS* 4, 172, n. 404) already noted that, since the text says it is not complete (rev. 10), is it likely that the original tablet contained a separate entry concerning the lamentations performed during the *dīk bīti*-ceremony for the 20th of each month.

incomplete. Two lamentations on the 14th of every month after one lamentation on the 15th is not likely. First of all it would contradict the chronology of the whole text. Also, if the 14th and 15th were alternative days, one would expect Anu (the most important god of Hellenistic Uruk) to be celebrated first, and so the 14th would be dedicated to Anu, and the 15th to Ištar; compare the other alternative days in obv. 1–4, where the 1st day is dedicated to Anu, the 2nd to Ištar. Therefore the two lamentations on the 14th are probably special lamentations for Araḫsamna, together with the following lamentation on the 18th (rev. 9).

However, because in the text there is no reference to Araḫsamna, McEwan considered day 14 to refer to every month.[68] He suggested that the second day for every month in cycle A, dedicated to Ištar, is an alternative day for the 1st day, dedicated to Anu, and the 14th day in cycle B, dedicated to Ištar, referring to every month, is an alternative day for the 15th, dedicated to Anu. All the other days refer to both gods at the same time. Based on this he deduced a different cultic pattern for the Rēš-temple of Anu and Antu, and the Ešgal-temple of Ištar and Nanāja: (a) *taqribtu*-lamentations to Anu in the Rēš-temple on days 1, 7, 15 and 20, and to Ištar in the Ešgal-temple on days 2, 7, 15 and 20. (b): *taqribtu*-lamentations during the *dīk bīti*-ceremony to Anu in the Rēš-temple on days 1, 7, 15 and (20), and to Ištar in the Ešgal-temple on days 1, 7, 14 and (20).

We must conclude that, since day 14 is not an alternative day for day 15, the two cultic patterns of Anu in the Rēš-temple and Ištar (and Nanāja) in the Ešgal-temple differ from each other on only one day, the 1st/2nd.

McEwan identifies the four monthly festivals in *TU* 48, celebrated on the 1st/2nd, 7th, 15th and 20th days, with the monthly recurring clothing ceremony (*lubuštu*) and the often connected *ḫitpu*-offerings.[69] His first argument is that *TU* 48, obv. 14 refers to *lubuštu*. Unfortunately the data for the days on which *lubuštu* is celebrated in the Neo-Babylonian and Hellenistic periods do not exactly match the days of *TU* 48.[70] Furthermore, McEwan argues, we know that the *ḫitpu*-offerings in the Neo-Babylonian period were made on four regular recurring days, for which also alternative days are attested. But again, these days also do not exactly match the days mentioned in *TU* 48.[71] However, we must keep in mind that, apart from *TU* 48, we have only one more dated reference to *lubuštu* from the Hellenistic period; from the Neo-Babylonian period we have more, but we cannot exclude the possibility that major changes concerning *lubuštu* may have occured after the Neo-Babylonian period. So, although McEwan may be right, the only certain reference in *TU* 48 to *lubuštu* is the one on day 20 of every month (obv. 14). Whether the other days refer to *lubuštu* cannot (for now) be established with certainty.

Comparing the three texts, we find that *TU* 48 is in many ways very similar to K 2724 + and BM 50503:

---

68 Although he also noted the 'generally laconic nature of the text', cf. *FAOS* 4, 172–3, with n. 405.
69 *FAOS* 4, 173.
70 For the data of *lubuštu* see II.3.3.
71 For the data of *ḫitpu* see II.3.3.

1. *TU* 48, BM 50503 and K 2724 + deal with all the months, although the Assur-text only mentions the months Šabaṭu, Addaru and Nisannu. The latter text is not complete, however. Apparently the Assur- and Sippar-texts have a different cult schedule for every month, while the Uruk-text uses one month as the model for the entire year; the days referred to in BM 50503 (1[?!]–8–15–20) and *TU* 48 (1–7–15–20) are similar, but not completely identical. The *dīk bīti*-ceremony is used in both K 2724 + and *TU* 48 with the *taqribtu*-lamentations ^{d}UTU.GIN$_7$ È.TA,[72] UD.DAM KI ÀM.MU.ÚS[73] and AM.E/ME AMAŠ.A.NA,[74] although for different days. Furthermore, *TU* 48 has the same *taqribtu* for the first day of every month as BM 50503, ABZU PE.EL.LÁ.ÀM,[75] but in the latter text not during the *dīk bīti*-ceremony (here instead ^{d}UTU.GIN$_7$ È.TA), while the *taqribtu*s for days 8 and 15 in the BM-text (U$_4$.DAM KI ÀM.MU.ÚS and AM.E AMAŠ.A.NA) are performed in *TU* 48 during the *dīk bīti*-ceremony on days 7 and 15.[76] Interestingly enough we have other texts, for instance the building rituals *TU* 45 and 46,[77] which enumerate lamentations, but do not mention the specific days and month on which they had to be recited; they only state: 'in an auspicious month, on a favourable day' (*ina* ITI *šal-mu ina* UD ŠE.GA).

2. Two *taqribtu*-lamentations, which are attested in *TU* 48 (rev. 1 and 6), are also mentioned in the New Year ritual *TU* 39 from Uruk. In this text the *dīk bīti*-ceremony is attested for 3 days of the month Tašrītu, although we must assume that the *dīk bīti*-ceremony was performed every cultic day. The first seven days of the New Year festival are presented in a very abbreviated version, with only one remark on day 6 (*TU* 39, obv. 6) and a few short remarks on day 7 (obv. 7–15), including a reference to the *dīk bīti*-ceremony (obv. 7); it was performed by the lamentation priests (as in *TU* 48), but no lamentation incipits are enumerated. In the same line the cook (*nuḫatimmu*) is also mentioned; although he is not referred to as one of the performers of the ceremony, it may indicate that, similar to the *pīt bābi*-ceremony (see below), foodstuffs were used during the ceremony (*TU* 39, obv. 7–10):

> '[7]Day 7: the awakening of the temple ceremony (performed) by the lamentation priests and the singers. (As to) the cook: food and songs of jubilation, [8]roasted meat, beef and mutton for the regular offerings, all sorts of fine beer, [9]including drawn wine and milk, date confection, fine mixed beer and *labku*-mixed beer, [10]*tirimtu*-cups(?), *dannu*- and *namḫaru*-vats (shaped like) raven(?) for Papsukkal and Guškinbanda'.

Days 8 to 11 are described extensively. Although the beginning of day 8 is preserved (*TU* 39, obv. 16 ff.) and the *pīt bābi*-ceremony is mentioned, the *dīk bīti*-ceremony is, strangely, not referred to here. The beginning of day 9 is lost. The *dīk bīti* ceremony is also mentioned for the last two days of the festival: on day 10 the *dīk bīti*-ceremony is performed by reciting the *taqribtu*-lamentations UMUN ŠE.ER.MA.AL AN.KI.A

---

[72] K 2724 +, obv. 10, *TU* 48, obv. 19.
[73] K 2724 +, obv. 14, *TU* 48, rev. 3.
[74] K 2724 +, obv. 18, *TU* 48, rev. 5.
[75] *TU* 48, obv. 1; BM 50503, obv. 1′.
[76] BM 50503, obv. 5′ and 9′; *TU* 48, rev. 3 and 5.
[77] See II.6.

and AN E.LU$_4$.UM.MA (*TU* 39, rev. 10–11). The latter is also attested in *TU* 48 (rev. 6) for the 15th day of every month. On day 11 the *dīk bīti*-ceremony is performed by reciting AM.E AMAŠ.AN.NA and E.LUM DI.DI.RA (*TU* 39, rev. 15–16). The latter is also attested in *TU* 48 (rev. 1) for the first day of every month. For day 10 and 11 the moment when the ceremony was performed is further indicated by *ina mūši* 'in the night'; for these days the text also records that the ceremony takes place shortly before the *pīt bābi*-ceremony. This agrees with *TU* 48, where (as we already noted above) the lamentations were recited 'in the morning watch' (obv. 18).

As Cohen noted, because on days 10 and 11 of the New Year festival an assembly of the gods took place, in which the fate for next year was determined, the recitation of the *taqribtu*s and their *eršemakku*s in order to appease the anger of the gods was of great importance.[78]

Table I: *dīk bīti*-ceremonies from Hellenistic Uruk

day	month(s)	text
7	VII	*TU* 39, obv. 7
[9]	[VII]	*TU* 40, obv.
10	VII	*TU* 39, rev. 11
11	VII	*TU* 39, rev. 16
1	I/XII	*TU* 48, rev. 1
7	I/XII	*TU* 48, rev. 3
15	I/XII	*TU* 48, rev. 5
14	⟨VIII⟩	*TU* 48, rev. 7
(20)	I/XII	*TU* 48

II.2.3. *pīt bābi*

The *pīt bābi* 'opening of the gate'-ceremony is known from the Old Babylonian period on.[79] Although it remains unclear how exactly the ceremony was performed, we know that the ceremony took place just before dawn in the temples, after the *dīk bīti*-ceremony and together they formed the beginning of all cultic activities inaugurating the new day. We must assume that the *pīt bābi*-ceremony (just like the *dīk bīti*-ceremony) was performed on every cultic day of the year. It was probably not a ceremony for special occasions, nor was its first aim to let the people enter the temple on the occasion of a feast, as suggested by Landsberger[80] and Weidner,[81] but rather the opening of the gate(s) indicates the time in the morning when all the priests and craftsmen who had to perform their usual duties in the temple (*ērib bīti*) were allowed to enter the temple.

---

[78] *Eršemma*, 50.

[79] See B. Landsberger, *Kult. Kalender*, 3–4, 87, 112; G. Furlani, *Riti*, 121; E. Weidner, *GDBT*, 25, n. 97; G.J.P. McEwan, *FAOS* 4, 165–6. Cf. also *bābu* in *CAD*, B, 20a, b', and *AHw*, 95a, 1; *petû* in id., 859a, 1, a and *pītu* in id., 871a, 1.

[80] *Kult. Kalender*, 3–4, 87, 112.

[81] *GDBT*, 25, n. 97.

From the pre-Hellenistic periods we have a few references to the day(s) on which the ceremony was performed: a sheep is slaughtered on the 11th before Sîn for the *pīt bābi*-ceremony in *KAJ* 199.[82] The ceremony is celebrated on the 4th of Ulūlu in the letters *LAS* I, no. 285,[83] and *ABL* 496,[84] and on the 4th, 5th and 6th of Ulūlu in *LAS* I, no. 287.[85] The fourth month Du'ūzu is identified as the 'month of the opening of the gate' (*araḫ pīt bābi*).[86]

Uruk

For the Hellenistic period *pīt bābi* is attested in several ritual texts from Uruk. The gate referred to in texts from Uruk is the *bābu ša Anu u Antu*, i.e. the gate of the Anu-Antu-temple in the Rēš-complex.[87] In *TU* 38 *pīt bābi* is one of the ceremonies enumerated in the list of ceremonies.[88] This text also informs us that loaves and date cakes and oxen and sheep are used during the ceremony.[89] In the ritual text *TU* 39–40 we have attestations of *pīt bābi*-ceremonies for the 8th, 10th and 11th days of the month Tašrītu.[90] The beginning of day 9, probably with the *pīt bābi*-ceremony, is lost. As we already saw in the previous paragraph, the first seven days are presented in an abbreviated form. Although the *dīk bīti*-ceremony is mentioned for the 7th day, the *pīt bābi*-ceremony is not referred to here. The *pīt bābi*-ceremony is also known from *TU* 41, describing special ceremonies during the vigil held during the night of the 16th and 17th of Ṭebētu(?).[91] When the night was over, after all the necessary ceremonies were performed, the gate was opened and the vigil ended.[92] In *BRM* 4, 6, the *pīt bābi*-ceremony is performed on the day after the eclipse of the moon.[93]

The *pīt bābi*-ceremony is also known from other texts from Hellenistic Uruk. In two calendar texts (VAT 7816 and 7815[94]) the *pīt bābi*-ceremony is attested for days 4, 6 and 7 of Nisannu,[95] and for days 4, 5 and 30 of Kislīmu.[96]

---

[82] Obv. 3.
[83] A, 7'.
[84] Obv. 10.
[85] Rev. 3–5. Cf. S. Parpola, *LAS* II, 187.
[86] See S. Langdon, *Menologies*, 44 sub 3 with text references.
[87] Cf. A. Falkenstein, *Topographie*, 24. Also referred to as: *bābu ina pani Anu u Antu* (*TU* 39, obv. 16, *TU* 41, rev. 28); *bābu ša Anu* (*BRM* 2, 3, obv. 3–4: KÁ *šá* ᵈLX *ù* KÁ *né-re-bi* 'the Gate of Anu and the entrance gate'; *nērebu* is the KÁ.MAḪ 'Grand Gate', the entrance gate of the Rēš-complex, cf. A. Falkenstein *Topographie*, 10); *bābu rabû* (KÁ.GAL) 'Great Gate' (*VS* 15, 48, obv. 3 and 4: É *mu-ter-tu₄ šá* KÁ.GAL-*ú* [*šá* ᵈLX] 'the portico of the Great Gate [of Anu]', also in *VS* 15, 36, obv. 4 and W 521, I, 2, see A. Falkenstein, *Topographie*, 14); or simply *bābu* (*TU* 39, rev. 11).
[88] Obv. 36, rev. 36. See II.1.
[89] Obv. 35, rev. 36.
[90] *TU* 39, obv. 16; rev. 11, 16.
[91] See I.2.
[92] Rev. 28–9.
[93] Rev. 31.
[94] See E. Weidner, *GDBT*, 41 ff. and 45 ff.
[95] VAT 7816, obv. 11, 17 and 21.
[96] VAT 7815, obv. 8, 11 and rev. 8.

In a legal document (a sale of *ērib bītūtu*- and *ṭābiḫūtu*-prebend shares) from Uruk, J. Oppert, J. Ménant, *Doc. jur.*, no. 5 (BM 93004),[97] we perhaps have a reference to the *pīt bābi*-ceremony (obv. 13), but the reading is not certain:

Obv.

11 … GIŠ.ŠUB.BA-*šú šá qa-a-a-i-tu*$_4$

12 *šá* 6 NINDA *tak-ka-su-ú u šá*[98] Ì.GIŠ 30 *as-né-e u* GIŠ.KUN *šá* UDU.NÍTA *ina* UD.13.KAM SA.SAL

13 *šá* BAD KÁ(?)[99] *šá a-na* ^{giš}BANŠUR *šá* ^{d}LX *u An-tu*$_4$ E$_{11}$-*ú* …

'[11] … her prebend (i.e. Rubuttu's, who sells the prebends) of parched barley, [12]of the 6 *takkasû*-pastries and of the oil, 30 Dilmun dates and a thigh piece of a sheep on day 13, (together with) the back(?) portion [13]of the *pīt bābi*-ceremony(?), which are brought up to the table of Anu and Antu (monthly) …'

If this reading is correct, then apparently part of the income of the *ērib bītūtu*- and *ṭābiḫūtu*-prebend consisted of foodstuffs, which were also used as offerings during, and therefore associated with, the *pīt bābi*-ceremony. This is quite possible, since the foodstuffs which are mentioned here remind us of the date cakes and oxen and sheep, used for (amongst others) the *pīt bābi*-ceremony mentioned in *TU* 38.

Finally, the *pīt bābi*-ceremony is also attested in an astrological text from Hellenistic Uruk, which concerns the zodiacal system.[100] From the twelve signs of the zodiac eight signs (Leo, Virgo, Libra, Scorpius, Aries, Taurus, Gemini, and Cancer) are associated with the opening of the gate ceremonies of various gods. See the following schedule:

Leo (Abu)	*pīt bābi*	Enlil
Virgo (Ulūlu)	*pīt bābi*	Sîn, Ištar
Libra (Tašrītu)	*pīt bābi*	Sîn, Šamaš, Ištar, Anu, Enlil, Ea, Ningirsu
Scorpius (Araḫsamna)	*pīt bābi*	Allatu, Nergal
Sagittarius (Kislīmu)	*pīt bābi*	Pabilsag, Ninurta
Aries (Nisannu)	*pīt bābi*	Marduk, Ninurta
Taurus (Ajjaru)	*pīt bābi*	Ninurta
Gemini (Simānu)	*pīt bābi*	Sîn, Šamaš, Nergal
Cancer (Du'ūzu)	*pīt bābi*	Šamaš, Šulpae

However, Weidner pointed out that instead of referring to the twelve months of the year, the cultic instructions may also refer to the twelve parts of the month, of 2 1/2 days each.[101]

---

[97] See also II.3.1.

[98] Following G.J.P. McEwan, *FAOS* 4, 77, contra L.T. Doty, *CAHU*, 412 and B. Funck, *Uruk zur Seleukidenzeit*, 162, who read: 10 NINDA.Ì.GIŠ '10 oil-breads'.

[99] While L.T. Doty (*CAHU*, 413) and B. Funck (*Uruk zur Seleukidenzeit*, 162) both read 'BAD EDIN(?)', G.J.P. McEwan (*FAOS* 4, 77), who was the last to collate the text, suggested BAD KÁ.

[100] *TU* 12, obv., second row; the sign-names on ib., rev., row three. Cf. E. Weidner, *GDBT*, 24–26 ('Reihe B'). For the reconstruction of the text see ib., 20–21.

[101] *GDBT*, 26.

Table II: *pīt bābi*-ceremonies from Hellenistic Uruk

day	month(s)	place	text
4	I	Uruk	VAT 7816, obv. 11
6	I	Uruk	VAT 7816, obv. 17
7	I	Uruk	VAT 7816, obv. 21
8	VII	Uruk	*TU* 39, obv.16
[9]	[VII]	Uruk	*TU* 40, obv.
10	VII	Uruk	*TU* 39, rev. 11
11	VII	Uruk	*TU* 39, rev. 16
4	IX	Uruk	VAT 7815, obv. 8, 14-X-120 (Antiochus)
5	IX	Uruk	VAT 7815, obv. 11, 14-X-120 (Antiochus)
30	IX	Uruk	VAT 7815, rev. 8, 14-X-120 (Antiochus)
17	X(?)	Uruk	*TU* 41, rev. 28
–	I/XII	Uruk	*TU* 12, obv., second row
–	–	Uruk	*TU* 38, obv. 36, rev. 36
–	–	Uruk	*BRM* 4, 6, rev. 31
(?)	–	Uruk	J. Oppert, J. Ménant, *Doc. jur.*, no. 5, obv. 13, 151–161 (Demetrius)

Babylon

We only have a few references to the ceremony from Babylon. In the New Year text (*Racc.*, 127 ff.), on days 2, 3, 4 and 5 of the month Nisannu, the high priest washes himself, says a prayer to Bēl, and then performs the opening of the gate ceremony (written: ^{giš}IG.MEŠ BAD-*te*) in Esagila.[102] Further on in the same text, on day 5, the *pīt bābi*-ceremony is referred to immediately after the *eššēšu*-ceremony, in a only partly preserved speech of the high priest to the king.[103] Finally, the ritual text BM 32206 + mentions at the beginning of the second column for the fourth day of the month Kislīmu the *pīt bābi*-ceremony, performed probably by the high priest.[104] Note that 2 days attested in Babylon, day 4 of Nisannu and day 4 of Kislīmu, are also known in Uruk.

Table III: *pīt bābi*-ceremonies from Hellenistic Babylon

day	month(s)	place	text
2	I	Babylon	*Racc.*, 130, 37
3	I	Babylon	*Racc.*, 132, 184
4	I	Babylon	*Racc.*, 136, 276
5	I	Babylon	*Racc.*, 140, 334; 145, 440
4	IX	Babylon	BM 32206 +, II, 55

102 *RAcc.*, 130, 37 (restored); 132, 184; 136, 276; 140, 334.
103 *RAcc.*, 145, 440.
104 G. Çağirgan, W.G. Lambert, *JCS* 43–45 (1991–1993), 95, II, 55.

II.3. Monthly ceremonies

The twelve months of the Babylonian year lasted 29 or 30 days each and they began with the first sighting of the crescent of the new moon in the evening.[105] During every month special ceremonies were celebrated which were connected with certain fixed days of the month. See for example *TU* 38, which refers to a purification, the cleansing of the hands ceremony (*tēbibtu qāti*)[106]: it was celebrated every month (*arḫussu*) on day 16 for Anu and Antu, exactly as was a special yearly celebrated ceremony on day 16 of the tenth month Ṭebētu (rev. 32–34, see the Appendix):

> '[32]On day 16, monthly, [34](the priest) will offer [32]10 first-quality sheep, fat (and) pure, whose horns and hooves are perfect, [33]for Anu and Antu of Heaven and the 7 planets, as cooked meat, on occasion of [34]the cleansing of the hands ceremony (*te-bi-ib-tu*$_4$ ŠU^{II}), in the Baramaḫ on the temple tower of Anu, just like on day 16 of Ṭebētu'.

Some monthly ceremonies are only identified by the name(s) of the god(s) for which the ceremony is celebrated. Other monthly ceremonies which are attested in the texts are specifically named (*eššēšu*, *lubuštu*, *bajjātu*, *nubattu*, *šalām bīti*); it is usually not specifically stated that they were performed monthly and the days are also often not mentioned in the Hellenistic period.[107] However, as we shall see, it is clear from texts of earlier periods and from the context in which they appear that they were monthly ceremonies. Also, we have an indication that a regular pattern of days used for cult activities was in practice in Hellenistic Babylon: an astronomical diary states that on days 1, 3, 7, 15, and 16 of the twelfth month Addaru a ritual procedure (*nēpešu*) was performed, for which *maḫḫuru*-offerings were presented (*maḫ-ḫu-ru un-daḫ-ḫi-ru*).[108] On the obverse of the tablet the eleventh month is discussed, and here we find a ritual procedure of the gods (*né-peš šá* DINGIR.MEŠ), for which *maḫḫuru*-offerings are also presented; the passage continues with a reference to the chief singer of dirges, who recites(?) *eršaḫungû*-tablets. Whether these two ritual procedures are identical is difficult to say, because of the damaged state of the passages. Nevertheless, the days mentioned here remind us of the days attested for the monthly ceremonies discussed here; although the name of the ritual procedure is lost, one of the above-named monthly ceremonies seems a likely candidate.

We will begin this section by describing the known unspecified monthly ceremonies and then turn our attention to the monthly celebrated ceremonies which are known by a specific name: *eššēšu*, *lubuštu*, *bajjātu*, *nubattu*, *šalām bīti*.

---

105 See P.-A. Beaulieu, *ZA* 83 (1993), 66 ff.

106 See III.6.3.

107 Cf. G.J.P. McEwan, *FAOS* 4, 171 ff.

108 A.J. Sachs–H. Hunger, *Diaries*, no. -229, B, rev. 13′. The *maḫḫuru*-offering is discussed in III.7.2.

II.3. Monthly ceremonies

II.3.1. *Unspecified monthly ceremonies*

Most of the unspecified monthly ceremonies come from legal documents concerning prebend shares.[109] Several unnamed monthly ceremonies for Anu, Antu, Enlil, Ištar, Nanāja, Bēlet-ša-Rēš, Bēlet-māti, Bēlet-ṣēri, Papsukkal, and also for the statues of the kings, are attested in the Hellenistic prebend texts from Uruk. The reference to the monthly recurring character of a ceremony is presented in several different ways, which we will illustrate with a few examples.[110]

1. A ceremony can be referred to without a date or any other further specification. In *OECT* 9, 42,[111] obv. 12, before two annual ceremonies for Papsukkal and Antu,[112] a monthly ceremony for Enlil and Ištar is mentioned, but no reference is made to the monthly recurring character of this ceremony, and a specific day is also not indicated:

10 3[0(?)]-*ʾ-ú ina* GIŠ.ŠUB.BA ^{lú}KU$_4$ É *pi-riš-tu$_4$-ú-tú u* ^{lú}KÙ.[DIM]-*ú-tú* MU.MEŠ
11 *ina* UDU.NÍTA.MEŠ *šá ḫi-it-pi*.MEŠ *šá* ^{túg}*lu-bu-uš-tu$_4$-a-tú*.MEŠ *ina* UZU *b*[*a-á*]*š-lu*
12 [*u*] *ina* UZU *ba-al-ṭu šá* UDU.NÍTA.MEŠ *šá a-na* ^{giš}BANŠUR *šá* ^{d}EN.LÍL *u* ^{d}INNIN E$_{11}$-*ú*
13 *ina* GU$_4^{ḫá}$ MUŠEN^{ḫá} *u* UDU.SILA$_4$ *šá ina* UD.17.KAM *šá* ^{iti}DU$_6$ *a-na* ^{giš}BANŠUR *šá* ^{d}PAP.SUKKAL
14 E$_{11}$-*ú ina* GU$_4$$^{⟨há⟩}$ MUŠEN$^{⟨há⟩}$ *u* UDU.SILA$_4$ *šá ina* UD.8.KAM *šá* ^{iti}ŠE *a-na* ^{giš}BANŠUR *šá An-tu$_4$*
15 E$_{11}$-*ú*

'[10]one-thirtieth of these *ērib bīt pirištūtu*- and *kutimmūtu*-prebends [11]in the sheep of the *ḫitpu*-offerings of the clothing ceremonies, in the cooked [12]and raw mutton, which are brought up to the table of Enlil and Ištar (monthly), [13]in the beef, birds and lamb, which [14]are brought up [13]to the table of Papsukkal (once a year) on day 17 of Tašrītu, [14]in the beef, birds and lamb, which [15]are brought up [14]to the table of Antu (once a year) on the day 8 of Addaru, ...'.

2. In *OECT* 9, 45, obv. 10 // 46, obv. 9,[113] before two annual ceremonies for Papsukkal and Antu, a monthly ceremony for Enlil is celebrated, this time on the monthly recurring *eššēšu*-days[114]:

9 ... *ina* UZU *ba-áš-lu ù ina* UZU *bal-ṭu šá* UDU.NÍTA
10 *šá ina* UD.ÈŠ.ÈŠ.MEŠ *a-na* ^{giš}BANŠUR *šá* ^{d}EN.LÍL E$_{11}$-*ú ina* UZU GU$_4$
11 UDU.NÍTA MUŠEN *ù* UDU.SILA$_4$ *ù šá qa-ʾ-i-tu$_4$ šá ina* UD.17.[KAM]

---

[109] I.e. income shares in one of the crafts or offices exercised in the temple for service of a deity. Most legal documents concerning prebend shares are from Uruk, see L.T. Doty, *CAHU*, 119–138; G.J.P. McEwan, *FAOS* 4, 67–120; B. Funck, *Uruk zur Seleukidenzeit,* 56–277. So far no prebend documents from Babylon are known, but we do have two deeds concerning bakers' prebends from Nippur, see R.J. van der Spek, in: Maria de Jong-Ellis (ed.), *Nippur at the Centennial*, 250–260.

[110] For a complete list see the Table at the end of this sub-paragraph.

[111] 14 [+x]-XI-?, Seleucus.

[112] For the unnamed annual ceremonies see II.4.1.

[113] 21-VIII-111, Antiochus (III).

[114] The *eššēšu*-ceremony is discussed below in paragraph II.3.2.

12 *šá* ^{iti}DU$_{6}$ *a-na* ^{giš}BANŠUR *šá* ^{d}PAP.SUKKAL E$_{11}$-*ú ina* UZU *šá* GU$_{4}$ UDU.NÍTA
13 MUŠEN$^{!}$ UDU.SILA$_{4}$ *šá qa-ʾ-i-tu*$_{4}$ *šá ina* UD.8.KAM *šá* ^{iti}[ŠE] *a-na*
14 ^{giš}BANŠUR [*šá*] *An-tu*$_{4}$ E$_{11}$-*ú* ...

'^{9} ... (his portion) in the cooked and raw mutton ^{10}which on the *eššēšu*-days is brought up to the table of Enlil (monthly), (his portion) in the beef, ^{11}mutton, bird and lamb and (his portion) of parched barley, which (once a year) on day 17 ^{12}of Tašrītu are brought up to the table of Papsukkal, (his portion) in the beef, mutton, ^{13}birds, lamb (and his portion) of parched barley which (once a year) ^{14}are brought up to the table of Antu ^{13}on day 8 of [Addaru], ^{14} ...'.

3. Sometimes a text specifically states that the ceremony is celebrated *arḫussu* 'monthly'. In *OECT* 9, 68,[115] obv. 3–6, after a monthly ceremony for Enlil celebrated on the *eššēšu*-days, a monthly celebrated ceremony for Ištar is mentioned, followed by an annual ceremony for Antu:

3 ... *ina* UDU.[NÍTA(?)]
4 [x x *ina*(?) UD.ÈŠ.] ÈŠ.MEŠ *a-na* ^{giš}BANŠUR *šá* ^{d}EN.LÍL E$_{11}$-*ú ina* UZU *šá* UDU.[NÍTA(?)]
5 *šá* ITI-*us-su a-na* ^{giš}BANŠUR *šá* ^{d}[*Iš*]-*tar* E$_{11}$-*ú* ḪA.LA-*šú ina* UZU *šá* [...]
6 MUŠEN^{ḫá} [*šá*] *ina* UD.8.KAM *šá* ^{iti}ŠE *a-na* ^{giš}BANŠUR *šá An-tu*$_{4}$ E$_{11}$-*ú* ...

'^{3} ...(his portion) in the mut[ton(?)] ^{4} ... on(?) the *eššēšu*-days is brought up to the table of Enlil (monthly), (his portion) in the mut[ton(?)] ^{5}which is brought up to the table of Ištar monthly, his share of the [...] meat ^{6}(and) birds which are brought up to the table of Antu on day 8 of Addaru, ...'.

4. A text sometimes not only states that the ceremony is celebrated monthly (*arḫussu*), but also mentions the specific day. In *BRM* 2, 36,[116] obv. 2–5, a ceremony for Anu on day 27 of each month is recorded, together with a ceremony for the statues of the kings on day 27 of each month:

2 GIŠ.ŠUB.BA-*šú šá qa-a-a-tu*$_{4}$ *šá* É ^{I}NÍG.SUM.MU-^{d}INNIN ^{uzu}GIŠ.KUN *šá* UDU.NÍTA ^{uzu}*kar-šú* ^{u}[^{zu}...]
3 ... 30 *as-né-e šá ina* UD.27.KAM *šá* ITI-*us-su a-na* BANŠUR *šá* ^{d}LX E$_{11}$-[*ú*] [GIŠ.ŠUB.BA-*šú* (?)]
4 *šá qa-a-a-ut-tu*$_{4}$ *šá* É ^{I}NÍG.SUM.MU-^{d}INNIN *šá ina* UD.27.KAM *šá* ITI-*us-su a-na* ^{giš}BAN[ŠUR]
5 *šá ṣa-lam* LUGAL.MEŠ E$_{11}$-*ú* ...

'^{2}his prebend of parched barley from the house of Nidintu-Ištar, thigh piece of a sheep, stomach and [...] ^{3} ... 30 Dilmun-dates, which on day 27, monthly, are brought up to the table of Anu, [his prebend(?)] ^{4}of parched barley of the house of Nidintu-Ištar, which on day 27, monthly, ^{5}is brought up ^{4}to the table ^{5}of the statues of the kings, ...'.

---

115 Date lost.
116 12-III-131, Seleucus (IV).

5. Finally, the specific reference to the monthly character of the ceremony (*arḫussu*) can be left out, while the day of the month is mentioned. In J. Oppert, J. Ménant, *Doc. jur.*, no. 5 (BM 93004),[117] several monthly ceremonies (always without *arḫussu*) for different deities and one for the statues of the kings are mentioned. After a monthly ceremony for Bēlet-māti, and another for Anu and Antu (obv. 9–13[118]), and before a monthly ceremony for Nanāja on the *eššēšu*-days, and another for the statues of the kings on the *eššēšu*-days (obv. 17–19), two monthly ceremonies are mentioned for Bēlet-ṣēri on day 4 and for Papsukkal and Bēlet-ṣēri on day 13, and furthermore a monthly ceremony for Ištar on day 3 (obv. 13–17):

13 … GIŠ.ŠUB.BA-*šú* 1-*en* UZU *ba-áš-lu u bal-ṭu*
14 TA UDU.NÍTA *šá ina* UD.4.KAM (erasure) *a-na* ^{giš}BANŠUR *šá* ^{d}GAŠAN.EDIN E$_{11}$-*ú* GIŠ.ŠUB.BA-*šú šá* UZU *ba-áš-lu*
15 *u bal-ṭu* TA UDU.NÍTA.MEŠ *šá ina* UD.13.KAM *a-na* ^{giš}BANŠUR *šá* ^{d}PAP.SUKKAL *u* ^{d}GAŠAN.EDIN E$_{11}$-*ú*
16 PAP 3 *ḫa-an-zi-šú-nu šá* UZU^{há} MU.MEŠ GIŠ.ŠUB.BA-*šú mi-šil ina* ^{uzu}ÚR TA UDU.SILA$_4$
17 *šá ina* UD.3.KAM *šá a-na* ^{giš}BANŠUR *šá* ^{d}INNIN E$_{11}$-*ú* …

'^{13} … her prebend of one cut of cooked or raw meat ^{14}from the sheep, which on day 4 is brought up to the table of Bēlet-ṣēri (monthly) – her prebend of one cut of cooked ^{15}or raw meat from the sheep, which on day 13 is brought up to the table of Papsukkal and Bēlet-ṣēri (monthly): ^{16}total three fifths of them, (i.e.) of these cuts of meat – her prebend of one half in a thigh from a lamb ^{17}which on day 3 is brought up to the table of Ištar (monthly) …'.

Table IV: unnamed monthly ceremonies in prebend texts from Hellenistic Uruk

day(s)	god(dess)	text	date
–	[Anu]	*BiMes* 24, no. 2	23-III-108 (Antiochus [III])
eššēšu	Enlil	*OECT* 9, 45 // 46	21-VIII-111 (Antiochus [III])
eššēšu	Enlil, Bēlet-ša-Rēš	*OECT* 9, 50	28-?-128 (Seleucus [IV])
27 *arḫussu*	Anu	*BRM* 2, 36	12-III-131 (Seleucus [IV])
27 *arḫussu*	statues of the kings	*BRM* 2, 36	12-III-131 (Seleucus [IV])
eššēšu	Enlil, Ištar, Bēlet-ša-Rēš	*OECT* 9, 60	10-IV-153 (Demetrius [I])
–	Bēlet-māti	J. Oppert, J. Ménant, *Doc. jur.*, no. 5	(Demetrius)
–	Anu, Antu	*Doc. jur.*, no. 5	(Demetrius)
4	Bēlet-ṣēri	*Doc. jur.*, no. 5	(Demetrius)
13	Papsukkal, Bēlet-ṣēri	*Doc. jur.*, no. 5	(Demetrius)

[117] Date lost, Demetrius.
[118] For obv. 11–13, see also II.2.3.

day(s)	god(dess)	text	date
3	Ištar	*Doc. jur.*, no. 5	(Demetrius)
eššēšu	Nanāja	*Doc. jur.*, no. 5	(Demetrius)
eššēšu	statues of the kings	*Doc. jur.*, no. 5	(Demetrius)
–	Anu	*BiMes* 24, 5	?-XI-? (Seleucus)
6	Anu	*BiMes* 24, 17	?-V-?
–	Enlil, Ištar	*OECT* 9, 42	14 +?-XI-? (Seleucus)
–	Enlil	*OECT* 9, 44	6-VII-? (Antiochus)
–	Ištar	*OECT* 9, 44	6-VII-? (Antiochus)
eššēšu	Enlil	*OECT* 9, 68	–
arḫussu	Ištar	*OECT* 9, 68	–
eššēšu	Enlil(?)	*VS* 15, 37	7-VII-107 Arsaces (A.E. = 171 S.E.)[119]
8 *arḫussu*	Enlil(?)	*VS* 15, 37	7-VII-107 Arsaces
8	–	*VS* 15, 37	7-VII-107 Arsaces
eššēšu	Enlil	*VS* 15, 37	7-VII-107 Arsaces
8 *arḫussu*	Ištar	*VS* 15, 37	7-VII-107 Arsaces
8	Antu	*VS* 15, 37	7-VII-107 Arsaces

When we examine these texts, we find that many are documents concerning *ērib bīt pirištūtu- + kutimmūtu*-prebend shares (i.e. concerning the office of the person authorized to enter the secret room, and the goldsmith's craft).[120] These prebends are connected because, as Doty noted,[121] the goldsmith (*kutimmu*) was responsible for making, cleaning and repairing the ornaments on the garments of the statues of the gods, which were stored in the *bīt pirišti*, only accessible to the temple enterers (*ērib bīti*), and here we find the reason why many of the unnamed monthly ceremonies are attested in documents concerning *ērib bīt pirištūtu- + kutimmūtu*-prebend shares: the income for these prebends comes not only from unnamed monthly ceremonies, from a few annual ceremonies, and the monthly *eššēšu*-ceremonies, but also from the monthly clothing ceremonies (*lubuštu*).

In all the texts the foodstuffs which are served on the offering table, and serve as income for the prebend holders, primarily consist of meat of ox and sheep, with the exception of J. Oppert, J. Ménant, *Doc. jur.*, no. 5 (BM 93004), which also mentions lamb and duck, and furthermore records parched barley, *takkasû*-pastries, oil, and Dilmun dates. Interestingly fowl is not mentioned, although it is attested for the unnamed annual ceremonies.[122]

Many of the texts also mention the *eššēšu*-ceremony, discussed below: we find that the unnamed monthly ceremonies do not refer to a specific day, when they are celebrated on an *eššēšu*-day. When they are not celebrated on an *eššēšu*-day, then the specific day is mentioned. Thus, in *VS* 15, 37, six ceremonies are mentioned, of which four are dated

---

[119] Cf. S. Sherwin-White, A. Kuhrt, *From Samarkhand to Sardis*, 224.

[120] *OECT* 9, 42, 44, 45 // 46, 50, 60, 68 and *VS* 15, 37. J. Oppert, J. Ménant, *Doc. jur.*, no. 5 contains a sale of *ērib bītūtu + tābiḫūtu*-prebend shares; *BRM* 2, 36, *BiMes* 24, 5, and 17 concern not further specified prebend shares.

[121] *CAHU*, 126 f.; id., in: M. E. Cohen, D.C. Snell, D.B. Weisberg (eds.), *The Tablet and the Scroll. Near Eastern Studies in Honor of William W. Hallo*, Bethesda, 1993, 87–89.

[122] See II.4.1.

to a specific day, while the other two are celebrated on *eššēšu*-days. *BRM* 2, 36 only dates two ceremonies to specific days. J. Oppert, J. Ménant, *Doc. jur.*, no. 5 (BM 93004) dates five ceremonies to specific days, and two to the *eššēšu*-days.

II.3.2. *eššēšu*

eššēšu (written (UD) ÈŠ.ÈŠ) is a ceremony with a long history.[123] It is attested from the Ur III period up to the Hellenistic period.[124] ÈŠ.ÈŠ is according to Jacobsen best translated 'all temple' (ÈŠ = temple) or '"general" festival' rather than 'monthly festival' and in the Ur III period it was celebrated in all the temples.[125] The ceremony was held on days 1, 7 and 15 of each month, corresponding to the phases of the moon.[126] Between the Ur III and Old Babylonian periods, in texts from Ur, the number is raised to 4 by adding day 25. Because this day cannot easely be connected with a phase of the moon, from this moment on the *eššēšu*-days were apparently no longer linked to lunar phases.[127] In the Middle Babylonian period the days were changed to days 4, 8 and 17 of each month.

The Neo-Babylonian period

While in Assyria an *eššēšu*-day as a ceremony is not attested,[128] in the Neo-Babylonian period, especially in texts from Uruk, up to 11 days per month are connected with *eššēšu*, but they almost never mention the specific dates of these days. We will give two examples. The first is *GC* 1, 209,[129] a statement of honey used on *eššēšu*-days:

Obv.

1 8 NINDA^{há} LÀL^{há} *šá* [*gu-u*]*q*(?)-*qu*
2 *šá* 8 UD.ÈŠ.ÈŠ.MEŠ *šá*
3 ^{iti}GAN ^{I}DÚG.GA-IM-É.AN.NA
4 6 NINDA^{há} *ina* UD.ÈŠ.ÈŠ.ME
5 *šá* ^{kaš}*na-a-ši*
6 ^{I}*Kal-ba-a* A ^{I}ŠU GIŠ

'³Ṭāb-šār-Eanna ⁶has brought ¹8 *akalu* honey of the [*gu*]*qqû*-offerings(?) ²for 8 *eššēšu*-festivals of ³the (ninth) month Kislīmu ⁶(and) Kalba, son of Gimillu, ⁴6 *akalu* for the *eššēšu*-festivals ⁵for (making) *nāšu*-beer'.

---

[123] Cf. B. Landsberger, *Kult. Kalender*, 111 ff. (see also 109 ff. and 94 ff.) with older literature; F. Blome, *Opfermaterie*, 56–58, 61, 257, 322; G. Furlani, *Riti*, 24, 51, 105, 121, 124; D. Cocquerillat, *WdO* 7 (1973–74), 110, n. 15; W.W. Hallo, *HUCA* 48 (1977), 8. See also *CAD*, E, 373b.

[124] *CAD*, E, 371–3, and *AHw*, 258.

[125] Th. Jacobsen, *The Treasures of Darkness: A history of Mesopotamian Religion*, New Haven and London, 1976, 97 and 122.

[126] Cf. N. Schneider, *Or. NS* 18 (1925), 39 f.; Th. Jacobsen, *Treasures*, 122; W. Sallaberger, *Der kultische Kalender der Ur III-Zeit*, Berlin, New York, 1993, 41, 56–58.

[127] Cf. B.A. Levine, W.W. Hallo, *HUCA* 38 (1967), 45–6; W.W. Hallo, *HUCA* 48 (1977), 7–8.

[128] Cf. G. van Driel, *Cult of Aššur*, 167.

[129] 2-IX-40, Nbk.

Another example is *GC* 1, 289,[130] a receipt for honey used on *eššēšu*-days of the month Kislīmu:

1 15 1/2 NINDA^{ḫá} LÀL^{ḫá}
2 *ina* UD.ÈŠ.ÈŠ.MEŠ *šá* ^{iti}GAN
3 *šá qu-lu-pu* ^{I}*Li-ši-ru*
4 A ^{Id}AG-SUR-ZI.ME GIŠ
5 3 NINDA^{ḫá} *ina* LÀL^{ḫá}
6 *šá mut-ta-qu* ^{I}DÙ-*ia* GIŠ

> '[3]Lišīru, [4]son of Nabû-ēṭir-napšāti has brought [1]15 1/2 *akalu* honey [2]for the *eššēšu*-festivals of the (ninth) month Kislīmu [3]for (making) *qullupu*-cakes [6](and) Banīja has brought [5]3 *akalu* honey [6]for (making) *muttāqu*-cakes'.

Table V: *eššēšu*-ceremonies from Neo-Babylonian Uruk and Babylon[131]

number of *eššēšu*-days	date of *eššēšu*-days	place	text	date
1	–	Uruk	*YOS* 17, 182	23-II-17 (Nbk)
8	IX	Uruk	*YOS* 17, 175	1-IX-17 (Nbk)
1	X	Uruk	*YOS* 17, 175	1-IX-17 (Nbk)
1	VI	Uruk	*YOS* 17, 173	1-VI-18 (Nbk)
3[132]	IX	Uruk	*YOS* 17, 174	19-VIII-13 (Nbk)
8	IX	Uruk	*BIN* 2, 129	15-VIII-19 (Nbk)
4	X	Uruk	*BIN* 2, 129	15-VIII-19 (Nbk)
4	XI	Uruk	*BIN* 2, 129	15-VIII-19 (Nbk)
plur.	IX	Uruk	*GC* 1, 48	1-IX-22 (Nbk)
4	–	Uruk	*GC* 1, 83	3-XI-23(?) (Nbk)
7	VII–VIII	Uruk	*GC* 1, 193	30-VII-34 (Nbk)
7	–	Uruk	*GC* 1, 193	30-VII-34 (Nbk)
7	–	Uruk	*GC* 1, 162	2-VI-36 (Nbk)
8	IX	Uruk	*GC* 1, 209	2-IX-40 (Nbk)
plur.	–	Uruk	*GC* 1, 209	2-IX-40 (Nbk)
4	–	Uruk	*GC* 1, 127	2-XI-40 (Nbk)
4 1/2	IX	Uruk	*GC 1*, 199	7-IX-40(?) (Nbk)
5	–	Uruk	*GC 1*, 199	7-IX-40(?) (Nbk)
rēḫit	IX	Uruk	*GC 1*, 199	7-IX-40(?) (Nbk)
4	–	Uruk	*BIN* 1, 170	7-VI-3 (Nrgl)
4	–	Uruk	*YOS* 6, 39	5-X-3 (Nbn)
1	–	Uruk	*YOS* 6, 39	5-X-3 (Nbn)
5	IX	Uruk	C.S. Knopf, Hewett *AV*,[133] pl. 25 A	8-IX-4 (Nbn)

[130] 7-IX-7, Nbn.
[131] The list is not complete.
[132] Obv. 1–3 read: 1 BÁN ŠE.GIŠ.Ì *a-na mut-ta-qu šá* 3 U[D.ÈŠ.È]Š.ME *šá* ^{iti}GAN ...
[133] C.S. Knopf, in: *Seventieth Anniversary Volume Honoring Edgar Lee Hewett*, Albuquerque, N.M., 1939.

number of *eššēšu*-days	date of *eššēšu*-days	place	text	date
plur.	IX	Uruk	*GC* 1, 289	7-IX-7 (Nbn)
1	–	Uruk	*YOS* 6, 170	23-X-11 (Nbn)
7	–	Uruk	*YOS* 7, 52	24-IV-6 (Cyr)
2	–	Uruk	*YOS* 7, 52	24-IV-6 (Cyr)
11	–	Uruk	*SWU*, 2	–
4	–	Uruk	*SWU*, 2	–
10	–	Uruk	*SWU*, 27	–
7	–	Uruk	*SWU*, 32[134]	–
7	–	Uruk	*SWU*, 45[135]	–
2	–	Uruk	*SWU*, 62[136]	–
11	–	Uruk	*SWU*, 118	–
x] + 6(?)	–	Uruk	*SWU*, 118	–
6(?)	–	Uruk	*SWU*, 125	–
4	–	Uruk	*AUWE* 5, 80	–
1	–	Uruk	*AUWE* 5, 80	–
–	day 20	Uruk	*TCL* 9, 134	–
–	–	Uruk	*YOS* 3, 51	–
11	[X(?)]	Uruk[137]	*TCL* 13, 233	–
9	–	Uruk	*TCL* 13, 233	–
3(?)[138]	–	Babylon	*Mesopotamia* 10–11 (1975–76), 33	?-II-1 (Dar)
–	–	Babylon	J. MacGinnis, *AfO* 38–39 (1991-92), 89[139]	–
5	III	Babylon[140]	*VS* 6, 268	–

The texts usually record the foodstuffs (often also with the endproducts of these foodstuffs) used for the *eššēšu*-ceremonies: honey,[141] oil,[142] Dilmun dates,[143] Dilmun

134 = *AnOr.* 9, 23.

135 = *AnOr.* 9, 22.

136 = *AnOr.* 9, 21 and 29.

137 Uruk as the place of origin not certain.

138 ⌜*a-na*(?)⌝ 3 ÈŠ.ÈŠ.ME *šá na-a-šú* 'for 3 *eššēšu*-days for (making) *nāšu*-beer', rather than Owen's reading [UD.]3 ÈŠ.ÈŠ.ME NINDA *na-a-šú* 'bread given out for the *essšēšu*-festivals of the 3rd day'? Incidently, the damaged beginning of obv. 1 probably reads: [...] ⌜gišPÈŠ!⌝.UD.A (= *uribtu*(?) 'dried figs'), rather than Owen's reading [GIŠ.ḪAŠḪUR].UD.A (*sippirû*/*ḫašḫūru ablu*(?) 'dried apples').

139 = F.E. Peiser, *BV*, 107.

140 Place of origin not Sippar (cf. A. Ungnad, *VS* 6, p. XII, III, no. I, where a survey of texts belonging to the Sippar collection is given) but Babylon, cf. l. 1: d*Iš-ḫa-r*[*a* ...].

141 *GC* 1, 199 (for making *nāšu*-beer); 127; 209 (*nāšu*-beer); 162 (*nāšu*-beer); 193 (*muttāqu*-cake/*nāšu*-beer); 83 (*nāšu*-beer); 289 (*qullupu*-cake); C.S. Knopf, *Hewett AV*, pl. 25 A (*nāšu*-beer/*qullupu*-cake).

142 *GC* 1, 48.

143 *YOS* 7, 52; *YOS* 6, 170 (*mirsu*-confection); *YOS* 17, 173 (*nāšu*-beer); *SWU*, 2 (*muttāqu*-cake).

dates and raisins,[144] Dilmun dates, dried figs and raisins,[145] dried figs and raisins,[146] emmer,[147] sesame,[148] barley,[149] and meat.[150]

In four texts from the Neo-Babylonian period we find that the *eššēšu*-ceremony is connected with other ceremonies and offerings. In J. MacGinnis, *AfO* 38–39 (1991–92), 89 it is connected with the *bajjātu*-[151] and *šalām bīti*-ceremonies,[152] and with the *ginû*-, *guqqû*-, *niqê šarri*-, and *niqê kāribi*-offerings,[153] in *BIN* 2, 129 with the *lubuštu*-, *nabrû*- and *bajjātu*-ceremonies,[154] in *VS* 6, 268 also with the *šalām bīti*- and *bajjātu*-ceremonies, and in *GC* 1, 199 with the *kinūnu*-ceremony.[155] The connection between the *eššēšu*- and the *šalām bīti*-ceremony is clear from a Neo-Assyrian letter (*LAS* I, 280, rev. 16–18), where the regular offerings (*ginû*) are presented, and incense is poured onto a censer on the *eššēšu*-day (and?) at the *šalām bīti*-ceremony.

Although we must assume that the *eššēšu*-ceremony was performed during every month of the year,[156] only the months IV and VII/XI are attested in Uruk, and month III in Babylon, which, however, is not surprising considering the small number of texts that we have. The number of *eššēšu*-days, however, from one to eleven, is astonishing, because in the earlier periods we know of only three or four. Were these ceremonies celebrated for more than one god? Or is the month mentioned in the given text only the first month for the *eššēšu* in question? This does not seem very likely. There is another possibility: if, for example, we concentrate on the receipts of honey,[157] we see that these texts have as their central topic not the *eššēšu*-ceremonies. The ceremonies are mentioned only as secondary information, necessary to describe the amount of the relevant foodstuff, needed for a certain month. So perhaps we should re-translate the relevant section as: 'PN has brought x honey (to the amount) of x *eššēšu*-offerings (usually brought in) month x'.

Because the actual days are almost never recorded (only the letter *TCL* 9, 134 refers to day 20), it remains unclear whether the same days from earlier periods were used or not. One must assume that these days were well-known, and mentioning them was not considered necessary. In any case, it becomes clear that, especially in Neo-Babylonian Uruk, *eššēšu* was still a very frequently and regularly performed monthly ceremony.

---

144 *YOS* 6, 39 (*qullupu*-cake); *AUWE* 5, 80 ([*qullupu*-cake]).
145 *YOS* 6, 39 (*nāšu*-beer); *AUWE* 5, 80 ([*nāšu*-beer]); *BIN* 1, 170 (*nāšu*-beer).
146 *Mesopotamia* 10–11 (1975–76), 33 (*nāšu*-beer?).
147 *YOS* 17, 182.
148 *YOS* 17, 175 (*muttāqu*-cake); 174 (*muttāqu*-cake); *BIN* 2, 129; *TCL* 13, 233 (*qullupu*-cake/*muttāqu*-cake).
149 *SWU*, 2; 27; 32(?) (*nāšu*-beer); 45 (*n*[*āšu*-beer]); 62; 118 (*kuluttu*(?)); 125(?).
150 *VS* 6, 268; J. MacGinnis, *AfO* 38–39 (1991–92), 89 (oxen and sheep); *TCL* 9, 134 (birds). See also *CT* 22, 46 (ox), and BM 74620 (Bertin 2112) (sheep), both from Sippar.
151 See II.3.4.
152 See II.3.6.
153 See III.7.2.
154 For *lubuštu* see II.3.3. The *nabrû*-ceremony is not attested in texts from the Hellenistic period. Cf. M.E. Cohen, *Cultic Calendars*, 394–5.
155 See III.5.
156 The Sippar letter BM 74620 states that the ceremony was *ša kal šatti* 'for the whole year', which, however, does not mean that the ceremony was celebrated every month; compare the data on the clothing ceremonies (*lubuštu*) in Sippar (see II.3.3), which were performed during 6 months of the year.
157 *GC* 1, 83; 127; 162; 193; 199; 209; 289.

The Hellenistic period

For the Hellenistic period the *eššēšu*-ceremony is well attested, especially in texts from Uruk.[158] However, the texts do not provide us with complete information because, as in the Neo-Babylonian period, they never record the specific dates for the *eššēšu*-days, again probably because they were well-known. This is confirmed by our list of unnamed monthly ceremonies from Hellenistic Uruk, discussed above, which are not specifically dated when they are celebrated on an *eššēšu*-day. If the days from earlier periods were also used in the Hellenistic period, then we must, for example assume that the *šalām bīti*- and *bajjātu*-ceremonies, performed during the night of the sixteenth in Uruk, and described in *TU* 41,[159] were followed by an *eššēšu*-ceremony on day 17, since this was an *eššēšu*-day in earlier periods.

In prebend texts from Hellenistic Uruk the *eššēšu*-ceremony is attested many times, often mentioned as a pair with the *guqqû*-offerings, using the phrase:

> *šá* ITI-*us-su kal* MU.AN.NA *gu-uq-qa-né-e* UD.ÈŠ.ÈŠ.MEŠ
> 'monthly for the whole year, the *guqqû*- and *eššēšu*-offerings'.[160]

The commodities used for these ceremonies served substantially to provide an income for the prebend holders. However, the composition of these commodities is almost never described. Fortunately we have four prebend sales, which present us with some information. In chronological order, the first text is *OECT* 9, 50, obv. 8–9[161]:

> 8 … *mi-šil ina* 12-*'u-ú ina* UZU *ba-šal u bal-ṭu šá* UDU.NÍTA.MEŠ
> 9 *šá ina* UD ÈŠ.ÈŠ.MEŠ *gab-bi a-na* ^gišBANŠUR *šá* ^dEN.LÍL *u* ^dGAŠAN-*šá*-É.SAG E_{11}.MEŠ
>
> '[8]One half in one twelfth in the cooked or raw meat from the sheep [9]which is brought up to the table of Enlil and Bēlet-ša-Rēš on all the *eššēšu*-days'.

The second is J. Oppert, J. Ménant, *Doc. jur.*, no. 5 (BM 93004), obv. 17–19[162]:

---

158 Cf. G.J.P. McEwan, *FAOS* 4, 162.
159 This text is discussed in II.8.6.
160 *BRM* 2, 4, 3 (*še-šá-an-na*); 8, 6; 11, 6 (*še-šá-an-na*); 12, 3 (*eš-šá-an-na*); 13, 4; 15, 4; 16, 5; 19, 6; 22, 4; 29, 6; 40, 8; 46, 8; 47, 9; 55, 6.
K. Kessler, *BaM* 15 (1984), 273–81, W 18586, 6.
OECT 9, 8, 4; 14, 4; 15, 5; 19, 7; 20, 5; 21, 4; 23, 4; 25, 6; 28, 4; 30, 6; 31, 6; 32, 5; 34, 4 = 35, 4; 36, 7; 37, 6; 45, 10 // 46, 9; 50, 9; 51, 13; 59, 8; 60,9; 61, 9; 67, 7; 68, 9.
J. Oelsner, *WZJ* 19 (1970), 905–12, no. 748, 4.
J. Oppert, J. Ménant, *Doc. jur.*, nos. 1, 3 (= F.E. Peiser, *KB* 4, 314, 6); 5, 18; BM 30118, 5 (= *KB* 4, 314, 6).
G.Kh. Sarkisjan, *VDI*, 1955, 4, 6; 7, 6; 8, 6.
G.Kh. Sarkisjan, *FuB* 16 (1975), 2, 9; 9, 3; 23, 9.
L. Speleers, *Recueil*, 294, 5; 297, 7.
TCL 13, 236, 5; 237, 6; 238, 5; 242, 8; 243, 6; 244, 5; 245, 5; 247, 4 (*eš*(?)-*še-e-šá*-⌜*na*/*ni*(?)⌝).
VS 15, 4, 4; 10, 6; 16, 5, 7; 18, 6; 26, 4; 28, 9; 32, 6; 33, 8; 37, 5, 24.
BiMes 24, 1, 4; 10, 6; 12, 5.
161 28-?-125 S.E., Seleucus (IV).
162 Date lost, Demetrius.

17 … GIŠ.ŠUB.BA-*šú* 7-*ú ina re-bu-ú ina* UZ.TUR$^{\text{mu[šen]}}$
18 *šá ina* UD ÈŠ.ÈŠ.MEŠ *gab-bi šá a-na* ^{giš}BANŠUR *šá* ^{d}*Na-na-a* E_{11}-*ú u* GIŠ.ŠUB.BA-*šú* […]
19 *ina mi-šil* UDU.NÍTA *šá ina* UD ÈŠ.ÈŠ.MEŠ *gab-bi šá a-na* ^{giš}BANŠUR *šá ṣa-lam* LUGAL.MEŠ E_{11}-[*ú* …]

'^{17} … her prebend of one seventh in one fourth of the duck[s], ^{18}which on all *eššēšu*-days are brought up to the table of Nanāja (monthly) and her prebend […] ^{19}in one half of a sheep which on all *eššēšu*-days is brought u[p] the table of the statues of the kings (monthly)'.

The third text is *VS* 15, 16, obv. 1–8[163]:

1 ^{Id}LX-TIN-*su*-E A *šá* ^{I}GIN-*a* […]
2 *ina ḫu-ud lìb-bi-šú* GIŠ.ŠUB.BA 2 *ga*[*b-bi*(?) …]
3 *ina* 1-*en*(?) TA ^{uzu}GIŠ.KUN(?) ^{uzu}BA-x[…]
4 PAP 4 UZU^{ḫá} *ba-šal u ba*[*l-ṭu* …]
5 *ina* 1-*en*(?) UD ÈŠ.ÈŠ *a-na* 1-*en* TA x[…]
6 TA UDU.NÍTA.MEŠ *šá in-*⟨*né-*⟩*ep-pu-uš*.MEŠ […]
7 *šá ṣa-lam* LUGAL.MEŠ *šá ina* UD ÈŠ.ÈŠ.MEŠ E[$_{11}$(?) …]
8 4-*ta* UZU^{ḫá} *šá ṣa-lam* LUGAL.MEŠ *šá ina* [UD ÈŠ.ÈŠ.MEŠ …]

'^{1}Anu-balāssu-iqbi, son of Kīnā […] ^{2}of his own free will (has sold) a prebend, 2 […] ^{3} … meat of the thigh, meat of […] ^{4}in total 4 cuts of meat, cooked or ra[w …] ^{5}on 1 *eššēšu*-day for one(?) …[…] ^{6}of the sheep, which are offered […] ^{7}for the statues of the kings, which on the *eššēšu*-days are br[ought up(?),] ^{8}one-fourth of the meat (of the sheep offered) for the statues of the kings, which on the [*eššēšu*-day …]'.

And finally *VS* 15, 37, rev. 21–24[164]:

21 18-*ʾu-ú* GIŠ.ŠUB.BA-*šú* ^{lú}KU$_4$-É *pi-ri-iš-tu$_4$-ú-tú u* ^{lú}KÙ.DIM-*ú-tú*
22 18-*ʾu-ú ina* UDU.[NÍTA].MEŠ *šá ḫi-ta-tap* GEŠTIN ^{šim}LI ^{túg}*ḫu-ṣa-na-tu$_4$*
23 ^{túg}*ṣu-pat-ta* ŠIM.MEŠ *u* GIŠ.MEŠ 18-*ʾu-ú ina* UZU *ba-šal u bal-ṭu*
24 *šá a-na* BANŠUR *šá* ^{d}EN.⟨LÍL⟩ *ina* UD ÈŠ.ÈŠ.MEŠ E_{11} …

'^{21}One eighteenth of the prebend of the *ērib bīt pirištūtu* and the *kutimmūtu*: ^{22}one eighteenth in the sheep of the *ḫitpu*-offerings, wine, juniper, *ḫuṣannu*-garments, ^{23}strips of carded wool, perfumes and woods, one eighteenth in the cooked or raw meat, ^{24}which is brought up to the table of Enlil on the *eššēšu*-days. …'.

Based on these texts, the offerings presented on the *eššēšu*-days consisted of meat of ducks and of sheep, and are otherwise described as cooked or raw. We have, however, another source of information for the foodstuffs which were offered during the *eššēšu*-ceremony: the list of offerings and ceremonies recorded in the ritual text *TU* 38.[165] It records loaves and date cakes, which are supplied for a number of offerings and

[163] ?-II-100 [+ x] S.E. .
[164] 7-VII-107, Arsaces (A.E. = 171 S.E.). See also obv. 2–5.
[165] See II.1.

ceremonies, among which is the *eššēšu*-ceremony;[166] on the reverse[167] almost the same list of offerings and ceremonies is recorded, but here oxen and sheep are served.

Finally, from the prebend texts we know that the *eššēšu*-ceremonies were not connected with one particular god but were apparently celebrated for many if not all important deities of Uruk. See for instance *OECT* 9, 61, obv. 5–10[168]:

5 … GIŠ.ŠUB.BA MU.MEŠ *šá* I[GI]
6 [^{d}LX] *An-tu*$_4$ ^{d}EN.LÍL ^{d}IDIM ^{d}XXX ^{d}UTU ^{d}IM ^{d}AMAR.UTU ^{d}PAP.SUK[KAL]
7 [^{d}INNIN] ^{d}GAŠAN.EDIN ^{d}*Na-na-a* ^{d}GAŠAN-*šá*-SAG ^{d}*Šar-ra-a-ḫi-tu*$_4$ *u* DINGIR.MEŠ
8 [É-*šú-n*]*u*(?) GIŠ.ŠUB.BA MU.MEŠ *šá* ITI-*us-su u* MU.AN.NA-*us-su gu- uq-qa-né-e*
9 [UD È]Š.ÈŠ.MEŠ *u mim-ma gab-bi šá a-na* GIŠ.ŠUB.BA.[MEŠ] MU.MEŠ
10 [^{lú}BAPPI]R-*ú-tú ik-kaš-ši-du*

'^{5} … (amount) of these (brewer's) prebends, which are befo[re] ^{6}[Anu], Antu, Enlil, Ea, Sîn, Šamaš, Adad, Marduk, Papsuk[kal], ^{7}Ištar, Bēlet-ṣēri, Nanāja, Bēlet-ša-Rēš, Šarraḫītu and (all) the gods ^{8}of [thei]r [temples], these prebends, monthly and yearly, the *guqqû*-^{9}(and) *eššēšu*-offerings and whatever ^{10}pertains ^{9}to these prebends of ^{10}the brewer's, …'

From Babylon we have only one reference to the ceremony in the ritual text which describes the New Year festival of the first month Nisannu. The relevant passage, only partly preserved, concerns day 5. In a speech from the high priest to the king the *eššēšu*-ceremony is mentioned just before the *pīt bābi*-ceremony[169] (*RAcc.*, 144–45, 434–40, see the Appendix):

'^{434}Do not fear […] ^{435}What Bēl has ordered […] ^{436}Bēl [will listen(?)] to your prayer […] ^{437}He will magnify your lordship […] ^{438}He will extol your kingship. ^{439}At the *eššēšu*-day, do […] ^{440}At the opening of the gate ceremony, cleanse (with) [your] hands […]!'

II.3.3. *lubuštu*

The ritual clothing ceremonies of the divine statues (*lubuštu*)[170] are attested from the Old Akkadian period on.[171] The ceremony is not mentioned in Assyrian rituals,[172] but it is attested in the letter *LAS* I, 285,[173] where *lubuštu* is celebrated on day 3-VI for Bēl. *Lubuštu* is also recorded in administrative and ritual texts from the Neo-Babylonian period.

---

166 Obv. 35 ff.

167 36 ff.

168 16-?-153 S.E., Demetrius (I).

169 It is also interesting that in this text the *pīt bābi*-ceremony is mentioned, as in the above cited Uruk document J. Oppert, J. Ménant, *Doc. jur.*, no. 5 (see obv. 13).

170 Cf. B. Landsberger, *Kult. Kalender*, 117 f.; G. Furlani, *Riti*, 161; E. Matsushima, in: H.I.H. Prince Takahito Mikasa (ed.), *Cult and Ritual in the Ancient Near East*, 7; id., in: E. Matsushima (ed.), *Official Cult and Popular Religion in the Ancient Near East*, 209–219; id., *ASJ* 16 (1994), 177–200.

For *lubuštu* referring to the 'clothing, wardrobe', and not the 'clothing ceremony', see the dictionaries. Three examples of the former from the Hellenistic period are *CT* 44, 84, AB 248 (= G.J.P. McEwan, *Iraq* 43 (1981), 143), obv. 14, and A.J. Sachs–H. Hunger, *Diaries*, no. -261, C, rev. 11′.

171 *CAD*, L, 235, 4, and *AHw*, 561a, 2, d.

172 Cf. G. van Driel, *Cult of Aššur*, 167.

173 A, 6′. Dated to 670 B.C. by S. Parpola, *LAS* II, 282.

The Neo-Babylonian period

In his dissertation, Bongenaar discussed the clothing ceremonies of Šamaš in Sippar.[174] BM 91002, a royal inscription of Nabû-apla-iddina (ninth century)[175] contains such regulations for days 7-I, 10-II, 3-VI, 7-VII, 15-VIII and 15-XII of the year; thus six ceremonies a year are listed. Bongenaar has demonstrated that these data are very similar to the data found in Neo-Babylonian administrative clothing texts from Sippar.[176] We will compare these numbers with relevant texts from Neo-Babylonian Uruk and Babylon. One example, *BIN* 2, 129[177] reads:

1 15 BÁN 4 SÌLA ŠE.GIŠ.Ì
2 *šá* 8 *iš-še-šá-a-ni* EN *lu-bu-uš-tú*
3 *šá* ^iti^GAN 4 *šá* ^iti^AB
4 EN *nab-re-e*
5 4 *šá* ^iti^ZÍZ EN *ba-a-a-*[*tu*$_4$] Lo.E.
6 ^I^DÙG.GA-IM-É.⌜AN.NA⌝
7 A^!^ ^I^MU-^d^AG[178] GIŠ

'⁶Ṭāb-šār-Eanna ⁷son of Iddin-Nabû has brought ¹5 *sūtu* 4 *qa* sesame ²for the 8 *eššēšu*-ceremonies including the clothing ceremony ³of the (ninth) month Kislīmu, 4 of the (tenth) month Ṭebētu ⁴including the *nabrû*-festival, ⁵4 of the (eleventh) month Šabaṭu including the *bajjātu*-ceremony'.

Table VI: clothing ceremonies (*lubuštu*) from Neo-Babylonian Uruk and Babylon[179]

number of *lubuštu*-ceremonies	date of *lubuštu*-ceremonies	place	text	date
–	VII	Uruk	*BIN* 1, 152	16-V-10 (Nbp)
–	V	Uruk	*BIN* 1, 152	16-V-10 (Nbp)
–	1, 16-VI	Uruk	*BIN* 1, 152	16-V-10 (Nbp)
–	–	Uruk	*BIN* 1, 152	16-V-10 (Nbp)
–	–	Uruk	*YOS* 17, 79	27-VIII-17 (Nbk)
–	IX	Uruk	*BIN* 2, 129	15-VIII-19 (Nbk)
–	–	Uruk	*GC* 1, 60	15-V-20 (Nbk)
5	IV–VII	Uruk	*GC* 1, 242	12-VI-22 (Nbk)[180]
–	–	Uruk	*LKU*, no. 47	–

174 A.C.V.M. Bongenaar, *The Neo-Babylonian Ebabbar temple at Sippar*, 305–7.
175 See L.W. King, *BBst.* no. 36 and pl. 101. Cf. E. Matsushima, in: E. Matsushima (ed.), *Official Cult and Popular Religion in the Ancient Near East*, 211–13, 216–17.
176 A.C.V.M. Bongenaar, *The Neo-Babylonian Ebabbar temple at Sippar*, 306, presented a table with the relevant administrative clothing texts.
177 15-VIII-19, Nbk.
178 Copy reads: GIŠ MU ^d^AG. As E. Matsushima, *ASJ* 16 (1994), 197, already noted, this Ṭab-šar-Eanna, son of Iddin-Nabû is already known from *YOS* 17, 175, 182, and 188.
179 The list is not complete.
180 5 GÍN KÙ.BABBAR 5 BÁN ^šim^LI *šá* 5 *lu-bu-uš-še-e-ti* TA ^iti^ŠU *a-di* ^iti^DU$_6$ ^I^DÙ-^d^INNIN A ^lú^AZLAG *it-ta-ši*.

number of *lubuštu*-ceremonies	date of *lubuštu*-ceremonies	place	text	date
–	1-V	Uruk	*LKU*, no. 51	–
–	1-VI	Uruk	*LKU*, no. 51	–
–	1-VII	Uruk	*LKU*, no. 51	–
–	8-II	Uruk	*NCBT* 1132[181]	–
(?)	17-IV	Uruk	*NCBT* 1132	–
–	24-VIII	Uruk	*NCBT* 1132	–
–	28-X	Uruk	*NCBT* 1132	–
–	26-IX	Uruk	*NCBT* 1132	–
–	16	Uruk	*NCBT* 1132	–
–	3-VI	Babylon	*ABL* 496	–

The texts, all but one (*ABL* 496) from Uruk, are administrative documents with the exception of *LKU*, nos. 47 and 51, which are ritual texts and *ABL* 496, which is a Neo-Babylonian letter from Babylon, recording a *lubuštu* for Bēl on day 3-VI. Other gods which are attested for the *lubuštu* are Nergal for days 8-II; 17-IV; 28-X, Gula for day 24-VIII, and Aška'itu and Nergal for day 26-IX.[182] Furthermore a *lubuštu* for Šamaš and Aška'itu is recorded.[183] For the clothing ceremonies, oil,[184] sesame,[185] wool,[186] sheep,[187] and finally payments,[188] silver for *burāšu*-incense,[189] and *lubāru*-clothing are attested.[190]

The evidence is scarce. From Uruk, especially informative is *NCBT* 1132, which mentions 8-II, 17-IV, 24-VIII, 26-IX, 28-X, and day 16 of an unknown month. It does not mention *lubuštu* in month I and VI, as in Sippar, but it does mention month IV (also in *GC* 1, 242), IX (also in *BIN* 2, 129) and X, which are not found in the Sippar calendar in BM 91002 (referred to above). Furthermore, the ritual text *LKU*, no. 51 records the first day of month V, VI, and VII, and day 1, together with day 16 of month VI, is also attested in *BIN* 1, 152. The days attested for the clothing ceremony in Uruk are very different from the Sippar days, but they do not allow us to establish a clear monthly schedule of days on which the ceremony was celebrated. Although *lubuštu* is, as we will see below, connected with the *ḫitpu*-offerings in prebend texts from Hellenistic Uruk, which are performed on days 6/7, 13/14, 20/21 and 27/28 of each month, the attested data for Neo-Babylonian Uruk do not match this *ḫitpu*-sequence. It is clear, however, that, while the ceremony was celebrated in Sippar during six months of the year, in Neo-Babylonian Uruk eight months are attested; whether *lubuštu* was celebrated during every month remains unclear for now.

---

181 Published by P.- A. Beaulieu, *ZA* 83 (1993), 81–86.
182 All in *NCBT* 1132.
183 *BIN* 1, 152.
184 *NCBT* 1132.
185 *BIN* 2, 129.
186 *YOS* 3, 49.
187 *YOS* 17, 79.
188 *BIN* 1, 152.
189 *GC* 1, 242.
190 *GC* 1, 60.

As we saw, the only reference from Babylon, *ABL* 496, mentions day 3-VI, which is also attested in the letter *LAS* I, 285, and furthermore it is also one of the *lubuštu*-days in Sippar. Obviously this is not enough to draw any conclusions as regards the data of *lubuštu* in Babylon, but it may be an indication that the *lubuštu*-schedule in Babylon was more similar to that in Sippar than to that in Uruk.

The Hellenistic period

While from Hellenistic Babylon no references to *lubuštu* are known, the ceremony is well attested in texts from Hellenistic Uruk.[191] The following gods are connected with the clothing ceremony: Antu;[192] Anu, Enlil, Nanāja and Bēlet-ša-Rēš;[193] Anu, Antu and the great gods (*ilānu rabûtu*);[194] and Anu.[195] Apparently the ceremony was connected with all, or at least with the more important gods of the pantheon of Uruk, and was not confined to one god.

lubuštu is one of the ceremonies recorded in a list of offerings and ceremonies in the ritual text *TU* 38 (obv. 36, rev. 37), informing us that apparently loaves and cakes, and oxen and sheep were used during the ceremony.

Another reference to the clothing ceremonies is recorded in *TU* 48, a cultic calendar from Uruk,[196] which mentions day 20 of every month; this day is not attested in the Neo-Babylonian period.

lubuštu is also frequently mentioned in prebend texts from Hellenistic Uruk, but the dates of the days are never recorded. *OECT* 9, 40,[197] obv. 3 speaks of the clothing ceremonies for every year:

2 … *mi-šil ina* ^{uzu}ZAG.LU UDU.NÍTA *šá ḫi-it-pi*.MEŠ […](?)
3 [*šá lu*]-*bu-šá-a-tú gab-bi šá An-*tu_4 *šá* MU-*us-su gab-bi* …

'2 … one half of the shoulder in the sheep of the *ḫitpu*-offerings […](?) 3[of all the clo]thing ceremonies of Antu for every year, all (of it) …'.

All the relevant texts are *ērib bīt pirištūtu-* + *kutimmūtu*-prebend texts.[198] We already noted[199] that the reason for this is that the clothing ceremony is one of the income

191 Cf. G.J.P. McEwan, *FAOS* 4, 163–4.
192 *OECT* 9, 40.
193 *OECT* 9, 50.
194 *OECT* 9, 60.
195 *TU* 48, obv. 14.
196 Discussed in II.2.2.
197 Date lost.
198 *OECT* 9, 42, 45 // 46, 50, and 60. Other *ērib bīt pirištūtu* + *kutimmūtu* prebends do not mention *lubuštu*, but they are very damaged (*OECT* 9, 33; 44 (but with *ḫitpu*); 51; 57; 68; *VS* 15, 37 (but with *ḫitpu*)). Not damaged is *OECT* 9, 54 // 55, but this text is actually a quitclaim. *OECT* 9, 50, obv. 5–7, mentions the garments *kitû*, *ṣuppātu* and *ḫuṣanātu*, besides *ḫitapatū ša ana lubuštu*; which is a clear indication that the former were not mentioned in place of the latter in texts where *lubuštu* is missing. *OECT* 9, 40 may be a *kutimmūtu*-prebend (*šá* KI ^{lú}KÙ.DIM.MEŠ, cf. G.J.P. McEwan, *FAOS* 4, 89) and also mentions the *ḫitpu*-offerings of the *lubuštu*-ceremonies (obv. 2–3: *ḫi-it-pi*.MEŠ […] [*šá* $^{\text{(túg?)}}$*lu*]-*bu-šá-a-tú gab-bi šá An-*tu_4 …).
199 See II.3.1.

sources for these prebends; the goldsmith (*kutimmu*) was responsible for the ornaments and garments of the statues of the gods, stored in the *bīt pirišti*.

In these texts, *lubuštu* is mentioned in connection with the *ḫitpu*-offerings, using the phrase ‘the *ḫitpu*-offerings of (*ša*) the clothing ceremonies’; *ša* apparently has to be interpreted as ‘belonging to’, i.e. ‘offerings presented during the clothing ceremonies’. The reference to the ox in the New Year ritual text *TU* 39, obv. 12[200] may refer, as McEwan has pointed out,[201] to the *ḫitpu*-offerings, because here these offerings are also mentioned in connection with *lubuštu*. However, in the prebend texts the *ḫitpu*-offerings always consist of sheep. In *OECT* 9, 60,[202] obv. 7 it is specifically stated that the *ḫitpu*-offerings are performed on the *lubuštu*-days:

6 … 60-ʾ-*ú ina* GIŠ.ŠUB.BA ^{lú}KU$_4$ É AD.ḪAL-*ú-tú*
7 *u* ^{lú}KÙ.DIM-*ú-tú šá ina* UDU.NÍTA.MEŠ *šá ḫi-it-pi*.MEŠ *šá ina u*$_4$*-mu lu-* ⌜*bu*⌝*-šá-at*.MEŠ
8 *šá a-na* ^{d}LX *An-tu*$_4$ *u* DINGIR.MEŠ GAL.MEŠ *in-ip-pu-uš*.MEŠ ⌜E$_{11}$(?)⌝-*ú* …

‘[6] … one-sixtieth of the *ērib bīt pirištūtu*- [7]and *kutimmūtu*-prebends, in the sheep of the *ḫitpu*-offerings, which on the day(s) of the clothing ceremonies [8]are offered to Anu, Antu and the great gods, are brought up(?) (to the table monthly) …’.

Fossey has studied several texts belonging to a small archive of the Eanna-temple in Uruk, mostly dating from the reigns of Cyrus and Cambyses (539–522), in which offerings of sheep and goats in the temple for each day of one particular month are described.[203] Among these *ḫitpu*-offerings are often mentioned. As Beaulieu has shown,[204] they involved the offering of a kid at average intervals of seven days, four times a month, usually on days 6/7, 13/14, 20/21 and 27/28 of each month. However, other days for these *ḫitpu*-offerings are also attested and apparently the inconsistency of the system was caused by the fact that the *ḫitpu*-offerings were tied to the four lunar phases. These phases varied from 6.75 to 7.75 days and this could explain the variety in the intervals between the ceremonies. Thus the *ḫitpu*-offerings, and also other cultic events like the clothing ceremony, could take place a day earlier or later than the average seven days interval date, and since *ḫitpu* and *lubuštu* appear to be connected in the Hellenistic prebend texts, they might have taken place on the same day.

Although the only certain monthly date for *lubuštu* from Hellenistic Uruk is 20-I/XII (*TU* 48), it does fit the schedule of the *ḫitpu*-days, and therefore it is not unlikely that the clothing ceremony in Hellenistic Uruk was performed on days 6/7, 13/14, 20/21 and 27/28 of each month. Similar to the *eššēšu*-ceremony, the fact that the days are not mentioned in the texts probably means that these were well-known and that it was not necessary to mention them.

---

200 See II.4.2.
201 G.J.P. McEwan, *FAOS* 4, 164.
202 10-IV-153, Demetrius (I).
203 Ch. Fossey, Etats mensuels d’animaux répartis pour sacrifices: époque néo-babylonienne, *RES* 1936 (I) I–IX; W.W. Hallo, *HUCA* 48 (1977), 8–9; P.- A. Beaulieu, *ZA* 83 (1993), 80–81; in n. 32 he refers to a new study on this subject, which is being prepared by E. Robbins.
204 *ZA* 83 (1993), 80–81.

Table VII: clothing ceremonies (*lubuštu*) from Hellenistic Uruk

day/month	god(s)	text	date
–	–	*TU* 38	–
20-I/XII	Anu	*TU* 48	–
–	Antu	*OECT* 9, 40	–
–	–	*OECT* 9, 42	14 + ?- XI-?
–	–	*OECT* 9, 45 //46	21-VI-111 (Antiochus and Antiochus)
–	Anu, Enlil, Nanāja Bēlet-ša-Rēš	*OECT* 9, 50	28-?-128, (Seleucus)
–	Anu, Antu, *ilānu rabûtu*	*OECT* 9, 60	10-IV-153, (Demetrius)

II.3.4. *bajjātu*

bajjātu is a nocturnal ceremony, a vigil held during the night in the temple.[205] The ceremony is not mentioned in the Assyrian rituals,[206] but it is attested from the Neo-Babylonian period onwards, mainly in administrative documents from Uruk and Babylon.[207]

Table VIII: *bajjātu*-ceremonies from Neo-Babylonian Uruk and Babylon[208]

day/month	place	text	date
–	Uruk	*BIN* 1, 152	10(?)-V(?)-16(?) (Nbp)
XI	Uruk	*BIN* 2, 129	15-VIII-19 (Nbk)
17-IX	Uruk	*UCP* 9, 88, no. 23	17-IX-39 (Nbk)
VI	Uruk	*BIN* 1, 170	7-VI-33 (Nrgl)
–	Uruk	*YOS* 6, 39	5-X-3 (Nbn)
–	Uruk	*GC* 2, 371	23-XIIb-12
–	Uruk	*AUWE* 5, 80	–
–	Uruk	*SWU*, 27	–
–	Uruk	*SWU*, 35	–
–	Uruk	*SWU*, 37	–
–	Uruk	*SWU*, 62	–
–	Babylon	J. MacGinnis, *AfO* 38-39 (1991–92), 89	2-?-26 (Dar)
III	Babylon	*VS* 6, 268	–

The *bajjātu*-ceremony is connected with the other monthly ceremonies, such as *lubuš-*

205 *CAD*, B, 34; *AHw*, 97a. Cf. G. Furlani, *Riti*, 141, 143.

206 Cf. G. van Driel, *Cult of Aššur*, 168.

207 A rare example from Neo-Babylonian Sippar is *RT* 17, 31 (1-II-8, Kand), where sheep are for the offerings of, amongst others, the night vigil(s) (*ba-a-ta*).

208 The list is not complete. See also E.W. Moore, *Michigan Coll.*, 52, obv. 14, but the place where the tablet was written is not clear.

tu,[209] *eššēšu*,[210] *šalām bīti*,[211] and *nabrû*[212] (not attested in texts from the Hellenistic period), and with the offerings *niqê šarri*, *niqê kāribi*, *ginû*, and *guqqû*,[213] which clearly demonstrates the monthly character of the ceremony. The foodstuffs which were presented for the ceremony consisted of bread and butter,[214] Dilmun dates,[215] Dilmun dates(?) and raisins,[216] sesame,[217] barley,[218] and meat.[219]

The Hellenistic period

In texts from the Hellenistic period we have a few examples of *bajjātu*.[220] The ceremony is attested in an administrative document, *CT* 49, 150, from Babylon. The text contains a list of temple expenditures; the relevant passage[221] mentions 4 shekels for the *bajjātu*-ceremony of day 16 of month IX, and day 3 of month XI.[222]

We only have a few examples from Uruk, and only in ritual texts, but they are important because they provide us with insight into the way the ceremony was performed. Firstly *bajjātu* is recorded in *TU* 38, in the above mentioned list recording several offerings and ceremonies;[223] from this passage it becomes clear that loaves and cakes and oxen and sheep were apparently used during the ceremony. Secondly, in *TU* 39 we have a description of the vigil held during the night of days 9 and 10 of the seventh month Tašrītu, during the second New Year festival in Uruk: the relevant passage[224] describes that in the evening of day 9 the second meal of the morning is cleared, and the first main meal of the evening is served. After a censer is filled, offerings presented, and a recitation is performed by the singers, this meal is cleared and the second meal of the evening is served. The singers perform the same recitation again, the second meal is not yet cleared, the vigil goes on the entire night, and the gate is closed:

> '[9] ... (the meal) will not be cleared. The vigil will continue the entire night (*ba-a-a-at i-ba-at*). The gate will be closed'.

Then the description of day 10 begins: after two lamentations and the awakening of the temple ceremony (*dīk bīti*) are performed, the gate is opened and the vigil ends:

> '[11]At dawn the gate will be opened and the vigil will be ended (*ba-a-a-at* DUḪ-*ma*)'.

---

209 *BIN* 1, 152; *BIN* 2, 129.
210 *BIN* 2, 129; J. MacGinnis, *AfO* 38–39 (1991–92), 89; *VS* 6, 268.
211 J. MacGinnis, *AfO* 38–39 (1991–92), 89; *VS* 6, 268.
212 *BIN* 2, 129.
213 J. MacGinnis, *AfO* 38–39 (1991–92), 89; *GC* 2, 371. These offerings are discussed in III.7.2.
214 *UCP* 9, 88, no. 23.
215 *BIN* 1, 170; *YOS* 6, 39.
216 *AUWE* 5, 80.
217 *BIN* 2, 129.
218 *SWU* 27; 35; 37; 62.
219 *GC* 2, 371 (sheep); J. MacGinnis, *AfO* 38–39 (1991–92), 89 (oxen and sheep); *VS* 6, 268.
220 Cf. G.J.P. McEwan, *FAOS* 4, 161; 171.
221 Rev. 44.
222 See R.J. van der Spek, in: J. Wiesehöfer (ed.), *Das Partherreich und seine Zeugnisse*, 222 ff., who collated the text.
223 Obv. 37, rev. 37. See II.1.
224 Rev. 5 ff.

The text continues with the description of the rest of day 10. After the serving of the two meals of the morning and the evening the gate is closed and the day ends.

An extensive description of a night vigil is recorded in *TU* 41. The text describes a special nocturnal festival held in the Rēš-temple of Anu during the vigil of days 16 and 17 of an unknown month, perhaps the tenth month Ṭebētu.[225] The ceremonies celebrated during this night, including a procession with a torch, an extra meal, and a *šalām bīti*-ceremony, are probably ceremonies for a special occasion and were not performed during every vigil. These ceremonies will be discussed below,[226] but the standard proceedings of the vigil are the same as in *TU* 39: the evening meal is served but not cleared away, the vigil continues the entire night (*ba-a-a-at i-ba-at*),[227] and the gate is not closed. There is no mention of closing the gate at the end of the night,[228] but in the morning of day 17, 40 minutes after sunrise the gate is opened again and the vigil ends (*ba-a-a-at* DUḪ-*ár*).[229]

Thus the only data that we have of *bajjātu* in the Hellenistic period are, from Uruk, for days 9-VII (*TU* 39) and 16-X(?) (*TU* 41), and from Babylon for days 16-IX and 3-XI (CT 49, 150). Because we only have one day from the Neo-Babylonian period, day 17-IX from Uruk (*UCP* 9, 88, no. 23), there is obviously not enough information to reconstruct the monthly schedule of *bajjātu*-days, although days 9 and 16 may indicate a schedule of seven days intervals, similar to the above discussed *ḫitpu*-offerings.[230]

II.3.5. *nubattu*

nubattu 'vigil, evening', but also 'evening ceremony, evening meal' is well known from the Neo-Assyrian period, especially in ritual texts and in the hemerological series *inbu bēl arḫim* ('Fruit (= epithet of the moon god Sîn), lord of the month').[231] As van Driel noted,[232] in the ritual texts *nubattu* was mostly used together with *šērtu* 'morning', and should be translated 'evening meal' and 'morning meal'. In the *inbu*-series *nubattu* seems to refer to a ceremony which had to be performed on the evening before the day on which the *eššēšu*-ceremony was celebrated; attested days are 3, 7 and 16, dedicated to Marduk, followed by the *eššēšu*-ceremony on the days 4, 8 and 17 of the month, dedicated to Nabû.

The Hellenistic period

While from the Neo-Babylonian period examples of *nubattu* with the meaning 'evening ceremonies' are not known, in the Hellenistic rituals only one example is (perhaps) attested, in *TU* 40, obv. 10–11. The section, from which this passage is taken, describes

---

225 See I.2.
226 The text is discussed more extensively in II.8.6.
227 Obv. 13.
228 See my comment on rev. 26 in the Appendix.
229 Rev. 28–9.
230 See II.3.3.
231 *CAD*, N/II, 307–8; *AHw*, 799–800; see also *CAD*, E, 373b; S. Langdon, *Menologies*, 153–4, n. 1. For the series *inbu bēl arḫim* see the literature referred to in I.2, n. 11. For *nubattu* see B. Landsberger, *Kult. Kalender*, 108–9.
232 *Cult of Aššur*, 156–7.

day 9 of the seventh month, Tašrītu, during the second New Year festival in Uruk (see the Appendix):

> '[10]The sheep, which since the evening (ceremonies?) (*nu-bat-tu*$_4$) [was tied(?) to] the gate of the [Grant(?)] Courtyard, [11]its rites as for the eighth day ditto'.

Whether *nubattu* has to be translated here 'evening ceremony/ies', or simple 'evening', 'vigil', is difficult to determine. It is, however, clear that no connection can be made with the data of the Neo-Assyrian texts, unless day 9 is an alternative day for day 8. Because we have no other examples from the Hellenistic period, it is not even certain whether *TU* 40, obv. 10–11 refers to a monthly ceremony, on this occasion performed during the New Year festival, or a special celebration, taking place only during the New Year festival.

II.3.6. *šalām bīti*

The ceremony called *šalām bīti*[233] is best translated: 'the good-functioning (or completion) of the temple' ceremony.[234] I do not know of arguments which support the translation 'greeting of the temple' or 'early morning ceremonies',[235] and my translation is based on the basic meaning of the verb *šalāmu* 'to stay well, to be in good condition, intact'. Furthermore, in a ritual from Hellenistic Uruk, *TU* 39, rev. 5 and 8–9, an Akkadian lamentation incipit is recorded, which may support this interpretation, although the translation is difficult:

> É *i-šal-lim* SILIM^{im}.MA.ÁB(?)
>
> 'the temple will stay intact, keep it safe!'(?).

The interpretation of the incipit is based on the idea, that the temple will not be destroyed, or that it will be restored, and must be kept safe and sound. This lamentation incipit appears to refer to the *šalām bīti*-ceremony, hence my translation: 'the good-functioning of the temple'.[236]

The Neo-Babylonian period

While we have only a few references to the ceremony in texts from the Neo-Assyrian period,[237] many data are available from texts of the Neo-Babylonian period. In his dissertation, Bongenaar has discussed the *šalām bīti*-ceremony for Šamaš and other

---

233 Cf. F. Thureau-Dangin, *RA* 16 (1919), 132, n. 10; G. Furlani, *Riti*, 147; A.B. Moldenke, 2, no. 48, 135, n. 5; F. Joannès, *Textes économiques*, 212.

234 Cf. *AHw*, *šalāmu*, 1144a, 6, 'erhalten bleiben', b, 'in Function bleiben'; and id., *epēšu*, 225b, h: '(Hausvollendung)'. See also *GC* 1, 27, n. 1; G.J.P. McEwan, *FAOS* 4, 166 does not translate, but states that the ceremony 'seemingly was concerned with insuring the continued well-being of the temple'.

235 *CAD*, Š/I, 202b. A.R. George, *BTT*, 222, n. 3, probably follows *CAD* since he states that the ceremony 'is apparently an exuberant greeting of the city's temples in anticipation of the feast-day ahead'.

236 See also my comments on this incipit in the Appendix.

237 Cf. G. van Driel, *Cult of Aššur*, 168. See also the letter S. Parpola, *LAS* I, 280 (*ABL* 437), rev. 17.

gods in Neo-Babylonian Sippar.[238] It appears to be so that in Sippar thirteen *šalām bīti*-ceremonies for the whole year were celebrated on: 2-I, 6-I, 10-I, 12-II, 14-II, 19/20?-II, 12-III, 20-III, 8-VII, 18?-VIII, 27-VIII, 20-XII and 25-XII. However, it is not certain whether the ceremonies for Šamaš and the other gods took place on the same day. We will compare these days in Sippar with the data from Neo-Babylonian Uruk and Babylon.

Table IX: *šalām bīti*-ceremonies from Neo-Babylonian Uruk and Babylon[239]

day/month	place	text	date
–	Uruk	F. Thureau-Dangin, *RA* 16 (1919), 125	20-I-2 (Marduk-zākir-šumi)
–	Uruk	*GC* 1, 12	14-V-9 (Nbk)
–	Uruk	*GC* 1, 198	12-XI-39 (Nbk)
8[240]	Uruk	*GC* 1, 203	7-I-41 (Nbk)
–	Uruk	*AUWE* 5, 145[241]	8-IX-1 (Amel-Marduk)
–	Uruk	HE 145[242]	1-XII-6 (Nbn)
–	Uruk	*YOS* 6, 62	6-XII-6 (Nbn)
–	Uruk	*GC* 1, 379	15-I-10 (Nbn)
8-IX	Uruk	*YOS* 6, 192	7-IX-15 (Nbn)
8-VII	Uruk	*YOS* 6, 189	8-VII-17 (Nbn)
–	Uruk	*YOS* 7, 185	15-XI-6 (Camb)
–	Uruk	*OECT* 1, 20[243]	–
–	Uruk	*BIN* 1, 19	–
–	Babylon	*VS* 5, 74 // 75	24-I-11 (Dar)
–	Babylon	J. MacGinnis, *AfO* 38-39 (1991–92), 89	2-x-26 (Dar)
8-VII	Babylon	*VS* 6, 268	–
5(?)[244]-IX	Babylon	*VS* 6, 268	–

In texts from Neo-Babylonian Uruk and Babylon the ceremony is mentioned together with the *bajjātu*- and *eššēšu*-ceremonies,[245] and with the *ginû*-, *guqqû*-, *niqê šarri*-, and *niqê kāribi*-offerings.[246] We already referred to the letter *LAS* I, 280 where the connection between the *eššēšu*- and the *šalām bīti*-ceremony is attested.[247] The connection with

[238] A.C.V.M. Bongenaar, *The Neo-Babylonian Ebabbar temple at Sippar*, 120–122. Add: Graziani, *Bardiya*, 25 (10-VI-1), where the ceremony is attested for the first month Nisannu, *BRM* 1, 100, with months XII and I, and *VS* 6, 169 (Dar). We also have two examples from Dilbat: *VS* 5, 161 (28-I-11, Dar), and *VS* 5, 76 (28-VI-13, Dar). Where A.B. Moldenke thought, 2, 48 (22-VII-4, Nbn) was written is not clear.

[239] The list is not complete.

[240] *CAD*, Š/I, 203a cites the relevant lines obv. 6–7 (*a-na šá-lam* É *šá* UD.8.KAM) and mistakenly adds: '(of Nisannu)', perhaps because the text was written in the first month Nisannu?

[241] Obv. 6-rev. 7: ⌜1 *ma-aq-qu-ú* GUŠKIN⌝(?) *šu*⌜(-*ul*?)-*lum* É⌝.

[242] = F. Joannès, *RA* 75 (1981), 144.

[243] = G.J.P. McEwan, *Iraq* 45 (1983), 190, 85.

[244] Mistake for 8?

[245] *VS* 6, 268; J. MacGinnis, *AfO* 38–39 (1991–92), 89.

[246] J. MacGinnis, *AfO* 38–39 (1991–92), 89.

[247] Rev. 16–18. See II.3.2.

these monthly-occurring cultic activities clearly shows that *šalām bīti* is also a monthly ceremony. For the *šalām bīti*-ceremonies, flour,[248] meat,[249] vessels,[250] and payments[251] are attested.

Because we only have a few data for the ceremony, it is not possible to say much about the schedule of the *šalām bīti*-days in Neo-Babylonian Uruk and Babylon. It is interesting however, that of the five data that we have, four concern day 8, and that only months VII and IX are attested. *GC* 1, 203 from Uruk records day 8, but does not mention the month; *YOS* 6, 192 and 189 mention days 8-IX and 8-VII. *VS* 6, 268 from Babylon mentions two *šalām bīti*-ceremonies (*ina* 2 *ša-lam* É), one on day 8-VII and one on 5-VII, but the latter may well be a mistake for day 8.

It is clear that the Sippar-schedule does not completely agree with our data: *YOS* 6, 192 (Uruk) and *VS* 6, 268 (Babylon) mention month IX, which is not attested in the Sippar-texts, but the other days (8-VII in *YOS* 6, 189 and *VS* 6, 268) do agree with them.

The Hellenistic period

The *šalām bīti*-ceremony is attested only once in texts from the Hellenistic period;[252] in *TU* 41, rev. 16, the *šangû*-priests and the temple enterers (*ērib bīti*) perform the ceremony in the Rēš-temple of Anu in Uruk during the vigil preceding day 17 of (perhaps) the tenth month Ṭebētu[253] (see the Appendix):

> '[14] ... The *šangû*-priests of the temples of Tiranna (and) secondly the temple enterers (*ērib bīti*) of all the temples [15]will kindle a fire from the torch and they will carry (it) to their temple. Then [16]they will perform the the good-functioning of the temple ceremony (*šá-lam* É). They will kindle a brushwood pile at the gates of their temple'.

Day 17-X is not attested in texts from Neo-Babylonian Uruk and Babylon.

II.4. Annual ceremonies

The Babylonian year consisted of twelve months. However, because a lunar year of twelve months consists of 354 days, the lunar year is eleven days shorter than the solar year with 365.25 days. For this reason after c. 600 B.C. a series of second Ulūlus and second Addarus had to be added, that is seven months in every cycle of nineteen years.[254] Based on the agricultural cycle, the year started around the time of the spring

---

[248] *GC* 1, 12; 198; 203; A.B. Moldenke, 2, 48; *BIN* 1, 19.
[249] *OECT* 1, 20, J. MacGinnis, *AfO* 38–39 (1991–92), 89; *VS* 6, 268.
[250] F. Thureau-Dangin, *RA* 16 (1919), 125; *AUWE* 5, 145; HE 145 (F. Joannès, *RA* 75 [1981], 144); *YOS* 6, 62; 192; 189; *YOS* 7, 185.
[251] *GC* 1, 379.
[252] Cf. G.J.P. McEwan, *FAOS* 4, 166.
[253] See I.2.
[254] Cf. O. Neugebauer, *JNES* 1 (1942), 400 f.; R.A. Parker, W.H. Dubberstein, *Babylonian Chronology 662 B.C.–A.D. 75*, Providence, 1956, 2 f.; R. Borger, *JEOL* 18 (1964), 326–7; S. Smith, *Iraq* 31 (1969), 74 ff.; C.B.F. Walker, H. Hunger, *MDOG* 109 (1977), 33; A.J. Sachs–H. Hunger, *Diaries*, vol. I, 13 ff.

equinox.[255] While the first month of the civil year is Nisannu, beginning around the middle of March,[256] and ending around the middle of April, the religious year began in the seventh month Tašrītu (September/October);[257] as we will see, for this reason two New Year festivals were celebrated, one in Nisannu and one in Tašrītu.[258] The year ended with the month Addaru, around February/March.

During the Babylonian cultic year ceremonies were celebrated, which occurred only on a fixed (number of) day(s) of a particular month. The most important and well-known annual ceremonies were celebrated during the New Year festival. However, there were more, of which we often know only very little.

In this section the unspecified ceremonies, recorded in legal documents from Hellenistic Uruk concerned with prebend shares, will be discussed first, followed by the clothing ceremonies, the processions, and the divine marriage ceremonies. Then we will turn our attention to the New Year festivals of Uruk and Babylon, as known from texts from the Hellenistic period. Also, the brazier festivals will be discussed. Finally, all the collected data are brought together in two cultic calendars, one for Uruk, and one for Babylon.

II.4.1. *Unspecified annual ceremonies*[259]

Uruk

While the monthly ceremonies are usually not dated, the annual ceremonies often were given an exact date by referring to the day and month on which they were performed; often the text specifically adds: *šattussu* 'every year, yearly'. In Hellenistic legal documents concerning prebend shares from Uruk a ceremony is recorded for Papsukkal on day 17 of Tašrītu,[260] a ceremony for Antu on day 8 of Addaru, and a ceremony for Bēlet-ṣēri on day 10 of Addaru.

---

[255] The *rēš šatti* (SAG MU.AN.NA) 'beginning of the year' was either the period between approximately 15-XII and 15-I (cf. E.F. Weidner, *Handbuch*, 82 f.), or, more likely, the 'New Year's day' (cf. S. Parpola, *LAS* II, 15 and 54).

[256] In the Achaemenid and Hellenistic periods day 1-I fell approximately 14 days after the equinox (with variations of course), cf. H. Hunger, *WZKM* 67 (1975), 27.

[257] *rēš šatti* could also refer to the seventh month, cf. E.F. Weidner, *Handbuch*, 83 and S. Parpola, *LAS* II, 187. In ancient Israel a New Year in the first month Nisan and in the seventh month Tišri were also known, cf. A.J. Wensinck, *Acta Or.* 1 (1923), 168. A. Cavigneaux and F. Al-Rawi, *Iraq* 55 (1993), 96 f. noted an interesting parallel between Babylonia and Israel: in Babylonia the writing of the tablets of fates for the whole coming year on day 7-VII is paralleled in Israel by the sealing of the destinies at the same time of the year, on Yom Kippur. A Syrian text identifies Nisan as the 'beginning of the months' and Tišri as the 'beginning of the year', cf. S.P. Brock, *JSS* 30 (1985), 186. Also the Romans originally had two moments when the year began: the Idus of March and the Saturnalia in December, cf. H.S. Versnel, *Triumphus. An inquiry into the origin, development and meaning of the Roman triumph*, Leiden, 1970, 228. Note that the Akkadian name for the seventh month, Tašrītu, means 'beginning', cf. W.G. Lambert, *NABU* 1989, no. 90.

[258] See II.4.5.

[259] For the unspecified monthly celebrated ceremonies see II.3.1.

[260] Cf. P.-A. Beaulieu, *ASJ* 14 (1992), 60 f.

Table X: unspecified annual ceremonies from prebend texts of Hellenistic Uruk[261]

date	god	text/date
17-VII	Papsukkal	*OECT* 9, 40; 42 (14 + x-XI-x, Sel); 44 (6-VII-x, Ant and Ant); 45 // 46 (21-VI-111, Ant [III] and Ant); 60 (10-IV-153, Dem [I])
8-XII	Antu	*OECT* 9, 40; 42 (14 + x-XI-x, Sel); 44 (6-VII-x, Ant and Ant); 45 // 46 (21-VI-111, Ant [III] and Ant); 60 (10-IV-153, Dem [I]); 68
10-XII	Bēlet-ṣēri	*OECT* 9, 44 (6-VII-x, Ant and Ant); 60 (10-IV-153, Dem [I])

The foodstuffs which are presented here consist of ox, fowl and lamb,[262] ox, sheep, fowl, lamb and parched barley,[263] or only fowl.[264] Interestingly fowl is presented on these annual ceremonies, while it is not attested for the unspecified monthly ceremonies.[265]

Several more ceremonies are known, the nature of which is often not clear. Because the data are all from calendar texts, we must assume that all ceremonies collected here were celebrated yearly. Only a few are known from Uruk: five ceremonies on day 10 [+ x], 22, 26, 27 and 29 of the eleventh month Šabaṭu are attested in the calendar text K 3753,[266] but because of the damaged state of the passage the context is difficult.

Babylon

Most of the ceremonies come from Babylon, and all are attested in the calendar texts *SBH* VII // *BRM* 4, 25 and *SBH* VIII. However the relevant passages are often damaged, and the context of the attested ceremonies is in many cases difficult. Of the many references to ceremonies, often together with offerings, we will list here those which can form part of the cultic calendar.[267] We will enumerate the ceremonies in a chronological order.

A ceremony with Nabû in the (temple) garden on day 6 of the second month Ajjaru[268] is known, followed by a ceremony of Nabû on day 7 of Ajjaru in the garden of Anu, situated in Emeurur, which is probably the temple of Nanāja at Babylon.[269]

---

261 Perhaps two more unspecified (annual?) ceremonies are recorded in *OECT* 9, 40, but the relevant passage is damaged; first a ceremony for Antu in the first month Nisannu (obv. 3–4): 3. *ina* ^{iti}BAR […] 4.[…] ^{šim}LI *ù* 1-*en* GEŠTIN$^{!}$ *ṣu-up-pe-ti šá* ^{giš}*tal-lu šá An-tu*$_4$ ‘^{3}in Nisannu […] ^{4}from the juniper and one(?) (amount of?) wine, carded wool(?) for the carrying pole of Antu’. Secondly a ceremony for Antu in the seventh month Tašrītu (obv. 5–6): 5.[…] *ina* ^{iti}DU$_6$ … (the copy reads 70, which must be a mistake) 1/2 SÌLA ^{šim}LI *ù* 1-*en* GEŠTIN$^{!}$ *ṣu-up-pe-ti šá* ^{giš}*tal-l*u 6.[*šá A*]*n-tu*$_4$ … ‘^{5}[…] in Tašrītu … and a half *qû*(?) juniper and one (amount of?) wine, carded wool(?) for the carrying pole ^{6}[of A]ntu …’.

262 *OECT* 9, 40; 42.

263 *OECT* 9, 45 // 46; 60.

264 *OECT* 9, 68.

265 See II.3.1.

266 III, 3; 5; 6; 9.

267 See II.4.7.

268 *SBH* VIII, II, 22: UD.6.KAM *ana qé-reb* ^{giš}KIRI$_6$ *uš-te-ṣa-am-ma ú-kal-lam* x […] ‘On day 6 he is brought out to the garden and discloses […]’.

269 *SBH* VIII, II, 23–4: UD.7.KAM *ana* É.ME.UR.UR *uš-te-šir ana* É.AN.NA *el-*[*li*] *ana* ^{giš}KIRI$_6$ *uṣ-ṣa-a ana* ^{giš}KIRI$_6$ ^{d}*A-nù i-ru-um-ma uš-šá-b*[*u*(?) …] ‘On day 7 he marches on to Emeurur, to pure Eanna, he goes out to the garden, enters the garden of Anu and [they(?)] sit’. For Emeurur see A.R. George, *House Most High*, 126, no. 794.

Bēlet-ilī celebrated a ceremony on day 15 of the third month Simānu,[270] and a ceremony of Nabû and an unknown god was held on day 22 of Simānu.[271]

On day 18 of the eighth month Araḫsamna a ceremony with offerings for Šamaš and others in various temples, including a procession and a ceremony with a brazier (*kinūnu*) is recorded,[272] and on day 25-VIII, a ceremony with offerings for Zababa of Kiš and furthermore for the city Isin and the temple Esabad, including a ceremony with the *abgalgungunnu*-drum and the kettledrum (*lilissu*).[273]

We also know of several ceremonies of the ninth month Kislīmu, which all include offerings for a certain deity: for Marduk, Zarpanītu and others on day 4-IX,[274] which is confirmed by a reference to a ceremony before Marduk on the same day elsewhere;[275] for Enlils (dEN.LÍL.MEŠ) and Adads (dIM.MEŠ), and others on day 6/7-IX;[276] for Lugalbanda on day 8-IX;[277] for Lugalasal (Bēl-ṣarbati), including a ceremony with braziers on day 9-IX;[278] for Ea and others, including a ceremony with the *ḫalḫallatu*-drum on day 10-IX;[279] for Ištar of Babylon on day 12-IX;[280] for Anunītu and Šarrat-Sippar of Babylon on day 13-IX;[281] for Ašratu on day 14-IX;[282] for Anaššat(?)[283] and Bēlet-Agade on day 15-IX;[284] for Nabû and others, including a ceremony with braziers, on day 16/17-IX,[285] which is confirmed by another reference to a ceremony for Nabû on day 17 elsewhere;[286] for Uraš, including a ceremony with a brazier on day 22-IX;[287] for Lugalmar(a)da and others on day 25-IX;[288] and for Nergal on day 28/9-IX.[289]

Finally, for day 10 of the tenth month Ṭebētu a ceremony with offerings for Palil, including a ceremony with braziers, is attested.[290]

---

270 *SBH* VIII, III, 6 ff.: 6.TA UD.15.KAM E[N ...] 7. *šá* d*Be-let*-DINGIR.MEŠ x [...] 'From day 15 t[ill ...] of Bēlet-ilī ... [...]'.

271 *SBH* VIII, III, 2 ff.: UD.22.[KAM ...] dAG *u* d[...] 'On day 22 [...] Nabû and [...]'.

272 *BRM* 4, 25, obv. 4–10. See II.4.6.

273 *SBH* VII, obv. 1–7 // *BRM* 4, 25, obv. 11–17.

274 *SBH* VII, obv. 8 f. // *BRM* 4, 25, obv. 18 f.

275 *SBH* VIII, V, 9 ff. G. Çağirgan, *Festivals*, 169–70, concluded that col. V is concerned with the tenth month Ṭebētu. However, although this may be true for the last part of the column (35 ff.; the directly preceding lines are damaged), the preceding part must deal with month Kislīmu (the 28th day of this month is mentioned in line 28).

276 *SBH* VII, obv. 10 f. // *BRM* 4, 25, obv. 20 ff.

277 *SBH* VII, obv. 12 // *BRM* 4, 25, obv. 25.

278 *SBH* VII, obv. 13 // *BRM* 4, 25, obv. 26 ff.

279 *SBH* VII, obv. 14 ff. // *BRM* 4, 25, rev. 30 ff.

280 *SBH* VII, obv. 17 // *BRM* 4, 25, rev. 36.

281 *SBH* VII, obv. 18 // *BRM* 4, 25, rev. 37.

282 *BRM* 4, 25, rev. 38.

283 Cf. E. Unger, *Babylon*, 137; K. Tallqvist, *Götterepitheta*, 262.

284 *SBH* VII, obv. 19 // *BRM* 4, 25, rev. 39 f.

285 *SBH* VII, obv. 20 f. // *BRM* 4, 25, rev. 41 f.

286 *SBH* VIII, V, 21 ff.

287 *SBH* VII, obv. 22 // *BRM* 4, 25, rev. 46.

288 *SBH* VII, obv. 23 f. // *BRM* 4, 25, rev. 47 f.

289 *SBH* VII, obv. 25 // *BRM* 4, 25, rev. 49.

290 *BRM* 4, 25, rev. 50 ff.

From Babylon an (annual?) ceremony or festival, elsewhere unknown, in the temple of Nergal on day 15 of an unknown month is attested in the administrative text *CT* 49, 187, obv. 4′: UD.15.KAM *ak-ka-di-ia šá* É dU.GUR 'On day 15 a cock of the temple of Nergal'. Cf. W. von Soden, *Or*NS 46 (1977), 184, no. 173.

Table XI: unspecified annual ceremonies from Hellenistic Uruk and Babylon

date	god(s)	place	text
10 [+ x]-XI	–	Uruk	K 3753
22-XI	–	Uruk	K 3753
26-XI	–	Uruk	K 3753
27-XI	–	Uruk	K 3753
29-XI	–	Uruk	K 3753
6-II	Nabû	Babylon	*SBH* VIII
7-II	Nabû	Babylon	*SBH* VIII
15-III	Bēlet-ilī	Babylon	*SBH* VIII
22-III	–	Babylon	*SBH* VIII
18-VIII	Šamaš	Babylon[291]	*BRM* 4, 25
25-VIII	Zababa, Isin	Babylon[291]	*SBH* VII // *BRM* 4, 25
4-IX	Marduk, Zarpanītu	Babylon[291]	*SBH* VII // *BRM* 4, 25; *SBH* VIII
6/7-IX	Enlils, Adads	Babylon[291]	*SBH* VII // *BRM* 4, 25
8-IX	Lugalbanda	Babylon[291]	*SBH* VII // *BRM* 4, 25
9-IX	Lugalasal	Babylon[291]	*SBH* VII // *BRM* 4, 25
10-IX	Ea	Babylon[291]	*SBH* VII // *BRM* 4, 25
12-IX	Ištar	Babylon[291]	*SBH* VII // *BRM* 4, 25
13-IX	Anunītu, Šarrat-Sippar	Babylon[291]	*SBH* VII // *BRM* 4, 25
14-IX	Ašratu	Babylon[291]	*BRM* 4, 25
15-IX	Anaššat(?)	Babylon[291]	*SBH* VII // *BRM* 4, 25
16/17-IX	Nabû	Babylon[291]	*SBH* VII // *BRM* 4, 25; *SBH*VIII
22-IX	Uraš	Babylon[291]	*SBH* VII // *BRM* 4, 25
25-IX	Lugalmar(a)da	Babylon[291]	*SBH* VII // *BRM* 4, 25
28/29-IX	Nergal	Babylon[291]	*SBH* VII // *BRM* 4, 25
10-X	Palil	Babylon[291]	*BRM* 4, 25

II.4.2. *Annual clothing ceremonies*

While the data from the Neo-Babylonian and Hellenistic periods usually refer to the regularly celebrated monthly clothing ceremonies,[292] there is some evidence from Hellenistic Uruk and Babylon that *lubuštu* was also celebrated yearly on special occasions, as for example during the New Year festival,[293] although due to lack of information the 'annual' character of the ceremony is not always certain.

Uruk

We know of several clothing ceremonies from Uruk, which may have been celebrated only occasionally.

---

[291] And neighbouring towns/cities, see A.R. George, *BTT*, 222, n. 4.

[292] For the monthly celebrated *lubuštu*-ceremony see II.3.3.

[293] Cf. G.J.P. McEwan, *FAOS* 4, 164.

The ritual text *TU* 39, describing the New Year festival of the seventh month Tašrītu, refers to several gods being robed (*nalbušu*) on days 1 and 6 (obv. 1 and 6), and then records in a summarised version the clothing ceremonies (*lubuštu*) of Anu, Antu and Ištar on the seventh day of the festival; the passage also mentions clothing ceremonies which are performed before the *guqqû*-offerings (obv.11–13):

> '[11]As to the cella: the clothing ceremonies (^{túg}*lu-bu-šá-at*) of Anu and Antu and the clothing ceremonies of Ištar. [12]The setting in place of the ox. (Inside the room) between the curtains: songs by the singer and the lamentation priest. [13](The presentation of) *guqqû*-offerings which follow the clothing ceremonies (^{túg}*lu-bu-uš-*tu_4) and (the presentation of) the *siltu*-food (offerings). The consecration of the temple'.

A clothing ceremony of Anu and Adad on day 3 of the sixth month Ulūlu is recorded in the calendar text K 3753.[294] Furthermore *CLBT*, pl. 1 contains, in obscure context, a reference to a clothing ceremony.[295] W 18728[296] does not contain clothing ceremonies but gives instructions for the clothing of various cultic functionaries, including several priests,[297] and the king.[298] The text probably deals with clothing instructions for a special festival, because of a reference to 'the second day' (*ina* 2-*i* u_4-*m*[*u* ...]),[299] so apparently refers to a festival lasting several days.[300] No data are mentioned.

Babylon

From Babylon four clothing ceremonies are attested in the calendar text *SBH* VIII: a clothing ceremony of Marduk presumably on day 8 of the first month Nisannu, during the New Year festival,[301] a clothing ceremony of Nabû for the divine marriage ceremony on the second day of the second month Ajjaru,[302] a clothing ceremony perhaps of Marduk on day 3 of the ninth month Kislīmu,[303] and a clothing ceremony of an unknown god on day 16 of Kislīmu.[304]

---

294 E. Weidner, *GDBT*, pl. 11, I, 7: UD.3.KAM ^{d}*A-nù u* ^{d}IM *te-di-iq in-na-an-di-qu-ʾ nu-um-mu-ru zi-mu-šú-nu* 'On the third day (of Ulūlu) Anu and Adad are clothed with fine attire, their appearance is shining'.

295 I, 19: [... *l*]u_4(?) *a-na te-di-iq la-biš* '[...] he is robed with fine attire'.

296 A Falkenstein, *UVB* 15 (1959), 40–44, and pl. 29, 34.

297 Obv. 5 ff.

298 Rev. 8 ff.

299 Obv. 4′.

300 Cf. A. Falkenstein, *UVB* 15 (1959), 40. Perhaps we should connect these clothing instructions with the New Year festival, see rev. 8′: *lu-bu-uš-*tu_4 LUGAL *šá ina ṣa-bat* ŠU^{II} DINGIR.MEŠ *il-lab-biš* 'clothing of the king, which he will wear when he takes the gods by the hands'; the phrase *qātē ṣabātu* is well-known, especially in texts describing the New Year festival. For this phrase see my comments on *TU* 39, obv. 27 in the Appendix. On the other hand, the passage describing the clothing instructions for the lamentation priest with references to *lubāru*-clothing and the kettledrum (obv. 10′ff.) reminds us of the third version of the lunar eclipse ritual, dealing with the duties of the lamentation priest during this ritual, where the *lubāru*-clothing and the kettledrum are also mentioned. See II.7.3.

301 II, 3: [... *t*]*e-di-iq be-lu-ti-šú in-na-an-di-iq i-na-áš*⟨*-ši*⟩ *me-lam-mu* 'he is clothed with fine attire of his Lordship, he bears the *melammu*-splendor'. See also II.4.5.2.

302 II, 15: ^{d}AG *šá ḫa-da-áš-šu-tú in-na-an-di-iq te-di-iq* ^{d}*A-nu-tú* 'Nabû in (his) status as bridegroom is clothed with fine attire of Anuship'. For the divine marriage ceremony see II.4.4.

303 V, 8: UD.3.KAM [*t*]*e-di-iq be-lu-tu* [*in-na-an-di-iq*(?)] 'On the third day (of Kislīmu) [he (= Marduk?) is clothed] with fine attire of Lordship [...]'.

304 V, 19 f.: UD.16.KAM *te-di-iq be-lu-tu in-*[*na-an-di-iq* ...] 'On the sixteenth day (of Kislīmu) he [is

In the Esagila-ritual performed during the ninth month Kislīmu, BM 32206 +, several clothing ceremonies are recorded: a clothing ceremony of/by the *dumuniglala*-priest[305] on day 3 of Kislīmu;[306] a clothing ceremony of Bēltīja and Tašmētu on day 3 of Kislīmu;[307] a reference to a clothing ceremony of Bēl on day 7 of Tašrītu(?) is mentioned (i.e. during New Year festival[308]), together with a clothing ceremony of Ištar of Babylon on day 3 of Kislīmu .[309]

Table XII: annual clothing ceremonies from Hellenistic Uruk and Babylon

date	god(s)	place	text
3-VI	Anu, Adad	Uruk	K 3753
7-VII	Anu, Antu, Ištar	Uruk	*TU* 39
–	–	Uruk	*CLBT*, pl. 1
8-I	Marduk	Babylon	*SBH* VIII
2-II	Nabû	Babylon	*SBH* VIII
7-VII(?)	Bēl	Babylon	BM 32206 +
3-IX	–	Babylon	*SBH* VIII
3-IX	–	Babylon	BM 32206 +
3-IX	Bēltīja, Tašmētu	Babylon	BM 32206 +
3-IX	Ištar of Babylon	Babylon	BM 32206 +
16-IX	–	Babylon	*SBH* VIII

II.4.3. *Processions*

The processions in Assyria and Babylonia of the first millennium have been discussed by B. Pongratz-Leisten.[310] Here we will list those which are recorded in texts from Hellenistic Uruk and Babylon.

Uruk

From Uruk the procession of Anu for the first New Year festival of the month Nisannu is described in *KAR* 132, but on which day(s) this occurred is not certain – probably day 8. The procession of Anu, performed during the second New Year festival of the month Tašrītu, is attested in *BRM* 4, 7 and *TU* 39–40, and took place on day 8 and day 9.[311] Furthermore we have a procession during a festival for Ištar, *TU* 42 +, but no reference is made to the day(s) on which it occurred.[312] Also a procession of Anu took

clothed] with fine attire of the Lordship [...]'.

305 For the *dumuniglala*, an unknown priest, see G. Çağirgan, W.G. Lambert, *JCS* 43–45 (1991–1993), 90b.

306 I, 6–13.

307 I, 43.

308 See II.4.5.2.

309 II, 53–54.

310 *ina šulmi īrub*.

311 Both processions will be discussed more extensively in II.4.5.1.

312 This text will be discussed in II.8.5.

place during a nocturnal feast in the Rēš-temple, *TU* 41, on day 16 and 17, probably of the month Ṭebētu.[313]

More processions from Hellenistic Uruk are known. A procession of Mīšaru, from Eḫenunna, the temple of Adad, on day 5 of Araḫsamna is attested in the ritual text *TU* 39;[314] this procession is also attested for the same day in the calendar text K 3753.[315] In the latter a procession of Nusku and Ningal into the streets of Uruk, and a procession of Nusku through the squares (*rebītu*) of Uruk, during day 3(?) of the month Ulūlu is also recorded.[316] Lastly a procession of a god(?) from the presence of Anu to Šamaš, on day 18 of Araḫsamna is mentioned.[317]

Babylon[318]

The New Year procession to the *akītu*-temple during the month Nisannu in Babylon on day 8 is well-known from pre-Hellenistic texts, but from Hellenistic Babylon we only have two references, one in an astronomical diary,[319] and one in a calendar text.[320]

Other processions are also known. Three more processions are attested in the calendar text *SBH* VIII from Babylon: a marriage procession of Nabû and Ninkali (?= Nanāja?) from Ezida to Euršaba (the cella of Nanāja in Esagila),[321] on day 2 of Ajjaru,[322] a procession of Nabû to Emeurur, on day 7 of Ajjaru,[323] and a procession of Nanāja from Euršaba to the 'garden of the Mountain', on day 17 of Ajjaru.[324] A procession of the *assinnu*-priest to the House of Lament (*bīt sipittê*) for day 15 of Simānu, and a procession of the *kurgarrû*-priest to a cultic place called the Equlû is attested for day 16

---

313 This text will be discussed in II.8.6.

314 Rev. 26.

315 II, 2 ff. (damaged context).

316 I, 10 and 13.

317 II, 12 ff. (damaged context).

An indirect reference to a procession in Uruk can be found in AO 11080 (J.-M. Durand, *Textes babyloniens*, pl. 35 = F. Joannès, *Textes économiques*, no. 52) (dated 109 S.E.), apparently a list of persons connected to the statue of Anu and his chariot (*narkabtu*)(?).

318 A Greek procession (*πομπή*), attested in an astronomical diary from Babylon (A.J. Sachs–H. Hunger, *Diaries*, no. -168, A, obv. 14–15), is discussed in II.8.4.

319 A.J. Sachs–H. Hunger, *Diaries*, no. -204. See also II.4.5.2 and II.8.7.

320 *SBH* VIII, II, 4: [...]x *uš-te-šir ana qé-reb* É.SÍSKUR.RA 'He marches on to (the *akītu*-temple) *bīt ikrībi*'. See II.4.5.2.

321 Or the temple of Ištar as Nanāja in Borsippa, cf. A.R. George, *House Most High*, 157, nos. 1195 and 1196.

322 *SBH* VIII, II, 15–21: 15.ᵈAG *šá ḫa-da-áš-šu-tú in-na-an-di-iq te-di-iq* ᵈ*A-nu-tú* 16.TA *qé-reb* É.ZI.DA *ina šat mu-ši uš-ta-pa-a na-an-na-ri-iš* 17.*ki-ma* ᵈXXX *ina ni-ip-ḫi-šú ú-nam-mar ek-let* 18.*ina qé-reb* É.UR$_5$.ŠÀ.BA *uš-te-šir i-šad-di-ḫu nam-riš* 19.*i-ru-um-ma ana ma-ḫar* ᵈNIN KA LI *šit-ku-nu ana ḫa-da-a-*[*áš-šu-nu*] 20.*ina qé-reb* É.UR$_5$.ŠÀ.BA GIM *u$_4$-mu i-šak-kan na-mir-*[*tu*] 21.*ina ma-a-al-tu$_4$ mu-ši ṭa-a-bi it-ta-na-a-a-lu šit-ta* [*ṭābta*] '15.Nabû in (his) status as bridegroom is clothed with fine attire of Anuship. 16.He shines forth from Ezida at night like the (moon) light. 17.He brightens the darkness with his shining like the moon. 18.He marches in Euršaba, he proceeds brightly, 19.he enters in front of NIN KA LI to perform the wedding festival. 20.He makes the light like day in Euršaba. 21.In the bed of a pleasant night they lay down again and again in [sweet] sleep'.

323 Already cited in II.4.1.

324 *SBH* VIII, II, 27–28: 27.UD.17.KAM TA *qé-reb* É.UR$_5$.ŠÀ.BA ᵈ*Na-na-a i-ḫ*[*i-iš* ...] 28.[*ana*] ᵍⁱˢKIRI$_6$ *ḫur-sa-an-na uš-*[*te*]*-šir* x x [...] '27.On day 17 Nanāja rus[hes?] from Euršaba [...], 28.she marches on to the "mountain" garden'.

of Simānu, followed by a procession to the Uraš-gate.[325] A procession of 'the sons of Bēl' to Enamḫe, the temple of Adad in Babylon, is recorded for day 18 of Araḫsamna in a calendar text.[326]

More processions from Babylon during the month Kislīmu are attested in BM 32206 +.[327] The text first records several events concerning Bēl and several other cult-participants, including a slave, a bull, and Ea's vizier Usmû, on day 3 of Kislīmu in Esagila,[328] leading up to the journey of the latter three on day 4 of Kislīmu from the entrance of the cella (*bāb papāḫi*)[329] to the *akītu*-temple,[330] after which the return to Esagila on the same day is described.[331] Furthermore, the text records three days, day 8 of Tašrītu, day 4 of Kislīmu, and a third lost day, on which a procession of Ninurta and the statue of Bēl (or Enlil?) departs from their cellas and sits at a gate, the name of which is lost.[332] The text describes another procession(?) 'from the opposite bank' (*ultu aḫulâ*) on day 16 of an unknown month, but the context is not clear.[333]

Finally, in an administrative document from the Arsacid period, *BRM* 1, 99,[334] silver is paid for several groups of persons involved in a procession on day 1 of an unknown month: for the *kurgarrû*-actors, *assinnu*-singer and songstresses, for the brewers(?), for two unknown groups of people, for the millers and for the Borsippaeans. The procession possibly took place during the so-called 'Love Lyrics Ritual' of Ištar of Babylon in her temple Eturkalamma.[335]

Table XIII: processions from Hellenistic Uruk and Babylon

date	god(s)	place	text
(8-I)	Anu	Uruk	*KAR* 132
3-VI	Nusku, Ningal	Uruk	K 3753
3-VI	Nusku	Uruk	K 3753
8–9-VII	Anu	Uruk	*BRM* 4, 7; *TU* 39–40
5-VIII	Mīšaru	Uruk	*TU* 39
5-VIII	Mīšaru	Uruk	K 3753
18-VIII	–	Uruk	K 3753
16–17-(X?)	Anu	Uruk	*TU* 41
–	Ištar	Uruk	*TU* 42 +
8-I	Bēl	Babylon	*Diaries*, no. -204; *SBH* VIII

325 BM 32656 (A.R. George, *Studies W.G. Lambert*, no. 2, 270 ff.), IV, 13′ ff. See II.8.5.
326 *BRM* 4, 25, obv. 6.
327 See also II.5.1. and II.8.2.
328 BM 32206 +, I, 4–45, II, 48–54.
329 II, 57.
330 III, 92.
331 III, 93 ff.
332 IV, 164–66.
333 IV, 167–8. B. Pongratz-Leisten, *ina šulmi īrub*, 48–9 has extensively described this procession to and from the *akītu*-temple.
334 Rev. 37–44 (date: 14-XII²-218 S.E. = 15-IV-93 B.C.). See G.J.P. McEwan, *FAOS* 4, 143–46. For the latest discussion of the text see R.J. van der Spek, in: J. Wiesehöfer (ed.), *Das Partherreich und seine Zeugnisse*, 229 ff.
335 The reference to the *kurgarrû*-actors, *assinnu*-singer and songstresses constitutes indirect evidence for the Love Lyrics Ritual being performed in the Arsacid period; see II.8.5.

date	god(s)	place	text
2-II	Nabû	Babylon	*SBH* VIII
7-II	Nabû	Babylon	*SBH* VIII
17-II	Nanāja	Babylon	*SBH* VIII
15-III	–	Babylon	BM 32656
16-III	–	Babylon	BM 32656
8-VII	Ninurta, Bēl (Enlil?)	Babylon	BM 32206 +
18-VIII	Sons of Bēl	Babylon	*SBH* VII // *BRM* 4, 25
4-IX	slave, bull, and Usmû	Babylon	BM 32206 +
–	Ninurta, Bēl (Enlil?)	Babylon	BM 32206 +
4-IX	Ninurta, Bēl (Enlil?)	Babylon	BM 32206 +
1-?	Ištar of Babylon	Babylon	*BRM* 1, 99

II.4.4. *Divine marriage ceremonies*

The Mesopotamian divine marriage (ἱερὸς γάμος, Akk. *ḫašādu*) was originally an hierogamy during which the king functions as a substitute for the god Tammuz (Dumuzi) and a priestess for the goddess Ištar (Inanna).[336] The ceremony is known from the Ur III period on, and it appears to be connected with the New Year festival.[337] In later texts the king has apparently lost his predominant position. In these texts the statues of a god and goddess were 'married'; they were brought together in a special bed-chamber for the divine marriage and for determining the destinies for the next year.

The divine marriage is known from both Hellenistic Uruk and Babylon.[338] The rites (*parṣu*) of the divine marriage in connection with the New Year festival are attested in the Uruk text *TU* 39; the relevant passage is mentioned in a section dealing with the first day of the New Year festival of the month Tašrītu[339]:

> '[4]The rites of the divine marriage (*par-ṣi šá ḫa-šá-du*) [5]will be performed [4]in the Eḫilikuga-chapel, the bed-chamber of Eḫilianna, [5]the temple of Nanāja'.

The bed-chamber (É.NIR) mentioned here is also attested in another Uruk ritual, *TU* 41, but a marriage does not take place there.[340]

The rites of the divine marriage (GARZA.GARZA *ḫa-šá-du*) are also attested in *TU* 38, in a list of offerings and ceremonies from Hellenistic Uruk.[341] Furthermore a wedding ceremony (*ḫadaššūtu*) on day 3 of Ulūlu is recorded in the calendar text K

336 There is much debate about the origin and purpose of the divine marriage. Cf. J. Renger, in: *RlA* 4 (1972–75), 251 ff. with earlier literature. See also W.H.PH. Römer, in: *Festschrift J.P.M. van der Ploeg* (AOAT Bd. 211), Kevelaer, 1982, 411 ff., especially 416 ff.; E. Matsushima, *ASJ* 10 (1988), 95 ff. For the archaeological evidence see J.S. Cooper, in: *RlA* 4 (1972–75), 259 ff.

337 Despite the evidence from Hellenistic Uruk and Babylon presented below, according to Lambert there is no evidence for a divine marriage in the course of the New Year festival (*JSS* 13 [1968], 106 f.).

338 Cf. E. Matsushima, *ASJ* 10 (1988), 98 and 110 ff.

339 *TU* 39, obv. 4–5.

340 *TU* 41, obv. 6–7. For the bed-chamber see also my comment on *TU* 39, obv. 4 in the Appendix. For *TU* 41 see II.8.6.

341 Obv. 37; rev. 37.

3753.[342] It is probably the wedding ceremony of Ištar, because I, 9 specifically states that the whole month of Ulūlu deals with Ištar.

Another Hellenistic reference to the divine marriage ceremony during the New Year festival, this time from Babylon, is recorded in *SBH* VIII; the relevant passage informs us that on day 11 of the New Year festival a wedding festival (*ḫadaššūtu*), probably between Marduk and Zarpanītu, is celebrated.[343] This text also refers to Nabû as bridegroom in a wedding ceremony with Ninkali (?= Nanāja?) in her temple Euršaba during day 2 of the month Ajjaru.[344]

Table XIV: marriage ceremonies from Hellenistic Uruk and Babylon

date	god(s)	place	Text
3-VI	Ištar	Uruk	K 3753
1-VII	–	Uruk	*TU* 39
–	–	Uruk	*TU* 38
11-I	Marduk, Zarpanītu(?)	Babylon	*SBH* VIII
2-II	Nabû	Babylon	*SBH* VIII

II.4.5. *The New Year festival*

The New Year festival (*akītu*) is one of the oldest annual festivals. The earliest reference dates from the Fara period, probably referring to an *akītu*-building or ceremony in Nippur.[345] In the first millennium the New Year festival was celebrated twice a year, in the spring and in the autumn. The first forms more or less the beginning of the civil year, while the second opens the cultic year.[346]

The main purpose of the festival was for the ruler to be reaffirmed in his office by the gods, and for his people to be assured of another peaceful and prosperous year. During the festival this divine approval and assurance was celebrated by the whole community. The history of the New Year festival has been described extensively, most recently by Cohen and Pongratz-Leisten.[347]

In this paragraph an attempt is not made to present a complete new discussion of the festival, but rather an inventory of all the available sources from Hellenistic Uruk and Babylon is offered, in order to reconstruct the cultic calendar of the festival.

---

342 I, 19: x.A.BI [...] *iš-ša*[*k-k*]*an ḫa-da-šu-tù* '[...] the wedding ceremony will be performed'.

343 II, 7–8. Or Nabû?, cf. E. Matsushima, *ASJ* 10 (1988), 98. See also II.4.5.2.

344 II, 15–21. This passage is cited in II.4.3, n. 69. See also the Neo-Assyrian letters *ABL* 65 (a divine marriage for the third day of Ajjaru) and *ABL* 113 (for the fourth day of Ajjaru).

345 M.E. Cohen, *Cultic Calendars*, 401.

346 Cf. K. van der Toorn, *Suppl. VT* 43 (1991), 332. The Babylonian New Year festival is based on the Sumerian *akītu*-festival (Á.KI.TI), which probably originated in Ur; it was also held twice a year at the beginning of the spring-equinox (new moon festival) and autumn-equinox (new year festival) and celebrated the time of harvest and sowing. Cf. W.H.Ph. Römer, in: *Festschrift J.P.M. van der Ploeg*, 422; M.E. Cohen, *Cultic Calendars*, 401–6.

347 M.E. Cohen, *Cultic Calendars*, 400–453; B. Pongratz-Leisten, *ina šulmi īrub* (discussing the *akītu*-processions in the first millennium). Especially relevant are also: G. Furlani, *Sacrificio*, 246 ff. and id., *Riti*, 119 ff., 159 ff. and 185 ff.; A. Falkenstein, *Topographie*, 42 ff. (*akītu*-temple); P.-R. Berger, in: *CRRA* 17 (1970), 155 ff. (Neo-Babylonian chronicles).

II.4.5.1. Uruk

From Hellenistic Uruk there is clear evidence for two New Year festivals, in the first month Nisannu and the seventh month Tašrītu. We know some of the proceedings of these festivals, especially from *BRM* 4, 7, *TU* 39–40, *KAR* 132 and *TU* 43. The temple ritual texts describing the second New Year festival of the month Tašrītu concentrate on the ritual activities in the Rēš-temple of Anu and Antu, and perhaps also in the Ešgal-temple of Ištar, because, as we already saw, we have a reference to a divine marriage ceremony taking place in the Eḫilikuga, the bed-chamber of the Eḫilianna, the temple of Nanāja.[348] In the Neo-Assyrian and Neo-Babylonian periods the temple of Nanāja was part of the Eanna complex, but as Falkenstein already noted,[349] although during the Late Babylonian period Ištar and Nanāja moved from the old complex, Eanna, to the new, Ešgal, it is not certain whether the temple-name Eḫilianna passed to the new cella of Nanāja in the Ešgal,[350] or whether it remained to indicate Nanāja's sanctuary in Eanna.

During the festival a procession to and from the *akītu*-temple took place. The ritual texts describing the first New Year festival in the month Nisannu concentrate on the ritual activities taking place before and during the procession to the *akītu*-temple, and the events in the *akītu*-temple. Several *akītu*-temples are attested from Hellenistic Uruk.[351] *Akītu*-temples of Anu and Ištar are mentioned in texts from Uruk concerning the *itinnūtu* (office of building master)-prebend,[352] and the *nārūtu* (singers) -prebend.[353] The *akītu*-temples of Anu and Uruk are also often mentioned in the ritual texts, among which are a 'higher situated *akītu*-temple of Anu', and an '*akītu*-temple (named) *Bīt ikribi*'.[354] Falkenstein presumed that the Hellenistic buildings were at the same position as the Neo- and Late Babylonian sanctuaries.[355] An *akītu*-complex was excavated during the twelfth excava-

---

348 *TU* 39, obv. 4–5. See II.4.4.

349 *Topographie*, 36, 41.

350 And not to the Rēš-temple (M.E. Cohen, *Cultic Calendars*, 329, n. 2 and 428, n. 2).

351 Cf. A. Falkenstein, *Topographie*, 43–4. Several *akītu*-temples are also known from Neo- and Late Babylonian Uruk (cf. ib., 42–3): an *akītu*-temple of Bēlet-ša-Uruk (*YOS* 7, 89, Cyr), an *akītu*-temple of Uṣur-amassu (*BIN* 2, 31 // *YOS* 9, 74, and BM 113205, cf. J.A. Brinkman, *WdO* 5 [1969–70], 39 ff., both Nabunaṣir; perhaps also: *BIN* 1, 170, Ner), and an *akītu* (-temple) of the open country (*ṣēru*) (*AnOr* 9, 2: 64, Asb.; 3: 44, Kand., cf. G. Frame, *RA* 76 [1982], 159). In texts from the Neo-Babylonian and later periods a special datepalm orchard ('garden') is often mentioned, called *ḫallatu*. D. Cocqrerillat demonstrated that this is the garden which surrounded the *akītu*-temple (*WdO* 7 [1973], 96 ff.; see also id., in: *RlA* 4 [1972], 60 f.). This garden existed in several cities among which are Uruk and Babylon. In Uruk the garden is situated near the '*akītu* (-temple) of the open country', and offerings are presented in the temple of the 'Lady of the open country' (Bēlet-ṣēri) and other goddesses of Uruk (*WdO* 7 [1973], 106, 108, and 113 ff.; see also G.J.P. McEwan, *FAOS* 4, 102 f.). The garden of Babylon is called 'of Bēl' (*WdO* 7 [1973], 131 f.; R. Zadok, *RGTC* 8 [1985], 147 f.).

352 *BRM* 1, 98, // HSM 913.1.6 (cf. J. Oelsner, *Materialien*, 161), É *á-ki-tu*₄.MEŠ; *BRM* 2, 22 // *BiMes* 24, 1: É *a-ki-tu*₄ *šá* ᵈINNIN. For the *itinnūtu*-prebend see also III.4.3.

353 *VS* 15, 19, [É] *a-ki-tu*₄.MEŠ.

354 The *akītu*-temple of Anu: *TU* 39, obv. 3 (É *a-ki-i-tu*₄ *e-lit šá* ᵈLX); *BRM* 4, 7, 24 (É *á-ki-tu*₄ É *ik-rib*). See also *TU* 39, obv. 14; *KAR* 132, IV, 6, 7, 10; *BRM* 4, 7, rev. 28, 41. For the *akītu*-temple of Ištar see: *TU* 42 +, rev. 23′, 24′ (KISAL É *a-ki-tu*₄).

355 *Topographie*, 42.

tion season.[356] The large site with several temples confirms the assumption of Falkenstein 'daß die verschiedenen Festhäuser nur Teile eines großen Akītu-Komplexes sind'.[357]

The second New Year festival (Tašrītu)

Of the two New Year festivals celebrated in Uruk, the festival of the seventh month Tašrītu is best known. The festival lasted eleven days. *BRM* 4, 7 probably concerns the New Year festival of Tašrītu. The colophon contains a catch-line, indicating that the text is part of a series of Uruk temple ritual texts.[358] The text describes a program of the procession of Anu's statue during the New Year festival in Uruk, from his cella to the center of the Rēš-temple, and then going outside to the *akītu*-temple. Anu leaves the cella Enamenna (É.NAM.EN.NA 'House of Dominion') and arrives at the Grand Gate, and then the exorcists recite an incantation and the high priest, the exorcists, the other temple enterers (*ērib bīti*), and the brewers, harnessed to the carrying pole, say a prayer. This is repeated during the seven stages of the procession until they have reached the *akītu*-temple.[359]

Falkenstein and Pongratz-Leisten have reconstructed this procession.[360] The statue of Anu and the high priest departed from the Anu-cella (É.NAM.EN.NA É *papāḫa*) in the Rēš-temple, through the Grand Gate (KÁ.MAḪ), i.e. the NE gate of the Rēš-temple; then Anu was greeted by the high priest, the exorcists, the temple enterers and the brewers; the procession moved SE along the Street of the Gods (*sūqa ilāni*) until they reached the Pure Quay, wharf of the Boat of Anu, procession of the gods (KAR KÙ.GA *arammu ša* ^{giš}MÁ.AN.NA *mālak ilāni*); then NE along the Ištar(?)-canal, to the upper wharf of the Pure Quay (*arammu elû ša* KAR KÙ.GA), still in the city area; then they disembarked, the procession moved through the district of the Adad-gate, the district of the Ištar-gate, and the district of the Šamaš-gate, leaving the city through the Royal Gate (*abul šarri*), in the city wall, reaching finally (after crossing a branch of the Euphrates) the *akītu*-tempel *Bīt ikribi.* During all these stages several incantations had to be recited.[361]

On what day did this procession take place? To solve this problem we need to examine another text which deals with the New Year festival of Tašrītu, *TU* 39–40.[362] In this

356 Cf. H.J. Lenzen, *UVB* 12/13 (1956), 35–42; J. Oelsner, *Materialien*, 87–8, with literature.
357 *Topographie*, 44.
358 For the colophon see also I.2.
359 As we already noted (I.3), the brewers, mentioned after the *ērib bīti*s because they are not allowed to enter the temple, can join in as bearers of the carrying pole, because Anu has left the restricted temple area. In obv. 11, 15, 19, and 23 the text does not mention the brewers but refers to them indirectly by saying: 'the bearers of the carrying pole'. For this carrying pole see my comments on *TU* 39, obv. 19, in the Appendix.
360 A. Falkenstein, *Topographie*, 45 ff.; B. Pongratz-Leisten, *ina šulmi īrub*, 42 f.
361 Similar to Anu in Uruk also Marduk in Babylon has to pass through seven stages during the procession to the *akītu*-temple, see B. Pongratz-Leisten, *ina šulmi īrub*, 40 f. Evidence for this procession comes from other texts, one of which is the Ashurbanipal tablet K 9876 + (latest discussion by B. Pongratz-Leisten, *ina šulmi īrub*, 228–32, no. 8). Similar to *BRM* 4, 7 this text from Babylon also contains instructions for the recitations which have to be recited during the seven stages of the procession of Marduk (Bēl) to the *akītu*-temple. Especially on the obverse the songs of the Ištar-priests appear to be important.
362 And not for the month Nisannu (A.K. Grayson, *Chronicles*, 278 and S. Sherwin-White, *JHS* 103 [1983], 159, n. 40), see *TU* 39, obv. 1.

text almost all of the eleven days of the festival of Tašritu are preserved. Crucial is the interpretation of *TU* 39, obv. 1–15, describing days 1, 6 and 7. Cohen argued that the procession to the *akītu*-temple took place on the first day, after which during the first seven days of the festival Anu resided in the *akītu*-temple.[363] The two chariots of Anu transported all sorts of ritual goods to the *akītu*-temple during those seven days.[364] Anu probably remained at the *akītu*-temple during this period, since neither Anu nor any other gods are mentioned going to the *akītu*-temple. Then, Cohen argues, at the end of day 7 the great procession from the *akītu*-temple to the Rēš-temple inside the city walls took place.[365]

However, another interpretation of *TU* 39, obv. 1–15 is possible, which agrees more with the events described on days 8–11. After Enlil, Ea and the other gods are robed (for the procession on day 8), a silver chariot of Anu and a golden chariot of Anu (but not Anu himself) go to the *akītu*-temple every day until day 8, apparently to bring all sorts of ritual goods for the ceremony. After a divine marriage ceremony on day 1, four more gods are robed on day 6 (for the procession on day 8).

On day 7 more preparations follow: after the awakening of the temple ceremony (*dīk bīti*), food and drinks are prepared,[366] and then, after the other gods are all robed for the procession, it is Anu's, Antu's and Ištar's turn.[367] The room between the curtains (*birīt šiddī*) in front of the Anu-cella (Enamenna), the first station which Anu will pass on day 8 on his way to the *akītu*-temple,[368] is made ready, followed by offerings and the consecration of the temple.[369] Then probably a reference is made to preparations on the route of the procession, referred to in the text as 'the street processional way, the procession-ships and the *akītu*-temple'.[370] Finally, as on every cultic day, on day 7 the morning and evening meals are also served and cleared away.

For the scribe of *TU* 39–40 the first seven days are of less importance than what follows on the next days, which are described extensively. Probably there is no need to describe them in detail, because they are the same as the first seven days of the Nisannu version; indeed it is specifically stated that the ceremonies of day 7 of Tašrītu are the same as those of day 7 of Nisannu.[371] The very abbreviated form in which the events are described also points in this direction. Anu is not mentioned, apart from a short reference to the cella, where clothing ceremonies of Anu, Antu, and Ištar are performed;[372] as we would expect, at this time Anu is apparently still in his cella in the Rēš-temple.

Only on day 8 does Anu appear in the foreground as the leading figure of the procession.[373] All the gods come down from their seats and gather in the Grand Courtyard in the Rēš-temple facing Anu. Here the procession of Anu to the *akītu*-temple begins, but we are not able to follow the route taken, because the end of day 8 and the beginning

---

363 *Cultic Calendars*, 428; see also 329–30 and 405.
364 Obv. 2–3.
365 Obv. 14.
366 Obv. 7–10.
367 Obv. 11.
368 Described in obv. 29.
369 Obv. 12–13.
370 Obv. 14.
371 Obv. 15.
372 Obv. 11.
373 Obv. 16ff.

of day 9 are lost. Still on day 8 the gods and the cultic objects take their seats in the Grand Courtyard, in front of Anu. The king and the people are sprinkled with water, a meal is served and libations performed, after which Anu enters the room between the curtains, accompanied by Papsukkal, the exorcists and a temple enterer (*ērib bīti*), who carries the Scepter of Kingship.[374] A priest performs several offerings and libations and the king and people are sprinkled again. Then the text breaks off. The description of the procession to the *akītu*-temple must have followed here, and then the journey back to the Rēš-temple, either on day 8, or at the latest on day 9, since *TU* 40 already mentions several stations which had to be passed on the way back.[375]

On day 9,[376] after a hand-raising prayer is recited,[377] the king performs a libation and then Anu enters the Grand Gate (KÁ.MAḪ) and sits on the Dais of Destinies (*parak šīmāti*).[378]The same rites as on day 8 are performed, after which Anu enters the room between the curtains[379] and all the gods gather around him. The same offerings and libations as those of day 8 are performed. Then Anu leaves the room between the curtains and sits upon the Dais of Kingship (*parak šarrūti*)[380] in his cella, surrounded by the other gods, after which the king performes a libation, and enters Ubšukkinaku. The following passage is damaged.

The reverse of *TU* 39 describes the final events of day 9, and the events on day 10 and 11. A liver is placed on the Dais of Anu. The diviner and the *šangu*-priest of Adad take the liver. The main and second meal are served. A lamentation is recited. Since this is a special occasion the gate is not closed, as was common on normal cultic days. In the evening the last meal is cleared and the main and second meal of the evening are served, after which the same lamentation is recited again. The vigil continues the whole night and the gate is closed at the end of the night, before the beginning of day 10.

On the 10th day[381] at night, in Ubšukkinaku the awakening of the temple ceremony is performed by means of the lamentations ANA ELUME 'The honored one of Heaven'[382] and UMUN ŠERMAL ANKIA 'Lord, respected one of Heaven and Earth'.[383] At dawn the gate is opened and the vigil ended. During the day the two main and second meals are served and in the evening the gate is closed.

On the 11th day[384] the awakening of the temple ceremony is also celebrated by means of the lamentations AME AMAŠANA 'The bull in his fold'[385] and ELUM DIDARA 'The honored one who wanders about',[386] at night in Ubšukkinaku. At dawn the gate is opened and several gods gather around Anu in the Grand Courtyard. They sit upon their

---

374 Obv. 29.

375 B. Pongratz-Leisten, *ina šulmi īrub*, 42.

376 *TU* 40, obv. 1 ff.

377 Obv. 4–5: EN NIRGALLA, the complete incipit is mentioned in *TU* 43, rev. 19, where it had to be recited on the eleventh day of Nisannu during the New Year festival in Uruk.

378 Obv. 9.

379 Obv. 15.

380 *TU* 40, rev. 7.

381 *TU* 39, rev. 10 ff.

382 Rev. 10. Also in the Uruk eclipse of the moon ritual and, for the *dīk bīti*-ceremony, in the Uruk cultic calendar text *TU* 48, see II.2.2.

383 Rev. 10. Also in the Uruk building ritual text and an the Uruk *mīs pî*-ritual text.

384 Rev. 15 ff.

385 Rev. 15. Also in the eclipse of the moon ritual and, for the *dīk bīti*-ceremony, in *TU* 48, see II.2.2.

386 Rev. 15. Also mentioned for the *dīk bīti*-ceremony in *TU* 48, see II.2.2.

seats and wait for Lugalbanda and Ninsun. The main meal of the morning is served. As soon as Lugalbanda and Ninsun have arrived the main meal is cleared and a priest performs a libation with a golden libation bowl for Lugalbanda and Ninsun and all the other gods. Then the main and second meal of the last double hour of the day take place in the usual manner.

The text ends with a colophon, with the catch-line: 'The (eighth) month Araḫsamna, day 5: Mīšaru will rise from Eḫenunna, the temple of Adad and (will come here)',[387] which shows that *TU* 39–40 is part of a series of temple ritual texts covering the whole year.

What is striking is that, although the king clearly participates in the ritual activities,[388] he is only one of the participants, especially in the procession leading Anu back from the *akītu*-temple on day 9.[389] This appears to be different in the Nisannu version.

The first New Year festival (Nisannu)

KAR 132 deals with the New Year festival of the first month Nisannu, and contains an elaborate description of the ceremonies which took place shortly before the procession to the *akītu*-temple, and also describes the beginning of the ceremonies at the *akītu*-temple.

In the beginning of the text Anu has already left his cella and taken up position in the Grand Courtyard.[390] A number of gods enter the Grand Courtyard. Then Enlil and Ea enter this courtyard,[391] while several of the other gods take up position at the left side of the gate of the cella (of Antu?). Next, the king follows these gods to the cella of Antu, joined by several goddesses. In the presence of the exorcists, the lamentation priests, the singers, the linen curtain and the golden libation bowl, Antu is escorted from the cella to the Grand Courtyard.[392] After this the king, together with the exorcists, the lamentation priests, the singers, the linen curtain and the golden libation bowl, and with Nanāja and several other goddesses, goes to the temple Urugal and leads Ištar to the Grand Courtyard.[393]

Col. II and III up to l. 17 describe the putting in position of the other gods, cultic objects and priests. In col. III, 21 Anu is led from the Dais of Destinies in Ubšukkinaku by Papsukkal, Nusku, Usmû and the king, followed by the other gods. Probably, therefore, in the broken passage (after the end of col. II) the procession of Anu from the Grand Courtyard to the Dais of Destinies is described, which could take place only after the arrival of Antu and Ištar in the Grand Courtyard.

Next, the whole assembly proceeds and, with Anu up front, enters the *akītu*-temple and takes it seats.[394] Anu takes up position on the Great Dais in the courtyard of the

387 *TU* 39, rev. 26.

388 Together with other persons he is sprinkled by a priest (*TU* 39, obv. 23; 34; *TU* 40, obv. 20; rev. 4), and on occasion he performes a libation (*TU* 40, obv. 8; 13; rev. 5; 8; 12; 17).

389 *TU* 40, obv. [13], rev. 6, 9, and 13.

390 I, obv. 7.

391 And not the Anu-cella, as A. Falkenstein presumed (*Topographie*, 23), because, as we saw, Anu is already in the Grand Courtyard.

392 I, 1–22.

393 I, 23–30.

394 IV, 1 ff.

akītu-temple, followed by the other gods. Papsukkal and the king then lead Anu from the Great Dais to his cella. Again, the other gods follow. The carrying poles of Anu and the other gods are brought in, a hand-raising prayer is recited by the lamentation priest,[395] and more gods enter the cella. After this the text breaks off.

The text concentrates on the *akītu*-procession, and does not describe the days before and after this procession. It is more than probable, however, that *KAR* 132 is only one of a series of tablets describing all the days of the festival in Nisannu; because the beginning and end of the text are damaged, any reference to these tablets has been lost.

The text gives more details on the beginning of the procession, by carefully recording all the deities and cult objects involved in the festival. While the cultic events in the *akītu*-temple are not mentioned in the Tašrītu version, here a detailed description of what took place at the *akītu*-temple is presented. Furthermore, apart from Anu and Antu, Ištar plays an important role, and more other gods are also mentioned here than in the Tašrītu version. Finally, as we saw, the king has a leading part in the procession; he plays a more prominant role in the Nisannu version of the festival, than in the Tašrītu version, which is not surprising since the New Year festival of Nisannu coincides with the beginning of the civil year, the month Nisannu being the coronation month of the king.

More evidence for the New Year festival of Nisannu comes from *TU* 43. The main part of the text contains a *šuillakku*- (hand-raising) prayer, which has to be recited on the tenth day of the New Year festival to Anu (obv. 1–20, rev. 1–16). See rev. 17:

> '[17]Hand-raising prayer of Anu, which [they will recite] in the (first) month Nisannu, day 10, to A[nu]'.

It also records a *šuillakku*-prayer to be recited on the eleventh day:

> '[18]The (first) month Nisannu, day 11, when Anu [sits] on the Dais of Anu, on the Dais [of Kingship(?)], [19][the la]mentation priest will stand and [20][will recite] the hand-raising prayer [19]'Strong Anu, revered by [himself(?)], [20]who [alo]ne is Lord [19][in Heaven and on Earth'], [20]to the accompaniment of a lyr[e]'.[396]

The text does not inform us where the *šuillakku*-prayer on day 10 is recited, but for the prayer on day 11 we are back in the cella of Anu (Enamenna), in the Rēš-complex, because the text mentions the Dais of Anu (*parak Ani*),[397] and (probably) the Dais of kingship.

The number of days on which the events described in *KAR* 132 took place is not preserved. If the New Year festival of the first month paralleled that of the seventh

395 IV, 23: ANGALE 'O, Great Anu'.

396 This hand-raising prayer was also recited on the ninth day of Tašrītu during the Uruk New Year festival (*TU* 40, obv. 4–5).

397 Also known as BÁRA.NAM.LUGAL.LA 'Dais of the royal Lordship', cf. A. Falkenstein, *Topographie*, 18 ff.

month then all the events described would have taken place on day 8 and 9, as in the Tašrītu version. An indication that the Nisannu version is at least partly similar to the Tašrītu-version is found in *TU* 39, where at the end of the passage describing day 7, it is noted that the ceremonies, described only briefly, are the same as on day 7 of Nisannu.[398] Furthermore, the description of day 11 of Nisannu in *TU* 43 outlines activities in the Rēš-temple, and no reference is made to the *akītu*-temple, nor to the procession, which may indicate that the procession did not return to the Rēš-temple on day 11 of Nisannu (as is the case in the Nisannu version in Babylon, see below), but on day 9, as in the Tašrītu version of Uruk.

However, as Cohen noted, because the Nisannu festival celebrates the beginning of the civil year, while the Tašrītu festival opens the cultic year, this may have (partly) altered the nature of the festival.[399] An indication that this may be the case may be found in a building inscription from Hellenistic Uruk, *YOS* 1, 52 (68 S.E.), which refers to day 8 of Nisannu, although there is no mention of the New Year festival: the building of the Rēš-temple is completed, Anu and Antu enter the temple to dwell for ever in the Anu-cella Enamenna, and the regular offerings are performed.[400] The entering of Anu in his cella on day 8 of Nisannu, presumably during the New Year festival,[401] does not fit the Tašrītu version, where Anu leaves his cella on day 8 and returns on day 9 from the *akītu*-temple.[402]

However, although differences may have existed between the Nisannu and the Tašrītu versions, in general probably a very similar schedule was used.

II.4.5.2. Babylon

Two New Year festivals were also celebrated in Babylon, one during the first month Nisannu, and one during the seventh month Tašrītu.

---

398 Obv. 15.

399 M.E. Cohen, *Cultic Calendars*, 433–4.

400 Lines 16–18.

401 Apparently the celebration of the restored Rēš-temple coincides with the New Year festival, since it is hardly conceivable that on this occassion the New Year festival did not take place (from chronicle texts we know that only at a time of a serious crisis was the festival not celebrated; see for example the Nabonidus chronicle, cf. A.K. Grayson, *Chronicles*, no. 7, II, 5 f.; 10 f.; 19 f.; see also III, 8). However, does the entering of Anu on day 8-I in the Rēš-temple, attested in the building inscription, perhaps indicate that, because of the special festivities, the New Year festival celebrated in year 68 S.E. did not follow the usual order of cultic events?

402 The inauguration of temples in the month Nisannu is only indicated by the Hellenistic Uruk building inscriptions *YOS* 1, 52 and J. Jordan, *Uruk-Warka*. WVDOG 51, Leipzig, 1928, pl. 108, c, with 41 (2-I-110 [+?] S.E.). In the series *iqqur īpuš* (defining certain months as favorable or unfavorable for particular activities) the month Nisannu is favorable for, amongst other things, building a temple, renovating a sanctuary, and for organizing an *akītu*, cf. R. Labat, *Calendrier*, 92, § 32, 1 (cf. 228, 12), but this is also favorable in some other months. The later months III and V were more appropriate for the building of temples, cf. R.S. Ellis, *Foundation Deposits in Ancient Mesopotamia*, New Haven and London, 1968, 17 ff. Note that Sennacherib inaugurated a temple in Ḫuzurīna (Sultantepe) on day 8 of the seventh month Tašrītu, cf. J.N. Postgate, *Royal Grants*, 78, no. 40, obv. 9′. Although in Israel the temple of Salomo was also inaugurated in the seventh month Ethanim (1 Kings, 8, 2; cf. 2 Chron., 5, 3), the festival for the inauguration of the temple in Jerusalem (Chanukkah) is celebrated on day 25 of the ninth month Kislev.

The second New Year festival (Tašrītu)

For the second New Year festival of the seventh month Tašrītu no evidence has been preserved from the Hellenistic period,[403] with the exception perhaps of a short reference to a clothing ceremony of Bēl on day 7 of Tašrītu(?), and a reference to the arranging of the *alû*-drum (for the procession to the *akītu*-temple?) on day 8 of Tašrītu in BM 32206 +.[404] This may be explained partly by the fact that ritual texts from Hellenistic Babylon are rare, and furthermore because the second festival opened the cultic year, not the civil year, and therefore no references to this festival would have been made in non-cultic sources such as chronicles and astronomical diaries, unless something unusual had happened. In the astronomical diaries no clear references are made to the New Year festival or the *akītu*-temple for the month Tašrītu. Note however that diary no. -132 describes political and religious upheavels during the 7th month Tašrītu: in the midst of political turmoil and war(threat) it is stated that "the god Bēl has entered Babylon" (B, rev. 27). Men and women place offerings on a dais and celebrate opposite it. On the 11th Nanāja appears: "Nanāja has entered Ezida in Borsippa" (B, rev. 31, similar during the 6th month Ulūlu, cf. B, obv. 29). In Borsippa(?) more celebrations and cultic events seem to follow, Nanāja is mentioned in connection with a headband(?) and a chariot; the assembly (*kiništu*) appears. Apparently the people of Babylon and Borsippa are advised to resist plundering and (importantly) not to hand over the gods as booty to the enemy in order to save the city (Left edge, 2). Because the historical passages are very damaged and far from understandable, we do not know if they bear any relation to the New Year festival. However, although the tablet still needs to be studied in depth, it is already very clear from diary no. -132 that Babylonian religion and cult were very much alive as late as 133 B.C.[405] It is remarkable that a "sailor whose mind was deranged" invited the population to participate in the festivals and that they, "men and women" enthusiastically did so, and "enjoyed themselves".

The first New Year festival (Nisannu)

There is more evidence for the New Year festival of the first month Nisannu, both from cultic and non-cultic sources, from Hellenistic Babylon. We do not have much evidence for day 1 of Nisannu, the first day of the festival. There is a small (Late Babylonian?) fragment discussed by Çağirgan.[406] Although damaged, some of the events are clear: on the first of Nisannu at dawn an arranger of the offering table (*mubannû*)[407] enters the courtyard of Bēl with a key (*namzaqu*); a house (or temple) and water are mentioned.

---

403 Pre-Hellenistic evidence for the New Year festival in Babylon during the month Tašrītu is also rare. Important is *ABL* 956 (*LAS* 190). Cf. S. Parpola, *LAS* II, 186–87; M.E. Cohen, *Cultic Calendars*, 328–9, and 451. However, according to F. Reynolds (*BiOr* 53 [1996], 92) the evidence for this festival has been overestimated.

404 II, 53, and 57–8. But note that also in Uruk clothing ceremonies for Anu, Antu and Ištar are performed on day 7 of Tašrītu (*TU* 39, obv. 11, see also 13).

405 See also note 457 below.

406 *Festivals*, 1 (from his private collection, only in transliteration and translation, no copy).

407 See III.4.3.

Then the arranger goes to the Grand Gate with the key, opens the gate of the well and throws the key(?) into the water of the well(?). The function of the ceremony is not clear.

There is also, in a list of temple expenditures, a reference to meat for regular offerings on day 1 of Nisannu.[408]

Several ritual texts, which contain parts of tablets 22 and 23 of the ritual series concerning the New Year festival of the month Nisannu (DT 15 +) were published by F. Thureau-Dangin.[409] It is our most important source for the public cult of Marduk (here called Bēl) in Hellenistic Babylon. The text concentrates especially on the prayers which accompanied the cultic actions. The ritual instructions for the first day of Nisannu are lost. For the second to the fifth day we have several large fragments. The text contains a short reference to the sixth day, incorporated in the description of the third day, but the seventh to the eleventh days are lost.

The first cultic events are for all four days the same. The description of each day begins with a reference to the exact double hour of the night,[410] on which a high priest rises and washes himself with river water.[411] Then he approaches Bēl and his spouse Bēltīja (i.e. Zarpanītu) and removes the curtain in front of them.[412] After these introductory lines one or more (for each day different) prayers are always recited, followed by the opening of the gate ceremony (*pīt bābi*).[413] On each day, so the text records, the temple enterers (*ērib bīti*) also enter the cella and 'perform their rites as usual' (ME-*šú-nu* GIM *šá gi-na-a* DÙ.MEŠ), as do the lamentation priests and singers.[414]

After these standard procedures the different cultic events of each day are presented. For day 2 after a prayer to Bēl[415] and the *pīt bābi*-ceremony only a small part of a ceremony is preserved.[416]

For day 3 we know a little more. The prayer to Bēl is almost completely lost.[417] After the third hour of the morning the high priest calls in three craftsmen, a metalworker, a carpenter and a goldsmith, and gives them materials to make two figurines. They have to work on these figurines from day 3 to day 6. The payments for these craftsmen is also mentioned.[418] In the next section the shape of these figurines is described.[419] They are kept in the temple of Madānu and in Eḫursagtila, the temple of Ninurta in Babylon until day 6, and are used in a ceremony involving Nabû on day 6, which leads to their destruction, but the exact turn of events is not clear because the passage is partly damaged.[420]

---

408 AB 244, rev. 30, U.E. 31 (G.J.P. McEwan, *Iraq* 43 [1981], 132–34). For the most recent discussion of this text see R.J. van der Spek, in: J. Wiesehöfer (ed.), *Das Partherreich und seine Zeugnisse*, 234 f.

409 *RAcc.*, 127–154.

410 See II.2.1.

411 In line 286 specified as coming from the Tigris and the Euphrates.

412 Lines 1–3, 157–8 (the removing of the curtain is [erroneously] not mentioned for day 3), 217–19, 285–87.

413 Lines 37, 184, 276, 334.

414 Cf. 38–40 (for day 2: in front of Bēl and Bēltīja), 185–6, 276–8, 335–7. Also attested in the Hellenistic temple ritual fragment BM 41577 (A.R. George, *Studies W.G. Lambert*, no. 1, 260 ff.; see below), II, 12′–13′.

415 Lines 5 ff. In this prayer the power of Bēl over the other gods and the people is described and his mercy for Babylon, Esagila and its inhabitants. This text must remain a secret according to the subscript.

416 Lines 41 ff.

417 Lines 160 ff.

418 Lines 190 ff. The payments consists of meat 'from before Bēl' (*ištu pāni Bēl*), which means from offerings.

419 Lines 201 ff.

420 M. Stol made the following suggestion to me: both figurines lift up their right hand against (*ana*) Nabû,

On day 4 a hand-raising prayer (*šuillakku*) for Bēl,[421] and also a prayer for Bēltīja are recited by the high priest.[422] The actual festival begins when the high priest pronounces praise three times with the words 'ikû-star (Pegasus), Esagila, image of Heaven and Earth'.[423] Then, after the second meal in the late afternoon, *Enūma eliš* is recited or enacted by the high priest[424] to Bēl, and apparently this took the rest of the day, because no other cultic events are recorded.[425] The text does not describe the procession of the king on the fourth day from his palace to the temple of Nabû, near the palace, where the scepter was offered to him and the fate of the king was decreed, except in the prayers recited during this day.[426] Also no mention is made of the king's journey to Borsippa, to bring the statue of Nabû back to Babylon the next day.[427]

On day 5 prayers for Bēl and for Bēltīja are recited.[428] Then the king enters Babylon with Nabû, but before he goes into Esagila the text describes extensively how Esagila, including the cella of Bēl and the cella of Nabû (Ezida), are prepared for this visit by the high priest.[429] During these preparations the high priest goes out to the open country, leaving an exorcist and a slaughterer to purify the temple with the carcass of a sheep.[430]

---

one holding a snake, the other a scorpion. Apparently they represent enemies of Nabû, the son of Marduk. Leftovers of the offering table of Madānu are served to them, which suggests that they are in a prison with bad food. Then they are apparently burned. Here perhaps a myth concerning Nabû is expressed, in which he defeats two opponents. Indeed Nabû is known as a savior, and as the one who reaps glory for his father Marduk (cf. F. Pomponio, *Nabû*, Roma, 1978, 122 and W.G. Lambert, in: *Matouš Festschrift* II, 95 sub B 12). It is also possible that the figurines symbolize the exorcist and the slaughterer, who purify the temple on day 5 (cf. J.A. Black, *Religion* 11 [1981], 55).

421 Lines 222 ff. A hand-raising prayer is a personal prayer, here illustrated by the fact that the priest refers to himself in the prayer (l. 245). Also, in this prayer the power of Marduk and his mercy for the city and its people is described.

422 Lines 251 ff. Note that some of the epithets of Zarpanītu are parallel to those of Marduk in the preceding prayer (lines 223–251; 240–254; 245–262). First Zarpanītu is described as the most brilliant of the stars (252), probably refering to the planet Venus (see 325). Then the prayer describes Zarpanītu as protector of the poor, the captive, the fallen, the king, the citizens of Babylon, but also for the servant, that is the high priest who performs the prayer and who addresses himself in the third person (note that in his prayer to Marduk he did not dare to pray for himself).

423 Line 274. Cf. K. van der Toorn, *Suppl. VT* 43 (1991), 332, with n. 7.

424 See my comments on line 282 in the Appendix.

425 From BM 32206 +, II, 62–64, we know that the *Enūma eliš* was also recited on day 4 of the ninth month Kislīmu in Babylon, which may indicate that it was recited on the fourth of every month. If this is true then obviously there is no special connection of the Epic of Creation with the New Year festival as W.G. Lambert suggested (*JSS* 13 [1968], 107); we would then have to re-examine the function of *Enūma eliš* in this festival, which could alter our present ideas of the festival all together.

426 Lines 244 ff.

427 Cf. K. van der Toorn, *Suppl. VT* 43 (1991), 332–3, with n. 8–10.

428 Lines 288 ff. and 317 ff. In these prayers Marduk's power and Zarpanītu's protective role (see 326) again are important. Marduk is called 'Dimmerankia, who decrees the destinies' (301) and Zarpanītu is identified with 'Damkianna, lady of Heaven and Earth' (324), wife of Enki-Ea and mother of Marduk in *Enūma eliš*. Then the names of planets and stars are mentioned, with whom the two deities have to be identified. Note that Marduk is connected with the male heavenly bodies and Zarpanītu with the female heavenly bodies. At the end of the prayer to Marduk sun and moon are mentioned (314–5), perhaps to be identified with Marduk, similar to Venus who must be identified with Zarpanītu (see above). Note that the Sumerian ideograms used are explained by their Akkadian epitheta, cf. M. Stol, *NABU* 1989, no. 60.

429 Lines 338 ff.

430 Also incantations (*šiptu*) of the type 'The house is conjured' are recited by the exorcist. We have evidence from the astronomical diaries that during the month Nisannu and Ajjaru in Babylon incantations are recited, see A.J. Sachs–H. Hunger, *Diaries*, no. -226, A, obv. 4′ and 23′ (85 S.E.)., in the latter case in connection with the kettledrum, see II.5.2.

Afterwards the carcass is thrown into the river and they leave for the open country themselves, not to return as long as Nabû is in Babylon, that is, as long as the New Year festival lasts, until day 12. Clearly their presence would disturb the ceremony since they might endanger the purification process.[431]

After the temple is consecrated, during the morning the high priest and the craftsmen bring out the golden canopy from the treasury of Marduk and cover Ezida, the cella of Nabû in Esagila, and utter a cry of distress (*ikkillu*).[432]

After the craftsmen have left an offering table is set up in front of Bēl, after which a prayer is recited.[433] The offering table is brought to Nabû (presumably in Borsippa), after which he travels to Esagila by ship, probably accompanied by the king, although the (damaged) text does not say this.[434]

Then the king enters the scene. His hands are washed and he is led into Esagila, where he has to take part in a special ceremony.[435] The high priest takes away scepter, loop, mace, and the Crown of Kingship and places them upon a seat in front of Bēl in his cella. Then he goes out and strikes the king's cheek, leads him into the cella in front of Bēl, pulls him by his ears and makes him kneel down on the ground. The slap on the cheek is an accusation, and the king replies by saying that he has not neglected the gods, the city of Babylon, the temple Esagila, nor his subjects.[436]

After a break in the text, during which the king leaves the cella again, the high priest assures the king that Bēl will magnify his lordship, extol his kingship, and destroy his enemies. The king rediscovers his dignity and the high priest brings out scepter, loop, mace and crown from the cella and returns them to the king, after which he strikes the king's cheek again: if tears flow, Bēl is satisfied, if not, Bēl is angry and he will bring about the king's downfall.[437]

---

[431] McEwan has interpreted this passage as referring to separate *akītu*-festivals outside Babylon: *akītu ina ṣēri* (*FAOS* 4, 179 and 180, n. 419), since day 6–11, attested in Uruk (*TU* 39–40), are not attested in Babylon. But see *SBH* VIII, II, 1–11 (discussed below), which probably describes events on day 8 and 11 of Nisannu in the *akītu*-temple. Furthermore, the Babylon text does not actually mention an *akītu*-ceremony 'in the open country'. As we already saw we have some Neo-Babylonian references to *a-ki-tu*$_4$(!) *šá* EDEN (*AnOr* 9, 2, 64; see also 3, 44) but here clearly the *akītu* (-temple) of the open country is intended, and not *akītu*-festivals outside Babylon. Also, there is no need for such an interpretation: as long as Nabû is in Babylon, the exorcist and the slaughterer, who have performed the purification with the carcass of a sheep and apparently are unclean, are not allowed to be in Babylon, so that their 'unclean' presence may not bring into danger the divine rites. For the same reason the high priest may not observe this purification, because if he does, he is not pure (lines 364–5). Compare this with *KAR* 60, describing the Neo-Assyrian Assur-version of the kettledrum ritual (obv. 15–18, rev. 1–4), where the lamentation priest had to uncover his head and bow down (a typical position of penitence), necessary because the priest was responsible for a crime: the killing of the bull, a sacred animal, which makes him unclean. Also he has to decline three times the responsibility for killing the animal. Furthermore, apparently the lamentation priests were allowed to eat the meat, but not the chief singer of dirges (*galamāḫu*), because he was considered responsible for killing the bull. See II.5.2.

[432] Lines 366 ff.

[433] Lines 384 ff. Here Marduk is addressed as the god of the *akītu*-festival, and perhaps a reference is made to the procession to the *akītu*-temple named *Bīt ikribi* (400–1), which has to follow on day 8 (not described in this text).

[434] Lines 403 ff.

[435] Lines 413 ff.

[436] Cf. K. van der Toorn, *Suppl. VT* 43 (1991), 333.

[437] Lines 434 ff.

After a ceremony with a reed bundle and the divine bull, the function of which is not clear,[438] the text ends.[439]

More information on the events from day 8 on comes from other sources.[440] Before discussing the Hellenistic textual evidence, first briefly the events on days 8–11: on day 8[441] the procession of the king, 'taking Bēl by the hand', together with Nabû and all the other gods, who had gathered in Esagila, moved from Esagila to the *akītu*-temple situated 'in the open country' (*ina ṣēri*). We are not well informed about the events taking place in the *akītu*-temple. The procession returned on day 11, probably by the same route, back to Esagila, passing through several stations, among which the Dais of Destinies (*parak šīmāti*), where Bēl determined the destinies for the next year.[442] This was one of the highlights of the festival.

New textual evidence from the Hellenistic period has come available. We now have a Hellenistic fragment of a temple ritual, BM 41577, which may deal with the month Nisannu, and presents us with new evidence for the New Year festival in Babylon.[443] The main proceedings described in this fragment consist of a visit of the high priest to the cella of Bēl, where he recites a Sumerian blessing to Bēl. Then he enters the cella of Bēltīja, to recite another Sumerian blessing. He returns to Bēl and recites a blessing, this time in Akkadian, after which he enters the cella of Bēltīja again for another blessing also in Akkadian. The fragment probably deals with day 6 or 7 of Nisannu, as George suggested,[444] and the cultic activities must have preceded the procession to the *akītu*-temple on day 8.

---

438 Lines 453 ff. In line 458 a reference is made to the slaughtering(??) of a white bull, after which a blessing to the divine bull follows. Lines 463–71 are now partly available in BM 32485 (published in this study, see Plate I), but do not help to explain the ceremony because of the damaged state of the fragment. The bull and the king are mentioned several times and perhaps a thigh-piece of the bull is consumed.

According to Thureau-Dangin (*RAcc.*, 146, n. 1) this slaughtering(??) of the white bull symbolizes the beginning of the New Year, quoting Virgil (Georg. I, 217): 'with his gilded horns the white bull opens the year'. At the time when the ritual took place in the spring the sun would still be in the zodiacal sign of the Bull. Note that the ceremony took place after sunset, and if the bull indeed has astral meaning, we might have to think in terms of the rising of constellations before sunrise or after sunset, cf. W. Hartner, *JNES* 24 (1965), 1 ff., especially 5 ff.

439 For the lines 472 ff. see my comments in the Appendix.

440 Cf. K. van der Toorn, *Suppl. VT* 43 (1991), 333 f. and M.E. Cohen, *Cultic Calendars*, 438 ff. with the relevant textual evidence. The procession is extensively described by B. Pongratz-Leisten, *ina šulmi īrub*, 40 f. See also the Neo-Babylonian fragments *VS* 24, 108 (+) 109 // 110 (*ina šulmi īrub*, 236–39, nos. 10–11), which deal with Marduk's stay in the *akītu*-temple.

441 See K. van der Toorn, *Suppl. VT* 43 (1991), 336, with n. 28, contra P.-R. Berger, in: *CRRA* 17 (1970), 156, who suggested that the procession left on day 9 of Nisannu.

442 The place where the destinies are determined, the Dais of Destinies, is sometimes called the DU_6.KÙ the 'Pure Mound', originally the cosmic seat of the king of the gods of Heaven and Earth (Lugaldimmerankia) in the divine assembly, see for example *BRM* 4, 7, rev. 37 (see my comments on this line in the Appendix). In Babylon it is the seat of Marduk/Bēl as Lugaldimmerankia in Ubšukkinaku of Esagila (cf. A.R. George, *House Most High*, no. 180). In our text the passage with the Dais of Destinies is missing, but on day 5 Marduk is called ᵈDÌM.ME.ER.AN.KI.A *mu-šim* NAM.MEŠ '(Lugal)dimmerankia, who decrees the destinies' (*RAcc.*, 137, 301). Note that the second New Year month Tašrītu in the Nippur calendar is called DU_6.KÙ(.GA), the beginning of the religious year when the destinies were determined in the DU_6.KÙ (cf. B. Landsberger, *Kult. Kalender*, 34; A. Tsukimoto, *Untersuchungen zur Totenpflege*, Kevelaer, 1985, 204). Also in Uruk the seventh month Tašrītu is called DU_6.KÙ, see the New Year text *TU* 39, obv. 1 and rev. 25.

443 A.R. George, *Studies W.G. Lambert*, no. 1, 260 ff.

444 ib., 263.

Day 8 day of the New Year festival of Nisannu is not discussed in the Babylon text *RAcc.*, 127 ff., but we do have other references to this day in texts from Hellenistic Babylon. First there is the chronicle 13b.[445] The text describes food offerings for Bēl and Bēltija in Esagila on day 8 of Nisannu in year 88(?) S.E. These offerings are made by the administrator (*šatammu*) of Esagila, according to the command of the king. There are many problems with this text, which will be dealt with elsewhere.[446] Important here is that, although the king himself is not present during these offerings, Bēl and Bēltīja are still in Esagila on day 8 of Nisannu, which must mean that these activities took place just before the procession began.

Strong evidence for this procession on day 8 of Nisannu comes from an astronomical diary, a fragment from the reign of Antiochus III (107 S.E.)[447]:

14 … [ITI].BI UD.8.KAM ^{I}*An* LUGAL *u* ⌜^{lú} x⌝
15 [TA] É.GAL È-*ni a-na* KÁ SIKIL.[LA *šá* É].SAG.GÍL *ḫa-ru-ú šá* MU ⌜x⌝
16 [*a-n*]*a*? É.SAG.GÍL *ina* IGI.MEŠ-*šú-nu* DÙ-*uš* N[IDBA?] ⌜*a-na*⌝ $^{[Id]}$AMAR.UTU KAR? ⌜x⌝
17 […] ⌜x⌝ *šá li-pi-šú-nu* GAR-*nu-ʾ ana* É.UD.1.KAM KU$_4$ [x x]
18 […^{d}]XV TIN.TIR^{ki} *u bul-ṭu šá* ^{I}*An* LUGAL ⌜DÙ⌝ […]
19 […] ⌜x x x x⌝ *a-na* É [x] […]

'[14] … That [month,] on the 8th, king Antiochus and the […] [15]went out [from] the palace. In front of the Holy Gat[e of E]sagila he performed the *ḫarû*-ritual of … [16][fo]r(?) Esagila in their presence. Ce[real offerings(?)] [for] Marduk … [17][…] of their descendants(?) were placed, entered the Day-one (= *akītu*)-temple […] [18][…] performed offerings for] Ištar of Babylon and the life of king Antiochus.[…].[19][…] … to … […]'.

The passage clearly describes the king taking part in a procession from Esagila to the *akītu*-temple during the New Year festival.[448] Another diary passage referring to the 8th day of Nisannu[449] suggests that after the second meal of the morning (*tardennu ša šēri*)[450] Ištar of Babylon was taken by the hands and brought from the temple of Gula, probably to Esagila, where she was to join in with the other participants of the procession to the *akītu*-temple.

For day 8 and 11 of the festival we can turn to a calendar text, *SBH* VIII. The beginning of the second column (and a large part of the first column?) deals with the New Year festival during the month Nisannu: a clothing ceremony (of Marduk) is mentioned probably for day 8, since the text continues with a procession to the *akītu*-temple *Bīt ikribi*.[451] On day 11 a festival (*isinnu*)[452] is celebrated in the *akītu*-temple,

---

445 BM 35421, published by A.K. Grayson, *Chronicles*, 283 f. and pl. XI (collated).
446 See II.8.7.
447 A.J.Sachs–H.Hunger, *Diaries*, no.-204, C, rev. 14–19. Cf. also S. Sherwin-White, A. Kuhrt, *From Samarkhand to Sardis*, 130–1. See also II.8.7.
448 There is more (although very scanty) evidence in the astronomical diaries of religious festivities during the month Nisannu: incantations (*šiptu*) and offerings (*niqû*) are recorded in A.J. Sachs–H. Hunger, *Diaries*, no. -226, A, obv. 4′ and no. -170, A, obv. 1′.
449 A.J. Sachs–H. Hunger, *Diaries*, no. -140, A, obv. 21–22.
450 See also III.2.1.
451 II, 3–4. See also II.4.3.
452 Different names for the festival (*isinnu*) of *akītu* are known, especially in royal inscriptions. Sanherib

for which presents and gifts are brought in, and which includes a wedding festival (*ḫadaššūtu*), perhaps between Marduk and Zarpanītu.[453]

The recently published Late Babylonian, possibly Hellenistic fragment BM 47902 +, originally consisting of four columns, deals with events taking place in the *akītu*-temple *Bīt ikribi* during the Nisannu New Year fesival in Babylon.[454] Obverse I describes Bēl and the other gods taking up position in the *akītu*-temple. Part of column IV is duplicated by K 9876 +, which describes recitations which had to be performed during the festival, similar to the Uruk text *BRM* 4, 7.[455] BM 47902 + also mentions the twelfth day 'when Bēl rises' (*tebû*, obv. I, 20), which probably refers to events taking place in Esagila after Bēl had returned from the *akītu*-temple.[456]

More indirect evidence for the eleventh day comes from non-cultic sources. An astronomical diary may suggest that king Antiochus II Theos (together with his three sons) was in Esagila on day 11 of Nisannu (66 S.E.), perhaps returning from the *akītu* temple on the last day of the festival.[457] Also, in the already mentioned list of temple

---

speaks of a 'festival of the banquet (*i-sin-ni qé-re-ti*) of Aššur', *OIP* 2, 143, 8–9, see also 136, 25 (cf. B. Menzel, *Tempel* I, 55 with II, 53*, n. 659, cf. also I, 23 with II, 21*, n. 239). Assurbanipal mentions a 'festival of joy' (*isinnu ḫidâti*), R.C. Thompson, *Esarh*., pl. 18, VI, 11 (*i-*[*sin-n*]*i* ḪÚL.MEŠ). Neriglissar speaks of a 'festival of *akītu*' (*i-na i-sì-in-ni a-ki-ti*), *VAB* 4, 210, Ner. 1, I, 35 (the reconstruction follows H.G. Güterbock, *ZA* 40 [1931], 289–90). And Nabonidus mentions a 'festival of the *akītu*-temple' (*i-sin-nu* É *a-ki-ti*), *VAB* 4, 284, Nbn 8, IX, 42. For more examples see *CAD*, A/I, 267 ff. sub *akītu*. For a festival called *isin*(*nu*) *bīti* see II.8.1.

453 II, 6–8.

454 W.G. Lambert, *RA* 91 (1997), 52–56 (earlier edition by B. Pongratz-Leisten, *ina šulmi īrub*, 233–35, no. 9). In this article other Late Babylonian fragments dealing with the procession to the *akītu*-temple are also discussed by Lambert, but these are less relevant for our discussion here which aims at reconstructing the chronology of the New Year festival days in Hellenistic Babylon. Note however the small Late Babylonian fragment, BM 77028 (ib., 71–74): it was probably written in Borsippa, but, as Lambert suggests, the fragment presents a recitation belonging to a ritual which probably deals with the boat trip of Marduk and the king of Babylon, well-known to be part of the procession to the *akītu*-temple during the New Year festival in Babylon. No indication of the day on which this occurred is given. In the badly preserved colophon the tablet is referred to as 'tablet 25 of the series EN …' (rev. 4), which may suggest that is was part of the large series of tablets describing the New Year festival in Babylon, as known especially from *RAcc*.

455 See II.4.5.1.

456 Rather than indicating the departure of Bēl from the *akītu*-temple on day 12, as Lambert suggests, *RA* 91 (1997), 53.

457 A.J. Sachs–H. Hunger, *Diaries*, no. -245, A, obv. 12′–13′. Cf. R.J. van der Spek, in: H. Sancisi-Weerdenburg e.a. (eds.), *De Agricultura*, 72, who assumes that the king probably did not visit Babylon, but that offerings were made on behalf of the king and his sons. Another diary (no. -161, A_1,A_2, obv. 27′–29′) describes events on days 10 and 11 of Nisannu: the damaged passage refers to sheep and the *dudē* gate of Esagila, but no reference to the New year festival is made. Another diary, no. -77, A, 'Obv. 12', relates to the assembly (*kiništu*) and administrator (*šatammu*) of Esagila and mentions a festival (*isinnu*) during the first month Nisannu, but because of the broken context it is not clear whether this refers to the New Year festival.

We must be careful with these kind of references, even when they mention the *akītu*-temple, because this temple was not only used during the New Year festival of Nisannu, as is clear for example from BM 32206 +, where a procession of Usmû, a slave and a bull to the *akītu*-temple is recorded on day 4 of Kislīmu. See II.4.3. Also the astronomical diaries often record events taking place in the *akītu*-temple in months other than Nisannu, but usually the relevant passages are badly damaged and the context remains unclear. The month of the second New Year festival, Tašrītu, is not attested in connection with this festival, nor with the *akītu*-temple. For references to the *akītu*-temple (written É UD.1.KAM 'Day one temple' and used as alternative name, cf. R.J. van der Spek, in: J. Wiesehöfer (ed.), *Das Partherreich und seine Zeugnisse*, 225) and the astronomical diaries: no.-204, C, rev. 17 (mentioned above); no. -187, A, rev. 10′; no. -171, B, rev. 4′; no. -170, A, obv. 13′; no. -158, C, 6′–8′; no. -132, D, rev. 12′; no. -129, A_2, obv. 20; no. -126, A, rev. 4; no. -124, rev. 16′; no. -88, B, obv. 12′; and no. -79, obv.' 6, dated 233 S.E. (79/8 B.C.), which is the last reference to the *akītu*-temple in the diaries. The *akītu*-temple is attested in administrative documents as late as 219 S.E.

expenditures, which refers to day 1 of Nisannu (see above), sheep for the regular offerings in the *akītu*-temple on day 11 of Nisannu are also mentioned,[458] which presumably means that Bēl has returned from the *akītu*-temple and is back in Esagila.

Some concluding remarks

When we compare the data from Uruk and Babylon, we must conclude that for Hellenistic Uruk only the data for the Tašrītu version are reasonably certain. Here preparations for the procession took seven days, after which the procession left on day 8 and returned to the Rēš-temple on day 9. The festivities lasted another two days. Furthermore we have indications which suggest that in Uruk the Nisannu version of the festival was probably similar to the Tašrītu version, but no certain data have been preserved for the days on which the procession took place.

In Hellenistic Babylon the Nisannu version follows the schedule used in the Neo-Babylonian period: the procession left on day 8, and did not return to Esagila earlier than on day 11 of Nisannu. The Tašrītu festival in Babylon remains unclear. The fact that the days, on which certain cultic activities of the New Year festival are held, are not the same in the various cities, as seems to be the case in Hellenistic Uruk and Babylon, has already been established by others.[459]

Table XV: the New Year festival in Hellenistic Uruk and Babylon

date	god	place	text
7-I	Anu	Uruk	*TU* 39–40
(8-I)	Anu	Uruk	*KAR* 132
10-I	Anu	Uruk	*TU* 43
11-I	Anu	Uruk	*TU* 43
1–11-VII	Anu	Uruk	*TU* 39–40
(8-VII)	Anu	Uruk	*BRM* 4, 7
1-I	Bēl	Babylon	Çağirgan, *Festivals*, 1; AB 244
2–5-I	Bēl	Babylon	*RAcc.*, 127 ff.
6-I	Bēl	Babylon	*RAcc.*, 127 ff.
(6/7/8(?)-I)	Bēl	Babylon	BM 41577
8-I	Bēl	Babylon	*Diaries*, no.-204; *SBH* VIII; Grayson, *Chronicles*, no. 13b
11-I	Bēl	Babylon	*SBH* VIII; *Diaries*, no. -245; AB 244
7-VII(?)	Bēl	Babylon	BM 32206 +
8-VII	Bēl	Babylon	BM 32206 +

(93/2 B.C.), cf. AB 244, obv. 14 (G.J.P. McEwan, *Iraq* 43 [1981], 132–34). The *akītu*-temple is perhaps also mentioned in chronicle 10, rev. 22 (A.K. Grayson, *Chronicles*, 118).

458 AB 244, obv. 13–16.

459 See W.G. Lambert, *JSS* 13 (1968), 107, where he noticed that the day, on which the great battle between Marduk and Tiamat during the New Year festival in Nisannu could occur, varies in the texts from day 8, 10 or 11.

II.4.6. *The brazier festivals*

The *kinūnu* 'brazier, hearth' (KI.NE, rarely KI.NE.NE) is a cult object used in ceremonies and rituals throughout the year, but also special brazier festivals are known. Brazier festivals are attested in documents from the Ur III and Old Babylonian periods.[460] Ceremonies with the *kinūnu* are less well-known from the Neo-Assyrian and Neo-Babylonian periods.[461] For the Hellenistic period[462] we have a reference to the ceremonies with the brazier in the Uruk ritual text *TU* 38,[463] which lists several ceremonies and offerings under the classification *parṣu*. This text also informs us that loaves and cakes and furthermore oxen and sheep were apparently used during the ceremony with the *kinūnu*. The ceremonies with the *kinūnu* probably took place during night vigils, as in earlier periods.[464]

Cohen has suggested[465] that there is evidence for a brazier festival in the Eanna-temple in Late Neo-Babylonian Uruk in the ninth month Kislīmu,[466] and also for a brazier festival in the Esagila-temple in Hellenistic Babylon in the ninth month Kislīmu, but note that references to the *kinūnu* begin as early as the eight month Araḫšamna, and continued into the tenth month Ṭebētu (also known as Kinūnu the 'brazier month').[467] Note also that the months referred to are all winter-months.

Another brazier called *garakku* is not often mentioned in Hellenistic temple ritual texts. However, it plays an important role in the eclipse of the moon ritual from Uruk, described in *BRM* 4, 6.[468]

---

460 M.E. Cohen, *Cultic calendars*, 392 ff.

461 *CAD*, K, 395a and *AHw*, 481–2. Cf. G. van Driel, *Cult of Aššur*, 168 and A.C.V.M. Bongenaar, *The Neo-Babylonian Ebabbar temple at Sippar*, 21, n. 47.

462 See G.J.P. McEwan, *FAOS* 4, 163.

463 Obv. 37 and rev. 37.

464 Cf. *RMA* no. 151, rev. 7–10 (= H. Hunger, *SAA* VIII (1992), p. 211, no. 371, rev. 10), which mentions a *kinūnu*-ceremony taking place during the night of the nineteenth of Kislīmu. I already argumented against McEwan's idea (*FAOS* 4, 163), that this is confirmed by the list in *TU* 38, see II.1.

465 *Cultic calendars*, 393–4.

466 *LKU*, no. 51, rev. 13–18.

467 *BRM* 4, 25 // *SBH* VII, obv. 5 ff. (for day 18 of the eighth month Araḫšamna), obv. 26 ff. (for days 9, 10, 17 and 22 of the ninth month Kislīmu), obv. 50 ff. (for the tenth day of the tenth month Ṭebētu). There is more supporting evidence for brazier ceremonies on the fourth day of the ninth month Kislīmu, in the Esagila ritual text BM 32206 +, IV, 149, 152, 154, 155, 156, all on day four of Kislīmu (cf. Lambert's remark on p. 90a top).

Another occurrence of *kinūnu* was suggested by G.J.P. McEwan, *FAOS* 4, 87–88, and B. Funck, *Uruk zur Seleukidenzeit*, 217–17: *BRM* 2, 22, 7 // Weisberg, *BiMes* 24, no.1, 7, a private contract from Hellenistic Uruk, reads in obv. 7 (see also rev. 21):

... ḪA.LA *šá ina* ^{giš}KI.E.NE.NE.MEŠ *šá* ^{d}INNIN.MEŠ *gab-bi*

While Clay, *BRM* 2, p. 24 apparently already identified the correct logogram (he reads: ^{iṣ}*melultu*^{pl} *ša Ištarâti* 'the festivities(?) of Ashtoreth, all of it'), L.T. Doty (*CAHU*, 133 with n. 266) suggested ^{giš}KI.E.NE.DÈ = EŠEMEN = *keppû* 'jump rope'. This was however not followed by McEwan, who read ^{giš}*kinūni šá ištarāti*.MEŠ *gab-bi* 'the braziers of all the goddesses', and Funck, who preferred: *is-qí-e* BIL.BIL.MEŠ, 'den Anteil an den Feueropfern'. *keppû* 'skipping-rope' has to be preferred, because *kinunu* is usually written KI.NE or rarely KI.NE.NE, but never KI.E.NE.NE; furthermore, *keppû* has, unlike *kinūnu and mēlultu*, the determinative GIŠ and is often attested with ^{d}INNIN 'the goddess' (see the dictionaries for references); see also R. Borger, *ABZ*, 237a, who also gives EŠEMEN = KI.E.NE.DI, and ÉŠEMEN = KI.E.NE.DI.AN.MÙŠ or KI.E.NE.DI.^{d}INNIN. So, probably we should read in *BRM* 2, 22, obv. 7: '(his) share in the skipping-ropes of all the goddesses'.

468 Obv. 14–18, 29–30, rev. 37–38. It is well-known in texts from earlier periods, see for instance, T.G. Pinches, *Berens Coll.*, no. 110, obv. 2 and passim in this text; *LKU* no. 51, obv. 8 (*napīšu ina muḫḫi garakka*), 10, 19, 20. Cf. also A. Falkenstein, *LKU*, 18, n. 2.

Table XVI: brazier festivals in Uruk and Babylon

date	god	place	text
1, 2, 6, 7, 14,15-IX	gods of Eanna	Uruk	*LKU*, no. 51
18-VIII	Šamaš	Babylon[469]	*BRM* 4, 25//*SBH* VII
18-VIII	Šamaš	Babylon[469]	*BRM* 4, 25//*SBH* VII
4-IX	–	Babylon	BM 32206 +
9-IX	Lugalasal	Babylon[469]	*BRM* 4, 25//*SBH* VII
10-IX	Madānu, Gula	Babylon[469]	*BRM* 4, 25//*SBH* VII
17-IX	Nabû of Borsippa	Babylon[469]	*BRM* 4, 25//*SBH* VII
22-IX	Uraš	Babylon[469]	*BRM* 4, 25//*SBH* VII
10-X	Palil of Upî (Opis)	Babylon[469]	*BRM* 4, 25//*SBH* VII

II.4.7. *The cultic calendars*

An attempt is made here to bring together all collected data which refer to annual cultic activities, in order to reconstruct cultic calendars for Uruk and Babylon in the Hellenistic period.[470] Although for the second, third, fourth, fifth and ninth months in Uruk, and for the fourth, fifth, sixth, eleventh and twelth months in Babylon no data are available, we have enough to reconstruct two calendars. Data for the two intercalary months, intercalary Ulūlu and intercalary Addaru are not attested.

The cultic calendar of Uruk

Nisannu (I)

date	cult activity	text
7-I	New Year festival of Anu	*TU* 39–40
(8-I)	procession of Anu	*KAR* 132
(8-I)	New Year festival of Anu	*KAR* 132
10-I	New Year festival of Anu	*TU* 43
11-I	New Year festival of Anu	*TU* 43

Ajjaru (II) (no data)

Simānu (III) (no data)

Du'ūzu (IV) (no data)

Abu (V) (no data)

Attested only once in the Hellenistic temple ritual texts (*KAR* 132, III, 17) is the *ḫuluppaqqu* (^{dug}NÍG.TAB.-TUR.RA) a small brazier of clay or metal (*CAD*, Ḫ, 232; cf. *AHw*, 354–5).

[469] And neighbouring towns/cities, see A.R. George, *BTT*, 222, n. 4.

[470] A first attempt was made by G.J.P. McEwan, *FAOS* 4, 169–182.

Ulūlu (VI)

date	cult activity	text
3-VI	clothing ceremonies for Anu, Adad	K 3753
3-VI	procession of Nusku, Ningal	K 3753
3-VI	procession of Nusku	K 3753
3-VI	marriage ceremony of Ištar	K 3753

Tašītu (VII)

date	cult activity	text
1–11-VII	New Year festival of Anu	*TU* 39–40
1-VII	marriage ceremony	*TU* 39
7-VII	clothing ceremonies for Anu, Antu, Ištar	*TU* 39
(8-VII)	New Year festival of Anu	*BRM* 4, 7
8–9-VII	procession of Anu	*BRM* 4, 7; *TU* 39–40
17-VII	ceremony for Papsukkal	*OECT* 9, 40; 42; 44; 45 // 46; 60

Araḫsamna (VIII)

date	cult activity	text
5-VIII	procession of Mīšaru	*TU* 39, K 3753
18-VIII	procession	K 3753

Kislīmu (IX) (no data)

Ṭebētu (X)

date	cult activity	text
16–17-(X?)	procession of Anu	*TU* 41

Šabaṭu (XI)

date	cult activity	text
10 [+ x]-XI	ceremony	K 3753
22-XI	ceremony	K 3753
26-XI	ceremony	K 3753
27-XI	ceremony	K 3753
29-XI	ceremony	K 3753

Addaru (XII)

date	cult activity	text
8-XII	ceremony for Antu	*OECT* 9, 40; 42; 44; 45 // 46; 60; 68
10-XII	ceremony for Bēlet-ṣēri	*OECT* 9, 44; 60

The cultic calendar of Babylon

Nisannu (I)

date	cult activity	text
1-I	New Year festival of Bēl	Çağirgan, *Festivals*, 1; AB 244
2–5-I	New Year festival of Bēl	*RAcc.*, 127 ff.
6-I	New Year festival of Bēl	*RAcc.*, 127 ff.
(6/7/8(?)-I)	New Year festival of Bēl	BM 41577
8-I	New Year festival of Bēl	*Diaries*, no. -204; *SBH* VIII; Grayson, *Chronicles*, no. 13b
8-I	clothing ceremony for Marduk	*SBH* VIII
8-I	procession of Bēl	*Diaries*, no. -204; *SBH* VIII
11-I	New Year festival of Bēl	*SBH* VIII; *Diaries*, no. -245; AB 244
11-I	marriage ceremony of Marduk, Zarpanītu(?)	*SBH* VIII

Ajjaru (II)

date	cult activity	text
2-II	clothing ceremony for Nabû	*SBH* VIII
2-II	procession of Nabû	*SBH* VIII
2-II	marriage ceremony of Nabû	*SBH* VIII
6-II	ceremony for Nabû	*SBH* VIII
7-II	ceremony for Nabû	*SBH* VIII
7-II	procession of Nabû	*SBH* VIII
17-II	procession of Nanāja	*SBH* VIII

Simānu (III)

date	cult activity	text
15-III	ceremony for Bēlet-ilī	*SBH* VIII
15-III	procession	BM 32656
16-III	procession	BM 32656
22-III	ceremony	*SBH* VIII

Du'ūzu (IV) (no data)

Abu (V) (no data)

Ulūlu (VI) (no data)

Tašrītu (VII)

date	cult activity	text
7-VII(?)	New Year festival of Bēl	BM 32206 +
7-VII(?)	clothing ceremony for Bēl	BM 32206 +
8-VII	New Year festival of Bēl	BM 32206 +
8-VII	procession of Ninurta, Bēl (Enlil?)	BM 32206 +

Araḫsamna (VIII)

date	cult activity	text
18-VIII	ceremony for Šamaš	*BRM* 4, 25
18-VIII	procession of the 'Sons of Bēl'	*SBH* VII // *BRM* 4, 25
18-VIII	brazier festivals of Šamaš	*BRM* 4, 25//*SBH* VII
25-VIII	ceremony for Zababa, Isin	*SBH* VII // *BRM* 4, 25

Kislīmu (IX)

date	cult activity	text
3-IX	clothing ceremony	*SBH* VIII
3-IX	clothing ceremony	BM 32206 +
3-IX	clothing ceremonies for Bēltīja, Tašmētu	BM 32206 +
3-IX	clothing ceremony for Ištar of Babylon	BM 32206 +
4-IX	ceremony for Marduk, Zarpanītu	*SBH* VII // *BRM* 4, 25; *SBH* VIII
4-IX	procession of slave, bull, and Usmû	BM 32206 +
4-IX	procession of Ninurta, Bēl (Enlil?)	BM 32206 +
4-IX	brazier festival	BM 32206 +
6/7-IX	ceremony for Enlils, Adads	*SBH* VII // *BRM* 4, 25
8-IX	ceremony for Lugalbanda	*SBH* VII // *BRM* 4, 25
9-IX	ceremony for Lugalasal	*SBH* VII // *BRM* 4, 25
9-IX	brazier festival of Lugalasal	*BRM* 4, 25//*SBH* VII
10-IX	ceremony for Ea	*SBH* VII // *BRM* 4, 25
10-IX	brazier festival of Madānu, Gula	*BRM* 4, 25//*SBH* VII
12-IX	ceremony for Ištar	*SBH* VII // *BRM* 4, 25
13-IX	ceremony for Anunītu, Šarrat-Sippar	*SBH* VII // *BRM* 4, 25
14-IX	ceremony for Ašratu	*BRM* 4, 25
15-IX	ceremony for Anaššat(?)	*SBH* VII // *BRM* 4, 25
16-IX	clothing ceremony	*SBH* VIII
16/17-IX	ceremony for Nabû	*SBH* VII // *BRM* 4, 25; *SBH* VIII
17-IX	brazier festival of Nabû of Borsippa	*BRM* 4, 25//*SBH* VII
22-IX	ceremony for Uraš	*SBH* VII // *BRM* 4, 25
22-IX	brazier festival of Uraš	*BRM* 4, 25//*SBH* VII
25-IX	ceremony for Lugalmar(a)da	*SBH* VII // *BRM* 4, 25
28/29-IX	ceremony for Nergal	*SBH* VII // *BRM* 4, 25

Ṭebētu (X)

date	cult activity	text
10-X	ceremony for Palil	*BRM* 4, 25
10-X	brazier festival of Palil of Upî (Opis)	*BRM* 4, 25//*SBH* VII

Šabaṭu (XI) (no data)

Addaru (XII) (no data)

II.5. The kettledrum ritual

One of the instruments used during ceremonies and rituals was the kettledrum (Akk. *lilissu*).[471] The kettledrum, usually made of bronze, is attested from the Old Akkadian period on.[472] We must distinguish between, on the one hand, the kettledrum as a cultic object and used as a musical instrument as one of the means of averting divine anger, and on the other hand the ritual for the covering of the kettledrum: here the drum is also a cult object, but now it is the main protagonist of a ritual during which a bull is slaughtered and its hide is used to cover (*arāmu*) the drum. First we will discuss the different occurrences of the kettledrum, and then we will describe the ritual.

II.5.1. *The kettledrum*

In many ceremonies the kettledrum plays an important part. It is often connected with the verb *šakānu* 'to place', which however, depending on the context, can also mean 'to play'. In several ritual texts from the Neo-Assyrian period we find occasional references to days on which the kettledrums were played (*lilisāti*).[473] In a Neo- or Late Babylonian cultic calendar text from Sippar, BM 50503, the kettledrum is used to accompany the lamentation priest reciting *taqribtu*s and *eršemakku*s on the days [1?]-8–15–20 of every month in Ebabbar, the temple of Šamaš.[474] From the late Neo-Babylonian or early Achaemenid period we have one text from Uruk, *LKU*, no. 51, listing ceremonies for Bēlet-ša-Uruk, Uṣur-amassu and Aška'itu for all twelve months of the year. The kettledrum is used during these ceremonies on at least eight separate days: on one or more unknown days of month IV, on day 17-IV, on the days 1 and 2-VII, on day 2-XII, on day 3-XII, on day [4]-XII, and on day 5-XII.[475]

The kettledrum is also attested in ritual texts from Hellenistic Uruk, but none of the days mentioned in *LKU*, no. 51 is attested. During an Ištar festival described in *TU* 42 + a kettledrum is placed on a *šuḫḫu*-stand in the cella of Ištar in her *akītu*-temple outside of Uruk,[476] which can be connected with *LKU*, no. 51,[477] which informs us that on an unknown day during the first half of the fourth month Du'ūzu[478] Nanāja sits next to Bēlet-ša-Uruk (Ištar), the kettledrum is placed, and then lifted up again to take

---

471 Wr. LI.LI.ÌZ, LILIZ and syllabically. Besides the kettledrum we also find other instruments used in the cult: the *alû*-drum, the *balaggu*-harp, the *uppu*-drum, the *manzû*-drum, the *ḫalḫallatu*-drum, the *tigû*-drum, the *abgalgungunnû*-drum, the *mālilu*-flute and the *tibbuttu*/*timbûtu*-harp. However, not all are attested in texts from the Hellenistic period. For the drum types played by the lamentation priests see D. Brown and the present author in *RA* 91 (1997), 162 (note 1′).

472 Cf. *AHw*, 552 f.; *CAD*, L, 186 f. Many references to the kettledrum also in G. Furlani, *Sacrificio*, 222 f., and id., *Riti*, 67 ff. See also F.Thureau-Dangin, *RA* 16 (1919), 121 f.; D.O. Edzard, M. Krebernik, in: *RlA* 7 (1987–90), 22b.

473 VAT 13596, BM 121206 and K 5413a; for a discussion of the *lilisāti*-data in these texts see G. van Driel, *Cult of Aššur*, 140 ff., and 148 f.

474 The text, published by Stefan Maul in: *Munuscula Mesopotamica. Festschrift für Johannes Renger*, Münster, 1999, 285 ff., was discussed in II.2.2.

475 Cf. obv. 23, 24, 25; 28; rev. 6, 8; 27; 31; 32; 35.

476 Rev. 32′. The text is discussed in II.8.5.

477 Obv. 22–25.

478 This seems likely since the first attested day of Du'ūzu is day 17 (obv. 27).

part in a procession, after which the kettledrum is placed on a *šuḫḫu*-stand, perhaps in Bēlet-ša-Uruk's cella in Eanna.

The kettledrum is also used during the Uruk eclipse of the moon ritual, more specifically in the third version of the ritual, dealing with the duties of the lamentation priest.[479] As we will discuss elsewhere, in this ritual the kettledrum is used as a musical instrument, serving the purpose of averting the evil consequences of the lunar eclipse, and furthermore it plays an important part as a cult object in the ritual.[480]

In another Uruk ritual text, W 18728,[481] describing clothing instructions for cult personnel and the king, the consecrated lamentation priest (*kalû gullubu*), probably belonging to the regular personnel of the temple, is dressed with linen *lubāru*-clothing; as long as he wears this clothing he is not allowed to sit near the kettledrum. After a passage which deals with the unconsecrated lamentation priest (*kalû la gullubu*), the chief singer of dirges (*galamāḫu*) is mentioned who also must take off the *lubāru*-clothing before he can sit near the kettledrum. At first sight this passage seems clear: as long as he wears this clothing the kettledrum cannot be used to accompany him when he recites lamentations. This, however, appears to be contradicted in the eclipse ritual text mentioned above: during the eclipse, i.e. when there is a threat of imminent danger, the people of the land and the lamentation priests have to cover their heads with (torn) *lubāru*-clothing,[482] which by itself is not unexpected: the clothing is worn as a gesture of mourning. However, while in W 18728 the lamentation priest must not come near the drum as long as he wears the *lubāru*-clothing, in the eclipse text there is no reference to the lamentation priests taking off this clothing when they begin reciting the lamentations, presumably accompanied by kettledrum music. What the exact significance of the passage in W 18728 is remains unclear, but it is clear that the lamentation priest cannot approach the kettledrum wearing *lubāru*-clothing, indicating some kind of negative or unclean association with this clothing, while the kettledrum is generally assumed to be positive.[483]

The kettledrum is also mentioned in a ritual text from Hellenistic Babylon: BM 32206 +[484] describes ceremonies performed during days 3 and 4 of the month Kislīmu. First several events concerning Bēl and several other cult-participants on day 3 of Kislīmu in Esagila take place, leading up to the journey of a slave, riding on a bull, and Usmû to the *akītu*-temple on day 4, and their return on the same day to Esagila.[485] Taking part in the events in Esagila is the kettledrum of Bēl, and the kettledrum of Bēltīja.[486] No reference to the slaughtering of the bull, or the covering of the drum is made (as in the ritual with

---

479 *BRM* 4, 6, rev. 42 ff. // BM 134701, obv. 1 ff.
480 See II.7.3.
481 A. Falkenstein, *UVB* 15 (1959), 40, obv. 10′f. and 13′f.
482 *BRM* 4, 6, obv. 21 and rev. 43 f. // BM 134701, obv. 2 f.
483 M. Stol suggested to me: note that *lubāru* is only connected with the verbs *katāmu* 'to cover' and *ḫalāpu* 'to clad in', but not with *labāšu* 'to put on/to wear' (cf. *BRM* 4, 6, obv. 21′ and rev. 43′, W 18728, obv. 10′–11 and 13′). The first two indicate a temporary action, a sign of impurity. Perhaps the vocalisation (*fu'āl*) indicates a dirty cloth or clothing, see M. Stol in *Fs. Rykle Borger*, Groningen, 1998, 348–9.
484 G. Çağirgan, W.G. Lambert, *JCS* 43–45 (1991–1993), 89–106
485 See II.4.3. and II.8.2.
486 Col. I, 5, 18.

the kettledrum, discussed below), although a drum skin(?) (*ḫuppu*) is mentioned.[487] The function of the bull is probably to carry the slave to and from the *akītu*-temple, as is clear from col. III, 115, where the slave descends from the bull when he has arrived in Esagila. Another reference to the kettledrum follows,[488] and during the night of day 3 a kettledrum of Bēl and a kettledrum of Ea are used.[489] The description of day 4[490] contains the arranging of the *alû*-drum, in the same manner as for day 8 of Tašrītu.[491] No mention of the kettledrum is made until the procession is back in Esagila,[492] but the context is not clear because the relevant passage is partly damaged. Finally, in col. IV, 158 the text refers to a kettledrum (lamentation) 'It touches the Earth like a storm' (UD.D[AM K]I ÀM.ÚS), which however is not attested in the kettledrum ritual texts discussed below.[493]

Finally, according to a calendar text priests will beat a kettledrum, together with an *abgalgungunnu*-drum, on day 25 of the eighth month Araḫsamna, after which the former is removed.[494]

This leaves us with only three attested pieces of data for the kettledrum, day 25-VIII, and days 3–4-IX, all from Babylon.

II.5.2. *The ritual of the covering of the kettledrum*

The ritual of covering the kettledrum is described in texts from the Neo-Assyrian period (Assur, Nineveh), and from the Hellenistic period, but only from Uruk.[495] Although as we saw the kettledrum is attested in texts from Babylon, no ritual texts from Hellenistic Babylon are known which describe the covering of the kettledrum. However, we have two references in the astronomical diaries, which indicate that as we would expect the ritual was also practiced in Babylon. The ritual is mentioned in a diary for day 24 of the month Araḫsamna in the year 41 S.E. (271 B.C.):

> 13′ [... ^{lú}MA]Š.MAŠ.MEŠ *u* ^{lú}LAGAR.MEŠ *né-pe-šú šá a-ra-mu šá li-*[*li-si* DÙ-*u* (?)]
>
> '[... the e]xorcists and the lamentation priests [performed(?)] the ritual procedure for the covering of the kettle[drum]'.[496]

---

487 Col. I, 44.
488 Col. II, 48.
489 Col. II, 53.
490 Col. II, 55 ff.
491 Col. II, 57–8, see also 59, and col. III, 102–3.
492 Col. IV, 132–3.
493 It is mentioned in the Uruk building ritual *TU* 46, rev. 5, in the Uruk *mīs pî*-ritual text *Bagh. Mitt. Beih.* 2, no. 1 (+ //), 9; and in the Uruk cultic calendar text *TU* 48, rev. 3, see II.2.2.
494 *SBH* VII, 4–5 // *BRM* 4, 25, 14–15.
495 Neo-Assyrian period: *KAR* 60; *KAR* 50; IV R^2, 23, no. 1 +. Hellenistic Uruk: *TU* 44; *Bagh. Mitt. Beih.* 2, nos. 5, 6, 7, 8, 9. The *lilissu* is depicted on the reverse of the explanatory text *TU* 47 (A. Livingstone, *Mystical*, 187 ff.), from Hellenistic Uruk, and on two seal impressions found on the edges of cuneiform tablets from Hellenistic Uruk, see R. Wallenfels, *Uruk. Hellenistic Seal Impressions in the Yale Babylonian Collection. I. Cuneiform Tablets*, Mainz am Rhein, 1994 (AUWE 19), 19–20, nos. 51 and 52.
496 A.J. Sachs–H. Hunger, *Diaries*, no. -270, B, rev. 12′–13′. This passage was discussed by W. Horowitz, *RA* 85 (1991), 75 ff.

In another diary, dealing with the month Ajjaru of the year 85 S.E., a reference is made to the temple workshop (*bīt mummi*); then a sheep is bound(?), after which the kettledrum is mentioned. Finally incantations are recited, presumably by an exorcist.[497] The passage is damaged, but the reference to the temple workshop especially and to the incantations remind us of the covering of the kettledrum ritual, as we will see.

Here we will concentrate on the continuity of the kettledrum ritual: is it possible to see whether the ritual in the Neo-Assyrian period was different from the ritual in the Hellenistic period? We have several texts which give us good insight into the ritual, and generally they follow the same procedures, but there are also differences. We will first describe the ritual as it is described in the most important text, *TU* 44, which will be used here as the basis text, and compare this with other kettledrum ritual texts from the Neo-Assyrian and Hellenistic periods.

TU 44

The most elaborate version of the ritual, *TU* 44, was written in Hellenistic Uruk (the text is discussed in the Appendix.). The ritual begins with an *enūma*-phrase: 'When y[ou] want [to cover] the kettledrum (proceed as follows)'.[498] First, a knowledgeable expert (*ummânu*) selects a black bull.[499] Then 'on a favorable day' the bull is led into the workshop (*bīt mummi*), where it is ritually prepared for the slaughtering.[500] Twelve gods (figurines) are prepared. After this the kettledrum is positioned, the curtains are drawn shut, and the washing of the mouth ceremony (*mīs pî*) is performed on the bull. After a number of incantations and lamentations have been recited, the bull is slaughtered.[501]

Its heart is burned, the sinew from its left thigh, which will be used later, is removed, and part of the carcass of the bull is buried in a cloth. Aside from the sinew more is left unburied: the face of the bull is placed towards the West, and the hide is soaked in flour, water, beer and wine. More preparations with the hide follow (laying it in ghee from a pure cow, steeping it with madder and alum), and then the kettledrum is covered with it, using a linen rope, wooden pegs, and the sinew, after which the remainder of the tanned hide is buried.[502]

Next a short explanatory passage follows which enumerates three groups totalling twelve gods: the three great gods Anu, Enlil and Ea, the twins Lugalgirra and Meslamtaea, and the seven children of Enmešarra.[503] No explanation is given for these names here, but the duplicate IV R^2, 23, no. 1 +, I, 6 identifies the last group of seven gods as the sons of Enmešarra: 'The seven gods, sons of Enmešarra, are (represented by) heaps of flour'. The twelve gods are probably the same figurines mentioned above, and they are placed in the kettledrum before it is covered, as is clear from the comment in the

497 A.J. Sachs–H. Hunger, *Diaries*, no. -226, A, obv. 22′–23′. See W. Horowitz, *NABU* 1991, no. 80.
498 Col. I, 1.
499 Col. I, 2 ff.
500 Col. I, 7 ff.
501 Col. II, 4 ff.
502 Col. II, 16 ff.
503 Col. III, 1 ff. This passage is duplicated among others in the explanatory text *TU* 47, obv. 10 ff. (Hellenistic) and in IV R^2, 23, no. 1 +, I, 1–6 (Neo-Assyrian). See my comments on these lines in the Appendix.

following lines 7–8: 'You will lay down twelve bronze gods into the bronze kettledrum and (then) you will cover the kettledrum'.[504]

The ritual continues: on day 15 the kettledrum is brought out before Šamaš, five offering accoutrements are arranged for Ea, Šamaš, Marduk, Lumḫa (also written ᵈBALAG 'the divine harp' in the duplicate *KAR* 60, see the Appendix) and the (now) divine kettledrum (ᵈLILIZ), although only after this is the drum consecrated, purified, and the washing of the mouth ceremony performed on it. Then the drum is led before the gods and placed in a bed of barley seeds. After the lamentation LUGAL DIMMER ANKIA 'The king, god of Heaven and Earth'[505] the ritual ends.[506] At the end of col. III a warning is added for the user of the tablet not to reveal its contents to anyone who is not competent.[507] Finally col. IV enumerates all the materials and foodstuffs used during the ritual. The text ends with a colophon, which explicitly states that the text belongs to the ritual procedure (*nēpešu*) of the lamentation priest.[508]

Evidence from Nineveh and Assur: IV R², 23, no. 1 +, KAR 50 and KAR 60

The Nineveh text IV R², 23, no. 1 + is a catalogue of recitations, which had to be performed during the kettledrum ritual (the text is given in the Appendix.). It belongs to the corpus of the lamentation priest, as is specifically stated in the colophon.[509] The text enumerates several recitations which have to be performed during the kettledrum ritual, but it also records a few passages from the ritual itself.[510] The text carefully records at which moment during the ritual a specific recitation has to be performed. It concentrates for the most part on the recitations, but we know that it was the first of a series of tablets describing the entire ritual, because the catchline refers to the bull entering the workshop, which, as we saw in *TU* 44, is the first step in the ritual after it has been inspected. These procedures are enumerated on separate tablets, which constitute our kettledrum ritual texts.

Descriptions for the kettledrum ritual in the Neo-Assyrian period are recorded in two text from Assur, *KAR* 50 and *KAR* 60 (both texts are given in the Appendix).

On the obverse of *KAR* 50[511] we find a bilingual incantation for 'the choice bull, the creation of the great gods'. The reverse describes the actual ritual. The text is apparently a shorter version of the ritual, compared with *TU* 44. After describing several offerings and purifications, the text explicitly describes how the bull was led into the workshop

---

504 See also II, 8–9. Cf. W.G. Lambert, *JSS* 13 (1968), 109–10; A. Livingstone, *Mystical*, 201.

505 III, 28, presented in full in *BRM* 4, 8, bilingual hymn to Anu, 61 S.E; cf. M.E. Cohen, *Lamentations*, 728 ff. Cohen pointed out (*Eršemma*, 48–9) that this lamentation, which had to be recited on the fifteenth of the month, was sung after the covering of the kettledrum was completed, and not while the drum was still being repaired. Therefore the recitation of lamentation to the accompaniment of the kettledrum did not serve the purpose of neutralising the divine anger, but was a means of testing the new drum.

506 Col. III, 15 ff.

507 Col. III, 29 ff.

508 Col. IV, 36.

509 Col. IV, 26.

510 Cf. I, 7–8; III, 24–9; IV, 2; 24.

511 Part of the text is duplicated by the Nineveh texts K 6060 (*BBR* 2, no. 56) + K 10820 (unpublished, see Plate II). For details see the discussion of the text in the Appendix.

(described here as 'a secluded place', i.e. forbidden for outsiders)[512] 'in the morning, before sunrise'[513] (elsewhere not attested, although clear from the context). The text continues, in a very abbreviated passage, with the incantations which have to be recited, the slaughtering of the bull and the removing of the hide and sinew for the covering of the kettledrum.[514]

More important for the comparison with *TU* 44 is another kettledrum ritual text from the Neo-Assyrian period, *KAR* 60. It is clear that in general the same procedures are followed, but the Uruk text describes all the ceremonies up to the slaughtering of the bull much more extensively[515] than the Assur text.[516] In addition, the enumeration of all the foodstuffs and materials, used during the ritual, is only attested in *TU* 44.[517] Furthermore, only in *TU* 44 is a short explanatory passage given.[518]

There is one major difference between *TU* 44 and *KAR* 60. While the Uruk text first describes the slaughtering of the bull, and immediately continues with the covering of the kettledrum, the Assur text describes a special additional ceremony with the lamentation priest[519]: he must uncover his head, kneel down and stand at the head of the bull, where he has to recite the prayer 'He, who lies asleep' three times. Then he must say: 'these ritual acts the totality-of-the-gods has performed, I did not perform (them)'[520] three times, after which the lamentation priest opens the curtains and this special ceremony is ended.

This passage has been discussed by Oppenheim.[521] The uncovering of the head and kneeling down is a typical position of penitence, and was necessary here because the priest was responsible for the crime he has committed: the killing of the bull, a sacred animal. That is why first he has to recite a lamentation for the dead three times, and then he has to decline the responsibility for killing the animal three times. Furthermore, in rev. 14 we read that the head of the lamentation priests, the chief singer of dirges (*galamāḫu*) is forbidden to eat the meat from the bull. Apparently the lamentation priests were allowed to eat the meat, but not the chief singer of dirges, because he was considered to have been responsible for killing the bull. This is interesting because in *TU* 44 the animal was carefully buried.[522] The Uruk text also mentions the burial of the remainder of the tanned hide.[523]

Oppenheim concluded that the inclusion of this ceremony in the ritual and the reference to the chief singer of dirges clearly show that between the Neo-Assyrian and the Hellenistic period major changes took place. However, we now have evidence from Hellenistic Uruk which might suggest otherwise.

---

512 Rev. 8
513 Rev. 1–2.
514 Rev. 8 ff.
515 Col. I, 7-II, 16.
516 Obv. 1–15.
517 Col. IV.
518 Col. III, 1–14.
519 Obv. 17–18, rev. 1–4.
520 Rev. 3–4.
521 *OrNS* 11 (1942), 122, n. 1 (but note that he misinterpreted *KAR* 60, obv. 17).
522 Col. II, 19.
523 Col. II, 32.

More evidence from Hellenistic Uruk: Bagh. Mitt. Beih. 2, no. 5[524]

Apart from *TU* 44 we have another kettledrum ritual text from Hellenistic Uruk, *Bagh. Mitt. Beih.* 2, no. 5, which allows us to follow the ritual procedures closely. Surprisingly this text is closer to the older Assur version then the other Hellenistic Uruk version *TU* 44[525]: the ceremonies that follow after the leading of the bull into the workshop[526] are described in a much shorter version than in *TU* 44, and resemble more the Assur text. After this the bull was slaughtered in front of the kettledrum (*ina* IGI LI.LI.ÌZ).[527] Note that in the duplicate *KAR* 60 the bull was placed for Lumḫa (dBALAG) and then slaughtered.[528]

Next the bull's heart is scattered with juniper.[529] This interesting passage is paralleled by *KAR* 60,[530] but not by *TU* 44, where the heart is burnt in front of the kettledrum together with cedar, juniper and *maṣḫatu*-flour.[531] For this reason Thureau-Dangin, who did not know of *Bagh. Mitt. Beih.* 2, no. 5, suggested that *KAR* 60 should be restored to make it fit *TU* 44.[532] But if we assume that the restoration proposed by Thureau-Dangin is not necessary, then we have here another indication that *TU* 44 on the one hand and *KAR* 60 and *Bagh. Mitt. Beih.* 2, no. 5 on the other represent two separate versions of the ritual.

The next passage in *Bagh. Mitt. Beih.* 2, no. 5 is badly damaged,[533] but may have contained the special ceremony with the lamentation priest attested in *KAR* 60.[534] The hide is then prepared and the drum covered with it.[535]

There are also parallels with *TU* 44. *Bagh. Mitt. Beih.* 2, no. 5, like the other Uruk text *TU* 44, appears to begin with the *enūma*-phrase 'When y[ou want to cover the kettledrum (proceed as follows)]',[536] but we know that in the Neo-Assyrian period the *enūma*-phrase was also used, as is clear from the catchline in IV R², 23, no. 1 +, IV, 25.[537] More important, the end of the text describes, like *TU* 44, the burial of the carcass of the bull with the remainder of the hide,[538] which is, as noted above, not in accordance with the Assur text.

---

524 Not discussed here is a small badly damaged fragment, *Bagh. Mitt. Beih.* 2, no. 9, which perhaps also describes part of the kettledrum ritual; for a transliteration see my comments on IV R², 23, no. 1 +, I, 17, in the Appendix.
525 Already noticed by G.J.P. McEwan, *BiOr* 38 (1981), 639f. See also the commentaries on *KAR* 60 and *Bagh. Mitt. Beih.* 2, no. 5 in the Appendix, with many parallel passages.
526 Obv. 7ff.
527 Rev. 22.
528 Obv. 14. See also *TU* 47, rev.: dLILIZ for the representation of the kettledrum
529 Rev. 23.
530 Obv. 15–16.
531 Col. II, 16–18.
532 *RAcc.*, 53, n. 61. See my comment on *KAR* 60, obv. 15–16, in the Appendix.
533 Rev. 24–5.
534 Obv. 17–8, rev. 1–4. Cf. *ep-še-e-ti an-na-a-tú*/*ti* in *Bagh. Mitt. Beih.* 2, no. 5, rev. 25 // *KAR* 60, rev. 3, both followed by the removal of the water basin and the loosening of the curtains.
535 Rev. 27ff.
536 Obv. 1.
537 The beginning of *KAR* 60 is lost; *KAR* 50 has a different beginning of the ritual.
538 Rev. 31ff.

Another text from Hellenistic Uruk, *Bagh. Mitt. Beih.* 2, no. 7, also appears to follow the shorter version of *KAR* 60 and *Bagh. Mitt. Beih.* 2, no. 5.[539] Of special interest here is obv. 6′, which, if it follows the duplicate *KAR* 60,[540] refers to the chief singer of dirges, who may not eat meat from the bull. If restored correctly, this clearly shows that in Hellenistic Uruk the chief singer of dirges is also not allowed to eat meat from the bull, as in the Neo-Assyrian period. Oppenheim's conclusion, based on *KAR* 60, cannot stand any longer.

II.5.3. *Who performed the kettledrum ritual?*

The kettledrum ritual texts indicate that the ritual belongs to the text corpus of the lamentation priest (*kalûtu*), which explains the dominant position of lamentations in the ritual. The lamentation priest, who is usually addressed in the second person (the 'you'-figure),[541] was not only responsible for the lamentations, but also took charge of many of the other cultic activities, such as making offerings and libations, and performing consecrations and purifications.

However, the two passages in the astronomical diaries mentioned above clearly state that the kettledrum ritual was performed by exorcists and lamentation priests. Horowitz already pointed out that, with the exception of the passages in the astronomical diaries, the exorcist is not attested in connection with the kettledrum ritual.[542] Clearly in the kettledrum ritual texts the duties of the exorcist are not referred to, only those of the lamentation priest are described.[543] Furthermore, although we know that the exorcist played a major part in other temple rituals from Uruk and Babylon,[544] in the kettledrum ritual many of the tasks, which are usually connected with the exorcist, are apparently performed by lamentation priests.[545]

Some concluding remarks

It is clear that the kettledrum ritual texts demonstrate an astonishing continuity of this tradition. We have different versions of the ritual, a longer one from Hellenistic Uruk (*TU* 44), and a shorter one from both Assur and Hellenistic Uruk (*KAR* 60, *KAR* 50, *Bagh. Mitt. Beih.* 2, nos. 5 and 7), but although the relation between the two versions is not exactly clear (in particular, are both Uruk-versions based on one older composition?),

---

539 Obv. 2–9 is probably a duplicate of *KAR* 60, rev. 10–15 and *Bagh. Mitt. Beih.* 2, no. 5, rev. 29–31. For a transliteration of these lines see my comments on *KAR* 60, rev. 10–15, in the Appendix.

540 Rev. 14.

541 Note that in *KAR* 60 the 'you'-figure is mentioned together with the lamentation priest (in the third person).

542 *RA* 85 (1991), 76.

543 The same is true for the building ritual texts, see II.6.3. In the cultic calendar texts *TU* 48, K 2724 + (see II.2.2) and BM 50503 (recently published by St. M. Maul, in: *Munuscula Mesopotamica. Festschrift für Johannes Renger*, Münster, 1999, 285 ff., cf. his remark on p. 291) only the activities of the lamentation priests are described.

544 See I.3.

545 Note that in the Nineveh text IV R^2, 23, no. 1 + the two incantations, usually connected with the exorcist, are also performed by the 'you'-figure (I, 19 ff.), presumably the lamentation priest.

there is probably no major change in tradition between the Neo-Assyrian and Hellenistic periods as far as the general procedures of the ritual are concerned.

The highlight of the ritual was the procedure with the bull. This is underlined by the fact that the curtains were drawn shut before it was prepared (as we known from *TU* 44, *KAR* 50 and IV R^2, 23, no. 1 +), and were opened again when the bull was slaughtered and recitations were performed (*KAR* 60, *Bagh. Mitt. Beih.* 2, no. 5 and IV R^2, 23, no. 1 +).[546]

Finally, we do not have many data on days during which the kettledrum ritual was performed. Only day 15 in Uruk (*TU* 44), and days x-II-85 S.E. and 24-VIII-41 S.E. in Babylon (*Diaries*, nos. -226 and -270) are attested. This can be explained by the fact that the ritual for covering the kettledrum was not part of the regularly performed temple rituals, but was only performed when repairs on the kettledrum were necessary.[547] Some of the texts contain the reference 'in an auspicious month, on a favourable day' (*ina* ITI ŠE.GA UD ŠE.GA),[548] which indicates that it was an occasional ritual: the same phrase is also used in the building ritual texts[549] and we must assume that this ritual was only performed on the occasion of rebuilding a temple. The occasional character of the ritual is also confirmed by the fact that the lamentations, recited during the ritual, are not accompanied by an exact date, as known from other texts.[550] The lamentations were performed when a drum needed to be covered, and the days for this ritual were not set.

II.6. The building ritual

Within the Babylonian cult the ritual for the rebuilding of a temple was important.[551] From Hellenistic Uruk several major building ritual texts are known.[552] Although the colophons do not refer to older originals, these texts must have had parallels from the Neo- and Late Babylonian periods, of which one is preserved.[553] Although from Hellenistic Babylon no building ritual texts are known, we do have one example from the Late Babylonian period, which interestingly enough is to a large extent duplicated by the Uruk texts.[554] These texts form the basic material from which we have reconstructed the building ritual.[555]

---

546 The procedure with the curtains is explained in III.3.

547 Cf. W. Farber, *TUAT* II, 2, 234.

548 Cf. Neo-Assyrian period: *KAR* 60, rev. 12, and similar in *KAR* 50, rev. 1; rev. 1–2 adds: 'in the morning, before sunrise'. Hellenistic period: *Bagh. Mitt. Beih.* 2, no. 5, obv. 7, and no. 7, obv. 5′.

549 See II.6.

550 See K 2724 + and *TU* 48, discussed in II.2.2.

551 Cf. G. Furlani, *Sacrificio*, 212 f.; id., *Riti*, 239 ff.; R.S. Ellis, *Foundation Deposits in Ancient Mesopotamia*, New Haven and London, 1968, 5 ff.

552 *TU* 45, *TU* 46, *Bagh. Mitt. Beih.* 2, nos. 10 and 11. Cf. J. Oelsner, *Materialien*, 169 sub b, no. 2.

553 *SpTU* 4, no. 141.

554 F.H. Weissbach, *Misc.*, no. 12. It also contains the beginning of the recitation *Enūma Anu ibnû šamê*, see below.

555 We can trace the *kalûtu*-type building ritual back to the Neo-Assyrian period, cf. the small Ninevite fragment K 5260 (K.D. Macmillan, *BA* 5/V, LVI, cf. p. 702). *STT* 232, which is concerned with the rebuilding/restoration of a door (cf. E. Reiner, *JNES* 26 [1967], 188), has similarities with *TU* 45. Other types of building rituals are known. For a short survey see F.A.M. Wiggermann, *Mesopotamian Protective Spirits. The ritual texts*, Groningen, 1992, 127 f.

From the textual evidence it appears that there are two different versions of the building ritual. In this paragraph we will attempt to reconstruct these two versions.

II.6.1. *The first version*

We will start with the most elaborate version of the ritual, *TU* 45. On two occasions the ritual is identified as belonging to the ritual procedure (*nēpešu*) of the lamentation priest.[556]

The text has a special structure. It is divided into four sections, separated by a cross-line, each describing a day.[557] Furthermore, the days are separated into two sub-sections, introduced by 'on a favourable day'; the described events apparently take place during the night (*ina* GE$_6$), as is attested for the first and fourth days,[558] and 'in the morning' (*ina še-rì*), and they are also separated by a cross-line.[559] Only on the first day is the introduction of the sub-section referred to as 'in an auspicious month, on a favourable day',[560] and appears to follow without a cross-line.[561] The text is interrupted by either a line, in which the ritual is attributed to the lamentation priest,[562] or one or two omens.[563]

Like the kettledrum ritual, the building ritual *TU* 45 also begins with an *enūma*-phrase: 'When the wall of the temple of Anu buck[les, to demolish and renovate that temple] ...'.[564] Then, 'in an auspicious month, on a favourable day, in the night', offerings, libations, and lamentations are performed for the god of the temple (Anu), the goddess of the temple (Antu), and the protective spirit (*lamassu*) of the temple, and also for Ea and Marduk.[565] Similar procedures are performed in the morning, this time on the roof of the temple, for Ea, Šamaš and Marduk.[566] Then the curtains are drawn shut, indicating that now the most important part of the ritual is about to begin.[567] Four lamentations are recited to Ea, Šamaš and Marduk. The curtains are opened (loosened) again, and the ritual ends.[568]

Two omens follow, which conclude the description of the first day.[569]

On the second day similar procedures are followed during the night, but now the king takes part in the ritual: he has to recite a special lamentation and *eršemšaḫungû*-prayers.[570]

---

556 Obv. 15, rev. 2.
557 Obv. 2 ff.; 17 ff.; rev. 5 ff.; 17 ff.
558 Obv. 2 and rev. 17.
559 Obv. 20, rev. 8, 20.
560 Obv. 2.
561 Obv. 6.
562 Obv. 15, rev. 2.
563 Obv. 16, rev. 3 f., 14 ff.
564 Obv. 1.
565 Obv. 2 ff.
566 Obv. 6 ff.
567 Obv. 11 ff.
568 See also III.3 and III.9.
569 Obv. 16.
570 Obv. 17 ff. *eršaḫungû*-tablets are attested twice in the astronomical diaries from Babylon: a passage mentions ritual procedures of the gods, *maḫḫuru*-offerings (see II.7.2), and *eršaḫungû*-tablets, which were recited(?) by the chief singer of dirges (A.J. Sachs–H. Hunger, *Diaries*, no. -229, B, obv. 5′–11′); a lamentation priest is refered to, and the chief singer of dirges (recites?) *eršaḫungû*-tablets (no. -226, B, rev. 1′–2′).

After more offerings and libations, and a lamentation, *eršemšaḫungû*-prayers are recited by the king in the morning.[571] Then a special ceremony follows[572]: the king prostrates himself (*šukênu*), the barber shaves off the hair of his body, and puts it into a bottle, after which it is sent off to the enemy's border. The king returns to his palace. This ceremony has been the subject of much discussion, concentrating on the question whether the ceremony served the purpose of purifying the king, or whether it had the function of protecting the land from an enemy. According to Mayer the ceremony is an 'Abwehrritus'.[573] The hair, which represents the power of the king even when it is shaven off, has the purpose of holding back the enemy from the border in order to protect the land from disaster. Danger from an enemy outside or from trouble within the land has also been announced in the omen in obv. 16: '(An omen says:) if the earth quakes, (then) an enemy will rise and the dwellings of the land will not be secure. (Another omen says:) if the earth turns around, (then) there will be injustice in the whole land, the land will turn mad'. Furthermore, *TU* 45 informs us that lamentations and *eršemšaḫungû*-prayers are recited over the king's hem in each and every sanctuary; if these instructions are followed, evil will not approach the king.[574] Finally, although the ceremony is not repeated in *TU* 45, several more omens appear,[575] all announcing some kind of danger for the king, the city or the land. So, warding off danger appears to be at least one reason for the recording of this special ceremony with the omens.[576]

Two more omens follow, and the description of the second day ends.[577]

The third day again begins with offerings, libations, a lamentation, and *eršemšaḫungû*-prayers, to be recited over the king's hem, this time, for the god of the city (Anu), the goddess of the city (Antu), and the protective spirit (*lamassu*) of the city.[578] The procedures of the ritual continue 'in the open country or on the bank of a river, on a place where nobody sets foot', and similar procedures follow for Anu, Enlil and Ea, but also for the god of the open country and the goddess of the open country.[579]

A special interlinear line mentions the exorcist who, together with the lamentation priest, has to purify the city.[580] Three more omens conclude the description of the third day.[581]

The section concerning the fourth day begins with the same procedures as for the third day, for 'that god, that goddess' (= Anu and Antu?), Mašdub and Šamaš, but now the king himself has to perform the *eršemšaḫungû*-prayers again.[582] In the morning

---

571 Obv. 20 ff.
572 Obv. 24 f.
573 W. Mayer, *OrNS* 57 (1988), 150 ff. (for earlier discussions see ib., n. 9 and 10).
574 Obv. 26, rev. 1.
575 Rev. 3 f., 14 ff.
576 St.M. Maul (*Zukunftsbewältigung*, Mainz am Rhein, 1994, 76, n. 47; see also 78) pointed out that, while the hair indeed had the function of giving protection against any danger, at the same time in many rituals the shaving of the hair, an unclean element, served the purpose of purifying the person, in this case the king. According to J.S. Cooper (in: M.E. Vogelzang, H.J.L. Vanstiphout, *Mesopotamian Poetic Language*, Groningen, 1996, 53, n. 24) the ceremony has a mainly purifying function.
577 Rev. 3 f.
578 Rev. 5 ff.
579 Rev. 8 ff.
580 Rev. 12. For a discussion of this line see II.6.3.
581 Rev. 14 ff.
582 Rev. 17 ff.

purifications and offerings are performed on the roof of the temple for Ea, Šamaš and Marduk. After another lamentation is performed and the king recites *eršemšaḫungû*-prayers, the temple is consecrated, which must be the final goal of the ritual. After the king has performed another lamentation and made a gift, the ritual ends.[583]

We have two more text (fragments) from Hellenistic Uruk, *Bagh. Mitt. Beih.* 2, nos. 10 and 11 (the latter in fact consists of five smaller fragments). They are both clearly duplicates of *TU* 45, and appear to represent the first version of the ritual.[584] However, one of the fragments belonging to *Bagh. Mitt. Beih.* 2, no. 11[585] contains a ceremony concerning the building-master and the first brick, and (the incipit of) the prayer 'When Anu created Heaven'.[586] These are not mentioned in *TU* 45, but we encounter them in the texts belonging to the second version of the ritual, to which this fragment apparently belongs.[587]

II.6.2. *The second version*

Several building ritual texts are known, which are clearly different from the version described in *TU* 45 and parallels. Two of them, *TU* 46 and *SpTU* 4, no. 141, come from Uruk.

Uruk

The second building ritual text from Hellenistic Uruk, *TU* 46, is only partly paralleled by *TU* 45, and most of the text is quite different. For example, the special ceremony concerning the king and the omens, attested in *TU* 45, is missing here. The text is identified twice as belonging to the ritual procedure of the lamentation priest.[588]

The beginning of *TU* 46[589] appears to be a duplicate of the section describing the first day of the ritual, as recorded in *TU* 45.[590] The only difference in this part of the text follows the *enūma*-phrase ('[When] the wall of the temple buckles'): the diviner is mentioned, deconsecrating the emplacement (the building plot) of the temple.[591] After this the text follows the same procedures as described for the first day in *TU* 45. The ceremony behind the curtains is also described, although the reference to drawing the curtains shut[592] is erroneously left out.[593]

583 Rev. 20 ff.
584 For the corresponding lines see my comments on *TU* 45 in the Appendix.
585 Obv. fragment 1, 2′–8′. For a transliteration of this fragment 1, see my comments on *TU* 45, obv. 11–14, 15, 16, in the Appendix.
586 See lines 4′ and 7′.
587 *TU* 46 (obv. 13–20) and F.H. Weissbach, *Misc.*, no.12 (obv. 14 ff.). However, the lines 9′ff. of the fragment record omens similar to those attested in *TU* 45.
588 Obv. 20, rev. 14, see also rev. 1.
589 Obv. 1–13.
590 Obv. 1–14.
591 Obv. 2. See my comments on this phrase in de Appendix.
592 Compare *TU* 45, obv. 11–12.
593 Obv. 9 ff.

But now a new section begins, in which the ceremony concerning the first brick (*libittu maḫrîtu*), performed by the building-master (*itinnu*),[594] is described.[595] Ellis argues that this first brick is probably a former brick which was removed from the old temple, and then re-used in the construction of the new temple; because the brick embodied the essence of the temple, the house of the god, the continuity of worship was assured.[596] The building-master has to remove this first brick with an axe made of lead, and place it in a secluded temple. Offerings and libations are performed before the brick for the god of the foundation, who is not named, and the lamentation priest recites the prayer 'When Anu created Heaven' in front of the brick.

A supplement (? [DI]RI.GA) follows, in which the duties of the diviner are described[597]: the intestines of a lamb are inspected, and if the result is good, the demolishing and renovating of the temple will be for the good of the king and the land.

The reverse is apparently concerned with the second day of the ritual, describing the laying of a temple foundation.[598] These procedures include offerings, libations and lamentations, partly attested also in *TU* 45, for the god, goddess and the protective spirit (*lamassu*) of the temple. Again the curtains are drawn shut for the most important moment of the ceremony, which consists of reciting the lamentations, and also the *šuillakku*-prayer 'When Anu, Enlil and Enki created Heaven and Earth'.[599] Erroneously, no reference is made to opening the curtains again. After the foundation is laid, the temple is consecrated, and the ritual ends.

The text only describes a part of the ritual, because, as the catchline indicates,[600] it is only one of a series of tablets belonging to the building ritual. Because this catchline refers to the doorframes, apparently the other tablet(s) is/are concerned with the different parts of the temple, but no examples are preserved.

A Late Babylonian text from Uruk, *SpTU* 4, no. 141, also contains a part of the building ritual belonging to the text corpus of the lamentation priest (*kalûtu*); the text is much more similar to *TU* 46 than to *TU* 45. The obverse contains the prayer 'When Anu created Heaven', also referred to in *TU* 46.[601] The first part of the reverse contains either the continuation of the prayer 'When Anu created Heaven', or more likely another prayer, probably for the well-being of the land and its people.[602] The second part, concerned with the activities of the diviner[603] is duplicated by *TU* 46.[604] When in *TU* 46 the laying of the foundations is next described,[605] in *SpTU* 4, no. 141 only the introductory line to this passage is given, followed by the colophon,[606] which confirms what we already

594 Wr. [lú]ŠITIM (also attested in F.H. Weissbach, *Misc.*, no.12, obv. [14]), not [lú]DÍM = *mubannû*, the 'arranger (of the offering table)', see III.4.3.

595 Obv. 13 ff.

596 Cf. R.S. Ellis, *Foundation Deposits*, 29.

597 Obv. 21 ff.

598 Rev. 2 ff.

599 Rev. 10.

600 Rev. 15.

601 Obv. 19.

602 Rev. x + 1 ff.

603 Rev. 14 ff.

604 Obv. 21 ff.

605 Rev. 1 ff.

606 Lo. E. 20 f.

suggested on the basis of the catchline of *TU* 46, namely that the building ritual of the *kalûtu*-type from Uruk was described on a series of tablets.

Babylon

Another Late Babylonian building ritual text, this time from Babylon, is F.H. Weissbach, *Misc.*, no.12. This text is important for it shows that this particular building ritual of the *kalûtu*-type was not only used in Uruk but also in Babylon. The obverse of the text is parallel to the first part of *TU* 46.[607] However, although the same procedures are described, there are also differences. The lamentation priest is instructed to recite a lamentation, but the incipit is not given, while in *TU* 46 two lamentations, with the incipits are given.[608] Then the Babylon text refers to the singer, who must recite a *inḫu*-song.[609] The ceremony which includes reciting four lamentations by the lamentation priest behind the curtains is also given, but no reference is made to the curtains.[610] After this the ceremony with the building-master and the first brick is described,[611] which includes, after the removing of the first brick, the phrase (missing in *TU* 46): 'he will mourn [for] the temple, say "woe!"'.[612] Finally the incipit of the prayer 'When Anu created Heaven' is given, after which the prayer is presented in full.[613] Of the reverse of the Weissbach text only a small badly damaged part, perhaps containing the continuation of 'When Anu created Heaven', remains.

Clearly this text belongs to the version represented by *TU* 46 and *SpTU* 4, no. 141.

There is also evidence of the use of the second version of this ritual recorded in the astronomical diaries. A passage is preserved, which, as Horowitz has shown,[614] refers to a building ritual, performed on day 10 of the twelfth month Addaru, 41 S.E.[615]:

15′ ... ITI.BI UD.10.KAM [...]
16′ [^lú^MA]Š.MAŠ.MEŠ *u* ^lú^LAGAR.MEŠ *šá* É.SAG.GÍL *né-pe-šú šá e-nu-m*[*a* ^d^*A-nu ib-nu-ú* AN-*e*]
17′ ⌜*lìb*⌝*-bu-ú šaṭ-ri ina pa-ni-šú* DÙ-ʾ

'15′That month, day 10, [...] 16′[the ex]orcists and the lamentation priests of Esagila 17′performed 16′the ritual procedure of 'Whe[n Anu created Heaven] 17′as written in front of it'.

607 Obv. 1–19.
608 Obv. 6.
609 Obv.5.
610 Obv. 11 ff.
611 Obv. 14 ff.
612 Obv. 18.
613 Obv. 23, and 24 ff. (but only partly preserved) also referred to in *TU* 46, obv. 19, and recited in full (but also only partly preserved) in *SpTU* 4, no. 141, obv. 1 ff. See also my comments on F.H. Weissbach, *Misc.*, no.12, obv. 23 ff., in the Appendix.
614 *RA* 85 (1991), 76 f.
615 A.J. Sachs–H. Hunger, *Diaries*, no. -270, B, rev. 15′–17′.

Although the ritual of the kettledrum also begins with *enūma*, this ritual procedure is already referred to in the same passage, line 13′.[616] Therefore Horowitz is probably right in identifying the ritual with the ritual for the rebuilding of a temple beginning with: 'When the wall of the temple buckles' (*enūma igār bīt ili iqâpu*). In the Babylon text F.H. Weissbach, *Misc.*, no.12 the ritual ends with the prayer 'When Anu created Heaven' (*enūma Anu ibnû šamê*) and according to Horowitz it is this incipit which has to be restored in the diary. The phrase 'as written in front of it' in the diary must refer to the text F.H. Weissbach, *Misc.*, no.12, where the actual ritual (obv. 1–23) is described in front of (= preceding) the passage containing the prayer (obv. 24 ff.).

The existence of two separate versions has been clearly established. But how can we explain the differences between the two versions?

The king is prominently present in the first version of the ritual (*TU* 45 and parallels); he is mentioned several times, while there are no references to him in the second version texts. Why is the king so prominent in the first version, but not in the second?

The first section of *TU* 45[617] must perhaps be interpreted as a general introduction to the building ritual. Note that only this part of the text is duplicated in the second version. The rest of the first version does not deal with the general procedures of the ritual, but instead only contains a specific part of the ritual activities performed by the priest addressed in the second person (the 'you'-figure), namely that part in which the king also participates.[618]

Furthermore, divination is incorporated in the first version. We know that divination played an important part in decision-making before important events, such as the building of a temple, and that it was used to control the behaviour of kings and other important persons. We have several omens in the first version, which alert the king, the people and the land to dangers. These omens must be connected with the role of the king in the ritual. Apparently the first version contains a special programme not only for the leading priest of the ritual, the 'you'-figure, but also for the king.

The second version (*TU* 46 and parallels) begins with (almost) the same general introduction of the building ritual as the first version. But then the important passage concerning the building-master, who performed the ceremony with the first brick, follows. This passage is not mentioned in the first version; clearly the duties of the building-master were not relevant there. Furthermore it is interesting that, except for the *enūma*-phrase, no more references are made to the demolishing or renovating of the temple in the first version, which is very different from the second version. Only at the end of *TU* 45 do we learn that the temple is consecrated.[619] Apparently this process of demolishing or renovating was not relevant in this text.

But in the second version divination is equally incorporated in the ritual. While no omens are mentioned, the diviner is one of the participants performing the building ritual

---

616 Discussed in II.5.2.

617 Obv. 1–14.

618 The question who this 'you'-figure is will be addressed in II.6.3.

619 Rev. 23.

activities. He is mentioned immediately after the introductory line, and he even receives a separate section, which underlines how important divination was for the building of a temple. So, the second version texts also describe how the building ritual had to be performed, but concentrates on other persons: it gives instructions for the 'you'-figure, the diviner, and the building-master.

So we clearly have two different versions of one and the same ritual; the existence of the different versions is solely dependant on the participants in the ritual. Because their duties differ from each other they each received their own programme, their own set of instructions.

II.6.3. *Who performed the building ritual?*

On several occasions the texts indicate that the building ritual texts belong to the text corpus of the lamentation priest (*kalûtu*); the many lamentation incipits also clearly indicate that the lamentation priest, usually addressed in the second person, is the most important priest at this ritual.

However, for the building ritual we also have evidence from the astronomical diaries that both the exorcists and the lamentation priests performed the ritual activities: the astronomical diary, no. -270 can, as we saw, be connected with the second version of the building ritual. Furthermore, in the first version of the building ritual texts, on one occasion only, the exorcist is mentioned together with the lamentation priest. Both are addressed in the third person.[620] In the second version, the exorcist is not mentioned. As in the kettledrum ritual, the role of the exorcist in this ritual also appears to be less important. The building ritual texts only concentrate on the duties of the lamentation priest, while the tasks of the exorcist, referred to in the astronomical diary, are left out.[621]

II.6.4. *Building programmes in Uruk and Babylon*

We know that under royal supervision large building programmes in Uruk and Babylon were taking place in the Hellenistic period.[622]

Two Uruk building inscriptions[623] inform us that in 244 B.C. the Rēš-temple complex of Anu was reconstructed by the governor (*šaknu*) Anu-uballiṭ, who was given the second name Nikarchos by king Seleucus II, and was further extended in 202/1 B.C. during

---

620 *TU* 45, rev. 12. Note that this is an interlinear line, perhaps added after the text was written. The scribes of the building ritual texts usually address the leading lamentation priest in the second person, but on occasion change to the third person (as in the kettldrum ritual *KAR* 60), but there is no doubt that the 'you'-figure is always the lamentation priest, as becomes clear when we compare the texts. E.g. in F.H. Weissbach, *Misc.*, no.12, a ceremony which includes reciting four lamentations by the lamentation priest (here addressed in the third person) is described (obv. 11 ff.), while in the parallel text *TU* 46 these same lamentations are performed by the 'you'-figure (obv. 10 ff.). See also *TU* 46, obv. 18 f. and 28; F.H. Weissbach, *Misc.*, no. 12, obv. 4; *SpTU*, no. 141, rev. 19.

621 Contra W. Horowitz, *RA* 85 (1991), 76–7. See also II.5.3.

622 R.J. van der Spek, in: J. Wiesehöfer (ed.), *Das Partherreich und seine Zeugnisse*, 205 and n. 2 with earlier literature.

623 *YOS* 1, 52 (partly reedited by L.T. Doty, in: *Studies A. Sachs*, Philadelphia, 1988, 95–6) and J. Jordan, *Uruk-Warka*. WVDOG 51, Leipzig, 1928, pl. 108, c, with 41.

the reign of Antiochus III by another Anu-uballiṭ, whose second name was Kephalon. The large Ešgal-temple of Ištar was also built by this Kephalon, as we know from an Aramaic building inscription from around 200 B.C.[624]

From Babylon there is more evidence. Alexander planned to restore Esagila and started by removing the debris.[625] After his death this was continued by his successors: Chronicle 10 refers to the removing of the debris of Esagila during the fourth year of the reign of Philippus III, and the sixth and eighth years of Alexander IV.[626] The famous building inscription of Antiochus I, dated 268 B.C.,[627] refers to bricks which are brought to Babylon and Borsippa for renovating the temples Esagila and Ezida. Although the renovations of Esagila are not mentioned, there is evidence from other sources on this. Horowitz already referred to Chronicle 11[628] (debris is removed from Esagila), the astronomical diary no. -273 (bricks for the reconstruction of Esagila are made) and the diary, mentioned in II.6.2, no. -270, referring to the building ritual and which, as Horowitz correctly assumes, probably relates to the reconstruction of Esagila by Antiochus I.[629] Also, during the reign of Demetrius II repair work on Esagila was performed, as we known from diary no. -144.[630]

We know that reconstruction work on Esagila continued into the Arsacid period. An astronomical diary testifies to repair works on Esagila in 106 B.C..[631] Administrative documents belonging to the archive of the official Raḫimesu (94–92 v.C.) refer to removing debris, repair work and restorations of (parts of) Esagila.[632] Also debris on the roof of the *akītu*-temple (Day One temple) was removed.[633] One text mentions expenditures for the restoration of the temple of Madānu.[634]

Some concluding remarks

Just as with the kettledrum ritual texts, the building ritual texts do not mention the specific days and months on which the ritual was performed. The texts only use the phrase 'in

[624] A. Falkenstein, *Topographie*, 31. Cf. J. Oelsner, *Materialien*, 248.

[625] A.K. Grayson, *Chronicles*, 116, obv. 6. Grayson refers in his comments to this line to *CT* 4, 39c, which is now *CT* 49, 6. BM 78651 in Grayson is now *CT* 49, 5. See also A.J. Sachs–H. Hunger, *Diaries*, no. -321, obv. 13′–14′. Cf. J. Oelsner, *AoF* 5 (1977), 80; R. Zadok, *BiOr* 34 (1977), 79, below; G.F. Del Monte, *Testi dalla Babilonia Ellenistica, Volume I. Testi Cronografica*, Pisa, Roma, 1997, 13–16. Classical sources: Arrian 3.16.4–5; Strabo 16.1.5.

[626] A.K. Grayson, *Chronicles*, 117, rev. 13, 118, rev. 33.

[627] *VAB* 3, 12–35. Cf. A. Kuhrt, S. Sherwin White, *JHS* 111 (1991), 71–86. In this text Antiochus I assumes the same duties as Babylonian kings before him, taking care of the Babylonian temples and respecting the Babylonian gods, which must 'be understood as intentional Seleucid policy (from Seleucus I on) of using Babylonian kingship as a vehicle for rule in Babylonia', S. Sherwin-White, A. Kuhrt, *From Samarkhand to Sardis*, 37. See also I.3.

[628] A.K. Grayson, *Chronicles*, 120, obv. 2.

[629] W. Horowitz, *RA* 85 (1991), 75–77.

[630] Obv. 33′–35′.

[631] A.J. Sachs–H. Hunger, *Diaries*, no. 105, A14′-A15′, B30′; A, rev. 3′; 21′; 38′.

[632] *CT* 49, 154; K. Kessler, in *Festschrift J. Oelsner*, no. 16; *CT* 49, 155; *CT* 49, 163; K. Kessler, in *Festschrift J. Oelsner*, no. 10; AB 246 (G.J.P. McEwan, *Iraq* 43 [1981], 138 ff.); *CT* 49, 162. See the latest discussions of these texts by R.J. van der Spek, in J. Wiesehöfer (ed.), *Das Partherreich und seine Zeugnisse*, 205 ff., nos. 16, 17, 15, 22, 25, 28, and 29.

[633] *CT* 49, 154.

[634] *CT* 49, 157. See also K. Kessler, in *Festschrift J. Oelsner*, no. 9 and no. 15.

an auspicious month, on a favourable day' (*ina* ITI *šal-mu ina* UD ŠE.GA).[635] The only date that we have, day 10-XII-41, comes from the astronomical diary no. -270.[636] Because of the nature of the ritual, no specific regular set of data must be expected: we must assume that the ritual was only performed on the occasion of rebuilding a temple, and for this reason the lamentations, recited during the ritual, are also not accompanied by any such data. When it was necessary to appease the anger of the gods, as was the case when a temple was built, lamentations were used.[637]

One important observation concerning the lamentations was made by Cohen[638]: in the building ritual the lamentations were recited while the offerings and libations were being performed. Furthermore, they were chanted during the demolition of the old building and not during ceremonies which commemorated the erection of the new building. Apparently the lamentations served the same function as the offerings, according to Cohen: they had to appease the anger of the gods whose sacred buildings are being torn down. In the kettledrum ritual, by contrast, the recitation of lamentations did not serve the purpose of neutralising the divine anger, but was a means of testing the new drum.[639]

II.7. The eclipse of the moon ritual

From Uruk we have evidence of a ritual which was performed during the course of a lunar eclipse.[640] It was probably written during the Hellenistic period.[641] This ritual continued until the eclipse had ended, and served the purpose of neutralizing any evil consequences of such a lunar eclipse.[642] The eclipse ritual shows that Uruk as provincial capital of southern Babylonia was an important centre of learning. In this paragraph an attempt is made to explain the composition of the Uruk rituals.[643]

Although a great deal is known about how the Mesopotamians envisaged the moon and the lunar eclipse, the ritual from Uruk is quite unique and difficult to compare with other evidence on the lunar eclipse.[644] The substitute king (*šar pūḫi*) ritual, probably performed to avert evil portended by an eclipse on the head of state, is known from the Old Babylonian period on, and appears to have been practised up to the Hellenistic

---

[635] *TU* 45, obv. 2; see also 17, rev. 5 and 17; *TU* 46, obv. 2; 23; rev. 2; *Bagh. Mitt. Beih.* 2, no. 5, obv. 2; F.H. Weissbach, *Misc.*, no.12, obv. 3.

[636] The fact that *TU* 45 was written on day 22 of the twelfth month Addaru is probably a coincidence. Compare *TU* 46, which was written on day 28 of the third month Simānu (81 S.E.).

[637] Compare also my concluding remarks on the kettledrum ritual in II.5.

[638] *Eršemma*, 48–9.

[639] See II.5.

[640] *BRM* 4, 6 and its continuation in BM 134701. The BM text was published by D. Brown and the present author in *RA* 91 (1997), 147–166. For more details see also the Appendix, where both texts are discussed.

[641] For the date of these texts see I.2 and the above mentioned *RA* article by David Brown and the present author.

[642] See E. Cassin, Le semblable et le différent, 1987, 258–66.

[643] The ritual is extensively discussed by G. Furlani, *Riti*, 263 ff., and E. Cassin, *La splendeur Divine*, Paris, La Haye, 1968, 42 ff.

[644] The most recent discussion of the moon and the lunar eclipse is that of M. Stol, in: *Natural Phenomena. Their Meaning, Depiction and Description in the Ancient Near East* (D.J.W. Meijer ed.), Amsterdam, Oxford, New York, Tokyo, 1992, 245 ff. with references to earlier literature. For the lunar eclipse see 257 ff.

period.[645] In Neo-Assyrian letters there are allusions to the eclipse of the moon, but no extended descriptions of the ritual which had to be performed against the consequences of an eclipse are given there.[646] Such a ritual is found in the Neo-Assyrian text *CT* 4, pl. 5–6. It describes for the twelve months of the year what the king had to do against the evil consequences of a lunar eclipse.[647] *CT* 51, 190[648] is a *namburbû*, an apotropaic ritual for an individual directed against the evil consequences of, in this case, a lunar eclipse, and furthermore it is also directed at the god who sent the omen in order to obtain protection from him (in this case Sîn).[649]

The first part of the Uruk ritual is described in *BRM* 4, 6; a small part of this text is duplicated in col. B of *CLBT*, pl.1. The last part of *BRM* 4, 6[650] is duplicated by the first sixteen lines of BM 134701.[651] The rest of the obverse of BM 134701, and the beginning of the reverse appear to describe the continuation of the ritual, but probably in rev. 10 ff. a passage begins, which belongs to the well-known lunar eclipse myth, described in the handbook against the evil *utukku*-demons (*utukkū lemnūti*).[652]

Because the description of the ritual on the two tablets partly overlaps, it is unlikely that they belong together. However, in both texts the sign NAG is on one occasion written for GU_7 ,[653] and therefore it is not impossible that both tablets were written by the same writer.

The obverse of BM 134701 is inscribed with great care, unlike the reverse, perhaps because the writer noticed that he had more than enough space on the tablet for the final part of the text. Nevertheless the interpretation of BM 134701 is often difficult,[654] especially because to a large extent the beginning and the end of the lines are lost.

Both texts must be dated to the Hellenistic period, and come from Uruk: the script is Late Babylonian; the texts mention the city of Uruk (Tiranna) and its temples, referring first to the Rēš- and Ešgal-temples before they mention Eanna and the other temples,[655] and Anu appears to be the predominant deity; also the name of the owner of BM 134701 begins with Anu, as is clear from the (damaged) colophon. All this indicates that the text was written in the Hellenistic period, when Anu was the leading deity of the pantheon, and the Rēš-temple was the most important sanctuary in Uruk.[656] However, as is clear from the incipits of the lamentations, the text must have had its roots in earlier periods.[657]

---

645 See S. Parpola, *LAS* II, xxii-xxxii and J. Bottero, *Akkadica* 9 (1978), 2–24 = id., *Mesopotamia. Writing, reasoning, and the gods*, Chicago, London, 1992, 138–55 (chapter 9).

646 See the index in S. Parpola, *LAS* II, 533 with references.

647 See E. Cassin, Le semblable et le différent, Paris, 1987, 258–266.

648 See R. Caplice, *OrNS* 40 (1971), 166–8; St. M. Maul, *Zukunftsbewältigung*, 458–60.

649 For the use of the kettledrum during an eclipse, see the end of II.7.3.

650 Rev. 42 ff.

651 Obv. 1–16.

652 Cf. *CT* 16, pl. 19 ff. See A.D. Kilmer, *JAOS* 98 (1978), 372–4 and M. Stol, in: *Natural Phenomena*, 260, with references to earlier literature.

653 Compare *BRM* 4, 6, rev. 48 with BM 134701, obv. 10.

654 See for instance obv. 23 and rev. 9.

655 *BRM* 4, 6, obv. 22, 26, rev. 39; BM 134701, rev. 5.

656 See I.3.

657 Strangely enough in the BM card catalogue a date of composition has been given to BM 134701. The note reads 'Uruk 172 B.C.'; it is probably written in the hand of the ex-Keeper (a non-cuneiformist), so we have no idea even whose suggestion this date is.

BRM 4, 6 and BM 134701 contain in fact more than one version of the ritual, performed possibly at three or four places, and at the same time[658]: each version probably concentrates on the duties of one or more particular priests during the eclipse ritual. Therefore the text appears to be a programme or a set of instructions for the main priests of the ritual.[659] We will discuss the different versions here.

II.7.1. *The first version*

First, two rituals are performed, one during and one after the eclipse, in the gates of the temples of Uruk and on the main street. This first version is the most extensive description of the ritual, and very clearly expresses the most important function of the ritual: the neutralization of the evil consequences of a lunar eclipse. It also mentions most of the main performers of the ritual: the lamentation priests, a temple enterer (*ērib bīti*), a priest addressed in the second person, the people of the land, and the exorcists.[660]

Where the text becomes clear, we find first general instructions to the lamentation priests, although the duties of the lamentation priest are specified only in the third version of the ritual[661]: he has to perform 'the ritual procedure of the lamentation priest' (*né-peš šá* ŠU^{II} ^{lú}GALA) during the eclipse.[662] This procedure consists of reciting several lamentations to the moon(god).[663] Then the text mentions the incipits, in Akkadian, of several lamentations, which are clearly the Akkadian interlinear versions of bilingual Sumerian-Akkadian lamentations.[664]

We can distinguish eight units, which apparently are the first lines of the lamentations. The first unit[665] perhaps contains a reference to the moongod Sîn. It not only mentions Ningal, who is the wife of Sîn, but also the wild cow.[666] According to our text the cow has left(?) the temple. This indicates that times are hard and that war if it occurs destroys cities and it peoples. It is believed by the Mesopotamians that difficult times must be explained by the fact that, for whatever reason, the gods have left their temples and that the inhabitants are consequently left on their own to suffer. The link with the moongod is clear: when the evil consequences of a lunar eclipse are not properly dealt with, disaster also strikes.

The incipits of the other units which now follow[667] confirm this interpretation; they are concerned with the destruction of cities and the consequences of it for the cult of the gods, a well-known theme in the Sumerian lamentations. Although this theme by itself has nothing to do with the eclipse of the moon, in the context of our text it is clear

658 *BRM* 4, 6 contains four rituals, performed possibly at three places, according to G. Furlani, *Riti*, 263 ff.

659 Unlike the kettledrum ritual texts, the building ritual texts and the cultic calendar texts, which only describe the role of one particular priest (i.e. the lamentation priest), see II.5.3.

660 *BRM* 4, 6, obv. 1–30, rev. 31–37.

661 *BRM* 4, 6, rev. 42 ff. // BM 134701, obv. 1 ff.

662 Obv. 2, see also 17.

663 See obv. 14.

664 Cf. J. Krecher, *Kultlyrik*, 27, n. 50.

665 Obv. 3–4.

666 Perhaps a reference to the well-known narrative 'A cow of Sîn', an incantation for a woman in childbirth, which tells of the moongod Sîn and his cow, called Geme-Sîn? For the latest edition see N. Veldhuis, *A Cow of Sîn* (Library of Oriental Texts, volume 2), Groningen, 1991.

667 Obv. 5–6; 7–8; 9; 10; 11a; 11b; 12–13.

that the lamentations refer to the evil consequences of an eclipse. The composer of our text felt that it was appropriate to list the lamentation incipits in this context.[668] Note the incipit in obv. 8, which reads: 'A storm arose, covered the face with dust', which in the duplicate *CLBT*, col. II, 8–9 is extended by the explanatory remark: 'Of Sîn they said: "a storm arose, covere[d] the face with dust"'. The commentator apparently sees a parallel here with the covering of the moon.

After the enumeration of these lamentation incipits, the actual ritual begins.[669] First near the gates of the temples and on the main street, a *garakku*-brazier is set up by a priest who is addressed in the second person. Then the text reads: 'As soon as the eclipse begins',[670] clearly indicating that the Babylonians were able to calculate the moment when an eclipse would occur.[671]

A temple enterer (*ērib bīti*) enters the scene, setting fire to the *garakku*-brazier. This fire must remain burning until the eclipse has ended. Until the end of the eclipse the lamentation priest must perform his 'ritual procedure', which may consist of performing the lamentations mentioned above, but may also refer to the lamentations mentioned in the third version of the ritual, discussed below.

Then several proceedings are described, indicating that the moment of an eclipsed moon is a time of distress and mourning[672]: funerary offerings (*kispu*) are made,[673] possibly because a parallel is seen here with the situation as at the end of the month, when the moon does not shine; we know that in the cult for the dead offerings for the deceased were usually made at the end of the month.

The people of the land express their sorrow by removing their headdresses, covering their heads with clothing (*lubāru*), and uttering a special lament: 'May hardship, murder, rebellion and (the evil predicted by) the eclipse not reach Uruk, Rēš, Ešgal, Baramaḫ, Eanna and the (other) temples of Tiranna'.[674] This appears to be a regular apotropaic formula for averting all possible sorts of disasters for the city. Then seven soldiers utter the same formula.[675]

---

668 According to T. Podella, *Ṣôm-Fasten*, Kevelaer, 1989, 45–49, the moon has left the people, and mourning is appropriate in this crisis situation when the gods have left them.

669 Obv. 14 ff.

670 Obv. 16, see also rev. 43.

671 Two deposition documents from the Eanna-temple in Neo-Babylonian Uruk are known which are concerned with the use of a kettledrum in Uruk and Larsa during an expected eclipse, which however did not occur (A. Boissier, *RA* 23 [1926], 13 ff. and *YOS* 7, 71). For a discussion see P.-A. Beaulieu and J.P. Britton, *JCS* 46 (1994), 73 ff. and P.-A. Beaulieu, in *Festschrift J. Oelsner*, AOAT, Bd. 252, Münster, 2000, 7–8.

672 Obv. 19 ff.

673 In a metaphorical way (obv. 19′–20′): 'You will make funerary offerings for the fields that lie fallow, you will make funerary offerings for the canals that bring no water, you will make funerary offerings for the Anunnaki'. Evil spirits that wander around and above the fields and make them lie fallow, and empty canals of water, and also the Anunnaki, the gods of the nether world, are appeased by these funerary offerings. This is the only example of *kispu* in Hellenistic temple ritual texts. Cf. G. van Driel, *Cult of Aššur*, 168–9; A. Tsukimoto, *Untersuchungen zur Totenpflege*, Kevelaer, 1985, 197–8; G.J.P. McEwan, *FAOS* 4. 167.

674 Obv. 22 f.

675 Obv. 26 f. Possibly this lament is an Akkadian translation of a first millennium version of an Emesal lyric. If this is the case, then we have here evidence of Emesal repertoire which was performed by persons other than the lamentation priest; note that this lament is also uttered by the *šangû*-priest (*BRM* 4, 6, rev. 38 ff.), contra J.A. Black, *Eme-sal Cult Songs and Prayers*, 23. From *BRM* 4, 6, rev. 48 ff. // BM 134701, obv. 7 ff. it appears to be the case that not only lamentation priests utter Emesal lamentations. See D. Brown and the

As soon as the eclipse of the moon has come to an end, the fire on the *garakku*-brazier is put out with beer. The last line of the obverse refers to 'the next day' (*ina* 2-*i* u_4-*mu*), when the building-master (*itinnu*)[676] throws the *garakku*-brazier into the river. This is strange, because after a cross-line indicating that a new section begins,[677] another ritual is described, again introduced by 'On the next day', which had to be performed on the day after the eclipse had ended. Perhaps the reference to the *itinnu* before the cross-line indicates that he had to throw the brazier into the river on the next day, but before the end of the night vigil and before the *pīt bābi*-ceremony,[678] which was the first ceremony which was performed on the following day.[679] In any case it is clear that for the composer of the text the removal of the ritual necessaries by the *itinnu* belongs to the ritual of the first day, but was performed on the second.

In the ritual for the second day the gates, which had been placed under seal, are opened and a reed *urigallu*-standard, a magic circle of flour, and a white and black cord, which were in the temple, are thrown into the river by the 'you'-figure. Probably, the broken beginning of the text contained the instructions for placing these objects in the temple. All the temples and especially the Edumununna, the temple of Sîn, are purified, the statue of Sîn is dressed, and the holy water basins are set up.

The following lines refer to the well-known lunar eclipse myth, attested in the handbook against evil *utukku*-demons, already mentioned above. Here the moon is threatened by seven hostile monsters. In our text the 'you'-figure must say: 'Verily, by the life of Anu and Enlil they (i.e. the seven monsters) are conjured',[680] after which the exorcists recite the Sumerian incantations 'Storm of jubilating water' and 'Evil *utukku*-demons'. Finally the magic circle of flour, the *takpertu*-purification necessaries and the *garakku*-brazier are thrown into the river. Note that the removing of all the ritual equipment has to be done again on the next day, although here by the 'you'-figure and not by the *itinnu* as at the end of the last section.

It is strange that only here does the exorcist enter the scene,[681] unless the 'you'-figure, the leading priest in the ritual, is also an exorcist, which is possible, since it is he who is the most important officiant in rituals which are used to neutralize the evil affects of bad omens such as an eclipse.[682]

Another cross-line follows.

II.7.2. *The second version*

This time, another very short version of the ritual, introduced with 'alternatively' (*šaniš*), is described, in which the actions of the *šangû*-priests of the temples of Uruk at the time of an eclipse of the moon are discussed.[683] They have to light the *garakku*-brazier in

---

present author in *RA* 91 (1997), 151, n. 13.

676 For the reading *itinnu* ([lú]ŠITIM) instead of *mubannû* ([lú]DÍM), see III.4.3.

677 Rev.1 ff.

678 See II.2.3.

679 Rev. 31.

680 Rev. 34.

681 But see also BM 134701, rev. 16.

682 See also I.3. Another candidate could be the chief singer of dirges (*galamāḫu*).

683 *BRM* 4, 6, rev. 38–41.

the gates of the temples in the district Tiranna and utter the same apotropaic formula as stipulated in the first version for the people of the land and the seven soldiers, until the eclipse had ended.

II.7.3. *The third version*

The third version of the ritual also describes what had to be done during an eclipse, but now concentrates fully on the lamentation priests; it is performed near the BÁRA.KI.BALAG the 'Dais, place (of) the Harp', and apart from the lamentation priests a 'you'-figure is also mentioned, as in the first version.[684] Although the lamentation priests are mentioned twice before, in this version the duties of these priests are the main topic of interest, as is especially clear from the fact that several musical instruments, including the kettledrum, are mentioned. Also, only in this version does he actively participate in the ritual.[685] As we saw, in the first version the lamentation priest only receives a general instruction to perform his 'ritual procedure' during the eclipse, which is now specified in the third version.

First, several musical instruments (a bronze *ḫalḫallatu*-drum, a bronze *manzû*-drum, and a bronze kettledrum) are brought near the 'Dais, place (of) the Harp'. When the eclipse begins the lamentation priests put on a linen garment, cover their heads with torn *lubāru*-clothing, and 'raise' (*na-šu-ú*)[686] lamentations, wailings and mourning for the eclipsed moon. Then three heaps of flour are poured facing the kettledrum within the magic circle of flour. A jar which is filled with 'tears of the holy tamarisk' and water is placed at the right side of these heaps of flour within the magic circle of flour, facing the eclipsed moon 'for the procedures of the lamentation priests' (*a-na kun-nu* ŠU^{II} *a-na* ^{lú}GALA.MEŠ).[687] Then the text describes lamentations which have to be recited during the several phases of the eclipsed moon.[688] As soon as the eclipse has ended, the three main cult objects of the ritual, the kettledrum, the heaps of flour and the jar, are thrown into the river, just as in the first version, but here apparently this occurs on the same day as the other ritual proceedings, since no reference is made to the next day.

We have seen that the kettledrum plays an important part in this third version of the ritual. Warding off the evil effects of a lunar eclipse can be achieved in different ways: by lamentation priests singing a lamentation, by the people of the land and soldiers or *šangû*-priests uttering an apotropaic formula, or by exorcists reciting an incantation.[689]

---

684 *BRM* 4, 6, rev. 42–55 // BM 134701, obv. 1–16.

685 See rev. 43 ff.

686 *BRM* 4, 6, rev. 45 // BM 134701, obv. 4.

687 *BRM* 4, 6, rev. 47 // BM 134701, obv. 6. See my comments on this line in the Appendix.

688 *BRM* 4, 6, rev. 48 ff. // BM 134701, obv. 7 ff. No songs or actions are outlined for when the maximal phase of the eclipse is passed and the moon begins to reemerge from the earth's shadow. Supported by eclipse reports from Babylon and Uruk this could indicate that lamentation probably took place only while the eclipses grew to their greatest extent. See the article of D. Brown and the present author in *RA* 91 (1997), 151 f., n. 14. For the eclipse reports from Babylon see now vol. V of the astronomical diaries on lunar and planetary texts.

689 See M. Stol, in: *Natural Phenomena*, 258 f. contra E. Cassin, *La splendeur divine*, 41 f., and id., *Le semblable et le différent*, 1987, 259 ff.: according to Cassin the eclipse must be interpreted as a state of 'being silent' of the moon-god. This matches well with the fact that during this period the king remains quiet in his palace. Furthermore there is a clear opposition between the behavior on the street and in the house: in the house one is supposed to be quiet, on the street one has to make noise and light fires. It symbolizes the chaos

Making loud noises and music are also effective.[690] The use of the kettledrum during an eclipse is well attested.[691] The lamentation priest playing the kettledrum on the occasion of a solar(?) eclipse is attested in the Assur prayer VAT 13832.[692] In a Neo-Assyrian letter to Esarhaddon from 671 B.C. the kettledrum is used during an eclipse of the moon (*LAS* I, 278[693]). Furthermore, we already mentioned two deposition documents from the Eanna-temple in Neo-Babylonian Uruk, where the kettledrum is mentioned in connection with a eclipse during the eighth year of Cyrus (one that did not occur!).

The Uruk eclipse text does not specifically say that the kettledrum was used for playing, or more specifically for accompanying the lamentation priests while they sing their lamentations, because for the composer of the text this is self-evident. The text does, however, describe the use of the instrument as a cult object, taking part in the ritual together with other cult objects. On the day of the eclipse it is placed (for playing) together with two other drums near the 'Dais, Place (of) of the Harp'. It is used in a ceremony which involves three heaps of flour and a magic circle of flour, and at the end of the ritual, when it served its purpose, the kettledrum together with the heaps of flour and a jar were thrown into the river. Clearly the kettledrum was not only an instrument which was used to make music during a ritual in order to neutralize the evil effects of the lunar eclipse, but it also functioned as a cult object taking part in the ritual. Finally, in our discussion of the kettledrum we already referred to another Uruk ritual text, W 18728, where the consecrated lamentation priest and the chief singer of dirges are instructed to take off (*paṭāru* lit. "to loosen") the *lubāru*-clothing before they can sit near the kettledrum, which appears to be in contrast with the eclipse ritual text, where the lamentation priests are deliberately wearing *lubāru*-clothing during the eclipse, while reciting the lamentations and kettledrum music is played.[694]

On BM 134701 this section of the text is separated from the following by a cross-line.

II.7.4. *The fourth version*

Finally, in the last section another ritual is described in which, apart from the 'you'-figure, the king appears to play an important part.[695] Unfortunately the beginning and end of the lines on part of the obverse and the complete reverse of BM 134701 are lost, which makes it difficult to give a comprehensive interpretation of the text.

When the eclipse begins the king, wearing a *tillû*-uniform, is apparently in his palace. A person addressed in the second person performs a ceremony with a palm leaf and a multicolored cord; a similar cord was also mentioned in the first version of the ritual.[696]

---

of the eclipse of the moon as much as the silence in the houses, according to Cassin. Stol opposed by arguing that noise and fire will surely have had apotropaic purposes. Furthermore, there is no opposition: silence inside – noise outside, or: no fire inside – fire outside in our ritual text. Note however that in BM 134701, obv. 17, when the eclipse begins, the king apparently is in his palace, which may refer to this opposition inside -outside (unfortunately the context of this passage is not clear).

690 See P.-A. Beaulieu and J.P. Britton, *JCS* 46 (1994), 77 f.

691 The kettledrum and the ritual for covering the kettledrum are discussed in II.5.

692 E. Ebeling, *OrNS* 17 (1948), pl. 49, cf. pp. 416–22 (see l. 23).

693 = S. Parpola, *SAA* 10, no. 347. Cf. also S. Parpola, *LAS* II, p. 268.

694 See II.5.1.

695 BM 134701, obv. 17 ff.

696 *BRM* 4, 6, rev. 32.

Furthermore myrtle, *ēru*-wood(?), and strong boxwood are mentioned and flour is used; while in *BRM* 4, 6 the magic circle of flour and heaps of flour are mentioned, in BM 134701 different types of flour (*tappinnu*, *šegušše*) are recorded. The 'you'-figure sprinkles a temple after which its gate is sealed. Another ceremony concerning the multicolored cord follows. At the end of the obverse the king is involved in another ceremony.

The reverse refers to a ceremony involving the cella and furthermore flour, utensils(?) and regular offerings are used.[697] The Rēš-temple, the Ešgal-temple, the Baramaḫ, the Eanna-temple and the other temples of Uruk, and also the *bīt pirišti* (a storage room for the ornaments and garments of the divine statues in the temple) and the Ubšukkinaku are involved in some kind of ceremony.[698] The 'you'-figure surrounds the temples with a magic circle of *tappinnu*-flour, and he places the well and the great gates under seal. Something else is not placed under seal.[699]

Finally a literary passage follows which refers to the lunar eclipse myth attested in *CT* 16, pl. 19 ff.[700] Presumably these lines had to be recited during the ritual, and they served the same purpose as the incantations which the exorcists had to recite at the end of the first version of the ritual: to ward off the evil consequences of the eclipse.

More evidence for a lunar eclipse myth can be found in *CLBT*, pl.1, a text probably also from Uruk. From col. A only the end of the lines are preserved, which makes an interpretation very difficult, but col. B is better preserved; it contains a passage which duplicates *BRM* 4, 6,[701] but which is then followed by what appears to be a part of an eclipse myth.[702] The use of the verb *qabû* 'to say'[703] perhaps suggests that this passage is a commentary containing quotations of a lunar eclipse myth with some commentary remarks. Note also phrases like 'He does not know' (*ul i-de*)[704] and 'Or/Another possibility (*šá-niš*),[705] which support this interpretation.[706]

Some concluding remarks

We can conclude that the lunar eclipse ritual was celebrated not only on the day the eclipse occurred, but was continued the next day. Furthermore, the ritual was performed by the priest, addressed in the second person, presumably the exorcist, but also other officiants took part, among whom the lamentation priest, the *šangû*-priest and the king are especially important. Our Uruk ritual text does not present us with different eclipse rituals, but with four different versions of the same ritual. The composition of the eclipse

---

697 Rev. 2 ff.
698 Rev. 5 ff.
699 Rev. 7 ff.
700 Rev. 10 ff. For details see the Appendix.
701 Col. B, 1–14 // *BRM* 4, 6, obv. 5–11.
702 Col. B, 15 ff. Note for example the phrases where Sîn 'weeps' (*bakû*), a figure of speech for 'to eclipse'. See M. Stol, in: *Natural Phenomena*, 258.
703 Col. B, 8, 20, 22, 24, although the use of a present (*iqabbû*) in the latter three does not fit very well. See *CAD*, Q, 29 f. with examples of *qabû* used in commentaries.
704 Col. B, 21. Or perhaps "I do not know"?
705 Col. B, 22.
706 See M. Stol, in: *Natural Phenomena*, 260.

text was based on what duties were to be performed and by whom; it consists of four programmes each of which concentrates on one or more participants.

II.8. Other festivals

In this section several other festivals will be discussed, of which only little is known: a temple festival in Esabad, a so-called palm festival in Esagila, a *ḫarû*-ritual in Esagila, a Greek festival, festivals for Ištar of Babylon and for Ištar of Uruk, and a nocturnal festival celebrated in the Rēš-temple, and finally the ruler cults.

II.8.1. *A temple festival in Esabad*

In an Arsacid document from Babylon, dated year 154 A.E./218 S.E. (= 94 B.C.)[707] a reference is made to a temple festival (*isinnu bīti*)[708] of Esabad, the temple of Gula in Babylon, which was celebrated on day 25 of the third month, Simānu. The relevant passage reads:

6 2 1/2 GÍN *ana ši-me* 1-*en* UDU.NÍTA SÍSKUR
7 *šá ana* UD.25.KAM *šá* ^{iti}SIG *šá i-sin-nu* É
8 *šá* É.SA.BAD *ina* ŠU^{II} ^{Id}ŠÚ-MU-MU
9 A *šá* ^{Id}AG-PAP *na-din*

> '^{6}2 1/2 shekels for the purchase price of one offering sheep ^{7}for day 25 of Simānu, which is the temple festival ^{8}of Esabad, ^{9}was given ^{8}to (into the custody of, to be spent by) Marduk-šuma-iddin, ^{9}the son of Nabû-nāṣir'.

We have several texts from Neo-Babylonian Sippar also referring to expenditures for temple festivals (*isinnu*).[709] They deal with expenditures of mainly barley, flour for temple festivals of Bēlet-Sippar, Anunītu and Gula (*Nbn* 767, 2;[710] *Camb* 236, 3, 8;[711] *Nbn* 799, 11;[712] *Dar* 160, 2;[713] *CT* 56, 268, rev. [1], 3[714]). *Camb* 236 records a festival of the temple enterers (*ērib bīti*) and exorcists on day 12 of the third month; *Dar* 160

707 AB 248, cf. G.J.P. McEwan, *Iraq* 43 (1981), 141–3; R.J. van der Spek, in: J. Wiesehöfer (ed.), *Das Partherreich und seine Zeugnisse*, 215 f.

708 Perhaps originally a festival commemorating the founding day of the temple? For the general term *isinnu* 'festival', see I.3.

709 See G.J.P. McEwan, *FAOS* 4, 163 (already mentioning two texts).

710 l. 1–5: 4 GUR *qé-me a-na šá-lam* É *šá i-sin-nu* É *šá* ^{d}GAŠAN-*Sip-par*^{ki} ^{d}*A-nu-ni-tu*$_4$ *u* ^{d}ME.ME (12-III-14, Nbn). Cf. *CAD*, I/J, 196b.

711 l. 1–5: 4 (NIGIDA) 4 BÁN ŠE.BAR *re-ḫi ma-la-a-ta šá* ^{iti}BÁR ^{iti}GU$_4$ *u* ^{iti}SIG$_4$ *a-di-i* UD.12.KAM *šá i-sin-nu* É *šá* ^{lú}KU$_4$-É-*ú-tu u* ^{lú}ZABAR-*ú-tu a-na* ^{I}*Su-qa-a-a* A-*šú šá* ^{I}*Ba-ku-ú-a* SUM-*na* […]x GUR 4 1/2 (NIGIDA) 3 SÌLA ŠE.BAR *ma-la-a-ta šá* MU.3.KAM [… ^{I}*B*]*a-la-ṭu*$_4$ *šá tar-ra-ṣu* […]x *i-sin-nu* É [… *n*]*a* ^{Id}EN-*it-tan-nu* […] SUM-*na* (25-III-4, Camb).

712 l. 11–12: 3 BÁN ŠE.BAR *ina* GIŠ.BÁN *šá* 10 MA.NA 2-*ta* EN *ma-la-a-ta šá* ⟨*i-*⟩*sin-ni* É *šá* ^{d}GAŠAN-*Sip-par*$^{[ki]}$ *šá* UD.22.KAM *šá* ^{iti}SIG$_4$ *šá* ^{I}*La-a-ba-ši ina* IGI ^{I}*Ri*-[…] (22-VII-14, Nbn).

713 l. 1–4: *ma-la-a-ta šá a-na* […] *šá* UD.12.KAM *šá* ^{iti}SIG$_4$ *šá* ⌜*i-sin-nu* É⌝ *šá* MU.5.KAM *a-na* ^{d}GAŠAN-*Sip-par*^{ki} ^{d}*A-nu-ni-tu*$_4$ *u* ^{d}*Gu-la na-di-in* (12-III-5, Dar).

714 l. rev. 1–4: [… EZEN] É ^{d}GAŠAN-*Sip*-[*par*^{ki}]⌜x x *la* x⌝ UD.12.KAM *šá* EZEN É ^{d}*A-nu-ni-tu*$_4$ 1 (NIGIDA) 4 BÁN (4-III-9, Nbn).

names a festival of Bēlet-Sippar on the same day, while *Nbn* 799 mentions day 22 of the third month for a festival of Bēlet-Sippar. See also *CT* 56, 268, which mentions a festival of Bēlet-Sippar on day 12 (of the third month?).

As McEwan has noted, these documents are similar to the Hellenistic text, although the latter mentions sheep instead of barley and flour.[715] However, the little evidence that we have of *isinnu* in the Hellenistic period does not give us enough information to draw any conclusions as to the nature of this special festival.

II.8.2. *A palm festival*

In BM 32206 +,[716] which describes ritual activities performed on the third and fourth day of the ninth month Kislīmu in Babylon, several references are made to a festival in which date palm branches (*libbi gišimmari*) play an important part.[717] On day 4 of Kislīmu date palm branches are brought by boat from the temple of Ea within the Esagila-complex to the god Zāriqu in a tent near the river bridge; then they are taken back by the boatmen to the temple of Ea, where temple personnel place them in various places in this temple and elsewhere in Esagila.[718] During the activities of the fourth day, *Enūma eliš* is recited for Bēl by the singer (*nāru*),[719] and furthermore two lamentations are recited: the kettledrum (lamentation) UDAM KI AMUS 'It touches the Earth like a storm'[720] and ELUM GUSUN 'Honored one, wild ox'.[721]

For this festival there is more evidence from the text BM 78076, a tablet dated to Darius, which describes days 2–15 of Kislīmu in the Gula temple in Babylon, Esabad.[722] Probably also referring to the palm festival is a small unpublished fragment of a temple ritual, BM 54901: although the context is not fully clear, the mentioning of several deities (Zāriqu, Muštēšir, ^{d}KAŠ.DIN.NAM), also attested in the Esabad and Esagila texts, strongly points in the direction of this festival.[723] Finally, the date palm branch is also used during the eclipse of the moon ritual in Hellenistic Uruk, as we now know from BM 134701.[724]

On the basis of textual evidence from Mesopotamia and Israel, Lambert made some suggestions as to the significance of this palm festival.[725] He concluded that possibly 'there was an old and widespread custom in the ancient Near East of carrying branches of the palm (among others) at a harvest festival, of which we see differing relics in the Babylonian Kislev rites and the Jewish Feast of Tabernacles'.[726] This festival is not attested elsewhere in texts from the Hellenistic period.[727]

---

715 *FAOS* 4, 163.
716 G. Çağirgan, W.G. Lambert, *JCS* 43–45 (1991–1993), 89–106. See also II.4. 3 and II.5.1.
717 See I, 11; II, 51, 64; III, 93, 98, 104, 107, 117, 123.
718 BM 32206 +, III, 93 ff.
719 II 62–3.
720 IV, 158. Not attested, however, in our kettledrum ritual texts, see II.5.1.
721 IV, 162. Also known from the Uruk night vigil text *TU* 41, rev. 31, and *TU* 48, obv. 8, see II.2.2.
722 This tablet is published by A.R. George, *Studies W.G. Lambert*, no. 3, 280 ff. A short description of the contents was given by G. Çağirgan, W.G. Lambert, *JCS* 43–45 (1991–1993), 92, cf. also 89.
723 We will discuss this fragment more extensively in a separate study.
724 Obv. 18. See II.7.4.
725 *JCS* 43–45 (1991–1993), 92–3.
726 *JCS* 43–45 (1991–1993), 93.
727 See however the New Year text from Babylon, *RAcc.*, 133, 209, where several figurines are girded with

II.8.3. *A ḫarû-ritual*

Not much is known about the nature of a religious ceremony or ritual called *ḫarû*,[728] related to but not to be confused with the *ḫarû*-container.[729] It is well known from the Neo-Assyrian and Neo-Babylonian periods,[730] but not attested in the Hellenistic period, with the exception of a reference in an astronomical diary from Babylon: during the New Year festival on the eighth day of Nisannu the king takes part in a procession from Esagila to the *akītu*-temple and 'he performed the *ḫarû*-ritual of ... [fo]r(?) Esagila in their presence'.[731]

The *bīt ḫarê*,[732] the *ḫarû*-temple, is attested in a Hellenistic chronicle text from Babylon.[733] The *ḫarû*-house of the god Nabû is well-known from Assur[734] and Babylon,[735] but it is attested only twice in texts from Hellenistic Babylon, in a calendar text, where offerings were made on day 17 of Kislīmu,[736] and in an astronomical diary.[737]

II.8.4. *A Greek festival*

In an astronomical diary from Babylon[738] a festival called *puppē*, derived from the Greek word *πομπή* (procession)[739] is mentioned:

14 ... ITI.BI *al-te-e um-*[*ma*]
15 [I]*An* LUGAL *ina* URU.MEŠ *šá* [KUR]*Me-luḫ-ḫa šal-ṭa-niš* GIN.GIN-*a*[*k*][740] [lú]*pu-li-ṭe-e pu-up-pe-e u ép-še-e-tú šá* GIM *ú-ṣur-tú* [lú]*ia-a-man-nu* ⌜x⌝ [...]

---

a belt of palm leaves (*eri gišimmari*); compare also 145, 455.

728 *CAD*, Ḫ, 117b, 2; *AHw*, 328b, 2.

729 Attested in *TU* 41, rev. 1 and 4. For the container see *CAD*, Ḫ, 117, 1; *AHw*, 328b, 1; K. Deller, I.L. Finkel, *ZA* 74 (1984), 89.

730 See the dictionaries for examples; see also: *AUWE* 5, no. 110 (Nbk); *YOS* 17, 50 (Nbk); M.J. Geller, in: *Solving Riddles and Untying Knots. Biblical, Epigraphic, and Semitic Studies in Honor of Jonas C. Greenfield*, Winona Lake, Indiana, 1995, 532, obv. 7, cf. also 535 and 537 (Nbn). For Sippar see *CT* 55, 594; *CT* 57, 83.

731 A.J. Sachs–H. Hunger, *Diaries*, no. -204, C, rev. 15–16. This passage is also discussed in II.4.5.2.

732 *CAD*, Ḫ, 118 and *AHw*, 328 f.

733 *BHT* pl. 17, 25 = A.K. Grayson, *Chronicles*, 118, chronicle 10, rev. 25: É *ḫa-re-e* ŠU[II]*-su* NU KUR 'he did not touch (capture) the *ḫarû*-house'.

734 See B. Menzel, *Tempel*, I, 75 f. and II, 158, cf. A.R. George, *BTT*, 178 (sub 158) with 461; B. Pongratz-Leisten, *ina šulmi īrub*, 101 f.

735 See A. Cavigneaux, *Textes scolaires du temple de Nabû ša ḫarê* I (Texts from Babylon), Baghdad, 1981, and id., *Sumer* 37 (1981), 118 ff., with all Neo-Babylonian references to the *Nabû ša ḫarê*-temple. For the location see J.N. Postgate, *Iraq* 43 (1981), 173; J. Oelsner, *Materialien*, 118; A.R. George, *BTT*, 24 (sub 5), see also 58 (sub 15) and 225 (sub 7), cf. id., *House Most High*, no. 878, with a short history of the temple; B. Pongratz-Leisten, *ina šulmi īrub*, 103.

736 *BRM* IV, 25, rev. 43.

737 A.J. Sachs–H. Hunger, *Diaries*, no. -77, B, rev. 16. Cf. R.J. van der Spek, *Grondbezit in het Seleucidische rijk*, 75.

738 A.J. Sachs–H. Hunger, *Diaries*, no. -168, A, obv. 14–15.

739 With assimilation of mp 〉 pp in Akkadian, see R.J. van der Spek, in: A. Kuhrt and S. Sherwin-White (eds.), *Hellenism in the East*, 67 f. The festival was celebrated not only by the Greeks, but also by the Romans, see H.S. Versnel, *Triumphus*, 94 ff. with more literature.

740 Cf. R.J. van der Spek, *AfO* 44/45 (1997/98), 170, n. 13.

> '[14] ... In that month I heard as follows: [15]King Antiochus went victoriously into the cities of Meluḫḫa (i.e. Egypt), the citizens [performed?] a *πομπή* and ritual acts according to Greek custom ... [...]'.

This Greek festival probably celebrates Antiochus IV's victories of the first Egyptian campaign in 169 B.C. According to Polybius (XXX 26, 9) the spoils of this victory were displayed during a well-known festival held in Daphne, near Antioch, in 166 B.C. For this reason R.J. van der Spek argued that the festival referred to in the astronomical diary cannot be identified with the festival in Daphne.[741] However, M.J. Geller suggested that the festival is indeed the festival of Daphne, but contrary to the classical sources celebrated in 169 rather than in 166 B.C..[742]

Important for us is that we have here a Babylonian source which refers to a Greek festival, celebrated by Greeks (^lú^*pu-li-ṭe-e* = *πολῖται*) according to Greek custom (^lú^*ia-a-man-nu*).[743]

II.8.5. *Festivals for Ištar of Babylon and Ištar of Uruk*

Two well-known deities are Ištar of Babylon and Ištar of Uruk. The cults of both deities must each have had their own series of temple rituals, but for the Hellenistic period only fragments are preserved.

Ištar of Babylon: BM 32656

The cult of Ištar of Babylon in her temple Eturkalamma[744] is attested in a temple ritual fragment from Hellenistic Babylon dealing with the month Simānu, BM 32656, which is published by A.R. George.[745] The leading roles of the *kurgarrû* and the *assinnu* demonstrate an especially close affinity with the so-called 'Love Lyrics Ritual', known from several Late Assyrian and Late Babylonian fragments.[746] There is evidence that the Divine Love Lyrics text was known up to the Arsacid period.[747]

The following cult proceedings are described[748]: the preserved part of the ritual begins with day 3 of Simānu (col. III), when a *kurgarrû* goes to Eturkalamma and recites a

---

741 *Grondbezit in het Seleucidische Rijk*, Amsterdam, 1986, 75; id., in: A. Kuhrt and S. Sherwin-White (eds.), *Hellenism in the East*, 67 f.; id., *BiOr* 50 (1993), 99 f.; id., *Religieuze en economische politiek in het Seleucidische Rijk*, 32.

742 *BSOAS* 54 (1991), 1 ff.

743 Another festival, only known from Greek sources, as for example in an unplaced fragment of Book 1 of Berossus' Babyloniaca, is the festival of Sacaea (*Σάκαια*); it is celebrated in Babylon on days 16–20 of the fourth month Du'ūzu. It may be of Persian origin, according to S.M. Burstein, *The Babyloniaca of Berossus*. SANE 1/5, Malibu, 1978, 17, with n. 24.

744 This temple is also attested in *BRM* 1, 99, rev. 26; *CT* 49, 150, obv. 23; AB 246 (G.J.P. McEwan, *Iraq* 43 [1981], 138), obv. 7, all belonging to the Raḫimesu archive, cf. R.J. van der Spek, in: J. Wiesehöfer (ed.), *Das Partherreich und seine Zeugnisse*, 253. For Eturkalamma in Babylon see A.R. George, *BTT*, 307 f.

745 *Studies W.G. Lambert*, no. 2, 270 ff.

746 W.G. Lambert, in: H. Goedicke and J.J.M. Roberts (eds.), *Unity and Diversity*, Baltimore, London, 1975, 98 ff. Perhaps also *CT* 51, 101 deals with the cult of Ištar of Babylon, cf. A.R. George, *Studies W.G. Lambert*, 270, n. 21.

747 Ph.M. Hibbert, *WdO* 15 (1984), 93–95. See also G.J.P. McEwan, *FAOS* 4, 14.

748 For a detailed discussion see the article of George.

prayer to Šamaš. This section is described elsewhere as a ritual procedure of the morning (*nēpešu ša šēri*). After a break the text continues with the last line of another prayer; this section is identified as the ritual procedure of the afternoon (*nēpešu ša muṣlāli*), and could refer to days 3 to 8, since the next passage deals with day 9 (col. IV). In the morning the *kurgarrû* goes to the temple Emeurur (the temple of Nanāja at Babylon) and throws fruit at a wall behind which, according to George, lies the cella of Nanāja. In the afternoon more fruit is thrown at the cult-rooms of Ištar of Babylon's temple. As George suggests, this fruit symbolizes aphrodisiacs, and must be connected with the patronage of sexual love of Ištar and Nanāja.[749] The text continues with the afternoon of day 15 of Simānu. The *assinnu* places a brick in the House of Lament (*bīt sipittê*); after this the text describes several ceremonies, and the recitation of a Love Lyric by the *assinnu* follows. On day 16 the *kurgarrû* performs a similar ritual in a cultic place called the Equlû,[750] after which he proceeds to the Uraš-gate, reciting perhaps another Love Lyric. Most of col. V is lost.

Ištar of Uruk: TU 42 +

We do not have much detailed information on the cult of Ištar of Uruk, although her name is often mentioned, both in cultic and non-cultic texts from the Hellenistic period. Her importance is illustrated not only by the fact that a new temple, Ešgal, was built for her in the Hellenistic period,[751] but also by several fragments of a well-known myth, 'The Exaltation of Ištar', which were copied during the Hellenistic period.[752]

In *TU* 42 + a special festival for Ištar is described, which is celebrated in Uruk during an unknown month. The obverse describes the preparations for a procession of Ištar; the ceremonies are similar to those, which for days 8 and 9 of the New Year festival (*akītu*) of Anu, during the seventh month Tašrītu, are handed down to us (*TU* 39–40). The last part of the obverse and the whole of the reverse describe the actual procession of Ištar from (probably) the Ešgal to the *akītu*-temple,[753] and resembles the Anu-procession described in *KAR* 132.[754]

The beginning of the text is lost. When the text becomes understandable, several deities, among whom are many goddesses, take up position (*tarāṣu*) in front of Ištar, presumably in her cella in the Ešgal-temple (which was probably mentioned in the lost beginning of the text), while the king prepares for the procession by putting on a *tillû*-uniform. Meals are served to Ištar and the other deities.[755]

---

749 For fruit served during the divine meal as offering see III.7.1.
750 Or *bīt qūlu*, cf. *CAD*, Q, 303a.
751 See I.3.
752 See J. Oelsner, *Materialien*, 168 with an enumeration of all the texts and literature.
753 The procession was also briefly analysed by B. Pongratz-Leisten, *ina šulmi īrub*, 44. *TU* 42 was also discussed by G. Furlani, *Sacrificio*, 251 f. and id., *Riti*, 219 ff.
754 See II.4.5.1.
755 Obv. 19′ff.

Then she is escorted to the first station of the procession, the room between the curtains (*birīt šiddī*), and again the gods take up position in front of her.[756] After an offering and a libation by a priest, and a purification of the king and others who are present, first the Scepter of Kingship, and then Ištar herself go to the next station of the procession, the Dais of Destinies (*parak šīmāti*).[757]

The procession of Ištar and the Scepter of Kingship together with the other gods then makes its way to the procession-boat (^{giš}MÁ.GUR$_8$).[758] After they have arrived at the wharf (*arammu*), the god Usmû and the king lead Ištar and the Scepter of Kingship into the courtyard of the *akītu*-temple, where Ištar takes her place on the Great Dais (BÁRA.GAL), and the other gods follow.[759] Presumably when all the gods are in the courtyard, Usmû and the king lead Ištar and the Scepter of Kingship into the last station of the procession, Ištar's cella (*papāḫu*) in the *akītu*-temple.[760] The final lines of the text describe other gods following Ištar into her cella, and preparations for a ceremony in her cella, which include setting up several cult objects, such as Anu's armchair, chariots, a kettledrum, a carrying pole, and offering tables.[761]

Because this festival for Ištar is not known from other ritual texts,[762] it is difficult to establish the function and importance of *TU* 42 +. It is clear, however, that the text only contains part of the ritual, and at least one more tablet must have been used to describe the rest of the festival, probably including the journey back to, in this case, the Ešgal-temple in Uruk, just as Anu returned during the New Year festival. The importance of this ritual for Ištar is underlined by the fact that the king takes part in the ritual. Clearly the text provides us with no more than a glimpse of the Ištar cult in Uruk, paralleled as it is by the Anu cult of which we know more, especially owing to the New Year texts.

It is interesting that the text mentions the exorcists, the lamentation priests, the singers and a temple enterer (*ērib bīti*),[763] but there is no reference to a leading priest, addressed in the second person. This is not unusual in the temple ritual texts which belong to the large series of temple rituals covering the whole year, and *TU* 42 + apparently belongs to this series.

II.8.6. *TU 41: a nocturnal festival in the Rēš-temple*

As we already saw,[764] an important source for the good-functioning of the temple ceremony (*šalām bīti*) and the vigil (*bajjātu*) is the Uruk temple ritual text *TU* 41, which describes a nightly ritual for days 16 and 17 of perhaps the tenth month Ṭebētu.[765] The

[756] Obv. 26′–27′.
[757] Obv. 35′.
[758] Rev. 15′.
[759] Rev. 21′ff. Whether there is any connection between the reference to the *assinnu* and *kurgarrû* in rev. 25′ and the 'Love lyrics ritual' known from Babylon, is not clear from the context, but it is not impossible since *TU* 42 + also deals with the cult of Ištar.
[760] Rev. 27′f.
[761] Rev. 29′ff.
[762] But we do know of an *akītu*-temple of Ištar in Neo- and Late Babylonian Uruk, see II.4.5.1.
[763] Obv. 25′; rev. 6′; 7′; 30′.
[764] See II.3.4 and II.3.6.
[765] See I.2. The text was discussed by G. Furlani, *Sacrificio*, 226 f. and id., *Riti*, 137 ff.

beginning (probably mentioning the place where, and the moment when, the festival was held) and end of the text are not preserved.

When the text becomes understandable, the Scepter and a lamp in the shape of a shoe (*šēnu*), which symbolizes Nusku, god of light and fire,[766] descend to the Grand Courtyard and take up position facing Anu, who is in his cella, and where he remains during the entire ritual. The Scepter enters and Papsukkal, Nusku and Usmû go and sit in the courtyard of Anu. Then the Shoe enters the bed-chamber of the goddess Antu, the 'House with the golden bed' (É.NIR É gišNÚ GUŠKIN *šá An-tu*$_4$)[767] and is placed upon a footstool, while the goddesses Mārāt-Anu and Mārāt-Uruk sit in the courtyard of Anu. An evening meal is served but not cleared away, and the gate, in contrast with a normal cultic day, is not closed because the vigil continues the entire night.[768] Then a description follows of the ceremonies which were held during this vigil, including several offerings, libations, and recitations in the sanctuary on the top of the temple tower of the Rēš-temple.[769] Note that most of these proceedings are performed by a priest addressed in the second person (see below).

The ritual continues with a procession with the Torch (*gizillû*),[770] that is a divine Torch, upon which the washing of the mouth ceremony (*mīs pî*) has been performed.[771] First a *lumaḫḫu*-priest lights this Torch. The chief temple enterer (*ērib bīti rabû*), accompanied by exorcists, lamentation priests and singers, leads the Torch down from the temple tower, and he enters the Grand Courtyard by the Holy Gate, where the torch takes up position in front of Anu.

After a container is broken(?) in front of Anu, the procession of the Torch, now led by the temple enterer together with three gatekeepers, Papsukkal, Nusku, Usmû, and Messagunug, proceeds to the cella of Antu. Again a container is broken(?), now in front of Antu. The next station of the procession is Ubšukkinaku: an ox is killed near the Dais of Destinies, a brushwood pile (*abru*) is kindled from the Torch, and the right and left side of the pile are touched with the shoulder of the slaughtered ox.[772]

Then the procession leaves the Ubšukkinaku through the Grand Gate (KÁ.MAḪ), and the four gods encircle the temple, after which they re-enter, each god through his own gate: Papsukkal through the Grand Gate, Nusku through the Great Gate (KÁ.GAL), and Usmû through the Main Gate (KÁ.SAG).[773]

Although the text makes no reference to the Torch and Messagunug returning into the temple, this must have taken place as is clear from what follows.[774] The three gods remain at their gates until dawn and temple enterers (*ērib bīti*) light brushwood piles from the Torch in front of them. Then fires in the other temples of Uruk are kindled from the Torch by *šangû*-priests and temple enterers, after which they perform 'the good-

766 See my comments on *TU* 41, obv. 2 in the Appendix.
767 See also II.4.4 and my comments on *TU* 39, obv. 4 in the Appendix.
768 Obv. 13.
769 Obv. 13 ff.
770 The different stations of this procession with the Torch are discussed by B. Pongratz-Leisten, *ina šulmi īrub*, 45–47.
771 Obv. 28 ff.
772 Rev. 1 ff.
773 Rev. 8 ff. For the location of these gates see B. Pongratz-Leisten, *ina šulmi īrub*, 45.
774 Rev. 13 ff.

functioning of the temple' ceremony (*šalām bīti*) in the temples. After more brushwood piles are kindled at the gates of the temples, and two blessings are recited, the Torch and Messagunug return to the courtyard of Antu. The Torch is extinguished by an exorcist. Messagunug remains in the Ubšukkinaku and Adad, Sîn, Šamaš and Bēlet-ilī in the courtyard until daybreak.

The people of the land kindle brushwood piles in their homes, serve a banquet for Anu, Antu and the other gods, and recite the same blessing as before.[775] The city guardians kindle brushwood piles in the streets and crossroads, and they also plant standards left and right of the city gates. Brushwood piles will burn here until dawn.[776]

There is no mention of closing the gate at the end of the night,[777] but in the morning of day 17, 40 minutes after sunrise, the gate is opened again and the vigil ends.[778] The main and second meals of the morning are served for Anu, Antu and the other gods. After censers have been filled, and more offerings and a recitation by the singers are performed (among which is the lamentation ELUM GUSUN 'Honored one, wild ox'[779]) Adad, Sin, Šamaš, Messagunug and Bēlet-ilī are led into the room between the curtains (*birīt šiddī*).[780] The rest of the text is lost.

Some concluding remarks

This text is especially interesting because it gives us more detailed information about the proceedings during the night vigil than the other sources which were discussed elsewhere.[781] However, the ritual which is described in *TU* 41 was probably held for a special occasion and the different ceremonies celebrated during the nocturnal ritual cannot be used as a standard schedule for a normal vigil. This is confirmed by the appearance of the priest addressed in the second person; this 'you'-figure is not attested in the texts belonging to the large series of temple ritual text covering the whole year. We do know of the 'you'-figure, especially from other occassional rituals, which belong to the corpus of the lamentation priest (the kettledrum ritual and the building ritual).[782] The most likely candidate for the 'you'-figure in *TU* 41 is the exorcist; he is mentioned more often than the other participants in the ritual. Moreover we know that he participated in many temple rituals performing all sorts of ritual activities.[783]

II.8.7. *Ruler cults*

As we saw, the Macedonian kings and their representatives in Babylon and Uruk took an active part in the Babylonian cults.[784] However, on several occasions we also referred to

---

775 Rev. 22 ff.
776 Rev. 24 ff. Note that, with the exception of the eclipse of the moon ritual (see II.7), this is the only other example in our corpus of Hellenistic temple ritual texts of the people participating in a ritual.
777 See my comment on rev. 26 in the Appendix.
778 Rev. 28 f.
779 Rev. 31.
780 Rev. 29 ff.
781 See II.3.4.
782 See II.5.3 and II.6.3.
783 See I.3.
784 See I.3.

a special cult *for* the king and his family; the royal family appears to have been the object of offerings in the Babylonian temples. In this paragraph we will discuss the evidence for this cult and examine whether it can be connected with the Hellenistic ruler cults.

Evidence from Hellenistic Babylonia

Susan Sherwin-White and Amélie Kuhrt have extensively discussed the so-called ruler cults in the Seleucid empire.[785] They emphasize the distinction which has to be made between on the one hand a centrally imposed and organised state cult, instituted by Antiochus III for himself and former rulers (*πρόγονοι*), together with a separate royal cult of his wife Laodice, and on the other hand civic ruler cults, established by the Greek cities on their own initiative without direct orders from the king.[786] As far as Babylonia is concerned, they argue, there is no evidence of any ruler cult (state nor civic) for Seleucid kings. There are many references in the Hellenistic text corpus from Babylonia to offerings, prayers or dedications 'for the life of the king'. In an earlier article Sherwin-White discussed these passages[787] and concluded that they constitute not a new development but an old Babylonian practice, which was only concerned with the physical and mental well-being of the king. Furthermore, the practice of offering before the statues of ruling and deceased kings cannot be connected with ruler cults, because deification of the king is not implied here. Also, offerings made by or on behalf of the king only indicate the participation of the king in the temple cult, and have nothing to do with a royal cult of the Seleucid monarchs.

Let us examine the Babylonian evidence of the Hellenistic period.

Uruk

An Uruk building inscription[788] from 244 B.C. dedicates the reconstruction work on the Rēš-temple complex of Anu to the reigning kings. Line 15 reads: *a-na bul-ṭu šá* ^I^*An-ti-ʾ-i-ku-su u* ^I^*Se-lu-ku* LUGAL.MEŠ DÙ-*uš-ma ú-šak-lil* '[15]for the life of Antiochus and Seleucus, the kings, he built (all this) in its entirety'. Similarly, in another Uruk building inscription from the year 202/1 B.C.;[789] lines 10–12: *a-na muḫ-ḫi* [*bul-ṭu šá*] ^I^*An-ti-ʾ-i-ku-su* LUGAL *b*[*e-el-ia*] *te-me-en-na-šú-nu-ti* SUMUN DAGAL '[10] … for the sake of the [life of] [11]Antiochus, the king, my lord, [12]I have extended their old foundations'. Another example is an Arsacid fragment, a contract from Uruk, which records the dedication of a slave girl[790]:

[785] *From Samarkhand to Sardis*, 116 ff.; 202 ff.
[786] This distinction was already made by E. Bickerman, *Institutions des Séleucides*, Paris, 1938, 236–57.
[787] S. Sherwin-White, *JHS* 103 (1983), 156–9. But see also R.J. van der Spek, *BiOr* 42 (1985), 557–61; revised in id., *BiOr* 50 (1993), 100–101 and id., BSOAS 57 (1993), 367–8.
[788] *YOS* 1, 52 (see L.T. Doty, in: *Studies A. Sachs*, Philadelphia, 1988, 95–6).
[789] J. Jordan, *Uruk-Warka*. WVDOG 51, Leipzig, 1928, pl. 108, c, with 41. See also II.6.4.
[790] *BRM* 2, 53.

1. [[I]*Ni-ka-nu-ur*] A *šá* [I]*Di-e-mu-uk-ra-te-e ina ḫu-ud lìb-bi-šú*
2. [[sal]*A-ra-ḫ*]*u-na-ʾ* SAL.KUR-*su šá ta-tur-ru*[791] DUMU.SAL *šá* MU.5 MU.MEŠ
3. [*a-na mu*]*ḫ-ḫi bul-ṭu šá* LUGAL *a-na muḫ-ḫi bul-ṭu šá* NÍ-*šú*
4. [*a-na mu*]*ḫ-ḫi bul-ṭu šá* UN.MEŠ *u a-na muḫ-ḫi bul-ṭu šá*
5. [A.MEŠ(?)]-*šú a-na* DÙ-*uš dul-lu*$_4$ IM[ḫá] *šá* É DINGIR.MEŠ *šá*
6. ⌜UNUG⌝[ki] *a-na* [d]LX *u An-tu*$_4$ *u* DINGIR.MEŠ GAL.MEŠ *šá* UNUG[ki]
7. *a-na u*$_4$*-mu ṣa-a-tú it-ta-din* …

> ‘[1][Nikanor] son of Demokrates, of his own free will [7]has given [2][Araḫ]ne, his slave girl, five years old, [3][fo]r the sake of the life of the king, for the sake of his own life, [4][fo]r the sake of the life of the people and for the sake of the life of [5]the (lit. his) [children(?)], for doing the work in clay for the temples of [6]Uruk, for Anu and Antu and the great gods of Uruk [7]in perpetuity. …’.

More examples are known.[792] They clearly show that the phrase *ana* (*muḫḫi*) *bulṭu* means ‘for (the sake of) the (physical and mental) health of’, and is in no way different from similar phrases use in pre-Hellenistic times. So far we can agree with Susan Sherwin-White and Amélie Kuhrt.

We already discussed Hellenistic legal documents from Uruk concerning prebend shares (all dated to the second century B.C.), which refer to offerings brought up ‘to (the table of) the statues of the kings’.[793] Unlike the passages discussed above, these references are unusual. We know that on rare occasions, particularly during the Ur III-period, statues of deified kings received offerings, but from the Old Babylonian period on deified kings are unknown in Mesopotamia. In the Neo-Babylonian and Achaemenid periods the statue of the legendary Sargon of Akkad was also honored with special offering gifts,[794] but note that in these texts Sargon was usually referred to by name, unlike the Hellenistic kings.

The question is whether the text passages from Hellenistic Uruk refer to statues of living kings of the Seleucid dynasty, or to statues of former rulers like Sargon. As van der Spek noted, there are parallels for deified kings honored as *σύνναοι θεοί* in native temples.[795] Also, phrases in Hellenistic cuneiform sources like the *ana (muḫḫi) bulṭu*-examples mentioned above (but also those attested in the astronomical diaries from Babylon discussed below) all refer to living Seleucid kings. We may therefore safely assume that the statues are also of living Seleucid rulers.

For now there is no hard evidence which connects the Hellenistic text passages with a ruler cult practice in Hellenistic Uruk, instigated by a Seleucid king, but, in view of

---

[791] According to G.J.P. McEwan, *RA 75* (1981), 91–2 and repeated in M.J. Geller, H. Maehler (eds.), *Legal Documents of the Hellenistic World*, London, 1995, 22, *šá ta-tur-ru = ‘widow’,* but different in M. Roth, *JCS* 43–45 (1991–93), 4, n. 17. See also F. Joannès, *KTEMA* 22 (1997), 123, and M. Jursa, NABU 2001, no. 103.

[792] A similar phraseology is used in YBT 11633 (= L.T. Doty, *CAHU*, 87 ff., 100 + x S.E.= J. Oelsner, *XXXVIII R.A.I.*, Paris, 1992, 346–7); *BiMes* 24, 43 (x-I-184 S.E./120 A.E. = 128 B.C.); *BiMes* 24, 44 (4-III-179 S.E./115 A.E. = 133 B.C.). See also an obscure text from Tell ʿUmar (ancient Seleucia-on-the-Tigris), published by L.T. Doty in *Mesopotamia 13–14* (1978–79), 91–98, S_{11}-894 (87 S.E. = 225/4 B.C.). Discussed again by J. Oelsner in *XXXVIII R.A.*I., Paris, 1992, 345–6.

[793] *BRM* 2, 36, J. Oppert, J. Ménant, *Doc. Jur.*, no. 5 and *VS* 15, 16. See II.3.1 and II.3.2.

[794] See A.C.V.M. Bongenaar, *The Neo-Babylonian Ebabbar temple at Sippar*, 230 f., n. 205.

[795] *BiOr* 42 (1985), 560.

the fact that suddenly in cuneiform sources of the second century B.C. in Uruk offerings for the statues of rulers show up, seeing a connection is tempting.

Babylon

From Babylon we have one example in a chronicle text. Chronicle 13b[796] states that during the reign of king Seleucus III the administrator (*šatammu*) of Esagila established offerings within Esagila *a-na* ᵈEN *u* ᵈGAŠAN-*ia u* DINGIR.MEŠ GAL.MEŠ *ù a-na dul-lu*(?) *šá* ᴵ*Se*[-*lu*]-*ku* ⌜LUGAL⌝ *u* A.MEŠ-*šú* 'for Bēl and Bēltīja and the great gods and for the ritual(?) of Seleucus, the king, and his sons' (obv. 7–8).

The phrase used here is slightly different: the offerings are made for DN_1 and DN_2 and the great gods 'and for' (*u ana*) the ritual (if this reading is correct) of the king and his sons, indicating not a separation,[797] but a close connection between on the one hand the gods and on the other hand the king and his family. The latter are not seen as gods (therefore no *dinger* [= god] sign is used) but as superhumans. Here offerings are made 'for the gods *and* for the ritual(?) of the king', while in pre-Hellenistic times offerings were made to the gods to ensure the well-being of the king (using the phrase: *ana* DN *ana bulṭi šarri*/*ana balāṭ napšāti šarri* 'to the gods for the life/well-being of the king').

We frequently encounter a very similar expression in the astronomical diaries from Babylon.[798] They start during the reign of Antiochus III and continue into the Arsacid period. They all deal with offerings made in Esagila for Bēl, Bēltīja, sometimes Ištar of Babylon, the great gods 'and for the life' (*u ana bulṭi*) of the king, usually performed by a high military or temple official, although the broken context is often a problem. See, for example, this passage from the Arsacid period (no. -107, 108 B.C.): [*ana* ᵈEN] ⌜ᵈGAŠAN-*iá*⌝ DINGIR.MEŠ GAL.MEŠ *u ana bul-ṭu šá* LUGAL LUGAL.MEŠ DÙ *uš-kin-nu* 'He (i.e. an official from Subartu, who was the substitute of Orodes, the chief *kumar* of the temples) performed (the offerings) [for Bēl], Bēltīja, the great gods and for the life of the king of kings, (and) prostrated himself'.

It is important to observe that the connecting word *u* 'and' (often *u ana* 'and for'), attested in chronicle 13b, is also used in most of these passages in the astronomical diaries (in fact, it is only missing when the tablet is damaged), but is unknown in texts from pre-Hellenistic times. On two occassions (nos. -187 and -178) the offerings are also made for the king's wife and sons. We have three examples (nos. -171, -140, -107) in which the offerer prostrates himself (*šukênu*) after having offered to the great gods and for the life of the king. The verb *šukênu* is used to express worship of or submission to a deity, although it can also be used between human beings, like subject and ruler.[799]

The evidence at least leaves open the possibility that perhaps from Seleucus III on in the Esagila-temple of Babylon a special royal cult was practised side by side with the cult for the great Babylonian gods. The passages known from Babylon are all very

---

796 A.K. Grayson, *Chronicles*, 283 f. See also II.4.5.2.
797 S. Sherwin-White, A. Kuhrt, *From Samarkhand to Sardis*, 203.
798 A.J. Sachs–H. Hunger, *Diaries*, no. -204, C, rev. 18 (cited in II.4.5.2); no. -187, A, rev. 5′ and 8′; no. -178, C, rev. 21′; no. -171, B, rev. 7′; no. -160, A, obv. 2′; C, rev. 2′; no. -144, rev. 18; no. -140, A, U.E., 1; no. -133, B and C, obv. 24′; no. -132, A, rev. 4′; D_2, rev. 14′, 23′; no. -129, A_1, obv. 14′; A_2, obv. 19′; no. -126, B, rev. 8′; no. -107, C, rev. 18′.
799 See *CAD*, Š/III sub *šukênu* 1 and 2.

similar in context and formulation. A clear connection is made between the gods and the king (sometimes including his wife and sons) by the word 'and' (*u*). Hence, all these fragments suggest that after this time the kings received a special status. Furthermore, why do we find in many of these passages a reference to the *ilāni rabûti* 'the great gods'? This may very well be an attempt to emphasize the difference between the 'real' gods and the superhuman king.

Some concluding remarks

As far as Uruk is concerned we must conclude that, for now, there is no evidence which suggests that the phrase 'for the life of the king' in the examples from the Hellenistic period deals with anything other than the physical and mental well-being of the king, just as in pre-Hellenistic times. However, the passages which refer to offerings brought before the statues of the kings are unusual; the possibility of a *local* ruler cult for Seleucid kings during the second century B.C. cannot be excluded.

For Hellenistic Babylon we have attempted to show that the cuneiform sources possibly contain references to a royal cult. The fact that in the astronomical diaries of Babylon the *ana bulṭu*-expression is used only from Antiochus III on (and not before him), is striking. Because a reference to the king's wife and sons is sometimes made in this phrase, and yet for the state cult of Antiochus III only his wife, and never his sons are included, Sherwin-White and Kuhrt may be right in assuming that the Babylonian references cannot be connected with this state cult. However, it does not exclude the possibility that these references constitute a *local* royal civic cult in Babylon. The evidence from chronicle 13b suggests that such a local cult in Babylon may have been practised at least from the time of Seleucus III on. Whether it was initiated by the Babylonians or by the Seleucid king remains unclear.

This does not mean, however, that the kings became top gods. As van der Spek already stated: 'Ruler-cult or dynastic cult did not imply that the "deified" kings were treated in the same way as Olympian or other traditional gods. Ruler-cult was a method of honouring one or more kings in a superhuman manner, but it did not mean that these kings became the colleagues of Zeus or Marduk'.[800] The cuneiform sources may reflect an *interpretatio Babylonica* of a Greek cult: the scribes of Babylon simply used the old *ana bulṭi*-phrase to express the Hellenistic view on superhuman kingship.

[800] *BiOr* 42 (1985), 559–60.

III. THE DIVINE MEAL

III.1. Introduction

One important element of the cult is the offering. An offering[1] is a series of cultic acts which exist in almost all known religions. One brings something from a profane or secular place into a holy or sacred place, kills or destroys it, or eats it in the presence of others, in order to make a connection with the divine.

In Mesopotamian rituals the offering is predominant. In his article '*The origins of the sacrificial cult: new evidence from Mesopotamia and Israel*', W.W. Hallo examines the origin of the offering in Israel and Mesopotamia[2]: in Mesopotamia and in Israel similar conceptions of the origins of the offering practice existed, namely to sanctify the act of consumption by the deity. However, the cult and concept of offering of the Hebrews and the Mesopotamians evolved in entirely different directions. Since in Mesopotamia the ideology of the ritual is never expressed, the myths are used to explain the function of the offering[3]: there we find that mankind was created to take over the hard work from the gods and provide the gods with food and drinks. Since the gods needed food just like humans, offerings usually consisting of food, drinks and aromatics (fumigation) were presented in front of the statues of the gods. The cultic meals provided for this need.

As in the Greek and Roman world the principle of *do ut des* (I give, in order that you give) was important: one has to give the deities the honours they deserve, and in return the deities will protect the state and give prosperity. The 'feeding of the gods' remained the most important purpose of the divine meal in Mesopotamia. Although the foods and drinks offered were re-distributed after the offering ceremony to priests, temple personnel and others, an official cult maintained up to the end of Mesopotamian civilization the fiction that the divine meal was consumed by the gods, or rather their statues, and that the offerings served no other purpose.

In texts from Mesopotamia we do not find a clear definition of an offering. However, a general description of the offering practice in the temples of Hellenistic Uruk is known. As we already saw,[4] in *TU* 38 a list is presented, which appears to be an attempt to present a complete description of the regularly recurring offerings and ceremonies during the cultic year in Uruk. Obv. 35–38 mentions loaves and date cakes which are meant for several offerings and ceremonies. The list starts off with two groups of general

[1] I will take W.G. Lambert's advice (in: *OLA* 55 [1993], 191) and avoid the term 'sacrifice' (usually referring to the killing of an animal), which in modern usage 'is too dependent on Biblical institutions and concepts to be a suitable vehicle to express ancient Mesopotamian practices'. Relevant for the study of the Babylonian offering practice in the Hellenistic period are especially G. Furlani, *Sacrificio*, F. Blome, *Opfermaterie*, and G.J. P. McEwan, *FAOS* 4, 166 ff.
[2] In: P.D. Miller Jr., P.D. Hanson, S. Dean McBride (eds.), *Ancient Israelite Religion*, Philadelphia, 1987, 3–13.
[3] For the connection between myth and ritual see also II.1.
[4] See II.1.

offering gifts: the travel provisions for the procession of (the statues of) the gods (*ṣidītu ilāni*),[5] and the monthly *guqqû*-offerings,[6] apparently here mentioned instead of *ginû* or *sattukku*, perhaps because further on in the list the *eššēšu*-festivals, with which they are connected, are mentioned.

At the end of the list a third group, the offerings of the *kāribu*-citizen, and a fourth group, the additional offerings, which the king had to perform (*tardīt šarri*), are mentioned.[7] No attempt has been made to enumerate all the specific offerings; instead they are summarized in four larger groups: one specific group of offerings performed by priests for the gods when they leave the temple for a procession, one general group of offerings performed by priests for the gods when they are in the temple, and two specific groups of offerings for the gods offered by *kāribu*-citizen and the king.

As for the divine meal, a sequence of events can be distinguished. At the place chosen as an offering site, an offering table is set up, and water is brought in for washing. Then the table is arranged. Meat, liquids and sometimes fruit are served, and fumigation and purifications are performed. The offering side is consecrated. Behind closed curtains recitations are performed, after which the table is cleared away. Here the divine meal ends.

Although not necessarily in this order, these are the basic elements of the divine meal. In this chapter we will first describe which cultic meals are attested in texts from Hellenistic Uruk and Babylon. Then we will describe the different elements of the divine meal.

III.2. Cultic meals

The income of the temple, which consisted of agricultural and meat products, was not only used as payment for the priests, administrators and other personnel in the temple, or stored away for future need. Most importantly, it served as food which was offered daily in front of the divine statues in the temple. In the temple ritual texts from Hellenistic Uruk and Babylon the cultic meals are described extensively. In this section we will first examine which cultic meals are attested. Then we will discuss *TU* 38, a text describing in detail the daily offering practice in the Rēš-temple and other sanctuaries of Hellenistic Uruk, and one which is therefore important for our understanding of the cultic meals.

III.2.1. *Terminology*

In the Hellenistic period[8] *naptanu* and *tardennu*[9] are known as the formal main and second ritual meals offered on a stand in front of the statues of the gods in the temples; they were prepared and served by priests during various ceremonies and rituals. This

[5] See III.2.2.
[6] See III.7.2. and II.3.2.
[7] See III.2.2. and III.7.2.
[8] Cf. G. Furlani, *Sacrificio*, 252 ff.; G.J.P. McEwan, *FAOS* 4, 165
[9] See J.J. Glassner's article 'Mahlzeit', in *RLA* 7 (1987–90), 259 ff. For the (cultic and secular) use of *naptanu* in older periods see E. Kingsbury, *HUCA* 34 (1963), 22 f.; B.A. Levine, W.W. Hallo, *HUCA* 38 (1967), 46 ff. and 55 sub kin-sig; R. Frankena, *Tākultu*, 54 ff.; G. van Driel, *Cult of Aššur*, 159 f.

combined use of main and second meal is also known in Neo-Babylonian Uruk.[10] In the Hellenistic temple ritual texts, both meals are used during the daily offering practice in Uruk,[11] the New Year festival in Uruk,[12] the Uruk night vigil festivities[13] and the festival for Ištar of Uruk.[14] Also during the festivities of the month Kislīmu in Babylon meals are served.[15] No meals are mentioned in the ritual texts of the lamentation priest, i.e. the kettledrum ritual and the building ritual texts.

Normally four meals were presented during the day: the main and second meal in the morning (*naptan rabû ša šēri, tardennu ša šēri*)[16] and the main and second meal in the evening ((*naptan*) *rabû u tardennu ša līlât*).[17] Sometimes additional indications for the times of the meal are given, e.g. a main and second (meal) of the (last) double hour of the day (GAL-*ú ù tar-den-nu šá bi-ru* u_4-*mu*),[18] or in the afternoon: on the fourth day of the New Year festival of the month Nisannu in Babylon, after a second meal in the late afternoon ([EGIR *tar*]-*den-nu šá ki-iṣ* u_4-*mu*) was served, *Enūma eliš* was recited.[19] Usually however the texts simply refer to these meals as *naptanu* and *tardennu*.

Other words for 'meal' e.g. *līlâtu*, *mākālû*, *qerītu*, *nubattu* and *tākultu* are, as far as the Hellenistic period is concerned, rare and usually only attested in (Emesal) incantations and prayers.[20]

The main and second meal are described extensively in the temple ritual text *TU* 38.

---

10 See the Late Neo-Babylonian Uruk ritual text *LKU*, no. 51, where ceremonies for the whole year involving the goddesses Bēlet-ša-Uruk, Uṣur-amassu and Aška'itu in the Eanna-temple are described (passim in this text).

11 *TU* 38, passim.

12 *TU* 39 +, passim.

13 *TU* 41, obv. 12 (KIN.SIG), 14; rev. 29, 30.

14 *TU* 42 +, obv. 19′, 20′.

15 G. Çağirgan, W.G. Lambert, *JCS* 43–45 (1991–93), I, 44, II, 58–59.

16 The main meal in the morning (*šēru*, written syll.): *TU* 38, obv. 1, 28; rev. 3, 4, 7; *TU* 39, rev. 12, 19; *TU* 41, rev. 29; the second meal in the morning: *TU* 38, obv. 6, 28; rev. 13; *TU* 39, obv. 2. The latter meal is also attested in the astronomical diaries from Babylon, A.J. Sachs–H. Hunger, *Diaries*, no. -140, A, obv. 21–22. See also II.4.5.2.

17 The main meal in the evening (*līlâtu*, written syll. or KIN.SIG): *TU* 38, obv. 6, 7, 29; rev. 18; *TU* 39, rev. 6, 14; the main meal in the evening: *TU* 38, obv. 6, 7, 29; rev. 21; *TU* 39, rev. 14. The main and second meals of the evening are also attested in a diary from Babylon, A.J. Sachs–H. Hunger, *Diaries*, no. -156, A, obv. 20′, on the 24th, 25th and 27th of Nisannu (context not clear).

18 *TU* 39, rev. 23. See also *LKU*, no. 51, obv. 26: 'the main (meal) of the (last) double hour of the day' (*ra-bu-ú šá bi-ri* u_4-*mu*).

19 *RAcc*., 136, 280. See II.4.5.2.

20 - *līlâtu* (written syll. and KIN.SIG) 'evening, evening meal', cf. B.A. Levine, W.W. Hallo, *HUCA* 38 (1967), 51 sub á-u_4-te-na, and 55 sub kin-sig; see also the dictionaries; in the Hellenistic text corpus only the meaning 'evening' is attested (often in connection with *naptanu* or *tardennu*, see above), with the exception of one Sumerian incipit of an incantation mentioned in *BRM* 4, 7, rev. 30.

– *mākālû* 'meal'. We have one example of *mākālû* in a Hellenistic Uruk ritual text, written syllabically, *TU* 38, obv. 46–47, in a partly Sumerian incipit of a blessing.

– *qerītu* (written syll. and KAŠ.DÉ.A), 'banquet', 'festival', cf. E. Kingsbury, *HUCA* 34 (1963), 25; see also the dictionaries. While it is well-known from Assyrian rituals (cf. G. van Driel, *Cult of Aššur*, 161–2), in Hellenistic ritual texts it only occurs once: in combination with *nīqu* it is mentioned in the Uruk ritual text *TU* 41, rev. 23. Other examples of *qerītu* in obscure context, in a Hellenistic cultic calendar text from Babylon: *SBH* VIII, rev. col. v, 10, and 22.

– for *nubattu* 'vigil, evening', but also 'evening ceremony, evening meal', see II.3.5.

– *tākultu* is not attested in texts from the Hellenistic period.

III.2.2. *TU 38*

TU 38 contains ritual instructions for the daily offerings in the temples of Anu, Ištar, Nanāja and the other gods in Hellenistic Uruk, and dates from the beginning of the second century B.C.[21] It describes very explicitly and in detail the immense quantity of products which were brought into the temples for the regular offerings (*ginû*).[22] They were used for the four daily meals. A main meal followed by a second meal were served in the morning; they took place at the beginning of the day when the temple was opened. Another main and second meal were served in the evening and apparently took place before the temple was closed.

liquids

Lines obv. 1–16 of the text begin to describe all sorts of liquids: barley-beer, *labku*-beer, *nāšu*-beer, *zarbābu*-beer, milk, and drawn wine, and first quality beers, which were brought in containers (*šappu*), containers used as libation bowls (*maqqû*), and vases (*tilimtu*) for the four daily meals to the table of Anu.

For the main meal of the morning we first find eighteen *šappu*-containers, which are not used as libation bowls, with their contents (obv. 1–5):

6 golden *šappu*-containers	barley-beer
5 golden *šappu*-containers	*labku*-beer
1 golden *šappu*-container	*nāšu*-beer
1 golden *šappu*-container	*zarbābu*-beer
1 alabaster *šappu*-container	milk
4 golden *šappu*-containers	drawn wine

For the second meal of the morning and the main and second meal of the evening the list is the same, with exception of the alabaster *šappu*-container with milk, which is not served during the evening meals (obv. 6–7). The first section of the text ends with 5 golden *šappu*-containers with a *zarīnu*-stand of *algamišu*-stone (obv. 8).

After a cross-line, five *šappu*-containers, which are used as libation bowls, with their contents are listed (obv. 9–16):

1 *šappu*-container used as libation bowl	barley-beer
1 *šappu*-container used as libation bowl	*labku*-beer
1 *šappu*-container used as libation bowl	*nāšu*-beer
1 *šappu*-container used as libation bowl	drawn wine
1 *šappu*-container used as libation bowl	*zarbābu*-beer(?)

Then a *šappu*-container with wine from Izallu and 4 *tilimtu*-vases are mentioned (obv. 11–16), after which a second cross-line follows, indicating the end of the second section.

The 5 *šappu*-containers used as libation bowls mentioned in the second section are additional to the 18 containers mentioned in obv. 1–5, as is clear from obv. 1: *e-lat šap-*

[21] See the introduction of the text in the Appendix.
[22] See III.7.2.

pi.MEŠ *šá ma-aq-qa-né-e* 'in addition to the *šappu*-containers belonging to the libation bowls'. This is what distinguishes section one from section two. As we will see, similar distinctions (indicated by *elat* 'in addition to/not included are') are given throughout the text.

Although Anu is mentioned together with Antu in obv. 16 (the context is not clear since the end of obv. 15 and 16 is damaged), it is evident that the first and second section (obv. 1–16) are only concerned with Anu (cf. obv. 2; see also the reference to the cella of Anu in obv. 12 and probably also in obv. 9). This is also confirmed by the fact that the following section, obv. 17–18, is concerned with Antu, Ištar and Nanāja:

14 golden *šappu*-containers	first quality beer	Antu
12 golden *šappu*-containers	(first quality beer)	Ištar
10 golden *šappu*-containers	(first quality beer)	[Nanāja]

In addition to these *šappu*-containers obv. 19 mentions golden *šappu*-containers used during the offering service of the whole year for the other gods living in Uruk. And, separated by another cross-line, obv. 20 (the fourth section) refers to 2 more golden *šappu*-containers with travel provisions for the procession of the gods (*ṣidītu ilāni*), and 2 *tilimtu*-vases. We will have more to say about these travel provisions shortly.

ṣidītu ilāni

The travel provisions of the gods are mentioned directly after the section concerned with the liquids (obv. 1–19), but separated by a cross-line, and directly before the section concerned with flour used to make loaves, also separated by a cross-line (obv. 21–47). So, what did they consist of? *Ṣidītu* was written syllabically and with the Sumerogram NINDA.KASKAL 'bread for the road' (Akkadian *akal ḫarrāni*[23]) which gives us some idea what these travel provisions, at least originally, consisted of. In the first millennium bread or flour (*qēmu*) must also have been a main component, next to beer, chick-peas and barley; the examples of flour connected with *ṣidītu* in Neo-Babylonian administrative texts confirm this.[24] The Hellenistic text discussed here, *TU* 38, also mentions the travel provisions once more (obv. 36); *ṣidītu ilāni* is listed here together with the offerings and ceremonies, for which large(?) loaves and date cakes are distributed. Exactly the same list of offerings and ceremonies, but without *ṣidītu ilāni*, is mentioned in rev. 36–38, but here oxen and sheep meat are distributed. So, apparently, in this case meat did not belong to the travel provisions of the gods. However, in a prebend sale of the *ērib bītūtu* (office of the temple enterer) a share in the mutton for the *ṣidītu ilāni* was also part of the sale.[25]

[23] Cf. the lexical list *Proto-Diri*, 374 f.: NINDA.KASKAL.[LA] = *ṣi-di-*[*tum*], *a-ka-al ḫar-*[*ra-nim*]. For the gods traveling see J. van Dijk, in: *RlA* 3 (1957-), s.v. 'Gott', § 4: 'Götterreisen'.

[24] Cf. *CAD*, Ṣ, 172–73 sub c-g, and for the Neo-Babylonian period 173 sub h.

[25] J. Oppert, J. Ménant, *Doc. jur.*, no. 2 (5, 7, 12, 20). L.T. Doty will publish two texts mentioning sales of rights to *ṣidītu ilāni*, NCBT 1963 and NCBT 1975, in *YOS* 20; apparently they also consist of mutton, cf. L.T. Doty, *CAHU*, 198. The *ṣidītu ilāni* is also attested in the ritual fragment *Bagh. Mitt. Beih.* 2, no. 14, 5′ (see my comments on *TU* 44, I, 8 in the Appendix).

flour and loaves

Lines obv. 21–35 (the fifth section) are concerned with barley flour and emmer flour (explicitly called flour in obv. 25), which the miller has to deliver every day to the bakers for the regular offerings (*ginû*, obv. 22), and are used to provide the loaves and cakes for the four divine meals of Anu, Antu, Ištar and Nanāja, and all the other gods in Uruk.[26] The amount of flour is described very accurately: the contents of 1 *pūru*-bowl = 3 kor and 3 *pānu* of barley and [emmer] flour = (in sexagesimal ciphers) 1,48 seah (*sūtu*) = (in decimal ciphers) 108 seah, in accordance with a fixed standard for the regular offerings: the seah-measure of 10 *manû* (*ina* ^gišBÁN *šá* 10 MA.NA). This is then further specified: the 108 seah flour consist of 81 seah barley flour and 27 seah emmer flour. This means that, by the Neo-/Late-Babylonian standard of 1 seah = 6 litres, the immense amount of 648 litres of flour was brought into the temple every day of the year, i.e. 486 litres of barley flour and 162 litres of emmer flour.[27]

The flour was used by the bakers to make 243 *ṣibtu*-loaves. Of these loaves 168 were supplied for the four daily offerings (obv. 26–33) in front of Anu, Antu, Ištar, Nanāja, for some divine symbols and for the ziqqurrat, as follows:

8 *ṣibtu*-loaves	the main meal of the morning	Anu
8 *ṣibtu*-loaves	second meal of the morning	Anu
7 *ṣibtu*-loaves	the main meal of the evening	Anu
7 *ṣibtu*-loaves	the second meal of the evening	Anu
30 *ṣibtu*-loaves	the four meals	Antu
30 *ṣibtu*-loaves	the four meals	Ištar
30 *ṣibtu*-loaves	the four meals	Nanāja
12 *ṣibtu*-loaves	the four meals	the seat of Anu and the household god of the cella of Antu
4 *ṣibtu*-loaves	the four meals	the 2 tiaras of Anu
16 *ṣibtu*-loaves	the four meals	the ziqqurrat and the household god of the ziqqurrat
16 *ṣibtu*-loaves	the four meals	the wings(?) of the cella of Anu and Antu

The 30 loaves for Antu, Ištar and Nanāja clearly must have been divided in the same manner as those of Anu: 8 loaves each for the main and second meal of the morning, and 7 each for the main and second meal of the evening. After specifying these 168 loaves there are 75 loaves for the four daily meals left (distinguished by *elat*) for the other gods from Uruk in their temples, making a total of 243 loaves (obv. 34–35).

In addition to (*elat*) these 243 loaves the text also mentions large(?) loaves (*ṣi-ba-at rab-bu-ú*) and the date cakes (*a-kal ma-ak-kàs*), which are used for the travel provisions for the processions of the gods and also during some other ceremonies and offerings (obv. 35–38): the *guqqû*-offerings, the *eššēšu*-ceremonies, the opening-of the gate ceremonies, the clothing ceremonies, the holy water (basin) ceremonies, the night

[26] See G. Furlani, *Riti*, 1 ff.
[27] Cf. *RAcc.*, 81, n. 4.

vigil ceremonies, the brazier ceremonies, the rites of the divine marriage, the offerings of the *kāribu*-citizen and the additional offerings of the king (*tardītu šarri*).[28]

It is not unlikely that the products mentioned next (obv. 38–43: red cakes (*sāmūtu*), *takkasû*-cakes, 1200 *kusīpu*-loaves, pressed oil, and *masḫatu*-flour) refer to the additional offerings of the king. In the almost identical list in rev. 36–38 (in a section which is concerned with meat) these additional offerings are also the last to be mentioned, but here they are not specified further.[29]

The fifth section ends with a reference to two recitation-incipits; these recitations have to be performed by the miller and the baker.

Dates, figs, raisins, ḫiṣṣaṣātu-cake

The last section of the obverse (obv. 48–50) describes the amount of choice dates, Dilmun-dates, figs, raisins, which 'in addition to *ḫiṣṣaṣātu*-cakes(?) and the table-arrangement (*tabnītu*)' (obv. 49) are needed for the four meals, and which are served to Anu, Antu, Ištar, Nanāja and the other gods of Uruk. The total of these products amounts to (in sexagesimal ciphers) 1, 48 seah or (in decimal ciphers) 108 seah, i.e. 648 litres, precisely as much as the amount of 648 litres of flour mentioned in the fifth section (obv. 21 ff.).

meat

The reverse of the tablet is concerned with meat deliveries for the regular offerings (*ginû*),[30] especially oxen and sheep. In total 13 sections are indicated by cross-lines. The introduction (rev. 1–3) states that these regular offerings will be served daily throughout the year to Anu, Antu, Ištar, Nanāja and the other gods residing in the Rēš-temple, the Ešgal-temple and the Ešarra-temple (the sanctuary, also called Baramaḫ, on the temple tower of Anu). Note that the Eanna-temple and the other temples of Tiranna (= Uruk) are addressed later (rev. 35).

Lines rev. 4–9 are concerned with the main meal of the morning. Then the text refers to the incipit of a blessing and perhaps to a prayer (rev. 10–12), which had to be recited during the slaughtering by the butcher (see rev. 8–9 and 11), after which the second meal of the morning is described (rev. 13–17). After this follow the main (rev. 18–20) and second (rev. 21–23) meals of the evening. The meat-products for these four daily meals are[31]:

main meal of the morning (rev. 4–9)	second meal of the morning (rev. 13–17)
7 first-quality sheep	6 fat, pure sheep
1 *kālû*-sheep suitable for the *ginû*	1 (*kālû*-) sheep suitable for the *ginû*
1 full-grown ox	5 fat sheep of lesser quality
1 suckling calf	1 full-grown ox

[28] For this list see also II.1 and III.1. For the *kāribu*-citizen see III.7.2.
[29] The *tardītu šarri* will be discussed in see III.7.2.
[30] Cf. rev. 1, 5, 6, 8, 15, 18, 20, 21, 23, 25, 35.
[31] See my comments on these lines of *TU* 38 in the Appendix.

main meal of the morning (rev. 4–9)	second meal of the morning (rev. 13–17)
10 fat sheep of lesser quality	8 lambs
	5 ducks
	2 ducks of lesser quality
	3 geese
	4 *ušummu*-mice
	30 *marratu*-birds
	20 turtledoves
	3 ostrich eggs
	3 duck eggs
main meal of the evening (rev. 18–20)	**second meal of the evening (rev. 21–23)**
4 fat, pure sheep	4 fat, pure sheep
1 *kālû*-sheep suitable for the *ginû*	1 *kālû*-sheep suitable for the *ginû*
5 sheep of lesser quality	5 sheep of lesser quality
10 turtledoves	10 turtledoves

Lines rev. 24–28 then give the totals of animals used for the two meals of the morning and the evening:

21 first-quality sheep	30 turtledoves
4 *kālû*-sheep	3 geese
25 sheep of lesser quality	5 ducks
2 full-grown oxen	2 ducks of lesser quality
1 suckling calf	4 *ušummu*-mice
8 lambs	3 ostrich eggs
30 *marratu*-birds	3 duck eggs

Furthermore in rev. 29–31 two special offerings to the planets are mentioned. First, in the *bīt maḫazzat*, an unknown room in the sanctuary,[32] 10 sheep are slaughtered 'for Anu and Antu, of the heaven, (for) Jupiter, Venus, Mercury, Saturn (and) Mars, (at?) sunrise and the appearance of the moon, to be offered as a voluntary(?) offering in the *bīt maḫazzat*'.

Secondly (rev. 32–34), every month on day 16 in the Baramaḫ (the name of the temple on the temple tower of Anu), 10 sheep are again offered for Anu and Antu of the heaven, and for Jupiter, Venus, Mercury, Saturn, Mars, the sun and the moon (here referred to as 'the seven planets'), this time on the occassion of the cleansing of the hands ceremony (*te-bi-ib-tu*$_4$ ŠU^{II}) exactly as on day 16 of the tenth month Ṭebētu.[33]

While so far the text has been concerned with offerings in the Rēš-temple, the Ešgal-temple and the Ešarra-temple, in the beginning of the next section sheep are mentioned as offerings in the Eanna-temple and the other temples of Uruk (rev. 35).

Furthermore the list already mentioned in obv. 36–38 is repeated, indicating here that oxen and sheep are also used for these offerings and ceremonies. The fact that the

[32] See my comments on rev. 31 in the Appendix.
[33] See my earlier remarks on this passage in I.2 and in the introduction of II.3.

travel provisions of the gods are not mentioned here indicates that meat products were not used for these provisions. Also, we already noticed above that the products which are probably used for the last offerings mentioned in the list, the additional offerings of the king (obv. 38 f.), are not further specified here. Finally, as discussed elsewhere, at the end of the section the list is explained as a description of the Urukaean cults.[34]

In a new section the text mentions a few restrictions on the meat-menu of four specific gods: Šakkan, Ningublaga, Bēlet-ṣēri and Ereškigal (rev. 40–42).[35]

The text ends with a most interesting colophon (rev. 43–50).[36]

Some concluding remarks

As Lambert already noted with regard to *TU* 38, because the gods deserve only the best, the offerings mentioned in the text only consist of the best food and liquids, while cheaper products such as pork, goat meat and fish are missing, as are fruits and vegetables, probably because these were not available throughout the year.[37]

As one would expect Anu, as the city god of Uruk and most important resident of the Rēš-temple, receives most of the offerings. See for example the total amount of liquids for Anu (obv. 1–16) which is much more than the liquids for Antu, Ištar Nanāja and the other gods (obv. 17–20). Also, the offerings for Anu are sometimes more accurately described than the offerings for the other gods: see obv. 28–29 which specifies the loaves for the two morning and evening meals for Anu, while for the other gods only the total numbers are mentioned.

Can we determine any differences between the four meals? The different kinds of liquids are the same for the morning and evening meals, except for the milk, which is missing in the main and second meal of the evening (obv. 6–7); the serving of fresh milk only during the morning meals probably reflects general custom.[38] Furthermore, while the main and second meal of the morning receive 8 loaves each, the main and second meal of the evening receive seven each (obv. 28–29).

As far as the meat offerings are concerned, from our table it becomes clear that there are many differences between the four meals. First of all, there is a remarkable difference between the meat products for the main and second meal of the morning: the first meal has more sheep, of which only seven in the morning meal are of first-quality, while the second meal contains ducks, geese, *marratu*-birds, turtledoves, ostrich eggs and duck eggs. A suckling calf is mentioned only in the main meal, while eight lambs are mentioned only in the second meal. The main and second meals of the evening are exactly the same, and the total amount of meat offerings is less then in the morning meals.

Also quality differences exist so far as the meat offerings go: sheep which have been fed with barley are of a higher quality than those not fed with barley; and ducks which

---

34 See II.1.

35 Cf. F. Blome, *Opfermaterie*, 59–60, who considers some food taboos for certain deities. W.G. Lambert, in: *OLA* 55 (1993), 199 has given some suggestions for explaining these taboos.

36 See I.3.

37 ib. For fruit see also III.7.1.

38 Fresh milk cannot be kept for more than a few morning hours, when it is cool, see M. Stol, in *RLA* 8 (1994), 192.

are fed with dough are of a higher quality than those not fed with dough, but both the ones fed with barley and those not fed with barley are offered for all four meals.

We can conclude that the difference between the morning and the evening meals lies apparently more in the quantities than in the qualities of the foodstuffs and liquids. The quantity of offerings is higher in the morning meals then in the evening meals, while perhaps the mentioning of more loaves and first-quality sheep only in the morning meal also suggests that the main meal of the morning is more important than the second.[39]

TU 38 does not state who performed the ritual instructions. Only in the beginning of the text a priest, addressed in the second person, appears (obv. 1, 2, 17). This person could be either the *mubannû* 'the arranger of the offering table',[40] or he could be the exorcist (*āšipu*), which is more likely, because the scribe of the text, Šamaš-ēṭir, is an exorcist. Furthermore, the *mubannû* is attested only rarely in the temple ritual texts, while the exorcist played a major part in many of the rituals from Uruk and Babylon.[41]

TU 38 very extensively describes what and how much was used for the meals, and furthermore where, when, and for which deities the foodstuffs were served. It also presents an elaborate list of ceremonies and offerings and in addition a description of the Urukaean cult is given in the colophon. As we saw, Falkenstein already dismissed this colophon as propaganda of the Urukaean priesthood for the Late Babylonian Anu-cult,[42] and indeed the scribe's elaborate description of the food products, ceremonies and offerings clearly shows that the text was written for propaganda purposes. Nevertheless this does not disqualify the entire text as unreliable. The scribe Šamaš-ēṭir may have exaggerated, but he did not invent what was not there. There is no reason to believe that the meals were not served in the Urukaean temples along the line as described in *TU* 38. Certainly, the foodstuffs used and the quantities referred to in the text may have differed in time and from temple to temple, but having said this, the text gives us a unique insight into the offering practices in Hellenistic Uruk.

III.3. The offering site

The location where the food and drink offerings in front of the statue of one or more gods were placed, and where the offering table and the offering accoutrements were set up,[43] was sometimes called KI SÍSKUR GABA.RI 'the place where (the god) is made

[39] Note also the fact that the sheep of lesser quality, which have not been fed with barley, are only called 'fat' in the section of the main (rev. 6) and second (rev. 15) meal of the morning, but not in the section concerned with the evening meals (rev. 20, 23), which could suggest a dominance of the morning over the evening meals. However, since the adjective is also missing in the enumeration of the four meals (rev. 26), it could merely reflect the slovenliness of the writer.
[40] See III.4.3.
[41] See I.3.
[42] See I.3.
[43] See G. Furlani, *Sacrificio*, 341 f.

to accept the offering'.[44] It had to be a secluded site,[45] away from daily secular life and safe from any intrusion of evil.

The temple ritual texts often only mention the temple(name) as the place where offerings took place, but sometimes a certain place in the temple is referred to, like for example the courtyard (*kisallu*) or the Grand Courtyard (*kisalmaḫḫu*) in the Rēš-temple,[46] or more specific places like the workshop (*bīt mummi*) in the Rēš-temple,[47] or the roof of the Anu-temple.[48] Sometimes offerings were placed outside the temple, as for example 'in the open country or on the bank of a river, on a place where nobody sets foot'.[49]

curtains

Sometimes the temple ritual texts refer to curtains (*šiddu*) which are used to isolate the offering place, or to the *birīt šiddī* '(the room) between the curtains',[50] which is the passage way between the cella, where the statue resides, and the ante-cella.[51] By using this curtain the offering table and the statue were hidden from human eyes during the ritual of the divine meal. Although this practice may have originally reflected palace protocol, in the temple its main purpose was not to disclose to outsiders that the gods did not really consume the offerings and that after the divine meal was finished it was the priests who disposed of the food and drinks, which as substantial 'leftovers' were presented to the priests and other temple personnel.

The normal procedure with regard to the curtains was as follows: first offering preparations, purifications and fumigations, after which offerings and libations were performed; then the curtains were drawn shut (*šiddā šadādu*),[52] after which lamentations were recited. When the recitations have ended the curtains were loosened (*šiddī nuḫḫu*) and the procedure was completed.[53]

Apparently the gods also spent the night behind closed curtains. This is at least the case for Bēl in Esagila during the New Year festival in Babylon.[54]

---

44 *TU* 39, obv. 30. See my comments on this line in the Appendix. See also *TU* 42 +, obv. 28′, 30′.

45 See for example *TU* 46, obv. 15 and F.H. Weissbach, *Misc.*, no.12, obv. 19 (É *pár-si* 'a secluded room'). Cf. *KAR* 50, rev. 8 (KI *par-si* 'a secluded place').

46 For example during the New Year festival in Uruk (*TU* 39–40) or during a night vigil in Uruk (*TU* 41).

47 For example during the kettledrum ritual (*TU* 44 and parallels).

48 For example during the building ritual (*TU* 45 and parallels).

49 *TU* 45, rev. 8 // *Bagh. Mitt. Beih.* 2, no. 11, rev., fragment 2, 3′ (KI GÌR^II^ *pár-kat*).

50 For references to these curtains or the *birīt šiddī*, in Neo-Assyrian temple ritual texts: *KAR* 60, rev. 4; *KAR* 50, rev. 7; IV R², 23, no. 1 +, IV, 1; 2; 24; also in the Neo-Babylonian temple ritual *LKU* no. 51, rev. 28; see also the dictionaries *AHw*, 128b, sub 2, c, *CAD*, B, 254b, mng. 3b–6′, and *CAD*, Š/II, 408a sub b.

In Hellenistic temple ritual texts: from Uruk *TU* 39, obv. 12; 29 (2x); *TU* 40, obv. 15; 16; rev. 6; *TU* 41, rev. 33; *TU* 42 +, 26′; *KAR* 132, I, 18; 26; *TU* 44, II, 8; *Bagh. Mitt. Beih.* 2, no. 1 (+ //), [23], no. 5, rev. 26; *TU* 45, obv. 11; 14; *TU* 46, obv. 13; rev. 7; *Bagh. Mitt. Beih.* 2, no. 1 (+ //), 23, no. 10, obv. 16; 20.

51 Cf. A. Falkenstein, *Topographie*, 20; B. Pongratz-Leisten, *ina šulmi īrub*, 40 ff. A place surrounded by a linen curtain is also found in the *akītu*-temple outside Uruk, cf. *TU* 42 +, rev. 24′.

52 Entirely different in St. M. Maul, *Zukunftsbewältigung*, 55 f. 'Mehllinien ziehen'.

53 See for example the building ritual text *TU* 45, obv. 1–14.

54 See the temple ritual *RAcc.*, 129, 3; 133, 218; 137, 287: at the beginning of the day the high priest removes (*dekû*) the *gadalû*-curtain in front of Bēl and Bēltīja.

flour and standards

Another way of secluding the site was by using heaps of flour (*zidubdubbû*), which were often connected with the verb *nadû* 'to throw/pour',[55] or by using a magical circle of flour (*zisurrû*), which 'served as a barrier to demonic entry' as Lambert pointed out.[56] Also *urigallu*-standards were set up; this is attested in ritual texts from the pre-Hellenistic periods,[57] but in the eclipse ritual text *BRM* 4, 6, rev. 31–33 we have perhaps an indication that this was also custom in the Hellenistic period:

> '31′On the next day, before sunrise, you will open the gates which you have placed under seal. You will moisten (l. 32′) the reed *urigallu*-standard, the magic circle of flour, 32′(and) a white and black cord (and) throw (it) into the river. You will purify (l. 33′) all the temples (with) *takpertu*-purifications 33′and (especially) Edumununna, the temple of Sîn'.

Because the *urigallu*-standard is mentioned here together with the circle, we may assume that both, together with the white and black cord, had the function of creating a secluded offering site.

III.4. The offering preparations

Several terms which are used in connection with the preparations of offerings are attested in the temple ritual texts. The offerings were made on offering tables (*paššūru*, *paṭīru*), which were set up in front of the divine statue(s) in the cella. On the table offering arrangements (*tabnītu*) were placed. The offering table was set by the 'arranger of the offering table' (*mubannû*). Finally the texts refer to the offering accoutrements (*riksu*). In this section we will discuss these terms.

III.4.1. *paššūru and paṭīru*

Often in the temple ritual texts the description of the preparation of the ceremony begins with the offering table (*paššūru*),[58] usually of gold (*ḫurāṣu*),[59] which was brought in and set up (*kunnu*) in front of the statue.[60] One temple ritual text refers to seven large offering

---

[55] *zidubdubbû* is attested in the Hellenistic eclipse of the moon ritual *BRM* 4, 6, rev. 45 (see also 46). See also *Bagh. Mitt. Beih.* 2, no. 1 (+ //), 23 (*mīs pî*) (Hellenistic period), and *KAR* 50, rev. 7 (kettledrum ritual, Neo-Assyrian example). Another Neo-Assyrian example from the kettledrum ritual, IV R², 23, no. 1 +, I, 6, is paralleled by the Hellenistic example *Bagh. Mitt. Beih.* 2, no. 5, obv. 11, in the latter connected with the verb *sarāqu* 'to scatter'. See my comments on this line in the Appendix. For *sarāqu* see III.4.1.

[56] *JSS* 13 (1968), 111. Examples from Hellenistic temple ritual texts from Uruk: the kettledrum ritual text *TU* 44, II, 13 and *Bagh. Mitt. Beih.* 2, no. 5, rev. 18. The eclipse of the moon ritual text: *BRM* 4, 6, rev. 31, 37, 45, 47. In BM 134701, rev. 7′, the flour of this magic circle is identified as *tappinnu*-flour.

[57] *AHw*, 1429–30 with references.

[58] Written: ᵍⁱˢBANŠUR. See also the lexical list Sᵃ Fragment M 14 (*MSL* III, 65): [...] BUR = *ni-q*[*u-ú*] = MIN = *naptanu* = MIN = *pa-áš-š*[*u-ru*].

For the table in general, cf. A. Salonen, *Möbel*, 174–203, for *paššūru*, 176–192.

[59] But see *TU* 42 +, rev. 33′, where a silver offering table (ᵍⁱˢBANŠUR KÙ.BABBAR) is mentioned.

[60] *TU* 41, obv. 17–18; *Bagh. Mitt. Beih.* 2, no. 1 (+ //), 14. Perhaps also in *TU* 42 +, rev. 33′: [ᵍⁱˢBANŠUR?] GUŠKIN *ina pa-ni* ᵈINNIN *uk-tan-nu* 'A golden [offering table(?)] will be set up before Ištar'.

tables (*paššurmāḫu*)[61] made of gold. Sometimes, however, we find that the offering table is not specifically mentioned at the beginning of the ceremony, and the text immediately concentrates on the cultic meal. Either the scribe refrains from mentioning this apparently self-evident information, or, less likely, the table is already (permanently?) placed in the temple in front of the statue.[62]

paššūru is also mentioned many times in Hellenistic prebend texts from Uruk, where during monthly and yearly ceremonies foodstuffs as prebend income are brought up (*elû* Š-stem) to the offering table in front of one or more deities.[63]

Several verbs are used in the temple ritual texts in connection with *paššūru*. Most important are *rakāsu* 'to arrange',[64] and *paṭāru* 'to clear (away)',[65] but other verbs are also attested.[66]

Also mentioned many times is the *paṭīru* (GI.DU$_8$),[67] an offering table or small altar,[68] which was made of reed, as becomes clear not only from the logogram (GI = *qanû* 'reed'), but also from kettledrum ritual text *TU* 44, IV, 34, where it is mentioned as one of the utensils of the reed-worker:

> '[34]The utensils of the reed-worker (*udê adkuppi*): 24 offering tables (*paṭīru*), 24 reed baskets (*selli*), 5 [35]hand-baskets (*sella qāti*), 3 reed mats (*burû*), 3 reed covers (*kutummu*)'.

The *paṭīru* was brought in and set up (*kunnu*)[69] or placed (*šakānu*)[70] in front of the statue. It was arranged (*paṭīra rakāsu*),[71] but strangely enough *paṭīra paṭāru* 'to clear away the offering table' is not attested in Hellenistic temple ritual texts. Also not attested

---

61 ^{giš}BANŠUR.MAḪ, see *TU* 41, obv. 22, see also obv. 32. Cf. *AHw*, 845b, 'kostbarer Opfertisch'.

62 For example, the ritual text *TU* 41, obv. 8 ff. begins by describing an offering ceremony with the divine meal (obv. 12), without mentioning the offering table; however, the following ceremony, performed on the roof of the ziqqurrat (obv. 14 ff.) does mention the offering table (obv. 17).

63 See II.3.1 and II.4.1.

64 *TU* 38, obv. 2, 17; *TU* 41, obv. 19; obv. 24; *RAcc.*, 142, 386–7.

65 *TU* 41, obv. 32; *RAcc.*, 143, 403; see also IV R^2, 23, no. 1 +, obv. 18 (*pi-ṭir* ^{giš}BANŠUR).
Instead of *paššūru* the object of *paṭāru* can also be the meal (*TU* 39, obv. 14; *TU* 40, obv. 15; *TU* 39, rev. 3; 5; 7; 9; 13; 14; 21; *TU* 41, obv. 13; rev. 30), the vigil (*TU* 39, rev. 11; *TU* 41, rev. 29; see II.3.4) and the censer (*RAcc.*, 142, 356; see III.5).

66 *ana paššūri nadānu* 'to deliver on the offering table' (*TU* 38, obv. 27. Cf. also *RAcc.*, 143, 405–6); *ana paššūri našû* 'to lift up on the offering table' (*TU* 41, obv. 22); *ina*(?) *pāni paššūri šakānu* 'to place in(?) front of the offering table' (*RAcc.*, 142, 393; 143, 410); *ina muḫḫi paššūri šakānu* 'to place on the offering table' (*RAcc.*, 142, 392; 143–4, 412–13); *ana tarṣi paššūri tarāṣu* 'to take up position in the direction of the offering table' (*TU* 41, obv. 30); *riksu ša paššūri šalāmu* 'to complete the offering accoutrements of the offering table' (*RAcc.*, 140, 339); *piṭru paššūri qerēbu* and *piṭru paššūri našû* 'to serve/lift up the leftovers of the offering table' (*RAcc.*, 133, 211 and 143, 410–12. For *piṭru* see my comments on *RAcc.*,133, 211 in the Appendix).

67 But see also *MSL* VII, 45, 197: GI.ŠU.BIL.LÁ = *pa*-[*ṭi-ru*] and 198: GI.DIM = ditto.

68 Cf. A. Falkenstein, *LKU*, 17, n. 6; *AHw*, 851b, 'Tragaltärchen'. See also a representation of a *paṭīru* in St. M. Maul, *Zukunftsbewältigung*, 58.

69 Uruk kettledrum ritual text: *TU* 44, I, 17, II, 2, 5; see also IV R^2, 23, no. 1 +, III, 25 (Neo-Assyrian). Uruk building ritual texts: *TU* 45, obv. 7; *TU* 46, obv. 8. An example from Neo-Babylonian Nippur is the ritual text T.G. Pinches, *Berens Coll.* no. 110, obv. 6 and 8–9.

70 *TU* 45, rev. 20.

71 In the Uruk building riual *TU* 45, obv. 2; 20; rev. 5; 8; 11; 17; *TU* 46, obv. 15; *Bagh. Mitt. Beih.* 2, no. 10, 10. See also *Bagh. Mitt. Beih.* 2, no. 11, rev. fragm. 2, 3′ (broken context); also the Neo-Assyrian kettledrum ritual *KAR* 50, rev. 2 and in the late Neo-Babylonian Uruk text *LKU*, no. 48, containing a ritual for the king, obv. [2] and 7.

in these texts is the expression *ina muḫḫi paṭīri naptana qerēbu* 'to bring the meal on the offering table'.[72] Finally, the explanatory Uruk text *TU* 47 offers on the reverse the drawing of a rectangle with the subscript: *paṭīru šuklulu* (GI.DU$_8$ DU$_7$) 'perfect offering table'.[73]

It is difficult to determine what the differences in function are between the *paššūru* and the *paṭīru*. We can only ascertain that the *paššūru* is never mentioned together with the *paṭīru* in a temple ritual text and therefore they apparently excluded each other. Furthermore the *paṭīru* was used only in the rituals of the lamentation priest (*kalû*),[74] while the *paššūru* is mentioned in the other temple rituals.[75] Finally, while *paššūru* is always singular in the Hellenistic temple ritual texts, the examples of *paṭīru* are usually plural.

Other tables, such as the *maškittu*, known from the Neo-Assyian period, are not attested in Hellenistic rituals. The *guḫšû*, an altar made of reed, known from the Old Babylonian period on and mentioned only rarely in the Neo-Assyrian rituals, was replaced by the *paṭīru* after the Middle Babylonian period.[76]

III.4.2. *tabnītu*

Attested only once in the Hellenistic corpus is *tabnītu* 'table-arrangement'. *TU* 38, obv. 48 ff. reads:

> '[48]Every day of the year, for the 4 (daily) meals (in sexagesimal ciphers) 1,48 seah (or in decimal ciphers) 108 seah choice dates, [49]Dilmun-dates, figs and raisins, in addition to *ḫiṣṣaṣātu*-cakes(?) and the table-arrangement (*tab-ni-ti*), which will be served (l. 50) to Anu, [50]Antu, Ištar, Nanāja and the (other) gods, residing in Uruk'.

Examples from earlier periods show that this table-arrangement must have consisted of dishes, bowls and the like which were used for serving food and drinks on the offering table.[77] The table arrangement was prepared by the *mubannû*, discussed next.

III.4.3. *mubannû*

The *mubannû* 'arranger (of the offering table)' was responsible for decorating the offering table.[78] The *mubannû*, best known from Neo-Babylonian administrative docu-

---

[72] This phrase is attested for example in the late Neo-Babylonian Uruk ritual text *LKU* no. 51, obv. 6.
[73] See A. Livingstone, *Mystical*, 194.
[74] From Hellenistic Uruk: *TU* 44, *TU* 45, *TU* 46, *Bagh. Mitt. Beih.* 2, no. 10 and 11. Also in *KAR* 50 (NA), *LKU*, no. 51 (NB).
[75] From Hellenistic Uruk: *TU* 38, *TU* 39–40, *TU* 41, *TU* 42; from Hellenistic Babylon, in the New Year text *RAcc.*, 127 ff.
[76] *CAD*, G, 125b; *AHw*, 296b.
[77] See *AHw*, 1299a, I, 2; A.L. Oppenheim, *ArOr.* 17 (1949), 231, n. 7 with text references. See also the Late Babylonian ritual from Uruk W 22758/5 (a fragment belonging to the so-called Nippur compendium = A.R. George, *BTT*, no. 18, 145–62), obv. III, 1.
[78] Cf. *AHw*, 665a, 'der "schön macht", Opfertische herricht', and *CAD*, M/II, 158a, 'cook (who prepares, arranges, and serves food to the gods), temple cook'. Translated as such for the first time by F. Thureau-Dangin, *RA* 20 (1923), 109, n. 3.

ments,[79] is also found in the Hellenistic Uruk ritual *KAR* 132, III, 16 (see also III, 3), where, during the procession of Anu to the New Year temple, two *mubannû*'s (lú*mu-ban-nu-ú*) bring out cedar (shavings, burning) in a *ḫuluppaqqu*-brazier to Anu. From this passage it becomes clear that the *mubannû* not only prepared the bowls and dishes for the divine meal, but was also allowed to enter the temple.[80] This is confirmed by another passage describing a ceremony, which took place on the first day of Nisannu during the New Year festival in Babylon[81]: here the *mubannû* performs a ceremony involving a key in the courtyard of Bēl in Esagila.

We have another reference to the *mubannû* in a deed concerning a baker's prebend from Nippur (154 B.C.).[82] Obv. 5 reads:

P]N ⸢A⸣ PN_2 *šá ana muḫ-ḫi ba-nu-ú šá* É.MEŠ DINGIR.MEŠ lúLÙNG[A *a-na*? PN_3 …]

'PN [descendant] of PN_2, who [is] in charge of arranging (the offering tables) of the temples, the brew[er, to PN_3 …]'.

Finally we have evidence of a *mubannûtu*-prebend in a list of temple expenditures from Hellenistic Babylon (of which however no prebends are known), *CT* 49, 150, reads in obv. 16–17:

šá ⟨*put*⟩ *baṭ-lu šá* lú*mu-ban-nu-ú-tú i-na-áš-šu-ú*

'(X amount is given by PN) who is responsible for the (non-) interruption of the office of the arranger (of the offering table)'.[83]

These four cases are the only certain references to the *mubannû* in texts from the Hellenistic period.[84]

---

79 A.L. Oppenheim, *ArOr*. 17 (1949), 231, n. 7; J. MacGinnis, *AfO* 38–39 (1991–1992), 81, no. 2, obv. 11 (Neo-Babylonian prebend text from Sippar); A.C.V.M. Bongenaar, *The Neo-Babylonian Ebabbar temple at Sippar,* 292–94.

80 Compare A.C.V.M. Bongenaar, *The Neo-Babylonian Ebabbar temple at Sippar,* 292–93.

81 Attested in a small ritual fragment discussed by G. Çağirgan, *Festivals*, 1. The ceremony is discussed in II.4.5.2.

82 Published by R.J. van der Spek, in: Maria de Jong-Ellis (ed.), *Nippur at the Centennial*, 250–54, and 257–8, text 1 (UM 29–15–802).

83 After R.J. van der Spek, in: J. Wiesehöfer (ed.), *Das Partherreich und seine Zeugnisse*, 223. G.J.P. McEwan, *FAOS* 4, 47, reads *šá til-lu šá* lú*mu-ban-nu-ú-tú i-na-áš-šu* (not *šú*) *-ú* 'who is picking up the trappings(?) of the temple cooks', referring to *AHw*, 1358 f. *tillu* 'ein Behang'. *CAD* M/II, 158b, quoting this passage, reads *baṭ-lu*, but gives no translation.

84 If Doty is right in asserting that lúDÍM in some cases must not be read lúŠITIM = *itinnu* 'the building master (builder, director of the reconstruction)', but lúDÍM = *mubannû* (*CAHU*, 129–133), we would have more examples: the Hellenistic Uruk ritual text *BRM* 4, 6 (describing the eclipse of the moon ritual), obv. 30′, refers to the lúDÍM who has to throw a *garakku*-brazier into the river. Furthermore Doty mentions several private documents from Hellenistic Uruk which are concerned with a lúDÍM-*ūtu*-prebend. However, Doty's reading is followed neither by the dictionaries (cf. *AHw*, 404a; *CAD*, I/J, 298a and id., M/II, 158), nor by G.J.P. McEwan (*FAOS* 4, 87–89), B. Funck (*Uruk zur Seleukidenzeit*, 214 ff., see especially n. 335), nor by J. Oelsner (in: M.J. Geller, H. Maehler (eds.), *Legal Documents of the Hellenistic World*, London, 1995, 109, n. 13), who prefer lúDÍM-*ūtu* = lúŠITIM-*ūtu* = *itinnūtu* 'office of the building master'.

III.4.4. *riksu*

The temple ritual texts refer many times to *riksu* (KEŠDA) 'offering accoutrements'.[85] Sometimes *raksu* is attested, which may be a Late Babylonian variant of *riksu*.[86] It stood for a set of cult objects, such as an altar or table,[87] the holy water basin (*egubbû*), and the censer (*nignakku*), used for fumigations and purifications,[88] and all sorts of bowls, vessels and dishes used to serve the offerings. Furthermore, *riksu* also included the offerings themselves, as Blome has already suggested.[89]

riksu is cognate with the verb *rakāsu* (also written KEŠDA), which has as a basic meaning 'to bind'. The expression *riksa rakāsu* 'to arrange the offering accoutrements', used at the beginning of the offering ceremony, is well-known from pre-Hellenistic and Hellenistic temple ritual texts.[90]

When the ceremony had ended, the offering accoutrements were removed, expressed by *riksa paṭāru* 'to clear away the offering accoutrements'.[91] *Riksu* is also found in connection with the verb *ullulu* (D-stem of *elēlu*) 'to purify' in the kettledrum ritual,[92] and with *šalāmu* 'to complete', said of *riksu ša paššūri* 'the offering accoutrements of the offering table', in the New Year festival in Babylon.[93]

It is interesting that *riksu* is only attested in Uruk in the rituals of the lamentation priest, i.e. the kettledrum ritual and building ritual (*TU* 44 and *TU* 45 with parallels).

---

[85] Cf. *AHw*, 984b, B, 2, a ('Opferzurüstung'). Translated as 'a set table of offerings' by *CAD*, E, 244b sub b. See also the definition of *riksu* in St. M. Maul, *Zukunftsbewältigung*, 66, n.74. A rare Neo-Babylonian example exists in the ritual T.G. Pinches, *Berens collection,* no. 110, rev. 15.

[86] In a liturgical calendar text from Hellenistic Uruk, *TU* 48 (see II.2.2); the text refers to a *taqribtu*-lamentation incipit which has to be recited on day 1 of Nisannu, over the offering accoutrements (*rak-su*) to Anu (obv. 8–9). Perhaps also in *Bagh. Mitt. Beih.* 2, no. 1 (+ //), 10, 25.

[87] Both *paššūru* and *paṭīru*, since *riksu* is found not only in the rituals of the lamentation priest but also in other rituals. However, in the Neo-Assyrian ritual IV R², 23, no. 1 +, III, 25 the *paṭīru* is set up and the offering accoutrement is arranged (GI.DU$_8$ GIN-*an* KEŠDA [KEŠDA]), which suggests that perhaps in this case the *paṭīru* is not part of the *riksu*.

[88] Discussed in III.5 and III.6.

[89] *Opfermaterie*, 343, no. 314; see also the index p. 465 s.v. *riksa rakāsu* and *riksa paṭāru*. See also G. Furlani, *Riti*, 246.

[90] Cf. St. M. Maul, *Zukunftsbewältigung*, 51. See for example the Neo-Assyrian kettledrum ritual IV R², 23, no. 1 +, III, 25: 'you will [arrange] an offering accoutrement (KEŠDA)'; see also the late Neo-Babylonian rituals *LKU* no. 51, obv. 19, rev. 7, 32, 35, and F.H. Weissbach, *Misc.*, no. 12, obv. 6 (3 *ri-ik-si* for Ea, Šamaš and Marduk).

Hellenistic period: *TU* 44, II, 33: 'You will arrange (KEŠDA-*as*) 1 offering accoutrement (KEŠDA) in front of Lumḫa'; III, 16–18: you will arrange 5 offering accoutrements for Ea, Šamaš, Marduk, Lumḫa and divine kettledrum; *TU* 45, obv. 18: 2 offering accoutrements for his (the kings'?) god and goddess you will arrange; *TU* 46, rev. 3: 5 offering accoutrements (one for each god) for Sin, Marduk, Ninmaḫ, Kulla and Ninšubur the lamentation priest will arrange; 6: 3 offering accoutrements for the god of the temple, the goddess of the temple (and) the genius of the temple the lamentation priest will arrange; 8–9: you will prepare three offering accoutrements for Anu, Enlil and [Ea]; *Bagh. Mitt. Beih.* 2, no. 1 (+ //), 10, 25.

[91] *TU* 44, III, 25 KEŠDA.MEŠ DUḪ; *TU* 46, rev. 11 'You will clear away the offering accoutrements' (KEŠDA.MEŠ DUḪ-*ár*); *Bagh. Mitt. Beih.* 2, no. 1 (+ //), 59, 60 (KEŠDA.MEŠ).

[92] *TU* 44, II, 2: 'you will purify the offering accoutrements' (KEŠDA.MEŠ *tu-ul-lal*).

[93] *RAcc.*, 140, 338–40: 'When the first double hour of the morning (has passed), after the offering accoutrements of the offering table of Bēl and Bēltīja are completed (*šal-mu*), he will call for the exorcist and he will consecrate the temple'.

See also the cultic calendar text *BRM* 4, 25 // *SBH* VII, obv. 5 (broken context).

Riksu in connection with *epēšu* (cf. *CAD*, E, 217a) is not attested in the Hellenistic temple ritual texts.

For every god who participates in the ritual (in the kettledrum ritual also for the drum itself) an offering accoutrement is arranged. Part of the offering accoutrements is the offering table, which in these texts is only the *paṭīru*, since we already noticed that the *paššūru* is not attested in the rituals of the lamentation priest. However, in general there is probably no restriction of *paṭīru* to *riksu* in Hellenistic ritual texts, because in the only example from Babylon (mentioned above) *riksu* is indeed connected with the *paššūru*.

III.5. Fumigation

Fumigation[94] is a religious act, during which barley, aromatics, flour, incense and aromatic woods are scattered (*sarāqu*) on a censer; the burning of these materials results in smoke which, because of its pleasant smell, pleases the gods, just as did presenting of the food as offerings.[95] Therefore, fumigation is a form of offering, which is confirmed by the fact that *serqu* and *surqinnu*, cognates of the verb *sarāqu*, mean 'offering' (*CAD*) or 'Schüttopfer' (*AHw*) and are also used for food offerings.[96] Furthermore, although fumigation is not a secular table custom to dispel the odor of food,[97] it has a purifying function: the burning of aromatics and incense purifies the atmosphere.[98]

In the divine meal fumigation could be performed either before or after the foodstuffs and liquids were served. The instrument used for fumigation is the censer. While the use of the *šēḫtu*-censer and the *qutrīnu*-censer is restricted to earlier periods,[99] the *nignakku*-censer (NÍG.NA) is attested up to the Hellenistic period.[100] It was made of gold[101] or silver[102] and used in all known temple rituals.[103] Together with the torch (*gizillû*) and holy water-basin (*egubbû*) it was also used for consecrations and purifications.[104]

In this section we will first examine how fumigation was described in the temple ritual texts. Then we will discuss the different fumigation materials which are attested.

---

94 Cf. G. Furlani, *Sacrificio*, 353; F. Blome, *Opfermaterie*, 272–84.

95 The gods love the smell of the fumes, cf. P.A.H. de Boer, in: *Suppl. VT* 23 (1972), 46f.

96 See W.G. Lambert, in: *OLA* 55 (1993), 195–6.

97 As suggested by A.L. Oppenheim, *Ancient Mesopotamia*, 189.

98 In the same way as sweeping and water-sprinkling purifies the offering site, and washing purifies the person who offers. See III.6.

99 See the dictionaries *AHw* and *CAD* sub *šēḫtu* and *qutrīnu* with many examples.

100 See the dictionaries *CAD* and *AHw* sub *nignakku*. See also St. M. Maul, *Zukunftsbewältigung*, Register, s.v. Räuchergefäß.

Hellenistic period: *TU* 39, rev. 4, 6; *TU* 41, obv. 10, 21, rev. 30; *TU* 42 +, rev. 34′, 35′; *TU* 44, I, 30; II, 12; III, 20; 26; IV, 31, cf. *KAR* 60, obv. 9 and *KAR* 50, rev. 6; *Bagh. Mitt. Beih.* 2, no. 1 (+ //), 19; *Bagh. Mitt. Beih.* 2, no.5, rev. 19; *Bagh. Mitt. Beih.* 2, no. 10, obv. 13; *TU* 45, obv. 9; *RAcc.*, 140–142, 343, 347, 351, 356, 392. See also the cultic calendar text SBH VII, rev. 6.

101 *TU* 41, obv. 10, 21, 26, rev. 30; *TU* 42 +, rev. 34′, [35′]; *RAcc.*, 142, 392.

102 *RAcc.*, 140, 351.

103 But also attested for example in an astronomical diary, no. -209, D, obv. 16′ (102 S.E.), which mentions a censer situated on the throne(?) in which the food offerings for Bēl and the other great gods were placed.

104 See III.6.1.

III.5.1. *sarāqu and šakānu*

In Akkadian the most likely candidates for 'fumigation' are as mentioned *surqinnu* and *serqu*,[105] but in the Hellenistic temple ritual texts *surqinnu* is not attested at all, and for *serqu* we only have a few examples.[106]

However, the cognate verb *sarāqu* 'to scatter' is used many times in the context of offerings of meat and libations. We find that cedar needles, *maṣḫatu*-flour, aromatics and juniper are scattered upon the censer, which indicates fumigation. Also, the phrase *nignak(ki) burāši šakānu*, 'to place a censer (with) juniper' i.e. 'which burns juniper', is used.[107]

Are there other references to fumigation without the verb *sarāqu* and *šakānu*? We have several examples from Uruk of the expression *nignakka (ḫurāṣu) mullû* 'to fill (*malû* D-stem) the (golden) censer'.[108] On one occasion the Uruk *mīs pî*-ritual text states that the (in this case unfired) censer is filled with *ašāgu*-coals and scattered with boxtree.[109] In this text the verb *ṣênu* is also used: to heap *ašāgu*-coals, probably on the censer.[110] The expressions are always made in direct connection with meals and/or offerings of oxen and sheep.

The verb *qatāru*, in D-stem *qutturu* 'to cause something to smoke, to make an incense offering, to cense, fumigate, to fume incense' (*CAD*) appears to be missing from Hellenistic temple ritual texts.[111]

Finally, we add that the burning (*qalû*) of aromatics during burnt offerings of meat and other foodstuffs is not to be interpreted as fumigation.[112]

III.5.2. *Fumigation materials*

We already encountered most of the materials which were used for fumigation: we mentioned cedar needles (*lukšu*?), boxtree (*šimeššalû*), *maṣḫatu*-flour, aromatics (*riqqū*) and juniper (*burāšu*).

Strangely enough we find that *qutrīnu* 'incense',[113] nor *qutāru* 'fumigant', is attested

---

105 For *serqu* see B.A. Levine, W.W. Hallo, *HUCA* 38 (1967), 52 sub DUB.DUB (Old Bab.); G.J.P. McEwan, *FAOS* 4, 169.

106 *TU* 44, I, 10; *TU* 46, obv. 18 (with *sarāqu*) and 28 // *SpTU* 4, no. 141, rev. 18; see also the Late Babylonian parallel from Babylon, F.H. Weissbach, *Misc.*, no.12, obv. 20 (a *serqu*-offering is scattered on a censer). Also from Babylon: BM 32206 +, III, 111.

107 *TU* 41, obv. 21, 26–27; *Bagh. Mitt. Beih.* 2, no. 5, rev. 19, cf. *KAR* 60, obv. 9 and similar in *KAR* 50, rev. 6; *RAcc.*, 140, 351–52; 142–4, 392–94. Fumigation also in the *mīs pî*-ritual text *Bagh. Mitt. Beih.* 2, no. 1 (+//), 19 (NÍG.NA DUB-*aq*).

For these phrases with *saqāru* and *šakānu*, see W.R. Mayer, in *OrNS* 47 [1978], 453, in *OrNS* 56 [1987], 207 sub *nignakku* a, in *OrNS* 60 [1991], 112 sub *sarāqu* A, and in *OrNS* 63 (1994), 114.

108 *TU* 39, rev. 4; 6; *TU* 42 +, rev. 34′, 35′; *TU* 41, obv. 10–11; rev. 30, 32.

109 *Bagh. Mitt. Beih.* 2, no. 1 (+//), 18.

110 ib., 21–22.

111 Perhaps with one exception, in *TU* 40, obv. 12, see my comments on this line in the Appendix.

Compare Akk. *qatāru*/*qutturu* with Hebrew cognated verb קטר in the pi 'send offerings up in smoke' and hi. 'make (offerings) smoke'.

112 The burnt offering is discussed in III.7.3.

113 Cognate of the verb *qatāru*; see also קְטֹרֶת smoke of (burning) offering', also: incense, perfumes burned in the fire of offering. Cf. *AHw*, 930–31; *CAD*, Q, 324–5, sub 2. For *labānatu* 'frankincense', see the dictionaries *CAD*, L, 8b and *AHw*, 522a.

in the Hellenistic temple ritual texts,[114] which stands in contrast with Herodotus, who wrote (Histories, I, 183) that yearly 1000 talents of incense (λιβανωτός) were offered in the temple of Bēl in Babylon. We may presume however that aromatics in general (*riqqū*), at least in the Hellenistic period, also included incense.[115]

That the garden was the origin of these aromatics is well-known.[116] An indication whence the aromatics, used in the cult of Hellenistic Babylon, came, is given by an administrative text, *BRM* 1, 99, rev. 26–27 (// *CT* 49, 150, obv. 23–24): ^{giš}KIRI$_6$ ^{šim}LI *la-me-e* É {É} ^{d}*Gu-la* É.ḪUR.SAG.SIKIL.LA 'the garden of juniper surrounding the temple of Gula, Eḫursagsikilla'.[117]

As a source for the aromatics used in Hellenistic Uruk we have the garden of Eḫilianna, the shrine of Nanāja, probably in the Eanna-complex,[118] in *VS* 15, 13 (146 S.E.), obv. 3 and 6: ^{giš}KIRI$_6$ É.ḪI.IL.AN.NA 'the garden of Eḫil(i)anna'.[119]

III.6. Consecration, purification and washing

In order to perform the divine meal succesfully the offering site, and also everything which, and everyone who, participated in the meal had to be 'pure'. This was partly achieved by fumigation, which purifies the atmosphere,[120] but equally by performing consecrations, purifications, sweeping the ground and sprinkling with water, everything else was made pure. Furthermore, the priest who performed the ritual purified himself by washing.

According to the Hellenistic temple ritual texts these religious activities could take place at different moments during the divine meal.[121] In this section these activities will be discussed.

III.6.1. *Consecration*

The Hellenistic temple ritual texts on occasion refer to a ritual act called *ḫub bīti* 'the consecration of the temple'. It is well attested for the public cult in texts from the Neo-Assyrian[122] and Hellenistic periods.

---

114 Other than *Bagh. Mitt. Beih.* 2, no. 6, obv. 20 (NÍG.NA // *qutrīnu*), actually a Hellenistic bilingual *šuillakku-* (hand-raising) prayer, which therefore represents an older tradition and cannot be used as evidence for the Hellenistic period.

115 This is supported by the lexical list *LTBA* 2, 1 VI 22 f. // 2, 358 f.: *zi-i-bu* = *qut-rin/ri-in-nu*, *qutrinnu* = ^{giš}ŠIM.MEŠ/*ri-qu-u*. Note that some of the known aromatics, such as *ladnu*, *qunnabu*, *kaṣiṣiḫatu* and *suādu*, are mentioned in the Hellenistic kettledrum ritual text *TU* 44, IV, 5 ff.

116 Cf. *CAD*, K, 414–15 sub c and *AHw*, 485a.

117 See also A.R. George, *BTT*, 306. This garden is also known from the astronomical diaries from Babylon, cf. A.J. Sachs–H. Hunger, *Diaries*, no. -93, A, rev. 25 and no. -79, obv. 4′.

118 See A. Falkenstein, *Topographie*, 41.

119 See also my comments on *TU* 39, obv. 4. Note that in a recently published private document from Uruk, dated 11 S.E. (*SpTU* 5, no. 308), uncultivated lands (*nidûtu*) of Nanāja are turned into garden and arable land (rev. 15).

120 See III.5.

121 See G.J.P. McEwan, *FAOS* 4, 166.

122 See G. van Driel, *Cult of Aššur*, 169 and the dictionaries *CAD* and *AHw* sub *ḫâbu*. A rare Neo-Babylonian example is *LKU*, no. 51, rev. 28.

In Hellenistic Babylon during the New Year festival, on the fifth day of the month Nisannu, first the temple complex Esagila was consecrated (*ḫâbu*),[123] and then Ezida, the cella of Nabû, was consecrated, in the last case by using the censer (*nignakku*), the torch (*gizillû*) and the holy water-basin (*egubbû*).[124] In Hellenistic Uruk the Rēš-temple was consecrated during the second New Year festival on the seventh day of Tašrītu.[125] During the Uruk building ritual the temple was consecrated with *takpertu*-purifications,[126] which illustrates the close connection between consecration and purification.

Objects could also be consecrated. In the beginning of the Uruk text describing what occured during a night vigil, the Scepter, which plays an important part in the ritual, is consecrated by the exorcist (*āšipu*).[127] In the Uruk kettledrum ritual a censer and torch are used to consecrate the bull[128] and the kettledrum.[129]

III.6.2. *Purification*

The importance of purifications is underlined by the fact that they are mentioned in the colophon of *TU* 38, detailing the daily offering practice in Uruk. Rev. 44–45 mention 'the pure *šuluḫḫu*-purification rites' (ŠU.LUḪ.ḪA KÙ.MEŠ) and 'the divine *šuluḫḫu*-purification rites of the Rēš-temple, the Ešgal-temple, the Eanna-temple and the (other) temples of Tiranna' (ŠU.LUḪ.ḪA DINGIR.RA *šá* É *re-eš* ÈŠ.GAL É.AN.NA *ù* É.MEŠ TIR.AN.NA^{ki}).[130]

takpertu and kuppuru

We already referred to the *takpertu*-purifications in connection with the verb *ḫâbu*. However, *takpertu* is also used with the cognate verb *kuppuru* (D-stem of *kapāru*) 'to purify'. The earliest references go back to the Old Babylonian period, but the purification is best attested in the Neo-Assyrian and Neo-Babylonian periods.[131] In the Late Babylonian Uruk eclipse of the moon text the priest must purify all the temples, and especially Edumununna, the temple of the moongod Sîn, with *takpertu*-purifications. The next day these purifications, together with a magic circle of flour (*zisurrû*) and a *garakku*-brazier, are thrown into the river.[132]

---

123 *RAcc.*, 140, 340 ff.

124 *RAcc.*, 140, 346 ff. For the *gizillû* see the dictionaries and St. M. Maul, *Zukunftsbewältigung*, Register, s.v. Fackel. For the *egubbû* see III.6.2.

125 *TU* 39, obv. 13.

126 *TU* 45, rev. 23–4, and the parallel *TU* 46, rev. 13. In the latter the object is not the temple but 'that emplacement' (KI.BI). See also the Hellenistic astronomical omen-text *BRM* 4, 19 (// 20), rev. 30: '(it is a favourable day) to purify the temple' (É *ana ḫu-ub-bi*). For *takpertu* see III.6.2.

127 *TU* 41, obv. 4.

128 *TU* 44, I, 30–31; II, 12–13.

129 *TU* 44, III, 20–21; 26. See also BM 32206 +, I, 12 (context not clear).

130 *šuluḫḫu*-purification rites for Anu and Ištar on a unknown day of the 6th month Ulūlu are also attested in the Uruk cultic calendar text K 3753, obv. I, 15. A Graeco-Babyloniaca fragment from Babylon, VAT 412 (M.J. Geller, *ZA* 87 (1997), 78–9, no. 13), palaeographically dated to the time of Tiberius(!), reads perhaps in obv. 5′: ⸢*par-ṣi*⸣ ŠU.⸢LUḪ⸣.ḪA[.MEŠ]. However, because according to Geller VAT 412 is probably a school text (containing extracts copied from other sources) we cannot use this passage as evidence for Babylonian cult practices in the first century A.D.

131 See the dictionaries *CAD* and *AHw* sub *takpe/irtu* and *kapāru*.

132 *BRM* 4, 6, rev. 32–33 and 37. Note that *takpertu*-purifications together with burnt offerings are also attested

For the use of *kuppuru* without the noun *takpertu* we have two examples in the Hellenistic temple ritual texts. Firstly, in a Uruk building ritual text it is said that an exorcist and a lamentation priest will purify the city.[133] Secondly, in the Esagila ritual text describing the New Year festival of the month Nisannu in Babylon, after the consecration of Ezida, the cella of Nabû (see III.6.1), an exorcist purifies the cella by using the carcass of a sheep, after which it is thrown into the river.[134]

tēliltu and elēlu

For the purification called *tēliltu* we have many references from the Middle and Neo-Assyrian, but only a few from the Neo-Babylonian period.[135] For the Hellenistic period only two examples, both from cultic calendar texts, are known, but the context in both cases is not clear.[136] However, the cognate verb *elēlu* (in D- and Dt-stem) is attested several times in the Hellenistic corpus in connection with the temple. In the Uruk kettledrum ritual the bull, the hide of which is used to cover the kettledrum, and the kettledrum itself are purified.[137] In the Uruk building ritual the king purifies himself.[138]

šabāṭu and qadāšu

The ground had to be sweeped (*šabāṭu*) in order to clear the offering site. This is attested in the Uruk kettledrum ritual (*tašabbiṭ*, written SAR, 'you will sweep')[139] and is a form of purification, as is illustrated by the duplicate, which reads instead: *tu-⸢qád⸣-da-áš* 'you will make ritually clean' (*qadāšu* D-stem).[140] The ground is also sweeped in the Uruk *mīs-pî*-ritual,[141] and in the Uruk building ritual the roof of the temple is sweeped.[142] This activity is also attested in a late Neo-Babylonian Uruk ritual for the king.[143]

salāḫu and sarāqu

After the ground was sweeped, it was sprinkled with water, in order to make the dust settle; this makes sprinkling a part of the purification activities.

---

in Neo-Assyrian letters dealing with the substitute king (*šar pūḫi*) ritual, which are probably performed to avert evil portended by an eclipse on the king (see II.7), e.g. S. Parpola, *LAS* I, 167.

133 *TU* 45, rev. 12.

134 *RAcc.*, 140–41, 353 ff. Cf. W.G. Lambert, in *OLA* 55 (1993), 201.

135 *AHw*, 1344–45. The expression *te-lil-te ú-lal* 'he performs the purification' is not attested in the Hellenistic temple rituals. Cognate with *elēlu* is the *mullilu*, a sprinkler used for purification; it is used during the Hellenistic Babylon ritual of Kislīmu in Esagila (BM 32206 +, obv. I, 22).

136 *SBH* VIII, II, 2 (Babylon); K 3753, I, 21 (Uruk).

137 *TU* 44, II, 12; III, 21.

138 *TU* 45, obv. 17. We also find *elēlu* in *RAcc.*, 142, 378, in a 'cry of distress' (*ikkillu*), and in *BRM* 4, 7, rev. 30, the incipit of the incantation 'The temple has been purified', but these represent older traditions and cannot be used as evidence for the Hellenistic period.

139 *TU* 44, I, 8.

140 *Bagh. Mitt. Beih.* 2, no. 5, obv. 8.

141 *Bagh. Mitt. Beih.* 2, no. 1 (+//), 3. The *mīs-pî*-ritual is discussed in III.6.3.

142 *TU* 45, obv. [6] // *TU* 46, obv. [7] // *Bagh. Mitt. Beih.* 2, no. 10, obv. 8–9. See also my comments on these lines in the Appendix.

143 *LKU*, no. 48, obv. 1.

The verb *salāḫu* (SÙ) 'to sprinkle' is used in connection with several locations: the Esagila-temple and Ezida, the cella of Nabû, were sprinkled with water from a well along the Tigris and a well along the Euphrates during the New Year festivities in Babylon.[144] Pure water was sprinkled on the roof of a temple in the building ritual in Uruk,[145] and in the same ritual in the open country or on the bank of a river.[146] Pure water was also sprinkled during the kettledrum ritual on the ground in the workshop (*bīt mummi*), where the bull, whose hide was used to cover the kettledrum, is placed.[147] Also note that water from the holy water-basin was sprinkled on the bull.[148]

Furthermore in the Uruk kettledrum ritual cedar balsam (*dam erēni*) was sprinkled for purification purposes on the bull itself,[149] and on the (still uncovered) kettledrum.[150]

And finally, an unknown substance was used to sprinkle the temple during the last phase of the Uruk eclipse of the moon ritual.[151]

Also scattering (*sarāqu*) juniper on the heart of the bull during the Uruk kettledrum ritual must have had purification purposes.[152]

On two occasions *sarāqu* is used without object: during the Uruk New Year festival and during a special festival for Ištar of Uruk aromatics presumably were scattered 'on the place where (the god) is made to accept the offering', after which offerings follow.[153] If we assume correctly that aromatics are the object, then these two passages may be connected with purification.

Furthermore, good oil was sprinkled on the torch used during the night vigil festivities,[154] all kinds of aromatics (*riqqū kalama*) and powder(?) of cedar (*qēm erēni*) were scattered during the Uruk *mīs pî*-ritual.[155]

egubbû

In the descriptions of the divine meal we often encounter the holy water-basin (*egubbû*, dugA.GÚB.BA). Water from this basin was used for purifying everything which was used during the divine meal.[156]

---

144 *RAcc.*, 140, 341–2 and 348–9.

145 *TU* 45, obv. 7; rev. 20, and the parallels *TU* 46, obv. 8, *Bagh. Mitt. Beih.* 2, no. 10, obv. 9, *Bagh. Mitt. Beih.* 2, no. 11, rev. fragment 2, 3′ (for this fragment see my comments on rev. 6–13 of *TU* 45, in the Appendix).

146 *TU* 45, rev. 8.

147 *TU* 44, I, 8 (cf. I, 35); *Bagh. Mitt. Beih.* 2, no. 5, obv. 8.

148 *Bagh. Mitt. Beih.* 2, no. 5, rev. 18; *KAR* 60, obv. 7.

149 TU *44*, II, 12.

150 *Bagh. Mitt. Beih.* 2, no. 5, rev. 22.

151 BM 134701, obv. 21.

152 *KAR* 60, obv. 15 (Neo-Assyrian), with the parallel *Bagh. Mitt. Beih.* 2, no. 5 (Hellenistic), rev. 23. Compare this with *saḫāpu* 'to overturn' a golden *malītu*-bowl of *maṣḫatu*-flour over the heart of an ox (*TU* 39, obv. 32, *TU* 40, rev. 2, *TU* 42 +, obv. 31′).

153 *TU* 39, obv. 30; *TU* 42 +, obv. 28′.

154 *TU* 41, obv. 29.

155 *Bagh. Mitt. Beih.* 2, no. 1 (+//), 8; 22.

156 Cf. *CAD*, E, 49bf.; ib., K, 171a, sub *kutunnu*; *AHw*, 17a, and 440b, with many references from earlier periods. See also St. M. Maul, *Zukunftsbewältigung*, Register, s.v. Weiwassergefäß (*agubbû*). For the Neo-Assyrian period see G. van Driel, *Cult of Aššur*, 167–8.

The holy water-basin-ceremony is well attested in temple ritual texts from the Hellenistic period. It is one of the ceremonies, mentioned in the Uruk text *TU* 38,[157] from which it becomes clear that loaves and cakes and oxen and sheep apparently were used during the ceremony. We also know of an incantation incipit 'From the pure holy water-basin', recited during the New Year festival of the month Tašrītu in Uruk.[158]

As we saw above, during the New Year festivities of Nisannu in Babylon it was used together with the censer and the torch to consecrate Ezida, the cella of Nabû in Esagila.[159] Furthermore, in the Uruk text which describes the night vigil festivities, the exorcist must extinguish the torch with water from the holy water-basin (together with beer, milk, wine and oil).[160] In the Uruk eclipse of the moon ritual first all the temples are purified, then the statue of Sîn is robed, after which a holy water-basin is set up and incantations are recited.[161]

Finally, the holy water-basin was used on a number of occasions during the Uruk kettledrum ritual: after two holy water-basins for the gods Kusu and Ningirim have been set up, offering tables are placed and food is served.[162] With water from the holy water-basin of Ningirim the offering accoutrements are purified,[163] and the bull is sprinkled with water from the holy water-basin.[164] After the bull is slaughtered the kettledrum itself, after being consecrated by using the censer and torch, is purified with water from the holy water-basin.[165]

III.6.3. *Washing*

In the Hellenistic temple ritual texts several kinds of washing activities are attested. Although we only have a few examples of washing expressed by the verbs *ramāku* or *mesû*, there are many references to hand-washing (*mê qāti*). This hand-washing was intended to cleanse the body of the priest who performs the ritual. It made the priest 'pure' and allowed him to proceed with the rest of the ritual, which sometimes contained another washing activity, the 'washing of the mouth' (*mīs pî*). This ritual had to be performed on the divine protagonist of the ritual, which could be either the statue of the god, an animal like the bull, or even an object like the torch. We will discuss these washing activities here.

---

157 Obv. 37; rev. 37; see II.1.
158 *BRM* 4, 7, obv. 13.
159 *RAcc.*, 140, 347. See III.6.1.
160 *TU* 41, rev. 19.
161 *BRM* 4, 6, rev. 33′.
162 *TU* 44, I, 16. Cf. also I, 28 and 34.
163 *TU* 44, II, 2.
164 Only attested in the duplicates *Bagh. Mitt. Beih.* 2, no. 5, rev. 18 // *KAR* 60, obv. 7.
165 *TU* 44, III, 21. Cf. IV, 29.
The context is less clear in W 18728 (A. Falkenstein, *UVB* 15 [1959], 40–44), rev. 16′. The holy water basin is also attested in the astronomical diaries from Babylon: No. -173, A, rev. 2–3, mentioned together with offerings; No. -200, A, rev. 16, in the cella of Bēl in Esagila.

Washing with river water

From the large temple ritual text describing days 2–5 of the New Year festival of the month Nisannu in Babylon, we know that at the beginning of every day the high priest (*aḫu rabû*) began by washing himself (*ramāku*, written TU_5) with river water, on one occassion specified as coming from the Tigris and Euphrates, after which he removes the curtain for the god Bēl and recites a prayer.[166]

Hand-washing

mê qāti našû

In Akkadian 'hand-washing' can be expressed in different ways. Firstly, there are references to *mê qāti našû* (written A.MEŠ $ŠU^{II}$ ÍL) 'to lift up the water (basin) for (the washing of) the hands'.[167] It is attested in the Uruk New Year festivals of Tašrītu[168] and Nisannu,[169] in the Uruk ritual text describing a special festival for Ištar,[170] and in the Uruk text describing the night vigil.[171] It is also attested in the Kislīmu ritual of Esagila in Babylon.[172] On one occassion the basins used are identified as 2 *kallu*-bowls and a golden *šulpu*-vessel.[173] They were probably placed on offering tables.[174]

These references state that the priest must 'lift up the water (basin) for (the washing of) the hands' for one or more deities after which, we assume, the priest proceeded by washing his hands; although this is never stated as such, it seems likely since often no further use of the water is indicated. We also assume that *mê qāti* is intended in the first place for the priest, as is specifically stated in one case.[175] However, the texts sometimes continue by indicating that the priest then 'sprinkles the king and the other persons'.[176] It is not impossible that *mê qāti* is also used for this, because there is a connection between *mê qāti* and the king: during the New Year festival of Nisannu in Babylon a water (basin) for (the washing of) the hands is moved in front of the king,[177] which may suggest that hand-washing was also performed by the king. Supporting evidence comes from a speech later on in the ritual, during which the high priest advises the king: 'At the opening of the gate ceremony, cleanse [your] hands [...]![178]'.

---

166 *RAcc.*, 129, 2; 132, 158; 133, 218; 136, 286 (in the later case: from the Tigris and Euphrates).

167 Cf. *CAD*, M/II, 155b, sub 3; *AHw*, 664b, 4, a. In the Assyrian rituals the expression *mê qāti ana* DN (*ana* LUGAL) *qurrubu* (instead of *našû*) is more common, e.g. in the rituals for the singer (*zammāru*), *BBR* 2, nos. 60–70.

168 *TU* 39, obv. 22, 29, 33; *TU* 40, obv. 3, 6, 20, rev. 3, 4; *TU* 39, rev. 12, 16.

169 *KAR* 132, I, 24, III,17, IV, 11.

170 *TU* 42 +, obv. 28′, 32′, rev. 26′.

171 *TU* 41, obv. 18, 24, 32.

172 BM 32206 +, II, 55, 81 and 83 (*šá* A.MEŠ 'the water rites'), III, 128, IV, 158 on day 4 of Kislīmu.

173 *TU* 40, rev. 4.

174 *TU* 41, obv. 22–24, 32, although this may not have been the rule.

175 Namely the chief singer of dirges (*galamāḫu*), in *TU* 40, obv. 3.

176 The verb *lapātu* (in D-stem) is probably used to expres 'to sprinkle': *TU* 39, obv. 23; 34; *TU* 40, obv. 20; rev. 4; *KAR* 132, III, 18; IV, 11; *TU* 42 +, obv. 32′; rev. 26′. For *lapātu* 'to sprinkle' instead of 'to smear' see my comments on *TU* 39, obv. 23 and *TU* 41, obv. 10, in the Appendix.

177 *RAcc.*, 144, 413.

178 *RAcc.*, 145, 440.

mê kunnu and mê našû

References to *mê qāti* are not attested in the Uruk temple rituals for the lamentation priest (*kalû*), i.e. the kettledrum ritual and the building ritual. We have instead in these texts many references to 'setting up the water (basin)' (*mê kunnu*) before drawing the curtains shut, and 'lifting up (i.e. removing) the water (basin)' (*mê našû*) after the curtains are loosened again.[179] Although the function of this water basin is never specifically indicated, we know that it was for hand-washing. In IV R^2, 23, no. 1 +, a Neo-Assyrian list of recitations, which had to be performed during the different stages of the kettledrum ritual, one section is concerned with setting up the water basin and drawing shut the curtains[180]: at this moment a bilingual recitation, beginning with the words:

> 3 [ŠU LUḪ.ḪA ME.E]N ŠU LUḪ.ḪA ME.EN 4 [*qa-ti-ka m*]*i-si qa-ti-ka mi-si*
> '3–4. [W]ash [your hands], wash your hands!'[181]

has to be performed, which clearly suggests a connection with hand-washing.

tēbibti qāti

The ceremony called 'the cleansing of the hands' (*tēbibti qāti*) is attested only once in Hellenistic temple ritual texts. We already referred to this ceremony taking place on the 16th of Ṭebētu in the sanctuary on top of the temple tower in Uruk.[182]

mīs pî

The statue of a god was made, i.e. given birth to, with great care. In order to endow the statue with life it was subjected to rituals and incantations. Two of these were the 'washing of the mouth' (*mīs pî*) and the 'opening of the mouth' (*pīt pî*), which together enabled the statue to eat the foodstuffs and drink the liquids served during the divine meal. While *pīt pî* is not attested in the Hellenistic temple ritual texts, we have some evidence for *mīs pî*.[183] Four texts from Uruk are known;[184] they probably fall into the

---

179 Kettledrum ritual: *TU* 44, II, 7 // *Bagh. Mitt. Beih.* 2, no. 5, obv. 15, rev. 26 // *KAR* 60, obv. 2, rev. 4. Building ritual: *TU* 45, obv. 11, 14 // *TU* 46, obv. 9, 13, rev. 7 // *Bagh. Mitt. Beih.* 2, no. 10, obv. 16, 20.

180 Cf. IV, 1 f. and 2 f.

181 The washing of the hands activities called *mīs qāti* are not attested elsewhere in the Hellenistic temple ritual texts.

182 In the Uruk text *TU* 38, rev. 32–34, see the introduction of II.3. For *tēbibtu* see *AHw*, 1341b. *Tēbibtu* is found in an Uruk *mīs pî*-ritual text: we learn that not only priests, but also the king and people could perform the *tēbibtu*, *Bagh. Mitt. Beih.* 2, no. 1 (+ //), 27. It is also attested for an unknown day of the 6th month Ulūlu, in the Uruk cultic calendar text K 3753, obv. I, 21 (broken context). The cognate verb *ebēbu* (in Dt-stem) is also used, in the Uruk building ritual *TU* 45, obv. 17 // *Bagh. Mitt. Beih.* 2, no. 1, fragment 2, 5′. One example of *tēbibtu* from Babylon is known: in the astronomical diary A.J. Sachs–H. Hunger, *Diaries*, no. 141, C, obv. 11′–12′, the cleansing ceremony is mentioned in connection with the lamentation priests. It was performed on the 17th of the second month Ajjaru, but the context is not clear.

183 Cf. *CAD*, M/II, 112a, b; *AHw*, 659a, 3, with references. See V. Hurowitz, *HUCA* 60 (1989), 48–73 and A. Berlejung, *Die Theologie der Bilde*r, Orbis Biblicus et Orientalis 162, Freiburg Schweitz, 1998, 178 ff. with earlier literature. See also P.J. Boden, *The Mesopotamian Washing of the Mouth* (*mīs pî*) *Ritual*, Baltimore, 1998. For the Hellenistic period see G.J.P. McEwan, *FAOS* 4, 164–5.

184 *Bagh. Mitt. Beih.* 2, no. 1 // no. 2 // no. 3, and no. 4, cf. W.R. Mayer, *OrNS* 47 (1978), 443–458.

Hellenistic period,[185] and describe the end of the *mīs pî*-ritual. Although the ritual appears to be in many ways unchanged in comparison with the earlier Assur version of the ritual, there are also some new elements,[186] in particular the appearance of the brushwood pile (*abru*), which is set on fire,[187] the references to lamentations, which have to be recited by the lamentation priest,[188] and the appearance of the king with or without the people.[189]

The *mīs pî*-ritual could also be performed on objects other than the statue of a god.[190] In the Uruk text *TU* 41, describing the festivities performed during a night vigil, the *mīs pî*-ritual was performed on a large torch, which was one of the protagonists in the night vigil festivities;[191] the interpretation of the ritual in this case is difficult. Furthermore, in the Uruk kettledrum ritual the *mīs pî*-ritual could be performed on a bull, the hide of which was used the cover the kettledrum,[192] and on the kettledrum itself.[193] The Neo-Assyrian catalogue of recitations which had to be performed during the kettldrum ritual, IV R^2, 23, no. 1 +, also describes (III, 23) which recitations had to be performed when the washing of the mouth ritual on the kettledrum was to be performed.

III.7. Offerings and libations

An important phase in the divine meal was the presentation of foodstuffs and liquids as offerings. In this section we shall first analyse how and what was served to the deities in the temples. Then we shall examine which offerings and libations are attested, concentrating on the terminology used in the Hellenistic temple ritual texts. We shall discuss the food and drink offerings and the burnt offering.[194]

---

185 According to W.R. Mayer, *Bagh. Mitt. Beih.* 2, p. 13.

186 Especially *TuL*, no. 27, cf. W.R. Mayer, *OrNS* 47 (1978), 444, with n. 37.

187 Attested in the Uruk text *TU* 41, describing the night vigil, and the Uruk building ritual (*TU* 45 and parallels).

188 Well-known from the Uruk building ritual and the eclipse of the moon ritual.

189 Passim in all the Uruk New Year texts, but also in the Uruk building ritual and the eclipse of the moon ritual.

Several lamentations are attested in the *mīs pî*-ritual texts, which are also known from other texts:

taqribtu: NIRGAL (LU) EDE 'Respected one, manifest one', in *Bagh. Mitt. Beih.* 2, no. 1 (+ //), 29. Also attested in K 2724 +, obv. 2; see M.E. Cohen, *Lamentations*, 21 ff. and 468 ff.; URSAGGAL ANNI ŠERMALLA ILLA 'Great warrior, hero in the Heaven, elevated', in *Bagh. Mitt. Beih.* 2, no. 1 (+ //), 12. As *taqribtu* in K 2724 +, obv. 12, as *eršemakku* in IV R^2, 53, III, 17.

eršemakku: DILMUN NIGINNA 'Important one, who wanders abound', in *Bagh. Mitt. Beih.* 2, no. 1 (+ //), 24; 26; also in the kettledrum ritual and the building ritual texts, see II.5 and 2.6; EŠABḪUNGATA 'The heart of the temple will be calmed down', in *Bagh. Mitt. Beih.* 2, no. 1 (+ //), 24; 26; (+ //), 30 f. Also attested in the building ritual texts, see II.6; UMUN BARAKUGA 'Lord of the pure Dais' (*Bagh. Mitt. Beih.* 2, no. 1 (+ //), 9); also in the building ritual text *TU* 46; UŠUM GUD NUA 'Dragon, recumbent (resting) bull', in *Bagh. Mitt. Beih.* 2, no. 1 (+ //), 12, cf. W.R. Mayer, *OrNS* 47 (1978), 452, n. 42; M.E. Cohen, *Eršemma*, 42–47.

190 See A. Berlejung, *Die Theologie der Bilde*r, Orbis Biblicus et Orientalis 162, Freiburg Schweitz, 1998, 182 ff.

191 Obv. 29.

192 *TU* 44, II, 8 // *Bagh. Mitt. Beih.* 2, no. 5, rev. 18 // *KAR* 60, obv. 7.

193 *TU* 44, III, 23.

194 The *ḫitpu*-offering was already discussed in connection with the *lubuštu*-ceremony, see II.3.3. For the funerary offering (*kispu*) see II.7.1. *Taklīmu* 'shew offering' is not attested in Hellenistic temple ritual texts; we only have an example in a Hellenistic bilingual hymn to Šamaš (W 18828, A. Falkenstein, *UVB* 15 [1959], 36 ff., obv. 13). Not attested in texts from the Hellenistic period are the *qinītu*-offering (*AHw*; *CAD*: *kīnajātu*)

III.7. *Offerings and libations*

III.7.1. *The presentation of the offerings*

Serving foodstuffs and liquids as offering

There are several verbs which are used to describe the presentation of the offerings before the god in the temple.[195]

Sarāqu 'to scatter' is used in the descriptions of the Uruk kettledrum ritual, in connection with dates and *sasqû*-flour,[196] loaves of barley and emmer bread and a *mirsu*-confection (made with honey, ghee, dates and *sasqû*-flour),[197] and barley seed.[198] It is also used in the Uruk building ritual texts, in connection with emmer bread, dates and *sasqû*-flour;[199] and all (kinds of) barley seed (*zēru kalama*).[200] And it is attested in the Uruk *mīs pî*-ritual, in connection with barley seed.[201]

Šakānu 'to place' in general is used with the same food products. In the kettledrum ritual it is used with barley bread and emmer bread and a *mirsu*-confection (made with honey, ghee, dates and *sasqû*-flour),[202] and furthermore with barley and emmer malt,[203] and with beer.[204] In the building ritual and the *mīs pî*-ritual it is used with the *mirsu*-confection made with honey, ghee, dates, *sasqû*-flour and pressed oil.[205]

---

and the *zību*-offering. *Siltu* is some kind of food which can be presented as an offering (*CAD*, S, 267, *AHw*, 1044a). It is attested only once in the Hellenistic ritual text corpus, in *TU* 39, obv. 13, together with the *guqqû*-offering. Perhaps *siltu* is cognate with the Hebrew/Aramaic noun סֹלֶת 'wheat groats'.

195 In the Hellenistic prebend texts from Uruk we often find the verb *elû* (E_{11}) 'to come up, to go up' in the Š-stem 'to bring up', in the context of bringing food up to the table (*paššūru*) in front of the divine statue(s). See II.3.1 and II.4.1 where the relevant passage have been discussed.

196 Only in the Aššur duplicate *KAR* 50, rev. 3 (Neo-Assyrian).

197 *Bagh. Mitt. Beih.* 2, no. 5, obv. 12–13, and IV R², 23, no. 1 +, III, 26–27 (Neo-Assyrian).

198 *TU* 44, II, 4.

199 Only in the Babylon duplicate F.H. Weissbach, *Misc.*, no. 12, obv. 7–8 (Late Babylonian).

200 *TU* 45, obv. 9–10; *TU* 46, obv. 9; 16; rev. 4; *Bagh. Mitt. Beih.* 2, no. 10, obv. 13–14; the Late Babylonian parallel F.H. Weissbach, *Misc.*, no. 12, obv. 10.

Blome suggested (*Opfermaterie*, 274–76) that *zēra sarāqu* (ŠE.NUMUN DUB) and *zēra kalama sarāqu* (ŠE.NUMUN DÙ.A.BI DUB) are general phrases: the object ŠE.NUMUN stands for 'offering material for fumigation' and the verb DUB for 'burning on a censer'. However, barley seed belongs to the food products and not to the aromatics, which explains why it is never mentioned in connection with the censer. Furthermore, we always find the expression in the context of offerings of meat and libations. Also, almost always before the scattering of barley seed, the phrase *nignak(ki) burāši šakānu* is used (see III.5.1), which indicates that only the latter phrase refers to fumigation.

201 *Bagh. Mitt. Beih.* 2, no. 1 (+ //), 16; *Bagh. Mitt. Beih.* 2, no. 3 (duplicate of *Bagh. Mitt. Beih.* 2, no. 1), 2′.

202 *TU* 44, I, 17–18; *KAR* 50, rev. 4.

203 *Bagh. Mitt. Beih.* 2, no. 5, obv. 14.

204 *TU* 44, I, 15.

205 *TU* 45, obv. 8; *Bagh. Mitt. Beih.* 2, no. 10, obv. 11–12; *Bagh. Mitt. Beih.* 2, no. 1 (+ //), 14–15(1?).

Rakāsu 'to arrange' is attested in the Uruk night vigil ritual with beef, mutton, and fowl;[206] in the *mīs pî*-ritual with emmer bread;[207] and in the Uruk description of the daily offerings with beer and wine.[208]

The use of *ṭuḫḫû* (D-stem of *ṭeḫû*)' to bring near'[209] is restricted to shoulder, *ḫimṣu*-omentum, roasted meat. Only in the Uruk temple rituals is it used for the lamentation priest in the context of the kettledrum ritual,[210] the building ritual,[211] and the *mīs pî*-ritual.[212]

Qerēbu 'to be served' is attested with food products such as milk, loaves, cakes, oil, dates, figs, raisins, and meat like oxen, sheep, mutton, beef, fowl, in the Uruk description of food offerings,[213] in one of the Uruk New Year texts[214] and in the description of the night vigil ritual[215] in connection with meals,[216] and in the Babylon New Year text it is used in connection with leftovers of the offering table of Madānu.[217]

Qurrubu 'to serve' (D-stem of *qerēbu*) is also attested in one of the Uruk New Year texts, this time in connection with meal and hot roasted meat,[218] and in a description of a special festival for Ištar of Uruk, also with meal and hot roasted meat.[219] Examples of *qerēbu* / *qurrubu* used with liquids are rare in Hellenistic temple ritual texts, contrary to the case with Neo-Assyrian rituals.[220]

Finally, the verb *kunnu* (D-stem of *kânu*) 'to set up' is only connected with (containers holding) beer, wine, and milk, and is attested in the Uruk description of daily offerings,[221] in the night vigil ritual text,[222] in the kettledrum ritual texts,[223] the building ritual texts[224] and in the *mīs pî*-ritual text.[225]

Šūtuqu and šubū'u

We have listed several ways in which the texts describe the serving of foodstuffs and liquids to the gods. However, Oppenheim pointed out that offered food was sometimes

---

206 *TU* 41, obv. 19, 25.
207 *Bagh. Mitt. Beih.* 2, no. 1 (+ //), 14.
208 *TU* 38, obv. 2, 17.
209 In Middle and Neo-Assyrian rituals for *ṭuḫḫû* usually *apālu* 'to present food offerings' is used, see the dictionaries *CAD* and *AHw* for examples.
210 *TU* 44, I, 31–32, II, 3–4, 6, 34–35, III, 19; *Bagh. Mitt. Beih.* 2, no. 5, obv. 14; *KAR* 50, rev. 5; IV R^2, 23, no. 1 +, III, 28.
211 *TU* 45, rev. 9–10; 22; *Bagh. Mitt. Beih.* 2, no. 10, obv. 3–4.
212 *Bagh. Mitt. Beih.* 2, no. 1 (+ //), 6–7; 10–11; 21; 25–26; 33–34. *Bagh. Mitt. Beih.* 2, no. 3 (dupl. of *Bagh. Mitt. Beih.* 2, no. 1), 7′–8′, 8′–9′(?). See also the late Neo-Babylonian ritual for the king *LKU* 48 (VAT 14521), obv. 4 and 10.
213 *TU* 38, obv. 7, 35, 42, 50, rev. 3, 39, 40, 41; 42.
214 *TU* 39, rev. 4, 6, 8, 12, 13, 14, 20.
215 *TU* 41, obv. 12, 14, rev. 29, 30.
216 See also the Neo-Babylonian ritual *LKU* 51 (VAT 14524), obv. 6, 25, rev. 9 (meal).
217 *RAcc.*, 133, 212.
218 *TU* 39, obv. 25.
219 *TU* 42 +, obv. 20′, 21′.
220 E.g. in the rituals for the singer (*zammāru*), *BBR* 2, nos. 60–70.
221 *TU* 38, obv. 20 (vases).
222 *TU* 41, obv. 20; 25.
223 *TU* 44, I, 19; *Bagh. Mitt. Beih.* 2, no. 5, obv. 13.
224 *TU* 45, obv. 9; *Bagh. Mitt. Beih.* 2, no. 10, obv. 13.
225 *Bagh. Mitt. Beih.* 2, no. 1 (+ //), 15.

also presented 'with a solemn ritual gesture, passing it in a swinging motion before the staring eyes of the image', comparing this with offering practices described in Egyptian religious texts and the Old Testament.[226] But what exactly was he referring to?

In the Mesopotamian ritual texts, we do know of several passages with *šūtuqu* (Š-stem of *etēqu*) 'to pass (objects) on, to move (objects) past (a person or another object)'.[227] Several occurrences of *ú-še-ti-iq* with *ana pa-ni* in Hellenistic ritual texts are attested.[228] However, on closer examination these cannot be the phrases which Oppenheim refers to. They all describe the passing on of offering dishes etc., which are in front of, or passed (from) before (*pāni*) one god, to (*ana pāni*) other gods, as for example in *TU* 39, obv. 25:

> '[25]He will pass the golden dish (from) before (*pa-ni*) Anu to (*ana pa-ni*) the (other) gods, who are in the Grand Courtyard'.

In texts from the Middle and Neo-Assyrian periods *šūtuqu* corresponds to the Babylonian verb *šubū'u* (*bâ'u* Š-stem) 'to move (an object) alongside (a person for ritual purposes)',[229] but the relevant examples of *šubū'u* in the Hellenistic temple ritual texts do not describe moving offerings in a swinging motion in front of a statue, but the moving of a censer and torch inside the temple,[230] or the moving of a water (basin) for (washing of) the hands in front of the king, and do not therefore parallels OT and Egyptian practices either.[231]

Fruit

Sometimes fruit (*inbu*) was used during the divine meal, 'adding an esthetic touch'.[232] See for example the Uruk temple ritual text *TU* 41, describing the night vigil festivities: after a golden offering table is set up for Anu and Antu of Heaven, and a water basin is brought for the washing of the hands, the table is arranged with meat, beer and wine. Then the text reads (obv. 20):

> 'You will provide all (kinds of) garden fruits (*inib kirî*) in abundance (*tu-šar-ra-aḫ*)'.

The text follows with the scattering of cedar needles(?) and *maṣḫatu*-flour on a golden censer. The ritual ends with a libation of wine. Then follows a similar ritual conducted on seven large golden offering tables for the seven planets (Jupiter, Venus, Mercury, Saturn, Mars, Moon and Sun), after which fruit from the garden plants is again used

---

226 A.L. Oppenheim, *Ancient Mesopotamia*, 192.
In the OT we find that not only placing an offering in front of a god, but also waving (תְּנוּפָה) and lifting up (תְּרוּמָה) in front of God or the altar was practised.

227 *CAD*, E, 391a, c.

228 *TU* 39, obv. 25; *KAR* 132, I, 2; 3; 4; *TU* 42 +, obv. 22′; 23′.

229 Cf. *CAD*, B, 181b sub 3, a; *AHw*, 117a, Š, 3.

230 *RAcc.*, 140, 343.

231 *RAcc.*, 144, 413.

232 A.L. Oppenheim, *Ancient Mesopotamia*, 188.

(obv. 26). A similar phrase is used in *TU* 12, an astrological text from Hellenistic Uruk, which is concerned with the zodiacal system.[233]

To slaughter an animal for offerings

To offer an animal for meat offerings means first having to slaughter it. Akkadian has several words for 'slaughtering' sacrificial animals, of which *nakāsu*,[234] *maḫāṣu*,[235] and *palāqu*[236] are attested in the Hellenistic temple rituals.[237] They are, however, unlike in ancient Israel,[238] 'entirely secular in overtones since there was no Kosher slaughtering in ancient Babylonia, and no custom of burning slaughtered victims to ashes'.[239]

III.7.2. *Food and drink offerings*

niqû-offerings

The Akkadian word most often used for 'offering' is *niqû*,[240] written syllabically and SISKUR or SÍSKUR. Often it is preceded by UDU.NÍTA, indicating that it usually consisted of sheep, although oxen and goats were also used. It is cognate with the verb *naqû* (BAL) 'to pour out (as a libation), to offer'. It is well-known from the Neo-Assyrian temple rituals, and Neo-Babylonian and Achaemenid administrative texts.[241]

In the Hellenistic temple ritual texts both sheep and cattle are attested as *niqû*-offering. We have a few examples of the phrases *niqâ naqû* 'to make an offering' (SÍSKUR BAL) and *niq alpi u immeri naqû* 'to make an offering of ox and sheep' (SÍSKUR GU_4 ù UDU.NÍTA BAL). They are all from Uruk and are attested in texts describing the New Year of the month Tašrītu, the special festival for Ištar, and the night vigil.[242] For the phrase *niqê naqû* 'to make a sheep offering' (udu.[níta].SÍSKUR BAL) there is more

[233] Obv. lower part, col. VI, last line reads: [GURUN] gišKIRI$_6$ *tu-šar-ra-aḫ* 'You will provide garden fruit in abundance'. For *TU* 12 see also II.2.3. For the garden see also III.5.2.

For fruit symbolizing aphrodisiacs, as George suggests, in a fragment related to the so-called Divine Love Lyrics, see II.8.5.

[234] *TU* 38, rev. 9; 11. Cf. the Neo-Babylonian temple ritual text VAT 14524, obv. 9, 17.

[235] *TU* 41, rev. 6.

[236] *TU* 44, II, 16; *Bagh. Mitt. Beih.* 2, no. 5, rev. 23; cf. he Neo-Assyrian parallel KAR 60, obv. 15.

[237] Not attested in Hellenistic temple ritual texts, although well-known from Assyrian rituals (see the dictionaries *CAD* and *AHw*) are *nasāḫu* and *ṭabāḫu*.

[238] Although there was both secular and sacred slaughtering, in a sense all slaughtering was religious, since meat with blood was not allowed to be eaten by humans (Gen. 9, 4; Lv. 3, 17; 7, 27; 27, 10). This is because blood (דָּם) is the soul, the power of life (Lv. 17, 14; Deut. 12, 23), or is the location of the soul (Lv. 17, 10–11); when blood is flowing out of the body, man or animal will die. Therefore all slaughtering was religious and had to be performed in a kosher manner. This 'blood consciousness', as Oppenheim called it (*Ancient Mesopotamia*, 192), is not paralleled in Mesopotamia. The concept of 'the life being in the blood' was known, but there was no general prohibition on the consuming of blood, nor of offering it, as, for example, was done by the king in *KAR* 146, rev. I, 10′.

[239] W.G. Lambert, in: *OLA* 55 (1993), 194.

[240] Cf. G.J.P. McEwan, *FAOS* 4, 169.

[241] See the dictionaries *CAD* and *AHw* sub *niqû* and *naqû*. An example of *niqû* from a Neo-Babylonian temple ritual text is VAT 14521, obv. 4.

[242] SÍSKUR: *TU* 39, obv. 30; *TU* 42 +, obv. 28′, 30′; *TU* 41, rev. 23. SÍSKUR GU_4 ù UDU.NÍTA: *TU* 39, rev. 6–7; *TU* 41, obv. 11; rev. 30–31 and 32.

evidence, but it is only attested in the Uruk temple rituals of the lamentation priest, i.e. the kettledrum ritual,[243] the building ritual,[244] and the *mīs pî*-ritual.[245]

Finally, from administrative documents,[246] chronicles[247] and the astronomical diaries[248] from Babylon we known that *niqû* remained important well into the Arsacid period. We find that in the diaries just as in the temple ritual texts sheep offerings are used side by side with offerings of cattle; together they are often referred to as *nindabû* 'food offering' (see below). These offerings are in most cases provided by a high official of Esagila, such as the administrator (*šatammu*) or his representative (*kūm šatammi*), sometimes performed in a specific place in the temple, e.g. the *dudē*-Gate or the 'Gate of the Son of the Prince'. Sometimes the offerings are used for the cult of the king and his family.[249]

naqû-libations

The verb which is usually used for libations[250] is *naqû* (BAL) 'to pour out'. It is well-known especially from the Assyrian rituals.[251]

In the Hellenistic temple ritual texts from Uruk we find *naqû*[252] with wine, beer, milk, honey, ghee, oil and cedar oil, in several different combinations. It is interesting that, with one exception,[253] all examples come from temple rituals for the lamentation

---

243 *TU* 44, II, 3; 5; 33; III, 18; *Bagh. Mitt. Beih.* 2, no. 5, obv. 13; cf. IV R², 23, no. 1 +, III, 27 (Nineveh, Neo-Assyrian).

244 *TU* 45, obv. [2]; [4]; 10; 18; 20; 25 (ᵘᵈᵘSÍSKUR GAL-ú); rev. 6; 9; 11; 17; 21; *TU* 46, 3; 5; 9; 16; rev. 4; *Bagh. Mitt. Beih.* 2, no. 10, obv. 3; 6; 14; *Bagh. Mitt. Beih.* 2, no. 11, obv. fragment 1, 5′; [7′](?); obv. fragment 2, 6′ (these fragments are discussed in my comments on *TU* 45, in the Appendix); F.H. Weissbach, *Misc.*, no. 12, obv. 4, 11 (Babylon, Late Babylonian).

245 *Bagh. Mitt. Beih.* 2, no. 1 (+ //), 6 (ᵘᵈᵘSÍSKUR ŠU.DU₇.MEŠ [*šuklulu*]); 10; 20; 25; 32 (⁽ᵘᵈᵘ⁾SÍSKUR GAL-*ú*); 33; *Bagh. Mitt. Beih.* 2, no. 3 (duplicate of *Bagh. Mitt. Beih.* 2, no. 1), 6′.

246 See for example *CT* 49, 151 (218 S.E.), an administrative text from the Arsacid period belonging to the so-called Raḫimesu archive (94–93 B.C.), which contains texts recording the income and expenditures of the temples. Obv. 6 refers to the 'offerings of the Day One temple', i.e. the *akītu*-temple (SÍSKUR.MEŠ *ina* É UD.1.KAM). Many of these administrative texts refer to (regular) offering sheep, indicating that for the temple expenditures sheep were primarily used as meat offering, e.g. AB 248 (= G.J.P. McEwan, *Iraq* 43 [1981], 141 ff.), obv. 6; *CT* 49, 150, obv. 29, rev. 39, 41, *CT* 49, 156, obv. 11; *BRM* 1, 99, obv. 11, rev. 31, 33, 45, 46; AB 244 (= G.J.P. McEwan, *Iraq* 43 [1981], 132 ff.), obv. 7, 13. The Raḫimesu archive was discussed by R.J. van der Spek, in: J. Wiesehöfer (ed.), *Das Partherreich und seine Zeugnisse*, 205–258.

247 See the Hellenistic chronicle 13b (A.K Grayson, *Chronicles*, 283 f., see II.4.5.2 and II.8.7), where 'The portions of the oxen and those (other) offerings (*niqû*) he designated for(?) the lamentation priests and the administrator (*šatammu*)' (8–9).

248 A.J. Sachs–H. Hunger, *Diaries*, no. -226, A, rev. 18; no. -204, C, rev. [18]; no. -187, A, rev. 5′, 13′; no. -178, C, rev. 20′; no. -173, A, rev. 3′; no. -171, B, rev. 6′; no. -170, A, obv. 1′; no. -160, C, obv. 6′(?); no. -158, C, obv. 6′; no. -144, rev. 18; no. -137, D, rev. 23, 27; no. -133, B and C, obv. 23′, 24′; no. -132, D_2, rev. 13′, 22′; no. -129, A_2, obv. 18′; 24′; no. -126, A, obv. 9, rev. 4, B, r ev. 7′; no. -125, A, rev. 6; no. -124, B, obv. 5′; rev. 19′; no. 111, B, 9′, 10′; no. -107, C, rev. 17′; no. -105, obv. A14′, B13′; no. -87, A, rev. 15′; no. -82, B, rev. 2′; no. -77, A, obv. 27′, 29′, rev. 30, B, rev. 15′.

249 See II.8.7.

250 For libations in general see F. Blome, *Opfermaterie*, 298–341; J. Danmanville, *RA* 49 (1955), 57–68 (concentrating on monuments which depict libations); W. Heimpel, *RLA* 7 (1987–1990), 1–5.

251 See the dictionaries *AHw*, 744 f. and *CAD*, N/I, 337 f. An example from a Neo-Babylonian temple ritual is *LKU*, no. 48 (VAT 14521), obv. 5, [10] and rev. 10.

252 In G-stem; *nuqqû*, the D-stem, is attested only twice: in the Uruk building ritual *TU* 46, obv. 19 and *Bagh. Mitt. Beih.* 2, no. 11, obv. fragment 1, 7′.

253 The ritual describing the night vigil: wine and oil (*TU* 41, obv. 9).

priests.[254] No examples from Babylon are known. The verb *nadû* 'to pour' is used to express a libation with water during the special festival of Ištar in Uruk.[255] Other verbs which express pouring liquids as libation are not attested in Hellenistic temple rituals either.[256]

maqqītu- and maqqû-libations

Two nouns which are cognates of *naqû* are *maqqītu* 'libation' (with liquids), or 'offering', attested from the Old Babylonian period on, and *maqqû* 'libation bowl',[257] known from Mari texts and from the Middle Babylonian and Middle Assyrian periods on.[258]

In the temple ritual texts from Hellenistic Uruk *maqqītu* is attested only once. In a building ritual text it is said that the lamentation priest (*kalû*) must continue with *serqu*-offerings, *maqqītu*-libations (*ma-aq-qa-a-tú*) and recitations.[259] Furthermore, during the Babylon Esagila ritual, on day 4 of Kislīmu, offerings ([*m*]*a-qa-a-tu*$_4$) of *maṣḫatu*-flour are scattered on the brazier by the high priest (*aḫu rabû*).[260]

The *maqqû*-libation bowl, usually made of gold, belongs to the category of the *šappu*-containers.[261] It is mentioned many times in Hellenistic temple rituals. It is placed on a offering table (*paššūru*) in front of the statue of the god in the temple.[262] The expression usually used is *maqqê redû* 'to make a libation with the libation bowl'.[263] While (as we saw) the libation expressed by *naqû* is almost exclusively used in the Uruk rituals for the lamentation priest, we find libations with the *maqqû*-libation bowl in the other Uruk

254 The kettledrum ritual: beer, wine, milk, cedar oil, honey and ghee (*TU* 44, I, 11, 29–30, 32; II, 4, 7, 35; III, 20; *Bagh. Mitt. Beih.* 2, no. 5, 19, 23); the building ritual: beer, wine, milk, honey, ghee, oil (*TU* 45, obv. 3, 5, 11, 21; rev. 6, 10, 12, 18, 22; *TU* 46, obv. 4, 6, 17, 19; rev. 5; *Bagh. Mitt. Beih.* 2, no. 10, 5, 7, 16; *Bagh. Mitt. Beih.* 2, no. 11, rev. fragment 2, 4′, 6′(?); H. Weissbach, *Misc.*, no. 12, obv. 9, 21–22 (Late Babylonian); the *mīs pî*-ritual: beer, wine and milk (*Bagh. Mitt. Beih.* 2, no. 1 (+ //), 7, 20 (a *miḫ*[*ru*]-offering(?)), 23, 34; the duplicate *Bagh. Mitt. Beih.* 2, no. 2, 7′(?); [9′]).

255 *TU* 42 +, rev. 31′. *nadû*, literally 'to throw', is also used in connection with flour (see III.3) or oil (*TU* 44, II, 20, cf. also I, 33), but not as libation. Water is used for libation in an astrological text from Hellenistic Uruk, *TU* 12, obv., second row. For this text see II.2.3.

256 *miḫḫa naqû* 'to pour out a libation of *miḫḫu*-beer' is known from a Neo-Babylonian ritual text (T.G. Pinches, *Berens Coll.*, no. 110, obv. 5, 8, 11). Also the verbs *karāru*, *ṣarāru* (in D-stem) and *tabāku* are well-known from Assyrian rituals, but not attested in Hellenistic temple ritual texts.

257 *CAD*, M/I, 253bf. Note that the *AHw*, 607b, 607–608 accepts *maqqītu* as 'offering bowl' and *maqqû* as 'offering' and offering bowl', but the examples of *maqqītu* in the dictionaries suggest a translation of 'libation' rather than 'libation bowl' or a bowl in the shape of a boat (*makkītu*). Cf. W. Heimpel, *RLA* 7 (1987–1990), 3a. For the boat *makkītu* see *KAR* 132, I, 24 and my comments on this line in the Appendix.

258 Cf. A. Salonen, *Hausgeräte*, II, 223 ('Libationskanne'); B.A. Levine, W.W. Hallo, *HUCA* 38 (1967), 52 sub dub-dub; G.J.P. McEwan, *FAOS* 4, 168.

259 *TU* 46, obv. 28 // *SpTU* 4, no. 141, rev. 18. In the Nabonidus chronicle (A.K. Grayson, *Chronicles*, 109, III, 7), possibly written in the Hellenistic period (J. Oelsner, *Materialien*, 204) a *maqqītu*- libation (written BALA-*tu*$_4$) of wine is attested.

260 BM 32206 +, rev. IV, 152. See also III.5.1.

261 See *TU* 38, obv. 1 ff. We know that these containers were used in secular and cultic context for keeping water, beer, milk, wine, oil, butter, honey, aromatics, vinegar and flour, see A. Salonen, *Hausgeräte*, II, 124 ff. Also the *tilimtu*-vases, mentioned in *TU* 38, obv. 11 ff. are used for libations, see the dictionaries and A. Salonen, *Hausgeräte* II, 232–234.

262 In two instances a libation is made on the head of a sheep: *TU* 39, obv. 33; *TU* 42 +, obv. 31′.

263 Cf. *AHw*, 965b, I, 6, c. See also Thureau-Dangin's comments on *redû* in *RAcc.*, 95, n. 4.

rituals, such as the description of the daily offering practice,[264] the New Year festival,[265] and the festival for Ištar;[266] no examples from Babylon are known. The liquids which are usually libated from the *maqqû*-libation bowl are wine, different types of beer and milk.

The expression *maqqê naqû* 'to pour out with the libation bowl' is mostly known from Assyrian rituals, but it is also attested in the Uruk ritual concerning the night vigil festivities.[267]

We have evidence from administrative texts belonging to the Raḫimesu archive (94–93 B.C.) from Babylon that both *maqqītu* and *maqqû* were used well into the Arsacid period.[268]

kāribu and tardīt šarri

The *kāribu*, perhaps not a priest but a citizen, a praying, private person, who offers on special occasions,[269] is attested from the Middle Babylonian and Middle Assyrian periods on.[270] *terdītu* 'additional offering' is known from the Middle and Neo-Babylonian periods on.[271] However, for the Hellenistic period they are only known from the Uruk description of the daily offering practice in *TU* 38. As we already saw, in this text a list of offerings and ceremonies is presented.[272] We suggested that the offerings mentioned here are in fact four general groups of offerings.[273] Among these four groups of offerings, there are two which are named: the offerings of the *kāribu*s and the additional offerings of the king (*tardīt šarri*). We also saw that the food products used for these offerings consisted of cakes, loaves, possibly oil and flour, and finally meat.[274]

This information supports McEwan's idea that *tardīt šarri* may be identified with the *niqī šarri* 'the offerings of the king' which are mentioned many times together with the *niqī kāribi* 'the offerings of the *kāribu*' in documents from the Neo-Assyrian and Neo-Babylonian periods.[275] The foodstuffs used in these documents, oxen and sheep, are also part of the products attested in *TU* 38 for the offerings of the *kāribu* and the

264 *TU* 38, obv. 1 and 9.

265 *TU* 39, obv. 23, 26, 32, 34, rev. 21; *TU* 40, obv. 8, 13, 21, rev. 2, 5, 8, 12, 17; *KAR* 132, I, 17, 19, 26, III, 19, IV, 4, 12.

266 *TU* 42 +, obv. 27′, 31′, 33′.

267 *TU* 41, obv. 22, 27–28.

268 *CT* 49, 150 (154 S.E.) is a list of temple expenditures, which informs us that Sosipatros was given 5 shekel for the purchase price of 5 vessels of wine for the libation (*ana ma-aq-qí-tú*) of the gates of Esagila for a certain period (Lo. E, 32). Similar in AB 244 (219 S.E.), rev. 26, and AB 248 (218 S.E.), obv. 11 (G.J.P. McEwan, *Iraq* 43 [1981], 132 ff. and 141 ff.), for the libations of Esabad. *CT* 49, 160 (219 S.E.), obv. 6 mentions *maqqû*-libation bowls together with *kallu*- and *šassu*-vessels.

269 Or perhaps a layman? Suggested to me by G. van Driel and A.C.V. M. Bongenaar (Leiden), based on an interpretation of L.W. King, *BBSt*. 36. See now also R. Da Riva, in *Festschrift Walker*, Dresden, 2002, 62–3.

270 Cf. *AHw*, 449a; *CAD*, K, 216.

271 *AHw*, 1348a, 2, b. Cognate of the verb *redû* D, 'hinzufügen, dazugeben'.

272 *TU* 38, obv. 36–38 and rev. 36–39. See II.1.

273 See III.1.

274 See III.2.2.

275 G.J.P. McEwan, *FAOS* 4, 167, 169, with text references; add: M. Ellis, *JCS* 36 (1984), 41, no. 6, obv. 4 (Kandalanu); F.E. Peiser, *Verträge*, 107, 4 (= J. MacGinnis, *AfO* 38–39 (1991–1992), 88–90, no. 7, 4) (Dar.); M. Jursa, *Das Archiv der Bēl-Rēmanni*, Istanbul, 1999, 144, obv. 7 (Dar.). See also F. Thureau-Dangin, *RA* 16 (1919), 132 sub n. 13; G. Furlani, *Sacrificio*, 345; B. Landsberger, *Brief*, 54–55 with n. 102.

additional offerings of the king. Moreover, the presentation of *niqī šarri* and *niqī kāribi* as a pair belonging together, is very similar to *kāribu* and *tardīt šarri* in *TU* 38. They represent the participation of a praying (private) person and the king in the Uruk cult activities, which corresponds with our assumption that *TU* 38 is intended to describe the complete daily offering practice in the temples of Uruk. The *tardīt šarri*-offerings are a part of the *sakkê šarrūtu* the 'ritual regulations of kingship' mentioned in the colophon of *TU* 38.[276]

merdītu

The *merdītu*-offering is known from Standard and Late Babylonian texts and is often used with its cognate verb *redû* 'to make a *merdītu*-offering'. The offering mainly consists of oxen and sheep.[277] In the Hellenistic temple ritual texts from Uruk we have a few examples.[278]

In the Uruk New Year texts of the seventh month Tašrītu, on the eighth and ninth day a *merdītu*-offering (written SÍSKUR *mer-de-e-tú*) consisting of ox and sheep is performed (*naqû*), after which the heart of the ox is scattered with flour and the head of the sheep is libated with wine.[279] In the Uruk text describing a special festival for Ištar, the same procedure is described (only here with the verb *redû*) for the eighth and ninth day of Tašrītu during the New Year festival.[280]

ginû and sattukku

Both *ginû* and *sattukku* are regular offerings i.e. they had to be performed every day, contrary to specific offerings, which had to be performed either on specific days of the month (e.g. *guqqû*, see below), or on a special occasions.[281] In the Neo-Babylonian period *ginû* and *sattukku* were interchangeable[282] and can refer to bread, dates, wine, beer, sheep, fish, oil, sesame, barley, pomegranates and juniper. For the Hellenistic period both are attested in temple ritual texts, building inscriptions, chronicles, and administrative and private documents, although the texts seem to favour *ginû*.

In the Uruk description of the daily offering practice *ginû* is (as expected in this text) dominantly present. As commodities, barley and emmer[283] and furthermore oxen and sheep are referred to.[284] The *ginû* used during the Uruk New Year festival of Tašrītu consisted of roasted meat, beef and mutton.[285] In the Uruk kettledrum ritual barley,

---

276 Rev. 44. See I.3.

277 See the dictionaries *AHw*, 645a, 2 and *CAD*, M/II, 20f. for examples. There is a different translation of *merdīta redû* in St. M. Maul, *Zukunftsbewältigung*, 56. *Merdītu* is also attested in the Late Babylonian explanatory text AO 17662 (J. Nougayrol, *RA* 41 [1947], 33), obv. 1, 4, 8, 12, rev. 18, a text very similar to those belonging to the so-called Nippur Compendium (A.R. George, *BTT*, 145ff.).

278 Cf. G.J.P. McEwan, *FAOS* 4, 168.

279 *TU* 39, obv. 30–31; *TU* 40, obv. 21.

280 *TU* 42 +, obv. 29′.

281 F. Joannès, *Textes économiques*, 57, 213.

282 A.C.V.M. Bongenaar, *The Neo-Babylonian Ebabbar Temple at Sippar*, 143.

283 *TU* 38, obv. 22.

284 *TU* 38, rev. 1; 5; 6; 8; 13; 15; 18; 20; 21; 23; 25; 35.

285 *TU* 39, obv. 8.

emmer, salt and juniper are mentioned, perhaps for the *ginû*, but the context is unclear.[286] In the New Year festival of Nisannu in Babylon no commodities are mentioned for the *ginû*[287] and the *sattukku*,[288] but again the context is unclear.

The building inscription *YOS* I, 52, from the year 244 B.C. (68 S.E.) is an inscription of Anu-uballiṭ, son of Anu-ikṣur, of the family Aḫûtu, who was given the Greek name Nikarchos. He was governor (*šaknu*) of Uruk during the reign of Seleucus II. The text describes an extensive building undertaking in the Rēš-temple, the temple of Anu and Antu in Uruk.[289] The end of the inscription records that the governor made Anu and Antu enter the Rēš-temple and take their seats in the cella Enamenna, where he established *ginû*- and *sattukku*-offerings as before (*gi-nu-ú sat-tuk-ku ki-ma maḫ-ri-im-ma ú-kin*[in]*-ni qé-reb-šú*) (18–19). No commodities are mentioned.

In the last passage of a Hellenistic chronicle regular offerings (*ginû*) are made in Ekišnugal, the temple of Sîn in Babylon.[290] An astronomical diary mentions a general (*rab uqu*) who gave a bull and sheep for the regular offering (*ginû*) of Bēl to the butchers of Esagila, after which they were offered to Bēl.[291]

In private documents from Uruk *ginû* is attested only rarely.[292] The administrative documents belonging to the Raḫimesu archive (94–93 B.C.) from Babylon refer to regular offering sheep, and cereals or meat for the regular offerings.[293]

guqqû

The *guqqû*-offering is attested in texts from the Neo-Babylonian, the Achaemenid and Hellenistic periods. It is unknown in Assyria. It was performed on a regular basis on certain days of certain months.[294] When no specific days are mentioned (*guqqû ša* [iti]MN), probably the total sum of all the *guqqû*-offerings of that month (*guqqānê*) are intended.[295] In the Neo-Babylonian and Achaemenid periods the *guqqû*-offerings consisted mainly of meat (sheep), dates, wine and beer.

---

286 *TU* 44, IV, 18.
287 *RAcc.*, 142, 388.
288 BM 32654 +, containing a line additional to *RAcc.*, 149, 72 (72a in my line numbering), see my comments on l. 69–79 in the Appendix.
289 A. Falkenstein, *Topographie*, 4–5. See L.T. Doty, in: *Studies A. Sachs*, Philadelphia, 1988, 95–6.
290 Antiochus I(?), A.K. Grayson, *Chronicles*, 26 f. and 119 ff., obv. 6.
291 A.J. Sachs–H. Hunger, *Diaries*, no. -273, B, obv. 12.
292 E.g. *VS* 15, 19 (109 S.E.), obv. 3, in connection with *akītu*-temples: [... É(?)] *a-ki-tu*$_4$.MEŠ *a-na gi-nu-ú* (see II.4.5.1); see also *BRM* 2, 47 (157 S.E.), obv. 15, where regular offering sheep (UDU.NÍTA.MEŠ *gi-né-e*) are mentioned.
293 *BRM* 1, 99 (218 S.E.), obv. 11, rev. 31, 33: regular offering sheep (UDU.NÍTA *gi-né-e*) of the *akītu*-temple, of Esabad, the Gula temple, rev. 28: cereals for the regular offerings (NINDA[ḫá] *gi-nu-ú*) of the Gula temple; AB 244 (219 S.E., G.J.P. McEwan, *Iraq* 43 [1981], 132 ff.), obv. 7: regular offering sheep of the *akītu*-temple, rev. 30: 2 cuts of meat for regular offerings (2 UZU(?) *gi-*[*nu*]*-ú*); *CT* 49, 156 (218 S.E.), obv. 12: offering sheep for the regular offerings ([udu]SÍSKUR *gi-nu-ú*), presented to the governor of Babylon; *CT* 49, 150 (218 S.E.), obv. 25: cereals for the regular offerings of the temple of Gula, rev. 41: regular offering sheep(?); 59: 5 cuts of meat for the regular offerings; rev. 43: here the expenditure consists of an advance payment of the *sattukku*-offering for a certain period.
294 F. Joannès, *Textes économiques,* 214; A.C.V.M. Bongenaar, *The Neo-Babylonian Ebabbar Temple at Sippar*, 145.
295 *AUWE* 5, 61–2.

In the Hellenistic temple ritual texts the *guqqû*-offerings are mentioned only rarely.[296] They are referred to together with clothing ceremonies and *siltu*-food, which had to be performed on the seventh day of Tašrītu during the New Year festival in Uruk.[297] Furthermore, the *guqqû*-offerings are one of the four groups of offerings listed in *TU* 38.[298] Here they precede the *eššēšu*-ceremonies with which they are connected. This connection is confirmed by the Uruk prebend texts where usually the *guqqû*-offerings are mentioned as a pair with the *eššēšu*-ceremonies. As we already suggested, the commodities used for the *guqqû*-offerings and *eššēšu*-ceremonies (loaves, cakes, oxen and sheep) served, together with the commodities of the monthly and yearly unspecified ceremonies,[299] to provide an income for the various prebends of the Hellenistic Uruk temples.[300]

nindabû

Nindabû 'cereal offering, food offering' is a Sumerian loanword (NIDBA),[301] and is attested from the Old Akkadian period on.[302] We find the offering usually in cultic context. It is a food offering, originally consisting of bread or cereal. However, McEwan already pointed out[303] that *nindabû* could also contain meat, as becomes clear from Hellenistic chronicle texts.[304] *Nindabû* is, together with *niqû*, the most frequently mentioned offering in the astronomical diaries from Babylon.[305] In these passages *nindabû* is used as a general term for food offering, usually consisting of bull and sheep (see my comments on the use of *niqû* above). From the Hellenistic temple ritual texts we have no examples of *nindabû*,[306] with exception of a reference in the eclipse of the moon ritual (*BRM* 4, 6, obv. 12′–13′). However, it is found in a literary passage, in an Akkadian quotation of a Sumerian lamentation, which had to be sung in front of Sîn at the time of an eclipse (see obv. 14). Because in this literary context *nindabû* is clearly distinguished from *niqû* as a different type of offering, in this passage the opposition of cereal offerings and meat offerings seems justifiable.

---

296 G.J.P. McEwan, *FAOS* 4, 166–7.

297 *TU* 39, obv. 13.

298 Obv. 36, rev. 36.

299 See II.3.1 and II.4.1.

300 See II.3.2.

301 For the etymology of the word see W.G. Lambert, in: *OLA* 55 (1993), 196, n. 3.

302 Cf. *CAD*, N/II, 236; *AHw*, 790b.

303 *FAOS* 4, 168.

304 In chronicle 11 (A.K. Grayson, *Chronicles*, 26 f. and 119 ff.) crown prince Antiochus I (?) presented a sheep as *nindabû* in Ekišnugal, the temple of Sîn in Babylon (obv. 8); in chronicle 13b (*Chronicles*, 283, 5 ff.) the administrator (*šatammu)* of Esagila established among other animals, oxen, ewes and ducks for the offering within Esagila for Bēl and Bēltīja and the great gods and for the ritual(?) of Seleucus, the king, and his sons. See also II.8.7.

305 A.J. Sachs–H. Hunger, *Diaries*, no. -209, D, obv. 16′; no. -204, C, rev. 16(?); no. -179, E, rev. 14′; no. -178, C, rev. 20′; no. -158, B, rev. 20′; 21′; no. -137, D, rev., 27; no. -136, C, rev. 13′; no. -133, B and C, obv. 25′; no. -132, B, obv. 27; rev. 27, 28; no. -126, B, rev. 5′; no. -124, rev. 20′; no. -123, B, 15′; no. -111, B, rev. 10′; no. -107, C, rev. 17′; no. -105, obv. A14′, B13′; no. -87, A, rev. 15′; no. -82, B, rev. 2′; no. -78, 13′; no. -77, A, obv. 27′, 30′, rev. 31, B, rev. 15′.

306 See also II.7.

muḫḫuru

Muḫḫuru, but also *maḫḫuru*, *miḫḫuru*, *miḫru* and *muḫru* all render the meaning 'offering'.[307] We know that in the Neo-Babylonian period *maḫḫuru*-offerings consisted of sheep and barley.[308] In Hellenistic temple ritual texts *muḫḫuru* is attested in the Uruk building ritual, where it is said that 'during the demolishing and renovating *muḫḫuru*-offerings (*mu-uḫ-ḫu-ru*) and *taqribtu*-lamentations (ÉR.MEŠ) will be performe[d]'.[309] Further on in the text it is stated: 'until (the completion of) that temple comes to an end, you will not stop performing the *muḫḫuru*-offerings (*mu-úḫ-ru*) (and) *taqribtu*-lamentations'.[310] Perhaps we also have an example of the *miḫru* (*meḫru*)-offering in the Hellenistic *mīs pî*-ritual text from Uruk.[311] In an astronomical diary a *maḫḫuru*-offering is mentioned on two occasions, together with rituals (*nēpešu*) of the gods and a chief singer of dirges (*galamāḫu*), who recites *eršaḫungû*-tablets, but the context is not entirely clear, and no information on the contents of the offerings is given.[312]

III.7.3. *Burnt offering*

Burning activities are frequently mentioned in the Hellenistic temple ritual texts. The night vigil description (*TU* 41), the building ritual (*TU* 45 and parallels), the *mīs pî*-ritual (*Bagh. Mitt. Beih.* 2, no. 1 and parallels) and the eclipse of the moon ritual (*BRM* 4, 6), all from Uruk, refer on many occassions to a brushwood pile (*abru*), sometimes using a torch (*gizillû*). For 'setting fire', the verbs *qâdu*,[313] *napāḫu*,[314] *nummuru* (D-stem of *namāru*),[315] and *šuṣbutu* (Š-stem of *ṣabātu*)[316] are used. Also fumigation is, as we have seen, a well-known practice.[317] However, unlike in Ancient Israel[318] or Assyria,[319]

---

307 See the dictionaries *CAD* and *AHw*.

308 E.g. *Cyr* 136, 4: sheep for the *maḫḫuru*-offering (*a-na maḫ-ḫu-ru*) of Anunītu were given. *Dar* 285, 10: barley for the *maḫḫuru*-offering of Anunītu are given. See also the Neo-Babylonian ritual text T.G. Pinches, *Berens Coll.*, no. 110, obv. 5: *maḫ-ḫu-ru tu-maḫ-ḫa-ru* 'you will present a *maḫḫuru*-offering'.

309 *TU* 46, obv. 27 // *SpTU* 4, no. 141, rev. 18.

310 Rev. 11–12. From the context it is clear that *mu-úḫ-ru* is not the *muḫru*-prayer (*CAD*, M/II, 177a), which is supported by similar passages e.g. in the *mīs pî*-ritual text K 224 (= E. Ebeling, *TuL*, 27), obv. 20: *mu-uḫ-ḫu-ru taqribtu ... ul i-kal-la.*

311 *Bagh. Mitt. Beih.* 2, no. 1 (+ //), 20: *mi-iḫ-*⌜*ri*?⌝ *ina* UGU SAG.DU UR.⌜MAḪ?⌝ BAL-*qí* 'You will pour out a *miḫru*-offering(?) on the head of the lion(?)'. If Mayer is correct in assuming that flour is poured out here (*OrNS* 47 [1978], 452), then my reading *mi-iḫ-*⌜*ri*?⌝ is not impossible, since flour is used with *miḫru* in Neo-Babylonian texts (thus *CAD*, M/II, 59b sub 5). Furthermore, Mayer's suggestion 'head of the lion' is supported by an example from the Neo-Assyrian royal inscriptions, where a *muḫḫuru*-offering is made over lions killed in a hunt (*CAD*, M/II, 176a sub 1, a).

312 A.J. Sachs–H. Hunger, *Diaries*, no. -229, B, obv. 7′; rev. 14′. For the interpretation of the historical passage in this diary, see R.J. van der Spek, *Religieuze en economische politiek in het Seleucidische Rijk,* 26.

313 *TU* 41, obv. 30, rev. 15.

314 *TU* 41, rev. 7 (N-stem), 16, 22, 25, 27; *TU* 45, rev. 7, 10, 22; *TU* 46, rev. 4; *Bagh. Mitt. Beih.* 2, no. 1 (+ //), 7, 11. Compare also the Neo-Babylonian temple ritual VAT 14521, obv. 5.

315 *TU* 45, obv. 4 with parallels *TU* 46, obv. 5 and *Bagh. Mitt. Beih.* 2, no. 10, obv. 5.

316 *TU* 41, rev. 13; *BRM* 4, 6, obv. 16, rev. 39. See also *šarāpu* 'to burn' (W 18828, rev. 2).

317 See III.5.

318 Well-known are אִשֶּׁה 'offerings made by fire', and כָּלִיל 'whole-offering', an offering of which the offerer does not eat, early replaced by עֹלָה 'whole burnt-offering', i.e. an offering which is burnt wholy. On the altar the animal would either be totally burnt as an offering to the god, or some of its flesh would be eaten and the rest burnt. By burning the food it could be consumed by the god through its scent.

319 E.g. *BBR* 2, no. 60, rev. 30: turtledoves are used as a burnt offering (*maqlūtu*), after which the heart of

burnt offerings (*maqlūtu*) are rare.[320] We have one example from the Uruk kettledrum ritual, where it is accompanied by burning aromatics: after cedar balsam(?) is kindled (*napāḫu*), the heart of the slaughtered bull is burnt (*qalû*) in front of the kettledrum with cedar, juniper and *maṣḫatu*-flour.[321]

---

a sheep is burnt. More often the burning of animals or meat on a brazier: VAT 16435 = F. Köcher, *ZA* 50 (1952), 192–202 (Middle Assyrian temple ritual), obv. 13–15; Bu 91–5–9, 104 = H. Zimmern, *Neujahrsfest* I, 131, n. 1 (Neo-Assyrian), 7′; K 3455 + = B. Menzel, *Tempel*, no. 43, rev. IV, 1–2.

320 Perhaps because of West Semitic influence, and so not typically Babylonian, according to W.G. Lambert, in: *OLA* 55 (1993), 194.

321 *TU* 44, II, 16–17, see my comments on *KAR* 60 obv. 15–16, in the Appendix. *maqlūtu* is perhaps attested in a passage from the lunar eclipse myth: *CLBT*, pl. 1 reads in Col. B, 26, in difficult context: *ma-qa-lu-*[*tú*(?)]. Note that burnt offerings are also attested in Neo-Assyrian letters dealing with the substitute king (*šar pūḫi*) ritual, which as we saw were also probably performed to avert evil portended by an eclipse on the king (see II.7), e.g. S. Parpola, *LAS* I, 167.

IV. CONCLUSION

We set out in this study to examine whether the temple ritual texts, which were copied during the Hellenistic period from older original compositions, are a reliable source of information on the cult practices of Hellenistic Uruk and Babylon. Having surveyed the textual evidence discussed in the previous chapters we can now conclude that there is enough evidence to suggest that the temple ritual texts do indeed describe the cultic activities as they took place during the Hellenistic period.

The extensive descriptions of festivals, rituals and offerings in the temple ritual texts show how important the public cults were in Hellenistic times, at least until the first century B.C. Daily ceremonies such as the 'awakening of the temple'-ceremony (*dīk bīti*) and the 'opening of the gate'-ceremony (*pīt bābi*) are well attested in ritual texts and cultic calendars. Many monthly ceremonies are also known, such as a ceremony called *eššēšu*, the monthly clothing ceremony (*lubuštu*), a nocturnal ceremony (*bajjātu*), an evening ceremony (*nubattu*), and a ceremony called 'the good-functioning of the temple'-ceremony (*šalām bīti*). The same is true for many of the annually celebrated ceremonies, such as the clothing ceremonies, the processions, the divine marriage ceremonies (*ḫašādu*), and the brazier festivals (*kinūnu*). Also, for the New Year festivals (*akītu*) of Uruk and Babylon there is substantial evidence to be gleaned from Hellenistic temple ritual texts. Many of the important temple rituals, such as the kettledrum ritual, the building ritual, the Uruk lunar eclipse ritual, festivals for Ištar of Uruk and Ištar of Babylon, and a nocturnal festival in the Rēš-temple in Uruk are extensively described; other less well-known temple rituals are also attested. They clearly show how active the Babylonians were on matters of religion and cult during the Hellenistic period. The large corpus of cult songs (particularly from Babylon) underlines this.

Admittedly, these literary texts are copies of older compositions, but the information of other, contemporary sources (chronicles, astronomical diaries, legal and administrative texts, building inscriptions) shows that the cults were still very important in the Hellenistic period. Moreover, some of the rituals (the kettledrum ritual, the building ritual) are referred to in the astronomical diaries. Although because of their damaged state the astronomical diaries are often very enigmatic, as far as the political and religious events described are concerned, they are nonetheless important evidence for the fact that Babylonian religion and cult were not yet dead; the numerous references to temples, gods and religious and cultic activities are firm evidence for the existence of the traditional Babylonian cults in the Hellenistic period. References to the New Year festival occur in all contemporary sources. The same is true for many offerings and libations, presented during the divine meal (*naptanu*).

The practice of using the names of deities in personal names is another important indication of the importance of Babylonian religion and cults in the Hellenistic period. The contemporary sources also refer on many occasions to different temples, not only the Rēš-temple in Uruk and the Esagila-temple in Babylon, but also to many other temples (e.g. Esabad, the temple of Gula in Babylon, Eturkalamma, the temple of Ištar of Babylon, and the temples of Zababa and Ninlil, of Nabû ša ḫarê, of Madānu, and the *akītu*-temples). We also found that building inscriptions refer to the restorations of temples.

Finally, administrative documents show how important the temples were as economic institutions; the prebendary system in Uruk cannot be explained if the cults were not functioning; it shows that the temple was not only an important religious center, but also an important economic institution.

The Babylonian cults practised in the temples of Uruk and Babylon in the Hellenistic period are, as far as we can see in the sources, not different from those in the pre-Hellenistic times. All the evidence clearly shows that the Babylonians held on to their old Babylonian traditions. The pantheon referred to in both religious and secular texts is entirely Babylonian. The terminology used for the cultic activities or the cult participants is not different from pre-Hellenistic times. Even the Macedonian rulership took part in the Babylonian cults; they did not attempt to change the cults but themselves adapted to Babylonian customs.

We found only one possible exception to this rule. In particular the astronomical diaries from Babylon contain some references to what may be a local ruler cult for the king and his family, a custom well-known to the Seleucid monarchies. In Babylon such a local ruler cult may have been in practice from the time of Seleucus III on. Also for Uruk we cannot exclude the possibility that certain texts contain references to a ruler cult practice, in which Seleucid kings were honored as superhumans; legal documents concerning prebend shares, dated to the second century B.C., which refer to offerings brought up 'to (the table of) the statues of the kings', may refer to this cult. Although the evidence remains scarce and dubious, this interpretation of the discussed text passages is possible. Hopefully new texts will help us to solve this difficult issue once and for all.

APPENDIX

THE TEMPLE RITUAL TEXTS[1]

[1] This appendix consists of a selection of temple ritual texts, of which only older or incomplete editions are available. The texts which are kept in the British Museum were collated by the present author. For a complete survey of all relevant temple ritual texts see I.2.

a. A description of the daily offerings in the temples of Uruk

TU 38 (AO 6451)[2]

This text describes the ritual instructions for the daily offerings in the temple of Anu (Rēš) and the other temples in Hellenistic Uruk. On the basis of prosopographic evidence we can date the text to the first half of the second century B.C.: the text is written by Šamaš-ēṭir, son of Ina-qibīt-Anu, son of Šibqat-Anu, who belongs to the family Ekur-zakir. He is also the scribe of the ritual text *TU* 39–40 (see *TU* 39, rev. 28–29). Furthermore he is known as the owner of several astronomical texts, two of which are dated 118 S.E. (194/3 B.C.)[3] Šamaš-ēṭir is also attested as the scribe of *VS* 15, 32 // HSM 913.2.181 (R. Wallenfels, *Seleucid Archival Texts*, no. VI), dated 119 S.E. (193/2 B.C.), and probably also of the much later *BRM* 2, 54 // *BiMes* 24, 28, dated 150 S.E. (162/1 B.C.) He is also mentioned as the father of the scribe Ina-qibīt-Anu in *BRM* 2, 49 and 50, both dated in the year 166 S.E. (146/5 B.C.), and probably also in *BiMes* 24, 12, dated 162 S.E. (150/49 B.C.) This indicates that Šamaš-ēṭir was probably at the end of his career around 155 S.E. (157/6 B.C.)

According to the colophon the high priest Kidin-Anu of the family Ekur-zakir made a copy of the original tablets, which Nabopolassar had carried off from Uruk to Elam, and brought them back to Uruk during the co-regency of either Seleucus I and Antiochus, which would have been during the period of 20–31 S.E. (292/1–281/0 B.C.), or during the co-regency of Antiochus I and his son Seleucus, 32–45 S.E. (280/79–267/6 B.C.). This Kidin-Anu is also known as the father of Anu-aḫa-ušabši, the owner of the tablet *BRM* 4, 7.[4]

The text is discussed in III.2.

Obv.

1 *u*$_4$*-mi-šam kal* MU.AN.NA *ina nap-tan* GAL-*ú šá še-e-ri e-lat šap-pi*.MEŠ *šá ma-aq-qa-né-e*
2 18 *šap-pi*.MEŠ GUŠKIN *ina* ^{giš}BANŠUR ^{d}LX *ta-rak-kás ina lìb-bi* 7 *šap-pi ana* XV
3 3 KAŠ ŠE.BAR 4 KAŠ *lab-ku* 7 *šap-pi a-na* 2,30 3 KAŠ ŠE.BAR 1-*en* KAŠ *lab-ku*
4 1-*en* KAŠ *na-a-šú* 1-*en* KAŠ *zar-ba-ba ù* GA *ina šap-pi* ^{na4}GIŠ.NU$_{11}$.GAL
5 4 {PA} *šap-pi*.MEŠ GUŠKIN *šá* GEŠTIN ŠUR.RA *a-na ma-ḫar* ^{d}*A-nù ta-rak-kás*
6 *šá tar-den-nu šá še-e-ri ù* GAL-*ú ù tar-den-nu šá li-lat* KI.MIN-*ma*
7 *ina* GAL-*ú ù tar-den-nu šá li-lat* GA *ul i-qar-rub ina šap-pi*.⸢MEŠ GUŠKIN⸣
8 *šá* ^{giš}BANŠUR 5 *šap-pi*.MEŠ GUŠKIN *šá za-ri-i-ni* ^{na4}[UD].SAL.[KA]B

---

9 5 *šap-pi*.MEŠ GUŠKIN *šá* 1 SÌLA.TA.ÀM *i-ṣab-bat ma-aq-qa-né-e šá* É *pa-pa-ḫa* [^{d}LX]

---

[2] Cf. *RAcc.*, 62–65, 74–86; E. Ebeling, in: H. Gressmann, *ATAT*^{2}, 305 ff.; A.J. Sachs, in: J.B. Pritchard, *ANET*^{2}, 343 ff.; W. Farber, *TUAT* II/2, 227 ff. See also R. Borger, *HKL* 1, 567 and 2, 297.

[3] O. Neugebauer, *ACT*, p. 17, F, l. 2; L, l. 23, which is dated 118 S.E. (194/3 B.C.); H, l. 2; O. Neugebauer, *ACT*, p. 18, M, l. 2, dated 118 S.E.; N, l. 9; 0, rev. 6; the colophons of these texts (except O. Neugebauer, *ACT*, p. 18, N) were collected by H. Hunger, *AOAT* 2, nos. 94, 103, 105, 118.

[4] See my introduction to *BRM* 4, 7, below. On Kidin-Anu see also R. Wallenfels, *Uruk. Hellenistic Seal Impressions in the Yale Babylonion Collection. I. Cuneiform Tablets*, Mainz am Rhein, 1994 (AUWE 19), 29, and 146, and id., *Seleucid Archival Texts in the Harvard Semitic Museum*, Groningen, 1998, 30.

10 *ina lìb-bi* 1-*en* KAŠ ŠE.BAR 1-*en* KAŠ *lab-ku* 1-*en* KAŠ *na-a-šú* 1-*en* GEŠTIN ŠUR.RA [*ù* 1-*en* GA]
11 *šap-pi šá* 5 NINDA^{há} *i-ṣab-bat šá* GEŠTIN ^{kur}*A-za-al-lu* 4 TI.L[IM.DÙ GUŠKIN]
12 *šá* É *pa-pa-ḫa* ^{d}LX *ina lìb-bi* 1-*et* TI.LIM.DÙ GUŠKIN *šá ši-iq-du* [*še-en-de-et*(?)]
13 1-*et* TI.LIM.DÙ GUŠKIN *šá a-a-ri še-en-de-et*
14 1-*et* TI.LIM.DÙ GUŠKIN *šá* DUR *ti-ik-ka-šú* NIGIN-*ú* 1-*et* TI.LIM.[DÙ GUŠKIN ...]
15 PAP 4-*ta* TI.LIM.DÙ GUŠKIN *ina muḫ-ḫi kan-du-ri-né-e* [...]
16 *šá* ^{d}*A-nù ù An-tu*$_{4}$ [...]

---

17 14 *šap-pi*.MEŠ GUŠKIN *ina* ^{giš}BANŠUR *An-tu*$_{4}$ *tar-kás* KAŠ SAG.MEŠ GI[M *šá* ^{giš}BANŠUR ^{d}LX]
18 12 *šap-pi*.MEŠ GUŠKIN IGI ^{d}INNIN 10 *šap-pi*.MEŠ GUŠKIN IGI [^{d}*Na-na-a*]
19 *e-lat šap-pi*.MEŠ GUŠKIN *šá kal* MU.AN.NA *šá* DINGIR.MEŠ *a-šá-bu-tu šá* [UNUG^{ki}]

---

20 *ù e-lat šap-pi*.MEŠ GUŠKIN *šá a-na ṣi-di-ti* DINGIR.MEŠ *ù* 2-*ta* TI.LIM.DÙ [...]⸢*ú*⸣-*kan-nu*(?)

---

21 *u*$_{4}$-*mi-šam kal* MU.AN.NA 1-*en* BUR 3 GUR 3 NIGIDA ŠE.BAR ⸢*ù*⸣ [ZÍZ.ÀM]
22 1, 48 ^{giš}BÁN.MEŠ 1 ME 8 ^{giš}BÁN SAG.DU *gi-né-e ina* ^{giš}BÁN *šá* 10 MA.NA [...]-*šú*(?)
23 *šá* ^{lú}ḪAR.MEŠ *ina* É ^{lú}MUḪALDIM.MEŠ *a-na* 1-*en u*$_{4}$-*mu a-na* 4 *nap-tan šá* ^{d}[LX] ⸢*An*⸣-*tu*$_{4}$
24 ^{d}INNIN ^{d}*Na-na-a ù* DINGIR.MEŠ *a-šá-bu-tu šá* UNUG^{ki} *a-na* ^{lú}MUḪALDIM.MEŠ *i-na*[*m-d*]*i-in*
25 *ina lìb-bi* 81 $^{giš!}$BÁN.MEŠ ZÌ ŠE.BAR 27 ^{giš}BÁN.MEŠ ZÌ ZÍZ.ÀM
26 *šá a-na* 2 ME 43 *ṣib-tu*$_{4}$ ^{lú}MUḪALDIM *ip-pu-ú šá* TA ⸢*lìb-bi*⸣ *a-na* 4 *nap-tan*
27 *a-na* ^{giš}BANŠUR *a-na* IGI ^{d}*A-nù* 30 *ṣib-tu*$_{4}$ ^{lú}MUḪALDIM *i-nam-din*
28 *ina* GAL-*ú ù tar-den-nu šá* KIN.NIM 8.TA.ÀM *ṣib-tu*$_{4}$ ^{lú}MUḪALDIM *i-nam-din*
29 *ina* GAL-*ú ù tar-den-nu šá* KIN.SIG 7.TA.ÀM *ṣib-tu*$_{4}$ ^{lú}MUḪALDIM *i-nam-din*
30 30 *ṣib-tu*$_{4}$ IGI *An-tu*$_{4}$ 30 *ṣib-tu*$_{4}$ IGI ^{d}INNIN 30 *ṣib-tu*$_{4}$ IGI ^{d}*Na-na-a* 12 *ṣib-tu*$_{4}$ IGI
31 *šu-bat* ^{d}LX *u* DINGIR É *šá* É *pa-pa-ḫa An-tu*$_{4}$ 4 *ṣib-tu*$_{4}$ IGI 2 AGA *šá* ^{d}*A-nù*
32 16 *ṣib-tu*$_{4}$ IGI *ziq-qur-rat ù* DINGIR É *šá ziq-qur-rat* 16 *ṣib-tu*$_{4}$ IGI *a-ḫa-nu šá pa-pa-ḫa* ^{d}LX
33 *ù An-tu*$_{4}$ PAP 1 ME 68 *ṣib-tu*$_{4}$ *šá a-na* 4 *nap-tan* ^{lú}MUḪALDIM SUM-*in*
34 *e-lat* 75 *ṣib-tu*$_{4}$ *šá a-na* DINGIR.MEŠ *a-šá-bu-tu šá* UNUG^{ki} *ina* É.MEŠ-*šú-nu*
35 *ina* 4 *nap-tan i-qar-rub e-lat ṣi-ba-at rab-bu-ú ù a-kal ma-ak-kàs*
36 *šá a-na ṣi-di-i-tu*$_{4}$ DINGIR.MEŠ *gu-uq-qa-né-e* UD ÈŠ.ÈŠ.MEŠ BAD-*te* KÁ.MEŠ *lu-bu-ša-at*
37 ^{dug}A.GÚB.BA.MEŠ *ba-a-a-at*.MEŠ KI.NE.MEŠ GARZA.GARZA *ḫa-šá-du ka-ri-bi*.MEŠ
38 *ù tar-di-i-tu*$_{4}$ LUGAL *sa-mu-tu šá ina* ^{gi}*se-li*.MEŠ *šá mun-ta-qu*
39 *tak-ka-su-ú šá ina* ^{gi}*se-li*.MEŠ *šá ma-ka-at ku-up-pu-šu es-pi*
40 *ù* 1 IGI 2 ME *ku-si-ip-e-ti* Ì.GIŠ *šá ina šu-pal ma-ak-kàs ù as-né-e*
41 *iš-šak-kan ù* Ì.GIŠ *ḫal-ṣa a-na muḫ-ḫi ka-lak šá* ^{d}LX *An-tu*$_{4}$ *u* DINGIR.MEŠ *šu-ut* UNUG^{ki}
42 *i-qar-rub ù* ZÌ.MAD.GÁ *šá ina ma-sap-pi ka-re-e*
43 *šá u*$_{4}$-*mi-šam kal* MU.AN.NA ^{lú}ḪAR *a-na* ^{lú}KU$_{4}$-É SUM-*in*
44 ^{lú}ḪAR *ina muḫ-ḫi ṭe*$_{4}$-*e-nu* ^{na4}ḪAR ^{mul}APIN *ina* EDEN ^{giš}APIN ŠE.NUMUN *iṣ-mi-du*
45 *naq-bit i-qab-bi ù* ^{lú}MUḪALDIM *ina muḫ-ḫi ba*$^{!}$-*la-la šá gi-ir-ṣi*
46 *ù ṭa-ḫu-ú šá em-mé-e-ti* ^{d}NISABA ḪÉ.EN.GÁL *du-uš-šu-ú*
47 *ma-ka-lu-ú el-lu naq-bi-tu*$_{4}$ *i-qab-bu-ú*

---

48 *u*$_{4}$-*mi-šam kal* MU.AN.NA *ina* 4 *nap-tan* 1, 48 ^{giš}BÁN.MEŠ 1 ME 8 ^{giš}BÁN *ma-ak-kàs*

49 *as-né-e* ^{giš}PÈŠ *ù mun-ziq e-lat ḫi-iṣ-ṣa-ṣa-at*(?) *ù tab-ni-ti šá a-na* ^{d}LX
50 *An-tu*$_4$ ^{d}INNIN ^{d}*Na-na-a ù* DINGIR.⸢MEŠ *a*⸣*-šá-bu-tu šá* UNUG^{ki} *i-qar-rub*

Rev.

1 GU$_4$.MEŠ *ù* UDU.NÍTA *gi-né-e šá u*$_4$*-mi-šam kal* MU.AN.NA *a-na* ^{d}LX *An-tu*$_4$ ^{d}INNIN ^{d}*Na-na-a*
2 *ù* DINGIR.MEŠ *a-šá-bu-tu šá* É *re-eš* É ÈŠ.GAL *ù* É.ŠÁR.RA BÁRA.MAḪ *ziq-qur-rat* ^{d}LX
3 *šá* TA UD.1.KAM *šá* ^{iti}BÁR *a-di* UD.30.KAM *šá* ^{iti}ŠE *ina nap-tan* GAL-*ú šá še-e-ri i-qar-rub*

---

4 *a-na nap-tan* GAL-*ú šá še-e-ri šá kal* MU.AN.NA 7 UDU.NÍTA *reš-tu-ú-tú ma-ru-tu*$_4$ DADAG.GA
5 *šá* 2-*ta* MU.AN.NA.MEŠ ŠE.BAR GU$_7$.MEŠ 1-*en* UDU *ka-lu-ú gi-né-e kab-ri šá* GA
6 PAP 8 UDU.NÍTA *gi-né-e* 1-*en* GU$_4$ GAL-*ú* 1-*en* ^{gu4}AMAR GA *ù* 10 UDU.NÍTA *kab-ru-tu*
7 *šá* EGIR.MEŠ-*šú-nu šá* ŠE.BAR *la* GU$_7$.MEŠ PAP *ina nap-tan* GAL-*ú šá še-rì šá kal* MU.AN.NA 18 UDU.NÍTA
8 *ina lìb-bi ina* 1-*en* UDU *ka-lu-ú gi-né-e šá* GA 1-*en* GU$_4$ GAL-*ú* 1-*en* ^{gu4}AMAR GA *ina muḫ-ḫi*
9 *na-ka-sa šá* GU$_4$ *ù* UDU.NÍTA ^{lú}GÍR.LÁ *naq-*[*b*]*i-tu*$_4$ *i-qab-bi*

---

10 DUMU ^{d}UTU *be-lu bu-lim ina* EDEN *ú-šab-šá-a ri-ʾ-i-ti*

---

11 *šá-niš a-na muḫ-ḫi na-ka-sa šá* GU$_4$ *ù* UDU.NÍTA ^{lú}GÍR.LÁ G[AL]-⸢*ú*⸣ *a-na* ^{d}LX *An-tu*$_4$ MUL.GAL
12 *ù* ^{d}*Dil-bad ba-la-ṭu i-qab*⟨*-bi*⟩*-ma a-na* DINGIR.MEŠ *šá-n*[*im-m*]*a ul i-qab-bi*

---

13 *nap-tan-nu tar-den-nu šá še-e-ri gi-nu-ú šá* ^{d}LX *An-tu*$_4$ *ù* DINGIR.MEŠ É.MEŠ-*šú-nu*
14 *šá* É *re-eš* É ÈŠ.GAL *ù* BÁRA.MAḪ *šá kal* MU.AN.NA 6 UDU.NÍTA *ma-ru-tú* DADAG.GA *šá* 2-*ta* MU.AN.NA.MEŠ ŠE.BAR GU$_7$.MEŠ
15 1-*en* UDU.NÍTA *gi-né-e kab-ri šá* GA *ù* 5 UDU.NÍTA *kab-ru-tú šá* EGIR-*šú-nu šá* ŠE.BAR *la* GU$_7$.MEŠ 1-*en* GU$_4$ GAL-*ú* 8 ^{udu}SILA$_4$ 5 UZ.TUR^{mušen} *šá* NÍG.SILAG.GÁ GU$_7$
16 2 UZ.TUR^{mušen} *šá* EGIR-*šú-nu* 3 KUR.GI^{mušen} *šá* ZÌ NÍG.SILAG.GÁ GU$_7$ 4 PÉŠ.GIŠ.GI
17 30 ŠEŠ^{mušen} 20 TU.KUR$_4$^{mušen} 3 NUNUZ GA.NU$_{11}$^{mušen} 3 NUNUZ UZ.TUR^{mušen}

---

18 *nap-tan* GAL-*ú šá* KIN.SIG *gi-nu-ú šá* ^{d}LX *An-tu*$_4$ *ù* DINGIR.MEŠ É.MEŠ-*šú-nu šá kal* MU.AN.NA
19 4 UDU.NÍTA *ma-ru-tú* DADAG.GA *šá* 2-*ta* MU.AN.NA ŠE.BAR GU$_7$.MEŠ 1-*en* UDU *ka-lu-ú*
20 *gi-né-e kab-ri šá* GA 5 UDU.NÍTA *šá-nu-ú-tú šá* EGIR-*šú-nu šá* ŠE.BAR *la* GU$_7$.MEŠ *ù* 10 TU.KUR$_4$^{mušen}

---

21 *nap-tan tar-den-nu šá* KIN.SIG *gi-nu-ú šá* ^{d}LX *An-tu*$_4$ *ù* DINGIR.MEŠ É.MEŠ-*šú-nu šá kal* MU.AN.NA
22 4 UDU.NÍTA *ma-ru-tú* DADAG.GA *šá* 2-*ta* MU.AN.NA ŠE.BAR GU$_7$.MEŠ 1-*en* UDU *ka-lu-ú*

23 *gi-né-e kab-ri*![5] *šá* GA 5 UDU.NÍTA *šá-nu-ú-tu šá* EGIR-*šú-nu šá* ŠE.BAR *la* GU$_7$.MEŠ

---

24 PAP *u*$_4$*-mi-šam kal* MU.AN.NA *a-na* 1-*en u*$_4$*-mu ina* 4 *nap-tan* 21 UDU.NÍTA *reš-tu-ú-tu ma-ru-tú*

25 DADAG.GA *šá* 2-*ta* MU.AN.NA.MEŠ ŠE.BAR GU$_7$.MEŠ 4 UDU *ka-lu-ú gi-né-e* 〈*kab-ri*〉 *šá* GA

26 25 UDU.NÍTA *šap-lu-ú-tú šá* EGIR-*šú-nu šá* ŠE.BAR *la* GU$_7$.MEŠ 2 GU$_4$ *rab-bu-tu*

27 1-*en* ^{gu_4}AMAR GA 8 ^{udu}SILA$_4$ 30 ŠEŠ^{mušen} 30 TU.KUR$_4$^{mušen} 3 KUR.GI^{mušen} *šá* NÍG.SILAG.GÁ GU$_7$〈.MEŠ〉

28 5 UZ.TUR^{mušen} *šá* ZÌ NÍG.SILAG.GÁ GU$_7$ 2 UZ.TUR^{mušen} *šá* EGIR-*šú-nu* 4 PÉŠ.GIŠ.GI 3 NUNUZ GA.NU$_{11}$^{mušen} 3 NUNUZ UZ.TUR^{mušen}

---

29 *u*$_4$*-mi-šam kal* MU.AN.NA 10 UDU.NÍTA *ma-ru-tu* DADAG.GA *šá* SI *ù* UMBIN *šuk-lu-lu*

30 *a-na* ^{d}LX *ù An-tu*$_4$ *šá* AN-*e* ^{d}SAG.ME.GAR ^{d}*Dil-bad* ^{d}GU$_4$.UD ^{d}GENNA ^{d}*Ṣal-bat-a-nu*

31 KUR-*ḫa* ^{d}UTU *ù* IGI.DU$_8$.ÀM ^{d}XXX *a-na na-qé-e lìb-bi ina* É *ma-ḫa-az-za-at in-né-ep-pu-uš*

---

32 UD.16.KAM *šá* ITI-*us-su* 10 UDU.NÍTA SAG-*ú-tú ma-ru-tú* DADAG.GA *šá* SI *u* UMBIN *šuk-lu-lu*

33 *a-na* ^{d}LX *ù An-tu*$_4$ *šá* AN-*e ù* ^{d}UDU.IDIM.MEŠ 7-*šú-nu a-na sa-al-qa i-na*

34 *te-bi-ib-tu*$_4$ ŠU^{II} *ina* BÁRA.MAḪ *ziq-qur-rat* ^{d}LX *ki-ma šá* UD.16.KAM *šá* ^{iti}AB DÙ-*uš*

---

35 *e-lat* UDU.NÍTA *gi-né-e šá kal* MU.AN.NA *šá* É.AN.NA *ù* É.MEŠ DINGIR.MEŠ ^{d}TIR.AN.NA^{ki}

36 *ù e-lat* GU$_4$ *ù* UDU.NÍTA *šá a-na gu-uq-qa-né-e* ÈŠ.ÈŠ.MEŠ BAD-*te* KÁ.MEŠ

37 ^{túg}*lu-bu-šá-at* ^{dug}A.GÚB.BA.MEŠ *ba-a-a-at*.MEŠ KI.NE.MEŠ GARZA.GARZA *ḫa-šá-du*

38 *ka-ri-bi*.MEŠ *ù tar-di-i-tu*$_4$ LUGAL *šá ina* GARZA *šá kal* MU.AN.NA *šaṭ-ri šá ina* É *re-eš*

39 É ÈŠ.GAL É.AN.NA *ù* É.MEŠ DINGIR.MEŠ TIR.AN.NA^{ki} *a-na* ^{d}LX *An-tu*$_4$ *u* DINGIR.MEŠ DÙ.A.BI *i-qar-rub*

---

40 *ina* É ^{d}UTU UZU UDU.NÍTA *a-na* ^{d}ŠÁKKAN *ul i-qar-ru-ub*

41 *ina* É ^{d}XXX UZU GU$_4$ *a-na* ^{d}NIN.GUBLAGA *ul i-qar-ru-ub*

42 UZU MUŠEN *a-na* ^{d}GAŠAN.EDEN *ul i-qar-rub* UZU GU$_4$ *ù* UZU MUŠEN *a-na* ^{d}EREŠ.KI.GAL *ul i-qar-rub*

---

43 *qàt* ^{Id}UTU-SUR A *šá* ^{I}*Ina-qí-bit*-^{d}LX A *šá* ^{I}*Šib-qát*-^{d}LX

44 ^{giš}DA GARZA ^{d}LX-*ú-tú* ŠU.LUḪ.ḪA KÙ.MEŠ *sak-ke-e* LUGAL-*ú-tú a-di* ŠU.LUḪ.ḪA DINGIR.RA *šá* É *re-eš* ÈŠ.GAL

45 É.AN.NA *ù* É.MEŠ TIR.AN.NA^{ki} *al-ka-ka-at* ^{lú}MAŠ.MAŠ.MEŠ ^{lú}GALA.MEŠ *u* ^{lú}NAR.MEŠ *ù* DUMU.MEŠ *um-man-nu*

46 *nap-ḫar-šú-nu šá* EGIR ^{lú}PAP(?) *a-na ma-še-e ma-la šá* ^{lú}ŠÁMAN.MAL.LÁ *kul-lu*$_4$ *ki-i pi-i ṭup-pi*.MEŠ

47 *šá* ^{Id}AG-A-URÙ LUGAL KUR *tam-tì* TA *qé-reb* UNUG^{ki} *iš-lu-lu-ma i-nu-uš* ^{I}*Ki-din*-^{d}LX ^{lú}UNUG^{ki}-*a*

48 ^{lú}MAŠ.MAŠ ^{d}LX *u An-tu*$_4$ ^{lú}ŠÀ.BAL.BAL ^{I}*É-kur-za-kir* ^{lú}ŠEŠ.GAL-*i šá* É.SAG *ṭup-pi*.MEŠ MU.MEŠ

---

[5] Copy: -*lu*.

49 *ina* KUR ELAM.MA^{ki} *ip-pal-lis-ma ina* BALA-*e* ^{I}*Se-lu-ku u* ^{I}*An-ti-ʾ-i-ku-su* LUGAL.MEŠ
50 *iš-ṭur-ú-ma a-na qé-reb* UNUG^{ki} *ú-bi-il*

Obv.

1 Every day of the entire year, for the main meal of the morning, you will arrange (l. 2), in addition to the *šappu*-containers belonging to the libation bowls,
2 18 golden *šappu*-containers on the offering table of Anu. Of these (18 containers) you will arrange in the presence of Anu (l. 5): 7 *šappu*-containers on the right,
3 3 with barley-beer, 4 with *labku*-beer, (and) 7 *šappu*-containers on the left, 3 with barley-beer, 1 with *labku*-beer,
4 1 with *nāšu*-beer, 1 with *zarbābu*-beer, and milk in an alabaster *šappu*-container,
5 (and) 4 golden *šappu*-containers with drawn wine.
6 For the second (meal) of the morning and the main and second (meal) of the evening ditto, but
7 no milk will be served for the main and second (meal) of the evening. Among the golden *šappu*-containers
8 for the offering table, there are 5 golden *šappu*-containers with a *zarīnu*-stand of *algamišu*-stone.

---

9 5 golden *šappu*-containers, each holding 1 litre, are the libation bowls of the cella [of Anu].
10 Of these (5 golden *šappu*-containers:) 1 with barley-beer, 1 with *labku*-beer, 1 with *nāšu*-beer, 1 with drawn wine [and 1 with milk].
11 The *šappu*-container holding 5 *akalu*, is for wine from the country Izallu. 4 [golden] *til*[*imtu*-vases]
12 belong to the cella of Anu. Of these 1 golden *tilimtu*-vase [is decorated(?)] with almonds,
13 1 golden *tilimtu*-vase, which is decorated with rosettes,
14 1 golden *tilimtu*-vase, which has a torque around its neck, 1 [golden] *tili*[*mtu*-vase, which …]
15 (This makes) a total of 4 golden *tilimtu*-vases on stands […]
16 of Anu and Antu […]

---

17 You will arrange 14 golden *šappu*-containers on the offering table of Antu (containing:) (the same) first-quality beers, exactl[y as those on the offering table of Anu].
18 12 golden *šappu*-containers (are to be set up) in front of Ištar, 10 *šappu*-containers in front of [Nanāja].
19 Not included are: the golden *šappu*-containers of the whole year for the (other) gods residing in [Uruk].

---

20 And not included are (also): the golden *šappu*-containers, which (are filled) with the travel provisions for (the procession of) the gods and the 2 *tilimtu*-vases, which […] will set up.

---

21 Every day of the entire year: 1 *pūru*-bowl (containing) 3 kor (540 litres), 3 *pānu* (108 litres) of barley and [emmer],
22 (in other words, in sexagesimal ciphers) 1,48 seah (or in decimal ciphers) 108 seah (648 litres), the original amount of the regular offerings, according to the seah-measure of 10 mina […]
23 which the millers in the (temple)kitchen will deliver (l. 24) every day for the 4 meals of [Anu], Antu,
24 Ištar, Nanāja and the (other) gods, residing in Uruk, to the bakers.

25 Of (these 108 seah-measures there will be) 81 seah (486 litres) of barley flour (and) 27 seah (162 litres) of emmer flour
26 which the baker will use in baking 243 *ṣibtu*-loaves. Of these (loaves) the baker will deliver (l. 27), for the 4 (daily) meals,
27 on the offering table before Anu 30 *ṣibtu*-loaves.
28 (That is specified:) for the main and second (meal) of the morning the baker will deliver 8 *ṣibtu*-loaves each;
29 for the main and second (meal) of the evening the baker will deliver 7 *ṣibtu*-loaves each.
30 (Furthermore,) 30 loaves in front of Antu, 30 loaves in front of Ištar, 30 loaves in front of Nanāja, 12 loaves in front of
31 the seat of Anu and the household god of the cella of Antu, 4 loaves in front of the 2 tiaras of Anu,
32 16 loaves in front of the temple tower and the household god of the temple tower, 16 loaves in front of the wings(?) of the cella of Anu
33 and Antu, totalling 168 *ṣibtu*-loaves, which the baker will deliver for the 4 (daily) meals.
34 Not included are the 75 loaves, which will be served (l. 35) to the (other) gods, residing in Uruk, in their temples
35 for the 4 (daily) meals. Not included are (also) the large(?) loaves and the date cakes
36 which are for the travel provisions of the gods, the *guqqû*-offerings, the *eššēšu*-ceremonies, the opening of the gate ceremonies, the clothing ceremonies,
37 the holy water (basin) ceremonies, the night vigil ceremonies, the brazier ceremonies, the rites of the divine marriage, (the offerings of) the *kāribu*s
38 and the additional offerings of the king (consisting of(?):) red (cakes), which are (collected) in reed baskets (usually used) for *muttāqu*-cakes
39 (and) *takkasû*-cakes, which are collected in reed baskets (usually used) for *makūtu*-cakes (and) *kubbušu*-cakes,
40 and (furthermore) 1200 *kusīpu*-loaves (baked in) oil, which are placed (l. 41) under the choice dates and the Dilmun-dates,
41 and pressed oil will be served (l. 42) upon the *kalakku*-container of Anu, Antu and the (other) gods of Uruk
42 and *maṣḫatu*-flour in *masappu*-baskets from the storage room,
43 which the miller will deliver every day during the whole year to a temple enterer.
44 The miller will say (l. 45), while grinding (flour) on the millstone, the blessing (l. 45) 'O Plow-star, they have hitched up the seeder-plow in the open country'
45 and the baker will say (l. 47), while kneading the pieces of dough,
46 and serving the hot (loaves), the blessing (l. 47) 'O Nisaba, rich abundance,
47 pure meal'.

---

48 Every day of the year, for the 4 (daily) meals (in sexagesimal ciphers) 1,48 seah (or in decimal ciphers) 108 seah (648 litres) choice dates,
49 Dilmun-dates, figs and raisins, in addition to *ḫiṣṣaṣātu*-cakes(?) and the table-arrangement, which will be served (l. 50) to Anu,
50 Antu, Ištar, Nanāja and the (other) gods, residing in Uruk.

Rev.
1 The oxen and sheep for the regular offerings, which will be served (l. 3) every day of the year to Anu, Antu, Ištar, Nanāja
2 and the (other) gods, residing in the Rēš-temple, the Ešgal-temple and the Ešarra-temple, (which is) the Baramaḫ on the temple tower of Anu,

3 from the first day of Nisannu through the thirtieth day of Adaru for the main meal of the morning:

---

4 For the main meal of the morning, during the whole year: 7 first-quality sheep, fat (and) pure,
5 which have been fed barley for 2 years; 1 *kālû*-sheep, for the regular offering, fattened with milk;
6 totalling 8 sheep for the regular offerings. (Furthermore) 1 full-grown ox, 1 suckling calf and 10 fat sheep,
7 of lesser quality, which have not been fed barley. Totalling, for the main meal of the morning, during the whole year: 18 sheep,
8 of which 1 is a suckling *kālû*-sheep for the regular offering, 1 full-grown ox (and) 1 suckling calf. While
9 slaughtering the oxen and sheep the butcher will say the ble[s]sing (beginning with the words:)

---

10 'The son of Šamaš, the lord of the cattle, will create in the open country a fertile meadow'.

---

11 Alternatively: while slaughtering the ox and sheep the he[ad]-butcher will say (l. 12) to Anu, Antu, the 'Big Star'
12 and Dilbat (a prayer for?) life, (but) he will not say (it) to the other gods.

---

13 (For) the second meal of the morning, the regular offerings for Anu, Antu and the (other) gods of their temples,
14 (i.e.) of the Rēš-temple, the Ešgal-temple and the Baramaḫ, during the whole year: 6 fat, pure sheep, which have been fed barley for 2 years;
15 1 (*kālû*-)sheep for the regular offering, fattened with milk and 5 fat sheep of lesser quality, which have not been fed barley; 1 full-grown ox; 8 lambs, 5 ducks, which have been fed dough;
16 2 ducks of lesser quality, 3 geese, which have been fed dough(!); 4 *ušummu*-mice;
17 30 *marratu*-birds; 20 turtledoves; 3 ostrich eggs (and) 3 duck eggs.

---

18 (For) the main meal of the evening, the regular offerings for Anu, Antu and the (other) gods of their temples, during the whole year:
19 4 fat, pure sheep, which have been fed barley for 2 years; 1 *kālû*-sheep,
20 for the regular offering, fattened with milk; 5 other sheep of lesser quality, which have not been fed barley, and 10 turtledoves.

---

21 (For) the second meal of the evening, the regular offerings for Anu, Antu and the (other) gods of their temples, during the whole year:
22 4 fat, pure sheep, which have been fed barley for 2 years; 1 *kālû*-sheep,
23 for the regular offering, fattened with milk; 5 other sheep of lesser quality, which have not been fed barley, and 10 turtledoves.

---

24 Totalling, every day during the whole year, for the 4 meals of the day: 21 first-quality sheep, fat,
25 pure, which have been fed barley for 2 years; 4 *kālû*-sheep, for the regular offering, ⟨fattened⟩ with milk;
26 25 'lower' sheep of lesser quality, which not have been fed barley; 2 full-grown oxen;

27 1 suckling calf; 8 lambs; 30 *marratu*-birds; 30 turtledoves; 3 geese, which have been fed dough;
28 5 ducks, which have been fed dough(!); 2 ducks of lesser quality; 4 *ušummu*-mice; 3 ostrich eggs (and) 3 duck eggs.

---

29 Every day during the whole year: 10 fat, pure sheep, whose horns and hooves are perfect,
30 will be slaughtered (l. 31) for Anu and Antu of the Heaven, (for) Jupiter, Venus, Mercury, Saturn (and) Mars,
31 (at?) sunrise and the appearance of the moon, to be offered as voluntary(?) offering in the *bīt maḫazzat*.

---

32 On day 16, monthly, (the priest) will offer (l. 34) 10 first-quality sheep, fat (and) pure, whose horns and hooves are perfect,
33 for Anu and Antu of Heaven and the 7 planets, as cooked meat, on occasion of
34 the cleansing of the hands ceremony, in the Baramaḫ on the temple tower of Anu, just like on day 16 of Ṭebētu.

---

35 Not included are the sheep for the regular offerings throughout the year in the Eanna-temple and the (other) temples of Tiranna,
36 and (also) not included are the oxen and sheep, which will be served (l. 39) for the *guqqû*-offerings and *eššēšu*-ceremonies, the opening of the gate ceremonies,
37 the clothing ceremonies, the holy water (basin) ceremonies, the night vigil ceremonies, the brazier ceremonies, the rites of the divine marriage,
38 (the offerings of) the *kāribu*s and the additional offerings of the king, which are written down in (the tablets of) the rites for the whole year, in the Rēš-temple,
39 the Ešgal-temple, the Eanna-temple and the (other) temples of Tiranna for Anu, Antu and all the (other) gods.

---

40 In the temple of Šamaš mutton will not be served to Šakkan.
41 In the temple of Sîn beef will not be served to Ningublaga.
42 Fowl will not be served to Bēlet-ṣēri; neither beef nor fowl will be served to Ereškigal.

(Colophon:)
43 (Written by) the hand of Šamaš-ēṭir, son of Ina-qibīt-Anu, son of Šibqat-Anu.
44 Wax-table (containing) the rites for the Anu-worship, the pure *šuluḫḫu*-purification rites, the ritual regulations of kingship, including(?) the divine *šuluḫḫu*-purification rites of the Rēš-temple, the Ešgal-temple,
45 the Eanna-temple and the (other) temples of Tiranna, the ritual activities of the exorcists, the lamentation priests, the singers and the craftsmen,
46 all of them, who are subservient to the …, not to mention all that concerns the apprentices, in accordance with the contents of the tablets,
47 which Nabopolassar, king of the Sealand, carried off from Uruk. And at that time(?) Kidin-Anu from Uruk,
48 the exorcist of Anu and Antu, descendant of Ekur-zakir, the high priest of the Rēš-temple,
49 saw these tablets (l. 48) in the land of Elam and during the reign of Seleucus and Antiochus, the kings,
50 he copied and brought (them) to Uruk.

Comments

Obv.

l. 3, the reading *labku* (cf. *RAcc.*, 75; *CAD*, L, 34a) is preferable to *ribku* (cf. *AHw*, 980b: 'ein (Drogen-)Absud'): see *SpTU* 3, no. 100, 5, where *labāku* is found in the context of brewing beer (reference of M. Stol).

l. 4 ff., for milk see M. Stol, in *RLA* 8 (1994), 192. See also obv. 10.

l. 5, 4 {PA} *šap-pi*.MEŠ, similar mistake in *Bagh. Mitt. Beih.* 2, no. 1, 18, see Mayer's comments on the latter in *OrNS* 47 (1978), 453.

l. 7 and passim in this and other Late Babylonian rituals: *i-qar-rub*, *qerēbu* is an *i*/*i*-verb but in the Neo- and Late Babylonian period often an *u*/*u*-verb. Cf. W. von Soden *GAG*, § 87, b.

l. 8, *za-ri-i-ni* na4[UD].SAL.[KA]B 'a *zarīnu*-stand of *algamišu*-stone', cf. *CAD*, Z, 68a.

l. 10, or, instead of milk: [KAŠ *zar-ba-ba*], *zarbābu*-beer?

l. 11, Azallu / Izallu. Wine imported from this country is famous, see A.L. Oppenheim, *JCS* 21 (1967), 244.

l. 19, 'the golden *šappu*-containers of the whole year', i.e. containers used for the offering service during the whole year.

l. 21, instead of BUR = *pūru*, W. Farber (*TUAT* II/2, 228 with n. 21, a) suggested BUR = *naptanu(*?) 'Speiselieferung'.

l. 24, *i-na*[*m-d*]*i-in*, a singular although a subjunctive in the plural (see the subject lúḪAR.MEŠ) is intended. In l. 33 and 43 a subjunctive ending *-u* is also missing.

l. 31, the 2 tiaras of Anu, see A. Falkenstein, *Topographie*, 19 with n. 3. Cf. also E. Unger, in *RlA* 2 (1938), 201 ff., especially p. 209–10; E. Douglas van Buren, *AnOr* 23, 104 ff.; *CAD*, A/I, 157a (commentary).

l. 31 (see also 32), DINGIR É 'household god' (cf. W. Farber, *TUAT* II/2, 229), i.e. the protective god of Antu's cella. For 'the 2 tiaras of Anu' see R. Wallenfels, *Uruk. Hellenistic Seal Impressions in the Yale Babylonion Collection. I. Cuneiform Tablets*, Mainz am Rhein, 1994 (AUWE 19), 135.

l. 32, *aḫānu* 'wings'(?), cf. *CAD*, A/I, 169b, B, 2. W. Farber, *TUAT* II/2, 229: 'Nebenkapellen'.

l. 35, *i-qar-rub*, the subjunctive ending *-u* is missing (see also l. 50, and rev. 3 and 39).

l. 37 (see also rev. 38), for the *kāribu*, see III.7.2.

l. 38–39, following *CAD*, K, *kubbušu*, 483b.

l. 41, *iš-šak-kan*, a singular N-stem, although a subjunctive in the plural is intended.

l. 41, 'upon the *kalakku*-container' (see *CAD*, K, 64a, 3, b and ib., Ḫ, 51a, 1). Or perhaps: 'at the expense of (*ana muḫḫi*) the silo' (following W. Farber, *TUAT* II/2, 229), see the following l. 42, where the storage room is mentioned.

l. 46, cf. *CAD*, E, 151a, c and *AHw*, 214b, 2, b. W. Farber (*TUAT* II/2, 229) translates: 'und wenn er (den Teig) auf die heißen (Backsteine) verstreicht'.

l. 49, *ḫiṣṣaṣātu*-cake(?), cf. *AHw*, 349a. See also *CAD*, Ḫ, 203b, '*ḫiṣṣaṣtu*-mats?' Or perhaps *ḫasisātu* (cf. *CAD*, Ḫ, 126b; *AHw*, 330b) bread in the form of an ear (suggestion M. Stol)?

Rev.

l. 2, É ÈŠ.GAL 'Ešgal-temple' (see also 14; 39; 44), the temple of Ištar in Hellenistic Uruk. It is also attested in *KAR* 132, I, 23 (written ÈŠ.GAL.LA ÚRU.GAL), and *BRM* 4, 6, obv. 22; 26; rev. 39. It is also known from private contracts from Hellenistic Uruk: L. Speleers, *Recueil*, 296, obv. 3 ([É] ÈŠ.GAL) and *VS* 15, 19, rev. 20. In other contracts it also refers to a city quarter of Uruk, see A. Falkenstein, *Topographie*, 36–39; add: *VS* 15, 27, obv. 3; G. Kh. Sarkisjan, *FuB* 16 (1975), 38, no. 25, obv. 3; 4.

The reading of this temple name has been much discussed. The reading ÈŠ.GAL is accepted widely (cf. *MSL* IV, 12 f., the dictionaries *CAD*, E, 364, 3, a, and *AHw*, 257a, 2, and recently A.R. George, *House Most High*, no. 270), contra IRI_{10-11}.GAL (cf. A. Falkenstein, *Topographie*, 31–34 and J.J.A. van Dijk, *AfO* 20 (1963), 162 f.).

l. 2, Rēš, it is not clear whether É = *bītu* has to be interpreted as the determinative ^{é}(Rēš) or whether we should read Bīt-Rēš; cf. J. Oelsner, *Materialien*, 330, n. 200 with literature. See also A.R. George, *House Most High*, no. 940.

l. 2 (see also 14, 34), the BÁRA.MAḪ 'Grand Dais', appellative of the sanctuary, named É.ŠÁR.RA 'House of the Universe', was the temple on top of the Anu-temple tower, cf. A. Falkenstein, *Topographie*, 27 ff.; A.R. George, *House Most High*, no. 1036. Cf. also *BRM* 4, 6, obv. 22; 26; rev. 40.

l. 5 (see also 8, 19, 22, 25), UDU *ka-lu-ú* 'sheep (pastured on) *kālû*-land', according to *CAD*, K, 105a, 2; ib., I-J, 131b, b'; or: *udukalû*-offering sheep, cf. *AHw*, 1402a. See also *TU* 39, obv. 8. I will follow the *CAD*. Note that attested in the same position in some Sippar texts is *pargallu* (*AHw*, 1582a), see F. Joannès, *RA* 82 (1988), 76 f.; Ungnad *NRV Glossar*, nos. 738–9, 745 etc.

l. 10, 'the lord of the cattle', i.e. Šakkan.

l. 11, 'Big Star', i.e. the planet Jupiter.

l. 12, 'Dilbat', i.e. the planet Venus.

l. 15, 1 (*kālû*-)sheep for the regular offering, fattened with milk (*gi-né-e kab-ri šá* GA): in l. rev. 5, 19 and 22 a *kālû*-sheep is mentioned for the main meal of the morning and the two meals of the evening, each time with the additional remark 'for the regular offering, fattened with milk'. In the summing up of all animals (l. rev. 24–28), however, 4 *kālû*-sheep are mentioned with this additional remark (however without the noun *kabri* 'fattened', which is probably a slovenlines of the scribe). Therefore the sheep mentioned in l. rev. 15 (for the second meal of the morning), with the same additional remark, is also a *kālû*-sheep; the scribe mistakenly wrote UDU.NÍTA for UDU *ka-lu-ú*.

l. 16 (see also 28), ZÌ NÍG.SILAG.GÁ: l. rev. 15 mentions 5 ducks which have been fed dough (NÍG.SILAG.GA, *līšu*), while l. 16 mentions 3 geese which have been fed ZÌ NÍG.SILAG.GA ('dough (and?) flour', according to *CAD*, Q, 207b, 9′). However, when the text sums up all the offering animals (l. 24–28), it refers back to the 3 geese, which have been fed dough, now written NÍG.SILAG.GA (without ZÌ, l. 27), and it refers back to the 5 ducks, which have been fed ZÌ NÍG.SILAG.GA, so now with ZÌ. (l. 28). It is clear that this is a scribal error (the scribe made another mistake in l. rev. 25, see my comment below), and in all cases we have to translate 'dough'. B. Landsberger (*WdO* 3 [1966], 252, with n. 25) already pointed out that *līšu* is written ZÌ.SILAG.GA. Cf. also B. Landsberger, O.R. Gurney, *AfO* 18 (1957–58), p. 330, l. 173: ZÌ.SILAG.GA = *li-e-*[*šu*].

l. 25, UDU *ka-lu-ú gi-né-e* ⟨*kab-ri*⟩ *šá* GA. *Kab-ri* 'fattened' is mistakenly omitted by the scribe. See my comment on l. rev. 15.

l. 31, see *CAD*, M/I, 89a. Or with W. Farber, *TUAT* II/2, 231: 'für *Herz-Opfer* im *Schlachthof* geschlachtet'? Cf. also *AHw*, 745a, 4, b and *CAD*, N/I, 340b, 3, b, but quoted without translation. For the *bīt maḫazzat* (or *bīt maḫaṣṣat*) see R. Zadok, *JAOS* 102 (1982), 116a: etymological evidence points into the direction of a 'wall, partitionwall', or 'a kind of gallery which is divided/set apart by a partition/compartment, apartment'.

l. 35 (see also 39; 45), $^{(d)}$TIR.AN.NA^{ki} is a Late Babylonian writing for Uruk. See also *TU* 39, rev. 29; *TU* 41, rev. 14; *BRM* 4, 6, obv. 23; 27; rev. 38; 40. Cf. A. Falkenstein, *Topographie*, 40, n. 4.

l. 41, probably ^{d}NIN.GUBLAGA (EZENxLA) is intended, although the copy reads ^{d}NIN.EZENxGU$_4$. See also *KAR* 132, I, 10. For l. 40–42 see also *CAD*, Q, 234b, 4. The god Ningublaga is the son of Nanna and resides in Kiabrig, in the temple É ^{d}NIN.EZEN (Å.W. Sjöberg, *TCS* III, p. 25–6, no. 11; cf. G. Selz, *Die Bankettszene*, Wiesbaden, 1983, 572), but he is also known from Ur (A.R. George, *House Most High*, nos. 295; 379; see also nos. 103, 294, 438, 499, 921). See also K.L. Tallqvist, *AGE*, 402 (NIN.EZEN+ḪÁR (GUD)). For the reading NIN.EZENxLA cf. R. Borger, *ABZ*, p. 242 and 386 with literature.

l. 43–50, for the colophon, see A. Falkenstein, *Topographie*, 8 f.; H. Hunger, *AOAT* 2, 46, no. 107; P.A. Beaulieu, *Studies W.W. Hallo*, Bethesda, 1993, 47.

l. 45, although in general ^{lú}MAŠ.MAŠ probably has to be read *āšipu*, we have evidence that in some literary texts for ^{lú}MAŠ.MAŠ (with the phonetic complements *-šu* or *-ši*) the learned reading *mašmaššu* is used (cf. *CAD*, A/II, 435a and M/I, 381b). For the Late Babylonian and Hellenistic periods both readings are attested. Based on the syllabic writings of *āšipu* in the clan list *VS* 15, 1, I, 8 and the prebend sale *YOS* 20, 84 (NCBT 1954, unpublished), 2 f. and 6, both from Hellenistic Uruk, G.J.P. McEwan (*FAOS* 4, 73) argued that the reading *mašmaššu* is to be excluded during the Hellenistic period. This seems to be supported by *CLBT*, pl. 1, col. B, 27 and possibly 29, where we find the syllabic writings *a-ši-pu* / *a-ši-*[*pu-ti*(?)]. However, from Late Babylonian Uruk we now also have evidence for the reading *mašmaššu*: *SpTU* 1, no. 56 (list), rev. 13: ^lú^*maš-maš-ši*, and *SpTU* 3, 111 (ḪAR.RA = *ḫubullu*), rev. VI, x + 1: ^lú(?)^*maš-maš-šu* (cf. J. Oelsner, in: *Šulmu IV, Papers Presented at the International Conference Poznan, 19–22 September, 1989*, 235).

l. 46, ^lú^ŠÁMAN.MAL (usually MÁL).LÁ *kul-lu*$_4$, see *CAD*, Š/I, 293b, 1′, contra H. Hunger, *AOAT* 2, 46, no. 107 (^lú^ŠAMÁN.MÁL.LÁ NUMUN.LUM 'lernender Opferschauer').

l. 47, *i-nu-uš*, see *CAD*, I-J, 163a, but not certain.

l. 48, ^lú^ŠEŠ.GAL-*i* 'the high priest', ^lú^ŠEŠ.GAL with the phonetic complements -*ú* or -*i* in texts from Hellenistic Uruk (see also *BRM* 4, 7, obv. 3, 7, 10, 14, 18, 22, 26, rev. 39, 45), and Babylon (see BM 32206 +, I, 20, 22; II, 75; III, 115; IV, 150; without the phonetic complements in *RAcc*., 127 ff. passim) probably has to be read *aḫu rabû* instead of *šešgallu*, cf. *CAD*, A/I, 204–5, ib., Š/II, 336b, and G. Çağirgan, W.G. Lambert, *JCS* 43–45 (1991–93), 101a. See also G. Frame, *ZA* 81 (1991), 42 and A.C.V.M. Bongenaar, *The Neo-Babylonian Ebabbar Temple at Sippar*, 149 f., with more references.

l. 50, *iš-ṭur-ú-ma* 'he has copied' (lit. 'written'), a plural although a singular is intended, see *ú-bi-il* in the same line.

b. The New Year ritual

TU 39 (AO 6459)[6] + *TU* 40 (AO 6465)[7]

These two tablets contain the ritual for the seventh month Tašrītu, the New Year festival (*akītu*) in Uruk. On the basis of prosopographical evidence we can give it an approximate date. Because *TU* 39–40 was written by the same scribe as *TU* 38, it can also be dated to the first half of the second century B.C. But we can be more precise here, by way of connecting the data on the scribe of *TU* 38 and *TU* 39–40, Šamaš-ēṭir, with the data on the owner of *TU* 39–40, Anu-uballiṭ, son of Nidintu-Anu, son of Ina-qibīt-Anu, of the family Ḫunzû. This Anu-uballiṭ is also known from two extispicy texts, dated 97 and 98 S.E. (215/4–214/213 B.C.),[8] and one astronomical text.[9] We also know more than one Anu-uballiṭ, son of Nidintu-Anu, of the family Ḫunzu from several private contracts.[10]

So, while the earliest date of scribe Šamaš-ēṭir is 118 S.E., the earliest date of owner Anu-uballiṭ is from 20 years before that, 97/98 S.E. Now, although the latest date of Šamaš-ēṭir is 150 S.E., it is not likely that Anu-uballiṭ was still alive at that time. Tablets *TU* 39–40 must have been written at least 20 years before 150 S.E., but not much earlier then 118 S.E., because at that time Šamaš-ēṭir could not have been working, considering his long career. Therefore *TU* 39–40 must have been written between approximately 115 and 130 S.E. (182/1 B.C.)

The text is discussed in II.4.5.1.

TU 39

U.E.
ina INIM ^{d}LX *u An-tu*$_4$ *liš-lim*

Obv.
1 ^{iti}DU$_6$.KÙ UD.1.KAM ^{d}EN.LÍL ^{d}*É-a ù šu-ut* UNUG^{ki} *il-lab-biš-ʾ*
2 ^{giš}GIGIR ^{d}LX KÙ.BABBAR ^{giš}GIGIR ^{d}LX GUŠKIN *u*$_4$*-mu* 1*-šú a-di* UD.8.KAM *it-ti tar-den-nu šá še-rì*
3 *a-na* É *a-ki-i-tu*$_4$ *e-lit šá* ^{d}LX GIN*-ak*.MEŠ*-ma* ^{lú}NAR.MEŠ *ina* IGI*-šú-nu* GIN*-ak*
4 *par-ṣi šá ḫa-šá-du ina* É ḪI.LI.KÙ.GA É.NIR *šá* É.ḪI.LI.AN.NA
5 É ^{d}*Na-na-a up-tar-ra-aṣ*

---

6 UD.6.KAM ^{d}IM ^{d}UTU ^{d}LUGAL.BÀN.DA *ù* ^{d}NIN.SÚN MU$_4$.MU$_4$*-ʾ ina* EN.NUN.USAN ^{dug}A.GÚB.BA *uk-tan-nu*

---

[6] Cf. *RAcc.*, 66–67, 89–90, 92–96, 98–99; G. Çağirgan, *Festivals*, 72–77, 87–81; W. Farber, *TUAT* II/2, 223 ff.; M.E. Cohen, *Cultic Calendars*, 431–33. See also R. Borger, *HKL* 1, 567.

[7] Cf. *RAcc.*, 72, 90–92, 96–97; G. Çağirgan, *Festivals*, 76–81; M.E. Cohen, *Cultic Calendars*, 431–33.

[8] R. Largement, *ZA* 52 (1957), 254, 116 (duplicate *TU* 4, but with different scribe), dated 97 (var. 99) S.E. i.e. 215/4 B.C. (213/2 B.C.); *BRM* 4, 12, 84 (duplicate no. 13, but with different scribe), dated 98 (var. 99) S.E. i.e. 214/3 (213/2) B.C.

[9] *TU* 11, rev. 38.

[10] *VS* 15, 36, dated 36 S.E., *OECT* 9, 11, dated 43 S.E., *BRM* 2, 21 (here with the grandfather, Labaši), 75 S.E.; *BRM* 2, 23, 78 S.E.; *OECT* 9, 57, dated 110 + S.E.; *BiMes* 24, 13, dated 137 S.E. In I 15, 26 the date is lost.

7 UD.7.KAM *di-ik* É *šá* ^{lú}GALA.MEŠ *ù* ^{lú}NAR.MEŠ ^{lú}MUḪALDIM *a-kal*.MEŠ *u* ŠÌR ḪÚL.LA
8 ^{uzu}*šu-me-e* UZU GU$_{4}$ *ù* UDU *ka-lu-ú gi-né-e* KAŠ SAG *nap-ḫar-šú-nu*
9 *a-di* GEŠTIN ŠUR.RA *ù* GA *ma-ak-kàs* KAŠ.Ú.SA SIG$_{5}$ *ù* KAŠ.Ú.SA *lab-ku*
10 *ti-ir-mat*$^{!}$.MEŠ *dan-nu-tu ù nam-ḫa-ri*.MEŠ *a-ri-bi šá* ^{d}PAP.SUKKAL *ù* ^{d}GUŠKIN.KÙ.BÀN.DA
11 *a-na* É *pa-pa-ḫa* ^{túg}*lu-bu-šá-at šá* ^{d}LX *ù An-tu*$_{4}$ *ù* ^{túg}*lu-bu-šá-at šá* ^{d}INNIN
12 *ta-ra-aṣ šá* GU$_{4}$ *ina bi-rit šid-di zi-im-ri šá* ^{lú}NAR *ù* ^{lú}GALA
13 *gu-uq-qa-né-e šá* EGIR ^{túg}*lu-bu-uš-tu*$_{4}$ *ù si-il-tu*$_{4}$ *ḫu-ub* É
14 *ma-la-ku su-qa*.MEŠ ^{giš}MÁ.GUR$_{8}$.MEŠ *ù* É *a-ki-i-tu*$_{4}$ KEŠDA *u* DUḪ-*ár*
15 *nap-tan šá še-e-ri ù li-lat ki-ma šá* UD.7.KAM *šá* ^{iti}BÁR KI.MIN

---

16 UD.8.KAM KÁ *ina pa-ni* ^{d}LX *ù An-tu*$_{4}$ BAD-*te-ma* ^{d}PAP.SUKKAL ZI-*ma a-na* KISAL.MAḪ E$_{11}$-*ma*
17 *ina* É.KA.KÉŠ.ḪU.ḪU *man-za-zi-šú a-na tar-ṣa* ^{d}LX *i-tar-ra-aṣ*
18 ^{d}NUSKU ^{d}ARA *ù* ^{d}KÙ.SÙ ZI.MEŠ-*nim-ma ina* DA ^{d}PAP.SUKKAL GUB-*zi-zu*
19 ^{giš}*tal-lu* GUŠKIN É-*a-ni a-na* ^{d}LX SUM-*in* ^{giš}TUKUL.MEŠ ^{d}UTU.MEŠ *ù* GIGIR.MEŠ ZI.MEŠ-*nim-ma*
20 *ina* KISAL.MAḪ *a-na* ^{d}LX LAL-*aṣ* ^{d}IM ^{d}ŠA.LA ^{d}XXX ^{d}UTU ^{d}MAŠ ^{d}MES.SAG.UNUG^{ki}
21 ^{d}IGI.DU ^{d}LUGAL.BÀN.DA *ù* ^{d}NIN.SÚN TA É.MEŠ-*šú-nu* ZI.MEŠ-*nim-ma*
22 *a-na* KISAL.MAḪ E$_{11}$.MEŠ-*ma a-na* ^{d}LX *i-tar-ra-aṣ* A.MEŠ ŠU^{II} *a-na* ^{d}LX *u An-tu*$_{4}$
23 ÍL-*ši-ma* LUGAL *u* UN.MEŠ *ú-lap-pat ma-aq-qu-ú* GUŠKIN *i-red-de-e-ma*
24 *nap-tan ù* ^{uzu}*šu-me-e ḫa-an-ṭu-tú ina muḫ-ḫi na-šap-pi* GUŠKIN *a-na* ^{d}LX
25 *ú-qar-rib na-šap-pi* GUŠKIN *pa-ni* ^{d}LX *ana pa-ni* DINGIR.MEŠ *šá ina* KISAL.MAḪ *ú-še-ti-iq*
26 ^{d}PAP.SUKKAL GIN-*ak-ma ina muḫ-ḫi* É.GÙ.BI.DÙG.GA GUB-*za-az* ^{lú}KU$_{4}$.É *ma-aq-qu-ú* GUŠKIN
27 *i-red-de-e-ma* ^{d}PAP.SUKKAL *ù* ^{lú}MAŠ.MAŠ.MEŠ ŠU^{II} ^{d}LX DAB-*bat*.MEŠ-*ma ina* ^{lú}MAŠ.MAŠ.MEŠ
28 È-*am-ma* 1-*en* ^{lú}KU$_{4}$.É *šá* ^{túg}ÍB.LÁ *rak-su* ^{giš}Ù.LUḪ NAM.LUGAL.LA *ina pa-ni-šú*
29 *na-ši-i-ma ki-ma šá* ^{d}LX *bi-rit šid-di ik-tal-du ina muḫ-ḫi šu-bat* GUŠKIN *ina bi-rit šid-di* DÚR-*ab* A.MEŠ ŠU$^{II!}$ ÍL
30 *ina muḫ-ḫi* KI SÍSKUR GABA.RI *i-sar-raq-ma* SÍSKUR *mer-de-e-tú* GU$_{4}$ *u* UDU.NÍTA
31 *ina pa-ni* ^{d}LX *i-naq-qa* ^{uzu}*lìb-bi šá* GU$_{4}$ *ù* SAG.DU *šá* UDU.NÍTA *ina pa-ni-šú i-šak-kan*
32 *ma-lit* GUŠKIN *šá* ZÌ.MAD.GÁ *a-na muḫ-ḫi* ^{uzu}*lìb-bi i-saḫ-ḫap ma-aq-qu-ú* GEŠTIN
33 ⸢*a-na*⸣ *muḫ-ḫi* SAG.DU UDU.NÍTA *i-red-de* A.MEŠ ŠU^{II} *a-na* ^{d}LX ÍL-*ši-ma*
34 [LUGAL *u* UN.MEŠ *ú-lap-pat m*]*a-aq-qu* GUŠKIN *i-red-de-e-ma* ^{d}PAP.SUKKAL *ù* ^{d}NUSKU
35 [...] ⸢^{lú}⸣MAŠ.MAŠ.MEŠ ⸢^{lú}N⸣[AR.MEŠ ...]
36 [...]

***TU* 40**

Obv.
1 [UD.9.KAM ... ^{lú}G]ALA.MAḪ GIN [...]
2 LÚ.MAḪ *ina* BA.AN.DU$_{8}$.DU$_{8}$ ⸢x⸣[...]
3 *šit-ti* A.MEŠ *a-na* ŠU^{II} ^{lú}GALA.⸢MAḪ⸣ [...]
4 ŠU^{II}-*su* LAL-*aṣ-ma* EN NIR.GÁL.LA [...]
5 ŠU.ÍL.LÁ.KAM *a-na* ^{d}LX ÍL-*ši* [...]
6 A.MEŠ ŠU^{II} *a-na* ^{d}EN.LÍL *ù* [^{d}*É-a* ÍL-*ši* ...]

7 ^{lú}DUMU *si-si-i pag-ri* GU$_4$ *su-uš-šú* [...]
8 LUGAL *ma-aq-qu-ú* GUŠKIN *i-red-de-*⸢*e*⸣[...]
9 KÁ.MAḪ KU$_4$-*ub-ma ina muḫ-ḫi* BÁRA NAM[.MEŠ DÚR-*ab*]
10 UDU.NÍTA *šá* TA *nu-bat-tu*$_4$ *it-ti* KÁ KISAL.[MAḪ(?) *rak-su*(?)]
11 *par-ṣi-šú ki-ma šá* UD.8.KAM KI.MIN KÁ ÈŠ.M[AḪ ...]
12 NU È *ina muḫ-ḫi* SAR-*ár* ^{giš}*tal-lu* GUŠKIN [...]
13 LUGAL *ma-aq-qu-ú* GUŠKIN *a-na* ^{d}LX *i-red-d*[*e-e* ^{d}PAP.SUKKAL LUGAL *u* ^{lú}MAŠ.MAŠ.MEŠ]
14 ŠU^{II} ^{d}*A-nù* TA BÁRA NAM.MEŠ DAB-*bat*.MEŠ-*ma n*[*ap-tan*(?)]
15 *ul* DUḪ-*ár ki-ma šá* ^{d}LX *bi-rit šid-du ik-t*[*al-du* ...]
16 *ina bi-rit šid-du pa-ni-šú a-na* ^{d}UTU.È.A GAR-*an-m*[*a* ...]
17 *ina muḫ-ḫi šu-bat* GUŠKIN DÚR-*ab* ^{d}IM KI.TUŠ GAL *ina* ŠÀ ⸢x⸣[...]
18 DINGIR.MEŠ *gab-bi ina man-za-zi-šú-nu* GUB-*zi-zu-ʾ* IGI.MEŠ-*šú-nu a-n*[*a* ^{d}LX GAR-*an*.MEŠ]
19 ^{d}INNIN.MEŠ *nap-ḫar-ši-na a-na pa-ni An-tu*$_4$ LAL-*aṣ*.MEŠ-*a-ma* [...]
20 A.MEŠ ŠU^{II} *a-na* ^{d}LX *ù An-tu*$_4$ ÍL-*ši-ma* LUGAL *ù* UN.MEŠ [*ú-lap-pat*]
21 *ma-aq-qu-ú* GUŠKIN *i-red-de-e-ma* SÍSKUR *mer-de-e-tú* GU$_4$ *u* UDU.NÍTA *ki-m*[*a šá* UD.8.KAM]

***TU* 40**

Rev.

1 ^{uzu}*lìb-bi šá* GU$_4$ *ù* SAG.DU *šá* UDU.NÍTA *ina pa-ni-šú* [*i-šak-kan*]
2 *ma-lit* GUŠKIN *šá* ZÌ.MAD.GÁ *a-na muḫ-ḫi* ^{uzu}*lìb-bi i-saḫ-ḫap ma-aq-q*[*u-ú* GEŠTIN *a-na*]
3 *muḫ-ḫi* SAG.DU UDU.NÍTA *i-red-de* A.MEŠ ŠU^{II} *a-na* ^{d}LX *ù An-t*[*u*$_4$ ÍL-*ši-ma*]
4 LUGAL *u* UN.MEŠ *ú-lap-pat ina* 2 *kal-lu*$_4$ *šul-pu* GUŠKIN A.MEŠ ŠU^{II} *a-n*[*a* ^{d}LX *u An-tu*$_4$]
5 KI *a-ḫa-a-meš* ÍL-*ši* LUGAL *ma-aq-qu* GUŠKIN [*i-red-de-e-ma*]
6 ^{d}PAP.SUKAL LUGAL *ù* ^{lú}MAŠ.MAŠ.MEŠ ŠU^{II} ^{d}LX TA *bi-rit šid-du* D[AB-*bat*.MEŠ-*ma*]
7 KU$_4$-*ma ina muḫ-ḫi* BÁRA NAM.LUGAL.LA *ina šub-ti-šú* DÚ[R-*ab* ...]
8 KU$_4$.MEŠ-*ma* XV *u* 2,30 GUB-*zi-zu* LUGAL *ma-aq-qu-ú* [GUŠKIN *i-red-de-e-ma*]
9 LUGAL ^{lú}MAŠ.MAŠ.MEŠ *u* ^{d}INNIN.MEŠ ŠU^{II} *An-tu*$_4$ DAB-*bat*.MEŠ-*ma a-*[*na* ...]
10 ^{d}*Be-let*-DINGIR.MEŠ ^{d}ŠA.LA ^{d}DUMU.SAL.MEŠ-^{d}LX ^{d}*A-a* [...]
11 *ina šu-tùm-mu šá* KISAL *An-tu*$_4$ DÚR-*ab ki-ma šá* ^{lú}[...]
12 LUGAL *ma-aq-qu-ú* GUŠKIN *a-na pa-ni* ^{d}EN.LÍL *ù* [^{d}*É-a i-red-de-e-ma*]
13 ^{d}NUSKU ^{d}KÙ.SÙ ^{d}ARA *ù* LUGAL ŠU$^{\text{[II}}$ ...]
14 DAB-*bat*.MEŠ-*ma* KÁ É *pa-pa-ḫa a-na pa-ni* [...]
15 ^{d}UTU ^{d}*A-a* ^{d}*Bu-ne-ne* ^{d}MAŠ ^{d}[...]
16 *ù* ^{d}ŠU.BU.LÁ ^{d}MES.SAG.UNUG^{ki} [...]
17 LUGAL *ma-aq-qu-ú* GUŠKIN *a-na pa-ni* [...]
18 LUGAL *a-di* UB.ŠU.UKKIN.NA.KI ⸢x⸣[...]
19 ^{lú}MAŠ.MAŠ.MEŠ ⸢^{lú}GALA.MEŠ⸣ [*u* ^{lú}NAR.MEŠ ...]
20 ⸢x⸣

b. The New Year ritual

***TU* 39**

Rev.

1 UZU [...]

2 *ina šub-ti-šú šá* KISAL DÚR-*ab* ^{uzu}KIN ÍL.MEŠ-*nim-ma ana* UGU BÁRA ^{d}LX *i-šak-kan-nu*

3 ^{lú}DUMU.AD.ḪAL *ù* ^{lú}SANGA ^{d}IM ^{uzu}KIN *i-leq-qu-ú* GAL-*ú* DUḪ-*ma*

4 *tar-den-nu i-qar-rub níg-na-qa*.MEŠ *ú-mál-le-e-ma* ^{lú}NAR.MEŠ *i-za-am-mu-ru*

5 É *i-šal-lim* SILIM^{im}.MA.ÁB(?) DUG$_4$.GA-*ma ul* DUḪ-*ár ina li-lat* DUḪ-*ár-ma*

6 *nap-tan* GAL-*ú šá li-lat i-qar-rub níg-na-qa* GUŠKIN *ú-mál-le-e-ma* ŠÍSKUR

7 GU$_4$ *ù* UDU.NÍTA *i-naq-qa* ^{lú}NAR.MEŠ *i-za-am-mu-ru* GAL-*ú* DUḪ-*ma*

8 *tar-den-nu i-qar-rub* ^{lú}NAR.MEŠ *i-za-am-mu-ru* É *i-šal-lim*

9 SILIM^{im}.MA.ÁB(?) DUG$_4$.GA-*ma ul* DUḪ-*ár ba-a-a-at i-ba-at* KÁ *ut-ta-dal*

---

10 UD.10.KAM *ina* GE$_6$ UMUN ŠE.ER.MA.AL AN.KI.A *a-na* ^{d}LX AN E.LU$_4$.UM.MA *a-na* DINGIR.DIDLI

11 *ina* UB.ŠU.UKKIN.NA.KI *di-ik* É *iš-šak-kan ina* ZÁLAG KÁ BAD-*te-ma ba-a-a-at* DUḪ-*ma*

12 A.MEŠ ŠU^{II} ÍL-*ši* Ì.GIŠ *iṣ-ṣa-bat nap-tan* GAL-*ú šá še-rì i-qar-ru-ub*

13 ^{lú}NAR.MEŠ *i-za-am-mu-ru* GAL-*ú* DUḪ-*ma tar-den-nu i-qar-rub tar-den-nu* DUḪ-*ma*

14 *nap-tan* GAL-*ú šá li-lat i-qar-rub* ^{lú}NAR.MEŠ *i-za-am-mu-ru tar-den-nu šá li-lat* DUḪ-*ma* KÁ *ut-ta-dal*

---

15 UD.11.KAM *ina* GE$_6$ AM.E AMAŠ {DIŠ}.AN.NA *a-na* ^{d}LX E.LUM DI.DI.RA *a-na* DINGIR.DIDLI

16 *ina* UB.ŠU.UKKIN.NA.KI *di-ik* É *iš-šak-kan ina* ZÁLAG KÁ BAT-*te-ma* A.MEŠ ŠU^{II} ÍL-*ši*

17 ^{d}IM ^{d}XXX ^{d}UTU ^{d}MAŠ ^{d}MES.SAG.UNUG^{ki} ^{d}PAP.SUKKAL ^{d}NUSKU ^{d}ARA *u* ^{d}KÙ.SÙ

18 ZI.MEŠ-*nim-ma ina* KISAL.MAḪ *a-na* ^{d}LX LAL-*aṣ ina* KISAL *ina muḫ-ḫi šu-bat*.MEŠ DÚR-*ab*.MEŠ-*ma*

19 *pa-ni* ^{d}LUGAL.BÀN.DA *u* ^{d}NIN.SÚN *i-dag-gal-la nap-tan* GAL-*ú šá še-e-ri*

20 *a-na* ^{d}LX *An-tu*$_4$ *ù* DINGIR.MEŠ DÙ.A.BI *i-qar-rub ki-ma šá* ^{d}LUGAL.BÀN.DA *u* ^{d}NIN.SÚN

21 *ik-tal-du a-na* KISAL ^{d}LX KU$_4$-*ma a-na* ^{d}LX LAL-*aṣ* GAL-*ú* DUḪ-*ár-ma ma-aq-qu-ú* GUŠKIN

22 *a-na* ^{d}LUGAL.BÀN.DA *ù* ^{d}NIN.SÚN *ù* DINGIR.MEŠ-*šú-nu-tú i-red-de-e-ma a-na*

23 *šub-ti-šú-nu* GUR-*ru*.MEŠ-*ma uš-šá-ba* GAL-*ú ù tar-den-nu šá bi-ru u*$_4$-*mu*

24 *ki-ma šá gi-né-e* KI.MIN-*ma*

---

25 *an-nu-ú* GARZA *šá* ^{iti}DU$_6$.KÙ AL.TIL

---

26 ^{iti}APIN DU$_8$.A UD.5.KAM ^{d}*Mi-šar-ri* TA É.ḪÉ.NUN.NA É ^{d}IM ZI-*am-ma*

27 TA ^{giš}DA SUMUN-*bar gaba-re-e* UNUG^{ki} SAR-*ma ba*-IGI IM ^{Id}LX-DIN-*iṭ* A *šá* ^{I}NÍG.SUM.MU-^{d}LX

28 A ^{I}*Ḫun-zu-ú* ^{lú}MAŠ.MAŠ ^{d}LX *u An-tu*$_4$ UNUG^{ki}-*ú* ŠU^{II} ^{Id}UTU-SUR A *šá* ^{I}*Ina-qí-bit*-^{d}LX A *šá* ^{I}*Šib-qát*-^{d}LX

29 ^{lú}ŠÀ.BAL.BAL ^{I}*É-kur-za-kir* ^{lú}MAŠ.MAŠ ^{d}LX *u An-tu*$_4$ TIR.AN.NA^{ki}-*ú*

***TU* 39**

U.E.
By the command of Anu and Antu may (this work) be successful.

Obv.

1 The (seventh) month Tašrītu, day 1: Enlil, Ea and those (other gods) of Uruk will be robed.

2 The silver chariot of Anu (and) the golden chariot of Anu will go (l. 3) each day until day 8, at the time of the second meal of the morning,

3 to the higher situated *akītu*-temple of Anu, and the singers will go in front of them.

4 The rites of the divine marriage will be performed (l. 5) in the Eḫilikuga-chapel, the bed-chamber of Eḫilianna,

5 the temple of Nanāja.

6 Day 6: Adad, Šamaš, Lugalbanda and Ninsun will be robed, at the first watch of the night the holy water-basin will be set up.

7 Day 7: the awakening of the temple ceremony (performed) by the lamentation priests and the singers. (As to) the cook: food and songs of jubilation,

8 roasted meat, beef and mutton for the regular offerings, all sorts of fine beer,

9 including drawn wine and milk, date confection, fine mixed beer and *labku*-mixed beer,

10 *tirimtu*-cups(?), *dannu*- and *namḫaru*-vats (shaped like) raven(?) for Papsukkal and Guškinbanda.

11 As to the cella: the clothing ceremonies of Anu and Antu and the clothing ceremonies of Ištar.

12 The setting in place of the ox. (Inside the room) between the curtains: songs by the singer and the lamentation priest.

13 (The presentation of) *guqqû*-offerings which follow the clothing ceremony and (the presentation of) the *siltu*-food (offerings). The consecration of the temple.

14 The street processional way, the procession-ships and the *akītu*-temple. The arranging and the clearing of

15 the meal of the morning and the evening, as for the seventh day of the month Nisannu ditto.

16 Day 8: the gate will be opened before Anu and Antu and Papsukkal will rise and come down (from his seat) to the Grand Courtyard and

17 will take up position in Ekakešḫuḫu, his station, in the direction of Anu.

18 Nusku, Usmû and Kusu will rise and stand next to Papsukkal.

19 The gold(-plated) carrying pole (for use) inside (the temple) will be given to Anu. The symbols, the sun disks and the chariots will rise and

20 take up position towards Anu in the Grand Courtyard. Adad, Šala, Sîn, Šamaš, Ninurta, Messagunug,

21 Palil, Lugalbanda and Ninsun will rise from their temples and

22 come down (from their seats) to the Grand Courtyard and take up position towards Anu. (The priest) will lift up (l. 23) the water (basin) for (the washing of) the hands to Anu and Antu

23 and he will sprinkle(?) the king and the (other) persons. He will make a libation with the golden libation bowl and

24 he will serve (l. 25) the meal and the hot roasted meat on the golden dish to Anu.

25 He will pass the golden dish (from) before Anu to the (other) gods, who are in the Grand Courtyard.

26 Papsukkal will go and stand up on Egubiduga. A temple enterer will, with the golden libation bowl,
27 make a libation and Papsukkal and the exorcists will lead Anu and he will go out (l. 28) and, accompanied by the exorcists,
28 and one temple enterer, who is girt with a girdle, he will lift up (l. 29) the Scepter of Kingship in front of him.
29 (Then), as soon as Anu has reached (the room) between the curtains, he will sit on the golden seat (in the room) between the curtains (while the priest) is lifting up the water (basin) for (the washing of) the hands.
30 He will scatter (aromatics) on the place where (the god) is made to accept the offering and he will make (l. 31) a *merdītu*-offering (consisting) of ox and sheep
31 in front of Anu. He will place the heart of the ox and the head of the sheep in front of him.
32 He will overturn a golden *malītu*-bowl with *maṣḫatu*-flour over the heart. With a libation bowl of wine
33 he will make a libation on the head of the sheep. He will lift up the water (basin) for (the washing of) the hands to Anu and
34 [sprinkl]e(?) [the king and the (other) persons]. He will make a libation with the golden libation bowl and Papsukkal and Nusku
35 […] the exorcists and the si[ngers …]
36 […]

***TU* 40**

Obv.

1 [(Day 9:) … the ch]ief lamentation priest will go […]
2 The *lumaḫḫu*-priest from the bucket […]
3 The rest of the water (basin) for (the washing of) the hands of the ⸢chief⸣ singer of dirges […]
4 He will stretch his hands and the hand-raising prayer (l. 5) 'Lord, Respected one' […]
5 he will recite to Anu […]
6 [He will lift up] the water (basin) for (the washing of) the hands to Enlil [and Ea …]
7 The charioteers […] the corpses of the oxen, … […]
8 The king will make a libation with the golden libation bowl […]
9 (Anu) will enter the Grand Gate and [sit] on the Dais of Destinie[s].
10 The sheep, which since the evening (ceremonies?) [was tied(?) to] the gate of the [Grand(?)] Courtyard,
11 its rites as for the eighth day ditto. The gate of the Ešm[aḫ …]
12 will not go out; he will write(?) on it. The gold(-plated) carrying pole […]
13 The king will make a libation with the golden libation bowl for Anu. [Papsukkal, the king and the exorcists]
14 will lead Anu from the Dais of Destinies. [The meal]
15 will not be cleared. When Anu has re[ached] (the room) between the curtains […]
16 (inside the room) between the curtains he will place his face towards the East a[nd …]
17 he will sit on the golden seat. Adad [will …] on the great seat in the middle of […]
18 All the gods will stand on their stations, they [will place] their faces t[owards Anu].
19 All the goddesses will take up position before Antu and […]
20 (The priest) will lift up the water (basin) for (the washing of) the hands, and [sprinkle(?)] the king and the (other) persons […]
21 He will make a libation with the golden libation bowl and a *merdītu*-offering (consisting of) ox and sheep as [for the eighth day ditto.]

TU 40

Rev.

1 [He will place] the heart of the ox and the head of the sheep in front of him.

2 He will overturn a golden *malītu*-bowl of *maṣḫatu*-flour over the heart. He will make(l. 3) a libation of [wine] with a liba[tion bowl]

3 on[to](l. 2) the head of the sheep. He [will lift up] the water (basin) for (the washing of) the hands to Anu and Ant[u and]

4 sprinkle(?) the king and the (other) persons. In 2 *kallu*-bowls (and) a golden *šulpu*-vessel he will lift up the water for (the washing of) the hands t[o Anu and Antu]

5 simultaneously [...]. The king [will make] a libation with the golden libation bowl [and]

6 Papsukkal, the king and the exorcists w[ill lead] Anu from (the room) between the curtains.

7 He will enter and sit on the Dais of Kingship, on his seat [...]

8 They will enter and stand on the right and the left, the king [will make a libation] with the [golden] libation bowl [and]

9 the king, the exorcist and the goddesses will lead Anu and t[o...]

10 Bēlet-ilī, Šala, Mārāt-Anu, Aja [...]

11 will sit in the storehouse of the courtyard of Antu. As soon as [...]

12 The king will make a libation with the golden libation bowl before Enlil and [Ea and]

13 Nusku, Kusu, Usmû and the king will lead (l. 14) [...]

14 and (from) the gate of the cella before [...]

15 Šamaš, Aja, Bunene, Ninurta, ... [...]

16 and Šubula, Messagunug [...]

17 The king [will make(?) a libation] with the golden libation bowl before [...]

18 The king [will go] up to Ubšukkinaku ...[...]

19 the exorcists, ⸢the lamentation priests⸣ [and the singers ...]

20 ⸢x⸣

TU 39

Rev.

1 meat ...[...]

2 He will sit on his seat in the courtyard. They will lift up and place the liver on the Dais of Anu.

3 The diviner and the *šangu*-priest of Adad will take the liver. The main (meal) will be cleared and

4 the second meal will be served. (The priest) will fill the censers and the singers will sing and (then)

5 'the temple will stay intact, keep it safe!'(?) they will say, and (the meal) will not be cleared. In the evening (the meal) will be cleared and

6 the main meal of the evening will be served. (The priest) will fill the golden censers and he will make (l. 7) offerings

7 of ox and sheep. The singers will sing (and) the main (meal) will be cleared. Then

8 the second (meal) will be served. The singers will sing and (then) 'the temple will stay intact,

9 keep it safe!'(?) they will say, and (the meal) will not be cleared. The vigil will continue the entire night. The gate will be closed.

---

10 Day 10: at night, (by means of the lamentations) 'Lord, respected one of Heaven and Earth' for Anu, (and) 'The honored one of Heaven' for the gods,

11 in Ubšukkinaku the awakening of the temple ceremony will be performed. At dawn the gate will be opened and the vigil will be ended. Then
12 a water (basin) will be lifted up for (the washing of) the hands. Oil will be taken, the main meal of the morning will be served.
13 The singers will sing. The main (meal) will be cleared and the second (meal) will be served. The second meal will be cleared. Then
14 the main meal of the evening will be served. The singers will sing. The second (meal) of the evening will be cleared and the gate will be closed.

---

15 Day 11: at night, (by means of the lamentations) 'The bull in his fold' for Anu, (and) 'The honored one who wanders about' for the gods
16 in Ubšukkinaku the awakening of the temple ceremony will be performed. At dawn the gate will be opened and a water (basin) will be lifted up for (the washing of) the hands.
17 Adad, Sîn, Šamaš, Ninurta, Messagunug, Papsukkal, Nusku, Usmû and Kusu
18 will rise and take up position towards Anu in the Grand Courtyard. In the courtyard they will sit on their seats and
19 wait for Lugalbanda and Ninsun. The main meal of the morning
20 will be served to Anu, Antu and all the (other) gods. As soon as Lugalbanda and Ninsun
21 have arrived, they will enter the courtyard and take up position towards Anu. The main (meal) will be cleared and with a golden libation bowl
22 (the priest) will make a libation for Lugalbanda and Ninsun and all those (other) gods. Then
23 (Lugalbanda and Ninsun) will return to their seats and sit. The main and second (meal) of the (last) double hour of the day
24 in the usual manner ditto.

---

25 These are the rites of the (seventh) month Tašrītu; completed.

(Catchline:)
26 The (eighth) month Araḫsamna, day 5: Mīšaru will rise from Eḫenunna, the temple of Adad and (will come here).
(Colophon:)
27 From an older wax table, a copy from Uruk. Copied and collated. Tablet of Anu-uballiṭ, son of Nidintu-Anu,
28 descendant of Ḫunzû, the exorcist of Anu and Antu, from Uruk. (Written by) the hand of Šamaš-ēṭir, son of Ina-qibīt-Anu, son of Šibqat-Anu,
29 descendant of Ekur-zakir, the exorcist of Anu and Antu, from Tiranna.

Comments

TU 39

U.E.

For the invocational formula see H. Hunger, *AOAT* 2, 12 ff.; J. Oelsner, *Materialien*, 210, n. 779 and 224 with n. 829; M.T. Roth, *JSS* 33 (1988), 1–9.

Obv.

l. 2, *it-ti* 'at the time of' (the second meal of the morning), following W. Farber, *TUAT* II/2, 224, seems better than translating literally 'with'.

l. 3, GIN-*ak* a singular although a plural is intended.

l. 4, the É.ḪI.LI.KÙ.GA 'House of Pure Luxuriance' is the name of the bed-chamber (É.NIR) of Nanāja (see M. Stol, in *RlA* 9 (1998), s.v. Nanaja), situated in the É.ḪI.LI.-AN.NA 'House of the Luxuriance of Heaven', the shrine of Nanāja. The É.ḪI.LI.AN.NA is also attested in *VS* 15, 13, a contract from Hellenistic Uruk concerning the sale of a plot of land, obv. 3 and 6 (gišKIRI$_6$ É.ḪI.IL.AN.NA 'the garden of Eḫil(i)anna'). Probably it has to be located not in the Ešgal, but in the Eanna-temple. Cf. A. Falkenstein, *Topographie*, 26, with. n. 2; 36 and 41; A.R. George, *House Most High*, nos. 459 and 464.

The É.NIR 'bed-chamber' (perhaps representing *É A.NIR = *bīt tānēḫi* 'House of Weariness', see A.R. George, *House Most High*, no. 899), is also mentioned in the Hellenistic ritual *TU* 41, obv. 6, here the bed-chamber of Antu in the Rēš-temple. It is also attested in a Late Babylonian (perhaps Hellenistic) list from Uruk enumerating different sections of temples, *SpTU* 1, no. 136, obv. 8′: É.NIR.MAḪ [KI] U$_8$.ZÉ.EB.BA.MU 'Exalted Bed-chamber, place where the sleep is made pleasant'.

l. 6, dugA.GÚB.BA *uk-tan-nu* 'the holy water-basin will be set up'; in similar context also in *BRM* 4, 6, rev. 33. *uk-tan-nu* is not a plural, but rather a Dt-stem present with 'überhängende Vokal' -*u* (cf. W. von Soden *GAG*, § 104, g; see also § 82, e and § 18, e): we have two more examples of *uk-tan-nu* where it is clearly connected with a singular subject. See *TU* 42 +, rev. 33′(2x). Furthermore we have several examples in Hellenistic rituals of a D-stem present singular *tu-kan-nu*. See *TU* 41, obv. 18; 20; 26; *Bagh. Mitt. Beih*. 2, no. 5, obv. 15.

l. 7, lúMUḪALDIM *a-kal*.MEŠ or perhaps lúMUḪALDIM.A.KAL.MEŠ 'bread bakers'? Cf. lúMU.NINDA, *MSL* 12, 234. Suggestion M. Stol.

l. 7, ŠÌR ḪÚL.LA 'songs of jubilation', cf. *CAD*, Z, 119a, a, although it looks out of place here together with the cook and several sorts of food.

l. 7, 'mutton', lit. '(meat of) *kālû*-sheep'.

l. 10, *ti-ir-mat*.MEŠ, *tirimtu*-cups(?), cf. *AHw*, 1361a.

l. 10, *dannu*- and *namḫaru*-vats, (shaped like) raven (*a-ri-bi*), following W. Farber, *TUAT* II/2, 224. *CAD*, A/II, 265b, 1, a is not certain. Perhaps similar to: 5 *ṣa-bit* '5 gazelle (shaped) vessels'(??), in *TU* 44, IV, 32 (but also not certain)? M.E. Cohen, *Cultic Calendars*, 431 (he only gives a translation) probably reads *e*!-*re-bi* and translates: 'the entering' (of DN$_1$ and DN$_2$).

l. 10, for dGUŠKIN.BÀN.DA the text reads dGUŠKIN.KÙ.BÀN.DA.

l. 16 (see also 20; 22; 25; *TU* 40, obv. 10(?); *TU* 39, rev. 18), KISAL.MAḪ 'Grand Courtyard' of the Rēš-temple. See also *TU* 41, obv. 3; 34; *TU* 42 +, obv. 2; *KAR* 132, I, 2; 7; 20; 30. The Grand Courtyard of Esagila is mentioned in *RAcc*., 136, 273 and 146, 456. The location of the Grand Courtyard (*kisalmaḫḫu*), situated by A. Falkenstein (*Topographie*, 22) in the 'Hof I', is now questioned by A.R. George, suggesting that 'either one of the several other courtyards in the temple's annexes or the principal courtyard of an outer precinct' is more likely (*BiOr* 53 [1996], 372).

l. 18, GUB-*zi-zu* (see also *TU* 40, rev. 8, and *TU* 40, obv. 18: GUB-*zi-zu-'*), probably a G-stem perfect plural *ittazizzū* (var. *ittašizzū*) with present meaning (see *CAD*, M/I, 236b, c), not (contra *AHw*, 409b, II, 1, b) *izzizū*, a G-stem preterite plural, in Late Babylonian also used as present, because a present is attested below l. obv. 26: GUB-*za-az*.

The verb *izuzzu* in G- and Š-stem (cf. W. von Soden, *ZA* 50 (1952), 163–69; id., *GAG*, § 107a-h; *AHw*, 408–9, 410a, sub 'Formen') is attested many times, with different spellings. To illustrate the variation in spellings attested in the Hellenistic rituals, we will give here a short survey of *izuzzu*:

1. G-stem (to stand):
   a. present singular masculine:
      - GUB-*za-az*: *TU* 39, obv. 26.
      - GUB-*za*: *TU* 42 +, obv. 32′ (GUB-[*za*(?)]); rev. 23′ (GUB-*z*[*a*(?)]); rev. 28′; *KAR* 132, II, 10 (or a plural femine, as in l. 6, 9, 15?); IV, 20; 23 (GUB-*za-ma*).
      - GUB-*az-ma*: *TU* 43, rev. 19 (see also *KAR* 60, obv. 18).
      - see also *TU* 44, II, 14 (GUB).
      - *iz-za-a*[*z*]: *TU* 43, obv. 8.
   b. present plural masculine:
      - GUB-*zu*: *TU* 42 +, rev. 24′ (GUB-*zu*!, copy has GUB-*za*); *KAR* 132, II, 2 ([GUB-*zu*]); 4.
      - GUB-*zu*.MEŠ: *KAR* 132, I, 11; 13.
      - GUB-*zi*.MEŠ: *KAR* 132, I, 21; IV, 11.
   c. present plural femine:
      - GUB-*za*: *KAR* 132, II, 6 (GUB-[*za*]); [9]; 15.
   d. a preterite, *iz-zi-za-ma*, but in the Late Babylonian period used as present, is attested once: *Bagh. Mitt. Beih.* 2, no. 6, obv. 18.
   e. perfect plural, with present meaning:
      - GUB-*zi-zu*: *TU* 39, obv. 18; *TU* 40, rev. 8; *TU* 42 +, obv. 19′; *KAR* 132, II, 16.
      - GUB-*zi-zu-'*: *TU* 40, obv. 18; *KAR* 132, II, 13.
   f. Furthermore a precative, *li-iz-zu-ka* (for *lizziz*(*z*)*ūka*, *TU* 43, rev. 4) is attested.
2. Š-stem (to make stand), all written syllabically:
   a. present singular masculine:
      - *tuš-za-za-ma*: *TU* 44, I, 14; *Bagh. Mitt. Beih.* 2, no. 14, 5′ (*tuš-za-za*).
      - *tuš-za-zi*: *Bagh. Mitt. Beih.* 2, no. 5, obv. 10.
      - *tuš-za-as-su-ma*: *Bagh. Mitt. Beih.* 2, no. 5, obv. 17.
      - see also in Neo-Assyrian texts: *tuš-za-za-a-ma* (*KAR* 60, obv. 6) and *tuš-za-az-ma* (*KAR* 50, rev. 8).
   b. We have one example of a preterite: *uš-ziz* (*Bagh. Mitt. Beih.* 2, no. 6, rev. 30).

l. 19, [giš]*tal-lu* 'carrying pole' see also *TU* 40, obv. 12. Also attested in the Uruk rituals *KAR* 132, IV, 20, 22, *TU* 42 +, obv. 18′, rev. 8′, 19′, 32′, and playing a major role in *BRM* 4, 7, obv. 4, 7, 11, 15, 19, 23, 26, rev. 40. Also known from Babylon: BM 47902 + (W.G. Lambert, *RA* 91 [1997], 52–56), I, 12–19. In his comments (ib., 56) Lambert suggested that the *tallu* might have been (or included) a portable incense altar. Note, however, that in *TU* 42 +, rev. 32′ff. a *tallu* of Ištar is mentioned before offering tables are placed in front of Ištar and the other gods and censers are filled, indicating perhaps that the *tallu* was not used for fumigation but had a different function. Evidence from Neo-Babylonian Sippar supports the translation 'carrying pole' (cf. A.C.V.M. Bongenaar, *The Neo-Babylonian Ebabbar Temple at Sippar*, 21, n. 247),

See also *RAcc.*, 141, 370, where based on the context for *tallu* a crossbeam in the top of Ezida, the cella of Nabû, is probably intended. For *tallu* = 'crossbeam(s) supporting a false ceiling below the roof itself', see A.R. George, *BTT*, 218.

l. 20, LAL-*aṣ*, a singular although a plural is intended. Other examples where a singular is written (usually LAL-*aṣ*), although from the context it is clear that a plural is intended: *TU* 39, obv. 22 (*i-tar-ra-aṣ*); *TU* 40, obv. 19; *TU* 39, rev. 18; 21 (KU_4-*ma* … LAL-*aṣ*, both singular).

l. 20 (see also *TU* 40, rev. 16; *TU* 39, rev. 17), ^{d}MES.SAG.UNUG^{ki} is a later writing of ^{d}MES.SANGA.UNUG^{ki}. For the latest information on this god see M. Krebernik, in *RlA* 8 (1993), 94–5. Cf. also *TU* 41, rev. 3, 5, 9, 10, 18, 20, 33; *KAR* 132, IV, 25.

l. 23 (see also 34, *TU* 40, obv. 20; rev. 4), *ú-lap-pat* 'sprinkle'(?) is probably better than 'smear' (for the latter see *TU* 41, obv. 10, see my comments on this line; *RAcc.*, 140, 350), following *CAD*, L, 92a, j. Cf. also *TU* 42 +, obv. 32′; rev. 26′; *KAR* 132, III, 18; IV, 11–12.

l. 27, ^{d}PAP.SUKKAL *ù* ^{lú}MAŠ.MAŠ.MEŠ ŠU^{II} ^{d}LX DAB-*bat*.MEŠ-*ma* 'Papsukkal and the exorcists will lead Anu', lit. 'will seize the hands of' (cf. *CAD*, Ṣ, 31a, b, 3′, c and 4′); the singular is usually written DAB-*bat-am-ma* or DAB-*bat-ma*. For more examples of the phrase *qātē ṣabātu* see for Uruk: *TU* 40, obv. 14; rev. 6; 9; 14. See also *TU* 41, obv. 34; rev. 3; 34(?); *TU* 42 +, obv. 25′ (unusual spelling of plural: DAB-*bat-ú-ma*); 34′; rev. 22′ (see also 32′); 27′ (DAB-*bat-ma*, a singular, although a plural is intended); *KAR* 132, I, 19; 27; III, 21; IV, 6; 13; *TU* 44, III, 27; *Bagh. Mitt. Beih.* 2, no. 1 (+ //), 30; W 18728 (A. Falkenstein, *UVB* 15 [1959], 40–44), rev. 8′. For Babylon see *RAcc.*, 143, 400. For a discussion see A.K. Grayson, in: *CRRA* 17, Ham-sur-Heure, 1970, 164 ff.; B. Pongratz-Leisten, *ina šulmi īrub*, 171 ff. with more text references. See also II.4.2.

l. 28, for ^{giš}Ù.LUḪ NAM.LUGAL.LA, see also *TU* 42 +, obv. 32′; rev. 16′, 22′–23′, 28′, and *Bagh. Mitt. Beih.* 2, no. 14, 4′.

l. 29, ŠU^{II}, the copy reads: *šu-ut*, see *RAcc.*, 90. n. 4.

l. 30, KI SÍSKUR GABA.RI 'the place where (the god) is made to accept the offering' (*šumḫuru*), cf. *AHw*, 579b, *maḫāru* Š; *CAD*, M/I, 68 f., *maḫāru* 10. See also *TU* 42 +, obv. 28′; 30′.

***TU* 40**, Obv.

l. 4–5, the complete incipit of this hand-raising prayer (*šuillakku*) is attested in *TU* 43, rev. 19.

l. 7, for *su-uš-šú* see *CAD*, S, 418–19, but no translation is suggested.

l. 9, KÁ.MAḪ 'Grand gate', cf. A. Falkenstein, *Topographie*, 10–11. See also *TU* 41, rev. 9; 12; *BRM* 4, 7, obv. 2. This gate is also mentioned in the building inscription *YOS* 1, 52, l. 4.

l. 9 (see also 14), BÁRA NAM.[MEŠ], 'Dais of Destinies'. See also *TU* 41, rev. 6; *TU* 42 +, obv. 32′; 35′; *KAR* 132, III, 21. The Dais of Destinies is most likely not located in the Grand Courtyard (courtyard I, cf. A. Falkenstein, *Topographie*, 22 f.; B. Pongratz-Leisten, *ina šulmi īrub*, 59 f.), but rather in the Ubšukkinaku, the large central courtyard in front of the Anu-Antu-temple, in the Rēš-complex (Falkenstein's courtyard VI, cf. ib., 10, 13, 22 ff.), according to A.R. George, *BiOr* 53 [1996], 373 f.

l. 10, KISAL.[MAḪ(?) *rak-su*(?)], following A. Falkenstein, *Topographie*, 23, n. 1.

l. 11, the ÈŠ.MAḪ, located in the Rēš-temple, is also attested in *KAR* 132, II, 16; 17. Cf. A. Falkenstein, *Topographie*, 24; A.R. George, *House Most High*, no. 281.

l. 12, *ina muḫ-ḫi* SAR-*ár* 'he will write(?) on it', this is rather sudden and strange in this context. Perhaps we should read *uqattar* 'he will make a fumigation on it' (suggestion M. Stol)?

l. 14, *n*[*ap-tan*], although the copy before the break reads AN, the context makes it clear that here a meal was mentioned. However, whether this was the main or the second meal is not clear.

***TU* 40**, Rev.

l. 4, *šulpu*-vessel, cf. *CAD*, Š/III, 257–8 (see also *AHw*, 1269b: 'Metalröhrchen'), but contra *CAD*, K, 83a, c: 'handle', which seems less likely since on other occasions *kallu* and *šulpu* are cleary separated by *u* 'and' (*CT* 51, 95, obv. 14); strong evidence can be found in the Late Babylonian ritual *LKU*, no. 51, rev. 5 where *kallu* and *šulpu* are also seperated by *u*, and furthermore both are preceded by the determinative DUG.

l. 6, D[AB-*bat*.MEŠ-*ma*], reconstruction following *TU* 39, obv. 27; *TU* 40, obv. 14; *TU* 40, rev. 9; 14. See my comment on *TU* 39, obv. 27, above.

l. 7, BÁRA NAM.LUGAL.LA 'Dais of Kingship', perhaps also in *TU* 43, rev. 18. Cf. A. Falkenstein, *Topographie*, 19.

l. 11, KISAL *An-tu*$_4$ 'courtyard of Antu'; for the latest discussion of KISAL see A.R. George, *BiOr* 53 (1996), 370 ff. (contra A. Falkenstein, *Topographie*, 21 with n. 6, and B. Pongratz-Leisten, *ina šulmi īrub*, 40, who translate 'Vorzella'). While A. Falkenstein situated the courtyard of Antu in 'Raum 16', the antechamber of the cella of Antu (*Topographie*, 25), A.R. George, ib., 372 suggested that the courtyard in front of this antechamber (Falkenstein's 'Hof I a') is more likely.

l. 18 (see also *TU* 39, rev. 11; 16), for the Ubšukkinaku (UB.ŠU.UKKIN.NA.KI), also attested in *TU* 41, rev. 5; 7; 9; 20; *KAR* 132, I, 4; *Bagh. Mitt. Beih.* 2, no. 12, obv. 12, see my comments on *TU* 40, obv. 9.

***TU* 39**, Rev.

l. 2 (see also 3), ^{uzu}KIN 'liver' (cf. *AHw*, 1351a, c, *CAD*, B, 122a, e' and Š/I, 382a, 3′). It is not attested elsewhere in Late Babylonian ritual texts.

l. 2, BÁRA ^{d}LX 'Dais of Anu', cf. A. Falkenstein, *Topographie*, 19. See also *TU* 43, rev. 18.

l. 5 (see also 8–9), É *i-šal-lim* SILIM^{im}.MA.ÁB, an Akkadian recitation incipit, but the translation is difficult: 'the temple will stay intact (or: will be completed), keep it safe!'(?) (suggestion M. Stol). Cf. *CT* 16, 7, 272: SILIM.MA.AB.

Less likely for the second part of the incipit is: SILIM^{-im}-*ma ma-lit* 'she is filled with peace'. Cf. M.E. Cohen, *Cultic Calendars*, 432–3, who does not transliterate but translates: 'He is reconciled (to) the house. *She is filled with peace*'. However, the problem here is that *malit* refers to a feminine subject while *bītu* (É) is masculine. See II.3.6.

l. 10, the lamentation 'The honored one of Heaven' is also attested in the Uruk eclipse of the moon ritual *BRM* 4, 6, rev. 51 and [53] and the duplicate BM 134701, obv. 11 and 13. Also mentioned for the *dīk bīti*-ceremony in the Uruk cultic calendar text *TU* 48, rev. 6, see II.2.2. The lamentation 'Lord, respected one of Heaven and Earth' is also mentioned in the Uruk building ritual text *TU* 46, rev. 9, an the Uruk *mīs pî*-ritual text *Bagh. Mitt. Beih.* 2, no. 1 (+ //), 24; 25. See M.E. Cohen, *Lamentations*, 413 ff.

l. 11 (see also 16), in my interpretation the *dīk bīti*-ceremony is the subject of *iššakkan*, but the lamentations in l. 10 can also be subject (cf. W. Farber, *TUAT* II/2, 226).

l. 15, the lamentation 'The bull in his fold' is also attested in *BRM* 4, 6, rev. 48, 49, 51, 52, and the duplicate BM 134701, obv. 7, 9, 11, 13. Also mentioned in connection with the *dīk bīti*-ceremony in *TU* 48, obv. 13, rev. 5, see II.2.2. The lamentation 'The honored one who wanders about' is also mentioned in connection with the *dīk bīti*-ceremony in *TU* 48, rev. 1, see II.2.2.

l. 19, *i-dag-gal-la* is a mistake for *i-dag-gal-lu*.

l. 23, *uš-šá-ba* is either a mistake for *uš-šá-bu* (plural) or a rare example of a dualis.

l. 23, *bi-ru* u_4-*mu*, see *AHw*, 130b, 3, b. See also II.2.2.

l. 27, *ba*-IGI (cf. *CAD*, G, 2b, b, 1) or BA.IGI (cf. H. Hunger, *AOAT* 2, 42, no. 99, 3) for *bari* is not attested elsewhere. The logogram IGI is used often, alone or in combination with KÁR, TAB, LAL and BAR, cf. H. Hunger, *AOAT* 2, 4 and index, 160a.

TU 43 (AO 6461)[11]

This text from Hellenistic Uruk contains part of a ritual for the New Year festival (*akītu*) of the month Nisannu. The text presents a *šuillakku*- (hand-raising) prayer, which has to be recited on the tenth day of the New Year festival, and a *šuillakku*-prayer on the eleventh day.

The text is discussed in II.4.5.1.

Obv.

1 ⸢^{giš}NÍG.GIDRU⸣ GAM.MA BAL.E NAM.LUGAL.LA NAM.BÍ.IN.S[A$_4$ …]
2 *ta-mi-ḫi ḫaṭ-ṭu kip-pat u pa-la-a na-bu-ú šar-ru-ú-tú*
3 NIR.GÁL DÌM.ME.ER.E.NE UKKIN.NA GAR.RA DÌM.ME.ER GAL.GAL.E.NE KA.TA.È.A.NI.ŠÈ SUN$_x$(BÚR).NA AK.AK.DA
4 *e-tel-lu* DINGIR.MEŠ *šá ina pu-ḫur šak-na šá* DINGIR.MEŠ GAL.MEŠ *šit-lu-ṭu ṣi-it pi-i-šú*
5 EN AGA KA.SILIM.MA U$_6$.BI.DI LA.LA SA$_5$.A
6 *be-lu a-gu-ú taš-ri-iḫ-tu$_4$ šá a-na tab-rat la-la-a ma-lu-ú*
7 U$_5$ UG.GAL.GAL.LA BÁRA NAM.LUGAL.LA.KE$_4$ NIR.GÁL.LA.BI.TA U$_6$.DI GUB.BA
8 *ra-kib u$_4$-mu rab-bu-tu šá ina pa-rak-ku šar-ru-tu a-na tab-rat e-tel-liš iz-za-a*[*z*]
9 KA.AB.BA.ZU.ŠÈ KA.KÙ.GA.TA ^{d}NUN.GAL.E.NE ZA.RA GEŠTUG^{II}.BI BAR.RA.A.NI (l.10:) IGI Ì.MA.AL
10 *a-na e-piš pi-i-ka el-lu* ^{d}Í.GÌ.GÌ *uz-na-ši-na ba-šá-a*
11 ^{d}A.NUN.NA.KE$_4$.E.NE NIGIN.NA.BI NÍ.BI ḪA.RA.AN.DÉ(!?).E
12 ^{d}*A-nun-na-ki nap-ḫar-šú-nu pal-ḫi-iš i-ba-ʾu-ka*
13 DÌM.ME.ER KÌLIB.BI.IR.RA DUG$_4$.GA.BI.ZU.ŠÈ GI U$_x$ (GIŠGAL).LU. GIN$_x$ (GIM) MU.UN.SÌG.SÌG.GA.E.NE
14 *a-na qí-bit-ka* DINGIR.MEŠ *nap-ḫar-šú-nu ki-ma* GI-*né-e me-ḫe-e i-šu-ub-*⟨*bu*⟩
15 E.NE.ÈM.ZU IM.GIN$_x$(GIM) IR.RA.BI Ú NAG.GÁ ŠÁR.RA
16 *a-mat-ka ki-ma šá-a-ri i-zi-iq ri-ʾ-i-tu$_4$ u maš-qí-tu$_4$ ud-da-áš*
17 DUG$_4$.GA.BI.TA KA.È.A.ZU.TA DÌM.ME.ER ŠÀ.DAB.BA.MU KI.TUŠ NAM.MU.UN.AN.GUR.RU
18 *ina qí-bit-ka* DINGIR.MEŠ *ze-nu-tu a-na šub-ti-šú-nu i-tur-ru*
19 DÌM.ME.ER AN.KI.A KÌLIB.BI.IR MÁŠ.DA.RA NÍG.ŠÀ.A IGI.ZU ḪÉ.EN.SI.SÁ.E.NE
20 DINGIR.MEŠ *nap-ḫar-šú-nu šá* AN-*e u* KI-*tì ina ir-bi u kat-re-e li-iš-te-šir ma-ḫar-ka*

Rev.

1 LUGAL KUR.KUR.E.NE GUN DUGUD.DA MU.UN.NA.AN.TÙM.MA.ZU
2 LUGAL.MEŠ *šá* KUR.KUR GUN-*su-nu ka-bit-ti li-bi-il-ú-ka*
3 A.ZA.LU.LU SÍSKUR KIR$_4$ ŠU MAR.RA UD.ŠÚ.UŠ ḪÉ.EN.LAḪ$_4$.LAḪ$_4$.GI.ZU
4 *te-né-še-e-ti ina ni-qa-a ut-ten-nen-ni u la-ban ap-pi u$_4$-mi-šam* (l. 5:) *li-iz-zu-ka*
5 ŠÀ.ḪUN.GÁ.ZU.ŠÈ DÌM.ME.ER GAL.GAL.E.NE NÍ.BI IN.TUR.TUR.RA
6 *a-na nu-uḫ lìb-bi-ka* DINGIR.MEŠ GAL.MEŠ *li-te-nu-ʾu-ú-ka*
7 BAR.ZU ḪÉ.EN.ŠED$_7$.DA.ZU.ŠÈ UN DA.MA.AL A.RA.ZU DÈ.RA. AB.B[A]
8 *a-na šu-up-šu-uḫ ka-bat-ti-ka* UN.MEŠ *da-ád-me tés-lit liq-bu-ú-k*[*a*]
9 DIMMER.GAL.GAL.E.NE UL A.RA.ZU.TA ŠÀ.ZU ḪÉ.EN.ḪUN.G[Á]
10 DINGIR.MEŠ GAL.MEŠ *ina an-na u tés-lit lìb-ba-ka li-ni-ḫ*[*i*]
11 KA.SÌ.SÌ.GA.TA KIR$_4$ ŠU MAR.R[A.TA] BAR.⸢ZU⸣ ḪÉ.EN.ŠED$_7$.E[.NE]

---

[11] Cf. *RAcc.*, 70–71, 108–111.

12 *ina te-me-eq u la-ban ap-pi* [*ka-bat-t*]*a-ka l*[*i-šap-ši*]*-iḫ*
13 UNUG.KI ÚRU.ZU NIGIN.NA.TA [...] ⸢x x⸣ [...]
14 *a-na Ú-ruk a-lu-ka ni-is*[...] ⸢x⸣ [...] ⸢x⸣ *ma ki* [...]
15 AN.GU.LA KI.BAL.ŠÈ ŠU ÚRU.ZU MU.UN.[GI...]
16 ^{d}*A-nù* GAL-*ú ina* KUR *nu-kúr-tu*$_{4}$ *gi-mil a-lu-k*[*a te-er*]

---

17 ŠU.ÍL.LÁ AN.NA.KE$_{4}$ *šá ina* ^{iti}BÁR UD.10.KAM *a-na* ^{d}⸢*A*⸣-[*nù i-na-aš-šu-ú*]

---

18 ^{iti}BÁR UD.11.KAM *ki-ma šá* ^{d}*A-nù ina muḫ-ḫi* BÁRA ^{d}LX *šá* BÁRA [NAM.LUGAL.LA(?) DÚR(*-bu*)]
19 [^{lú}G]ALA GUB-*az-ma* AN.NA Á.GÁL.LA MÍ.DUG$_{4}$.GA IM.R[A.BI.ŠÈ AN.KI.A]
20 [AŠ.E].NE NIR.GÁL.LA ŠU.ÍL.LÁ.KAM *ina muḫ-ḫi pa-la-ag-g*[*i* ÍL(*-ši*)]

---

21 [AN.NA Á.GÁL].⸢LA MÍ.DUG$_{4}$.GA IM.R⸣A.BI.ŠÈ AN.KI.A AŠ.E.NE [NIR.GÁL.LA]
22 [...] ⸢x⸣ *šá e-diš-ši-šú ina* AN-⸢*e*⸣
23 [...] ⸢*u*⸣ KI-*tì e-tel-lu*

Obv.

1–2 (You) (Anu) who holds the scepter, the loop, and the bala-symbol, who decrees kingship,
3–4 lord of the gods, whose utterance prevails in the established assembly of the great gods,
5–6 master of the crown of splendor, which is full of amazing decoration,
7–8 who rides the great storms, who stands on the Dais of Kingship in amazing lordly splendor,
9–10 the Igigi heed any command coming from your pure mouth;
11–12 all the Anunnaki gods come to meet you respectfully;
13–14 at your command all the gods tremble like reeds in a violent storm;
15–16 your word, when it blows like a wind, creates abundance in pasture and watering place;
17–18 the angry gods return at your command to their dwelling place;
19–20 may all the gods of Heaven and Earth proceed into your presence with gifts and presents!

Rev.

1–2 May the kings of all (foreign) lands bring you their substantial tribute!
3–4 May mankind stand by you every day through offering, prayer, and supplication!
5–6 May the great gods pray to you to calm your heart!
7–8 May the people of (all) inhabited regions address (their) invocation to you to appease your mind!
9–10 May the great gods make your heart relent through approval and invocation!
11–12 M[ay they appea]se your [min]d by intense prayer and supplication!
13–14 for/to Uruk, your city, ...[...] ...[...]
15–16 O, great Anu, [avenge] your city in enemy land!

---

17 Hand-raising prayer of Anu, which [they will recite] in the (first) month Nisannu, day 10, to A[nu].

---

18 The (first) month Nisannu, day 11, when Anu [sits] on the Dais of Anu, on the Dais [of Kingship(?)],

19 [the la]mentation priest will stand and [will recite] the hand-raising prayer (l. 20) 'Strong Anu, revered by [himself(?)], who [alo]ne is Lord (l. 20) [in Heaven and on Earth'],

20 to the accompaniment of a lyr[e].

21–22–23 ['Strong Anu], revered by himself(?), who alone is Lord in Heaven and on Earth'.

Comments

obv.

l. 1–2, GAM.MA // *kip-pat* 'loop' (cf. *CAD*, K, 398, c), or perhaps better 'ring', as one of the royal insignia (cf. *AHw*, 483a, 4, b)? Cf. also *RAcc.*, 137, 302; 144, 415; 145, 448.

l. 1–2, BAL.E // *pa-la-a*, cf. *AHw*, 817a, 3, a. Or mantle(?), cf. *CAD*, N/I, 32b lex. section.

l. 6 and 8, *a-na tab-rat* 'amazing', see *AHw*, 1299b, 3: 'zum Staunen', but cf. also *CAD*, L, 49a lex. section: 'pleasing to look at'.

l. 9–10, following *CAD*, B, 145a lex. section. See also *AHw*, 113a, G, 1, c and 2, c.

l. 11, ḪA.RA.AN.DÉ.E, we transliterate DÉ, following *CAD*, B, 179a lex. section (see also *CAD*, N/I, 292b lex. section): the copy has MÚRU, which is not *bâ'u*, nor any other verb. For *bâ'u* one would expect DIB (see for example *RAcc.*, 144, 413). Because MÚRU is a sign very similar to DÉ, *CAD* probably interpreted MÚRU as a mistake for DÉ (which is usually *šasû* and *abālu*), being an variant spelling of DIB elsewhere not attested.

l. 13–14, see *CAD*, Š/I, 18a, 1, b; however, the copy does not read KILIB (= LAGAB) but KÌLIB (= NIGIN) (see also l. 19).

l. 15–16, the translation of the first part follows the Sumerian. The Akkadian line reads: 'your word, when it blew like a wind' (preterite *zâqu*). Cf. *CAD*, Z, 64a lex. section.

l. 18–19, IGI.ZU ḪÉ.EN.SI.SÁ.E.NE // *li-iš-te-šir ma-ḫar-ka* 'may ... proceed into your presence', not *li-iš-te-'u* (contra *RAcc.*, 109; *CAD*, I-J, 174a lex. section; ib., K, 32b lex. section; ib., Š/II, 355b lex. section). The copy clearly reads *šir*, not *'u*. Furthermore, SI.SÁ is *ešēru*, not *še'û*. An identical writing is attested in the conjuration *CT* 17, 26, rev. 82–83 (ḪÉ.EN.SI.SÁ.E // *liš-te-šir*). See also the incantation *KAR* 223, obv. 12 (*lu-uš-te-šir ma-ḫar-ka* 'may I prosper in your presence') and the Neo-Assyrian ritual text IV R^2, 23, no. 1 +, III, 15–22 (SI.SÁ.BI // *šu-te-šir*) (damaged; see below in this Appendix). A problem is that the Sumerian verb is plural, while the Akkadian verb is singular, but this is a mistake which is also attested elsewhere in this text (cf. obv. 13–14: MU.UN.SÌG.SÌG.GA.E.NE // *i-šu-ub* and probably also, if restored correctly, in rev.11–12: ḪÉ.EN.ŠED$_7$.E[.NE] // *l*[*i-šap-ši*]-*iḫ*).

rev.

l. 3–4, for KIR$_4$ ŠU MAR.RA // *la-ban ap-pi* see also l. 11–12.

l. 4, *ut-ten-nen-ni* 'prayer' is missing in the Sumerian line. Cf. *AHw*, 1444, *utnēnu* I, 2, a. For the verb *utnēnu* see l. 6.

l. 4, *li-iz-zu-ka* for *lizziz(z)ūka* (cf. *RAcc.*, 109, n.2). See my comment on *TU* 39, obv. 18.

l. 5–6, for *li-te-nu-ʾ-ú-ka* (or *li-te-⟨nen(?)⟩-nu-ʾ-ú-ka*), see *RAcc.*, 109, n. 3; *AHw*,1444b, *utnēnu* II, 2, a; W. von Soden *GAG*, § 107, v; id., *ZA* 50 (1952), 181.

l. 8 and 10, *tés-lit* 'invocation / prayer', or perhaps *taṣ-lit* (see *RAcc.*, 109), because the cognate verb *sullû* 'to pray' and the noun *sullû* 'prayer' are also attested with the variant *ṣullû*.

l. 12, *l*[*i-šap-ši*]*-iḫ*, probably a Š-stem has to be restored, see rev. 8: *šu-up-šu-uḫ* (but cf. *RAcc.*, 109: *l*[*i-pa-saš-ši*]*-iḫ*). It is singular, although the subject of the verb is clearly 'the great gods', mentioned in l. 9–10. See my comment on obv. 18–19.

l. 18–21, also translated by M.E. Cohen, *Cultic Calendars*, 436.

l. 18, BÁRA [NAM.LUGAL.LA(?), following A. Falkenstein, *Topographie*, 19 (contra *RAcc.*, 109: BÁRA [NAM.MEŠ). See my comment on *TU* 40, rev. 7.

KAR 132 (VAT 7849)[12]

This text from Hellenistic Uruk describes the route for the procession of Anu's statue to the *akītu*-temple outside the city during the New Year festival (*akītu*) of the first month Nisannu.

The text is discussed in II.4.5.1.

I.

Obv.

1 […] ⌜x x *na*!⌝[13]*-šap-pi* GUŠKIN(?)⌝ […]

2 [*pa-ni* ^{d}LX *a-na pa-ni* ^{d}EN.L]ÍL *ù* DINGIR.MEŠ *ma-la ina* KISAL.MAḪ *ú-še-ti-iq*

3 [*na-šap-pi*] GUŠKIN *pa-ni An-tu*$_{4}$ *a-na pa-ni* ^{d}INNIN.MEŠ *šá ina* KISAL *ú-še-ti-iq*

4 [*na-šap-pi*] GUŠKIN *pa-ni* ^{d}INNIN *a-na pa-ni* DINGIR.MEŠ *ma-la ina* UB.ŠU.UKKIN.NA.KE$_{4}$ *ú-še-ti-iq*

5 [^{d}EN.LÍL ^{d}*É*]*-a* ^{d}IM ^{d}XXX ^{d}UTU DINGIR.MEŠ DÙ.A.BI ^{giš}TUKUL.MEŠ ^{d}UTU.MEŠ

6 [*ù*] ^{giš}GIGIR.MEŠ ⌜TA⌝ *šub-ti-šú-nu ina ma-ak-ki*![14]*-tu*$_{4}$ *šá na-mur-tu*$_{4}$ LUGAL ZI.MEŠ-*nim-ma*

7 [*a-n*]*a* KISAL.MAḪ E$_{11}$.MEŠ-*ma a-na* ^{d}*A-nù* LAL-*aṣ*.MEŠ ^{d}EN.LÍL KU$_{4}$-*ma*

8 [*i-na mu*]*ḫ-ḫi* KI.AGA.ZI.DA *a-na* XV ^{d}*A-nù* DÚR-*ab* ^{d}*É-a* KU$_{4}$-*ma*

9 [*ina mu*]*ḫ-ḫi* KI.AGA.KÙ.GA *a-na* 2,30 ^{d}*A-nù* DÚR-*ab* ^{d}XXX ^{d}ŠUL.PA.È.A

10 [^{d}]MAŠ ^{d}*Mi-šar-ri* ^{d}NUSKU ^{d}INNIN.LÀL *ù* ^{d}NIN.GUBLAGA

11 [*ina* X]V KÁ *pa-pa-ḫa ina* DA ^{d}IM GUB-*zu*.MEŠ ^{d}UTU ^{d}*Bu-ne-ne*

12 [^{d}]GIŠ.BAR ^{d}*Za-ba*$_{4}$*-ba*$_{4}$ ^{d}U.GUR ^{d}LUGAL.GÌR.RA ^{d}DINGIR.MAR.TU(?) ^{d}KÙ.SÙ

13 [*ù*] ^{d}ARA *ina* 2,30 KÁ *pa-pa-ḫa* GUB-*zu*.MEŠ LUGAL *a-na pa-pa-ḫa An-tu*$_{4}$ GIN-*ma*

14 [*uš*]*-kin-ni* ^{d}*Be-let*-DINGIR.MEŠ ^{d}ŠA.LA ^{d}DUMU.SAL.MEŠ-^{d}LX ^{d}*A-a* ^{d}*Gu-la*

15 [^{d}N]IN.ÈŠ.GAL ^{d}AMA.SÁG.NU.DU$_{7}$ ^{d}SA.DÀR.NUN.NA ^{d}*Aš-rat*

16 [*ù*] ^{d}*Šar-rat*-AN-*e* TA *šub-ti-ši-na ina ma-ak-ki-tu*$_{4}$ *šá na-mur-tú* LUGAL

17 [ZI].MEŠ-*nim-ma a-na An-tu*$_{4}$ LAL-*aṣ*.MEŠ LUGAL *ma-aq-qu-ú* GUŠKIN *a-na An-tu*$_{4}$

18 [*i-r*]*ed-de-e-ma* ŠU^{II} *An-tu*$_{4}$ *ina* ^{lú}MAŠ.MAŠ.MEŠ ^{lú}GALA.MEŠ ^{lú}NAR.MEŠ *šid-di* GADA

19 [*ù*] *ma-aq-qu* GUŠKIN DAB-*bat-am-ma An-tu*$_{4}$ GIN-*ak-ma ina man-za-zi-šú*

20 [*ina* K]ISAL.MAḪ *ina muḫ-ḫi šu-bat* GUŠKIN *pa-ni-šú a-na* ^{d}UTU.È.A GAR-*an-ma* DÚR-*ab*

21 [^{d}INNIN].MEŠ *nap-ḫar-ši-na a-na tar-ṣi An-tu*$_{4}$ GUB-*zi*.MEŠ

22 [^{lú}MAŠ.MA]Š.MEŠ ^{lú}GALA.⟨MEŠ⟩ *ù* ^{lú}NAR.MEŠ *ina pa-ni-šú i-par-ra-su*

23 [LUGAL] *ù* ^{lú}KU$_{4}$-É *a-na* ÈŠ.GAL.LA ÚRU.GAL (UNU.GAL) GIN-*ak*.MEŠ-*ma*

24 [^{lú}K]U$_{4}$-É A.MEŠ ŠU^{II} *a-na* ^{d}INNIN ÍL-*ši-ma* LUGAL *ma-ak-ki-tu*$_{4}$ *šá na-mur-tú*

25 [*a-n*]*a pa-ni* ^{d}INNIN DAB-*bat-ma* ŠU^{II} ^{d}INNIN *ù šu-bat* ^{d}LX *šá* É *pa-pa-ḫa* ^{d}INNIN

26 [*ina* ^{lú}MAŠ.MA]Š.MEŠ ^{lú}GALA.MEŠ ^{lú}NAR.MEŠ *šid-di* GADA [*ù*] *ma-aq-qu* GUŠKIN

27 [DAB-*ba*]*t-am-ma* ^{d}*Na-na-a* ^{d}NIN.SI$_{4}$.AN.NA ^{d}NIN.IGI^{II}.ZI.BAR.RA

28 [^{d}*I-š*]*ar-tu*$_{4}$ ^{d}NIN.ME.UR.UR $^{d!}$[15]ÁB.É.TÙR.RA ^{d}ŠÀ.GE.PÀ.D[A]

29 [^{d}DUMU.SAL.MEŠ]-UNUG^{ki} ^{d}DUMU.SAL.MEŠ-É.AN.NA ^{d}NIN.SÚN *ù* ^{d}*Šar-rat*-[BÁRA]

30 [*a-na* ^{d}INNIN] ⌜LAL.MEŠ⌝-*ṣa-nim-ma* ^{d}INNIN *a-na* KISAL.MAḪ E$_{11}$-*ma ina man-za-zi-šú* [DÚR-*ab*]

---

[12] Cf. *RAcc.* 99–108; E. Ebeling, in: H. Gressmann, *ATAT*², 314 ff.; H. Zimmern, *Neujahrsfest* 2, 20 ff.; G. Çağirgan, *Festivals*, 50–63; M.E. Cohen, *Cultic Calendars*, 434–36. See also R. Borger, *HKL* 1, 99.

[13] Copy: *ab*.

[14] Copy: *ni*.

[15] Copy: *ni*.

II

Obv.

1 ^{d}XXX ^{d}[ŠUL.PA.È.A ^{d}MAŠ ^{d}*Mi-šar-ri* ^{d}NUSKU ^{d}INNIN.LÀL *ù* ^{d}NIN.GUBLAGA]
2 *ina* DA ^{d}IM [GUB-*zu* ^{d}UTU ^{d}*Bu-ne-ne* ^{d}GIŠ.BAR ^{d}*Za-ba*$_4$*-ba*$_4$ ^{d}U.GUR]
3 ^{d}LUGAL.GÌR.RA ^{d}DINGIR.M[AR.TU(?) ^{d}KÙ.SÙ *ù* ^{d}ARA …]
4 *ina* DA ^{d}IDIM GUB-*zu* ^{d}*Be-*⸢*let*-DINGIR⸣.MEŠ ^{d}ŠA.LA ^{d}[DUMU.SAL.MEŠ-^{d}LX ^{d}*A-a*]
5 ^{d}ME.ME ^{d}BA.BA$_6$ ^{d}NIN.ÈŠ.GAL ^{d}AMA.SÁG.NU.D[U$_7$ ^{d}SA.DÀR.NUN.NA]
6 ^{d}*Aš-rat ù* ^{d}*Šar-rat*-AN-*e* EGIR *An-tu*$_4$ GUB-[*za* ^{d}*Na-na-a* ^{d}NIN.SI$_4$.AN.NA]
7 ^{d}NIN.IGI^{II}.ZI.BAR.RA ^{d}*I-šar-*⸢*tu*$_4$ ^{d}NIN.ME.UR⸣.[UR ^{d}ÁB.É.TÙR.RA]
8 *ù* ^{d}ŠÀ.GE.PÀ.DA ^{d}DUMU.SAL.[MEŠ-UNUG^{ki} ^{d}DUMU.SAL.MEŠ-É.AN.NA ^{d}NIN.SÚN]
9 *ù* ^{d}*Šar-rat*-BÁRA GIN-*ak-a-*[*ma* EGIR ^{d}INNIN GUB-*za* …]
10 GIN-*ak-ma a-na* XV ^{d}*Na-na-a* GUB-*za* ^{d}[…]
11 ^{d}LUGAL.BÀN.DA ^{d}IMIN.BI ^{d}IGI.DU ^{d}MEŠ.LAM.T[A.È.A …]
12 ^{d}ḪENDUR.SAG.GÁ *ù* ^{d}ŠU.BU.LÁ *ina maḫ-ri pa-ni-šú* […]
13 *iš-šak-kan-nu-ma* GUB-*zi-zu-*ʾ ^{d}URÙ-INIM-*su* ^{d}[…]
14 ^{d}NIN.ÚR.BU ^{d}NIN.IMMÀ ^{d}ŠILAM.KUR.RA […]
15 EGIR ^{d}NIN.SI$_4$.AN.NA GUB-*za* ^{d}[…]
16 *šá* KÁ ÈŠ.MAḪ GUB-*zi-zu* ^{d}[…]
17 *bi-*ʾ *šá* ÈŠ.MAḪ *ina pa-ni-šú* […]
18 *rak-su* ^{lú}GÍR.LÁ […]
19 *ip-par-su a-na* […]
20 *šá* DUG […]
21 KÁ x[…].

III

Rev.

1 EGIR-*šú* 2 […]
2 EGIR-*šú* 4 […]
3 EGIR-*šú* 2 ^{lú}*mu-*⸢*ban*(?)*-nu*(?)*-ú*(?)⸣[…]
4 EGIR-*šú* ^{mul}GIGIR ^{giš}GIGIR-*su* […]
5 EGIR-*šú* ^{giš}GIGIR ^{d}MAŠ ^{giš}G[IGIR …]
6 EGIR-*šú* ^{giš}GIGIR ^{d}UTU *ù* ^{giš}GIGI[R …]
7 *an-na-a* ^{giš}GIGIR.MEŠ ^{lú}ÉRIN-*ni* […]
8 *iš-pat*.MEŠ GUŠKIN *šá* ^{d}LX *ù An-t*[*u*$_4$ …]
9 *it-ti* ^{giš}GIGIR ^{d}LX GIN-*ak*.MEŠ EGI[R-*šú* …]
10 *ù* ^{d}LUGAL.BÀN.DA EGIR-*šú* ^{d}IMIN.BI ^{d}IGI.[DU … ^{d}ḪENDUR.SAG.GÁ]
11 *ù* ^{d}ŠU.BU.LÁ EGIR-*šú* ^{d}LUGAL.GÌR.RA ^{d}MES.LA[M.TA.È.A …]
12 ^{d}INNIN.LÀL *ù* ^{d}NIN.GUBLAGA ^{d}MAŠ.TAB.BA ^{d}*Tu-ma-mu*[…] ⸢ME(?)⸣ […]
13 EGIR-*šú* ^{d}MAŠ ^{d}*Bu-ne-ne ù* ^{d}*Za-ba*$_4$*-ba*$_4$ EGIR-*šú* ^{d}UTU *u* ^{d}I[M …]
14 EGIR-*šú* ^{d}PAP.SUKKAL ^{d}NUSKU ^{d}GIŠ.BAR ^{lú}NAR.MEŠ *ù* ^{lú}GALA.MEŠ
15 EGIR-*šú* ^{lú}EN.NA ^{d}DINGIR.MAR.TU(?) ^{d}KÙ.SÙ ^{d}SIRSIR(?) *ù* ^{lú}MAŠ.MAŠ.[MEŠ]
16 XV *u* 2,30 *šá* ^{lú}MAŠ.MAŠ.MEŠ 2 ^{lú}*mu-ban-nu-ú* GIŠ.GÌR ZA.GÌN.NA GAR.RA GÍD ^{giš}ERE[N]
17 *ina* ^{dug}NÍG.TAB.TUR.RA *ina pa-ni-šú* È.MEŠ-*nim-ma* EGIR-*šú* A.MEŠ ŠU^{II} *a-na* ^{d}LX
18 *ù An-tu*$_4$ ÍL-*ši* LUGAL *ù* UN.MEŠ *ú-lap-pat* ^{d}PAP.SUKKAL
19 ^{d}NUSKU *ù* ^{d}ARA *a-na* ^{d}*A-nù* LAL-*aṣ*.MEŠ-*ma* LUGAL *ma-aq-qu-ú* GUŠKI[N]
20 *a-na pa-ni* ^{d}*A-nù i-red-de-e-ma* ^{d}PAP.SUKKAL ^{d}NUSKU ^{d}ARA *ù* LUGAL
21 ŠU^{II} ^{d}*A-nù* TA BÁRA NAM.MEŠ DAB-*bat*.MEŠ-*ma* ^{d}EN.LÍL *ina* XV-*šú ù* ^{d}[*É-a*]
22 *ina* 2,30-*šú* GIN-*ak*.MEŠ-*ma* 2-*ú-ta a-na na-mis-su* EGIR-*šú An-*[*tu*$_4$ ^{d}INNIN]
23 *ù* ^{d}*Na-na-a* EGIR-*šú* ^{d}NIN.SI$_4$.AN.NA ^{d}ŠA.LA *ù* [^{d}DUMU.SAL.MEŠ-^{d}LX]

24 EGIR-*šú* {d}*A-a* {d}ME.ME {d}BA.BA6 *ù* {d}NIN.È[Š.GAL]
25 EGIR-*šú* {d}AMA.SÁG.NU.DU7 {d}SA.DÀR.NUN.NA {d}*Aš-rat* [*ù* {d}*Šar-rat*-AN-*e*]
26 ⸢EGIR-*šú*(?) {d}x.x.AN.NA *u*(?) {d}UTU(?) x⸣ [...] ⸢x x⸣ [...] ⸢x x⸣ [...]

IV
Rev.
1 [... *k*]*i-ma šá* {d}*A-nù ina muḫ-ḫi a-ra-am*
2 [*e-lu-ú šá* KAR KÙ.GA *ik-tal-du*(?)] x-*ú* DINGIR.MEŠ *gab-bi a-na pa-ni-šú* LAL-*aṣ*
3 [...] {giš}*qa-ru-ú ir-rak-kas-ma*
4 [... LUG]AL *ma-aq-qu-ú* GUŠKIN *a-na pa-ni* {d}*A-nù*
5 [*i-red-de-e-ma* {d}P]AP.SUKKAL *ù* LUGAL *a-na* {d}*A-nù* LAL-*aṣ*.MEŠ-*ma*
6 [ŠU{II}] ⸢{d}LX DAB⸣.MEŠ-*ma a-na* KISAL É *á-ki-tu4* KU4-*ma ina muḫ-ḫi*
7 [BÁR]A.GAL *ina* KISAL É *á-ki-tu4 pa-ni-šú ana* {d}UTU.È.A GAR-*an-ma* DÚR-*ab*
8 [{d}E]N.LÍL *ù* {d}*É-a* KU4.MEŠ-*ma* XV *u* 2,30 DÚR-*ab An-tu4* {d}INNIN
9 *ù* {d}*Na-na-a ina muḫ-ḫi šu-bat*.MEŠ EGIR {d}LX DÚR-*ab* {d}IM *ina* DA
10 {d}EN.LÍL *ana* XV {d}LX DÚR-*ab* DINGIR.MEŠ *nap-ḫar-šú-nu* KU4.MEŠ-*ma ina* KISAL É *a-ki-tu4*
11 *ina pa-ni-šú* GUB-*zi*.MEŠ A.MEŠ ŠU{II} *a-na* {d}LX *ù An-tu4* ÍL-*ma* LUGAL *u* UN.MEŠ
12 *ú-lap-pat* LUGAL *ma-aq-qu-ú* GUŠKIN *a-na* {d}LX *u An-tu4 i-red-de-e-ma*
13 ⸢{d}⸣PAP.SUKKAL *ù* LUGAL ŠU{II} {d}⟨*A*⟩-*nù* TA BÁRA.GAL DAB-*bat*.MEŠ-*ma* KU4-*ma ina pa-pa-ḫa-šú*
14 [DÚR]-*ab* EGIR-*šú* {d}EN.LÍL *ù* {d}*É-a* KU4.MEŠ-*ma* XV *u* 2,30 DÚR-*ab*
15 [*An*]-*tu4* KU4-*ma ina muḫ-ḫi šub-ti-šú* DÚR-*ab* {d}ŠA.LA *ù* {d}DUMU.SAL.MEŠ-{d}LX
16 [X]V *u* 2,30 *šá An-tu4* DÚR-*ab* {d}INNIN KU4-*ma ina muḫ-ḫi šub-ti-šú* DÚR-*ab*
17 [{d}]*Na-na-a ù* {d}NIN.SI4.AN.NA XV *ù* 2,30 *šá* {d}INNIN DÚR-*ab*
18 [{d}]IM KU4-*ma ina* DA {d}EN.LÍL *a-na* XV {d}*A-nù* DÚR-*ab*
19 [{d}]UTU KU4-*ma ina* DA {d}*É-a a-na* 2,30 {d}*A-nù* DÚR-*ab*
20 [{d}]PAP.SUKKAL *ina ku-bur-ru-ú* KÁ *pa-pa-ḫa* GUB-*za* {giš}*tal-lu* GUŠKIN [{d}*A*]-*nù*!
21 *ú-še-el-lu-ú šá* {d}EN.LÍL {d}IDIM {d}*An-tu4* {d}INNIN {d}IM *u* {d}UTU KI.MIN-*ma*
22 [*ki-m*]*a šá* {giš}*tal-lu ik*![16]-*tal-du* {d}PAP.SUKKAL GIN-*ak-ma ina muḫ-ḫi šub-ti-šú* DÚR-*ab*
23 [{lú}GAL]A ⸢*ina* DA⸣ GUB-*za-ma* AN.GAL.E ŠU.ÍL.LÁ.KÁM *a-na* {d}LX ÍL-*ši*
24 [... GIN-*ak*].MEŠ-*ma ina šub-ti-šú-nu šá* KISAL DÚR-*ab* {d}*I-šum* GIN-*ak-ma*
25 [*ina* D]A(?) LUGAL *a-na* XV DÚR-*ab* {d}MES.SAG.UNUG{ki} GIN-*ak-ma*
26 [*ina* D]⸢A⸣(?) {d}LX *a-na* 2,30 DÚR-*ab*
27 [...]⸢x⸣ {d}LX *ina pa-ni-šú-nu i-sal-li-ʾ*
28 [... -*šú*(?)]-*nu it-ta-*⸢*šab* x x GUŠKIN⸣

I.
Obv.
1 [...] ... a golden dish(?) [...]
2 [(from) before Anu], he will pass to Enlil, and whatever gods are in the Grand Courtyard.
3 He will pass a golden [dish], (from) before Antu, to the (other) goddesses who are in the courtyard.
4 He will pass a golden [dish], (from) before Ištar, to whatever gods are in the Ubšukkinaku.
5 [Enlil, E]a, Adad, Sîn, Šamaš (and) all of the (other) gods, the symbols, the sun disks,
6 [a]nd the chariots will rise from their seats in the towboat, which is a gift of the king, and

16 Copy: *it*.

7 they will come down to the Grand Courtyard and take up position towards Anu. Enlil will enter and
8 sit on (the dais called) Kiagazida to the right side of Anu. Ea will enter and
9 sit on (the dais called) Kiagakuga to the left side of Anu. Sîn, Šulpaea,
10 Ninurta, Mīšaru, Nusku, ^{d}INNIN.LÀL and Ningublaga
11 will stand at the right side of the gate of the cella next to Adad. Šamaš, Bunene,
12 Girra, Zababa, Nergal, Lugalgirra, Il-Amurri(?), Kusu
13 [and] Usmû will stand at the left side of the gate of the cella. The king will go to the cella of Antu and
14 will [pro]strate himself. Bēlet-ilī, Šala, Mārāt-Anu, Aja, Gula,
15 NinEšgal, Amasagnudu, Sadarnunna, Ašrat
16 [and] Šarrat-šamê [will rise (l. 17)] from their seats in the towboat, which is a gift of the king,
17 and take up position towards Antu. The king [will make] a libation with the golden libation bowl to Antu
18 and he will lead (l. 19) Antu, accompanied by the exorcists, the lamentation priests, the singers, the linen curtain
19 and the golden libation bowl, and Antu will go (from the cella) and, at her station
20 in the Grand Courtyard, on the golden seat she will place her face towards the West and sit.
21 All [the goddess]es will stand in the direction of Antu.
22 [The exorcis]ts, the lamentation priests and the singers will stop (their procession) in front of her.
23 [The king] and the temple enterers will go to the great temple Urugal and
24 [a te]mpel enterer will lift up the water (basin) for (washing of) the hands to Ištar. Then the king will take (l. 25) the towboat, which is a gift,
25 [be]fore Ištar. He will [lea]d (l. 27) Ištar and Anu's seat, which is in the cella of Ištar,
26 [accompanied by the exorci]sts, the lamentation priests, the singers, the linen curtain and the golden libation bowl.
27 Nanāja, Ninsianna, Ninigizibarra,
28 [Iš]artu, Ninmeurur, Abeturra, Šagepada,
29 Mārāt-Uruk, Mārāt-Eanna, Ninsun, and Šarrat-[parakki]
30 will take up position [towards Ištar] and Ištar will come down to the Grand Courtyard and [sit] at her station.

II.
Obv.

1 Sîn, [Šulpaea, Ninurta, Mīšaru, Nusku, INNIN.LÀL and Ningublaga]
2 [will stand] next to Adad. [Šamaš, Bunene, Girra, Zababa, Nergal,]
3 Lugalgirra, Il-Amur[ri(?), Kusu and Usmû ...]
4 will stand next to Ea. Bēlet-ilī, Šala, [Mārāt-Anu, Aja,]
5 Gula, Baba, NinEšgal, Amasagnud[u, Sadarnunna,]
6 Ašrat and Šarrat-šamê will sta[nd] behind Antu. [Nanāja, Ninsianna,]
7 Ninigizibarra, Išar⸢tu, Ninmeur⸣[ur, Abeturra,]
8 and Šagepada, Mār[āt-Uruk, Mārāt-Eanna, Ninsun,]
9 and Šarrat-parakki will go [and stand behind Ištar. ...]
10 will go and stand by the right side of Nanāja. [...]
11 Lugalbanda, Sebettu, Palil, Meslamt[aea ...]
12 Ḫendursagga and Šubula before her [...]
13 will be placed and stand (there). Uṣur-amassu, [...]
14 Ninurbu, Ninimma, Šilamkurra [...]

15 will stand behind Ninsianna. [...]
16 will stand by the gate of the Ešmaḫ. [...]
17 the (wall) opening of the Ešmaḫ, in front of him/her [...]
18 is/are bound. The (ritual) butcher [...]
19 they stayed away, to [...]
20 of a [...]-container [...]
21 the gate [...]

(In the following break the procession of Anu from the Grand Courtyard to the Dais of Destinies in Ubšukkinaku was probably described.)

III.
Rev.
1 Next, 2 [...]
2 Next, 4 [...]
3 Next, 2 arrangers(?) (of the offering table) [...]
4 Next, (the constellation) Auriga, its chariot [...]
5 Next, the chariot of Ninurta (and) the cha[riot of ...]
6 Next, the chariot of Šamaš and the chari[ot of ...]
7 These are the chariots (and) the personnel [...]
8 The golden quiver(s) of Anu and Ant[u ...]
9 They will go alongside the chariot of Anu. Nex[t ...]
10 and Lugalbanda. Next Sebettu, Pal[il ... Ḫendursagga]
11 and Šubula. Next Lugalgirra, Mesla[mtaea ...]
12 ^{d}INNIN.LÀL and Ningublaga, ^{d}Māšu, Tu'āmu [...]
13 Next Ninurta, Bunene and Zababa. Next Šamaš and Ad[ad]
14 Next Papsukkal, Nusku, Girra, the singers and the lamentation priests.
15 Next the En-priest, Il-Amurri(?), Kusu, Sirsir(?) and the exorcist[s].
16 To the right and left of the exorcists, 2 arrangers (of the offering table) will 'pull (out?)' a footstool, mounted in lapis-lazuli.
17 They will bring out cedar (shavings, burning) (l. 16) in a *ḫuluppaqqu*-brazier in front of him (Anu). Next (the priest) will lift up a water (basin) for (the washing of) the hands to Anu
18 and Antu; he will sprinkle(?) the king and the (other) persons. Papsukkal,
19 Nusku and Usmû will take up position towards Anu and the king will make a libation (l. 20) with a golden libation bowl
20 before Anu. Then Papsukkal, Nusku, Usmû and the king
21 will lead Anu from the Dais of Destinies. Enlil will go at his right and [Ea]
22 will go at his left, and for a second time ... Next An[tu, Ištar]
23 and Nanāja. Next Ninsianna, Šala and [Mārāt-Anu.]
24 Next Aja, Gula, Baba and Nine[šgal]
25 Next Amasagnudu, Sadarnunna, Ašrat [and Šarrat-šamê.]

IV.
Rev.
1 [... As soon] as Anu [has reached (l. 2)] the [upper] wharf
2 [of the Pure Quay(?)] ... all the gods will take up position before him.
3 [...] The *karû*-stand will be put together and
4 [... the ki]ng will make a libation (l. 5) with a golden libation bowl befor Anu.
5 [Then P]apsukkal and the king will take up position towards Anu, and

6 they will lead Anu. Then (Anu) will enter the courtyard of the *akītu*-temple and on
7 the Great [Dai]s in the courtyard of the *akītu*-temple, he will place his face towards the East and sit.
8 [E]nlil and Ea will enter and sit at the right and the left side. Antu, Ištar
9 and Nanāja will sit on the seat behind Anu. Adad
10 will sit next to (l. 9) Enlil at the right side of Anu. All the gods will enter and stand in front of him (l. 11) in the courtyard of the *akītu*-temple.
11 (The priest) will lift up a water (basin) for (the washing of) the hands to Anu and sprinkle(?) (l. 12) the king and the (other) persons.
12 The king will make a libation (l. 20) with a golden libation bowl for Anu and Antu and
13 Papsukkal and the king will lead Anu from the Great Dais. Then he will enter his cella and
14 sit. Enlil and Ea will enter and sit at the right and left side.
15 [An]tu will enter and sit on her seat. Šala and Mārāt-Anu
16 will sit at the right and left side of Antu. Ištar will enter and sit on the seat.
17 Nanāja and Ninsianna will sit at the right and left side of Ištar.
18 Adad will enter and sit at the right side of Anu next to Enlil.
19 Šamaš will enter and sit at the left side of Anu next to Ea.
20 Papsukkal will stand by the *kuburrû*-doorframe of the cella. They will bring up (l. 21) the gold(-plated) carrying pole of [A]nu.
21 As far as (the carrying poles of) Enlil, Ea, Antu, Ištar, Adad and Šamaš are concerned, ditto. Then,
22 [as soon a]s the carrying pole has arrived, Papsukkal will go and sit on his seat.
23 [The lamentation priest] will stand to the side and recite the hand-raising prayer 'O, Great Anu' to Anu.
24 [... will com]e and sit on their seats in the courtyard. Išum will come and
25 will sit [at the side of] the king on the right. Messagunug will go and
26 will sit [at the side of] Anu on the left.
27 [...] ... Anu he will ... in front of them.
28 [... on the]ir [...] he sat ... gold

Comments

I.
Obv.

l. 1–4, the restoration follows *TU* 39, obv. 24–25 and *TU* 42 +, obv. 19′–23′.

l. 8, KI.AGA.ZI.DA 'Place of the True Crown', socle of Enlil in the Grand Courtyard of the Rēš-temple, cf. A.R. George, *House Most High*, no. 584.

l. 9, KI.AGA.KÙ.GA 'Place of the Pure Crown', socle of Ea in the Grand Courtyard of the Rēš-temple, cf. A.R. George, *House Most High*, no. 583.

l. 10, for ^{d}INNIN.LÀL see A. Deimel, *Pantheon Babylonicum*, Romae, 1914, 225, no. 2762. For Ningublaga see my comment on *TU* 38, rev. 41.

l. 12 (see also II, 3; III, 15), we know that AN.AN.MAR.TU (or ^{d}DINGIR.MAR.TU?) and ^{d}MAR.TU i.e. the god Amurru, are identical, cf. M. Stol, *JCS* 31 (1979), 178, but the reading remains uncertain; perhaps Il-Amurri, following *RAcc.*, 100? Cf. also J.-R. Kupper, *L'iconographie du dieu Amurru dans la glyptique de la Ire dynastie babylonienne*, Bruxelles, 1961, 69 f.; F. Thureau-Dangin, *TCL* I, 59 f.

l. 15, Amasagnudu, this goddess, already known from the Old Babylonian period on, is also attested twice in private contracts from Hellenistic Uruk: *TCL* 13, 242, obv. 5 (^{d}AMA.SÀG.NU.DU$_{7}$); *BRM* 2, 29, obv. 4 and rev. 22 (^{d}*Ama-saq-qa-nu-úl*). See P.-A. Beaulieu, *ASJ* 14 (1992), 47–53.

l. 22, 'the priests) will stop (*i-par-ra-su*) (their procession)', cf. *AHw*, 831a, 6, g.

l. 23, ÈŠ.GAL.LA ÚRU.GAL (UNU.GAL) 'the great temple Urugal', i.e. the Ešgal-temple. See my comment on *TU* 38, rev. 2.

l. 24, *ma-ak-ki-tu*$_{4}$ towboat', or, with B. Pongratz-Leisten, *ina šulmi īrub*, 59b: *ma-aq-qí-tu*$_{4}$ 'Opfergefäß'? Pongratz-Leisten argues that, since a libation bowl (written *ma-aq-qu-ú*) is already mentioned in l. 26, the reading *maqqītu* is more probable. However, the different spelling makes it more likely that *makkītu* was intended.

l. 25–27, ŠU^{II} ^{d}INNIN … [DAB-*ba*]*t-am-ma*. See my comment on *TU* 39, obv. 27.

II.
Obv.

l. 4–8 (see also III, 22–25), the gods mentioned here are also enumerated in another small fragment from Hellenistic Uruk, *Bagh. Mitt. Beih.* 2, no. 13:

x +
1′ […] x […] UŠ ⸢x x⸣ […]
2′ […] ^{d}*Na-na-a* […]
3′ […] ⸢^{d}⸣ŠA.LA *ù* ^{d}⸢DUMU.SAL⸣.MEŠ-^{d}LX […]
4′ […] $^{[d]}$BA.BA$_{6}$ *ù* ^{d}NIN.ÈŠ.GAL […]
5′ […] $^{[d]}$SA.DÀR.NUN.NA ^{d}*Aš-rat u* ^{d}*Šar*-[*rat*-AN-*e* …]
6′ […] ⸢^{d}⸣NIN.IGI^{II}.⸢ZI.BA⸣R.RA *ù* ^{d}[*I*]-⸢*šar-tu*$_{4}$⸣(?) […]
7′ […^{d}Á]B.É.TÙR.⸢RA(?)⸣ *u* ^{d}ŠÀ.⸢GE⸣.P[À.DA …]

l. 6, GUB-[*za*] (cf. also l. 9; 15), with a feminine plural ending (see also GIN-*ak-a*-[*ma* in l. 9), because the subjects of the verb are all goddesses (cf. GUB-*zu* in l. 4, referring to masculine gods; see also l. 2). Difficult is GUB-*za* in l. 10, because the subject or subjects at the end of l. 9 is/are lost. However, since GIN-*ak-ma* at the beginning of l. 10 is singular, and furthermore there does not seem to be much space left at the end of l. 9 for more than one god(dess), GUB-*za* here appears to be singular, as in IV, 20 and 23. See also my comment on *TU* 39, obv. 18 and *TU* 42 +, obv. 32′.

l. 16 (see also 17), ÈŠ.MAḪ, also attested in *TU* 40, obv. 11; see my comment on this line.

III.
Rev.

l. 3 (see also 16), for the *mubannû* see III.4.3.

l. 15, ^{d}Sirsir: the sign looks more like SIRSIR (cf. R. Borger, *ABZ*, no. 371a, but written with an extra A in it. See B. Landsberger, *WdO* 1 (1947–52), 362 ff.) than ^{d}ASILAL$_{4}$

(EZENxA.LÁL, cf. R. Borger, *ABZ*, no. 160. See E. Ebeling, in *RlA* 1 (1932), 176b; Ch. Fossey, *Manuel* II, Paris, 1926, 391).

l. 16, GIŠ.GÌR, *kilzappu* 'footstool', usually written (GIŠ.)GÌR.GUB(.BU), but also GIŠ.GÌR is attested. See J.A. Knudtzon, *EA*, no. 241, 7; D.J. Wiseman, *Alalakh*, pl. XLI, no. 418, 1, 3 and 5 (3 GIŠ.GÌR). *Kilzappu* is also attested in the Late Babylonian cultic text AO 17662, obv. 3 (GIŠ.GÌR.GUB) and the Hellenistic ritual text *TU* 41, obv. 7 (GÌR.GUB.BU).

Another possibility is GIŠ.GÌR = *kurṣû* 'foot fetters', links' (*CAD*, K, 568b) (suggestion M. Stol), but this does not help to explain the specific meaning of the verb *šadādu* (GÍD) in this context.

IV.
Rev.

l. 1–2, cf. *BRM* 4, 7, obv. 12 ff., especially l. 20. The restoration was suggested by A. Falkenstein, *Topographie*, 48, n. 2. It seems to fit the context, since Anu has reached the other side of the river, and proceeds to the *akītu*-temple. But see also M.E. Cohen, *Cultic Calendars*, 435, who translates: '[They place the throne] of Anu on the ramp of [the ...-sanctuary].'

l. 2, LAL-*aṣ*, a singular, although a plural is intended, as in I, 7, 17, 30, III, 19 and IV, 5.

l. 3, for the *karû*-stand (^{giš}*qa-ru-ú*), see *CAD*, K, 229a, a with commentary.

BRM 4, 7 (MLC 1873)[17]

This tablet contains part of the ritual for probably the second New Year festival (*akītu*) in Uruk during the seventh month Tašrītu. The text describes the route for the procession of Anu's statue from his cella in the Rēš-temple to the *akītu*-temple outside the city. The colophon informs us that the text was written by Anu-balāssu-iqbi, son of the owner of the tablet, Anu-aḫa-ušabši, son of Kidin-Anu, of the family Ekur-zakir. It is dated 24(?)-IV-61 S.E. (251 B.C.). This Anu-aḫa-ušabši is also attested elsewhere.[18] The colophon also tells us that the tablet is a copy of an older original.

The text is discussed in II.4.5.1.

U.E. *ina a-mat* ^{d}LX *u An-*tu_4 *liš-lim*

Obv.

1 [… *ki-m*]*a šá* ^{d}*A-nù* TA É.NAM.EN.NA É *pa-pa-ḫa it-ta-ṣa-a*
2 [*a-*]⸢*na*⸣ KÁ.MAḪ KUR-*ád* ^{lú}MAŠ.MAŠ.MEŠ *gab-bi* ÉN LUGAL *it-ta-ṣa-a* 3-*šú* ŠID-*nu-ú*
3 $^{[l]ú}$MAŠ.MAŠ.MEŠ *i-kal-lu-i-ma* EGIR-*šú* ^{lú}ŠEŠ.GAL-*ú* ^{lú}MAŠ.MAŠ.MEŠ
4 ^{lú}KU$_4$-É.MEŠ *u* ^{lú}LÙNGA.MEŠ *šá* ^{giš}*tal-lu ṣa-an-du*
5 ^{d}*A-nù* GAL-*ú* AN-*e u* KI-*tì lik-ru-bu-ka a-na* ^{d}LX *i-kar-rab*

---

6 EGIR *ka-ra-bi* ^{lú}MAŠ.MAŠ.MEŠ ÉN LUGAL *it-ta-ṣa-a a-di su-qa* DINGIR.MEŠ 4-*ší* ŠID-*nu-ú*
7 ^{lú}ŠEŠ.GAL-*ú* ^{lú}MAŠ.MAŠ.MEŠ ^{lú}KU$_4$-É.MEŠ *u* ^{lú}LÙNGA.MEŠ *šá* ^{giš}*tal-lu ṣa-an-du*
8 ^{d}*A-nù* GAL-*ú* AN-*e u* KI-*tì lik-ru-bu-ka a-na* ^{d}*A-nù i-kar-rab*

---

9 EGIR *ka-ra-bi ina su-qa* DINGIR.MEŠ ^{lú}MAŠ.MAŠ.MEŠ ÉN LUGAL.E AN.KI.A LUGAL.TA È.A
10 4-*šú* ŠID-*nu-ú* ÉN *i-kal-lu-i-ma* ^{lú}ŠEŠ.GAL-*ú* ^{lú}MAŠ.MAŠ.MEŠ ^{lú}KU$_4$-É.MEŠ
11 *ù na-še-e* ^{giš}*tal-lu ki-ma maḫ-ri-im-ma a-na* ^{d}*A-nù i-kar-rab*

---

12 EGIR *ka-ra-bi* ^{lú}MAŠ.MAŠ.MEŠ ÉN LUGAL.E EZEN ŠI.IN.MU.UN.DU
13 *u* ÉN A.GÚB.BA KÙ.GA.TA *a-di* KAR KÙ.GA *a-ram-mu šá* ^{giš}MÁ.AN.NA
14 *ma-la-ki* DINGIR.MEŠ 7.TA.ÀM ŠID-*nu-ú* ÉN *i-kal-lu-i-ma* ^{lú}ŠEŠ.GAL-*i*
15 ^{lú}MAŠ.MAŠ.MEŠ ^{lú}KU$_4$-É.MEŠ *u na-še-e* ^{giš}*tal-lu a-na* ^{d}*A-nù i-kar-rab*

---

16 *ki-ma šá* ^{d}*A-nù a-na muḫ-ḫi a-ram-mu šá* ^{giš}MÁ.AN.NA *ik-tal-du*
17 ^{lú}MAŠ.MAŠ.MEŠ *u* ^{lú}KU$_4$-É.MEŠ ÉN ^{giš}MÁ.GUR$_8$ MU.UN.U$_5$ ŠU.ÍL.LÁ.KE$_4$
18 *a-na* ^{d}*A-nù* ÍL-*ú* EGIR-*šú* ^{lú}ŠEŠ.GAL-*ú* ^{lú}MAŠ.MAŠ.MEŠ ^{lú}KU$_4$-É.MEŠ
19 *ù na-še-e* ^{giš}*tal-lu ka-ra-bi ki-ma maḫ-ri-im-ma ana* ^{d}LX *i-kar-rab*

---

20 TA *muḫ-ḫi a-ram-mu e-lu-ú šá* KAR KÙ.GA *a-di* KÁ.GAL LUGAL
21 ^{lú}MAŠ.MAŠ.MEŠ ÉN LUGAL.TA.È.A SIL.A KÙ.GA BA.DIB.A.TA 7-*šú* ŠID-*nu-ú*

---

[17] Cf. E. Ebeling, in: H. Gressmann, *ATAT*^{2}, 313 f.; A.J. Sachs, in: J.B. Pritchard, *ANET*^{2}, 342 f.; F. Thureau-Dangin, *RA* 20 (1923), 107 ff.; A. Falkenstein, *Topographie*, 45 ff.; G. Çağirgan, *Festivals*, 64–71; M.E. Cohen, *Cultic Calendars*, 429–30. See also R. Borger, *HKL* 1, 57 and 2, 34.

[18] As the owner of the tablets *BRM* 4, 8, dated 61 S.E., *UCP* 9 (1931), 399, rev. 30, not dated, W 18828, dated 62 S.E., and K 3753, dated 65 S.E. See also the chronicle text *SpTU* 1, no. 2 (dated 61 S.E.), and the astronomical text *TU* 19, 84 S.E. See furthermore the private documents *OECT* 9, 12 // 13, date lost, *BRM* 2, 17, dated 67 S.E. and no. 21, dated 75 S.E. Perhaps also *BiMes* 24, 42, date lost. See also I.2.

22 ÉN *i-kal-lu-i-ma ina* KÁ.GAL LUGAL ^{lú}ŠEŠ.GAL-*ú* ^{lú}MAŠ.MAŠ.MEŠ ^{lú}KU$_4$-É.MEŠ
23 *ù na-še-e* ^{giš}*tal-lu ka-ra-bi ki-ma maḫ-ri-im-ma ana* ^{d}LX *i-kar-rab*

---

24 TA KÁ.GAL LUGAL *a-di* É *á-ki-tu*$_4$ É *ik-rib* ^{lú}MAŠ.MAŠ.MEŠ
25 *ki-ma šá ina šu-ú-qu* DINGIR.MEŠ ÉN.MEŠ ŠID-*nu-ú* ÉN.MEŠ *i-kal-lu-i-ma*
26 ^{lú}ŠEŠ.GAL-*i* ^{lú}MAŠ.MAŠ.MEŠ ^{lú}KU$_4$-É.MEŠ *u* ^{lú}LÙNGA.MEŠ *šá* ^{giš}*tal-lu*
27 *ṣa-an-du ka-ra-bi a-di* 7-*šú ú-šal-la-mu-ma ana* ^{d}LX *i-kar-rab*

Rev.
28 *ki-ma šá* ^{d}*A-nù* É *á-ki-tu*$_4$ *ik-tal-du* ^{lú}MAŠ.MAŠ.MEŠ
29 ÉN É KÙ.GA É DIMMER.RE.E.NE ÉN AN LUGAL.MU ŠÀ.DÙG.GA.ZU.ŠÈ
30 ÉN ÚNU(TE.UNUG) KIN.SIG AN.NA.KE$_4$ ÉN ME.TE BÁRA.MAḪ ÉN *ú-tal-lil* É
31 *ù* ÉN *šub-tu*$_4$ *šá* DINGIR.MEŠ GAL.MEŠ ŠID-*nu-ú*

---

32 ^{d}*A-nù ra-bu-ú* AN-*e u* KI-*tì lik-ru-bu-ka*
33 ^{d}EN.LÍL ^{d}*É-a u* ^{d}*Be-let*-DINGIR.MEŠ *ḫa-diš lik-ru-bu-ka*
34 DINGIR.MEŠ *ki-lal-la-an* ^{d}XXX *u* ^{d}UTU *ina* IGI.DU$_8$.ÀM-*šú-nu lik-ru-bu-ka*
35 ^{d}U$^{!}$[19].GUR *u* ^{d}IMIN.BI *ina kun-nu lìb-bi-šú-nu lik-ru-bu-ka*
36 ^{d}Í.GÌ.GÌ *šá* AN-*e u* ^{d}*A-nun-na-ki šá* KI-*tì lik-ru-bu-ka*
37 DINGIR.MEŠ *šá ap-si-i u* DINGIR.MEŠ *šá* DU$_6$.KÙ *lik-ru-bu-ka*
38 *u*$_4$-*mu* ITI *u* MU.AN.NA *u*$_4$-*mi-šam lik-ru-bu-ka*

---

39 *an-na-a ka-ra-bi* ^{lú}ŠEŠ.GAL-*i* ^{lú}MAŠ.MAŠ.MEŠ ^{lú}KU$_4$-É.MEŠ
40 *ù* ^{lú}LÙNGA.MEŠ *šá* ^{giš}*tal-lu ṣa-an-du iš-tu* É *re-eš*
41 *a-di* É *á-ki-tu*$_4$ *a-na* ^{d}*A-nù* 7-*šú i-kar-rab*

---

42 ÉN LUGAL *it-ta-ṣa-a* LUGAL *it-ta-ṣa*$^{!}$[20]*-a*
43 *ki-ma* SUMUN-*šú* SAR-*ma ba-rù ù up-puš*$_4$ *gaba-re* ^{giš}DA SUMUN-*bar* NÍG.GA ^{d}LX *u An-tu*$_4$
44 IM ^{Id}LX-ŠEŠ-GÁL-*ši* A *šá* ^{I}*Ki-din*-^{d}LX ⟨^{lú}⟩ŠÀ.BAL.BAL ^{I}*É-kur-za-kir* ^{lú}MAŠ.MAŠ ^{d}LX *u An-tu*$_4$
45 ^{lú}ŠEŠ.GAL-*i šá* É *re-eš* UNUG^{ki}-*ú* ŠU^{II} ^{Id}LX-DIN-*su*-E DUMU-*šú ana a-ḫa-a-zi-šú*
46 GÍD.DA UD.MEŠ-*šú* DIN ZI-*tì-šú u kun-nu* SUḪUS.MEŠ-*šú* SAR-*ma ina* UNUG^{ki} *u* É *re-eš*
47 É EN-*ú-ti-šú ú-kin pa-liḫ* ^{d}LX *u An-tu*$_4$ *ina šur-qu* NU TÙM-*šú*
48 ⸢UNUG⸣^{ki} ^{iti}ŠU UD.⸢24⸣(?).KAM MU.61.KAM ^{I}*An-ti-ʾ-ku-su* LUGAL KUR.KUR

U.E. By the command of Anu and Antu may (this work) be successful!

Obv.
1 [… Afte]r Anu has gone out from the cella Enamenna,
2 and arrives at the Grand gate, all the exorcists will recite the incantation 'The king has gone out' three times.
3 The exorcists will stop and after this the high priest, the exorcists,

[19] Copy: *eš*.
[20] Copy: *è*.

4 the temple enterers and the brewers, who are harnessed to the carrying pole,
5 will pronounce praise to Anu (saying) 'Great Anu, may Heaven and Earth greet you'.

---

6 After the prayer the exorcists will recite the incantation 'The king has gone out', up to the Street of the Gods four times.
7 The high priest, the exorcists, the temple enterers and the brewers, who are harnessed to the carrying pole,
8 will pronounce praise to Anu (saying) 'Great Anu, may Heaven and Earth greet you'.

---

9 After the prayer in the Street of the Gods the exorcists will recite (l. 10) the incantation 'The king, who in Heaven and Earth surpasses all (other) kings'
10 four times. They will stop the incantation and the high priest, the exorcists, the temple enterers
11 and the bearers of the carrying pole will pronounce praise to Anu as before.

---

12 After the prayer the exorcists will recite (l. 14) the incantation 'The king is coming to the festival',
13 and the incantation 'From the pure holy water-basin', up to the Pure Quay, the wharf of the Boat of Anu,
14 (along) the procession of the gods, seven times. They will stop the incantation and the high priest,
15 the exorcists, the temple enterers and the bearers of the carrying pole will pronounce praise to Anu.

---

16 As soon as Anu has reached the wharf of the Boat of Anu,
17 the exorcists and the temple enterers will recite (l. 18) the incantation 'He has boarded the *makurru*-boat', a hand-raising prayer,
18 to Anu. After this the high priest, the exorcists, the temple enterers
19 and the bearers of the carrying pole will pronounce the (same) prayer to Anu as before.

---

20 From the upper wharf of the Pure Quay up to the Royal Gate
21 the exorcists will recite the incantation 'He who surpasses all kings, after he has passed by in the Pure Street' seven times.
22 They will stop the incantation and at the Royal Gate the high priest, the exorcists, the temple enterers
23 and the bearers of the carrying pole will pronounce the (same) prayer to Anu as before.

---

24 From the Royal Gate up to the *akītu*-temple (named) *Bīt ikribi*, the exorcists
25 will recite the (same) incantations as in the Street of the Gods. They will stop the incantations and
26 the high priest, the exorcists, the temple enterers and the brewers, who are harnessed (l. 27) to the carrying pole,
27 will pronounce the prayer to Anu seven times in its entirety.

Rev.
28 When Anu has reached the *akītu*-temple, the exorcists
29 will recite (l. 31) the incantation 'Pure house, house of the gods', the incantation 'Anu, my king, your good heart',

30 the incantation 'The evening meal of Anu', the incantation 'The proper Grand Dais', the incantation 'The temple has been purified'

31 and the incantation 'The dwelling of the great gods'.

---

32 'Great Anu, may Heaven and Earth greet you!

33 May Enlil, Ea and Bēlet-ilī greet you in joy!

34 May the pair of gods Sîn and Šamaš greet you in their appearances!

35 May Nergal and Sebettu greet you in their steadfast hearts!

36 May the Igigi of Heaven and the Anunnaki of Earth greet you!

37 May the gods of the Subterranean Water and the gods of the Pure Mound greet you!

38 May they greet you daily, (each) day, month and year!'

---

39 This is the prayer which the high priest, the exorcists, the temple enterers

40 and the brewers, who are harnessed to the carrying pole, will pronounce to Anu (l. 41) from the Rēš-temple

41 up to the *akītu*-temple, seven times.

(Catchline:)

42 Incantation: 'The king has gone out, the king has gone out'.

(Colophon:)

43 Copied, collated and 'made' in accordance with its original. A copy of an older tablet, property of Anu and Antu.

44 Tablet of Anu-aḫa-ušabši, son of Kidin-Anu, descendant of Ekur-zakir, the exorcist of Anu and Antu,

45 the high priest of the Rēš-temple in Uruk. (Written by) the hand of Anu-balāssu-iqbi, his son. He has written (the tablet) (l. 46) for his (own) instruction,

46 his long days, his well-being and the permanence of his position and set (it) up (l. 47) in Uruk and in the Rēš-temple,

47 the temple of his lordship. He who honors Anu and Antu, will not take it away by means of theft.

48 Uruk, the (fourth) month Du'ūzu, day 24(?), year 61, Antiochos, king of the lands.

Comments

Obv.

l. 1, the Enamenna is the cella of Anu in the Rēš-temple in Uruk. It is also attested in the building inscription *YOS* 1, 52, 17. Cf. A. Falkenstein, *Topographie*, 18–20; A.R. George, *House Most High*, no. 837.

l. 3, the unusual spelling *i-kal-lu-i-ma*, also attested in l. obv. 10; 14; 22; 25, does not occur elsewhere, although the verb *kalû* is attested often in Hellenistic ritual texts: *TU* 45, obv. 14; *TU* 46, obv. 13; 28; rev. 12; *Bagh. Mitt. Beih.* 2, no. 10, obv. 20; *Bagh. Mitt. Beih.* 2, no. 11, obv. fragment 1, 3′; *BRM* 4, 6, obv. 7 // *CLBT*, pl. 1, col. II, 5′. See also F.H. Weissbach, *Misc.*, no. 12, obv. 14.

l. 4 (see also 7, 26, rev. 40), 'the brewers, who are harnessed to the carrying pole', referred to only indirectly in obv. 11, 15, 19, and 23, as 'the bearers of the carrying pole'.

l. 5 (see also 8), the prayer is given in full in rev. 32–38.

l. 5, *i-kar-rab*, a singular, although a plural is intended; see also l. 8, 11, 15, 19, 23, 27 (cf. *ú-šal-la-mu-ma* in this line), rev. 41.

l. 9, 'The king of Heaven and Earth, who surpasses all (other) kings', similar in l. 21.

l. 13, the passage in which Anu, on his way to the *akītu*-temple, sets foot on the boat, is not described. Also the part from 'the Pure Quay, the wharf of the Boat of Anu', up to 'the upper wharf of the Pure Quay' is not mentioned (see *KAR* 132, IV, 1–2; *TU* 42 +, rev. 19′). Cf. F. Thureau-Dangin, *RA* 20 (1923), 110, n. 3 and A. Falkenstein, *Topographie*, 48.

l. 20 (see also 22; 24), KÁ.GAL LUGAL, the 'Royal Gate', see F. Thureau-Dangin, *RA* 31 (1934), 145 f., where he suggests that the royal gate is the gate of the *akītu*-temple. Against this A. Falkenstein, *Topographie*, 48 argues that the procession had to be long enough to recite a number of incantations; so the gate in question must have been one of the gates in the city wall.

l. 21, 'He who surpasses all kings, after he has passed by in the Pure Street', the second part of the incipit probably belongs to the incipit of this incantation, although it looks like a reference to the route which the procession had to take. See F. Thureau-Dangin, *RA* 20 (1923), 110 and A. Falkenstein, *Topographie*, 47. See also the incipit in l. obv. 9, which is very similar to the first part of the incipit here.

l. 24, É *ik-rib* (usually written É.SÍSKUR) 'House of Blessing', an epithet of the *akītu*-temple of Anu in Uruk. It is also the name of the *akītu*-temple in Babylon, see the Hellenistic *akītu*-ritual, *RAcc.*, 143, 401: [ina É.SÍS]KUR É *ik-ri-bi*. See also the ritual calendar text from Hellenistic Babylon, *SBH* VIII, II, 4 and 7. Cf. A.R. George, *House Most High*, no. 993.

Rev.

l. 30, 'The evening (*līlâtu*, KIN.SIG) meal (*mākālû*, ÚNU) of Anu'. Or, with M.E. Cohen (*Cultic Calendars*, 430): '(In) the Banquet Hall (ÚNU), at the Evening Meal (KIN.SIG) of Anu'?

l. 35, *ina kun-nu lìb-bi-šú-nu* 'in their steadfast hearts', cf. *CAD*, K, 543, 2.

l. 37, the DU_6.KÙ 'Pure Mound' is the cosmic seat of the king of the gods of Heaven and Earth (Lugaldimmerankia) in the divine assembly, cf. B. Pongratz-Leisten, *ina šulmi īrub*, 56; A.R. George, *House Most High*, no. 178; E.J. Wilson, *'Holiness' and 'Purity' in Mesopotamia* (AOAT, Band 237), Kevelaer, 1994, 19–20, who suggestes KÙ to be translated 'holy' rather than 'pure'. DU_6.KÙ is also another name for the Dais of Destinies (*parak šīmāti*), where the destinies were determined during the New Year festival. The DU_6.KÙ is known especially from Nippur, Babylon and Girsu (Lagaš), cf. A.R. George, *House Most High*, nos. 179, 180 and 181. See also II.4.5.2.

l. 43–49, for the colophon, see H. Hunger, *AOAT* 2, 37–38, no. 87.

l. 43, *up-puš*$_4$ 'made', see H. Hunger, *AOAT* 2, 3b, with *AHw*, 227b, D, 3, b ('richtig b(ehandeln) od mit Kolophon abschließen?'), but contra *CAD*, E, 232b, 5′ ('to copy'). *uppušu* usually follows *šaṭāru*, so the translation 'to copy' is less likely.

l. 48, UD.⌜24⌝, or ⌜25⌝?

RAcc., 127–154 (DT 15, DT 109) + BM 32485[21] (DT 114, MNB 1848)[22]

The ritual texts contain parts of the twenty-second and twenty-third tablets of the ritual series concerned with the New Year festival (*akītu*) of the month Nisannu in Hellenistic Babylon. The ritual instructions for the first of Nisannu are lost; for the second to the fifth day we have several large fragments; the sixth to the eleventh day are also lost. For the date and composition of the text see I.2.

The text is discussed in II.4.5.2.

1 [DIŠ] *ina* ^{iti}BÁR UD.2.KAM 1 DANNA GE$_{6}$
2 $^{[lú]}$ŠEŠ.GAL ZI-*ma* A.MEŠ ÍD TU$_{5}$
3 [*ana*] IGI ^{d}EN KU$_{4}$-*ma* ^{túg}GADA.LAL *ina* IGI ^{d}EN
4 [*i-d*]*e-ek-ku ana* ^{d}EN ŠÙD.BI DUG$_{4}$.GA

---

5 UMUN.MU NU.ZA.PA.ÁG.BI GIŠ.BU E.NE
6 ^{d}EN *šá ina uz-zi-šú ma-ḫi-ir* NU TUK-*ú*
7 UMUN.MU BÁRA.SIG$_{5}$.GA UMUN.MU KUR.KUR.RA
8 ^{d}EN LUGAL *dam-qa* ^{d}EN KUR.KUR.MEŠ
9 KÁR.KÁR Á.DÚRU.NA KI.A.A NU.ZU
10 *mu-tir* SILIM.ME *šá* DINGIR.DINGIR GAL.GAL
11 EN.A.NI UMUN.MU A.NA UMUN.MU AN ḪUN.GÁ
12 ^{d}EN *šá ina né-kel-mi-šú ú-šam-qit dan-nu-tú*
13 ^{d}BÁRA LÚ.LÚ ^{d}BÁRA LÚ.TUK.A
14 ^{d}EN LUGAL.MEŠ ZÁLAG LÚ-*tú mu-za-ʾ-iz is-qé-e-tú*
15 UMUN.MU TUŠ.MU.ŠU GIŠ.GÁL.LA Ú.AGA KI.IN.NIR
16 ^{d}EN *šub-ta-ku* E^{ki} *Bar-sip a-gu-ku*
17 [A]N.AN.MU AN.AN.ŠÀ.BI PEŠ.E
18 AN-*e rap-šu-tú gi-mir ka-bat-ti-ku*
19 $^{[d]}$EN *ina* IGI^{II}-*ku ta-bar-ri gim-re-e-tú*
20 [*ina*] UR$_{5}$.ÚŠ.MEŠ-*ka ta-ḫa-ṭu* UR$_{5}$.ÚŠ.MEŠ
21 [*ina*] *né-kel-me-ku ta-nam-din ur-tu*$_{4}$
22 [*in*]*a la-pa-*⟨*ti*⟩*-ka ta-qam*(?)*-mu dan-nu-tú*
23 [*l*]*a* GI-*ka ta-kam-mu ina* ŠU^{II}
24 [*ina*] *nap-lu-si-ka ta-ra-áš-šá-šú-nu-tú* ARḪUŠ
25 [*t*]*u-kal-lam-šú-nu-tú* ZÁLAG *i-dab-bu-bu qur-di-ku*
26 ^{d}EN KUR.KUR ZÁLAG ^{d}Í.GÌ.GÌ *qa-bu-u* SIG$_{5}$.MEŠ
27 *man-nu šá ka-a-šú la i-dab-bu-bu qur-di-ku*
28 *la i-qab-bi ta-nit-ku la ú-šá-pa-a* ^{d}EN-*ut-ku*
29 ^{d}EN KUR.KUR *a-šib* É.U$_{4}$.UL *ṣa-bit* ŠU^{II} *na-as-ku*
30 *ana* URU-*ku* E^{ki} *re-še-e* ARḪUŠ
31 *ana* É.SAG.ÍL É-*ku suḫ-ḫir* IGI-*ku*
32 *šá* DUMU.MEŠ E^{ki} ^{lú}ÉRIN *ki-din-nu šu-kun šu-bar-ru-šú-nu*

---

[21] This unpublished fragment (see Plate I) covers lines 235–8 (almost entirely lost) and 463–471.

[22] For the concordance, see *RAcc.*, 128–9. DT 15, 109 and 114 are collated. A photo of MNB 1848 is to be found in B. André-Leicknam, *Naissance de l' écriture*, Paris 1982, 223, no. 165. Cf. also: E. Ebeling, in: H. Gressmann, *ATAT*^{2}, 295 ff.; A.J. Sachs, in: J.B. Pritchard, *ANET*^{2}, 331 ff.; G. Çağirgan, *Festivals*, 2–39; W. Farber, *TUAT* II/2, 212 ff.; M.E. Cohen, *Cultic Calendars*, 441–47. See also R. Borger, *HKL* 1, 567 and 2, 297.

33 21 MU.ŠID.BI URÙ-*tú* É.SAG.ÍL
34 [*pa-li*]*ḫ* ^{d}EN *al-la* ^{lú}ŠEŠ.GAL É.TUŠ.A
35 [*l*]*a ú-kal-lam*

---

36 [TA] *naq-bit an-na-a* DUG$_4$.GA-*ú*
37 [^{giš}IG.MEŠ BAD]-*te* ^{lú}KU$_4$-É.MEŠ
38 [ZI]-*ú* ME-*šú-nu* GIM *šá gi-na-a*
39 [*ina* IGI] ^{d}EN *u* ^{d}GAŠAN-*iá* DÙ.MEŠ
40 [^{lú}GALA.MEŠ *u* ^{lú}]NAR.MEŠ KI.MIN

Now a very damaged part follows.

41 [...]
42 [...]
43 [...]
44 [...]
45 [...]
46 GIŠ [...]
47 KI.TUŠ x [...]
48 TA LU MA [...]
49 GAR-*an* $^{\text{na4}}$KIŠIB x [...]
50 *ina* AGA *šá* ^{d}L[X ...]
51 *šá* UD.2.KAM *ina mu*[*ḫ-ḫi*/UGU ...]
52 *ina* IGI-*šú-nu* GAR-*an* ⌜x⌝ [...]
53 3-*šú* DUG$_4$.GA [...]

---

54 *za-ma-nu lem-nu-tú* [...]
55 *šá ina dan-nu-ti-šú-*[*nu* ...]
56 *an-na-a šá ina* E[^{ki}...]
57 *šá* NAM.BÚR.BI [...]
58 *áš-šú* ^{lú}KÚR *u ḫab-b*[*i-lu* ...]
59 ^{d}EN GAL-*ú* ^{d}ŠÚ [...]
60 ÁŠ NU BÚR *i-r*[*u-ur* ...]
61 NAM NU GUR *i-*[*šim* ...]
62 *šá* ^{d}EN EN-*iá* [...]
63 *šá* EN KUR.KUR [...]
64 *šá* E^{ki} [...]
65 *ina qé-reb* KI-*t*[*ì* ...]
66 *šá* É.U$_4$.UL [...]
67 *ub-bu-ub* [...]
68 GIM AN-*e u* [KI-*tì* ...]
69 UNUG^{ki} *u* E[N.LÍL^{ki} *qa-ma-a u ka-ma-a*]
70 *na-si-iḫ t*[*e-me-en-ši-na na-di ana* A.MEŠ]
71 É.KUR.MEŠ *šá q*[*er-*⟨*bi*⟩*-ši-na* Ú.TU-*šu-nu* x ...]
72 *ma-áš* ME-*šú-nu* [*ana u*$_4$-*mu*.(MEŠ SUD.MEŠ)]
72a [*ul i-kan-nu* SÁ.DUG$_4$-*šu-*⟨*nu*⟩ x ...]
73 *sa-pi-iḫ* GI[Š.ḪUR-*šu-*(*nu*) ...]
74 UN.MEŠ *a-šib* [... *iḫ*-x ...]

75 GÉME.GÉME *si*-[…]
76 *šá* E^{ki} [… *dan*-x …]
77 *šá* É.U$_4$.U[L … *dan*-x …]
78 *ik-me-ku-nu*-[*ti* …*ḫi*(?)…]
79 *ra-ma-tu*[-*nu* …]

about 75 lines (2 columns) missing.

156 AL […]

---

157 DIŠ *ina* ^{iti}BÁR UD.[3.KAM 1 1/3 DANNA GE$_6$ ^{lú}ŠEŠ.GAL]
158 Z[I-*ma* A.MEŠ ÍD] TU[$_5$ …]
159 *ana* [^{d}E]N Š[ÙD.BI DUG$_4$.GA]

---

160 UMUN.MU ^{d}LÚ.LÚ […]
161 ⸢x x x x⸣ […]
162 ⸢x x⸣ […]
163 AL. […]
164 SAG […]
165 […]
166 ⸢x⸣[…] ⸢x⸣ […]
167 ⸢x⸣ […] ⸢x⸣ […]
168 UMUN.MU SIPA Á x […]
169 […] KUR […]
170 ⸢x⸣ […] ⸢x x⸣ […]
171 ⸢x LU(?)⸣ […] ⸢x⸣ […]
172 *na-din* […]
173 MU.LU ^{d}NISABA […]
174 *šá* UN.⟨MEŠ⟩ *ṣal-mat* SAG.DU […]
175 *ta-ḫa-ṭ*[*u*(?)] UD(?) ⸢*a-na*(?)⸣ […]
176 TA […] ⸢x⸣ UD(?) ⸢*a-na*(?)⸣ […]
177 ⸢x⸣ […]⸢x⸣ UD DI(?) […]
178 […] BAD […] ⸢x⸣ […]
179 […] LUGAL UMUN GÌR.NÍTA […]
180 *ina* KA *ṣal-mat* SAG.DU […]
181 *šá* É.SAG.ÍL [É-*ku* …]
182 *šá* E^{ki} URU-*ku* […]
183 *ana qa-bu-u* SIG$_5$ […]

---

184 ^{giš}IG.MEŠ BAD-[*te* ^{lú}KU$_4$-É.MEŠ]
185 KU$_4$.MEŠ-*m*[*a* ME-*šú-nu* GIM *šá gi-na-a*]
186 DÙ.M[EŠ ^{lú}GALA.MEŠ *u* ^{lú}NAR.MEŠ KI.MIN]
187 […]

Possibly 2 lines missing.

190 [*e-nu-m*]*a* 1 1/2 DANNA ME NIM-*a* ^{lú}GUR.GUR
191 [GÙ-*m*]*a* NA$_4$ *ni-siq-tú u* GUŠKIN

192 [TA] NÍG.GA ^{d}AMAR.UTU *ana* DÙ-*eš šá* 2 NU.MEŠ
193 *ana* UD.6.KAM *i-na-an-din-šú* ^{lú}NAGAR GÙ-*ma*
194 ^{giš}EREN *u* ŠINIG (GAD.ŠÚ.NAGA) SUM-*šú*
195 ^{lú}KÙ.DIM GÙ-*ma* GUŠKIN SUM-*šú*
196 TA UD.3.KAM EN UD.6.KAM TA *pa-ni* ^{d}EN
197 *ana* ^{lú}GUR.GUR 〈GIŠ〉.KUN *ana* ^{lú}KÙ.DIM GABA
198 *ana* ^{lú}NAGAR ZAG *ana* ^{lú}UŠ.BAR TI *an-na-a*
199 TA IGI ^{d}EN *ana* ^{lú}ŠEŠ.GAL É.⸢TUŠ.A⸣
200 *ana* ^{lú}DUMU.MEŠ *um-man ú-šeb-b*[*i-lu*]

---

201 NU.MEŠ *šu-nu-tú* 7 SI *la-an-šú-nu*
202 1-*en šá* ^{giš}EREN *u* 1-*en šá* ^{giš}ŠINIG
203 ⸢4(?)⸣ GÍN GUŠKIN *iḫ-zu-us-su-nu*
204 ⸢4(?)⸣ ^{na4}DUḪ.ŠI.A *ana muḫ-ḫi-šú-nu i-lu*
205 [1-*en*] *ina* ŠU^{II} 2,30-*šú* MUŠ *šá* ^{giš}EREN *na*-[*ši*]
206 [ŠU^{II}]-*šu šá* XV *ana* ^{d}AG *na-ši šá-nu-ú* [*ina* ŠU^{II}]
207 [2,30]-*šú* GÍR.TAB *na-ši* ŠU^{II} XV-*šú*
208 [*ana* ^{d}A]G *na-ši* TÚG SA$_5$ *lab-šu-ú*
209 [*ina e*]-*ri* ^{giš}GIŠIMMAR *qab-li-šú-nu*
210 [*rak-s*]*u* EN UD.6.KAM *ina* É ^{d}DI.[KUD]
211 [GAR].MEŠ DUḪ ^{giš}BANŠUR *šá* ^{d}DI.K[UD]
212 *i-qar-ru-ub-šú-nu-tú* UD.6.KAM [...]
213 ^{d}AG É.ḪUR.SAG.TI.LA *ina* KUR-[*šú*]
214 ^{lú}GÍR.LÁ *kar-ri* SAG.DU-*su-nu* SÌ[G-*a*]*ṣ-ma*
215 *ina* IGI ^{d}AG *tur-ru*(?) MÚ.MEŠ-*nim-ma*
216 *ana* ŠÀ *tur-ru*(?) ŠUB.M[EŠ]

216a IM 22.KAM-*ma* EME.GIR$_{15}$.DU$_7$.⸢E NU TI⸣
216b IM *šá* EGIR-*šú ina* ^{iti}BÁR UD.4.KAM

216c *ina a-mat* ^{d}EN *u* ^{d}GAŠAN-*iá liš-lim*
217 DIŠ *ina* ^{iti}BÁR UD.4.KAM 1 2/3 DANNA GE$_6$
218 ^{lú}ŠEŠ.GAL ZI-*ma* A.MEŠ ÍD TU$_5$ ^{túg}GADA.LAL
219 *ina* IGI ^{d}EN *u* $^{(d)}$GAŠAN-*iá i-de-*〈*ek*〉-*ku*
220 ŠU.ÍL.LÁ *an-na-a ana* ^{d}EN *i-na-áš-ši*
221 *ana* ^{d}EN ŠÙD.BI DUG$_4$.GA

---

222 UMUN.MU UMUN.MU.NA UMUN.MU UMUN.MU.NA
223 *be-lu gaš-ri* ^{d}Í.GÌ.GÌ *ṣi-rì šá* DINGIR.DINGIR GAL.ME
224 UMUN.MU SUM.SUM UMUN.MU NU.KEŠDA.MU.NA
225 *be-lu kib-rat* LUGAL DINGIR.DINGIR $^{(d)}$ŠÚ *mu-kin* GIŠ.ḪUR
226 ALIM NU.ZA.PA.ÁG.BI UMUN.E MU.NA
227 *kab-tu ṣi-rì šá-qu-u e-tel-lu*
228 LÁ.A.KE$_4$ UŠUMGAL(GAL+UŠUM) NU.RA A.RI.A
229 *na-šu-u* LUGAL-*tú ta-mi-iḫ* UMUN-*tú*
230 [ZÁL]AG.GA NU.NU ZÁLAG.GA NU É.U$_4$.UL TUŠ
231 [*nu-u*]-*ri nam-ri* ^{d}AMAR.UTU *a-šib* É.MIN
232 [...]x SAḪAR KUR.NU.TUK
233 [...] *sa-pi-nu* KUR *a-a-bi*
234 [...] x E.NE

Several lines missing.

237 [....] x x x RU UD [...]
238 [...] x x x [...]
239 ⸢DINGIR(?)⸣ x x x [...] x
240 *e-bir* AN-*e* LÁ-*ṭi*$^{!}$ KI-*tì*
241 *ma-di-di* A.MEŠ *tam-tim mu-ur-riš* APIN-*tú*
242 *a-šib* É.U$_{4}$.UL EN E^{ki} ^{d}AMAR.UTU MAḪ
243 *mu-šim* NAM.MEŠ *šá* DINGIR.MEŠ DÙ.A.BI
244 *na-din* ^{giš}NÍG.PA KÙ-*tì ana* LUGAL *pa-liḫ-ḫi-šú*
245 *ana-ku* ^{lú}ŠEŠ.GAL É.TUŠ.A E-*u* SIG$_{5}$-*ku*
246 *ana* URU-*ku* E^{ki} *nap-šìr*
247 *ana* É.SAG.GÍL É-*ku ri-še-e* ARḪUŠ
248 *ina* KA-*ka ṣir-tú* EN DINGIR.DINGIR GAL.GAL
249 *ana* IGI ^{lú}DUMU.MEŠ E^{ki} *liš-šá-kin* ZÁLAG-*tú*

---

250 TA IGI ^{d}EN È-*ma ana* ^{d}GAŠAN-*iá* ŠÙD.BI DUG$_{4}$.GA

---

251 *gaš-rat i-lat ṣi-rat* ^{d}XV.MEŠ
252 ^{d}*Zar-pa-ni-tu*$_{4}$ *na-bat* MUL.⟨MEŠ⟩ *a-ši-bat* É.U$_{4}$.UL
253 *kaz*$^{!}$-*bat*(?) *i-lá-a-tú šá* IZI.GAR *lu-bu-ši-šú*
254 *e-bi-rat* AN-*e* LÁ-*at*$^{!}$ KI-*tì*
255 ^{d}*Zar-pa-ni-tu*$_{4}$ *šá man-za-zu šá-qu-u*
256 *nam-rat* ^{d}GAŠAN-*iá ṣi-rat u šá-qát*
257 *ina* ^{d}XV.MEŠ *ul i-ba-ši* GIM *šá-a-šú*
258 *a-ki-lat kar-ṣu ṣa-bi-tat a-bu-tú*
259 *mu-lap-pi-nát* ^{lú}NÍG.TUKU *mu-šá-áš-rat* ^{lú}ÚKU
260 *mu-šam-qí-tat* ^{lú}KÚR *la a-dir* DINGIR-*ti-šú*
261 *e-ṭi-rat ka-mi-i ṣa-bi-tat* ŠU^{II} *na-as-ku*
262 *šá* ^{lú}ÌR E-*u* SIG$_{5}$ MU-*ku qí-bi-i* SIG$_{5}$-*šú*
263 *ana* LUGAL *pa-liḫ-ḫi-ku* NAM-*šú* NAM
264 *ana* ^{lú}DUMU.MEŠ E^{ki} ^{lú}ÉRIN *ki-din-nu šú-ruk-šú-nu-tú* DIN
265 *ina* IGI LUGAL DINGIR.DINGIR ^{d}AMAR.UTU *ṣa-bat a-bu-su-nu*
266 *liq-bu-ú ta-nit-ku lu-šar-bu-u* UMUN-*ut-ku*
267 *lid-bu-bu-ú qur-di-ku li-šá-pu-u zik-ri-ku*
268 *ana* ^{lú}ÌR *qa-bu-u* SIG$_{5}$-*ku* TUKU-*e* ARḪUŠ
269 *ina pu-uš-qa u dan-nát ṣa-bat* ŠU^{II}-*šú*
270 *ina* GIG *u ta-ni-ḫu šu-ruk-šú* DIN
271 *lit-tal-lak* DIŠ-*a ina ḫi-da-a-tú u ri-šat*
272 *lid-bu-ub qur-di-ku ana* UN.MEŠ *kal* DÙ.DÙ.A

---

273 *ana* KISAL.MAḪ È-*ma* IGI-*šú ana* IM-2 GAR-*an-ma*
274 ^{mul}AŠ.IKU É.SAG.ÍL *tam-šil* AN *u* KI
275 3-*šú ana* É.SAG.ÍL *i-kar-rab*
276 ^{giš}I[G].MEŠ BAD-*te* ^{lú}KU$_{4}$-É.MEŠ *gab-bi*
277 K[U$_{4}$.M]EŠ-*ma* ME-*šú-nu* GIM *šá* DIŠ-*a* DÙ.MEŠ
278 ^{lú}[GAL]A.MEŠ *u* ^{lú}NAR.MEŠ KI.MIN

---

279 [*e-nu-m*]*a an-na-a i-te-ep-šú*
280 [EGIR *tar*]-*den-nu šá ki-iṣ u*$_{4}$-*mu e-nu-ma e-liš*

281 [TA *re-š*]*i*(?)-*šú* EN TIL-*šú* ^{lú}ŠEŠ.GAL É.TUŠ.A
282 [*ana* ^{d}EN *i*]-*na-áš-ši ma-la šá* UD *e-liš*
283 *ana* ^{d}EN [*i*]-*na-áš-šu-u* IGI *šá* AGA *šá* ^{d}LX
284 *u* KI.TUŠ *šá* ^{d}EN.LÍL *ku-ut-tu-mu-u*

---

285 DIŠ *ina* ^{iti}BÁR UD.5.KAM 2 DANNA GE$_{6}$ ^{lú}ŠEŠ.GAL
286 ZI-*ma* [A.MEŠ] ÍD ^{íd}IDIGNA *u* ^{íd}BURANUN^{ki}
(interlinear:) *i*-TU$_{5}$
287 [*ana* IGI ^{d}EN KU$_{4}$-*ma*] ^{túg}GADA.LAL *ina* IGI ^{d}EN *u* ^{d}GAŠAN-*iá i-de-*⟨*ek*⟩*-ku*
288 [*ana* ^{d}EN] ŠÙD.BI DUG$_{4}$.GA

---

289 UMUN.MU E.[N]E UMUN.MU E.NU.NU
290 UMUN.MU NI [...] UMUN.MU NU.MU.NA
291 UMUN.MU ŠU(?) [...] UMUN.MU BÁRA.KUR.KUR
292 UMUN.MU GIŠ.[...].NA UMUN.MU GIŠ.EN.NA
293 UMUN.MU NU [...] ÁG UMUN.MU NU.GÍD.EN
294 UMUN.MU ⌜x⌝ [...] ZAL UMUN.MU A.A.AL.NI
295 UMUN.MU [...] UMUN.MU KÉŠDA.DA
296 UMUN.MU [...] ⌜x⌝ UMUN.MU TUŠ É.U$_{4}$.UL
297 UMUN.MU [...] UMUN.MU NU.DIB.DIB
298 UMUN.MU [...] ⌜x⌝ UMUN.MU ZÉ.ÈM
299 UMUN.M[U ...] ⌜x⌝ UMUN.MU BÁRA.TUŠ.A
300 UMUN.M[U ...] ⌜x⌝ UMUN.MU UMUN.MU E.NE
301 ^{d}DÌM.ME.ER.AN.KI.A *mu-šim* NAM.MEŠ UMUN.MU UMUN.MU ḪUN
302 ^{múl}MU.BU.KÉŠ.DA *šá* ^{giš}GIDRI *u* ^{giš}GÚR *na-šu-*⟨*u*⟩ UMUN.MU UMUN.MU ḪUN
303 ^{múl}ERIDU(NUN)^{ki} *šá er-šu-tú aḫ-zu* UMUN.MU UMUN.MU ḪUN
304 ^{d}ASAR.RI *šá-ri-ik* APIN-*tú* UMUN.MU UMUN.MU ḪUN
305 ^{múl}BABBAR *na-áš ṣa-ad-du ana* DÙ.DÙ.A UMUN.MU UMUN.MU ḪUN
306 ^{múl}GU$_{4}$.UD *mu-šá-az-nin* ŠÈG UMUN.MU UMUN.MU ḪUN
307 ^{múl}GENNA MUL *kit-tú u mi-šar* UMUN.MU UMUN.MU ḪUN
308 ^{múl}AN ^{d}GIBIL$_{6}$ *ez-zu* UMUN.MU UMUN.MU ḪUN
309 ^{múl}KAK.SI.[SÁ] *ma-di-di* A.MEŠ *tam-tì* UMUN.MU UMUN.MU ḪUN
310 ^{múl}ŠU.PA EN ^{d}EN.LÍL.MEŠ UMUN.MU UMUN.MU ḪUN
311 ^{múl}NE.NE.GAR *šá ina* NÍ-*šú* DÙ-*u* UMUN.MU UMUN.MU ḪUN
312 ^{múl}NU.MUŠ.DA *muš-tab-ru-u* ŠÈG UMUN.MU UMUN.MU ḪUN
313 ^{múl}GABA.GÍR.TAB *ka-bi-is* GAB *tam-tì* UMUN.MU UMUN.MU ḪUN
314 ^{d}UTU ZÁLAG *kib-rat* UMUN.MU UMUN.MU ḪUN
315 ^{d}XXX *mu-nam-mir* {*mir*} *ik-let* UMUN.MU UMUN.MU ḪUN
316 UMUN.MU DIMMER.MU UMUN.MU EN.MU UMUN BAR.RA.NA

---

317 *ana* ^{d}GAŠAN-*iá* ŠÙD.BI DUG$_{4}$.GA

---

318 GAŠAN.MU GI$_{4}$.GI$_{4}$ GAŠAN.MU ḪUN.A
319 GAŠAN.MU NU.KÉŠ.DA GAŠAN.MU ḪUN.A
320 GAŠAN.MU SÌ.SÌ GAŠAN.MU DÙG.DÙG
321 GAŠAN.MU LAL.E.EN GAŠAN.MU DÙG.DÙG
322 GAŠAN.⟨MU⟩ ḪUN.NU.KÉŠ.DA GAŠAN.MU ŠUB.A.KE$_{4}$
323 GAŠAN.MU A.RA.ZU GAŠAN.MU ŠUB.A.KE$_{4}$
324 ^{d}DAM.KI.AN.NA *bé-lat* AN *u* KI GAŠAN.MU MU.NE

325 ^{múl}DIL.BAD *na-bat* MUL.⟨MEŠ⟩ GAŠAN.MU MU.NE
326 ^{múl}BAN ŠUB-*át dan-nu-tú* GAŠAN.MU MU.NE
327 ^{múl}ÙZ *ba-rat* AN-*e* GAŠAN.MU MU.NE
328 ^{múl}ḪÉ.GÁL.A MUL *nu-uḫ-šú* GAŠAN.MU MU.NE
329 ^{múl}BAL.TÉŠ.A MUL *bal-tú* GAŠAN.MU MU.NE
330 ^{múl}MAR.GÍD.DA *mar-kàs* AN-*e* GAŠAN.MU MU.NE
331 ^{múl}E$_4$.RU$_6$ *ba-nát re-ḫu*$^{!}$[23]*-tú* GAŠAN.MU MU.NE
332 ^{múl}NIN.MAḪ BA-*át* DIN GAŠAN.MU MU.NE
333 GAŠAN.MU GAŠAN.MU.NA GAŠAN.MU NU.MU.NE

---

334 TA *naq-bit iq-bu-ú* ^{giš}IG.MEŠ BAD-*te*
335 ^{lú}KU$_4$-É.MEŠ *gab-bi* KU$_4$.MEŠ-*ma*
336 ME-*šú-nu* GIM *šá* DIŠ-*a* DÙ.MEŠ
337 ^{lú}GALA.MEŠ *u* ^{lú}NAR.MEŠ KI.MIN

---

338 *e-nu-ma* 1 DANNA ME NIM-*a* TA *rik-su*
339 *šá* ^{giš}BANŠUR *šá* ^{d}EN *u* ^{d}GAŠAN-*iá šal-mu*
340 ^{lú}MAŠ.MAŠ GÙ-*ma* É *i-ḫab-ma*
341 A.MEŠ PÚ ^{íd}*Ì-diq-lat u* PÚ ^{íd}BURANUN^{ki}
342 É *i-sal-làḫ* NÍG.KALA.GA URUDU *ina* ŠÀ É
343 *ú-ḫal-lal* NÍG.NA GI.IZI.LÁ *ina* ŠÀ É *uš-ba-'*
344 [... *ina lìb*(?)]-*bi* TÙR BA(?) *ana pa-pa-ḫi šá* ^{d}EN
345 *u* ^{d}GAŠAN-*iá* NU KU$_4$ *e-nu-ma ḫu-up* É
346 *šal-mu ana* É.ZI.DA *ana pa-pa-ḫi* ^{d}AG
347 KU$_4$-*ma ina* NÍG.NA GI.IZI.LÁ A.GÚB.BA
348 É *i-ḫap-ma* É *pa-pa-ḫi* A.⟨MEŠ⟩ PÚ *Ì-diq-lat*
349 *u* PÚ ^{íd}*Pu-ra-at*$^{!}$[24]*-tú i-sal-làḫ*
350 ^{giš}IG.MEŠ *šá pa-pa-ḫi gab-bi* Ì.GIŠ EREN TAG
351 *ina* MÚRU KISAL *šá pa-pa-ḫi* NÍG.NA KÙ.BABBAR GAR-*ma*
352 ŠIM^{ḫá} *u bu-ra-šú ina muḫ-ḫi i-sár*$^{!}$*-raq*$^{!}$
353 ^{lú}GÍR.LÁ GÙ-*ma* SAG.DU UDU.NÍTA *i-bat-taq-ma*
354 *ina pag-ri* UDU.NÍTA ^{lú}MAŠ.MAŠ É *ú-kap-par*
355 ÉN.MEŠ *šá tùm-mu* É *i-man-nu*
356 *pa-paḫ gab-bi* EN NIGIN-*ti-šú i-ḫab-ma* NÍG.NA DUḪ
357 *pag-ri* UDU.NÍTA *šú-a-tì* ^{lú}MAŠ.MAŠ *i-na-áš-ši-ma*
358 *ana* ÍD GIN-*ak* IGI-*šú ana* ^{d}UTU.ŠÚ.A GAR-*an*
359 *pag-ri* UDU.NÍTA *šú-a-tú ana* ÍD ŠUB-*di*
360 *ana* EDEN È ^{lú}GÍR.LÁ SAG.DU UDU.NÍTA KI.MIN
361 ^{lú}MAŠ.MAŠ *u* ^{lú}GÍR.LÁ *ana* EDEN È.MEŠ *ma-la*
362 *šá* ^{d}AG *ina* E^{ki} *ana* E^{ki} NU KU$_4$.MEŠ
363 TA UD.5.KAM EN UD.12 *ina* EDEN DÚR.MEŠ
364 *ḫu-ub-bu šá* É ^{lú}ŠEŠ.GAL É.TUŠ.A NU IGI-*mar*
365 BAD-*ma i-mu-ru* NU KÙ
366 EGIR *ḫu-ub šá* É *e-nu-ma* 1 2/3 DANNA
367 ME NIM-*a* ^{lú}ŠEŠ.GAL É.TUŠ.A È-*ma*
368 DUMU.MEŠ ^{lú}*um-man-nu* DÙ.A.BI-*šú-nu* GÙ-*si*
369 AN-*e* GUŠKIN TA NÍG.GA ^{d}AMAR.UTU

---

23 Copy: *ri*.
24 Copy: *ri*.

370 È-*ma* É.ZI.DA *pa-pa-ḫi* ^{d}AG TA ⌜^{giš}⌝*tal-lu*
371 *a-di iš-di* É *ir-ri-mu-ú*
372 ^{lú}ŠEŠ.GAL É.TUŠ.A *u* ^{lú}DUMU.MEŠ *um-man-nu*
373 *ik-kil-lu*$_4$ *an-na-a i-qab-bu-u*
374 É *ul-la-lu-ú*
375 ^{d}ASAL.LÚ.⟨ḪI⟩ DUMU ERIDU(NUN)^{ki}.KE$_4$ É.U$_4$.UL DÚR.DÚR
376 ^{d}KÙ.SÙ GIŠ.ŠÚ.A.NA ^{d}KÙ.SÙ
377 ^{d}NIN.GÌRIM(A.ḪA.⟨KUD⟩.DU) A.RA.⟨ZU⟩ GIŠ.TUK.TUK
378 ^{d}AMAR.UTU *ul-lal* É
379 ^{d}KÙ.SÙ *uṣ-ṣir* GIŠ.ḪUR
380 ^{d}NIN.GÌRIM *i-nam-di* ÉN
381 *mim-ma lem-nu šá ina* É *e-ṣu*
382 *gal-lu-ú* GAL-*ú li-nar-ku* ^{d}EN
383 KI.TUŠ GAR.RA.AŠ ḪU.NI.IB.DA.TAR.AM$_6$

---

384 ^{lú}DUMU.MEŠ *um-man-nu* DÙ.A.BI-*šú-nu ana* KÁ È

---

385 [...] *u*$_4$*-mu* ^{lú}ŠEŠ.GAL *ana* IGI ^{d}EN
386 [KU$_4$*-ma*(?) ...]⌜-*šú*(?)⌝ *i-de-*⟨*ek*⟩*-ku*(?) ^{giš}BANŠUR GUŠKIN
387 [*i-rak-kas*(?) ^{uz}]^{u}KA.NE.MEŠ *ina* UGU GAR-*an*
388 [... *ina* UG]U GAR-*an* 12 *gi-nu-ú ina* UGU GAR-*an*
389 [... GUŠ]KIN MUN SA$_5$-*ma ina* UGU GAR-*an*
390 [... GUŠK]IN LÀL SA$_5$-*ma ina* UGU GAR-*an*
391 [...] *ina muḫ-ḫi* GAR-*an* 4 *šap-pi* GUŠKIN
392 [... *ina mu*]*ḫ-ḫi* ^{giš}BANŠUR GAR-*an* NÍG.NA GUŠKIN
393 [... *ina*(?)] IGI ^{giš}BANŠUR GAR-*an* ŠIM *u* LI
394 [*ina muḫ-ḫi i-sar-raq*] GEŠTIN *i-na-aq-qí*
395 [ŠÙD *an-n*]*a-a i-qab-bi*
396 [^{d}AMAR.UTU EN].MAḪ *šá* DINGIR.MEŠ-*a-nu*
397 [DÚR É.SAG.Í]L *ba-nu-ú ki-na-a-tú*
398 [...] *ana* DINGIR.DINGIR GAL.MEŠ
399 [...] x-*ku ra me-dil ka-a-ri*
400 [*li-iḫ-du*(?)] *lìb-bi-ku ana ṣa-bat* ŠU^{II}-*ku*
401 [*ina* É.SÍS]KUR É *ik-ri-bi*
402 [*ina*(?) ...]x *aš-ri-ku li-iš-šú* SAG-*su*
403 [TA *na*]*q-bit* E-*u* ^{giš}BANŠUR DUḪ-*ár*
404 [^{lú}DUMU.MEŠ] *um-man-nu* DÙ.A$^{!}$.BI-*šú-nu* GÙ-*si*
405 ^{giš}BANŠUR *gab-bi ana* ^{lú}DUMU.MEŠ *um-man-nu*
406 [SUM-*i*]*n-ma ana* ^{d}AG *ú-šeb-bil-šú*
407 [^{lú}DUMU.ME]Š *um-man-nu* TI.MEŠ-*ma ina* KI KAB ṢAB/PI(?) GAG
408 [*ina* GÚ ^{í}]^{d}*ku-nát a-mat-su*(?) GIN.MEŠ *e-nu-ma* ^{d}AG
409 [*ina* KI KAB ṢA]B/PI(?) GAG *ina ka-ša-di-šú ana* ^{d}AG *ú-bar-ru-šú*
410 [*ana* IGI(?)] ^{giš}BANŠUR *ina* IGI ^{d}AG GAR.MEŠ-*šú* DUḪ ^{giš}BANŠUR
411 [*ki-ma*] *šá* ^{d}AG TA ^{giš}MÁ ÍD.DA.ḪÉ.DU$_7$
412 [È *i*]*-na-áš-šu-nim-ma ina* UGU ^{giš}BANŠUR
413 [GAR.MEŠ] A.MEŠ ŠU^{II} LUGAL DIB-ʾ-*nim-ma*
414 [*ana* É.SAG].ÍL KU$_4$.MEŠ-*šú* DUMU.MEŠ *um-man-nu ana* KÁ È.MEŠ
415 [*ana* IGI ^{d}]EN *ina* KUR-*šú* ^{lú}ŠEŠ.GAL È-*ma* ^{giš}NÍG.GIDRU ^{giš}GÚR
416 $^{[giš]}$TUKUL.DINGIR
417 [*šá* ŠU^{II} LUGAL(?)] ÍL-*ši* AGA LUGAL-*ú-ti-šú i-na-áš-ši*

418 [*ana* IGI ^{d}E]N *ú-še-rib-šú-nu-tú ina* IGI ^{d}EN
419 [*ina* UGU] KI.TUŠ GAR-*an-šú-nu-tú* È-*ma* TE LUGAL SÌG-*aṣ*
420 [LUGAL(?)] EGIR-*šú* GAR-*an ana* IGI ^{d}EN *ú-še-rib-šú*
421 [EGIR-*šú*(?)] GEŠTUG^{II}-*šú i-šad-dad ina* KI *ú-šá-kam-su*
422 [*adi*/KI(?)] LUGAL 1-*šú an-na-a* DUG$_4$.GA
423 [*ul ah*]-*ṭu* EN KUR.KUR *ul e-gi ana* DINGIR-*ti-ku*
424 [*ul ú-ḫa-a*]*l-liq* E^{ki} *ul aq-ṭa-bi* BIR-*šú*
425 [*ul ú-ri*]*b-bi* É.SAG.GÍL *ul ú-ma-áš-*⟨*ši*⟩ ME-*šú*
426 [*ul am-da*]*ḫ-ḫa-aṣ* TE ^{lú}*ṣab-bi ki-din-nu*
427 [… *ul*] *áš-kun qa-lal-šú-nu*
428 [*ú-pa-a*]*q ana* E^{ki} *ul a-bu-ut šal-ḫu-šú*
429 IM *šá* EGIR-*šú*
430 […] ⸢DIŠ(?)⸣ *ina* ^{iti}BÁR UD.5.KAM

About 5 lines missing.

434 ⸢*la ta-pal-làḫ*⸣ […]
435 *šá* ^{d}EN *iq-ta-bi* […]
436 ^{d}EN *ik-ri-ib-ka* [*i-šem-me*(?)]
437 *ú-šar-bi* UMUN-*ut-ka* […]
438 *ú-šaq-qa* LUGAL-*ut-ka* […]
439 *ina* UD ÈŠ.ÈŠ *e-pu-u*[*š* …]
440 *ina* BAD KÁ *ub-bi-ib* ŠU[^{II}-*ka* …]
441 *ur-ri u* GE$_6$ *lu*-⸢x⸣ […]
442 *šá* E^{ki} URU-*šú* […] E […]
443 *šá* É.SAG.GÍL É-*su* […] BI […]
444 *šá* DUMU.MEŠ E^{ki} ^{lú}ÉRIN *ki-din-*[*ni* …] AṢ […]
445 ^{d}EN *i-kar-rab-ku* KI [… *a-n*]*a da-ri-*[*iš*]
446 *ú-ḫal-laq* ^{lú}KÚR-*ku ú-šam-qát za-ma-an-*⸢*ku*⸣
447 *e-nu-ma* E-*u* LUGAL *ka-bat* KIR$_4$ DIŠ-*ú-šú i-*[…]
448 ^{giš}NÍG.GIDRU ^{giš}GÚR ^{giš}TUKUL.DINGIR AGA È-*ma ana* LUGAL [SUM-*in*]
449 TE LUGAL *i-maḫ-ḫa-aṣ e-nu-ma* TE-*su* [*im-ḫa-ṣu*]
450 *šum*$_4$-*ma di-ma-tu-šú il-lik* ^{d}EN *sa-l*[*im*]
451 *šum*$_4$-*ma di-ma-tu-šú* NU GIN.MEŠ ^{d}EN *e-zi-i*[*z*]
452 ^{lú}KÚR ZI-*am-ma i-šak-kan* ŠUB-*su*

---

453 *e-nu-ma an-na-a i-pu-šú* KI XX ŠÚ MAN(?) ^{lú}ŠEŠ.GAL
454 40 GI.MEŠ *šá* 3 KÙŠ.ÀM NU BAR.MEŠ
455 NU ḪAŠ.MEŠ GIŠ.MEŠ-*ma šá rik-su ina e-ri* GIŠIMMAR
456 *i-rak-ka-as-šú-nu-tú ina* KISAL.MAḪ PÚ BAD.MEŠ-⸢*ma*⸣
457 *ina* PÚ *ú-kan* LÀL Ì.NUN Ì.GIŠ [SAG(?) *ina* UGU *i-naq-qa*(?)]
458 PA *ina*! IGI! *nag-be* GAR-*an* GU$_4$ BABBAR *ana* I[GI PÚ(?) …]
459 LUGAL IZI.GAR *ina* GI *ana lìb-bi-šú ú-*[*šá-aṣ-bat*(?)]
460 *naq-bit an-na-a* LUGAL *u* [^{lú}ŠEŠ.GAL *i-qab-bu-u*]
461 ^{d}GU$_4$ ZÁLAG *nam-ri mu-n*[*am-mir ik-le-ti*]
462 *qa-mu-ú šá* ^{d}*A-nù* […]
463 ^{d}GIBIL$_6$.MEŠ ⸢x x⸣ GAR-*nu*
464 TA *u-mi-šú-nu-ti-ma* x […]
465 *i-nu-ú ana di-na-ni* x […]

466 *a-di-na-ni-šú i-nu-ú* x [...]
467 ^{d}GU$_{4}$ DÙ.A.BI-*šú* LUGAL [...]
468 *ana* ^{d}EN ÚR *i-kal* x [...]
469 *e-nu-ma* ^{d}GU$_{4}$ x [...]
470 LUGAL *ana šu-tùm* ⸢DINGIR(?) x x⸣ [...]
471 *mi*-x x [...]

472 ^{im}DUB 23 EME.⸢GIR$_{15}$.DU$_{7}$.E⸣ [NU TI]
473 ^{im}DUB *šá* EGIR-⸢*šú*⸣

---

474 DIŠ *ina* ^{iti}BÁRA UD.5.KAM IGI.TAB *u* IGI.KÁR

---

475 *pa-liḫ* ^{d}AMAR.UTU *u* ^{d}*Zar-pa-ni-tu*$_{4}$
476 *ana* ŠU^{II} NU È *šá ana* ŠU^{II} È-*u*
477 DINGIR.DINGIR *ma-la ina qé-reb* ^{uru}E^{ki}
478 *ba-šu-u li-ru-ru-šú*

The rest is lost.

1 In the (first) month Nisannu, day 2, at the last double hour of the night,
2 [the h]igh priest will rise and wash (himself) with river water.
3 He will enter [be]fore Bēl and remove (l. 4) the *gadalû*-curtain in front of Bēl.
4 He will say the following prayer to Bēl:

5–6 Bēl, who in his anger has no rival,
7–8 Bēl, good king, lord of the lands,
9–10 who returns the favour of the great gods,
11–12 Bēl, who overthrows the strong ones by his angry look (alone),
13–14 lord of kings, the light of mankind, who allotted the portions:
15–16 Bēl, Babylon is your seat, Borsippa is your crown,
17–18 the whole of your mind is (like) the vast Heaven.
19 Bēl, you watch over everything with your (own) eyes:
20 you explore (the implications of all) omina [through] the omina you (give),
21 [with] your angry look you give orders,
22 [with] your touch you burn(?) the strong ones,
23 you capture the [u]nsubmissive(?) with (your) hands,
24 [with] your glance you grant mercy to them,
25 you show them the light, they talk of your heroism.
26 Lord of the lands, light of Igigi, who speaks favourably,
27 who, (when speaking) of you, will not talk of your heroism,
28 will not speak of your praise, will not proclaim your lordship?
29 Lord of the lands, who resides in Eu(d)ul,who helps the fallen,
30 to your city Babylon, grant mercy!
31 To Esagila, your temple, turn your face!
32 Establish freedom from service for the citizens of Babylon, (your) privileged subjects!

---

33 21 lines, secret of Esagila.
34–35 [He who revere]s Bēl will [n]ot show it (l. 35) (to anyone) but the high priest of Etuša.

---

36 [After] he has said this blessing,
37 [he will op]en [the gates]. The temple enterers
38 [will ris]e, (and) perform (l. 39) their rites as usual
39 [in front] of Bēl and Bēltīja.
40 [The lamentation priests and the] singers ditto.

---

41 […]
42 […]
43 […]
44 […]
45 […]
46 … […]
47 seat […]
48 … […]
49 He will place, the seal […]
50 on the tiara of An[u …]
51 of the second day, u[pon …]
52 he will place in front of them … […]
53 he will say three times […]

---

54 The wicked enemies […]
55 who, in their strength […]
56 this, which is in Babylo[n …]
57 of a *namburbû*-ritual […]
58 because the enemy and lawless [persons …]
59 The great lord, Marduk […]
60 has utte[red] a irremovable curse […]
61 has decreed a irrevocable fate […]
62 of Bēl, my lord […]
63 of the lord of the lands […]
64 of Babylon […]
65 on Earth […]
66 of Eu(d)ul […]
67 is cleansed […]
68 like Heaven and [Earth …]
69 Uruk and Ni[ppur are burnt and captured],
70 th[eir foundation] is removed [and thrown into the water],
71 the temples in [their midst, their …]
72 their rites are forgotten [to distant days …]
72a [their regular offerings do not take place …]
73 [their] div[ine decrees] are scattered […]
74 the people who reside […] … […] … […]
75 the servant girls … […]
76 of Babylon […]
77 of Eu(d)u[l …]
78 he captured you […]
79 you sit down […]

Approximately 76 lines (2 columns), with the rest of the ceremonies for the second day of Nisannu, are missing.

156 … […]

---

157 In the (first) month Nisannu, day 3, [at 1 1/3 double hours of the night, the high priest]
158 will ri[se and] wash (himself) [with river water].
159 [He will say the following pray]er to [Bēl]:

---

160 My lord, Lulu […]
161 … […]
162 … […]
163 … […]
164 … […]
165 […]
166 … […] … […]
167 … […] … […]
168 My lord, the shepherd … […]
169 […] … […]
170 … […] … […]
171 … […] … […]
172 who gives […]
173 … Nisaba […]
174 of the dark-headed people […]
175 you watch over(?) … […]
176 … […] … […]
177 … […] … […]
178 […] … […] … […]
179 […] king, lord, governor […]
180 in the mouth of the dark-headed […]
181 of Esagila [your temple …]
182 of Babylon your city […]
183 to speak well […]

---

184 (The high priest) will ope[n] the gates. [The temple enterers]
185 will enter [and] perform (l. 186) [their rites as usual].
186 [The lamentation priests and the singers ditto].
187 […]

3 lines lost.

190 [Whe]n 1 1/2 double hours of daytime have passed,
191 he will call for the metalworker (l. 190) and give him (l. 193) precious stones and gold
192 from the treasury of Marduk to make 2 figurines
193 for (the ceremony of) the sixth day. He will call for the carpenter and
194 give him cedar and tamarisk.
195 He will call for the goldsmith and give him (some) gold.
196 From the third day to the sixth day, from (the offering table) before Bēl (the meat has to be distributed as follows):

197 the thigh piece to the metalworker, the breast to the goldsmith [...],
198 the shoulder piece to the carpenter, the rib(s) to the weaver. This
199 they will bring (l. 200) from (the offering table) before Bēl to the high priest of Etuša
200 (and?) to the craftsmen.

201 The size of these figurines is 7 fingers.
202 One (has to be made) of cedar and one of tamarisk.
203 4(?) shekels of gold (will be) their mountings.
204 4(?) *dušû*-stones will go up on them.
205 [One] will lift [up] a snake of cedar in its left hand
206 (and) it will lift up its right [hand] to Nabû. The second
207 will lift up a scorpion [in] its [left hand] (l. 206), (and) it will lift up (l. 208) its right hand
208 [to N]abû. They will be robed in red garment(s),
209 their hips [will be gir]t (l. 210) with (a belt of) palm leaves.
210 [They will be plac]ed (l. 211) in the temple of Ma[dānu] until the sixth day.
211 The leftovers of the offering table of Mad[ānu]
212 will be served to them. On the sixth day [...],
213 when Nabû reaches Eḫursagtila,
214 the slaughterer and seller (of prepared meat dishes) will strike their heads. Then
215 they will kindle the ashes(?) in front of Nabû and
216 thro[w] (the figurines) into the ashes(?).

(Colophon and catchline:)
216a The twenty-second tablet. Perfect Sumerian. Not finished.
216b Tablet, that follows: in the (first) month Nisannu, day 4.

216c By the command of Bēl and Bēltīja may (this work) be successful.
217 In the (first) month Nisannu, day 4, at 1 2/3 double hours of the night,
218 the high priest will rise and wash (himself) with river water.
219 He will remove the *gadalû*-curtain (l. 218) in front of Bēl and Bēltīja.
220 He will recite this hand-raising prayer to Bēl,
221 he will say the following prayer to Bēl:

222–3 Powerful lord of the Igigi, most exalted of the great gods,
224–5 lord of the world regions, the king of the gods, Marduk, who establishes the divine decrees,
226–7 honorable, exalted, sublime, lordly,
228–9 who carries kingship, who holds lordship,
230–1 bright light, Marduk, who resides in Eu(d)ul,
232–3 [...] who overwhelms the lands of the enemies.

Several lines missing

237 [...] ... [...]
238 [...] ... [...]
239 ... [...] ...
240 who crosses the Heaven, who watches over the Earth,
241 who measures out the water of the sea, who plants (every) cultivated field,

242 who resides in Eu(d)ul, the lord of Babylon, exalted Marduk,
243 who decrees the destinies of all the gods,
244 who gives the pure scepter to the king who reveres him.
245 I am the high priest of Etuša, who speaks well of you:
246 be forgiving to your city, Babylon,
247 grant mercy to your temple, Esagila,
248 with your exalted word, lord of the great gods,
249 may light be set (again) before the citizens of Babylon.

---

250 He will go out (from) before (the statue of) Bēl and will say the following prayer to Bēltīja:

---

251 Most powerful of the female deities, most exalted of the goddesses,
252 Zarpanītu, most brilliant of the stars, who resides in Eu(d)ul,
253 most attractive(?) of the female deties, whose garment is light,
254 who crosses the Heaven, who watches over the Earth,
255 Zarpanītu, whose (heavenly) station is sublime,
256 bright is Bēltīja, exalted and sublime!
257 There is none like her among the goddesses,
258 who denounces, who intercedes,
259 who impoverishes the rich, who makes the poor rich,
260 who overthrows the enemy, who does not fear her divinity,
261 who saves the captive, who helps the fallen:
262 speak well of the servant who speaks well of your name,
263 decree the fate of the king who reveres you,
264 prolong the life of the citizens of Babylon, (your) privileged subjects,
265 intercede for them in front of the king of the gods, Marduk,
266 may they speak of your praise, may they magnify your lordship,
267 may they talk of your heroism, may they proclaim your fame,
268 grant mercy to the servant who speaks well of you,
269 help in distress and hardship,
270 prolong his life from sickness and suffering,
271 may he always walk amongst rejoicings and jubilation,
272 may he talk of your heroism to all people.

---

273 (Then) he will go out to the Grand Courtyard and he will place his face towards the North, and (with the words)
274 'ikû-star, Esagila, image of Heaven and Earth'
275 he will pronounce praise to Esagila three times.
276 (Then) he will open the ga[te]s. All the temple enterers
277 w[ill en]ter and perform their rites as usual.
278 The [lam]entation priests and the singer ditto.

---

279 [Whe]n they have done this,
280 [after the] second meal in the late afternoon,
281 the high priest of Etuša will 'raise' (l. 282)(?) *Enūma eliš* (l. 280) [from its beg]inning to its end
282 [to Bēl]. While he 'raises' (l. 283) *Enūma eliš*
283 to Bēl, the front part of Anu's tiara
284 and Enlil's seat will remain covered.

285 In the (first) month Nisannu, day 5, at 2 double hours of the night, the high priest
286 will rise and wash (himself) (interlinear) with river water from the Tigris and the Euphrates.
287 [He will enter before Bēl and] remove the *gadalû*-curtain in front of Bēl and Bēltīja.
288 He will say the following prayer [to Bēl]:

289 My lord is he! Is he not my lord?
290 My lord … Is his name not 'My lord'?
291 My lord …, my lord is king of the lands,
292 My lord …, my lord …,
293 My lord …, my lord …,
294 My lord …, my lord …,
295 My lord […], my lord …,
296 My lord […], my lord who resides in Eu(d)ul,
297 My lord […], my lord …,
298 My lord […], my lord …,
299 M[y] lord […], my lord who sits on a throne,
300 M[y] lord […], my lord, he is my lord!
301 Dimmerankia, who decrees the destinies, my lord, my lord, be calm.
302 Mubukešda-star, who carries scepter and loop, my lord, my lord, be calm.
303 Eridu-star, who possesses wisdom, my lord, my lord, be calm.
304 Asari, who bestows cultivated land, my lord, my lord, be calm.
305 Jupiter, who carries a sign for all, my lord, my lord, be calm.
306 Mercury, who brings rain, my lord, my lord, be calm.
307 Saturn, star of truth and justice, my lord, my lord, be calm.
308 Mars, fierce fire (god), my lord, my lord, be calm.
309 Siri[us], who measures the water of the sea, my lord, my lord, be calm.
310 Šupa-star, the lord of the highest-ranking gods, my lord, my lord, be calm.
311 Nenegar-star, who was created by himself, my lord, my lord, be calm.
312 Numušda-star, who makes the rain last long, my lord, my lord, be calm.
313 'Breast of Scorpion'-star, who walkes upon the 'breast' of the sea, my lord, my lord, be calm.
314 Sun, light of the world regions, my lord, my lord, be calm.
315 Moon, who illuminates the darkness, my lord, my lord, be calm.
316 My lord is my god, my lord is my lord, (is there) a lord without him?

317 He will say the following prayer to Bēltīja:

318 My lady …, my lady, be calm.
319 My lady …, my lady, be calm.
320 My lady, who gives, my lady, who is very good.
321 My lady, …, my lady, who is very good.
322 My lady, …, my lady, …
323 My lady, …, my lady, …
324 Damkianna, lady of Heaven and Earth, whose name is 'My lady'.
325 Venus, most brilliant of the stars, whose name is 'My lady'.
326 Bow-star, who fells the strong ones, whose name is 'My lady'.
327 Goat-star, who watches over Heaven, whose name is 'My lady'.

328 Ḫegalla-star, the star of abundance, whose name is 'My lady'.
329 Balteša-star, the star of dignity, whose name is 'My lady'.
330 Wagon-star, the center of Heaven, whose name is 'My lady'.
331 Erū(a)-star, who creates progeny, whose name is 'My lady'.
332 Ninmaḫ-star, who gives life, whose name is 'My lady'.
333 My lady is indeed 'My lady'! Is her name not 'My lady'?

---

334 After he has said the blessing, he will open the gates.
335 All the temple enterers will enter and
336 they will perform their rites as usual.
337 The lamentation priests and singers ditto.

---

338 When the first double hour of daytime has passed, after the offering accoutrements
339 of the offering table of Bēl and Bēltīja are completed,
340 he will call for the exorcist and he will consecrate the temple. Then,
341 with the water from a well along the Tigris and from a well along the Euphrates,
342 he will sprinkle the temple. He will sound (l. 343) the copper *nigkalagû*-drum inside the temple.
343 He will move the censer (and) the torch inside the temple.
344 [... i]n the courtyard(?) ... He will not enter (l. 345) the cella of Bēl
345 and Bēltīja. When the consecration of the temple
346 is completed, he will enter (l. 347) Ezida, the cella of Nabû,
347 and consecrate the temple (l. 348) with censer, torch (and) holy water-basin
348 and sprinkle (l. 349) the cella with the water from a well along the Tigris
349 and from a well along the Euphrates.
350 He will smear all the doors of the cella (with) cedar oil.
351 He will place the silver censer in the middle of the courtyard of the cella and
352 scatter aromatics and the juniper on it.
353 (The high priest) will call for the slaughterer and he will cut off the head of the sheep and
354 the exorcist will purify the temple with the carcass of the sheep.
355 He will recite incantations (of the type): 'The house is conjured'.
356 He will consecrate the whole cella to its full extent, and clear away the censer.
357 The exorcist will lift up the carcass of that sheep and
358 go to the river. He will place his face towards the West.
359 He will throw the carcass of that sheep into the river.
360 He will go out to the open country. The slaughterer with the head of the sheep ditto.
361 The exorcist and the slaughterer will go out to the open country; as long as
362 Nabû is in Babylon, they will not (re)enter Babylon.
363 From the fifth day until the twelfth day they will stay in the open country.
364 The high priest of Etuša will not observe the consecration of the temple.
365 If he observes (it) he is not pure.
366 After the consecration of the temple, when 1 2/3 double hours
367 of daytime have passed, the high priest of Etuša will go out and
368 call for all the craftsmen.
369 They will bring out (l. 370) the golden canopy from the treasury of Marduk
370 and they will cover (l. 371) Ezida, the cella of Nabû, from (its) crossbeam
371 to the foundation of the temple.
372 The high priest of Etuša and the craftsmen
373 will utter this cry of distress:

374 'They will purify the temple.
375 Asalluḫi, the son of Eridu, who resides in Eu(d)ul,
376 Kusu, who is on his stool(?), Kusu,
377 Ningirim, who listens to the invocation,
378 Marduk purifies the temple,
379 Kusu establishes the divine decrees,
380 Ningirim casts the spell:
381 Any evil, which is in the temple, go forth!
382 Great demon, may Bēl kill you!
383 May he expel you to your abode!'

---

384 All craftsmen will go out to the gate.

---

385 [...] the (same) day(?), the high priest [will enter (l. 386)(?)] before Bēl.
386 [and] he will remove(?) his [...]. [He will arrange (l. 387)(?)] the golden offering table.
387 He will place [r]oasted meat on (it).
388 He will place [... o]n (it). He will place 12 regular offerings on (it).
389 He will fill the golden [...] with salt and he will place on (it).
390 He will fill the golden [...] with honey and he will place on (it).
391 He will place [...] on (it). 4 golden *šappu*-containers
392 [...] he will place [o]n the offering table. The golden censer
393 [...] he will place [in(?)] front of the offering table. Aromatics and juniper
394 [he will scatter on it]. He will make a libation of wine.
395 He will say [th]is [prayer]:
396 [Marduk], exalted [lord] of the gods,
397 [who resides in Esagi]la, who is the creator of orderliness,
398 [...] to the great gods,
399 [...] ... the bolt of the quay,
400 [May] your heart [rejoice(?)] for the one whom you take by the hand,
401 [in E]sizkur, the (*akītu*-temple named) *Bīt ikribi*,
402 [in...], your place, may he raise his head!
403 [After] he has said the [bles]sing he will clear the offering table.
404 He will call for all the [crafts]men.
405 [He will give (l. 406)] all of the offering table to the craftsmen
406 and he will make them bring it to Nabû.
407 [The crafts]men will take (it) and they will go (l. 408) to the ...-place,
408 [on the bank of the] Kunat-amassu-[c]anal. When Nabû
409 arrives [at the...] ... [place], they will usher him (the king) in for Nabû.
410 They will place him [before(?)] the offering table in front of Nabû. They will lift up (l. 412) the leftovers of the offering table,
411 [as soon as] Nabû [goes out] from (l. 412) the ship Iddaḫedu, and
412 [place (them)] (l. 413) on the offering table.
413 They will move a [wa]ter (basin) for (the washing of) hands (in front of) the king and
414 make him enter [Esag]ila. The craftsmen will go out to the gate.
415 When (the king) has arrived [before] Bēl, the high priest will go out (of the cella) and
416 lift up (l. 417) the scepter, the loop, the mace
417 [of the king(?)]. He will (also) lift up the Crown of Kingship.
418 He will make them enter [before Bē]l (and), in front of Bēl,
419 he will place them [on] a seat. He will go out and strike the cheek of the king.
420 He will place [the king(?)] behind him. He will make him enter before Bēl.

421 [After this(?)] he will pull his ears, make him kneel on the ground.
422 [Together w]ith(?) the king he will say this once:
423 [I have not] sinned, lord of the lands, I have not neglected your divinity,
424 [I have not] ruined Babylon, I have not ordered its dissolution,
425 [I have not] made Esagila tremble, I have not forgotten its rites,
426 [I have not] struck the cheek of any privileged subject,
427 [...] I have [not] brought about their humiliation,
428 [I have been taking ca]re of Babylon, I have not destroyed its outer walls!
(Catchline:)
429 Tablet, that follows:
430 [...] In the (first) month Nisannu, day 5.

About 5 lines are missing, which must have contained an instruction to the king to leave the cella again, and the beginning of a speech of the high priest to the king.

434 Do not fear [...]
435 What Bēl has ordered [...]
436 Bēl [will listen(?)] to your prayer [...]
437 He will magnify your lordship [...]
438 He will extol your kingship.
439 At the *eššēšu*-day, do [...]
440 At the opening of the gate ceremony, cleanse [your] hands [...]!
441 Day and night may [...]
442 Concerning Babylon, his city [...] ... [...]
443 Concerning Esagila, his temple [...] ... [...]
444 Concerning the citizens of Babylon, his privileged subjec[ts ...] ... [...]
445 Bēl will bless you with(?) [... f]orev[er].
446 He will ruin your enemy (and) overthrow your adversary.
447 When he has spoken (this), the king [will rediscover(?)] his normal dignity.
448 (The high priest) will bring out the scepter, the loop, the mace (and) the crown and [will give] (them) to the king.
449 He will strike the king's cheek (again). When [he has struck] his cheek,
450 if his tears flow, Bēl is well disposed,
451 if his tears do not flow, Bēl is angry,
452 the enemy will rise and bring about his downfall.

---

453 When he has done this, as soon as it is one-third (of the double hour) of sunset(?) the high priest will tie together (l. 456)
454 40 reeds, of 3 cubits each, peeled,
455 unbroken, straight, which (are suitable for) a belt, with palm leaves.
456 They will dig a hole in the Grand Courtyard and
457 set up (the belt) into the hole. [He will make a libation of] honey, ghee, [fine(?)] oil [over it(?)].
458 He will place a branch in front of the bundle. A white bull in [front of the hole(?) ...]
459 The king [will light(?)] a fire by means of a reed to it.
460 The king and [the high priest will say] this blessing:
461 O divine bull, the bright light, which [illuminates the darkness],
462 the burning one of Anu [...]
463 Divine fires ... are placed.

464 At that time(??) … […]
465 When for the sake of … […]
466 On account of him, when … […]
467 The divine bull, all of it, the king […]
468 For Bēl he will eat (its) thigh … […]
469 When the divine bull … […]
470 The king to the storehouse of the god(?) … […]
471 … […]

(Colophon and catchline:)
472 The twenty-third tablet. Perfect Sumerian. [Not finished]
473 Tablet, that follow[s:]

---

474 in the (first) month Nisannu, day 5. Collated and checked(?)

---

475 He who reveres Marduk and Zarpanītu,
476 will ensure that (this tablet) does not leave the hands; he who makes (this tablet) leave the hands,
477 may all the gods, who are (l. 470) in Babylon,
478 curse him.

Comments

l. 15–16, see *CAD*, A/I, 154a, lex. section. The Sumerian is obscure.

l. 16, *šub-ta-ku* and *a-gu-ku*, the possessive pronominal suffix *-ku* (passim in this text) in Late Babylonian often stands for *-ka* (see l. 20: UR$_5$.ÚŠ.MEŠ-*ka*). Cf. W. von Soden *GAG*, §42, j and k.

l. 17–18, *ka-bat-ti-ku* 'your mind' (cf. also W. Farber, *TUAT* II/2, 213) rather than 'your inside' (see *CAD*, K, 12a, 1).

l. 19, *gim-re-e-tú* 'everything', or: 'the universe'?

l. 20, 'you explore (the implications of all) omina [through] the omina you (give)', see *CAD*, Ḫ, 160a, 2.

l. 22, [*in*]*a la-pa-*⟨*ti*⟩*-ka ta-qam*(?)*-mu*, for this reading see *RAcc.*, 130 and W. Farber, *TUAT* II/2, 213, n. 22a.

l. 23, [*l*]*a* GI-*ka* 'the [u]nsubmissive(?)' (see *CAD*, K, 130a), or: 'those who are [no]t loyal to you'.

l. 29, É.U$_4$.UL (or UD.UL) the temple of Marduk (here Bēl-mātāti) in Esagila, is also attested in 66, 77, 230–1, 242, 252, 296 and 375, and furthermore in BM 41577 (A.R. George, *Studies W.G. Lambert*, no. 1, 260 ff.), col. III, 27. See A.R. George, *House Most High*, no. 1141.

l. 29, *ṣa-bit* ŠU^{II} 'who helps', lit. 'taking the hands of', cf. also l. 261, 269 and 400.

l. 33, URÙ-*tú* É.SAG.ÍL 'secret of Esagila', cf. P.-A. Beaulieu, *ZA* 82 (1992), 108, with n. 37.

L. 37–9 (see also 184–86, 276–77, 335–36), this phrase is also attested in BM 41577 (A.R. George, *Studies W.G. Lambert*, no. 1, 260 ff.), col. II, 12′–13′.

l. 69–79, these lines are duplicated by the fragment BM 32654 + 38193, rev. col. III, 18–30. This mythical text, which goes back to an older original, will be published by W.G. Lambert. BM 32654 was published by T.G. Pinches, *PSBA* 30 (1908), 53 ff. and 77 ff. BM 38193 is unpublished.

l. 74, UN.MEŠ *a-šib* [... *iḫ*-x ...], BM 32654 + reads: UN.MEŠ *šá qer-*⌜*bi*⌝ [...].

l. 157, 1 1/3 DANNA GE_6, because the second day started with the last double hour of the night (l. 1), the fourth day with 1 2/3 double hours of the night (l. 217), and the fifth day with two double hours of the night (l. 285), it is most likely that the third day started with 1 1/3 double hours of the night.

l. 175, *ta-ḫa-ṭ*[*u*(?)]', as in l. 20?

l. 179, LUGAL UMUN GÌR.NÍTA, or perhaps LUGAL u GÌR.NÍTA 'king and governor'?

l. 190 (see also 338 and 367), [*e-nu-m*]*a* 1 1/2 DANNA ME NIM-*a* "[Whe]n 1 1/2 double hours of daytime (read *ūmu išqâ*) have passed", following *CAD*, Š/II, 20a, 2′, a'.

l. 201, *ubānu* (SI), usually written ŠU.SI, see *RAcc.*, 133, n. 1.

l. 203 and 204, ⌜4⌝, contra *RAcc.*, 133, who reads: *šá*.

l. 207, *aqrabu* (GÍR) is usually written GÍR.TAB.

l. 209, '(a belt of) palm leaves', see also l. 455.

l. 211 (see also 410), in DUḪ gišBANŠUR 'the leftovers of the offering table', DUḪ probably has to be read *piṭru*, see the parallel K 9876, obv. 18 (*pi-ṭir* gišBANŠUR). Cf. *AHw*, 871b, 3: 'Abräumung, Abgeräumtes'. Less likely candidates are *tuḫḫu* (cf. *AHw*, 1366b, 3; M. Stol, *BiOr* 28 [1971], 170 f.) and *kupsu* (var. *kuspu*), despite *Ugaritica* 5, no. 168, 17 (*ku-su-up* gišBANŠUR), which must have a similar meaning, but this literary text stands far away from Hellenistic Babylonian ritual texts and cannot be used as parallel.

The reading DUḪ = *piṭru* is also supported by the fact that the cognate verb *paṭāru* (DUḪ[-*ár*]) is used several times in the ritual texts in similar context:

– 'to clear away (the offering table)', *TU* 41, obv. 32; *RAcc.*, 143, 403.
– 'to clear away (the meal)', cf. *TU* 39, obv. 14; *TU* 40, obv. 15; *TU* 39, rev. 3; 5; 7; 9; 13; 14; 21; *TU* 41, obv. 13; rev. 30.

For a discussion of *paṭāru* and *piṭru* see also III.4.1.

l. 214, lúGÍR.LÁ *kar-ri* 'slaughterer and seller (of prepared meat dishes)', see *CAD*, K, 222a.

l. 214, SÌ[G-*a*]*ṣ-ma* 'strike', i.e. 'cut off', see also l. 353.

l. 215–216, *tur-ru* probably stands for for *tumru*, see *CAD*, N/I, 265a, c and W. Farber, *TUAT* II/2, 215 with n. 26a, contra *AHw*, 1397a, 1.

l. 216a (see also 464), EME.GIR$_{15}$.DU$_{7}$.E, this reading was suggested by G. Çağirgan, *Festivals*, 13 and 39 (with GIR$_{14}$ for GIR$_{15}$). H. Hunger, *AOAT* 2, 65, no.182 reads: EME.KU.UL.E, but he does not give a translation.

l. 216c, this invocational formula is also attested in the astronomical diaries from Babylon, e.g. A.J. Sachs–H. Hunger, *Diaries*, no. -158, A, obv. 1; no. -142, B, U.E. 1; no. -137, E, obv. 0. See also the beginning of my comments on *TU* 39 +, U.E.

l. 240 (see also 254), LAL-*ṭi* KI-*tì* 'who watches over the Earth' (*ḫâṭu*), following W. Farber, *TUAT* II/2, 216 with n. 24a and 217 with n. 38a, contra *RAcc.*, 134, 135 and *CAD*, Š/I, 414b, 6′: LÁ-*ku* KI-*tì* 'who heaps up the earth' (*šapāku*).

l. 253, *kaz*[!]-*bat*(?), following W. Farber, *TUAT* II/2, 216 with n. 37a.

l. 265, LUGAL DINGIR.DINGIR, in DT 114, obv. II, 1 (*RAcc.*, 135, 265), but DINGIR DINGIR.DINGIR in the duplicate MNB. 1848, obv. III, 7 (*RAcc.*, 153, 265), cf. *RAcc.*, 135, n. 4.

l. 280, *šá ki-iṣ u*$_{4}$*-mu* 'in the late afternoon', lit. 'that of the cool of the day', i.e. the evening.

l. 282 (see also 283), *i-na-áš-ši*, 'raise', i.e. 'recite'? Cf. W. Farber, *TUAT* II/2, 217, n. 66–67a. A similar use perhaps as in *BRM* 4, 6, rev. 45. Usually the verb *našû* can have the meaning 'to recite' only when referring to a hand-raising prayer (*šuillakku*), cf. *CAD*, N/II, 109a. Or should we interpret *našû* here as 'to enact'?

l. 289–300 is written in difficult Sumerian and for the most part is not clear. M.E. Cohen attempted a translation, cf. *Cultic Calendars*, 444.

l. 301, [d]DÌM.ME.ER.AN.KI.A, 'god of Heaven and Earth', one of the 50 names of Marduk in *Enūma eliš*, usually: [d]LUGAL.DÌM.ME.ER.AN.KI.A. We also known the *taqribtu*-lamentation LUGAL.E DÌM.ME.ER AN.KI.A, see *TU* 44, III, 28, presented in full in *BRM* 4, 8, a bilingual hymn to Anu.

l. 302–332 mention several stars or constellations. Most of them are discussed in F. Gössmann, *Planetarium Babylonicum*, Rom, 1950: Mubukešda 'the hitched Yoke' = a Draconis? Cf. H. Hunger–D. Pingree, *MUL.APIN*, 137 (cf. 24: I, i, 19); see F. Gössmann, no. 282; for Eridu, an unknown star (or constellation), see no. 306; for the Šupa-star, Boötes, see no. 385; for the Nenegar-star (Aldebaran?), see no. 301; for Numušda, an unknown star (or constellation), see no. 305, cf. D.O. Edzard, *WM* I, 116; for the 'Breast of Scorpion'-star, part of the constellation Scorpius, see no. 60; for the Bow-star, Canis major or Sirius, see no. 47; for the Goat-star, Lyra, see no. 145; Ḫegalla and Balteša are unknown stars; for Erūa, also a surname of Zarpanītu (see l. 252, 255, 467), see D.O. Edzard, *WM* I, 119; W. Farber, *TUAT* II/2, 219, n. 115a; for the Ninmaḫ-star, see no. 324, for the mother goddess Ninmaḫ see D.O. Edzard, *WM* I, 105. For the stars see also E. Reiner, *Astral Magic in Babylonia*, Philadelphia, 1995, 138–9.

The Akkadian epithets, which follow the Sumerian names of stars and constellations, mentioned in this section of the text, are based on explanations of the ancient philologists. Several were analyzed by M. Stol in *NABU* 1989, no. 60.

l. 304, Asari is one of the fifty names of Marduk in *Enūma eliš*, VII, 1, cf. F.M.Th. de Liagre Böhl, *AfO* 11 (1936/1937), 201; J. Bottéro, in: *Finkelstein Mem. Vol.*, 5.

l. 309, for Sirius see J. Koch, *Neue Untersuchungen zur Topographie des babylonischen Fixsternhimmels*, Wiesbaden, 1989, 74.

l. 318–323 is written in difficult Sumerian and for the most part is not clear. M.E. Cohen attempted a translation, cf. *Cultic Calendars*, 444.

l. 324, Damki(an)na, also known as Damgalnunna, see E. Ebeling, in *RlA* 2 (1938), 105–6; D.O. Edzard, *WM* I, 50.

l. 331, *ba-nát*, following *RAcc.*, 139 with n. 5. See M. Stol, *NABU* 1989, no. 60, n. 1. *ba-nit* according to *CAD*, B, 87b, 3, a, 1′.

l. 351, KISAL *šá pa-pa-ḫi* 'the courtyard of the cella', see A.R. George, *BiOr* 53 (1996), 371.

l. 370, ⸢^{giš}⸣*tal-lu* 'crossbeam' rather than ⸢*ku*⸣-*tal-lu* 'rear' (contra *CAD*, A/II, 229b, f; see also W. Farber, *TUAT* II/2, 220 with n. 154a): because *išdu* 'foundation' refers to the lowest part of the temple, the 'crossbeam' in top of Ezida seems more appropriate than the 'rear'.

l. 376, ^{d}KÙ.SÙ GIŠ.ŠÚ.A.NA ^{d}KÙ.SÙ 'Kusu, who is on his stool, Kusu', but M.E. Cohen, *Cultic Calendars*, 446 translates different: 'Kusu, who adorns the clear sky from his (Chapel-of)-the-Darkening Sky', perhaps interpreting GIŠ.ŠÚ as GISSU 'shadow'?

l. 379, 'Kusu establishes the divine decrees', or perhaps better 'Kusu makes the drawing/plan (of the temple)', following W. Farber, *TUAT* II/2, 220?

l. 382, 'Great demon, may Bēl kill you!', but see W. Farber, *TUAT* II/2, 221, who translated differently: 'Der große Dämon Bel möge dich umbringen!'.

l. 383, 'to', because of the terminative in GAR.RA.AŠ, contra W. Farber, *TUAT* II/2, 221, who translated: 'Von deinem Sitzplatz'.

l. 394, [*ina muḫ-ḫi i-sar-raq*], for the restoration see l. 352.

l. 396, [^{d}AMAR.UTU EN].MAḪ, the restoration follows *RAcc.*, 143; see 134, 242.

l. 399, *me-dil ka-a-ri*, following *CAD*, M/2, 3.

l. 407 (see also l. 409), *ina* KI KAB ṢAB/PI(?) GAG 'on the …-place', not clear to me, but see M.E. Cohen, *Cultic Calendars*, 446: 'the place of the heroic one'.

l. 408, [*ina* GÚ ^{i}]^{d} *ku-nát a-mat-su*(?), following W. Farber, *TUAT* II/2, 221, but this restoration is not certain.

l. 410, GAR.MEŠ-*šú* 'They will place him', -*šú* referrring to the king (as in l. 409: *ú-bar-ra-šú*) rather than the offering gifts on the offering table (see l. 405), contra *RAcc.*, 143, and W. Farber, *TUAT* II/2, 221. [LUGAL] *šakānu* is probably also attested in l. 420.

l. 421, *ú-šá-kam-su* for *ušakmassu*.

l. 422, '[Together w]ith', this restoration was suggested by W. Farber, *TUAT* II/2, 222.

l. 423–5, see P. Michalowski, in: *Studies W. Moran*, Atlanta, 1990, 393.

l. 428, '[I have been taking ca]re of Babylon', see *AHw*, 879b (*puqqu*). M.E. Cohen, *Cultic Calendars*, 447 different.

l. 442, 'Concerning Babylon, his city [...] ... [...]'. For the second damaged part of the sentence W. Farber, *TUAT* II/2, 222, suggested: 'spr[ich] nicht [...]'. Although the copy appears to read E (= *qabû*), the rest of the traces remain unclear to me.

l. 445, 'Bēl will bless you with(?) [... f]orev[er]'; W. Farber, *TUAT* II/2, 222, suggested: 'Bel wird dich *mit einem Segen auf ewig* segnen', perhaps reading ŠÙD in the break, although the copy does not leave enough space for this.

l. 450, *il-lik*, a singular, although a plural (*illika*) is intended, see l. 451 (GIN.MEŠ).

l. 453, KI XX ŠÚ MAN = as soon as it is one-third (of the double hour) of sunset (= forty minutes after sunset)?, following *CAD*, Š/III, 384b. See also *CAD*, E, 258b and G. Çağirgan, *Festivals*, 36–37. Different in W. Farber, *TUAT II/2, 223: ki Šamaš* (XX) *irbû* (ŠÚ-*u)* ⟨⟨*u*⟩⟩ "sobald die Sonne untergegangen ist". Perhaps similar phrase in BM 41577 (A.R. George, *Studies W.G. Lambert*, no. 1, 260 ff.), col. III, 23: GIM 1 DANNA DIŠ x x AN UD lúŠEŠ.GAL.

l. 455, GIŠ.MEŠ-*ma* 'straight'. M. Stol suggested to me: GIŠ = *našû*, G or Gtn, thus translating 'he will carry and', since one would expect a verbal form before *-ma*.

l. 456, BAD.MEŠ-*ma* 'They will dig', lit. 'They will open' (*ipettûma*).

l. 458, PA *ina*! IGI! *nag-be* GAR-*an*, following W. Farber, *TUAT* II/2, 223, n. 239a.

l. 459, IZI.GAR ... *ú*-[*šá-aṣ-bat*(?)], the restoration is not certain, but perhaps similar to *BRM* 4, 6, rev. 39 (*nu-ur ú-šá-aṣ-bat*).

l. 463–471 are attested in the unpublished BM 32485, reverse. See Plate I.

l. 472–478, these lines, attested in DT 114, rev., VI (*RAcc.*, 152), contain the colophon and the catchline of day 5-I (not given at the end of the description of day 4-I, after l. 284). Cf. H. Hunger, *AOAT* 2, 65–6, no.182.

l. 474, IGI.TAB *u* IGI.KÁR, both ideograms have the meaning *barû* 'to collate', so here one of them has to be translated differently, perhaps *sanāqu* 'to check', cf. H. Hunger, *AOAT* 2, 3, with other examples.

c. A festival for Ištar

TU 42 (AO 7439) + AO 8648 + AO 8649[25]

The text describes a special festival for Ištar, and was written in Uruk. In what month this festival was celebrated is not clear. The obverse contains the same ceremonies as those, which for the eighth and ninth day of the New Year festival (*akītu*) of Anu, during the seventh month Tašrītu, have been handed down to us (see *TU* 39–40). The end of the obverse and the reverse describe the procession of Ištar from the Ešgal to the *akītu*-temple, which resembles the Anu-procession described in *KAR* 132.

The text is discussed in II.8.5.

Obv.

1′ [...] *ina* KISAL [...]

2′ [... *a-na*] KISAL.MAḪ ⸢E$_{11}$⸣[...]

3′ [...] ^{d}A.DA.PÀ [...]

4′ [...] É.UL.MAŠ [...]

5′ [... ^{lú}KUR].GAR.RA(?) TA É.SAG [...]

6′ ^{d}ŠÀ.GE.PÀ.DA ^{d}*Áš-ka-*[...]

7′ [...]⸢^{d}⸣GALGA.MU.NA.SUM.MU ^{d}IGI.DU ^{d}[...]

8′ [^{d}URÙ].INIM-*su* 2 ^{d}ŠEŠ.GAL *ù* 3 ^{d}AḪ-[LA-MAT(?)...]

9′ [^{d}*Be-l*]*i-li ù* ^{d}*Ba-ri-ri-i-tu*$_{4}$ TA É.LÍL[.LÁ(?) ...]

10′ [...] 4 UR.MAḪ LÚ.U$_{18}$.LU TA É ^{d}LÀMA.EDEN ^{d}DUMU.SAL.MEŠ É.AN.NA *ù* [^{d}DUMU.SAL.MEŠ UNUG^{ki}]

11′ [*ù*] ^{d}LÀMA.SIG$_{5}$.GA ZI.MEŠ-*nim-ma a-na* KISAL.ŠÀ.BA E$_{11}$.MEŠ-*ma i*[*na*(?)...]

12′ ^{d}IGI.LA.BÀD ^{d}IGI.BAR.LÚ.TI ^{d}KA.BI.LÚ.SIG$_{5}$ ^{d}A.DA ^{d}[É.SA.PÀR...]

13′ ^{d}NIN.ḪÉ.NUN.NA ^{d}EN.UR.AN.NA *ù* ^{d}ŠEŠ.AN.TU[R] ^{d}NIN.É.AN.NA *šá U*$_{4}$*-*[*dan-nu*...]

14′ ^{d}*Šar-rat-*AN-*e ù* ^{d}SA.DÀR.NUN.NA ^{d}NIN.ÌMMA ^{d}*Šar-rat-*BÁRA ^{d}*Mi-*[*šar-ri*(?) ...]

15′ *ù* ^{d}*I-šar-tu*$_{4}$ TA *šub-ti-šú-nu* ZI.MEŠ-*nim-ma ki-ma* ^{d}UTU KUR-*ḫa* DINGIR.MEŠ *nap-ḫar-šú-*[*nu*]

16′ *a-na pa-ni* ^{d}INNIN LAL-*aṣ* LUGAL ÍL-*ut* EN.NA DÙ-*uš til-le-e-šú eb-bu-tu il-lab-b*[*iš*]

17′ [...] ⸢^{d}*šá-ra-ḫi-i*⸣*-tu*$_{4}$ GIN-*ak-ma uš-ken* ^{d}*šá-ra-ḫi-i-tu*$_{4}$ ZI-*am it-t*[*i* ...]

18′ [...^{giš}]*tal-lu* GUŠKIN É-*a-ni a-na* ⸢^{d}INNIN SUM-*in*⸣ [...]

19′ [...KU$_{4}$.MEŠ(?)-*m*]*a* GUB-*zi-zu* ⸢*nap-tan ù* UZU *šu-me-e ḫa*⸣-[*an-ṭu-tu* ...]

20′ [*ina muḫ-ḫi na-šap-pi* GUŠKIN(?) *a-*]*na* ^{d}INNIN *ú-qar-rab nap-tan ù* UZU *šu-me-e ḫa-an-ṭu*[*-tu*]

21′ [*ina muḫ-ḫi na-šap-p*]i GUŠKIN(?) *a-*]*na* ^{d}*Na-na-a ù* ^{d}GAŠAN-šá-SAG *ú-qar-r*[*ab* ...]

22′ [*na-šap-pi* GUŠKIN *pa-ni* ^{d}INNIN(?) *a-*]*na* IGI DINGIR.MEŠ *ma-la ina* KISAL *ú-še-ti-i*⸢*q*⸣

23′ [*na-šap-pi* GUŠKIN *pa-ni* ^{d}... *a-*]*na* IGI ^{d}INNIN.MEŠ *šá ina* KISAL *ú-še-ti-i*⸢*q*⸣

24′ [... *ma-aq-qu-ú* GUŠKIN(?) *a*-na ^{d}]*Na-na-a ù* ^{d}GAŠAN-*šá*-SAG *i-red-de-e*

25′ ⸢^{d}NIN.IGI^{II}(?).ZI.BAR.RA⸣ [...ŠU]^{II} ^{d}INNIN DAB-*bat-ú-ma* ^{lú}MAŠ.MAŠ.MEŠ ^{lú}GALA.MEŠ *u* ^{lú}NAR.MEŠ

26′ *ú-šar-ru-ú* ^{d}INNIN *ina muḫ-*⸢*ḫi šub*⸣*-ti šá bi-rit šid-di šá ina* KÁ *pa-pa-ḫa* DÚR-*ab*

---

25 Obv. 1′–18′: AO 7439; obv. 19′–36′: AO 8648 + AO 8649; rev. 1′–18′: AO 8648 + AO 8649; rev. 19′–20′: AO 7439 + AO 8648 + AO 8649; rev. 21′–36′: AO 7439.

For *TU* 42 see *RAcc.*, 73, 111–118; M.E. Cohen, *Cultic Calendars*, 436–37. AO 8648 + 8649 were published by S. Lackenbacher, *RA* 71 (1977), 39–50. See also R. Borger, *HKL* 1, 567.

27′ DINGIR.MEŠ *nap-ḫar-šú-nu šá* KISAL *a-na pa-ni-šú* LAL-*ṣa ma-aq-qu-ú* GUŠKIN *i-red-de-e-ma*
28′ A.MEŠ ŠU^{II} ÍL-*ši ina muḫ-ḫi* KI SÍSKUR GABA.RI *i-sar-raq-ma*
29′ SÍSKUR *mer-de-e-ti* GU$_4$ *ù* UDU.NÍTA *ina pa-ni-šú i-red-de* UZU *lìb-bi šá* GU$_4$ *ù* SAG.DU *šá* UDU.NÍTA
30′ *ina muḫ-ḫi* KI SÍSKUR GABA.RI *i-šak-kan*[*-ma*] *ma-lit* GUŠKIN *šá* ZÌ.MAD.GÁ *a-na muḫ-ḫi lìb-bi*
31′ *i-saḫ-ḫap ma-aq-q*⸢*u-ú* GEŠTIN⸣ *a-na mu*[*ḫ-ḫi* SAG.DU] ⸢UDU.NÍTA⸣ *i-red-de* A.MEŠ ŠU^{II} *a-na* ^{d}INNIN
32′ ÍL-*ma* LUGAL UN.MES *ú-lap-pat* ^{giš}Ù[.LUḪ NAM.LUGAL.LA(?) …] *ina* DA BÁRA NAM.MEŠ GUB[*-za*(?)]
33′ LUGAL *ma-aq-qu-ú* GUŠKIN *a-na pa-ni* ^{d}INN[IN *i-red-d*e …Š]U^{II} ^{d}INNIN
34′ DAB-*bat*.MEŠ-*ma* ^{d}*Na-na-a ù* ^{d}GAŠAN[-*šá*-SAG …]⸢x⸣
35′ ^{d}INNIN GIN-*ak-ma ina muḫ-ḫi* BÁRA NAM.MEŠ *š*[*á*(?) …]
36′ […]-⸢*ma*(?)⸣ *šá* È(?) *a-na lìb-bi* AB[…]

Rev.
1′ ^{d}[…]
2′ EGIR-*šú* 2 ^{d}ŠEŠ.GAL 3 ^{d}AḪ-LA-MAT(?) ^{d}⸢x⸣[…]
3′ ^{d}KA.BI.LÚ.SIG$_5$ ^{d}A.DA *u* ^{d}É.SA.PÀR ⸢x⸣[…]
4′ EGIR-*šú* MUNUS *šá* SAG KAL-*tú* ^{d}URÙ.INIM-*su* ^{d}[…]
5′ EGIR-*šú* ^{d}PAP.SUKKAL ^{d}NUSKU ^{d}ARA *ù* ^{d}ME[S.SAG.UNUG$^{ki(?)}$ …]
6′ ^{lú}NAR.MEŠ ^{lú}GALA.MEŠ *ù* ^{lú}MAŠ.MAŠ.MEŠ ^{d}INNIN x[…]
7′ *a-di* ^{giš}GIGIR ^{d}LX 1-*en* ^{lú}KU$_4$-É *šá* ^{túg}ÍB.LÁ *rak-s*[*u* …] ⸢x x⸣ *ù*(?) $^{d(?)}$[…]
8′ *ina* GABA(?)-*šú* GAR-*an-ma ina bi-rit* ^{giš}*tal-lu šá* ^{d}INNI[N …] EGIR-*šú* ^{d}*Na-na-a u* ^{d}[GAŠAN-*šá*-SAG]
9′ EGIR-*šú* ^{giš}GU.ZA *šá* ^{d}LX *šá né-me-du* ^{d}DUMU.SAL.MEŠ UNUG^{ki} *ù* DUMU.SAL.MEŠ É[.AN.N]A
10′ EGIR-*šú* ^{d}NIN.SI.GAR.AN.NA ^{d}NIN.IGI^{II}.ZI.BAR.RA ^{d}ÁB.⸢É.TÙR.RA⸣ *ù* ^{d}ŠÀ.GE.⸢PÀ⸣.DA
11′ EGIR-*šú* ^{d}NIN.ME.UR.UR *ù* ^{d}NIN.SÚN EGIR-*šú* ^{d}NIN.É.AN.NA *šá U*$_4$*-dan-nu*
12′ [EGIR-*šú* ^{d}GAŠA]N(?)-AN-*e* ^{d}KA.NI.SUR.RA *ù* ^{d}*Ša*[*r-r*]*at*-BÁRA EGIR-*šú* ^{d}*A*(?)-*nun*(?)-*ni*(?)-*tu*$_4$ ^{d}NIN.ÌMMA
13′ [… ^{d}SA.DÀ]R.NUN.NA ^{d}ŠEŠ.AN.TUR *ù* ^{d}EN.ME.UR.AN.NA
14′ […] DINGIR.MEŠ *ki-ma* GÌR^{II}-*šú-nu ina* IGI-*šú u* EGIR-*šú il-lak*
15′ […]x *šá* (?) ^{giš}MÁ.GUR$_8$ TE(?)-*ḫi*(?)-*ma a-na* ^{giš}GIGIR EREN(?).NA
16′ […]x *it-ti-šú* E$_{11}$-*ma* ^{giš}Ù.⸢LUḪ.NAM.LUGAL.LA⸣ […]
(edge:) […*u*]*r-rad-ma it-ti-šú* E[$_{11}$(?)]
17′ […]-*tu*$_4$ ^{d}DUMU.SAL.MEŠ.UNUG.KI *ù* ^{d}DUMU.SAL.MEŠ.É.AN.N[A]
18′ […]x *a-di* ^{giš}GIGIR.MEŠ *it-ti ma-ṣi-ri ina pa-n*[*i-šú*-(*nu*)(?)]
19′ [… ^{giš}]*tal-lu* [GUŠKIN …*ki-ma*] *šá* ^{d}INNIN *ina muḫ-ḫi a-ra-a*[*m-mi*]
20′ […*i*(?)-*te*(?)-]⸢*lu*⸣-*ú* DINGIR.MEŠ *gab-bi ù* ⸢^{giš}GIGIR⸣.M[EŠ] [KU$_4$.MEŠ-*ma*] ⸢*a-na pa-ni-šú*⸣ LAL-*a*[*ṣ*…]
21′ [^{lú}D]UMU *bu*-⸢x⸣-*ú a-ma-ṣi-ri a-na* ŠU^{II} LUGAL GAR-*an-ma ru-ku-bu i-ki*-⸢*li*⸣ ^{d}ARA [*ù* LUGAL]
22′ [Š]U^{II} ^{giš}Ù.LUḪ NAM.LUGAL.LA *ù* ^{d}INNIN DAB-*bat*.MEŠ-*ma a-na* KISAL É *a-ki-i-tu*$_4$ KU$_4$-[*ma*]
23′ [*ina*] *muḫ-ḫi* BÁRA.GAL *ina* KISAL É *a-ki-tu*$_4$ DÚR-*ab* ^{giš}Ù.LUḪ NAM.LUGAL.LA *ina* DA-*šú* GUB-*z*[*a*(?) …]

24′ DINGIR.MEŠ *gab-bi* KU$_4$.MEŠ-*ma ina* KISAL É *a-ki-tu*$_4$ *ina pa-ni-šú* GUB-*za šid-di* GADA NIGIN.MEŠ-*šú*-[(*nu*(?))]
25′ $^{[lú]}$KUR.GAR.RA ^{lú}UR.MUNUS *šá til-le-e* ^{d}*Na-ru-du rak-su ki-ma maḫ-ri-i* TA ⸢2, 30⸣
26′ [*a-*]*na* XV NIGIN-*šú-nu-tú* A.MEŠ ŠU^{II} *a-na* ^{d}INNIN ÍL-*ši-ma* LUGAL *ù* UN.MEŠ *ú-lap-p*[*at*]
27′ [*m*]*a-aq-qu-ú* GUŠKIN *i-red-de-ma* ^{d}ARA *ù* LUGAL ŠU^{II} ^{d}INNIN DAB-*bat-ma* KU$_4$-*ma ina pa-pa-ḫa-šú* DÚR-[*ab*]
28′ $^{[g]iš}$Ù.LUḪ NAM.LUGAL.LA *a-na* DA-*šú* GUB-*za* ^{d}GAŠAN-*šá*-SAG KU$_4$-*ma ina pa-pa-ḫa* ^{d}INNIN *a-na* 2,30 [DÚR-*ab*]
29′ $^{[gi]š}$GU.ZA *šá* ^{d}LX *šá né-me-du ù* ^{d}*Na-na-a* KU$_4$.MEŠ-*ma ina* É *pa-pa-ḫa-šú-nu* DÚR-*ab* DINGIR.MEŠ *gab-b*[*i*]
30′ *ù* ^{giš}GIGIR.MEŠ KU$_4$.MEŠ-*ma ina šub-ti-šú-nu šá* KISAL DÚR-*ab* ^{lú}MAŠ.MAŠ *šá kap-pu a-na* ^{d}INNIN *u* DINGIR.MEŠ ⸢DÙ.A.BI⸣
31′ [ÍL]-*ši* A.MEŠ ŠUB.ŠUB-*am* LI.LI.ÌZ ZABAR *ina muḫ-ḫi šu-uḫ-*⟨*ḫi*⟩ G[UB-*za* ...]
32′ [...DA]B-*bat* LI.LI.ÌZ ZABAR ZI-*ma* ^{giš}*tal-lu* GUŠKIN *šá* ^{d}INNIN [...]
33′ [^{giš}BANŠUR(?)] GUŠKIN *ina pa-ni* ^{d}INNIN *uk-tan-nu* ^{giš}BANŠUR KÙ.BABBAR *ina pa-ni* DINGIR.MEŠ DÙ.A.BI [*uk-tan-nu*]
34′ [...]⸢x⸣ *níg-na-qa* GUŠKIN *ina pa-ni* ^{d}INNIN *ú-mál-le-e-*[*ma* ...]
35′ [*níg-na-qa* GUŠ]KIN *ina pa-ni* ^{d}*Na-na-a u* ^{d}GAŠAN-šá-SAG *ú-mál-l*[*e-e-ma* ...]
36′ [...] ⸢x⸣ DINGIR [...]

Obv.
1′ [...] in the courtyard [...]
2′ [...] will come down [to] the Grand Courtyard [...]
3′ [...] Adapa [...]
4′ [...] the Eulmaš temple [...]
5′ [... the *kur*]*garrû*-actor(?) from the Rēš-temple [...]
6′ Šagepada, Aška-[...]
7′ [...] Galgamunasummu, Palil [...]
8′ [Uṣur]-amassu, 2 divine high priests, and 3 ...[...]
9′ [Bel]ili and Barirītu from the Elil[la(?)-temple ...]
10′ [...] 4 ‘lion-men’ from the temple of Lama-eden, Mārāt-Eanna and [Mārāt-Uruk]
11′ [a]nd Lamasiga will rise and come down to the Inner Courtyard and i[n(?)...]
12′ Igilabad, Igibarluti, Kabilusig, Ada, [Esapar(?)]
13′ Ninḫenunna, Enuranna and Šešantur, Nineanna of (the city) U[dannu]
14′ Šarrat-šamê and Sadarnunna, Ninimma, Šarrat-parakki, Mī[šaru ...]
15′ and Išartu will rise from their seats and, as the sun rises, all the gods
16′ will take up position before Ištar. The king will perform the ceremony of the installation of the *ēnu*-priest(?), he will be robed in his clean *tillû*-uniform.
17′ [...] Šarraḫītu will come and prostrate herself. Šarraḫītu will rise, and wi[th...]
18′ [...] a gold(-plated) [car]rying pole (for use) inside (the temple) will be given to Ištar [...]
19′ [... they will enter(?) a]nd stand. He will serve (l. 20) the meal and ho[t] roasted meat [...]
20′ [on golden(?) dishes t]o Ištar. He will serv[e] (l. 21) the meal and ho[t] roasted meat
21′ [on golden(?) dishes t]o Nanāja and Bēlet-ša-Rēš. [...]
22′ [Golden dishes, (from) before Ištar], he will pass [t]o all the gods, who are in the courtyard.
23′ [Golden dishes, (from) before ...,] he will pass [t]o the goddesses, who are in the courtyard.
24′ [... with a golden libation bowl] he will make a libation [to] Nanāja and Bēlet-ša-Rēš.

25′ Ninigizibarra [...] will lead Ištar, and the exorcists, the lamentation priests and the singers
26′ will go down. Ištar will sit on the seat in (the room) between the curtains, which is near the gate of the cella.
27′ All the gods, who are in the courtyard, will will take position before her. (The priest) will make a libation with a golden libation bowl and
28′ will lift up a water (basin) for (the washing of) the hands. On the place where (the god) is made to accept the offering, he will scatter (aromatics) and
29′ he will make a *merdītu*-offering of ox and sheep in front of him. He will place (l. 30′) the heart of the ox and the head of the sheep
30′ on the place, where (the god) is made to accept the offering. [Then] he will overturn (l. 31) a golden *malītu*-bowl of *maṣḫatu*-flour over the heart.
31′ He will make a libation with the libation bowl on [to the head] of the sheep. He will lift up (l. 32′) the water (basin) for (the washing of) the hands to Ištar
32′ and sprinkle(?) the king (and) the (other) persons. The Sc[epter of kingship] will stan[d] next to the Dais of Destinies.
33′ The king [will make a libation] with a golden libation bowl befor Išt[ar. ...] will lead (l. 34′) Ištar
34′ and Nanāja and Bēlet-[ša-Rēš ...]
35′ Ištar will go and on Dais of Destinies o[f(?) ...]
36′ [...] and(?) he will go out(?) inside ... [...]

Rev.
1′ The god [...]
2′ Next, 2 divine high priests, 3 ... [...]
3′ Kabilusig, Ada and Esapar [...]
4′ Next, ‘the mighty woman of the Rēš-temple’(?), Uṣur-amassu, [...]
5′ Next, Papsukkal, Nusku, Usmû and Me[ssagunug(?) ...]
6′ The singers, the lamentation priests and the exorcists [...] Ištar [...]
7′ up to the chariot of Anu. A temple enterer, who is gir[t] with a girdle [...]
8′ will place on his chest, and between the carrying poles of Išta[r ...] Next, Nanāja and [Bēlet-ša-Rēš].
9′ Next Anu’s armchair, Mārāt-Uruk and Mārāt-E[ann]a.
10′ Next Ninsigaranna, Ninigizibarra, Abeturra and Šagi⸢pa⸣da.
11′ Next Ninmeurur and Ninsun. Next Nineanna of (the city) Udannu.
12′ [Next Šarra]t-šamê, Kanisurra and Ša[rr]at-parakki. Next Anunītu(?), Ninimma
13′ [... Sada]rnunna, Šešantur and Enmeuranna
14′ [and the rest of(?)] the gods will go according to their ranks in front of her/him or behind her/him.
15′ [...] of the procession-boat he will bring near(?) and for the chariot of cedar(?)[...]
16′ [...] he will come down with him/her, and the Scepter of Kingship [...] he will come down(?) and with him/her he will come [down(?).]
17′ [...] Mārāt-Uruk and Mārāt-Eann[a]
18′ up to the chariot with ... in front of [him/her/them]
19′ [... a gold(-plated) c]arrying pole [... When] Ištar [has arr]ived(?) (l. 20′) at the wharf
20′ [...], all the gods and chariot[s will enter and] will take up position before him. [...]
21′ [...].. will place ... in the hands of the king and ... a chariot ... Usmû [and the king]
22′ will lead the Scepter of Kingship and Ištar, and (Ištar) will enter the courtyard of the *akītu*-temple. [Then]
23′ she will sit [on] the Great Dais in the courtyard of the *akītu*-temple. The Scepter of Kingship will sta[nd] at her side.

24′ All the (other) gods will enter and stand before her in the courtyard of the *akītu*-temple. A linen curtain will encircle th[em].

25′ The *kurgarrû*-actor and the *assinnu*-singer, who are girt with the *tillû*-uniform of Narudu, will circle around them (l. 26′), as before, from le[ft]

26′ to right. (The priest) will lift up a water (basin) for (the washing of) the hands to Ištar and he will sprink[le(?)] the king and the (other) persons.

27′ He will make a libation with a golden libation bowl. Then Usmû and the king will lead Ištar and she will enter and si[t] in her cella.

28′ The Scepter of Kingship will stand at her side. Bēlet-ša-Rēš will enter and [sit] in the cella of Ištar on the left side.

29′ Anu's armchair and Nanāja will enter and they will sit in their cella. All the gods

30′ and the chariots will enter and sit on their seats in the courtyard. The exorcist, who [lifts] up (l. 31′) the *kappu*-bowl to Ištar and all the (other) gods,

31′ will repeatedly make a libation of water. The bronze kettledrum w[ill stand] on a *šuḫḫu*-stand [...]

32′ [...he will s]eize(?). The bronze kettledrum will rise and the gold(-plated) carrying pole of Ištar [...]

33′ A golden [offering table(?)] will be set up before Ištar. A silver offering table [will be set up] before all the gods.

34′ [...] (the priest) will fill the golden censer in front of Ištar [and ...]

35′ he will fill [the gold]en [censer] in front of Nanāja and Bēlet-ša-Rēš [and ...]

36′ [...] the god [...]

Comments

Obv.

l. 6′, ^{d}*Áš-ka*-[...], perhaps to be restored ^{d}*Áš-ka*-[*a-a-i-tu*], Aška'itu, as in the Late Babylonian ritual *LKU*, no. 51, obv. [1], 2, 5 and passim in this text, cf. A. Falkenstein, *LKU*, p. 17, n. 3, but see S. Lackenbacher, *RA* 71 (1977), 40, n. 2. ^{d}*Áš-du* according to M.E. Cohen, *Cultic Calendars*, 437.

l. 8′ (see also rev. 2), 3 ^{d}AḪ-[LA-MAT...], S. Lackenbacher (*RA* 71 [1977], 41, n. 4) suggested that perhaps we should read ^{d}*Aḫ-la-mat*, to be identified with Aḫlamītu (^{d}*Áḫ-la-mi-tu*$_4$), attested in Neo-Babylonian administrative texts from Sippar, *Nbn* 117, 3 and *VS* 6, 77, 5. Cf. *AHw*, *aḫlamû*, 21a. See also F. Joannès, *RA* 86 (1992), 161.

l. 9′, *Be-li-li*, or *Ki-li-li*? See E. Reiner, *Šurpu*, 56, sub 75.

l. 10′, 'lion-men' (*urmaḫlullû*), cf. W.G. Lambert, *AfO* 18 (1957–58), 112; A. Falkenstein, *LKU*, 20, n. 5; G.J.P.McEwan, *FAOS* 4, 14. For the latest discussion see F.A.M. Wiggermann, *Mesopotamian Protective Spirits. The ritual texts*, Groningen, 1992, 181–2 and id., in *RlA* 8 (1994), 243, no. 20.

l. 10′, the temple of Lama-eden, cf. A. Falkenstein, *Topographie*, 36; 52e (perhaps in the Ešgal-temple).

l. 13′, ^{d}EN.UR.AN.NA, also mentioned in l. rev. 13′, here written: ^{d}EN.ME.UR.AN.NA. See also *CT* 24, 50, coll. II, 4: ^{d}EN.ME.UR$_4$.AN.NA. Because it is difficult (if not impossible) to distinguish UR from UR$_4$ in Late Babylonian texts, we transliterate UR in this book.

l. 13′ (see also rev. 11′), dNIN.É.AN.NA *šá U₄-[dan-nu]*, cf. P.-A. Beaulieu, *OrNS* 61 (1992), 402–3.

l. 16′ (see also rev. 20′), LAL-*aṣ*, a singular, although a plural is intended. See also l. 27 (LAL-*ṣa*).

l. 16′, 'The king will perform the ceremony of the installation (*nišūt*) of the *ēnu*-priest (EN.NA)(?)', following *CAD*, E, 179a, 3′, ib., N/II, 299a and *AHw*, 220b, 2, b. Another translation was suggested by M.E. Cohen, *Cultic Calendars*, 437: 'The king performs the prayer "Ud-en-na"'. For the *ēnu*-priest see also *KAR* 132, III, 15 (lúEN.NA).

l. 16′ (see also rev. 25′), a similar reference of *tillû* is also attested in the eclipse text BM 134701, obv. 21; see also 17 and 19. For a discussion of *tillû*, see F.A.M. Wiggermann, *Mesopotamian Protective Spirits*, 53–4, 55, 56.

l. 17′, Šarraḫītu is also attested in the Kislīmu-ritual from Hellenistic Babylon, BM 32206 +, I, 16.

l. 20′–24′, these lines are partially parallelled in *TU* 39, obv. 24 ff. (cf. S. Lackenbacher, *RA* 71 (1977), 40 with n. 7). See also *KAR* 132, I, 1–4. These lines are also discussed in III.7.1.

l. 28 (see also 30′), for GABA.RI, see my comment on *TU* 39, obv. 30.

l. 32 (see also rev. 26′), for *ú-lap-pat* see my comment on *TU* 39, obv. 23.

l. 32′ (see also rev. 23′), the singular GUB-*za* is restored after l. rev. 28′. This singular is also attested in *KAR* 132, II, 10 and IV, 20, 23. However, GUB-*za* in l. rev. 24′ seems to be a mistake for GUB-*zu*, because the subject of the verb (DINGIR.MEŠ) is masculine. See my comment on *TU* 39, obv. 18.

For gišÙ[.LUḪ NAM.LUGAL.LA(?) ...], see also l. rev. 16′, 22′–23′, 28′, and furthermore *TU* 39, obv. 28 and *Bagh. Mitt. Beih.* 2, no. 14, 4′.

Rev.

l. 4, 'the mighty woman of the Rēš-temple'(?), following S. Lackenbacher, *RA* 71 (1977), 49 with n. 1.

l. 10′, for Ninsigaranna and Ninigizibarra, see S. Lackenbacher, *RA* 71 (1977), 49, n. 2 with further literature. Perhaps Ninsigaranna has to be identified with dNinsianna (= Inanna) in *KAR* 132, I, 27, who is mentioned here also together with Ninigizibarra. The latter is also mentioned in *Bagh. Mitt. Beih.* 2, no. 13, 6′.

l. 12′, for Kanisurra, see D.O. Edzard, in *RlA* 5 (1980), 389 with literature.

l. 14, *il-lak*, a singular although a plural is intended.

l. 15′, TE(?)-*ḫi*(?)-ma, he will bring near(?); see also the Neo-Assyrian ritual *KAR* 50, rev. 5, and the Hellenistic building ritual *TU* 45, rev. 1.

l. 15′, a 'chariot (model) of cedar' is parallelled with a 'boat (model) of cedar', cf. *CAD*, E, 276b, 2′ with examples.

l. 18′ and 21′, *ma-ṣi-ri* and *a-ma-ṣi-ri* not clear, cf. *AHw*, 42a; *CAD*, A/II, 27b. See S. Lackenbacher, *RA* 71 (1977), 45, n. 7 and 49 with n. 6.

l. 20′, DINGIR.MEŠ *gab-bi ù* ⌜gišGIGIR⌝.M[EŠ] [KU4.MEŠ-*ma*], paralleled in l. rev. 29′–30′.

l. 21′, *i-ki-li* is not clear. See S. Lackenbacher, *RA* 71 (1977), 50, n. 1.

l. 23′, BÁRA.GAL 'Great Dais', cf. A. Falkenstein, *Topographie*, 43–4. See also *KAR* 132, IV, 7 and 13.

l. 24, GUB-*za* is a mistake for GUB-*zu*.See my comment on l. obv. 32′ and on *TU* 39, obv. 18.

l. 25′, for the cultic performers *kurgarrû* (see also obv. 5′) and *assinnu* in the Hellenistic period, see I.3 and II.8.5.

l. 27′, DAB-*bat-ma*, a singular, although a plural is intended. See my comment on *TU* 39, obv. 27.

l. 29 (see also 30′), DÚR-*ab* is a singular, although a plural is intended.

l. 31′, [ÍL]-*ši*, although we would expect a subjunctive ending -*u*.

l. 31′, ŠUB.ŠUB-*am*, mistake for ŠUB.ŠUB-*ma*?

l. 31′, for the *šuḫḫu*-stand, see also the Late Babylonian ritual *LKU*, no. 51, obv. 25 (cf. A. Falkenstein, *LKU*, p. 18 with n. 12), and the Hellenistic calendar text *TU* 48, obv. 3, 12, 13.

d. A nocturnal festival in the Rēš-temple

TU 41 (AO 6460)[26]

The text contains part of a ritual for the sixteenth and seventeenth days of an unknown month, perhaps the tenth month Ṭebētu (see I.2), probably belonging to the same collection of instructions as *TU* 39–40. The text describes special ceremonies held during the vigil (*bajjātu*) in the Anu-temple in Uruk. The tablet belongs to an archive from Uruk, written in the Hellenistic period. The beginning and end of the text are not preserved.

The text is discussed in II.8.6.

Obv.

1 *ina muḫ-ḫi* ⸢x⸣ [...] ⸢x⸣ *pa-ni* ^{giš}NÍG.GIDRU *i-dag-gal ki-*⸢*ma*⸣ [...]

2 ^{giš}NÍG.GIDRU *ù še-e-nu* ZI.MEŠ-*nim-ma* DINGIR.MEŠ *ù* ^{d}INNIN.MEŠ *ki-ma maḫ-ri-*[*im-ma*]

3 *ina pa-ni-šú ù* EGIR-*šú* GIN-*ak a-na* KISAL.MAḪ E$_{11}$.MEŠ-*ma a-na* ^{d}LX LAL-⸢*aṣ*⸣

4 ^{lú}MAŠ.MAŠ ^{giš}NÍG.GIDRU *ú-ḫab*^{ab}-*ma* KU$_4$-*ma ina šub-ti-šú* DÚR-*ab* ^{d}PAP.SUKKAL ^{d}NUSKU

5 *ù* ^{d}ARA *ina* KISAL ^{d}LX *ina muḫ-ḫi šu-bat*.MEŠ DÚR-*ab ù še-e-nu* ^{d}DUMU.SAL.MEŠ-^{d}L[X]

6 *ù* ^{d}DUMU.SAL.MEŠ UNUG^{ki} GUR-*ru*.MEŠ-*nim-ma še-e-nu a-na* É.NIR É ^{giš}NÚ GUŠKIN

7 *šá An-tu*$_4$ KU$_4$-*ma ina muḫ-ḫi* GÌR.GUB.BU *iš-šak-kan* ^{d}DUMU.SAL.MEŠ-^{d}L[X]

8 *ù* ^{d}DUMU.SAL.MEŠ UNUG^{ki} *ina* KISAL *An-tu*$_4$ *ina muḫ-ḫi šu-bat*.MEŠ DÚR-*ab* GEŠTIN *ù* Ì.GIŠ DÙG.GA

9 *iš-te-niš* ḪE.ḪE-*ma ina* KÁ É *pa-pa-ḫa a-na* ^{d}LX *An-tu*$_4$ *ù* DINGIR.MEŠ DÙ.A.BI *i-naq-qa*

10 *sip-pi*.MEŠ *šá* KÁ É *pa-pa-ḫa* ^{giš}IG.MEŠ *ù* KÁ.MEŠ *ú-lap-pat níg-na-qa*.MEŠ GUŠKIN

11 *ú-mál-le-e-ma* SÍSKUR GU$_4$ *ù* UDU.NÍTA *a-na* ^{d}LX *An-tu*$_4$ *ù* DINGIR.MEŠ DÙ.A.BI BAL-[*qí*]

12 KIN.SIG *šá li-lat a-na* ^{d}LX *An-tu*$_4$ *ù* DINGIR.MEŠ DÙ.A.BI *i-qar-rub*

13 [*u*]*l* DUḪ-*ár ba-a-a-at i-ba-at* KÁ *ul ut-ta-dal a-na* DINGIR.MEŠ *ma-la ina* KISAL

14 [*aš-b*]*a*(?) *nap-tan i-qar-rub ina* EN.NUN.USAN *ina ú-ru* BÁRA.MAḪ *ziq-qur-ra*[*t*]

15 *šá* É *re-eš ki-ma šá* $^{mul\,d}$LX GAL-*ú šá* AN-*e it-tap-ḫa An-tu*$_4$ GAL-*tu*$_4$ *šá* AN-*e*

16 *ina* ^{mul}MAR.GÍD.DA *it-tap-ḫa a-na tam-šil zi-i-mu bu-un-né-e* MUL *šá-ma-mi*

17 ^{d}*A-nù* LUGAL *it-ta-ṣa-a ṣa-lam ba-nu-ú* ^{giš}BANŠUR GUŠKIN *a-na* ^{d}LX *u An-tu*$_4$

18 *šá* AN-*e tu-kan-nu* A.MEŠ ŠU^{II} *a-na* ^{d}LX *ù An-tu*$_4$ *šá* AN-*e* ÍL-*ši-ma*

19 ^{giš}BANŠUR *ta-rak-kás* UZU GU$_4$ UZU UDU.NÍTA *ù* MUŠEN^{ḫá} *ta-rak-kás* KAŠ *reš-tu-ú*

20 *a-di* GEŠTIN ŠUR.RA *tu-kan-nu* GURUN ^{giš}KIRI$_6$ DÙ.A.BI *tu-šar-ra-aḫ*

21 ^{giš}ERIN.SÍG *ù* ZÌ.MAD.GÁ *ina muḫ-ḫi níg-na-qa* GUŠKIN *ta-sar-raq-ma*

22 *ma-aq-qu-ú* GUŠKIN GEŠTIN ŠUR.RA *ta-naq-qa ina muḫ-ḫi* 7 ^{giš}BANŠUR.MAḪ GUŠKIN

23 *a-na* ^{d}SAG.ME.GAR ^{d}*Dil-bad* ^{d}GU$_4$.UD ^{d}GENNA *ù* ^{d}*Ṣal-bat-a-nu* ^{d}XXX

24 *ù* ^{d}UTU *ki-ma šá in-nam-mar* A.MEŠ ŠU^{II} ÍL-*ši-ma* ^{giš}BANŠUR *ta-rak-kás*

25 UZU GU$_4$ UZU UDU.NÍTA *ù* MUŠEN^{ḫá} *ta-rak-kás* KAŠ *reš-tu-ú a-di* GEŠTIN ŠUR.RA

[26] Cf. *RAcc.*, 68–69, 118–125; E. Ebeling, in: H. Gressmann, *ATAT*^{2}, 317 ff.; A.J. Sachs, in: J.B. Pritchard, *ANET*^{2}, 338–339.

26 *tu-kan-nu* GURUN ^{giš}KIRI$_6$ DÙ.A.BI *tu-šar-ra-aḫ ina muḫ-ḫi* 7 *níg-na-qa* GUŠKIN
27 ZÌ.MAD.GÁ *ù lu-uk-šú ta-sar-raq-ma ma-aq-qu-ú* GUŠKIN GEŠTIN ŠUR.RA
28 *ta-naq-qa* LÚ.MAḪ *šá* ^{túg}ÍB.LÁ *rak-su* GI.IZI.LÁ GAL-*ú šá* ŠIM^{ḫá}
29 *su-un-nu-uš* Ì.GIŠ DÙG.GA *sal-ḫu ù* KA.LUḪ.Ù UD.DA *šu-pu-uš*
30 *ina* IZI KI.A-^{d}ÍD *i-qa-dam-ma a-na tar-ṣi* ^{giš}BANŠUR *i-tar-ra-aṣ-ma*
31 ŠU^{II}-*su a-na* ^{d}*A-nù* GAL-*ú šá* AN-*e* ÍL-*ši-ma* $^{\text{mul d}}$LX *e-tel-lu šá-ma-mi*
32 *naq-bit i-qab-bi* ^{giš}BANŠUR.MAḪ DUḪ-*ár-ma* A.MEŠ ŠU^{II} ÍL-*ši*
33 ^{lú}KU$_4$-É GAL-*ú* ŠU^{II} GI.IZI.LÁ *ina* ^{lú}MAŠ.MAŠ.MEŠ ^{lú}GALA.MEŠ *ù* ^{lú}NAR.MEŠ
34 TA *ziq-qur-rat* DAB-*bat-am-ma* KÁ.SIKIL.LA *šá ku-tal pa-pa-ḫa a-na* KISAL.MAḪ KU$_4$-*ma*

Rev.
1 *it-ti* KI.ZÁLAG.GA *a-na* ^{d}LX LAL-*aṣ* ^{dug}*ḫa-ru-ú ina* IGI-*šú ib-bat-ta-qa*
2 *naq-bit i-qab-bi* ^{lú}KU$_4$-É ŠU^{II} GI.IZI.LÁ ^{d}PAP.SUKKAL ^{d}NUSKU ^{d}ARA
3 *ù* ^{d}MES.SAG.UNUG^{ki} DAB-*bat-ma a-na* É *pa-pa-ḫa An-tu*$_4$ GIN-*ak*.MEŠ-*ma*
4 *a-na An-tu*$_4$ LAL-*aṣ* ^{dug}*ḫa-ru-ú ina pa-ni-šú ib-bat-ta-qa* ^{d}PAP.SUKKAL
5 ^{d}NUSKU ^{d}ARA *ù* ^{d}MES.SAG.UNUG^{ki} *it-ti* GI.IZI.LÁ *ana* UB.ŠU.UKKIN. NA.KI
6 È.MEŠ-*nim-ma ina* DA BÁRA NAM.MEŠ GU$_4$ *ina pa-ni-šú-nu im-ma-ḫa-aṣ* IZI.ḪA.MUN
7 TA GI.IZI.LÁ *ina* UB.ŠU.UKKIN.NA.KI *in-nap-pa-aḫ* ^{uzu}ZAG.LU GU$_4$ *a-di* KUŠ-*šú*
8 *iṭ-ṭi-ir-ma* XV *u* 2,30 *šá ab-ri i-lap-pat* ^{d}PAP.SUKKAL ^{d}NUSKU ^{d}ARA
9 *ù* ^{d}MES.SAG.UNUG^{ki} *it-ti* GI.IZI.LÁ TA UB.ŠU.UKKIN.NA.KI KÁ.MAḪ
10 *a-na su-ú-qa* È.MEŠ-*nim-ma* ^{d}MES.SAG.UNUG^{ki} *ina pa-ni-šú* ^{d}PAP.SUKKAL ^{d}NUSKU
11 *ù* ^{d}ARA *it-ti-šú* GIN-*ak*.MEŠ-*ma* É NIGIN-*ú* GUR-*ru*.MEŠ-*nim-ma*
12 ^{d}PAP.SUKKAL *ina* KÁ.MAḪ ^{d}NUSKU *ina* KÁ.GAL *ù* ^{d}ARA *ina* KÁ.SAG
13 ^{lú}KU$_4$-É TA GI.IZI.LÁ IZI.ḪA.MUN *ina pa-ni-šú-nu ú-šá-aṣ-ba-at-ma*
14 *a-di* ZÁLAG DÚR-*ab* ^{lú}SANGA.MEŠ *šá* É.MEŠ DINGIR.MEŠ TIR.AN.NA^{ki} *šá-niš* ^{lú}KU$_4$-É DINGIR.MEŠ DÙ.A.BI
15 *nu-úr* TA GI.IZI.LÁ *i-qád-du-ú-ma a-na* É DINGIR.MEŠ-*šú-nu* ÍL-*ši-ma*
16 *šá-lam* É *ip-pu-uš* IZI.ḪA.MUN *ina* KÁ É DINGIR.MEŠ-*šú-nu i-nap*[27]*-pa-aḫ*
17 ^{d}LX *uš-ta-pa-a ina nap-ḫar* KUR.KUR *ù it-ta-ṣa-a ṣa-lam ba-nu-ú naq-bit i-qab-bu-ú*
18 GI.IZI.LÁ *ù* ^{d}MES.SAG.UNUG^{ki} GUR-*ru-nim-ma a-na* KISAL *An-tu*$_4$ KU$_4$-*ma*
19 *a-na An-tu*$_4$ LAL-*aṣ* ^{lú}MAŠ.MAŠ *ina* A.MEŠ ^{dug}A.GÚB.BA KAŠ SAG GA GEŠTIN *u* Ì.GIŠ
20 GI.IZI.LÁ *ú-na*{*-an*}*-aḫ* ^{d}MES.SAG.UNUG^{ki} GIN-*ak-ma ina* UB.ŠU.UKKIN.NA.KI
21 *a-di na-ma-ri* DÚR-*ab* ^{d}IM ^{d}XXX ^{d}UTU *ù* ^{d}*Be-let*-DINGIR.MEŠ *ina* KISAL
22 *a-di na-ma-ri* DÚR-*ab* UN.MEŠ KUR *ina* É.MEŠ-*šú-nu* IZI.ḪA.MUN *i-nap-pa-aḫ*
23 SÍSKUR *qé-re-e-ti a-na* ^{d}LX *An-tu*$_4$ *ù* DINGIR.MEŠ DÙ.A.BI *i-naq-qu-ú*
24 *naq-bit ki-ma maḫ-ri-im-ma i-qab-bu-ú* ^{lú}EN.NUN URU *ina su-ú-qa*.MEŠ
25 *ù* SILA.LÍM.MA IZI.ḪA.MUN *i-nap-pa-aḫ* KÁ.GAL.MEŠ UNUG^{ki} *a-di na-ma-ri*
26 *ul uḫ-ḫe-er*(?) ^{lú}EN.NUN KÁ.GAL.MEŠ ^{giš}URÌ.GAL.MEŠ XV *ù* 2,30
27 *šá* KÁ.GAL.MEŠ *ú-zaq-qa-pu ab*[28]*-ri a-na na-ma-ri ina* KÁ.GAL.MEŠ *i-nap-pa-*⸢*aḫ*⸣

---

28 UD.17.KAM 10 UŠ *u*$_4$*-mu* EGIR KUR-*ḫa* ^{d}UTU KÁ *ina pa-ni* ^{d}LX *u An-tu*$_4$ BAD-*te-ma ba-a-a-a*[*t*]
29 DUḪ-*ár nap-tan* GAL-*ú šá še-rì a-na* ^{d}LX *An-tu*$_4$ *ù* DINGIR.MEŠ DÙ.A.BI *i-qar-ru-ub*

---

[27] Copy: *ṣab*; cf. *RAcc.*, 120, n. 2.
[28] Copy: *nap*.

d. A nocturnal festival in the Rēš-temple

30 GAL-*ú* DUḪ-*ma tar-den-nu i-qar-ru-ub níg-na-qa*.MEŠ GUŠKIN *ú-mál-le-e-ma* ⸢SÍSKUR⸣
31 GU$_4$ *ù* UDU.NÍTA BAL-*qí* ^{lú}NAR.MEŠ *i-za-am-mu-ru* E.LUM GU$_4$ SÚN.NA *na*[*q*$^{!}$-*bit i-qab-bu-ú*(?)]
32 *ina* IGI DINGIR.MEŠ DÙ.A.BI *níg-na-qa*.MEŠ *ú-mál-le-e-ma* SÍSKUR GU$_4$ *ù* UDU.NÍTA BA[L-*qí*]
33 ŠU^{II} ^{d}IM ^{d}XXX ^{d}UTU ^{d}MES.SAG.UNUG^{ki} *ù* ^{d}*Be-let*-DINGIR.MEŠ *ina šid-di* ⸢GADA⸣ [...]
34 [DAB-*bat*]-⸢*am-ma*⸣(?) [...]

Obv.
1 on [...] he (the Shoe?) will wait for the Scepter, just as [...]
2 The Scepter and the Shoe will rise and the gods and goddesses, will, exactly as before,
3 go in front of him and behind him. They will come down to the Grand Courtyard and take up position towards Anu.
4 The exorcist will consecrate the Scepter. Then (the Scepter) will enter and sit on his seat. Papsukkal, Nusku
5 and Usmû will sit in the courtyard of Anu. Then the Shoe, Mārāt-Anu
6 and Mārāt-Uruk will return and the Shoe will enter (l. 7) the bed-chamber, the 'House with the golden bed'
7 of Antu and will be placed on a footstool. Mārāt-Anu
8 and Mārāt-Uruk will sit in the courtyard of Anu on the seats. (The priest) will mix (l. 9) wine and good oil
9 and will make a libation (with it) at the gate of the cella of Anu, Antu and all the (other) gods.
10 He will smear the doorframes of the gate of the cella, the doors and gates (with the wine and good oil). He will fill (l. 11) the golden censers
11 and he will make an offering of ox and sheep to Anu, Antu and all the (other) gods.
12 The evening meal will be served to Anu, Antu and all the (other) gods.
13 (The meal) will not be cleared. The vigil will continue the entire night. The gate will not be closed. To all the gods, who sit(?) (l. 14) in the courtyard,
14 the meal will be served. In the first watch of the night on the roof of the (topmost) sanctuary of the temple tower
15 of the Rēš-temple, when the star 'Great Anu of Heaven' rises (and the star) 'Great Antu of Heaven'
16 rises in the constellation Ursa maior, (he will recite) 'Rivaling the glow of the most beautiful of the stars of the sky' (and)
17 'Anu, the king, has risen, the beautiful constellation'. You will set up (l. 18) a golden offering table for Anu and Antu
18 of Heaven. You will lift up a water (basin) for (the washing of) the hands to Anu and Antu. Then
19 you will arrange the offering table. You will arrange beef, mutton and fowl. You will (also) set up (l. 20) fine beer
20 together with drawn wine. You will provide all (kinds of) garden fruits in abundance.
21 You will scatter cedar needles(?) and *maṣḫatu*-flour on a golden censer. Then
22 you will make a libation of drawn wine with a golden libation bowl. On 7 large golden offering tables you will lift up (l. 24),
23 for Jupiter, Venus, Mercury, Saturn and Mars, Moon
24 and Sun, as soon as they appear, a water (basin) for (the washing of) the hands, and you will arrange the offering table.

25 You will arrange beef, mutton and fowl. You will (also) set up (l. 26) fine beer together with drawn wine.
26 You will provide all (kinds of) garden fruits in abundance. On 7 golden censers
27 you will scatter *maṣḫatu*-flour and cedar needles(?). Then you will make a libation (l. 28) of drawn wine with a golden libation bowl.
28 The *lumaḫḫu*-priest, who is girt with a girdle, will light with sulphur fire (l. 30) the large Torch, studded (l. 29) with aromatics,
29 which has been sprinkled with good oil and on which the washing of the mouth ceremony has been performed.
30 Then he will take up position in the direction of the offering table and
31 he will raise his hands for 'Great Anu of Heaven' and he will say the blessing (l. 32) 'Anu, Lord of Heaven'.
32 You will then clear the large offering table and lift up a water (basin) for (the washing of) the hands.
33 The chief temple enterer will lead (l. 34) the Torch accompanied by the exorcists, the lamentation priests and the singers
34 from the temple tower and (then) he will enter (through) the Holy Gate, which is behind the cella, to the Grand Courtyard. Then

Rev.

1 at the side of the Kizalagga he will take up position towards Anu. In front of him a *ḫarû*-container will be broken(?).
2 He will say a blessing. The (head) temple enterer will (then) lead (l. 3) the Torch of Papsukkal, Nusku, Usmû,
3 and Messagunug and they will go to the cella of Antu. Then
4 (the Torch) will take up position towards Antu. In front of her a *ḫarû*-container will be broken(?). Papsukkal,
5 Nusku, Usmû and Messagunug will go out (l. 6) (from the Antu-cella) with the Torch to the Ubšukkinaku.
6 Next, near the Dais of Destinies an ox will be killed in front of them. A brushwood pile
7 will be kindled from the Torch in the Ubšukkinaku. (The priest) will take away (l. 8) the shoulder of the ox, together with its hide,
8 and (with it) he will touch the right and left of the brushwood pile. Papsukkal, Nusku, Usmû,
9 and Messagunug will go out (l. 10) with the Torch from the Ubšukkinaku, (through) the Grand Gate,
10 into the street. Then, with Messagunug at the head, Papsukkal, Nusku
11 and Usmû will go with him circling the temple. (Then) they will return and
12 Papsukkal (will enter) by the Grand Gate, Nusku by the Great Gate and Usmû by the Main Gate.
13 A temple enterer will light a brushwood pile from the Torch in front of them and
14 they will sit until dawn. The *šangû*-priests of the temples of Tiranna (and) secondly the temple enterers of all the temples
15 will light a fire from the Torch and they will carry (it) to their temple. Then
16 they will perform the good-functioning of the temple ceremony. They will kindle a brushwood pile at the gates of their temple.
17 They will say the blessing 'Anu will shine forth in all the lands' and 'He (Anu, the king) has risen, the beautiful constellation'.
18 The Torch and Messagunug will return and enter the courtyard of Antu. Then

19 they will stand before Antu. The exorcist will extinguish the Torch (l. 20) with water from the holy water-basin, fine beer, milk, wine and oil.
20 Messagunug will (again) go and sit (l. 21) in the Ubšukkinaku,
21 until daybreak. Adad, Sîn, Šamaš and Bēlet-ilī will sit (l.22) in the courtyard,
22 until daybreak. The people of the land will kindle the brushwood piles in their homes.
23 They will make offerings for the banquet for Anu, Antu and all the (other) gods.
24 They will say the (same) blessing, as before. The city guardians will kindle brushwood piles (l. 25) in the streets
25 and crossroads. The city gates of Uruk until daybreak
26 will not … The guardians of the city gates will plant (l. 27) standards on the right and left side
27 of the city gates (and) will kindle brushwood piles in the gates until dawn.

---

28 On the seventeenth day (of the month), 40 minutes after sunrise, in front of Anu and Antu the gate will be opened, and the vigil
29 will be ended. The main meal of the morning will be served to Anu, Antu and all the (other) gods.
30 The main (meal) will be cleared and the second (meal) will be served. (The priest) will fill the golden censers and he will make (l. 31) ⌜offerings⌝
31 of ox and sheep. The singers will sing. The b[lessing(?)] 'Honored one, wild ox' [they will say].
32 (The priest) will fill censers for all the gods and he will mak[e] offerings of ox and sheep.
33 [(The priest) will le]ad(l. 34)(?) Adad, Sîn, Šamaš, Messagunug and Bēlet-ilī to (the room between) the curtains […].
34 […]

Comments

Obv.

l. 2, a lamp in the shape of a shoe is the symbol of Nusku as god of light and fire. See D.O. Edzard, *WM* I, 116f. For the shoe see A. Livingstone, *Mystical*, 219, 83 (Marduk's Ordeal). It is also attested in a ritual from Babylon, BM 35019 (A.R. George, *BTT*, no. 45), obv. 1′.

l. 3, GIN-*ak*, a singular where a plural is intended (as in rev. 3 and 11). This kind of mistake has been made several times in this text:

- obv. 3, rev. 19, LAL-*aṣ*.
- obv. 5, 8, rev. 14, 22, DÚR-*ab*.
- obv. 24, *in-nam-mar*.
- rev. 15, ÍL-*ši-ma*.
- rev. 16, *ip-pu-uš*.
- rev. 16, 22, and 25, 27, *i-nap-pa-aḫ* (the subject of this verb in the last two cases, ^{lú}EN.NUN in 24 and 26, must be interpreted here as a plural, see *ú-zaq-qa-pu*, rev. 27).
- for *tu-kan-nu* in obv. 18, 20 and 26 see my comment on *TU* 39, obv. 6.

l. 6, GUR-*ru*.MEŠ-*nim-ma*, a masculine plural, although the subjects of this verb (*šēnu*, Mārāt-Anu, Mārāt-Uruk) are all feminine.

l. 10, 'he will smear' rather than 'he will sprinkle', for which in this text *salāḫu* is used (obv. 29), the translation follows *CAD*, D, 53–4, 1, a. To smear objects is also attested in *RAcc.*, 140, 350; *Bagh. Mitt. Beih.* 2, no. 5, rev. 30; BM 93046 (A.R. George, *BTT*, no. 44), rev. 3′ff. For *lapātu* 'to sprinkle' see my comment on *TU* 39, obv. 23.

l. 14, [*aš-b*]*a*(?), according to *RAcc.*, 119. Perhaps a ventive? Or a mistake for *aš-bu*?

l. 16, ^{mul}MAR.GÍD.DA, *eriqqu*, see *CAD*, E, 297b, 3.

l. 16, 'Rivaling the glow of the most beautiful of the stars of the sky', the translation of this incipit follows *CAD*, Z, 121b, 2.

l. 17, 'Anu, the king has risen, the beautiful constellation', the translation of this incipit follows *CAD*, Ṣ, 84b, c. The same incipit, but without ^{d}A-nù LUGAL, in rev. 17.

l. 21, ^{giš}ERIN.SÍG, *lukšu* 'needles of the cedar(?)', see *CAD*, 240b. Cf. *RAcc.*, 119, n. 2; *AHw*, 562a, *luk/gšu*, 'Holzspäne?'. See also below l. 27 (*lu-uk-šú*).

l. 34, KÁ.SIKIL.LA 'Holy Gate', cf. A. Falkenstein, *Topographie*, 12; A.R. George, *BTT*, 420 ff.

Rev.

l. 1, KI.ZÁLAG.GA, cf. A. Falkenstein, *Topographie*, 24, and A.R. George, *House Most High*, no. 643.

l. 1 (see also 4), ^{dug}*ḫa-ru-ú ina* IGI-*šú ib-bat-ta-qa* 'a *ḫarû*-container will be broken(?)', cf. *AHw*, 114b, N, 4 ('durchgeschlagen(?)'); see also A.J. Sachs in J.B. Pritchard, *ANET*^{2}, 338b. *CAD*, B, 165a, 10 and ib., Ḫ, 117a, 1, b translate 'will be/is opened', but this is not specific enough because for 'to open' the verb *petû* was usually used, as for example in *CT* 15, 44, 17 (see *CAD*, Ḫ, 117a, 1, b with more examples). For the religious ceremony called *ḫarû* see II.8.3.

l. 12, the KÁ.GAL 'Great Gate', is the station of Nusku. Cf. A. Falkenstein, *Topographie*, 11. It is also mentioned in the building inscription *YOS* 1, 52, 5. Compare the KÁ.GAL with the KÁ.MAḪ, the station of Papsukkal, see my comment on *TU* 40, obv. 9.

l. 12, the KÁ.SAG 'Main Gate', is the station of Usmû. Cf. A. Falkenstein, *Topographie*, 11–12.

l. 23, this is the only place where *qerītu* is attested in combination with *nīqu* (SÍSKUR). Or should we interpret SÍSKUR *qé-re-e-ti* here as a specific sort of offering? (see *CAD*, Q, 241a, b; B. Pongratz-Leisten, *ina šulmi īrub*, 45, n. 32).

l. 26, *ul uḫ-ḫe-er*, one expects a verb 'to close', cf. *TU* 39, rev. 9: after the vigil the gate was closed and at dawn after the *dīk bīti*-ceremony, it was opened again for a new cultic day. 'to close the gate' is not only *abullam/bābam edēlu* (in G-, D- and Dt-stem) (see *TU* 39, rev. 9; 14; *TU* 41, obv. 13; cf. *CAD*, E, 25–6; *AHw*, 185–6), but also *turrum* (cf. *AHw*, 1335a, 16, b). Perhaps *uḫ-ḫe-er* is a mistake for *ú-te*$^{!}$*-er* (suggestion of M. Stol)? B. Pongratz-Leisten, *ina šulmi īrub*, 45 suggests a D stative of *aḫāru* 'ließ er (der *maṣṣar ili*) nicht aus den Augen?'.

l. 28 10 UŠ '40 minutes', cf. *AHw*, 1289a and R. Borger, *ABZ*, no. 211.

l. 31, the *taqribtu*-lamentation 'Honored one, wild ox' is mentioned here, after which the text perhaps reads: *na*[*q-bit i-qab-bu-ú*], although one would expect *taqrībtu* (ÉR). According to F. Thureau-Dangin in *RAcc.*, 121, n. 2, the traces exclude such a restoration, but the sign before the break may very well be *naq*-. The lamentation is also mentioned in the Babylon Kislīmu ritual BM 32206 +, IV, 162 and in the Uruk cultic calendar text *TU* 48, obv. 8, see II.2.2.

l. 34, [DAB-*bat*]-⸢*am-ma*⸣(?), '[(The priest) will le]ad(?)'. See my comment on *TU* 39, obv. 27.

e. The kettledrum ritual

TU 44 (AO 6479)[29]

This text contains the most elaborate version of the kettledrum ceremony (*lilissu*). Although written in Hellenistic Uruk, the text is a copy of an older original, as the colophon specifically states. The owner of the tablet is Anu-aḫa-ittannu, son of Riḫat-Anu, probably, as Wallenfels suggested, of the family Sin-lēqe-unnīni (known from several private contracts dated ca. 68–73 S.E.), because the Anu-aḫa-ittannu of *TU* 44 is a chief singer of dirges (*galamāḫu*) and all attested lamentation priests (*kalû*) and chief singers of dirges are descendants of the family Sin-lēqe-unnīni.[30] The text is partially a duplicate of *KAR* 60 and *Bagh. Mitt. Beih.* 2, no. 5.

The text is discussed in II.5.

I

1 *e-nu-ma* LI.LI.ÌZ ZABAR *a-na a-*[*ra-mi* IGI-*k*]*a*

2 GU$_4$ *šuk-lu-lu* GE$_6$ *šá* SI.MEŠ *ù* ^{giš}U[MBIN].MEŠ *šal-mu* TA SAG.DU-*šú*

3 EN *ap-pi* KUN-*šu* ^{lú}UM.ME.A *m*[*u-d*]*u-ú it-ta-nap-la-as-su-ma*

4 *šum-ma zu-mur-šú* GIM ESIR (A.ÉSIR) GE$_6$ *a-na par-ṣi u* KI.DU.DU-*de-e*

5 *il-leq-qu šum-ma* 7 SÍG BABBAR-*tu*$_4$ GIM MUL *ta-kip ina* ^{giš}NÍG.GIDRU

6 *ma-ḫi-iṣ ina qin-na-zi la-pit ana par-ṣi u ki-du-de-e ul il-leq-qé*

---

7 *e-nu-ma* GU$_4$ *a-na* É *mu-um-mu tu-šèr-ri-bu ina* UD ŠE.GA

8 *ina* Á GU$_4$ ZI.GA KI SAR A KÙ SÙ É *mu-um-mu tu-ta-am-*⟨*ma*⟩

9 2-*ta* SIG$_4$ XV *u* GÙB *šá* KÁ É *mu-um-mu* ŠUB-*di*

10 *sìr-qí a-na* DÌM.ME.ER AN.NA DÌM.ME.ER AN.KI.A DINGIR.MEŠ GAL.MEŠ *ta-sar-raq*

11 KAŠ SAG BAL-*qí* GU$_4$ *a-na* É *mu-um-mu tu-še-rib*

12 ^{gi}KID.MÁ.ŠÚ.A ŠUB-*di* KI.TA ^{gi}KID.MÁ.ŠÚ.A *ba-aṣ-ṣa*

13 [DUB]-*ak* Á.MEŠ ^{gi}KID.MÁ.ŠÚ.A *ba-aṣ-ṣa* NIGIN-*mi* GU$_4$ *šá-a-šú*

14 [*ina mu*]*ḫ*-⸢*ḫ*⸣*i* ^{gi}KID.MÁ.ŠÚ.A *tuš-za-za-ma ina* ÉŠ.LÁ *šá* SÍG ÙZ

15 [*ina kin*]-*ṣi tar-kás* KAŠ.Ú.SA SIG$_5$$^!$ *ina* ÙB ZABAR *ina* IGI GU$_4$ GAR-*an*

16 [2 ^{dug}]⸢A⸣.GÚB.BA *a-na* ^{d}KÙ.SÙ *u* ^{d}NIN.GÌRIM (A.ḪA.KUD.DU) GUB-*an*

17 [2 GI.D]U$_8$ GUB-*an* 7.TA.ÀM NINDA^{ḫá} ŠE.BAR 7.TA.ÀM NINDA ZÍZ.ÀM

18 [NINDA.Ì.D]É.ÀM LÀL Ì.NUN.NA ZÚ.LUM.MA ^{zì}EŠA (A.TIR) GAR-*an*

19 [KAŠ GEŠTIN] GA GUB-*an* ^{dug}*a-da-kur-ru* GUB[-*an* …]-*a*

20 […]x ^{šim}LI

21 […] ^{dug}*maš-qu-ú* GUB-*an*

22 […] 1/3 MA.NA SÍG BABBAR.BABBAR

23 […] ⸢x⸣-*na* 7 1/2 SÍG ÙZ GAR-*an*

24 […]-*an* KAŠ.Ú.SA SIG$_5$$^!$

25 […-*m*]*a ḫur-da-at šá* ŠINIG (GAD.ŠÚ.NAGA)

26 […^{giš}GIŠIM]MAR GI.ŠUL.ḪI

27 […]-*ga* ^{giš}KIŠI$_{16}$ (Ú.GÍR)

---

[29] Cf. *RAcc.*, 3–6, 10–20; E. Ebeling, in: H. Gressmann, *ATAT*^{2}, 303 ff.; A.J. Sachs, in: J.B. Prichard, *ANET*^{2}, 334 ff. See also R. Borger, *HKL* 1, 567 and 2, 297.

[30] R. Wallenfels, *Uruk. Hellenistic Seal Impressions in the Yale Babylonion Collection. I. Cuneiform Tablets*, Mainz am Rhein, 1994 (AUWE 19), 19–20, and 146. See also G.J.P. McEwan, *FAOS* 4, 13.

28 [...^{du}]^{g}A.GÚB.BA ŠUB-*di*
29 [...] Ì ^{giš}EREN LÀL Ì.NUN.NA
30 [...ŠU]B-*di ina* NÍG.NA *u* GI.IZI.LÁ
31 [*tu-ḫab-bi-šú*...^{uz}]^{u}ZAG.LU ^{uzu}ME.ḪÉ
32 [*u* ^{uzu}KA.NE *tu-ṭaḫ-ḫi* KAŠ SAG GEŠTI]N GA BAL-*qí*
33 [... ŠU]B-*di*
34 [...] ^{dug}A.GÚB.BA
35 [...S]Ù *šu-šu-rat*
36 [... 1]2 SIG$_4$ ŠUB-*di*

II
1 12 GADA *ina muḫ-ḫi* ŠUB-*di* DINGIR.MEŠ 12-*šú-nu ina muḫ-ḫi tu-še-šeb*
2 A.MEŠ TA ^{dug}A.GÚB.BA *šá* ^{d}NIN.GÌRIM ÍL-*ma* KEŠDA.MEŠ *tu-ul-lal* 12 GI.DU$_8$ GUB
3 12 ^{udu}SÍSKUR BAL-*qí* ^{uzu}ZAG.LU ^{uzu}ME.ḪÉ *u* ^{uzu}KA.NE
4 *tu-ṭaḫ-ḫi* KAŠ GEŠTIN GA BAL-*qí* ŠE.NUMUN DUB-*aq* LI.LI.ÌZ GUB-*an*
5 1 SIG$_4$ *a-na* ^{d}*Lum-ḫa* ŠUB-*di* 1 GI.DU$_8$ GUB-*an* $^{udu.níta}$SÍSKUR
6 BAL-*qí* ^{uzu}ZAG.LU ^{uzu}ME.ḪÉ *u* ^{uzu}KA.NE *tu-ṭaḫ-ḫi*
7 KAŠ SAG GEŠTIN GA BAL-*qí* A.MEŠ *ina maḫ-ri-šú-nu* GUB-*an*
8 *šid-di* GÍD.DA GU$_4$ *šá-a-šú* LUḪ KA *tu-še-pis-su*
9 ÉN GU$_4$.GAL GU$_4$.MAḪ Ú KI.ÚS KÙ.GA *ina* ^{gi}SAG.KUD GI DÙG.GA
10 *ana lìb-bi* GEŠTUG^{II} XV-*šú tu-làḫ-ḫaš* ÉN GU$_4$ *i-lit-tu*$_4$ *An-zi-i at-ta-ma*
11 *ina* ^{gi}SAG.KUD GI DÙG.GA *a-na lìb-bi* GEŠTUG^{II} GÙB-*šú*
12 *tu-làḫ-ḫaš* ÚŠ ^{giš}EREN SÙ-*šú ina* NÍG.NA *u* GI.IZI.LÁ
13 *tu-ḫa-bi-šú* ZÌ.SUR.RA-*a ta-lam-miš ina* SAG GU$_4$
14 GUB-*ma* DILMUN^{ki} NIGIN.NA *ina* ŠEM$_4$ ZABAR *ta-za-am-mur*
15 EGIR-*šú* ⸢DÌM.ME.ER GAL.GAL.E.NE AN.KI.A MU.UN.DÍM.MA⸣
16 ⸢ŠID-*nu*⸣ GU$_4$ *šá-a-šú ta-pal-laq-ma* ⸢^{giš}ÚŠ(?) ^{giš}EREN MÚ⸣ *lìb-ba-šu*
17 *ina* ^{giš}EREN ^{šim}LI ZÌ.MAD.GÁ *ina* IGI LI.LI.ÌZ
18 *ta-qal-la* SA ⸢^{uzu}GIŠ⸣.KUN GÙB-*šú* ÍL-*ma*
19 AD$_6$ (LÚ.BAD) GU$_4$ *šá-a-šú ina* 1-*en* TÚG.KUR.RA SA$_5$ *ta-qeb-bir*
20 Ì.GIŠ *gu-un-nu a-na muḫ-ḫi-šú* ŠUB-*di* IGI-*šú ana* ^{d}UTU.ŠÚ.A
21 GAR-*an* KUŠ GU$_4$ *šá-a-šú ta-leq-qé-e-ma ina* ZÌ KUM
22 ^{d}NISABA KÙ.GA *ina* A.MEŠ KAŠ SAG GEŠTIN *te-re-es-si-in*
23 *ina* Ì.NUN.NA ^{GU_4}⟨ÁB⟩ KÙ.GA *u* ŠIM.MEŠ *lìb-bu* ^{ú}SAR-*šú-nu it-ti* 4 SÌLA ZÌ MUNU$_4$ 4 SÌLA
24 ZÌ *bit-qa ana sad-ru* ŠUB-*di ina* ^{giš}ḪAB *u* NA$_4$.KUR.RA *šá* ^{kur}*Ḫat-ti*
25 *ta-ṣar-ra-pu* LI.LI.ÌZ ZABAR *tar-rim*
26 1-*en* ÉŠ.LÁ *šá* GADA *ana muḫ-ḫi* GÍD.DA ^{giš}GAG.MEŠ
27 *šá* ^{giš}MES.MÁ.KAN.NA ^{giš}TASKARIN ^{giš}EREN ^{giš}ESI
28 *u re-eḫ-tu*$_4$ *sik-kat*.MEŠ *gab-bi* ^{giš}*maš-tu-ú*
29 *a-na* LI.LI.ÌZ ZABAR *ina* ŠE.GÍN KÙ.GA ⟨...⟩
30 *ina* SA ^{uzu}GIŠ.KUN GÙB-*šú ba-ab-šu ta-šap-pi*
31 ÉŠ.LÁ DUḪ-*ma a-na muḫ-ḫi nap-du-ú* ŠUB-*di*
32 DIRI-*rat* KUŠ.TAB.BA *ta-qeb-bir*
33 1 KEŠDA *a-na* ^{d}*Lum-ḫa* KEŠDA-*as* $^{udu.níta}$SÍSKUR
34 BAL-*qí* ^{uzu}ZAG.LU ^{uzu}ME.ḪÉ ^{uzu}KA.NE
35 *tu-ṭaḫ-ḫi* KAŠ SAG GEŠTIN *u* GA BAL-*qí*

III

1 ^{d}*A-nù* ^{d}EN.LÍL *u* ^{d}*É-a* DINGIR.MEŠ GAL.MEŠ

---

2 ^{d}LUGAL.GÌR.RA *u* ^{d}MES.LAM.TA.È.A

---

3 ^{d}ZI.SUM.MU NIBRU^{ki} ŠÀ.GA.KE$_4$
4 ^{d}NIN.IMMA$_x$ *šá qé-reb Ni-ip-pú-ru*
5 ^{d}BI.GÌR.ḪUŠ ⟨ENGUR⟩.RA.KE$_4$
6 ^{d}ŠU.ZI.AN.NA *šá ap-si-i*
7 ^{d}ŠENBAR.RA.GIM$_4$.GIM$_4$.ME A.ŠÀ MAR.RA.KE$_4$
8 ^{d}EN.NU.GI *šá-kin eq-li*
9 ^{d}ÙR.BÀD.DA EN SUKUD.DA.KE$_4$: ^{d}KÙ.SÙ *be-lu šá-qu-u*
10 ^{d}ÙR.BÀD.ḪUM.ḪUM DUMU É.ŠÀ.BA.KE$_4$: ^{d}NIN.ŠAR DUMU É.ŠÀ.BA
11 ^{d}GUB.BA.GA.RA.RA.È DUMU URU.GIBIL$_4$.LA.KE$_4$
12 ^{d}NIN.KA.SI DUMU URU *eš-ši*
13 ^{d}A.BAR.RA.LAḪ$_5$ DUMU UD.30.KAM UD.NÁ.ÀM
14 ^{d}NUSKU DUMU *še-la-še-e bu-um-bu-li*

---

15 *a-na* UD.15.KAM LI.LI.ÌZ ZABAR *ana* IGI
16 ^{d}UTU *tu-še-eṣ-ṣi* 5 KEŠDA *a-na* ^{d}*É-a*
17 ^{d}UTU ^{d}ASAL.LÚ.ḪI ^{d}*Lum-ḫa u* ^{d}LILIZ
18 KEŠDA-*as* $^{udu.níta}$SÍSKUR BAL-*qí*
19 ^{uzu}ZAG.LU ^{uzu}ME.ḪÉ ^{uzu}KA.NE *tu-ṭaḫ-ḫi*
20 KAŠ SAG GEŠT[IN GA] BAL-*qí ina* NÍG.NA *u* GI.IZI.LÁ
21 *tu-ḫa-ba* [*ina*(?) A.MEŠ ^{dug}A].GÚB.BA *tul-lal*
22 ^{d}EN.KI ^{d}UTU ^{d}x[...] ZA DÉ DÉ
23 3-*šú* ŠID-*nu* LUḪ KA [...]
24 *tu-še-pis-su* Ì.NUN.NA *u* Ì.GIŠ BÁR.GÉ ŠÉŠ-*s*[*u* $^{!}$]^{ú} ⸢GALA.MAḪ⸣ [...]
25 *ana* UGU LI.LI.ÌZ ZABAR ŠUB-*di* KEŠDA.MEŠ DUḪ
26 *ina* NÍG.NA *u* GI.IZI.LÁ *tu-ḫab-bi-šú* ŠU^{II} LILIZ *ana* IGI DINGIR.ME
27 DAB-*ma ina* ŠE.NUMUN.MEŠ GUB-*an*
28 LUGAL.E DÌM.ME.ER AN.KI.A ÉR GAR-*an*
29 DÍM.DÍM.MA *an-na-a šá te-ep-pu-uš* Á.È
30 IGI *a-ḫu-ú la* DUMU EN GARZA NU IGI-*mar*
31 UD.MEŠ-*šú* LÚGUD.DA.MEŠ ZU-*ú a-na* ZU-*ú*
32 *li-kal-lim la* ZU-*ú* NU IGI *ina* NÍG.GIG ^{d}LX ^{d}EN.LÍL
33 *u* ^{d}IDIM DINGIR.MEŠ GAL.MEŠ

IV

1 [...UD.MEŠ]-*šú* GÍD.DA.MEŠ

---

2 [...LI.]LI.ÌZ ZABAR
3 [...^{gi}]^{š}ŠUR.MÌN 1/2 MA.NA ^{šim}GÍR
4 [...ŠI]M.ŠAL 1/2 MA.NA GI DÙG.GA
5 [...] *lad-nu* 10 GÍN ^{šim}*qu-an-na-bu*
6 [...] ^{šim}*ka-ṣi-ṣi-ḫa-tu*$_4$
7 [...] GÍN ^{šim}GIG
8 [...^{ši}]^{m}MAN.DU 2 SÌLA Ì.GIŠ *ḫal-ṣa*
9 [...]-*na* 2 SÌLA GEŠTIN
10 [...] ⸢x⸣ ZÌ *bit-qa* 4 SÌLA ZÌ MUNU$_4$

e. The kettledrum ritual

11 [...]-*nu* 1/2 SÌLA ÚŠ ^{giš}EREN
12 [...^{ú}*a*-]*ṣu-ṣe-e-tú* ŠE.GÍN
13 [...] *lap-pi šá* ^{giš}GAG.MEŠ

---

14 [...] TÚG.KUR.RA BABBAR-*ú* 1 TÚG.KUR.RA SA$_5$
15 [...] MA.NA SÍG^{ḫá} 7 MA.NA
16 [...] 7 MA.NA ^{síg}ZA.GÌN.NA
17 [...SÍG Ù]Z 2 GUR 4 NIGIDA ŠE.BAR 1 ŠE.NUMUN.MEŠ
18 [...ZÍ]Z.ÀM MUN *u* ^{šim}LI 1 *gi-nu-ú*
19 [...] LAL *ú-de-e*
20 ⌜AN.BAR⌝ [...] 1/2 MA.NA
21 IM.SAḪAR.NA$_4$.KUR.RA *šá* ^{kur}*Ḫat-ti* 1 MA.NA ŠE.GÍN ZÁLAG-*tu*$_4$
22 ^{giš}GAG.MEŠ 3-*ta šá* ^{giš}MES.MÁ.KAN.NA 3-*ta*
23 *šá* ^{giš}TASKARIN 3-*ta šá* ^{giš}EREN 3-*ta šá* ^{giš}ESI
24 3-*ta šá* ŠINIG *re-eḫ-tu*$_4$ *sik-kat*.MEŠ *gab-bi maš-tu-u*
25 10 ÉŠ.LÁ *šá* GADA *šá* 1-*en* ÉŠ.LÁ 10 KÙŠ GÍD.DA
26 1 ÉŠ.LÁ *šá* GADA *šá* 1 ME KÙŠ GÍD.DA 10 ÉŠ.LÁ
27 *šá* SÍG ÙZ *šá* 4 KÙŠ GÍD.DA 1 ÉŠ.LÁ *šá* GU$_4$
28 *ina lìb-bi* KEŠDA 1-*en* ^{túg}*su-ḫat-tu* 1 *ku-tu-um-mu*

---

29 *ú-de-e* ^{lú}BÁḪAR 4 ^{dug}A.GÚB.BA 4 ^{dug}*kan-du-ru-u*
30 4 ^{dug}*saḫ-ḫa-ri* 24 ^{dug}*a-da-kur-ru* 24 ^{dug}*ḫa-bu-u*
31 1 ME 20 ^{dug}*ma-lit-tu*$_4$ 3 ME ^{dug}*ba-gur-ru* 60 NÍG.NA
32 5 *ṣa-bit* 6 *ag-gan-nu* 6 *ni-sip* 2 *ṣi-in-du-u* 2 *nam-ḫa-ri*
33 *ú-de-e* ^{lú}NAGAR 1 ^{giš}*ku-um-mu* 4 ^{giš}GAG AN.BAR *iṣ-ṣi ana* ^{giš}GAG.MEŠ
34 *ú-de-e* ^{lú}AD.KID 24 GI.DU$_8$ 24 ^{gi}*sel-li* 5-*ta*
35 $^{[g]i}$*sel-la* ŠU^{II} 3 ^{gi}KID.MÁ.ŠÚ.A 3 ^{gi}*ku-tu-um-mu*

---

36 [*né-pe*]-*šú šá* ŠU^{II} ^{lú}GALA: IM ^{Id}LX-ŠEŠ-MU-*nu* A šá ^{I}*Ri-ḫat*-^{d}LX
37 ^{lú}GALA.MAḪ ^{d}LX *u An-tu*$_4$ UNUG^{ki}-*ú* GIM SUMUN-*bar-šú* SAR-*ma ba-rù u up-puš*

I

1 When y[ou] want [to cover] the kettledrum (proceed as follows).
2 A knowledgeable expert will carefully inspect (l. 3) an ungelded black bull, whose horns and hooves are intact, from its head
3 to the tip of its tail;
4 if its body is black as pitch, it will be taken (l. 5) for the rites and rituals.
5 If it is spotted with 7 white tufts (which look) like stars, (or if) it has been struck (l. 6) with a stick
6 (or) touched with a whip, it will not be taken for the rites and rituals.

---

7 When you want to make the bull enter the workshop, on a favourable day
8 you will step up to the side of the bull, you will sweep the ground, you will sprinkle pure water, (and) you will conjure the workshop.
9 You will lay down 2 bricks on the right and left side of the door of the workshop.
10 You will scatter a *serqu*-offering for the gods of Heaven (and) the gods of Heaven and Earth, (i.e.) the great gods.
11 You will make a libation of first-quality beer. You will make the bull enter the workshop.
12 You will lay down a reed mat. Underneath the reed mat you will [heap] up (l. 13) sand.

13 You will surround the sides of the reed mat with sand. You will make that bull stand (l. 14)
14 [o]n the reed mat and (then), with a rope of goat hair,
15 you will tie (its) [le]gs. You will place fine mixed beer in a bronze *uppu*-drum in front of the bull.
16 You will set up [2 holy water]-basins for Kusu and Ningirim.
17 You will set up [2 offering tabl]es; you will place (l. 18) 7 loaves of barley bread, 7 loaves of emmer bread each,
18 (together with) a [*mir*]*su*-confection (made with) honey, ghee, dates (and) *sasqû*-flour.
19 You will set up [beer, wine] (and) milk. You will se[t up] an *adakurru*-container. [...] ...
20 [...] juniper
21 [...] you will set up a *mašqû*-vessel.
22 [...] 1/3 mina of white wool
23 [...] ... you will place 7 1/2 of goat's hair.
24 [...] ... fine mixed beer
25 [... a]nd a *ḫurdatu*-pole (made of) of tamarisk
26 [... young date]-palm, *šalālu*-reed,
27 [...] acacia,
28 [...] you will set up a holy water-basin.
29 [...] cedar oil, honey, ghee,
30 [... you will po]ur. With censer and torch
31 [you will consecrate it (the bull). ...] Shoulder, *ḫimṣu*-omentum,
32 [and roasted meat you will bring near]. You will make a libation [of first-quality beer, wi]ne (and) milk.
33 [... you will] pour.
34 [...] a holy water-basin
35 [...you will sprink]le(?). The sweepings
36 [...] you will lay down [1]2 bricks.

II
1 On (the 12 bricks) you will lay down 12 linen (cloths). On them you will make the 12 gods sit.
2 You will lift up the water (basin filled) from the holy water-basins of Ningirim and (then) you will purify the offering accoutrements (with it). You will set up 12 offering tables.
3 You will make 12 sheep offerings. You will bring near (l. 4) shoulder, *ḫimṣu*-omentum and roasted meat.
4 You will make a libation of beer, wine (and) milk. You will scatter barley seed. You will set up the kettledrum.
5 You will lay down 1 brick for Lumḫa. You will set up 1 offering table. You will make (l. 6) a sheep offering.
6 You will bring shoulder, *ḫimṣu*-omentum and roasted meat near.
7 You will make a libation of first-quality beer, wine (and) milk. You will set up a water (basin) before them (the gods).
8 You will draw the curtains shut. On the aforementioned bull you will perform the washing of the mouth ceremony.
9 Into its right ear you will whisper (l. 10), by means of a tube (made of) sweet reed, the incantation 'Great bull, choice bull, which treads on the pure meadow'.
10 You will whisper (l. 12) the incantation 'O bull, you are a descendant of Anzu'
11 into its left ear, by means of a tube (made of) sweet reed.
12 You will sprinkle it with cedar balsam. With censer and torch

13 you will consecrate it. (With) a magic circle of flour you will surround it. You will stand (l. 14) at the head of the bull
14 and you will sing (the *eršemakku*-lamentation) 'Important one, who wanders abound' to the accompaniment of a bronze *ḫalḫallatu*-drum.
15 After that, you will recite (l. 16) (the *šuillakku*-prayer)'Great gods, who have created Heaven and Earth'.
16 (Then) you will cut open that bull and you will kindle cedar balsam(?). You will burn (l. 18) its heart,
17 (together) with cedar, juniper, *maṣḫatu*-flour in front of the kettledrum.
18 You will remove the sinew from its left thigh and
19 you will bury the carcass of that bull in a red … cloth.
20 You will pour ordinary oil on it. You will place (l. 21) its face towards the West.
21 You will take the hide of that bull and soak (it) (l. 22) in *isqūqu*-flour
22 of pure grain, in water, first-quality beer (and) wine.
23 You will (then) lay (it) (l. 24) in the ghee from a pure cow and aromatics from their vegetables, (together) with 4 litres malt flour, (and) 4 litres of
24 *bitqu*-flour of standard quality. You will steep (it) (l. 25) with madder, and alum from the land of Ḫattu.
25 (Then) you will cover the bronze kettledrum (with it).
26 On (the kettledrum) you will pull (it) taut by means of a linen rope. ⟨You will paint (l. 29)(?)⟩ pegs
27 of sissoowood, boxwood, cedar, ebony
28 and the rest of the pegs, all of *martû*-wood
29 for the bronze kettledrum with pure paint.
30 With the sinew from its left thigh you will fasten its opening.
31 You will loosen the rope and you will lay (it) on the tie.
32 You will bury the remainder of the bulls hide.
33 You will arrange 1 offering accoutrement for Lumḫa. You will make (l. 34) a sheep offering.
34 You will bring (l. 35) shoulder, *ḫimṣu*-omentum and roasted meat
35 near. You will make a libation of first-quality beer, wine and milk.

III
1 Anu, Enlil and Ea, the great gods.

---

2 Lugalgirra and Meslamtaea

3–4 Zisummu nibruki šagake = Ninimma, who is in Nippur.
5–6 Bigirḫuš ⟨engur⟩rake = Šuzianna, of the Subterranean Water.
7–8 Šenbarragimgimme ašamarrake = Ennugi who cultivates the fields.
9 Urbadda en sukuddake = Kusu, the exalted lord.
10 Urbadḫumḫum dumu ešabake = Ninšar, the son of Ešaba
11–12 Gubbagararae dumu urugibillake =Ninkasi, the son of the New City.
13–14 Abarralaḫ dumu ud.30.kam udnaam = Nusku, the son of the thirtieth day (of the month), the day of non-appearance of the moon.

---

15 On the fifteenth day you will bring out (l. 16) the bronze kettledrum before
16 Šamaš. You will arrange (l. 18) 5 offering accoutrements in front of Ea,
17 Šamaš, Marduk, Lumḫa and the divine kettledrum.
18 You will make a sheep offering.
19 You will bring shoulder, *ḫimṣu*-omentum (and) roasted meat near.

20 You will make a libation of first-quality beer, wi[ne and milk]. With censer and torch
21 you will consecrate (the kettledrum). [With water from the holy] water-basin you will purify (the kettledrum).
22 Enki, Šamaš, … […] …
23 you will recite three times. You will perform (l. 24) the washing of the mouth ceremony […]
24 (on the kettledrum). (With) ghee and pressed oil you will anoint it. The chief singer of dirges will lay down (l. 25) […]
25 on the bronze kettledrum. You will clear away the offering accoutrements.
26 With censer and torch you will consecrate it (the kettledrum). You will lead (l. 27) the kettledrum before the gods
27 and set (it) up in (a bed of) barley seeds.
28 You will perform the *taqribtu*-lamentation 'The king, god of Heaven and Earth'.
29 This ritual procedure, which you perform, only the novice
30 may see (it); an outsider, someone who is not responsible for the rites, may not see (it),
31 (because if this happens) his days will be short. The one who is competent may show (l. 32) (the tablet only) to one who is (also) competent;
32 he who is not competent may not see (it). Taboo of Anu, Enlil
33 and Ea, the great gods.

IV

1 [… his day]s will be long.

---

2 [… the bron]ze kettledrum
3 […] cypress, 1/2 mina myrtle,
4 […box]tree, 1/2 mina sweet reed,
5 […] *ladnu*-aromatics, 10 shekel *qunnabu*-aromatics,
6 […] *cassia*,
7 […] shekel *kanaktu*-tree,
8 […] elder(?), 2 litres pressed oil,
9 […] 2 litres wine,
10 […] *bitqu*-flour, 4 litres malt flour,
11 […] 1/2 litre cedar balsam,
12 […] *aṣuṣimtu*-plant, *šindu*-colouring matter,
13 […] the wrappings of the pegs.

---

14 […] white … cloth, 1 red … cloth,
15 […] mina wool, 7 mina
16 […] 7 mina of blue wool,
17 […] goat's hair, 2 kor 4 *pānu* of barley, 1 (*pānu*) of barley seeds,
18 [… em]mer, salt and juniper, 1 regular offering,
19 […] utensils,
20 of iron […] 1/2 mina
21 alum from the land of Ḫattu, 1 mina of white paint,
22 3 pegs of the sissoowood, 3
23 of boxwood, 3 of cedar, 3 of ebony,
24 3 of tamarisk, the rest of the pegs, all of *martû*-wood,
25 10 linen ropes, of which each rope is 10 cubits long,
26 1 linen rope of 100 cubits long, 10 ropes
27 of goat hair 4 cubits long, among them 1 rope with which the bull

28 was tied, 1 *suḫattu*-cloth, 1 cover.

29 The utensils of the potter: 4 holy water-basins, 4 *kandurû*-containers,
30 4 *saḫḫarru*-bowls, 24 *adakurru*-containers, 24 *ḫabû*-jugs,
31 120 *malītu*-bows, 300 *bagurru*-scoops, 60 censers,
32 5 gazelle (shaped) vessels(??), 6 *agannu*-bowls, 6 *nēsepu*-containers, 2 *ṣindu*-containers, 2 *namḫaru*-vats.
33 The utensils of the carpenter: 1 *kummu*(?), 4 iron nails, pieces of wood for pegs.
34 The utensils of the reed-worker: 24 offering tables, 24 reed baskets, 5
35 hand-baskets, 3 reed mats, 3 reed covers.

(Colophon:)
36 [Ri]tual of the lamentation priest. Tablet of Anu-aḫa-ittannu, son of Riḫat-Anu,
37 the chief singer of dirges of Anu and Antu, citizen of Uruk.
Written in accordance with its original, collated and 'closed with a colophon'(?).

Comments

I

l. 2, for the use of *šuklulu* in Neo-Babylonian administration see G. van Driel, *BSA* 8 (1995), 220f.

l. 5, *il-leq-qu* is apparently a mistake for *il-leq-qé* (see I, l. 6).

l. 7, see *Bagh. Mitt. Beih.* 2, no. 5, obv. 7; *Bagh. Mitt. Beih.* 2, no. 7, rev. 7; IV R^2, 23, no. 1 +, IV, 25.

l. 8, *qaqqara tašabbiṭ mê ellūti tasallaḫ* (KI SAR A KÙ SÙ), a well-known phrase, see *RAcc.*, 48, n. 3, *BBR* 2, 196–7, n. b, *CAD*, Š/I, 9b, b, and *AHw*, 1119b, 3, with more examples.

We have several other examples from Uruk: see *LKU*, no. 48, obv. 2 (late Neo Babylonian or early Achaemenid period); the most important example from Hellenistic Uruk is *Bagh. Mitt. Beih.* 2, no. 10, obv. 9, paralleled by *TU* 45, obv. 6–7 (partly lost) and *TU* 46, obv. 7–8 (partly lost). And finally, perhaps the phrase is attested in a small fragment, which contains part of a ritual, *Bagh. Mitt. Beih.* 2, no. 14 (cf. G.J.P. McEwan, *BiOr* 38 (1981), 640):

1′ […] ⸢x⸣ […]
2′ [… KI *ta-šab*]-*biṭ* A.MEŠ K[Ù *ta-sal-làḫ*(?) …]
3′ [… *muḫ*]-*ḫi a-gur-ru* KÙ […]
4′ […^{giš}]⸢Ù⸣.LUḪ NAM.LUGAL.LA *u*(?)[…]
5′ [… *t*]*uš-za-za ṣi-di-i-t*[u_4 DINGIR.MEŠ(?) …]
6′ […] U BA(?) ⸢x⸣ […]

l. 3′, *a-gur-ru* KÙ 'the pure brick', or: *a-gur-ru* KÙ.[BABBAR 'the silver (coloured) brick' (cf. *VAB* 4, 158, VI, 36; *PBS* 15, 79, I, 61; *AnOr* 8, 25, 12)?

Similar to the phrase *qaqqara tašabbiṭ mê ellūti tasallaḫ* is also *Bagh. Mitt. Beih.* 2, no. 5, obv. 8: KI *tu-*⌜*qád*⌝*-da-áš* A KÙ SÙ-*uḫ*. See also my comment on *TU* 45, rev. 8.

l. 13, [DUB]-*ak* 'you will heap up' (*tašappak*), and probably not *tasarraq* (DUB-*aq*) (cf. *RAcc.*, 10). See *BRM* 4, 6, obv. 7, where *baṣṣu* is also attested with *šapāku*, in: *ba-aṣ it-taš-pak* 'sand is heaped up' (lamentation incipit). See the duplicates *Bagh. Mitt. Beih.* 2, no. 5, obv. 16 and *KAR* 60, obv. [4]. See also my comment on l. 18.

l. 15 (see also 24), KAŠ.Ú.SA $SIG_5^!$ is probably 'fine mixed beer' (*billatu*) (reading suggestion M. Stol), well attested in ritual texts; see for example *TU* 39, obv. 9; cf. also the dictionaries. Not: KAŠ ^{ú}*sa-pi-e* (see *RAcc.*, 10), which is otherwise unknown.

l. 16, here and in II, 2 the holy water-basin and Ningirim are mentioned together, a connection which is confirmed by A. Livingstone, *Mystical*, 176, 1.

l. 18, 'you will place' (GAR-*an*), this verb is also used in the parallels *KAR* 50, rev. 4, *TU* 45, obv. 8 and *Bagh. Mitt. Beih.* 2, no. 10, obv. 11–12. Other parallels have the verb *sarāqu* (DUB-*aq*): IV R^2, 23, no. 1 +, III, 26–27; *Bagh. Mitt. Beih.* 2, no. 5, obv. 13–14. One has to ask whether in some cases instead of *sarāqu* the verb *tabāku* (DUB) is intended, see R. Borger, *BiOr* 30 (1973), 178, 27: ZÚ.L[U]M(.MA) ^{zi}EŠA *ta-tab-bak-ma* (cf. *CAD*, S, 173b).

l. 19, based on the syllabic writing ^{dug}*a-da-kur-ru* (see also IV, 30) it is preferable to read ^{dug}A.DA.GUR_5 in Late Babylonian/Hellenistic ritual texts (see *TU* 45, obv. 9; *Bagh. Mitt. Beih.* 2, no. 10, obv. 13; F.H. Weissbach, *Misc.*, no. 12, obv. 9) as *adakurru* rather than *adagurru*.

l. 31, [*tu-ḫa-bi-šú*], the restoration is based on II, 13. See also III, 26 (*tu-ḫab-bi-šú*). One would of course expect *tu-ḫa-ab/ḫab-šú*. Cf. III, 21 (*tu-ḫa-ba*); *TU* 41, obv. 4 (*ú-ḫab*^{ab}*-ma*); *TU* 45, rev. 24 and *TU* 46, rev. 13 (*tu-ḫa-ab*).

l. 31, *ḫimṣu*-omentum, see D.A. Foxvog, in Å.W. Sjöberg, *AV*, 171b.

II

l. 9 ff., several recitations are referred to here, which are also attested elsewhere. First two incantations in II, 9 and 10: 'Great bull, choice bull, which treads on the pure meadow', also attested in the parallels *Bagh. Mitt. Beih.* 2, no. 5, rev. 19, and *KAR* 60, obv. 10, and 'O bull, you are a descendant of Anzû', also in *Bagh. Mitt. Beih.* 2, no. 5, rev. 21, and *KAR* 60, obv. 12. The incantation are recited in full in IV R^2, 23, no. 1 +, I, 9 ff. and 19 ff.

Then follows an *eršemma* in II, 14: 'Important one, who wanders abound', cf. M.E. Cohen, *Eršemma*, 110 ff.; also in the building ritual text *TU* 45, obv. 13 and parallels *TU* 46, obv. 11; rev. 9; *Bagh. Mitt. Beih.* 2, no. 10, 18, and no. 11, obv. fragment 1, 2′; F.H. Weissbach, *Misc.*, no. 12, obv. [11]; also in the Uruk *mīs pî*-ritual *Bagh. Mitt. Beih.* 2, no. 1 (+ //), 24; 26.

After this in II, 15 a hand-raising prayer (*šuillakku*) is recited: 'Great gods, who have created Heaven and Earth', recited in full in *Bagh. Mitt. Beih.* 2, no. 6, see W.R. Mayer, *OrNS* 47 (1978), 432–437.

l. 16, ⌜^{giš}ÚŠ(?) ^{giš}EREN MÚ⌝ 'you will kindle cedar balsam'(?) (*dam erēni*), as in l.

12? Compare also the parallel *KAR* 60, obv. 14 and *Bagh. Mitt. Beih.* 2, no. 5, rev. 22: cedar balsam is kindled (gišÚŠ EREN MÚ-*aḫ*) shortly before the slaughtering of the bull, while here in *TU* 44, II, 16, if the restoration is correct, the cedar balsam is kindled directly after the slaughtering of the bull.

l. 19 (see also IV, 14), the reading of TÚG.KUR.RA is not clear, see *CAD*, S, 130, 2′. Cf. A. Ungnad, *NRV Glossar*, 140; A.L. Oppenheim, *JCS* 4 (1950), 191 ff.; R. Borger, *OrNS* 26 (1957), 7; R.H. Sack, *Amēl-Marduk 562–560 B.C.*, Kevelaer + Neukirchen-Vluyn, 1972, 111; R. Borger, *ABZ*, no. 536, contra *CAD*, Ṣ, 225b (*sad-ru*).

l. 23, GU4⟨ÁB⟩ KÙ.GA ‘pure cow’, see the parallel *KAR* 60, rev. 7.

l. 23–24, ‘You will (then) lay it in the ghee from a pure cow and aromatics from their vegetables, (together) with 4 litres malt flour, (and) 4 litres of *bitqu*-flour of standard quality’, so this is another mixture in which the hide is laid to soak. We should not translate (with *CAD*, S, 19b, 2, b): ‘you will pour 4 litres *bitqu*-flour into (*ana*) the ordinary flour (*sadru*) with 4 litres malt flour’, because then we have the problem that this mixture is apparently not used for the soaking or for anything else, since the text continues (l. 24–25) to tell us that the hide is steeped (*ṣarāpu*) in madder and alum. See the parallels *Bagh. Mitt. Beih.* 2, no. 5, rev. 28 and *KAR* 60, rev. 7–8, where no mention is made of this mixture with *bitqu*-flour, but the hide is directly steeped in ghee, alum and madder.

For *ḫūratu* ‘madder’ (Rubia tinctorum), cf. M. Stol, in *RlA* 6 (1980–1983), 534 f.

l. 25, *ta-ṣar-ra-pu* ‘You will steep (it)’ (with *-u* ending, although a singular is intended, see I, l. 5). Cf. *CAD*, Ṣ, 105a, c.

l. 26–28 and IV, 22–24, *maš-tu-ú* ‘pegs’, necessary to stretch the hide over the kettledrum. See *BE* VIII, 154 (list of objects used in a ritual), obv. 12: 10 *sik-kat šá mar-tu-ú* ‘10 pegs of *martû*-wood’.

l. 32, KUŠ.TAB.BA ‘bulls hide’, see M. Stol, in *RlA* 6 (1980–1983), 528; K. Radner, *SAA Studies* VI (1997), 192–3.

III

l. 1–14, for the beginning of column III, see A. Livingstone, *Mystical*, 200 ff. It is partially duplicated by or related to several other texts, which are discussed by A. Livingstone, *Mystical*, 187–204187–204: AO 17626, rev.(!) 1–6; IV R2, 23, no. 1 +, I, 1–6; *CT* 24, pl. 4–5, 29–36 (series AN = *Anum*); *TU* 47, obv. 10 ff.

See also *Bagh. Mitt. Beih.* 2, no. 8. The obv. 1′ff. is a partial duplicate of *TU* 47, obv. 6–11(?) (see W.R. Mayer, *Bagh. Mitt. Beih.* 2, p. 16 sub no. 8); for the reverse, horizontal, 1′–4′, see *TU* 47, reverse, lower right side and AO 17626, rev. (! see A. Livingstone, *Mystical*, 198–9) 1–6:

Obv.
1′ [...] ⌜x⌝ DI(?) ⌜x x⌝ [...]
2′ [... *ip-qi*]*d-da-á*[*š-šú*]
3′ [...dME]Š.LAM.TA.È.A
4′ [...TUŠ] KI!-*tì*

5′ [...]⌜x⌝
6′ [...]⌜x⌝

Rev.
horizontal:
1′ [^{d}ÙR.BÀD.DA ^{d}GUB.BA.GA.RA.]RA.È
2′ [^{d}DUMU.ZI ^{d}*A-nù* ^{d}KI]N.GU.GU ^{d}EN.ME.⌜ŠAR⌝.RA
3′ [^{d}MU.UM.MU ^{d}PAP.SUKKAL/^{d}*Il-lab-rat* ^{d}]AL.LA AN.ŠÁR
4′ [^{d}Á.SÀG *An-tu*$_{4}$ ^{d}UB-*n*]*a* ^{d}[LUGAL.DU$_{6}$.KÙ]

vertical:
1′ [*šá* (...) ^{d}Š]U.ZI.AN.NA
2′ [IGI-*šú*(-*nu*) *ana* IM.MA]⌜R.TU⌝ GAR-*nu*

For a discussion of these lines see II.5.2.

l. 17, ^{d}*Lumḫa* also written ^{d}BALAG 'the divine harp' in the duplicate *KAR* 60, obv. 14. See *RAcc.*, 49, n. 13; D.O. Edzard M. Krebernik, in: *RlA* 7 (1987–90), s.v. Lumḫa = BALAG = harp; also the god of the lamentation priests in An = Anum, II, 307.

l. 24, *ḫalṣu* (BÁR.GÉ) 'pressed', is usually written BÁR.GA.

l. 29, *te-ep-pu-uš* is mistakenly written without the subjunctive ending *-u*.

l. 31–33, cf. P.-A. Beaulieu, *ZA* 82 (1992), 98–111.

IV

l. 3 ff., here the enumeration of all the products and instruments which are needed for the above described ceremonies begins.

l. 6, ^{šim}*ka-ṣi-ṣi-ḫa-tu*$_{4}$ 'cassia', see M. Jursa, *NABU* 1997, no. 34: *kaṣī'atu* / *kaṣīḫātu*? 'Kassia, Zimtblüten'.

l. 18, '1 regular offering' (*gi-nu-ú*), not *qanû* (GI-*nu-ú*), see *AHw*, 290a, 4, b, contra *RAcc.*, 18.

l. 32, 5 *ṣa-bit* '5 gazelle (shaped) vessels (*ṣabītu*)(?), see *CAD*, Ṣ, 43b, d. Perhaps similar to *nam-ḫa-ri*.MEŠ *a-ri-bi* '*namḫaru*-vats (shaped like) raven'(?), in *TU* 39, obv. 10 (but also not certain)?

l. 37, see H. Hunger, *AOAT* 2, 47. For *uppuš*, see my comment on *BRM* 4, 7, rev. 43.

KAR 60 (VAT 8022)[31]

This text, found in Assur, and copied in the seventh century B.C., from an older Babylonian tablet for the library of Assurbanipal, describes the kettledrum ceremony (*lilissu*). It appears to be a shortened version of *TU* 44.

The text is discussed in II.5.

Obv.

1 BAD x [...]
2 A.MEŠ *ina maḫ-ri-šú-nu* [GUB-*an*]
3 ^{lú}GALA *ina* ÙB ZABAR NI [...]
4 ^{gi}KID.MÁ.ŠÚ.A ŠUB-*di ina* KI.TA ^{gi}K[ID.MÁ.ŠÚ.A *ba-aṣ-ṣa* DUB-*ak*]
5 Á.MEŠ ^{gi}KID.MÁ.ŠÚ.A ⸢*ba-aṣ*⸣-*ṣa* NIGIN-*mi* GU$_4$ *šá-a-š*[*u*]
6 *ina* UGU ^{gi}KID.MÁ.MAḪ *tuš-za-za-a-ma*
7 A.MEŠ A.GÚB.BA SÙ-*šu* KA-*šu te-me-es-si*
8 ZÌ.SUR.RA-*a ta-lam-me-šú* SIG$_4$ *ina* IGI-*šú* LAL-*aṣ*
9 NÍG.NA ^{šim}LI *ta-sár-raq* KAŠ SAG BAL-*qí*
10 ÉN GU$_4$.GAL GU$_4$.MAḪ Ú KI.ÚS KÙ.GA *ina* ^{gi}SAG.KUD GI DÙG.GA
11 *ana* ŠÀ GEŠTUG^{II} ZAG-*šú tu-làḫ-ḫaš*
12 ÉN GU$_4$ *i-lit-ti An-zi-i at-ta-ma*
13 *ina* ^{gi}SAG.KUD GI DÙG.GA *ina* ŠÀ GEŠTUG^{II} GÙB-*šú tu-làḫ-ḫaš*
14 ⸢*ina* IGI⸣ ^{d}BALAG LAL-*ma* ^{giš}ÚŠ EREN MÚ-*aḫ*
15 [G]U$_4$ *šá-a-šú ta-pal-laq-ma* ŠÀ-*šu ina* IGI ^{d}BALAG
16 [*i*]*na* ^{šim}LI *ta-sár-raq* KAŠ BAL-*qí*
17 ^{lú}GALA SAG.DU-*su i-paṭ-ṭar-ma*
18 [*ina ki*]*m-ṣi i-kam-me-es-ma ina re-ši-šu* GUB-*az-ma*

Rev.

1 MU.LU NÁ.A KI.MIN 3-*šú* ŠID-*nu*
2 *ù* EGIR-*šú ki-a-am* 3-*šú i-qab-bi*
3 [*e*]*p-še-e-ti an-na-a-ti* DÌM.ME.ER KÌLIB.BA *i-tep-pu-uš*
4 *a-na-ku ul e-pu-uš* A.MEŠ ÍL-*ma šid-da tu-na-ḫi*
5 KUŠ *šá-a-šú te-leq-qé-e-ma i-na* ZÌ KUM NISABA KÙ-*tì*
6 *ina* A.MEŠ KAŠ *u* GEŠTIN *reš-ti-i te-re-es-si-in*
7 *ina* Ì.NUN.NA $^{\text{gu}_4}$ÁB KÙ.GA IM.SAḪAR.NA$_4$.KUR.RA *šá* ^{kur}*Ḫat-ti*
8 *u* ^{giš}ḪAB *ta-ṣar-rap-ma* LI.LI.ÌZ ZABAR *ta-rim*
9 *ina* SA GÙB *šá* ^{uzu}GIŠ.KUN *ba-ab-šú ta-šap-pi*
10 *ina* ^{síg}GA.ZUM.AK.A ^{giš}GAG.MEŠ LI.LI.ÌZ ZABAR *tál-pap*
11 ŠE.GÍN ZÁLAG.GA *ta-ṣap-pi-ma tu-ta-ri*
12 *ina* ITI ŠE.GA UD ŠE.GA *tam-mar-ma*
13 NÍG.DÍM.DÍM.MA *an-na-a-ti tep-pu-uš*
14 UZU GU[$_4$] *šá-a-šu* ŠÚ.MAḪ NU GU$_7$
15 Á.È *bà*-⸢*ri*⸣(??) [...] ⸢EN(?)⸣ RU(?) NU ZU NU IGI-*mar*

Obv.

1 ... [...]
2 [You will set up] a water (basin) before them [...]

---

[31] Cf. *RAcc.*, 20–23; A.J. Sachs, in: J.B. Pritchard, *ANET*^{2}, 336. See also R. Borger, *HKL* 1, 98.

3 the lamentation priest in a bronze drum [...]
4 You will lay down a reed mat. Underneath the r[eed mat you will heap up sand].
5 You will surround the sides of the reed mat with sand. You will make that bull
6 stand on the reed mat and you will sprinkle it (l. 7)
7 with water from the holy water-basin. You will wash its mouth.
8 You will surround it with a magic circle of flour. You will set in place a brick in front of it.
9 (On) a censer you will scatter juniper. You will make a libation of first-quality beer.
10 You will whisper (l. 11), by means of a tube (made of) sweet reed, the incantation 'Great bull, choice bull, which treads on the pure meadow'
11 into its right ear.
12 You will whisper (l. 13) the incantation 'O bull, you are a descendant of Anzu'
13 into its left ear, by means of a tube (made of) sweet reed.
14 You will set in place (the bull) in front of Lumḫa and you will kindle cedar balsam.
15 You will cut open that [b]ull and you will scatter (l. 16) its heart in front of Lumḫa
16 with juniper. You will make a libation of beer.
17 The lamentation priest will uncover his head,
18 kneel down and stand at its head.Then

Rev.
1 he will recite three times 'He, who lies asleep'
2 and after this he will say three times thus:
3 'these ritual acts the totality-of-the-gods has performed,
4 I did not perform (them)'. (Then) you will lift up the water (basin) and loosen the curtains.
5 You will take the aforementioned hide and soak (it) (l. 6) with *isqūqu*-flour of pure grain
6 in water, beer and first-quality wine.
7 You will steep (it) (l. 8) in ghee from a pure cow, alum from the land of Ḫattu
8 and madder and you will cover the kettledrum (with it).
9 With the sinew left from (its) thigh you will fasten its opening.
10 You will wrap the pegs of the bronze kettledrum with carded wool.
11 You will dip (them) in white paint and place (them) back (in the kettledrum).
12 In an auspicious month you will look for a favourable day and
13 you will perform these ritual acts.
14 The chief singer of dirges will not eat from the meat of that bull.
(Colophon:)
15 Collated by(??) the novice [...] ... the person who is not competent may not see (it).

Comments

Obv.

l. 2, A.MEŠ *ina maḫ-ri-šú-nu* [GUB-*an*], as in *TU* 44, II, 7?

l. 4, the reconstruction follows *TU* 44, I, 12–13.

l. 14, MÚ-*aḫ* "you will kindle", or perhaps, with Thureau-Dangin, *RAcc.*, 20 f., a mistake for SÙ-*aḫ* "you will sprinkle", as in the parallel *TU* 44, II, 12 (cf. *CAD*, S, 86b, 2′).

l. 15–16, F. Thureau-Dangin (*RAcc.*, 53, n. 61) suggested that the scribe mistakenly omitted several words, and, based on *TU* 44, II, 17–18 and *KAR* 60, obv. 9, he restored: [G]U$_4$ *šá-a-šú ta-pal-laq-ma* ŠÀ-*šu ina* IGI ^{d}BALAG [*i*]*na* ^{šim}LI ⟨^{giš}EREN ZÌ.MAD.GÁ *ta-qal-la* NÍG.NA ^{šim}LI⟩ *ta-sár-raq*.

See also *CAD*, S, 173a: *ina* ^{šim}LI ⟨*ta-qal-la* NÍG.NA ^{šim}LI⟩ *ta-sár-raq*. However, one must ask whether a restoration is necessary, since the short version in *KAR* 60 can also be found in the Hellenistic parallel text *Bagh. Mitt. Beih.* 2, no. 5, rev. 22–3:

GU$_4$ *šá-a-šú ina* IGI LI.LI.ÌZ *t*[*a-pal-la*]*q-ma lìb-bi-šu ina* IGI LI.LI.ÌZ ^{šim}LI DUB-*aq*.

Also, the restoration by Thureau-Dangin includes the scattering of the censer, which, incidentally, does not occur in *TU* 44. However, in *KAR* 60 (obv. 9) and *Bagh. Mitt. Beih.* 2, no. 5 (rev. 19) this scattering had already taken place, long before the relevant passage with the heart of the bull is described.

If we assume correctly that the restoration is not necessary, then we have, with the passage discussed here, an indication for two separate versions. In the Uruk version *TU* 44 the heart is burned (*qalû*) together with juniper, cedar and *maṣḫatu*-flour, while in the Assur version *KAR* 60 and the other Uruk parallel *Bagh. Mitt. Beih.* 2, no. 5 the heart is scattered (*sarāqu*) with juniper. For an analysis and comparison of these texts see II.5.2.

l. 17, 'The lamentation priest will uncover his head', see *AHw*, 849b, 5, a and *CAD*, Q, 103a, 6′. See also *CAD*, K, 93a, 3′: 'The lamentation priest makes his hair disheveled'.

Rev.

l. 1, MU.LU NÁ.A 'He, who lies asleep', the text is recited in full in IV R^2, 23, no. 1 +, I, 27–32. Cf. J. Krecher, *Kultlyrik*, 25, n.39.

l. 8, LI.LI.ÌZ ZABAR *ta-rim*, as in the parallel *TU* 44, II, 25 (*tar-rim*). Cf. *CAD*, A/II, 228b, 1, a, and *AHw*, 64b; not *ta-ḫap*, as in *CAD*, Ḫ, 20a, 1 and *AHw*, 306a. See also *Bagh. Mitt. Beih.* 2, no. 5, rev. 28 (restored) and IV R^2, 23, no. 1 +, I, 8 (*te-rim*).

l. 9, *ina* SA GÙB *šá* ^{uzu}GIŠ.KUN 'With the sinew left from its thigh', as in the parallel *Bagh. Mitt. Beih.* 2, no. 5, rev. 29. Different in *TU* 44, II, 30: *ina* SA ^{uzu}GIŠ.KUN GÙB-*šú* 'With the sinew from its left thigh'. See W. Farber, *TUAT* II/2, 236, l. 29.

l. 10–15, these lines are partially duplicated by *Bagh. Mitt. Beih.* 2, no. 5, rev. 29–31, and also by another fragment from Hellenistic Uruk, *Bagh. Mitt. Beih.* 2, no. 7, obv. 2–9:

Obv.
1′ […] x […]
2′ [*ina* ^{sig}]GA.ZUM.AK.[A ^{giš}GAG.MEŠ LI.LI.ÌZ ZABAR *tál-pap*]
3′ […] x NA Ù ŠÁ UD x[…]
4′ […] LI.LI.ÌZ ZA[BAR …]
5′ [… *ina* ITI ŠE.GA UD] ŠE.GA *tam-mar-ma* NÍG.[DÍM.DÍM.MA *an-na-a-ti tep-pu-uš*]
6′ [… UZU] GU$_4$ *šá-a-šú* [ŠÚ.MAḪ NU GU$_7$]
7′ […] NU ZU-*ú* N[U IGI …]
8′ […L]I.LI.Ì[Z ZABAR(?)…]
9′ […] GU$_4$ […]

l. 14, ŠÚ.MAḪ the 'chief singer of dirges' (*galamāḫu*) is lost in the duplicate *Bagh. Mitt. Beih.* 2, no. 7, obv. 6, but is also attested many times in Hellenistic rituals, although usually written $^{\text{(lú)}}$GALA (UŠ.KU).MAḪ, see *AHw*, 273–4 and *CAD*, G, 19–20 (here our reference *KAR* 60, rev. 14 is mistakenly transliterated LÚ.UŠ.KU.MAḪ). Cf. also *CAD*, Š/III, 120b, c. See also H. Hunger, *AOAT* 2, nos. 499, 5 and 524, 2, with two more examples of ŠÚ.MAḪ.

KAR 50 (VAT 8247)[32]

This Neo-Assyrian text, found in Assur, was copied from an older Babylonian text in the seventh century for the library of Assurbanipal. It is apparently a shortened version of the kettledrum ritual (*lilissu*). On the obverse we find a bilingual incantation for 'the choice bull, the creation of the great gods'. The reverse describes the actual ritual.

The text is discussed in II.5.

Obv.

1 ÉN GU$_4$.MAḪ ZA DÍM.MA DIMMER.GAL.[GAL.E.NE]
2 *at-ta gu-um-m*[*a-ḫ*]*u bi-nu-ut* [DINGIR.MEŠ GAL.MEŠ]
3 DÍM.ME.BI KIM$_x$.MA DIMMER.GA[L].GAL.E.N[E …]
4 *tab-ba-ni-ma ana š*[*i-pir* DING]IR.MEŠ GAL.[MEŠ …]
5 AN ALAM GARZA ^{d}A.NU.TA.KE$_4$ […]
6 *ina* AN-*e ṣa-lam-ka a-na pa-ra-aṣ* ^{d}*A-nu-*[*ti* …]
7 UD AN ^{d}EN.LÍL.LÁ ^{d}EN.KI ^{d}NIN.MAḪ NAM DIMMER.GAL.[GAL.E.NE …]
8 *i-nu* ^{d}MIN ^{d}MIN ^{d}MIN *u* ^{d}MIN *ši-mit* DINGIR.MEŠ GAL.MEŠ [*i-ši-mu*]
9 KUŠ.ZU SA ḪAL.GA DIMMER.GAL.GAL.E.NE NAM TAR.TAR […]
10 *ma-šak-ka ši-ir-an-ka ana pi-riš-ti* DINGIR.MEŠ GAL.MEŠ *iš-*⌜*šá*⌝*-a-mu*
11 UD.ḪAL.DIMMER.BI UD DA.IR.E[Š] ZA.GI.NA
12 *ina pi-riš-ti* DINGIR.BI *ana* UD.MEŠ *da-ru-ú-tú ku-ú-ni*
13 ALAM DIMMER KI.ŠEŠ.BI NAM TAR.TAR.E.NE
14 *ṣa-lam šu-ú it-ti* DINGIR.MEŠ ŠEŠ.MEŠ-*šú ši-mit ši-mu*
15 DIMMER.BI ⌜ZAG.GU⌝.LA.BI MU.UN.SIKIL MU.UN.DADAG
16 DINGIR *šu-ú e-šèr-ti-šú li-lil li-bi-ib*
17 EME.ḪUL.GÁL BAR.ŠÈ ḪÉ.EN.TA.GUB

Rev.

1 DÙ.DÙ.BI *ina* ITI SI.SÁ *ina u$_4$-mi* DÙG.GA *ina šèr-ti*
2 *la-am* ^{d}UTU KUR-*ḫa* 3 GI.DU$_8$ *ana* ^{d}*É-a* ^{d}UTU
3 *u* ^{d}ASAL.LÚ.ḪI *tar-kás* ZÚ.LUM.MA ^{zi}EŠA DUB-*aq*
4 NINDA.Ì.DÉ.A LÀL Ì.NUN.NA GAR-*an* 3 UDU.NÍTA.MEŠ BABBAR.MEŠ
5 BAL-qí ^{uzu}ZAG.LU *ḫi-in-ṣa u šu-me-e* TE-*ḫi*
6 NÍG.NA ^{šim}LI GAR-*an* ZÌ.MAD.GÁ *ta-sár-raq*
7 *šid-du* GÍD.DA-*ad* ZÌ.DUB.DUB.BU ŠUB.ŠUB-*di*
8 GU$_4$.MAḪ *ana* KI *par-si tuš-za-az-ma ana* ŠÀ GEŠTUG^{II} XV-*šú* (*u* 2,30-*šú*)
9 3.TA.ÀM *tu-làḫ-ḫàš gu-ma-ḫu* KUD-*is-ma*
10 ⌜*ma-áš-ku*⌝ *u šír-a-nu ana šip-ri šá-a-šú* [T]I-*qí*
11 ÉN KAR.ZA.GÌN.NA ⌜KAR x⌝ […]

Obv.

1–2 Incantation: You are the choice bull, the creation of [the great gods].
3–4 You were created for the wo[rk of the great go]ds.
5–6 In heaven your statue … for the rites of the Anu-worship.

[32] Cf. *RAcc.*, 22–25; A.J. Sachs, in: J.B. Pritchard, *ANET*^{2}, 336 f. See also R. Borger, *HKL* 1, 98. The text is partly duplicated by K 6060 (*BBR* 2, no. 56) + K 10820 (unpublished), see Plate II. For details see my comments on the text.

7–8 When Anu, Enlil, Enki and Ninmaḫ [decreed] the fate of the great gods,
9–10 your hide and your sinew have been assigned to the mystery of the great gods.
11–12 Abide for eternity in the mystery of that god!
13–14 The fate of that statue has been decreed (together) with its fellow gods.
15–16 May the sanctuary of that god become pure, become clean!
17 May the evil tongue stand aside!

Rev.
1 The pertinent ritual: in a proper month, on a good day, in the morning,
2 before sunrise, you will arrange (l. 3) 3 offering tables for Ea, Šamaš,
3 and Marduk. (On these tables) you will scatter dates (and) *sasqû*-flour.
4 You will place a *mirsu*-confection (made with) honey (and) ghee. You will offer (l. 5) 3 white sheep.
5 You will bring shoulder, *ḫimṣu*-omentum and roasted meat near.
6 You will place a censer (with) juniper; you will scatter *maṣḫatu*-flour.
7 You will draw the curtains shut. You will repeatedly pour heaps of flour.
8 You will make the choice bull stand in a secluded place and you will whisper (l. 9) in its right (and left) ear
9 three times (the 2 pertinent incantations). Then you will slaugter the choice bull and
10 you will [ta]ke (its) hide and sinew for that work.
11 Incantation: 'The Pure Quay' … […]'.

Comments

Obv.

l. 1–2, GU$_4$.MAḪ NÍG(!? Copy: ZA).DÍM.MA // *at-ta gu-um-m*[*a-ḫ*]*u bi-nu-ut*, see 4R 25, III, 58 f.: NÍG.DÍM.DÍM.MA // *bi-nu-ut* DINGIR 'divine creation'.

l. 3, the Sumerian differs from the Akkadian version: 'Whose creation is the work of the great gods'.

DÍM.ME.BI, for ME, which stands for MA, see A. Poebel, *Grundzüge der sumerischen Grammatik*, Rostock, 1923, p.12, § 16. Or simply a mistake as in obv. 8, 9, 11, 14?

l. 8 and 14, *ši-mit* perhaps a scribal error for *ši-mat*? The scribe made more mistakes, see my comments on obv. 9 and 11.

l. 9, ḪAL.GA // *pi-riš-ti*, normally written AD.ḪAL, or ḪAL. See also obv. 11.

l. 11 - rev. 10, these lines are duplicate of the Nineveh text K 6060 (*BBR* 2, no. 56) + K 10820 (unpublished), but obv. 11–12 and 13–14 appear to be interchanged in the duplicate. See plate II.

l. 11, or perhaps better: "*Be faithful* forever to that divine secret". UD stands for AD in AD.ḪAL // *pi-riš-ti*. IR in DA.IR stands for RÍ, as is clear from the duplicate K 10820, obv. x + 3: DA.R[Í.EŠ.

l. 13–14, *ši-mit ši-mu* "has been decreed", following *CAD*, Ṣ, 84, c, rather than *CAD*, Š, 361, 2′, a', where an imperative is assumed.

l. 15–16 = K 10820, obv. x + 5–6, the Sumerian differs from the Akkadian version, the precative prefix is missing: 'his sanctuary will become pure, become clean'. See also obv. 17.

l. 17, 'May the evil tong stand aside', i.e. 'leave'. The duplicate K 6060 + 10820 reads obv. x + 8: [...] *li-šá-nu le-mut-tú ina a-ḫa-t*[*i* GUB]. See *RAcc.*, 24, n. a, and *CAD*, L, 211b, c with more parallels.

Rev.

l. 1, *ina* ITI SI.SÁ *ina* u_4*-mi* DÙG.GA, usually written *ina* ITI *šal-mu*/*-me*/ŠE.GA (*ina*) u_4*-mu*/UD ŠE.GA, cf. *KAR* 60, rev. 12, and *KAR* 50, rev. 1; *Bagh. Mitt. Beih.* 2, no. 5, obv. 7; no. 7, obv. 5′; no. 10, obv. 2; *TU* 45, obv. 2; *TU* 46, obv. 2, 23, rev. 2; F.H. Weissbach, *Misc.*, no.12, obv. 3; *SpTU* 4, no. 141, rev. 15.

l. 8, *ana* KI *par-si* 'in a secluded place', see my comment to *TU* 45, obv. 6.

l. 8, (*u* 2,30-*šú*) is written only in K 6060 + 10820, rev. 4.

l. 9, '(the 2 pertinent incantations)', namely: GU_4.GAL GU_4.MAḪ Ú KI.ÚS KÙ.GA (cf. *TU* 44, II, 9; *Bagh. Mitt. Beih.* 2, no. 5, rev. 19; *KAR* 60, obv. 10) and GU_4 *i-lit-*tu_4 *An-zi-i at-ta-ma* (cf. *TU* 44, II, 10; *Bagh. Mitt. Beih.* 2, no. 5, rev. 21; *KAR* 60, obv. 12).

l. 11, KAR.ZA.GÌN.NA 'The Pure Quay' or 'The Quay of Lapis Lazuli', a sacred quay located at Eridu, Nippur, Ur and Lagaš, see A.R. George, *House Most High*, no. 568. See also Å.W. Sjöberg, *Mondgott*, 103; A.J. Ferrara, *Nanna-Suen's Journey*, Rome, 1973, 128–9; M.W. Green, *Eridu in Sumerian Literature*, Chicago, 1975, 185 (who, incidentally, reads the traces before the break as '[d]En-[ki]', but the copy does not allow this reading). For the É.KAR.ZA.GÌN.NA, the temple of Ea within Esagila at Babylon, see A.R. George, *House Most High*, no. 569. Also two É.ZA.GÌN.(NA)-temples are known, see A.R. George, *House Most High*, nos. 1219 and 1220.

Bagh. Mitt. Beih. 2, no. 5 (W 20030/4)[33]

This text from Hellenistic Uruk is a shortened version of the kettledrum ritual (*lilissu*). The owner of the tablet is Anu-bēlšunu, son of Nidintu-Anu, of the Sîn-lēqe-unnīni family, and is dated 10(?)-VII-150 S.E. (8-X-162 B.C.) He is also attested in *Bagh. Mitt. Beih.* 2, no. 89, dated 147 S.E. (165/4 B.C.) He is the grandson of Anu-bēlšunu who wrote *Bagh. Mitt. Beih.* 2, no. 12, dated 112 S.E., *TU* 45, with an incomplete date, and *TU* 46, dated 81 S.E. (see the introductions of these texts, below).[34] The text is partially duplicated by *TU* 44, I–II and *KAR* 60.

The text is discussed in II.5.

U.E.
[...] x x [...]
u šu-ut(?) [...]

Obv.
1 *e-nu-ma* ⸢LI⸣.[LI.ÌZ ZABAR *a-na a-ra-mi* IGI-*k*]*a*
2 GU$_4^!$ ŠU.DU$_7$ GE$_6$ ⸢*šá* ^{giš}UMBIN⸣.MEŠ *u* SI.MEŠ-*šú šal*-⸢*me*$^!$⸣
3 TA SAG.DU-*šú* EN *ap-pi* KUN-*šu* ^{lú}UM.ME.A *mu-du-ú it-ta-nap-la-su-ma*
4 *šum-ma* KUŠ-*šú* SÍG GE$_6$ *a-na* GARZA *u ki-du-de-e il-leq-qé*
5 *šum-ma* 7 SÍG BABBAR *ki-ma* MUL *ta-kip ina* ^{giš}NÍG.GIDRU *ma-ḫi-iṣ ina qin-na-zu la-pit*
6 ⸢*a-na*⸣ GARZA ⸢*u*⸣ *ki-du-de-e ul* TI-*qé*
7 [*e-nu-m*]*a* GU$_4$ *a-na* É *mu-um-mu tu-šèr-ri-ba ina* ITI *šal-me ina* UD ŠE.GA
8 [*ina* Á GU$_4$] ⸢ZI.GA⸣ KI *tu*-⸢*qád*⸣-*da-áš* A KÙ SÙ-*uḫ* 12 SIG$_4$ LAL-*aṣ*
9 [12 GADA] *ina muḫ-ḫi* ŠUB-*di* DINGIR.MEŠ 12-*šú-nu ina muḫ-ḫi tu-še-šeb*
10 [...]⸢x.MEŠ⸣ *tuš-za-zi* 2 DINGIR.MEŠ DINGIR GÍD.DA ŠU ⸢GÍD(?)⸣.DA ⸢GÍD(?)⸣.DA
11 [7 DINGIR.MEŠ DUMU ^{d}E]N.ME.ŠÁR.RA ZÌ.DUB.DUB.BU.MEŠ *tu-sar-raq*
12 [12] G[I.DU$_8$ GUB-*an*] 7.TA.A.⟨AN⟩ *šá* ŠE.BAR 7.TA.ÀM NINDA ZÍZ.ÀM NINDA.Ì.DÉ.ÀM
13 ⸢LÀL Ì.NUN.NA ZÚ.LUM.MA ^{zì}EŠA⸣ DUB-*aq* KAŠ *u* GEŠTIN GUB-*an*
12 ^{udu}SÍSKUR BAL-*qí*
14 ^{uzu}ZAG.LU ^{uzu}ME.ḪÉ *u* ^{uzu}K[A.NE *t*]*u-ṭaḫ-ḫa* ŠE.BAR ŠE.MUNU$_4$(?) ZÍZ.ÀM GAR-*an*
15 SÍG S[A$_5$(?) SÍ]G ZA.GÌN.NA x x x [...]x SIG$_4$.MEŠ DUB-*aq* A.MEŠ *maḫ-ri-šú-nu tu-kan-nu*
16 ^{gi}KID.MÁ.ŠÚ.A ŠUB-*di ina* KI.TA ^{gi}KID.MÁ.ŠÚ.A [*ba-a*]*ṣ-ṣa* DUB-*ak* Á.MEŠ ^{gi}KID.MÁ.ŠÚ.A ŠUB-*di*
17 [*ba-aṣ*]-*ṣa ta-lam-mi* GU$_4^!$ *šá-a-šú ina muḫ-ḫi* ^{gi}KID.MÁ.ŠÚ.A *tuš-za-as-su-ma*

Rev.
18 ⸢A.MEŠ⸣ ^{dug}A.GÚ[B.BA] ⸢*ta-sal*⸣-*làḫ-šú* KA-[*šú te-me-es-si* ZÌ.SUR.R]A *ta-lam-mi-iš* SIG$_4$ LAL-*aṣ*
19 NÍG.NA ^{šim}LI *ta-s*[*ár*]-*raq* KAŠ S[AG BAL-*q*]*í* ÉN ⸢GU$_4$⸣.GAL ⟨GU$_4$⟩.MAḪ Ú KI.⟨ÚS⟩ KÙ.GA {UŠ KU}
20 *ina* ^{gi}SAG.KUD GI DÙG.GA *a*-[*na lìb-bi* GEŠTU]G^{II} ZAG-*šú tu-làḫ-ḫaš* EGIR-*šú*

[33] Cf. W. Farber, *TUAT* II, 2, 234 ff.
[34] For both Anu-bēlšunu's see L. E. Pearce–L. T. Doty, in *Festschrift J. Oelsner*, AOAT, Bd. 252, Münster, 2000, 331–341.

21 ÉN GU$_4$! ⸢*i-lit-tu$_4$ An-zi*⸣-[*i at-t*]*a-ma ina* ^{gi}SAG.KUD GI DÙG.GA *a-na lìb-bi* GEŠTUG^{II} GÙB-*šú tu-làḫ-ḫaš*
22 LI.LI.ÌZ [ZABA]R ÚŠ ^{giš}EREN SÙ-*aḫ-šú* GU$_4$! *šá-a-šú ina* IGI LI.LI.ÌZ
23 *t*[*a-pal-la*]*q-ma lìb-bi-šu ina* IGI LI.LI.ÌZ ^{šim}LI DUB-*aq* KAŠ BAL-*qí*
24 [...]⸢x⸣ KU DU
25 [EGI]R(?)-*šú ep-še-e-ti an-na-a-tú*
26 ⸢A⸣.MEŠ ÍL-⸢*ma*⸣ *ŠID*-⸢*da*⸣ *tu*-⸢*na-ḫu*⸣
27 [KUŠ *šá*]-⸢*a*⸣-*šú ta-leq*!-*qé-e-ma ina* ZÌ KUM ^{d}NISABA KÙ *ina* A.MEŠ KAŠ GEŠTIN *reš-tú*!-*ú ta-re-es-si*-⸢*in*⸣
28 [*ina* Ì.NUN.NA ^{gu_4}ÁB] KÙ-*tì* IM.SAḪAR.NA$_4$.KUR.RA *šá* ^{kur}*Ḫat-ti u* ^{giš}ḪAB *ta-ṣar-rap-ma* LI.LI.ÌZ ZA[BAR (⸢UD⸣.[K]A.[BAR]) *tar-rim*]
29 ⸢*ina* SA GÙB⸣ *šá* ^{uzu}GIŠ.KUN KÁ-*šú ta*-⸢*šap*⸣-*pi* ⸢^{giš}⸣NAGAR ^{giš}GAG.MEŠ LI.LI.ÌZ [ZABAR *tál-pap*]
30 ŠE.⸢GÍN *ta-ṣab-bi* Ì.GIŠ(?) ZÁLAG.G⸣A *ta-lap-pat-ma a-na lìb-bi* LI.LI.ÌZ *tu-ta-a*-⸢*ri*⸣
31 *ina* ITI [*šal*]-*me* UD ŠE.GA [*ep-še-e*]-*ti an-na-a-ti tep-pu-uš* UZU GU$_4$! *šá-a-šú ina* 1-*en* T[ÚG.KUR.RA SA$_5$ *tál-pap*(?)]
32 *ta*-[...] x x x [...] Ì.GIŠ *gu*-⟨*un*⟩-*nu ana* ŠÀ-*šú* ⸢ŠUB⸣-*di ta-qeb*-[*bir* ...IGI-*šú*]
33 *a-na* IGI ^{d}[UTU.ŠÚ.A GAR-*an* DIRI-*rat* KUŠ.TA]B.BA(?) *it-ti-šu ta-qeb-bir*

R.E.
34 [I]M ^{Id}LX-EN-*šú-nu* A *šá* ⸢^{I}NÍG.SUM.MU-^{d}LX⸣ [A ^{Id}XXX-TI-ÉR] ⸢UNUG^{ki}(?)⸣ ^{iti}DU$_6$ ⟨UD⟩.10.KAM(?)
35 [MU].1 ME 50.KAM ^{I}*An-t*[*i-i-ku-su* LUGAL ...] ⸢x x x⸣-*šú*

U.E.
[...] ... [...]
... [...]

Obv.
1 When y[ou want to cover the kettledrum (proceed as follows)].
2 A knowledgeable expert will carefully inspect (l. 3) an ungelded black bull, whose horns and hooves are intact,
3 from its head to the tip of its tail;
4 if its hide (consists only) of black hair, it will be taken for the rites and rituals.
5 If it is spotted with 7 white tufts (which look) like stars, (or if) it has been struck with a stick (or) touched with a whip,
6 it will not be taken for the rites and rituals.
7 [Whe]n you want to make the bull enter the workshop, in an auspicious month, on a favourable day,
8 you will step up [to the side of the bull], you will make the ground ritually clean, sprinkle it with pure water. You will set in place 12 bricks.
9 On (the 12 bricks) you will lay down [12 linen] (cloths). On them you will make the 12 gods sit.
10 [...] ... you will make stand. 2 gods ... you will make long(?) ...
11 You will scatter [the 7 gods, sons of E]nmešarra (represented by) heaps of flour.
12 [You will set up 12] offering ta[bles]. You will scatter (l. 13) 7 loaves of barley (and) emmer bread each, (together with) a *mirsu*-confection (made with)
13 honey, ghee, dates (and) *sasqû*-flour. You will set up beer and wine. You will make 12 sheep offerings.

14 [Y]ou will bring shoulder, *ḫimṣu*-omentum and r[oasted meat] near. You will place barley (and) emmer malt.
15 (A piece of cloth of) r[ed(?)] and blue wool … […] you will scatter on the bricks. You will set up a water (basin) in front of them.
16 You will lay down a reed mat. Under the reed mat you will heap up [sa]nd. You will lay down the sides of the reed mat
17 (and) surround (it) with [sa]nd. You will make that bull stand on the reed mat and

Rev.
18 sprinkle it (with) water from the holy wat[er-basin]. You will [wash its] mouth. You will surround it with [a magic circle of flo]ur. You will set in place a brick (in front of it).
19 You will sc[at]ter a censer (with) juniper. [You will make a lib]ation of fir[st quality] beer. In[to its] right [ear] you will whisper, by means of a tube (made of) sweet reed (l. 20), the incantation 'Great bull, choice bull, which treads upon the pure meadow';
20 after this
21 you will whisper the incantation 'O bull, [yo]u are a descendant of Anzu' into its left ear, by means of a tube (made of) sweet reed.
22 You will sprinkle the [bronz]e kettledrum (with) cedar balsam. You will (then) c[ut ope]n (l. 23) that bull in front of the kettledrum
23 and you will scatter its heart in front of the kettledrum (with) juniper. You will make a libation of beer.
24 […] …
25 [After] this(?) (he will say three times thus)(?) 'these ritual acts (…)'.
26 (Then) you will lift up the water (basin) and loosen the curtains.
27 You will take [th]at [hide] and soak (it) with *isqūqu*-flour of pure grain in water, beer and first-quality wine.
28 You will steep (it) [in ghee from a] pure [cow], alum from the land of Ḫattu (and) madder and [you will cover] the bro[nze] kettledrum (with it).
29 With the sinew left from (its) thigh you will fasten its opening. [You will wrap] the pegs [of the bronze] kettledrum in acorn-shape.
30 You will soak (them) in paint and smear (them) with ritually pure oil(?) and place them back in the kettledrum.
31 In an [ausp]icious month, on a favourable day you will perform these [ritual ac]ts. (Then) [you will wrap(?)] the meat of that bull in a [red … cloth].
32 […] You will pour ordinary oil over it (and then) you will bur[y] (it) […].
33 [You will place its face(l. 32)] towards [the West. The remainder of the bulls hide(?)] you will bury with it.

R.E.
(Colophon:)
34 [Tab]let of Anu-bēlšunu, son of Nidintu-Anu, descendant of Sîn-lēqe-unnīni. Uruk, the (seventh) month Tašrītu, day 10(?),
35 year 150 of An[tiochus …] …

Comments

U.E.

u šu-ut, perhaps referring to the well known phrase *ṣâtu u šūt pî* 'explanatory words and comments'? Cf. *AHw*, 872b, B, m; ib., 1097a, B; *CAD*, Ṣ, 119, 2; G. Meier, *AfO* 12 (1937–39), 237 ff.; H. Hunger, *AOAT* 2, 173a and 177b.

Obv.

l. 2, GU$_4$!, the copy has GA (see also obv. 17; rev. 19; 21; 22; 31), but written correctly in obv. 7. The scribe made more mistakes, see for example obv. 12; rev. 19; 27; 32; R.E. 34.

l. 2, *šal-*⌜*me*!⌝, the copy reads: *šal-*⌜IGI⌝. Cf. *TU* 44, I, 2.

l. 7, see *TU* 44, I, 7; *Bagh. Mitt. Beih.* 2, no. 7, rev. 7; IV R^2, 23, no. 1 +, IV, 25.

l. 8, [ina Á GU$_4$] ⌜ZI.GA⌝, cf. *TU* 44, I, 8. W. Farber, *TUAT* II/2, 234 apparently reads: [Á.GÚ].ZI.GA, '(gleich) morgens …'

l. 8, *tu-*⌜*qád*⌝*-da-áš*, 'you will make ritually clean'; the duplicate (*TU* 44, I, 8) reads *tašabbiṭ* (SAR), 'you will sweep'.

l. 8, LAL-*aṣ*, a singular, although a plural is intended. See the correct singular in rev. 18 and the parallel *KAR* 60, obv. 8.

l. 11, this line, but without the verb, is also attested in IV R^2, 23, no. 1 +, I, 6. *Zidubdubbû* is often connected with the verb *nadû* 'to pour' (see *CAD*, N/I, 75; *AHw*, 707; see also *CAD*, Z, 107–108; St. M. Maul, *Zukunftsbewältigung*, 56). Because this line has the phrase ZÌ.DUB.DUB.BU.MEŠ *sarāqu*, McEwan suggests that ZÌ.DUB.DUB.BU.MEŠ should be interpreted here, and perhaps also in some other references, as *qēm serqi* 'flour offerings' rather than *zidubdubbû* 'heaps of flour', since the phrase *serqa sarāqu* is well-known (*BiOr* 38 [1981], 639–40). However, *nadû* and *sarāqu* render similar meanings, and the context much more suggests 'heaps of flour' as representatives of the seven children of Enmešarra then 'flour offerings'; this is confirmed by the seven circles on the reverse of *TU* 47, which stand for the seven children of Enmešarra (see obv. 10–15); these circles probably symbolize heaps of flour. So, in the case of *Bagh. Mitt. Beih.* 2, no. 5, obv. 11 we prefer the reading *zidubdubbû* for ZÌ.DUB.DUB.BU.

Zidubdubbû is also attested in the eclipse of the moon ritual *BRM* 4, 6, rev. 45 (see also 46), connected with the verb *nadû*. See also *Bagh. Mitt. Beih.* 2, no. 1 (+ //), 23 (with *nadû*), and *KAR* 50, rev. 7 (with *nadû*).

For the mythological background of pouring these heaps of flour, see W.G. Lambert, *JSS* 13 (1968), 104–112, especially 109 ff.

l. 12–13, for *tasarraq* (DUB-*aq*), 'you will scatter', the duplicate (*TU* 44, I, 18) has *tašakkan* (GAR-*an*), 'you will place', which in this context with loaves seems better. See my comment on *TU* 44, I, 18.

Rev.

l. 22, *ina* IGI LI.LI.ÌZ, see the duplicate *KAR* 60, obv. 14: *ina* IGI ^{d}Lumḫa (BALAG). Cf. also *TU* 47, rev., where ^{d}LILIZ is the representation of the kettledrum (*lilissu*).

l. 23, see my comment on *KAR* 60, obv. 15–16.

l. 24–25, these incomplete lines seem to contain a shorter version of the duplicate *KAR* 60, obv. 17–18, rev. 1–4: 'The lamentation priest will uncover his head, kneel down and stand at its head.Then he will recite three times: 'He, who lies down' and after this he will say three times thus: "these ritual acts the totality-of-the-gods has performed, I did not perform (them)"'. Cf. W. Farber, *TUAT* II/2, 235 with n. 24–25a.

l. 26, *tu-*⸢*na-ḫu*⸣, although the parallel *KAR* 60, rev. 4 has *tu-naḫ-ḫi*, the sign here appears to be -*ḫu*.

l. 27, *ta-leq*$^{!}$*-qé-e-ma*, the copy reads: *di*.

l. 27, *reš-tú*$^{!}$*-ú*, the copy reads: *reš-te-ú*.

l. 28, '[you will co]ver the bro[nze] kettledrum (with it)', see the duplicates *TU* 44, II, 25 and *KAR* 60, rev. 8.

l. 29, ⸢^{giš}⸣NAGAR 'in acorn-shape' (*allānu*). See W. Farber, *TUAT* II/2, 236, who translates: 'in Zäpfchenform'.

l. 30, ŠE.⸢GÍN *ta*⸣-[*ṣab-bi* Ì.GIŠ(?) ZÁLAG.G]A *ta-lap-pat-ma*, see W. Farber, *TUAT* II/2, 236: '[tränkst sie] mit Farbe, schmierst (sie) [mit rei]nem [*Öl*]'. See also *KAR* 60, rev. 11: ŠE.⸢GÍN⸣ [ZÁLAG.G]A *ta-ṣap-pi-ma* (in the Neo-Assyrian dialect *ṣapû* stands for *ṣabû*).

l. 31, *ina* ITI [*šal*]-*me* UD ŠE.GA [*ep-še-e*]-*ti an-na-a-ti tep-pu-uš*. There is not enough space for *tam-mar-ma* or IGI-*ma* as in the duplicate *KAR* 60, rev. 12–13:

> *ina* ITI ŠE.GA UD ŠE.GA *tam-mar-ma* NÍG.DÍM.DÍM.MA *an-na-a-ti tep-pu-uš*
>
> 'In an auspicious month you will look for a favourable day and perform these ritual acts'.

See also *Bagh. Mitt. Beih.* 2, no. 7, obv. 5′: [… *ina* ITI *šal-me*/ŠE.GA UD] ŠE.GA *tam-mar-ma* NÍG.[DÍM.DÍM.MA *an-na-a-ti tep-pu-uš*].

l. 31–33, see the duplicate *TU* 44, II, 19–21. In l. 31 we have restored: *ina* 1-*en* T[ÚG.KUR.RA SA$_5$ *tál-pap*(?)], although the duplicate has *ta-qeb-bir* (l. 19), because the burying of the meat is described in the following line 32. See W. Farber, *TUAT* II/2, 236: 'wicke[lst] du' (*lapāpu*).

l. 33, DIRI-*rat* KUŠ.TAB.BA 'the remainder of the bulls hide'(?), see the duplicate *TU* 44, II, 32.

Pinches, IV R^2, 23, no. 1 (K 4806)[35] + K 9421[36]

This text is a partly bilingual ritual text from Nineveh and was copied from an older Babylonian tablet. Several recitations, known from the kettledrum ritual texts, are presented here in full.

The text is discussed in II.5.

I.[37]

1 [^{d}ÙR.BÀD.ḪUM.ḪUM DUMU É.ŠÀ.BA.KE$_4$: ^{d}NIN.ŠAR DUMU É.ŠÀ.BA]
2 [^{d}GUB.BA.GA.RA.R]A.È DU[MU URU.GIBIL$_4$.LA].KE$_4$
3 [^{d}NIN].KA.[SI] DUMU URU *eš-ši*
4 ^{d}É.BAR.RA.LAḪ$_5$ DUMU UD.30.KAM UD.NÁ.ÀM
5 ^{d}NUSKU DUMU *še-la-še-e bu-ub-bu-lu*$_4$

---

6 7 DINGIR.MEŠ DUMU ^{d}EN.ME.ŠÁR.RA ZÌ.DUB.DUB.BU

---

7 12 DINGIR.MEŠ ZABAR *a-na* ŠÀ LILIZ ZABAR ŠUB-*ma*
8 LILIZ ZABAR *te-rim*

---

9 GU$_4$.GAL GU$_4$.MAḪ Ú KI.ÚS KÙ.GA
10 GU$_4$.GAL-*lu*$_4$ GU$_4$.MAḪ-*ḫu ka-bi-is ri-te* KÙ-*tì*
11 ŠÀ.TÚM DIB.DIB.A ḪÉ.GÁL DAGAL.LA
12 *ib-ta-ʾ qer-bé-ti mu-kil* ḪÉ.GÁL-*li*
13 ^{d}DU$_7$.ŠÁR.RA URU$_4$.A A.GÀR ḪI.LI.A
14 *e-ri-iš* ^{d}NISABA *mu-šáḫ-li-lu* A.GÀR
15 ŠU.MU DADAG.GA IGI.ZU BAL.BAL.E
16 *qa-ta-a-a* KÙ.MEŠ *iq-qa-a ma-ḫar-ka*

---

17 INIM ABZU *šá* ŠÀ GEŠTUG^{II} GU$_4$ *šá* ZAG *šá* LILIZ ZABAR *a-ra-mi*
18 *i-na* ^{giš}SAG.KUD GI DÙG.GA *tu-làḫ-ḫaš*

---

19 GU$_4$ *i-lit-ti An-zi-i at-ta-ma*
20 *a-na par-ṣi ki-du-de-e na-šu-ka*
21 *a-na da-riš* ^{d}NIN.GIZ.ZI.DA *ib-ri-ka*
22 *a-na* DINGIR.MEŠ GAL.MEŠ GIŠ.ḪUR.MEŠ *ú-ṣu-ri*
23 *a-na* DINGIR.MEŠ *mu*(?)-*ši-im par-ṣi šá* AN-*e ù* KI-*tì*
24 [GU]$_4$ *an-nu-u ana* ^{d}BALAG *lip-pa-qid-ma*
25 [...]-*šú* ÙB-*šú* DA DIŠ ŠE *a-na* ^{d}EN *liq-da-ʾ-iš*

---

26 [INIM A]BZU *šá* ŠÀ GEŠTU[G^{II} G]U$_4$ *šá* GÙB *šá* LILIZ ZABAR *a-ra-mi*

---

27 [MU.LU] NÁ.A E.LUM MU.LU NÁ.A ÈN.ŠÈ BA.AN.NÁ.A
28 [*šá*] *ṣal-lu be-lu*$_4$ *šá ṣal-lu*$_4$ *a-di ma-ti ṣa-lil*

---

35 Collated. Cf. F. Thureau-Dangin, *RAcc.*, 24–33; A.J. Sachs, in: J.B. Pritchard, *ANET*^{2} 337f. See also R. Borger, *HKL* 1, 403.

36 This is an unpublished fragment (cf. R. Borger, *BiOr* 30 [1973], 176a), covering lines I, 22–27, and IV, 6–15. See plate III.

37 The copy does not show the first lost line; so col. I, 1 in the copy is here col. I, 2. See *RAcc.*, 24–5.

29 KUR.GAL A.A ^{d}MU.UL.LÍL.LÁ MU.LU NÁ.A ÈN.ŠÈ
30 KUR-*ú* GAL-*ú a-bu* ^{d}MIN *šá ṣal-lu*$_4$ *a-di mat*
31 SIPA NA.ÁM.TAR.TAR.RA MU.LU NÁ.A ÈN.ŠÈ
32 *re-ʾ-ú mu-šim ši-ma-a-ti šá ṣal-lu*$_4$ *a-di mat*

II.[38]
1 [...]
2 ^{d}[MU.UL.LÍL URÚ.ZU BA.AN.ZÉ.ÈM UR.RE.EŠ BA.AN.GU$_7$.E]
3 ^{d}[*Mullil šá* URU *šá id-di-nu-ma iš-te-niš i-tak-ka-lu*]
4 TÚG.GAL.GAL.[LA ŠED$_7$.DÈ BA.AN.GÚR]
5 *la-biš ṣu-*[*ba-a-ti ra-bu-ú-ti*]
ina ku-[*ṣi uš-mi-it*]
6 GÁN.GAL.GAL.LA Š[À.MAR.RA.AŠ BA.AN.GÚR]
7 *šá mi-riš-ti* [*ra-pa-áš-ti*]
ina bu-[*bu-ti uš-mi-it*]

---

8 KI.ŠÚ.BI.IM [*šá* 12 DINGIR.MEŠ ZABAR]
9 *a-na* ŠÀ LILIZ ZABAR [*na-de-e*]

---

10 SIPA ZI.DA SIPA [ZI.DA]
11 *re-ú ki-nu re-ú* [*ki-nu*]
12 ^{d}EN.LÍL.LA SIPA [ZI.DA]
13 ^{d}EN.LÍL *re-ú* [*ki-nu*]
14 UMUN GÚ KALAM.MA SIPA [ZI.DA]
15 *be-el nap-ḫar ma-a-ti re-ú* [*ki-nu*]
16 UMUN GÚ ^{d}I.GI$_4$.GI$_4$ SIPA ZI.[DA]
17 *be-el nap-ḫar* ^{d}MIN *re-ú ki-*[*nu*]
18 UMUN GÚ DIMGUL (MÁ.MUG) SIPA ZI.[DA]
19 *be-el tar-kul-li re-*[*ú ki-nu*]
20 UMUN MA.A.NI GIŠ.ḪUR.RA UMUN MA.[A.NI ...]
21 *be-lu*$_4$ *mu-uṣ-ṣir* KUR-[*šú be-lu*$_4$ ... KUR-*šú*]
22 UMUN MA.A.NI GIŠ.ḪUR.RA [...]
23 *be-lu*$_4$ *mu-uṣ-ṣir* [KUR-*šú* ...]
24 MU.UN.GA MA.AL.LA K[ÚR.RE BA.AN.ZÉ.ÈM]
25 *ma-ak-ku-ri šak-na* [*ana nak-ri ta-ad-din*]
26 GIL.SA.A MA.AL.LA [KÚR.RE BA.AN.ZÉ.ÈM]
27 *šu-kut-ta šá-kin-ta* [*ana nak-ri ta-ad-din*]
28 TUŠ KÙ.GA [KÚR.RE BA.AN.DA.TUŠ]
29 *šu-ub-ta* KÙ-*tì* [*nak-ri it-ta-šá-ab*]
30 KI KÙ.GA [KÚR.RE BA.AN.DA.TUŠ]
31 *áš-ru el-lu*$_4$ [*nak-ri it-ta-šá-ab*]
32 KI.NÁ KÙ.GA [KÚR.RE BA.AN.DA.NÁ]
33 *tap-šá-ḫa el-lu*$_4$ [*šá-nu-um-ma i-ni-il*]

III.
1 ÚRU.È.A [MU.LU KÚR.RA A.GIM MU.UN.NA.ZÉ.ÈM]
2 *a-lu*$_4$ *šu-pu-u* [*ana nak-ri ki-i ta-ad-din*]

[38] As in col. I, the copy does not show the first lost line; so col. II, 1 in the copy is here col. II, 2. See *RAcc.*, 28–9.

3 UMUN ^{d}EN.KI LUGAL AB[ZU ŠÀ.ZU ḪÉ.EN.ḪUN.E(?)]
4 *be-lu*$_4$ ^{d}*É-a* LUGAL [ABZU *lìb-ba-ka li-ni-iḫ*(?)]
5 UMUN ^{d}ASAL.LÚ.ḪI [BAR.ZU ḪÉ.EN.ŠED$_7$.DÈ(?)]
6 *be-lu*$_4$ ^{d}AMAR.UTU [*ka-bat-ta-ka li-pa-áš-ši-iḫ*(?)]
7 UMUN A.A ^{d}IŠKUR.RA [ŠÀ.ZU(?)]
8 *be-lu*$_4$ *a-bu* ^{d}MIN [*lìb-ba-ka*(?)]
9 UMUN ŠUL ^{d}UTU [BAR.ZU(?)]
10 *be-lu*$_4$ *eṭ-lu* ^{d}UTU [*ka-bat-ta-ka*(?)]
11 UMUN ^{d}URAŠ.A.KE$_4$ [ŠÀ.ZU(?)]
12 *be-lu*$_4$ ^{d}NIN.URTA [*lìb-ba-ka*(?)]
13 UMUN MAḪ ^{d}ŠUL.PA.È.A [BAR.ZU(?)]
14 *be-lu*$_4$ *ṣi-ru* ^{d}MIN.A [*ka-bat-ta-ka*(?)]
15 ŠU SI.SÁ.BI ŠU S[I.SÁ.BI]
16 *qa-ta šu-te-šir qa-t*[*a šu-te-šir*]
17 ŠU SI.SÁ.BI KI.ÚS.MU [SI.SÁ.BI]
18 *qa-ta šu-te-šir kib-sa* [*šu-te-šir*]
19 DUG$_4$.GA.BI SI.SÁ DUG$_4$.GA.[BI SI.SÁ]
20 *qí-bi-ta šu-a-tu*$_4$ *šu-te-šir* [*qí-bi-ta šu-a-tu*$_4$ *šu-te-šir*]
21 LI.LI.ÌZ ZABAR DUG$_4$.GA.BI [SI.SÁ]
22 LI.LI.ÌZ *qí-bit-su šu-*[*te-šir*]

---

23 KI.ŠÚ.BI.IM KA.LUḪ LILIZ ZABA[R (DÙ)(?)]

---

24 *i-na* IGI ^{d}BALAG *ù* LILIZ Z[ABAR]
25 GI.DU$_8$ GUB-*an* KEŠDA [KEŠDA]
26 NINDA.Ì.DÉ.A LÀL Ì.NUN.NA Z[U.LUM.MA]
27 ^{zì}EŠA DUB-*aq* ^{udu}SÍSKUR [BAL-*qí*]
28 ^{uzu}ZAG ^{uzu}ME.ḪÉ *u* ^{uzu}K[A.NE *tu-ṭaḫ-ḫa*]
29 ⸢^{šim}LI(?)⸣ […]

IV.
1 [KI.ŠÚ.BI.I]M *ša* A.ME *kun-ni šid-du šá-da-di*
2 [A.ME *ina kun-ni*] ^{túg}*šid-du* GÍD-*ad*

---

3 [ŠU LUḪ.ḪA ME.E]N ŠU LUḪ.ḪA ME.EN
4 [*qa-ti-ka m*]*i-si qa-ti-ka mi-si*
5 [ŠU LUḪ.ḪA ME].EN ^{d}EN.LÍL.LÁ ME.EN
6 [^{d}EN.LÍL *at-ta qa-t*]*i-ka mi-si*
7 [ŠU LUḪ.ḪA ME].EN ^{d}NIN.LÍL ME.EN
8 [^{d}NIN.LÍL *at-ta qa-t*]*i-ka mi-s*[*i*]
9 [ŠU LUḪ.ḪA ME.E]N ^{d}EN.KI ^{d}UTU ^{d}INNIN ME.EN
10 [^{d}*É-a* ^{d}UTU] ^{d}*Iš-tar* ⟨*at-ta*⟩ *qa-ti-ku-nu m*[*i*(?)]*-sa-a*
11 [ŠU LUḪ.ḪA ME].EN ^{d}ASAL.LÚ.ḪI ME.EN
12 [^{d}ASAL.LÚ.ḪI *at-ta*] *qa-ti-ka mi-si*
13 [ŠU LUḪ.ḪA ME].EN ^{d}IM(?) x […] ME.EN
14 [^{d}IM(?)…*at-ta*] ⸢*qa*⸣-[*ti-ka*] *mi-si*
15 […] AD(?) ME.EN […]x ME.EN
16 […] x-*ka* KI-*tì* MIN
17 […] ḪÚL.LA.ME.EN
18 [DINGIR.MEŠ] *nap-ḫar-šú-nu li-iḫ-du-ka*

19 [^{d}ASAL.LÚ.ḪI] LUGAL.ZU.ŠÈ Ì.DU$_8$ MA.RA.AB
20 [^{d}AMAR.UTU] *ana šar-ri-ka paṭ-ra-ta ri-ši-šú*
21 ^{d}IŠKUR.RA LUGAL.ZU.ŠÈ Ì.DU$_8$ MA.RA.AB
22 ^{d}MIN *ana šar-ri-ka paṭ-ra-ta ri-ši-šú*

---

23 KI.ŠÚ.BI.IM *šá* A.ME *na-še-e* DUG$_4$.GA-*ma*
24 A.ME *ina* ÍL-*ma šid-di tu-na-aḫ*

---

25 *e-nu-ma* GU$_4$ *a-na* É *mu-um-mu tu-še-ri-bu*
26 *né-pe-ši* NAM.GALA.KAM
27 LIBIR.RA.BI GIM AB.SAR.ÀM BA.AN.È

I.
1 [Urbadḫumḫum dumu ešabake = Ninšar, son of Ešaba]
2–3 Gubbagararae du[mu urugibilla]ke = Ninkasi, son of the New City.
4–5 Abarralaḫ dumu ud.30.kam udnaam = Nusku, son of the thirtieth day (of the month), the day of non-appearance of the moon.

---

6 The 7 gods, sons of Enmešarra, are (represented by) heaps of flour.

---

7 You will lay down 12 bronze gods into the bronze kettledrum and
8 (then) you will cover the kettledrum.

9–10 Great bull, choice bull, which treads upon the pure meadow,
11–12 he walkes across the pastures, bringing abundance.
13–14 He, who sows the grain, who makes the fields thrive,
15–16 my pure hands made an offering in your presence!

---

17 (This is) the word of the Subterranean Water which you will whisper (l. 18) into the right ear of the bull, which (will be used) for covering the bronze kettledrum,
18 by means of a tube (made of) sweet reed.

---

19 O bull, you are a descendant of Anzu,
20 for the rites and rituals they have lifted you up.
21 Ningizzida is your friend for ever.
22 For the great [god]s, guard the divine decrees!
23 For the gods, who establish(?) the rites of Heaven and Earth,
24 may this [bu]ll be entrusted to Lumḫa,
25 may its […], its *uppu*-drum … be presented to Bēl!

---

26 [(This is) the word of the Sub]terranean Water, which (you will whisper) into the left ea[r of the b]ull, which (will be used) for covering the bronze kettledrum.

27–28 He, who lies asleep, the lord, who lies asleep, how long will he stay asleep?
29–30 Great mountain, father, Mullil, who lies asleep, how long (will he stay asleep)?
31–32 The shepherd, who decrees the fates, who lies asleep, how long (will he stay asleep)?

II.
1 […]
2–3 [Mullil of the city which he has given (away) so that they eat it at once].

4–5 [He killed] with co[ld] the one who wears [heavy] gar[ments].
6–7 [He killed] with hun[ger] the one who has [large], cultivated fields.

---

8 (End of) the stanza (which you will say when) [the 12 bronze gods (figurines)]
9 [are laid down] in the bronze kettledrum.

10–11 Loyal shepherd, [loyal] shepherd,
12–13 Enlil, [loyal] shepherd,
14–15 lord of all lands, [loyal] shepherd,
16–17 lord of all Igigi, lo[yal] shepherd,
18–19 lord of all mooring poles, lo[yal shepherd],
20–21 the lord, who 'draws' [his] land, [the lord, who … his land],
22–23 the lord, who 'draws' [his land …],
24–25 [you gave] the stored treasures [to the enemy],
26–27 [you gave] the stored jewelry [to the enemy].
28–29 [An enemy has occupied] the Pure Dwelling.
30–31 [An enemy has occupied] the Pure Place.
32–33 [A stranger lies down] in the Pure Resting Place.

III.
1–2 [How could you give] the splendid city [to the enemy]?
3–4 [May] the lord, Ea, the king of the Subter[ranean water, calm your heart(?)]!
5–6 [May] the lord, Marduk, [appease your mind(?)]!
7–8 (May) the lord, the father, Adad, [(calm) your heart(?)]!
9–10 (May) the lord, the young man, Šamaš, [(appease) your mind(?)]!
11–12 (May) the lord, Ninurta, [(calm) your heart(?)]!
13–14 (May) the exalted lord, Šulpaea [(appease) your mind(?)]!
15–16 Make the hand right, [make] the ha[nd right]!
17–18 Make the hand right, [make] the step [right]!
19–20 Make those words right, [make those words right]!
21–22 Make the utterance of the bronze kettledrum [right]!

---

23 (End of) the stanza (which you will say when) the washing of the mouth ceremony of the bronze kettledrum [(has been performed)(?)].

---

24 In front of Lumḫa and the br[onze] kettledrum
25 you will set up an offering table (and) [you will arrange] the offering accoutrements.
26 You will scatter (l. 27) a *mirsu*-confection (made with) honey, ghee, da[tes (and)]
27 *sasqû*-flour. [You will make] a sheep offering.
28 [You will bring] shoulder, *ḫimṣu*-omentum and ro[asted meat] [near].
29 juniper(?) […]

IV.
1 [(End of) the stan]za (which you will say when) the setting up of the water (basin) (and) the drawing shut of the curtains (has been performed).
2 [(After) the setting up of the water (basin)], you will draw the curtains shut.

3–4 [W]ash [your hands], wash your hands!
5–6 [You are Enlil], wash your h[ands]!
7–8 [You are Ninlil], was[h] your [han]ds!

9–10 You are [Ea, Šamaš], Ištar, wash your hands!
11–12 [You are Asalluḫi], wash your hands!
13–14 [You are Adad(?) …], wash [your hands]!
15–16 […] the Earth ditto.
17–18 May all [the gods] rejoice over you!
19–20 [O Marduk,] recite(?) for your king (the prayer) 'You are released'.
21–22 O Adad, recite(?) for your king (the prayer) 'You are released'.

---

23 (End of) the stanza which you will say when the water (basin) is lifted up. Then,
24 (after) the lifting up of the water (basin) you will loosen the curtains.

(Catchline:)
25 When you want to make the bull enter the workshop.
(Colophon:)
26 (This is) the ritual procedure for the lamentation priesthood.
27 Copied and collated in accordance with an older tablet.

Comments

I.

l. 1–5, see *TU* 44, III, 10–14, and my comments on these lines. See also II.5.2.

l. 6, this line is duplicated by *Bagh. Mitt. Beih.* 2, no. 5, obv. 11, but here *tu-sar-raq* 'you will scatter' is added at the end of the sentence.

l. 7, '12 bronze gods', apparently 12 small figurines. See also col. II, 8.

l. 9–10, the incipit is also mentioned in *TU* 44, II, 9, *Bagh. Mitt. Beih.* 2, no. 5, rev. 19 and *KAR* 60, obv. 10.

l. 13–14, see *CAD*, E, 287b, 12′; lit. 'who causes the fields to resound with shouts of *alāla*', cf. *CAD*, A/I, 331b lex. section. For *mu-šáḫ-li-lu* see also *AHw*, 680b.

l. 17 (see also 26), for other occurences of *amat apsî* see R. Borger, *BiOr* 30 (1973), 176a sub IV, 26. This line is perhaps duplicated by *Bagh. Mitt. Beih.* 2, no. 9, 4′. This small fragment from Hellenistic Uruk perhaps also contains a part of the kettledrum ritual:

1′ […] ⌜x⌝ […]
2′ […LI.LI.ÌZ(?)] ZABAR […]
3′ […] ⌜x⌝ *at-ta* […]
4′ […LI.LI.ÌZ(?)] ZABAR *a-ra*[*-mi*(?)…]
5′ […] ⌜x⌝ *re-ʾ-ú ki-nu* […]
6′ […] MEZE ZABAR […]

l. 19, see *TU* 44, II, 10, *Bagh. Mitt. Beih.* 2, no. 5, rev. 21 and *KAR* 60, obv. 12.

l. 22–27, the beginning of these lines are partly preserved in the unpublished fragment K 9421, obverse. See Plate III.

l. 22, *ú-ṣu-ri*, a corrupt form, perhaps for *uṣur*, the imperative of *naṣāru*? Cf. *RAcc.*, 27.

l. 23, perhaps *mu*(?)-*ši-im* (as in col. I, 31–32), an irregular participle G-stem of *šâmu* (cf. W. von Soden *GAG*, § 104, k). See *CAD*, Š/I, 360a, 1′.

l. 27–28, this prayer is referred to in *KAR* 60, rev. 1. While the Akkadian version has 'the lord' (*be-lu*$_4$), the Sumerian version reads 'the honored one' (E.LUM).

l. 29–30 (see also col. II, 2–3), Mullil is Emesal Sumerian for Enlil.

l. 31–32, NA.ÁM.TAR.TAR.RA // *mu-šim ši-ma-a-ti*, see also *Bagh. Mitt. Beih.* 2, no. 6, obv. 5–6.

II.

l. 2–7, these three bilingual lines are also mentioned in the *taqribtu*-lamentation EN-EMANI ILU ILU, cf. M.E. Cohen, *Lamentations*, 189, 34 ff. (see also p. 24a and 26a with n. 65) = *SBH* 44, rev. 29 ff. The incipit of this lamentation is also attested in the Hellenistic calendar text *TU* 48, rev. 4. See II.2.2.

l. 2–3, '[Mullil of the city which he has given (away) so that (*-ma*) they eat it (*i-tak-ka-lu*) at once]', this line is problematic: the Akkadian apparently has a Gtn-stem preterite *ītakkalu*, but this is a problem because 'at once' (*ištēniš*) does not fit an iterative form. One would expect 'so that it is eaten at once' (*innakkalu*), because the Sumerian line has the passive form (B[A.AN].GU$_7$.E). Also, note that the copy *SBH* 44, rev. 30 has *it-tak-ka-lu* (not *i-tak-ka-lu*), an N-stem perfect. Cf. *CAD*, I-J, 280a lex. section (disregards *-ma* and subjunctive *-u*), *RAcc.*, 28 and 55, n. 73, and M.E. Cohen, *Lamentations*, 189, 34 (translation follows the Sumerian).

l. 4–5 and 6–7, not only paralleled in *SBH* 44, rev. 33 ff. but also similar in *SBH* 58 (IMMAL GUDEDE), obv. 15 ff. (cf. M.E. Cohen, *Lamentations*, 616, c + 214 f.): [UD.D]È TÚG.GAL.GAL.LA ŠED$_7$.DA BA.AN.[GÚR] // *u*$_4$*-mu la-biš ṣú-ba-ti* GAL-*ti i-na ku-ṣi* [...], GÁN.NI GÁN.DA.MA.AL.LA ŠÀ.MAR.RA.AŠ [BA.AN.GÚR] // *šá me-reš-ti ra-pa-áš-ti ina bu-bu-ti uš-m*[*i-it*].

l. 8 (see also col. III, 23; col. IV, 1 and 23), KI.ŠÚ.BI.IM: M.E. Cohen, *Lamentations*, 31a, translates 'It is its *kišû*', *kišû* indicating the end of the lamentation. According to *CAD*, K, 464b *kišubû*, a Sumerian loan word of KI.ŠÚ.BI(.IM), is: 'final part of a hymn'. Whether KI.ŠÚ(.BI) = *kīlu*, LB *killu* (see *AHw*, 476 'Festhalten; Haft') is connected with this, is not clear to me; the cognate verb *kalû* can also mean 'to stop', see my comments on *TU* 45, obv. 14.

Related to *kišubû* is *kirugu*. *kirugu* (KI.RU.GÚ, cf. M.E. Cohen, *Lamentations*, 29a with n. 80) is tuning up an instrument, *Kišubû* is tuning down an instrument; this happens each time between the ritual acts, after a song; in this way perhaps *kišubû* came to mean 'stanza' (suggestion Th.J.H. Krispijn, Leiden).

l. 20–21 and 22–23, 'the lord, who "draws" his land', GIŠ.ḪUR.RA // *uṣṣuru*, in this context perhaps 'who establishes (the rules of) his land'? Cf. *CAD*, E, 348b, 2, a, 3′, and 2, b.

l. 24–27, see *SBH*, p. 70, no. 39, obv. 8 f. (similar in *SBH*, p. 84, no. 47, rev. 8 f. and 115, no. 60, rev. 6 f.). See also col. III, 2.

l. 32–33, similar in *SBH* p. 70, no. 39, obv. 13 f. (MU.NÁ.BI KÙ.GA KÚR.RE BA.AN.-DA.NÁ // *ina er-ši-šú el-lu*$_4$ *šá-nu-um-ma i-ni-il*).

III.

l. 1–2, similar in *SBH*, p. 70, no. 39, obv. 15 f.: É.ZU MU.LU KÚR.RA A.GIM MU.UN.NA.ZÉ.ÈM // É-*ka ana*! (copy: *šá*) *nak-ri ki-i ta-ad-din*). See my comment on col. II, 24–27.

l. 3–14, F. Thureau-Dangin gave a reconstruction of these lines based on F. Delitzsch, *AL*^{3}, 136, 9 ff. (cf. *RAcc.*, 55) // *SBH* 53, rev. 56 ff. // *BRM* 4, 10, rev. 31 ff., but the reconstruction is not certain.

l. 21–22, 'bronze' (ZABAR) only in the Sumerian version.

IV.

l. 6–15, partly preserved in the unpublished fragment K 9421, reverse. See Plate III.

l. 15–22, these lines are duplicated by *Bagh. Mitt. Beih.* 2, no. 7, rev. 1′–5′ (cf. W.R. Mayer, *Bagh. Mitt. Beih.* 2, p. 16 sub no. 7), but only the Sumerian version is given there. This fragment from Hellenistic Uruk contains a part of the kettledrum ritual. The obverse is partially a duplicate of *KAR* 60, rev. 10–15 (see my comments on these lines):

Rev.
1′ [...]x ME.EN x[...]
2′ [...]x ḪÚL.LA.M[E.EN]
3′ [...]x ME.EN: DINGIR [...]
4′ [...] ⌜ḪÚL.LA⌝[.ME.EN(?)]
5′ [^{d}IŠKUR.RA LUGAL.ZU.Š]È Ì.DU$_8$ ⌜MA⌝.[RA.AB]

6′ [...] *ana* ⌜LI⌝.LI.⌜ÌZ *ta*⌝-[*na-ad-di*(?)]

7′ [*e-nu-ma*(?) GU$_4$] *ana* É *mu-um-mu* ⌜*tu*⌝-[*še-ri-bu*]
8′ [...] *ina* ^{iti}⌜SIG$_4$⌝ [...]
9′ [...] ⌜x⌝ [...]

l. 6′ appears to differ from IV R^2, 23, no. 1 +, IV, 23–24, but the traces are not clear. For l. 7′, see IV R^2, 23, no. 1 +, IV, 25; *TU* 44, I, 7; *Bagh. Mitt. Beih.* 2, no. 5, obv. 7.

l. 19–22, MA.RA.AB // *ri-ši-šú* 'recite', in the Sumerian version lit. 'place it'; the use of the verb GAR (Emesal MAR) with the meaning 'to recite' is not uncommon, for example in the phrase *taqribta šakānu* (ÉR GAR) (see the dictionaries). However, the use of what appears to be the imperative of *rašû* (lit. 'receive it') in the Akkadian translation is unusual. Cf. the duplicate *Bagh. Mitt. Beih.* 2, no. 7, rev. 5 (see my comments on col. IV, 15–22).

l. 25, see *TU* 44, I, 7; *Bagh. Mitt. Beih.* 2, no. 5, obv. 7; id., no. 7, rev. 7.

f. The building ritual

TU 45 (AO 6472)[39]

This text was written in Uruk, and dates from the Hellenistic period. The owner and scribe of the tablet is Anu-bēlšunu, son of Nidintu-Anu, but the colophon contains an incomplete date; the scribe mistakenly omitted the year number. However, in other documents he is mentioned with his family name: Anu-bēlšunu, son of Nidintu-Anu, of the family Sin-lēqe-unnīni, is attested in the building ritual *TU* 46, dated 81 S.E. (231/0 B.C., see below), the *šuillakku*-prayer *Bagh. Mitt. Beih.* 2, no. 12, dated 112 S.E. (200/199 B.C.), the kettledrum ritual *Bagh. Mitt. Beih.* 2, no. 5, dated 150 S.E. (162/1 B.C., see above) and the list *Bagh. Mitt. Beih.* 2, no. 89, dated 147 S.E. (165/4 B.C.).[40] The Anu-bēlšunu of *Bagh. Mitt. Beih.* 2, no. 5 and no. 89 is the grandson of Anu-bēlšunu, who wrote *Bagh. Mitt. Beih.* 2, no. 12, *TU* 46 and *TU* 45.

The text describes the rituals which had to be performed for the rebuilding of a temple, after it had fallen into ruin. It is partially duplicated by *TU* 46, *Bagh. Mitt. Beih.* 2, nos. 10 and 11 and F.H. Weissbach, *Misc.*, no. 12.

The text is discussed in II.6.

Obv.

1 *e-nu-ma* É.GAR$_8$ É ^{d}LX *i-qa-p*[*u a-na na-qa-rim-ma uš-šu-ši šá* É *šu-a-tu*]

2 *ina* ITI *šal-mu ina* UD ŠE.GA *ina* GE$_6$ 3 GI.D[U$_8$ *a-na* DINGIR É ^{d}INNIN É *u* ^{d}LAMMA É *tar-kás* ^{udu}SÍSKUR]

3 BAL-*qí* ^{uzu}ZAG.LU ^{uzu}ME.ḪÉ *u* ^{uzu}KA[.NE *tu-ṭaḫ-ḫa* KAŠ GEŠTIN GA BAL-*qí*]

4 *ab-ru a-na* ^{d}*É-a u* ^{d}ASAL.LÚ.ḪI *tu-*[*nam-mar* ^{udu}SÍSKUR *a-na* ^{d}*É-a u* ^{d}ASAL.LÚ.ḪI]

5 BAL-*qí* KAŠ SAG GEŠTIN GA BAL-*qí* ^{d}UTU.GIN$_7$ ⸢È⸣.[TA ÉR]

6 Ù.Ù' A.BA MU.ḪUL ÉR.ŠEM$_4$.MA ŠÌR *ina še-rì* [*ina* ÙR É DINGIR *šu-a-tu a-šar ta-šab-biṭ*]

7 A KÙ.MEŠ *ta-sal-làḫ* 3 GI.DU$_8$ *a-na* ^{d}*É-a* ^{d}UTU *u* ^{d}A[SAL.LÚ.ḪI GUB-*an* 3 GADA]

8 *ina muḫ-ḫi* KI.TUŠ.MEŠ GAR-*an* NINDA.Ì.DÉ.ÀM LÀL Ì.NUN.NA [ZÚ.LUM.MA ^{zì}EŠA]

9 Ì.GIŠ BÁR.GA GAR-*an* 3 ^{dug}A.DA.GUR$_5^{!}$ KAŠ SAG GEŠTIN GA GUB-*an* [NÍG.NA ^{šim}LI]

10 GAR-*an* ŠE.NUMUN DÙ.A.BI DUB-*aq* 3 ^{udu}SÍSKUR BAL-*qí* ^{uzu}ZAG.LU ^{uz}[^{u}ME.ḪÉ]

11 *u* ^{uzu}KA.NE *tu-ṭaḫ-ḫa* KAŠ SAG GEŠTIN GA BAL-*qí* A.MEŠ GUB-*an* ^{túg}*šid-du*

12 GÍD.DA-*ad* É.ZI GUL.GUL.LU.DÈ NÍ.BI.ŠÈ ÉR IM.ŠE$_8$.ŠE$_8$ *ina ter-ṣi*

13 É ŠÌR EGIR-*šú* DILMUN^{ki} NIGIN.NA ^{d}UTU LUGAL.ÀM É.ŠÀ.AB.ḪUN.GÁ.TA *ina ḫal-ḫal-la-tú*

14 *a-na* ^{d}*É-a* ^{d}UTU *u* ^{d}ASAL.LÚ.ḪI ŠÌR *i-kal-la* A.MEŠ ÍL-*ma* ^{túg}*šid-du tu-na-ḫa*

---

15 *né-pe-ši šá* ŠU^{II} ^{lú}GALA

---

[39] Cf. *RAcc.*, 7–8, 34–40; A.J. Sachs, in: J.B. Pritchard, *ANET*^{2}, 339 f. See also R. Borger, *HKL* 1, 567 and 2, 297.

[40] Anu-bēlšunu is also known from other texts, in chronological order: in the Esagila tablet *TU* 32, dated 83 S.E.; in the astronomical text O. Neugebauer, *ACT*, 18, M, dated 118 S.E.; as the father of Anu-aba-utēr in the astronomical text *TU* 25, dated 130 S.E.; in the private documents *BRM* 2, 37 // *BiMes* 24, 23, dated 133 S.E., and *BRM* 2, 38, dated 139 S.E.; and finally in the astronomical texts O. Neugebauer, *ACT*, 16, D, and 20, Zd, but both are without a date.

---

16 DIŠ KI *i-nu-uš* ZI KÚR KI.TUŠ KUR *ul i-kan*: DIŠ KI BAL-*it ina* KUR DÙ.A.BI NU GI.NA GÁL UŠ$_4$ KUR MAN-*ni*

---

17 *ina* UD ŠE.GA LUGAL *li-tu-lil li-te-bi-ib ši-gu-ú a-na* ^{d}LX ^{d}EN.LÍL *u* ^{d}IDIM GÙ-*si*
18 EGIR-*šú* 2 KEŠDA *a-na* DINGIR-*šú u* ^{d}INNIN-*šú tar-kás* ^{udu}SÍSKUR BAL-*qí* ÉR GAR-*an*
19 ÉR.ŠEM$_4$.ŠÀ.ḪUN.GÁ.MEŠ-*šú-nu a-na* LUGAL *tu-šad-bab*

---

20 *ina še-rì* ⸢3⸣ GI.DU$_8$.MEŠ *a-na* ^{d}*A-nù* ^{d}EN.LÍL *u* ^{d}*É-a tar-kás* ^{udu}SÍSKUR BAL-*qí*
21 ^{uzu}ZAG.LU ^{uzu}ME.ḪÉ *u* ^{uzu}KA.NE *tu-ṭaḫ-ḫa* KAŠ SAG GEŠTIN GA BAL-*qí* ÉR GAR-*an*
22 BAR.RA UMUN.E TA MA NÍGIN AN.NAM ÉR.ŠEM$_4$.ŠÀ.ḪUN.GÁ *a-na* ^{d}*A-nù*
23 ME.E U.MU.UN.MU.ŠI ŠIM *a-na* ^{d}EN.LÍL *a-na* ^{d}IDIM ME.E AN.ŠAR *a-na* ^{d}UTU
24 *a-na* LUGAL *tu-šad-bab uš-ken* ^{lú}ŠU.I-*su* DÙ-*uš* MÚNŠUB (SÍG.LAM.SUḪUR) SU-*šú ina* ^{dug}LA.ḫA.AN SÁḪAR
25 *ta-kam*(!)-*mis-ma a-na mi-ṣir* ^{lú}KÚR TAG$_4$-*šu a-na* É.GAL-*šú* SI.SÁ ^{udu}SÍSKUR GAL-*ú*
26 *ana* ^{d}*A-nù* BAL-*qí* ÉR GAR-*an* EGIR-*šú* ÉR.MEŠ *u* ÉR.ŠEM$_4$.ŠÀ.ḪUN.GÁ.MEŠ-*šú-nu ina* TÚG.SÍG LUGAL 〈ŠID-*nu*〉

Rev.
1 *ina kul-lat* KI.ŠU.PEŠ$_5$.MEŠ DÙ.DÙ-*uš an-nam*$^{a\text{-}am}$ DÙ.DÙ-*uš-ma* ḪUL *ana* LUGAL NU TE-*ḫi*

---

2 *né-pe-ši šá* ŠU^{II} ^{lú}GALA

---

3 DIŠ UR.GI$_7$ *ana* É DINGIR KU$_4$ DINGIR.ME *ana* KUR AMA$^{!}$ NU GAR.MEŠ
4 DIŠ *ú-ma-mu* EDEN BAR-*ú aq-ru ana* ŠÀ URU KU$_4$-*ma* IGI-*ir mim-ma ú-šal-pit* ŠUB-*e* URU
(interlinear:)[41] ZÁḪ UN.MEŠ-*šú*

---

5 *ina* UD ŠE.GA 3 GI.DU$_8$.MEŠ *a-na* DINGIR URU ^{d}INNIN URU$^{!}$[42] ^{d}LAMMA URU KEŠDA
6 ^{udu}SÍSKUR BAL-*qí* ^{uzu}ZAG.LU ^{uzu}ME.ḪÉ *u* ^{uzu}KA.NE *tu-ṭaḫ-ḫa* KAŠ SAG GEŠTIN GA BAL-*qí*
7 *ab-ru* MÚ-*aḫ taq-rib-tu*$_4$ GAR-*an* ÉR.ŠEM$_4$.ŠÀ.ḪUN.GÁ.MEŠ-*šú-nu ina* TÚG.SÍG LUGAL ŠID-*nu*

---

8 *ina še-rì ina* EDEN *lu-u ina* GÚ ÍD KI GÌR^{II} *pár-kat* KI SÙ A KÙ SÙ 3 GI.DU$_8$.MEŠ
9 *a-na* ^{d}*A-nù* ^{d}EN.LÍL *u* ^{d}IDIM *tar-kás* ^{udu}SÍSKUR BAL-*qí* ^{uzu}ZAG.LU ^{uzu}ME.ḪÉ *u* ^{uzu}KA.NE
10 *tu-ṭaḫ-ḫa* KAŠ SAG GEŠTIN GA BAL-*qí ab-ru* MÚ-*aḫ taq-rib-tu*$_4$ GAR-*an* ÉR.ŠEM$_4$.ŠÀ.ḪUN.GÁ.MEŠ-*šú-nu*
11 *ina* TÚG.SÍG LUGAL ŠID-*nu* EGIR-*šú a-na* DINGIR EDEN ^{d}INNIN EDEN 2 GI.DU$_8$.MEŠ KEŠDA ^{udu}SÍSKUR
12 BAL-*qí* ^{uzu}ZAG.LU ^{uzu}ME.ḪÉ *u* ^{uzu}KA.NE *tu-ṭaḫ-ḫa* KAŠ SAG GEŠTIN GA BAL-*qí* ÉR GAR-*an*
(interlinear:) ^{lú}MAŠ.MAŠ *u* ^{lú}GALA URU.BI *ú-kap-ru-*ʾ

---

[41] The interlinear line between rev. 4 and 5 (see also between rev. 12–13 and 14–15) is marked by 3 successive separation signs (:).
[42] Copy: É.

---

13 *an-nam*$^{a\text{-}am}$ *te-ep-pu-uš-ma* ḪUL *a-na* LUGAL NU TE.ME

---

14 DIŠ ALAM LUGAL KUR.BI *lu-u* ALAM AD-*šú* *lu-u* ALAM AD AD-*šú* ŠUB-*ut-ma* ḪAŠ-*ir lu-u bu-un-na-an-ni-šú uk*$^{!}$-*kil*
(interlinear:) LUGAL KUR.BI UD.MEŠ-*šú* LÚGUD.DA.MEŠ

---

15 DIŠ *ina* É.KUR *tab-lu* TÙM-*ma* I.^{d}UTU DINGIR NÍG.GA LUGAL *a-na ki-di* È
16 DIŠ GISKIM ḪUL-*tu*$_{4}$ GISKIM BAR-*tu*$_{4}$ *ina* É DINGIR IGI-*ir ina* É DINGIR.BI GÌR^{II} KUD-*as*: GIR UB

---

17 *ina* UD ŠE.GA(!?) *ina* GE$_{6}$ 3 GI.DU$_{8}$.MEŠ *a-na* DINGIR.BI ^{d}INNIN.BI ^{d}MAŠ.DÚB ^{d}UTU KEŠDA ^{udu}SÍSKUR
18 BAL-*qí* ^{uzu}ZAG.LU ^{uzu}ME.ḪÉ *u* ^{uzu}KA.NE *tu-ṭaḫ-ḫa* KAŠ SAG GEŠTIN *u* GA BAL-*qí*
19 ÉR GAR-*an* ÉR.ŠEM$_{4}$.ŠÀ.ḪUN.GÁ.MEŠ-*šú-nu a-na* LUGAL *tu-šad-bab*

---

20 *ina še-rì ina* ÙR É DINGIR MU.MEŠ KI SÙ A KÙ SÙ 3 GI.DU$_{8}$.MEŠ *a-na* ^{d}IDIM ^{d}UTU
21 *u* ^{d}ASAL.LÚ.ḪI GUB-*an* 3 GADA *ina* UGU KI.TUŠ.MEŠ GAR-*an* ^{udu}SÍSKUR BAL-*qí*
22 ^{uzu}ZAG.LU ^{uzu}ME.ḪÉ *u* ^{uzu}KA.NE *tu-ṭaḫ-ḫa* KAŠ SAG GEŠTIN GA BAL-*qí ab-ru* MÚ-[*aḫ*]
23 ÉR GAR-*an* ÉR.ŠEM$_{4}$.ŠÀ.ḪUN.GÁ.MEŠ-*šú-nu a-na* LUGAL *tu-šad-bab tak-per*$^{!}$-*tu*$_{4}$ É DINGIR.B[I]
24 *tu-ḫa-ab* EGIR-*šú* LUGAL *ši-gu-ú* GÙ-*si* NÍG.BA *a-na* DINGIR.BI B[A]

---

25 IM ^{Id}LX-EN-*šú-nu* A *šá* ^{I}NÍG.SUM-*tu*$_{4}$-^{d}LX ŠU^{II} NÍ-*šú* UNUG^{ki} ^{iti}ŠE UD.22.KAM ^{I}*Se-l*[*u-ku* LUGAL]

Obv.

1 When the wall of the temple of Anu buck[les, to demolish and renovate that temple],
2 [you will arrange] in an auspicious month, on a favourable day, in the night 3 offering [tables for the god of the temple, the goddess of the temple and the protective spirit (*lamassu*) of the temple]. You will make (l. 3) [a sheep offering].
3 [You will bring] shoulder, *ḫimṣu*-omentum and roa[sted meat [near]. You will make a libation of beer, wine (and) milk].
4 You will set fir[e to] a brushwood pile for Ea and Marduk. You will make (l. 5) [a sheep offering for Ea and Marduk].
5 You will make a libation of first-quality beer, wine (and) milk. You will sing (l. 6) [the *taqribtu*-lamentation] 'Come out like the sun'
6 (and) the *eršemakku*-lamentation 'Woe, who has destroyed (the temple)?'. In the morning, [on the roof of the temple, you will sweep (this) place],
7 you will sprinkle pure water. [You will set up] 3 offering tables in front of Ea, Šamaš and Ma[rduk]. You will place (l. 8) [3 linen (cloths)]
8 on the seats. You will place (l. 9) a *mirsu*-confection (made with) honey, ghee, dates, *sasqû*-flour.
9 (and) pressed oil. You will set up 3 *adakurru*-containers (with) first-quality beer, wine (and) milk. You will place (l. 10) [a censer with juniper].
10 You will scatter all (kinds of) barley seed. You will make 3 sheep offerings. You will bring near (l. 11) shoulder, [*ḫimṣu*-omentum]
11 and roasted meat. You will make a libation of first-quality beer, wine (and) milk. You will set up a water (basin). You will draw (l. 12) the curtains shut.

12 You will sing (l. 13) 'Because of the destruction of the old house, they spontaneously utter a *taqribtu*-lamentation', in the direction of

13 the temple. After this you will sing (l. 14) (the *eršemakku*-lamentations) 'Important one, who wanders abound', 'Utu is king' (and) 'The heart of the temple will be calmed down' to the accompaniment of a *ḫalḫallatu*-drum

14 for Ea, Šamaš and Marduk. He will (then) stop (singing). You will lift up the water (basin) (for the washing of the hands) and loosen the curtains.

---

15 (This is) the ritual procedure of the lamentation priest.

---

16 (An omen says:) if the earth quakes, (then) an enemy will rise and the dwellings of the land will not be secure. (Another omen says:) if the earth turns around, (then) there will be injustice in the whole land, the land will turn mad.

---

17 On a favourable day may the king purify and cleanse himself (and) cry a *šigû*-lamentation for Anu, Enlil and Ea.

18 After this you will arrange 2 offering accoutrements in front of his god and his goddess. You will make a sheep offering (and) perform a *taqribtu*-lamentation.

19 You will make the king recite their (the gods') *eršemšaḫungû*-prayers.

---

20 In the morning you will arrange 3 offering tables for Anu, Enlil and Ea. You will make a sheep offering.

21 You will bring shoulder, *ḫimṣu*-omentum and roasted meat near. You will make a libation of first-quality beer, wine (and) milk. You will perform a *taqribtu*-lamentation.

22 You will make the king recite (l. 24) the *eršemšaḫungû*-prayers 'O lord, what turned about in my mind? It is Anu'(?) to Anu,

23 'I want to offer my life to my lord' to Enlil (and) Ea, (and) 'I want to speak a prayer to Šamaš' to Šamaš.

24 He will (then) prostrate himself. He submits to treatment by the barber. (Then) you will gather (l. 25) the hair of his body into a porous(?) *laḫannu*-bottle

25 and send it off to the enemy's border. He will (then) go straightaway to his palace. You will make (l. 26) a large sheep offering

26 for Anu. You will perform a *taqribtu*-lamentation. After this ⟨you will recite⟩(?) the *taqribtu*-lamentations and their *eršemšaḫungû*-prayers over the king's hem.

Rev.

1 In each (and) every sanctuary you will do (this). You will do this each time, and evil will not approach the king.

---

2 (This is) the ritual procedure of the lamentation priest.

---

3 (An omen says:) if a dog enters a temple, (then) the gods will show no mercy to the land.

4 (Another omen says:) if a wild animal, strange and rare, enters the city and is seen and defiles something, (then) ruin of the city,
dispersal of its inhabitants.

---

5 On a favourable day you will arrange 3 offering tables in front of the god of the city, the goddess of the city(!) and the protective spirit (*lamassu*) of the city.

6 You will make a sheep offering. You will bring shoulder, *ḫimṣu*-omentum and roasted meat near. You will make a libation of first-quality beer, wine, (and) milk.

7 You will kindle a brushwood pile. You will perform a *taqribtu*-lamentation. You will recite their *eršemšaḫungû*-prayers over the king's hem.

---

8 In the morning, in the open country or on the bank of a river, on a place where nobody sets foot, you will sprinkle the ground, you will sprinkle pure water. You will arrange (l. 9) 3 offering tables
9 for Anu, Enlil and Ea. You will make a sheep offering. You will bring (l. 10) shoulder, *ḫimṣu*-omentum and roasted meat
10 near. You will make a libation of first-quality beer, wine (and) milk. You will kindle a brushwood pile. You will perform a *taqribtu*-lamentation. You will recite (l. 11) their *eršemšaḫungû*-prayers
11 over the king's hem. After this you will arrange 2 offering tables in front of the god of the open country (and) the goddess of the open country. You will make (l. 12) a sheep offering.
12 You will bring shoulder, *ḫimṣu*-omentum and roasted meat near. You will make a libation of first-quality beer, wine (and) milk. You will perform a *taqribtu*-lamentation.
The exorcist and the lamentation priest will purify that city.

---

13 You will do this, and evil will not approach the king.

---

14 (An omen says:) if a statue of the king of that land or a statue of his father or a statue of his grandfather falls over and breaks, or if its features become indistinct, (then) the days of the king of that land will be short.

---

15 (An omen says:) if (stolen) goods are taken away from the temple, and there is a complaint from the god, (then) the royal property will go out (from the city).
16 (Another omen says:) if an evil sign, a strange sign, is seen in the temple, (then) access to that temple will be blocked. …

---

17 On a favourable(?) day, during the night, you will arrange 3 offering tables for that god, that goddess, Mašdub (and) Šamaš. You will make (l. 18) a sheep offering.
18 You will bring near shoulder, *ḫimṣu*-omentum and roasted meat. You will make a libation of first-quality beer, wine and milk.
19 You will perform a *taqribtu*-lamentation (and) you will make the king recite their *eršemšaḫungû*-prayers.

---

20 In the morning, on the roof of that temple you will sprinkle the ground. You will sprinkle pure water. You will set up (l. 21) 3 offering tables in front of Ea, Šamaš
21 and Marduk. You will lay down 3 linen (cloths) on the seats. You will make a sheep offering.
22 You will bring shoulder, *ḫimṣu*-omentum and roasted meat near. You will make a libation of first-quality beer, wine (and) milk. You will kindle a brushwood pile.
23 You will perform a *taqribtu*-lamentation (and) you will make the king recite their *eršemšaḫungû*-prayers. You will consecrate (l. 24) th[at] temple with *takpertu*-purifications.
24 After this the king will cry a *šigû*-lamentation (and) he will ma[ke] a gift to that god.

(Colophon:)
25 Tablet of Anu-bēlšunu, son of Nidintu-Anu, (written by) his own hand, Uruk, the (twelfth) month Addaru, day 22, Sel[eucus being king].

Comments

Obv.

l. 2, the reconstruction is based on *TU* 46, obv. 2–3 and rev. 6. See also my comments on *TU* 46, obv. 3.

l. 5–6, the *taqribtu* 'Come out like the sun' is also attested in the parallels *TU* 46, obv. 6; *Bagh. Mitt. Beih.* 2, no. 10, 7; also in the Uruk cultic calendar *TU* 48, obv. 19, see II.2.2; the accompanying *eršemakku*: 'Woe, who has destroyed (the temple)?' also in the parallel *Bagh. Mitt. Beih.* 2, no. 10, 8.

l. 6–7, *ina še-rì* [*ina* ÙR É DINGIR *šu-a-tu a-šar ta-šab-biṭ*] A KÙ.MEŠ *ta-sal-làḫ*, this phrase is only partly preserved in the parallel *TU* 46, obv. 7 (see also F.H. Weissbach, *Misc.*, no. 12, obv. 5); however, we now have a complete parallel in the duplicate *Bagh. Mitt. Beih.* 2, no. 10, obv. 8–9: *ina še-rì ina* ÙR É DINGIR.MEŠ *šu-a-tu a-šar ta-ši-biṭ* (= *tašabbiṭ*) A KÙ.MEŠ *ta-sal-*⌜*làḫ*⌝. For the well-known phrase *qaqqara tašabbiṭ mê ellūti tasallaḫ* (KI SAR A KÙ SÙ) see my comments on l. rev. 8 below, and on *TU* 44, I, 8.

F. Thureau-Dangin's reconstruction in *RAcc.*, 34 (*ina še-rì* [*ina* ÙR É DINGIR *šu-a-tu a-šar* GÌR^{II} KUD-*at* (= *parsat*)] 'In the morning, [on the roof of the temple, a place to which access is blocked]') is not based on parallels, but is only conjecture. Phrases similar to the latter are attested in *TU* 45, rev. 16 // *Bagh. Mitt. Beih.* 2, no. 11, rev., fragment 2, 16′: GÌR^{II} KUD-*as* (= *ipparras*). See also *TU* 45, rev. 8 // *Bagh. Mitt. Beih.* 2, no. 11, rev., fragment 2, 3′: KI GÌR^{II} *pár-kat* (see my comments on rev. 6–13, below). Compare also *TU* 46, obv. 15 (*ina* É *pár-si*) and *KAR* 50, rev. 8 (*ana* KI *par-si*). Cf. *RAcc.*, 55, n. 83 and 54, n. 68, *CAD*, Š/II, 304a and *AHw*, 830b, G,1, b, b, with more examples.

l. 7, for the restoration see rev. 21 and *Bagh. Mitt. Beih.* 2, no. 10, obv. 11.

l. 9, GUR$_5$$^{!}$ (= URUxGU), the copy has BANŠUR (URUxURUDU). For the restoration of this line see *Bagh. Mitt. Beih.* 2, no. 10, obv. 13.

l. 11–14, 15, 16, these lines are duplicated by a fragment from Hellenistic Uruk, *Bagh. Mitt. Beih.* 2, no. 11, obv. fragment 1, 1′–3′, 8′, 10′a and 11′a (for fragment 1, obv. 4′ and 7′, see also the duplicate F.H. Weissbach, *Misc.*, no. 12, obv. 15–17, 22 f. Lines 2′–8′ of fragment 1 are duplicated in *TU* 46, obv. 11–20. Lines 9′ff. of fragment 1 contain several omen texts, of which two (10′a and 11′a) are also attested in *TU* 45, obv. 16):

Bagh. Mitt. Beih. 2, no. 11, obv. fragment 1:

1′ [… KAŠ] SAG GEŠTIN G[A BAL-*qí* …]

2′ [… *ina te*]*r-ṣi* É ŠÌR EGIR-*šú* DILMUN^{ki} N[IGIN.NA …]

3′ [… ^{d}ASAL.L]Ú.ḪI ŠÌR *i-kal-la* A.MEŠ ÍL-*ma* ^{túg}*ši*[*d-du tu-na-ḫa*]

4′ [… ḪAR AN.NA] *ina* ŠU^{II}-*šú* GAR-*an ḫa-ṣi-in* A.GAR$_5$ ÍL-*ma* SIG$_4$ ⌜*maḫ*⌝-[*ri-ti*]

5′ [… 1-*en* GI.DU$_8$] *a-na* IGI SIG$_4$ *a-na* DINGIR URU$_4$$^{!}$ KEŠDA ^{udu}SÍSKUR BAL-*qí* ^{uzu}[ZAG.LU]

6′ [… *uš-k*]*en a-di na-qa-ri u e-pe-ši-ka* A A AM SAR ⌜KA(?) x⌝ […]

7′ [… *ina*] UGU *ú-naq-qu* ^{lú}GALA *e-nu-ma* ^{d}*A-nu* [*ib-nu-ú* AN-*e* …]

8′ [... ŠU^II] ^lú^GALA
9′ [DIŠ ...] *ši-si-it* LUGAL *dan-nu ina* KUR GÁL-*ši*: DIŠ AN-*ú*.GÙ-*ú-m*[*a*...]
10′ [DIŠ KI *i*]-*nu-uš* ZI KÚR KI.TUŠ KUR *ul i-kan*: DIŠ KI ⌈GÙ⌉-*ma* [...]
11′ [DIŠ K]I BAL-*it ina* KUR DÙ.A.BI NU GI.NA GÁL ⌈UŠ4 MAN(?): DIŠ⌉ KI [...]
12′ [DIŠ KI] ⌈*i*⌉-*nu-uš* LU RU UD *lu-u* ⌈x x⌉ SI KUR AN-*ú* [...]
13′ [DIŠ KI] *lu-u ú-pa-ṭa lu-u* LÀL *lu-u* GA *lu-u* [...*i-ḫi-il*(-*ma*)]
14′ [...]⌈-*qu*(?)⌉ LUGAL *dan-nu* LÚ *ma-qit*(?) ⌈x x⌉ [...]
15′ [...] ⌈x x⌉ KÁ ⌈x⌉ [...]

For URU4 in l. 5′ the copy reads MAḪ.
For KEŠDA in l. 5′ the duplicate *TU* 46, obv. 16 has *tar-kás*.
L. 5′–6′ differs from duplicate *TU* 46, obv. 16–17: for ŠE.NUMUN DÙ.A.BI DUB-[*aq*] the fragment at the end of l. 5 clearly reads UZU, so we must assume that here the three well-known meat portions, many times attested in *TU* 45 and *TU* 46, are brought near (^uzu^[ZAG.LU ^uzu^ME.ḪÉ *u* ^uzu^KA.NE *tu-ṭaḫ-ḫa*]).
L. 6, A A AM SAR ⌈KA(?) x⌉ (lost in *TU* 46, obv. 17) is not clear to me. The duplicate *TU* 46, obv. 18 has additionally: [...]-*ma sír-qu* ^lú^GALA *i-sar-raq*, but there does not seem to be enough room here.
L. 7′, ^d^*A-nu*, the duplicate *TU* 46, obv. 19 has ^d^LX.
L. 11′, ⌈UŠ4(?)⌉ [MAN(?)], the parallel *TU* 45, obv. 16 has UŠ4 KUR MAN-*ni*, but there does not seems to be enough room here.

Although the omen texts in this fragment (9 ff.) and in *TU* 45 (obv. 16, rev. 3–4, 14–16) remind us of *šumma ālu*, as far as I known they are not attested elsewhere.

l. 12–13, four lamentations are recited to Ea, Šamaš and Marduk, which are also attested elsewhere:

‘Because of the destruction of the old house, they spontaneously utter a wail’, see also the parallels *TU* 46, obv. 10, *Bagh. Mitt. Beih.* 2, no. 10, 16–17, and F.H. Weissbach, *Misc.*, no. 12, obv. 13); the interpretation of the incipit was suggested to me by Th.J.H. Krispijn (Leiden).

In obv. 13, the *eršemakku*’s:

‘Important one, who wanders abound’, also in the parallels *TU* 46, obv. 11; rev. 9; *Bagh. Mitt. Beih.* 2, no. 10, 18; *Bagh. Mitt. Beih.* 2, no. 11, obv. fragment 1, 2′; F.H. Weissbach, *Misc.*, no. 12, obv. [11]. Furthermore it is attested the Uruk kettledrum ritual text *TU* 44, II, 14, and the Uruk *mīs pî*-ritual text Bagh. Mitt. Beih. 2, no. 1 (+ //), 24; 26; cf. M.E. Cohen, *Eršemma*, 110 ff.;

‘Utu is king’, see *TU* 46, obv. 11; *Bagh. Mitt. Beih.* 2, no. 10, 18, F.H. Weissbach, *Misc.*, no. 12, obv. [11]. Also as *taqribtu*, cf. M.E. Cohen, *Lamentations*, 423 ff.;

‘The heart of the temple will be calmed down’, see *TU* 46, obv. 12, rev. 7, *Bagh. Mitt. Beih.* 2, no. 10, obv. 18, F.H. Weissbach, *Misc.*, no. 12, obv. [11]; and the Uruk *mīs pî*-ritual text *Bagh. Mitt. Beih.* 2, no. 1 (+ //), 30. In the Neo-Assyrian calendar text K 2724 +, obv. 24, rev. 17 and in T.G Pinches, IV R^2, 53, III, 11, it is classified as an *eršemakku*.

l. 17–18, these lines are duplicated by *Bagh. Mitt. Beih.* 2, no. 11, obv. fragment 2, 5′–6′:

1′ […] ⸢x⸣ […]
2′ […] ⸢x x x⸣ […]
3′ […] ⸢MA(?)⸣ DINGIR.RA.ÀM-*šú* d*É*-⸢*a*(?)⸣[…]
4′ […]⸢x⸣ KI KUR BI IT AD [x][…]

5′ [… *li-te-bi*]-*ib ši-gu-ú a*-[*na* dLX …]
6′ [… *tar-ká*]*s* uduSÍSKUR BAL-[*qí* …]

7′ […] ⸢x⸣ […]

l. 22, BAR.RA UMUN.E TA MA NÍGIN AN.NAM ‘O lord, what turned about in my mind? It is Anu’(?), similar in *SBH*, p. 8, no. 4, 65, 67 (ŠÀ.GA ÀM.NIGIN.NÉ // *ina qer-bé-e-ti i-ṣa-ad*); *SBH*, p. 4, no. 2, 22, 24; J.A. Craig, *ZA* 10 (1895), 276, pl. II, 13, 14. The interpretation of the incipit was suggested to me by Th.J.H. Krispijn (Leiden). Cf. also St. M. Maul, *Herzberuhigungsklagen*, 73.

l. 23, ME.E U.MU.UN.MU.ŠI ŠIM (cf. St.M. Maul, *Herzberuhigungsklagen*, 82; 122) is probably the *eršaḫungû* no. 11: [ME.E UMUN (?) MU.RA ŠI.M]U DA.AN.NA.AB.DE$_{6}$ ‘I want to offer my life to my lord’ (St.M. Maul, *Herzberuhigungsklagen*, 127–30). ME.E AN.ŠAR is probably ME.E dUTU.RA A.RA.ZU GA.AN.NA.AB.DUG$_{4}$ ‘I want to speak a prayer to Šamaš’ (St. M. Maul, *Herzberuhigungsklagen*, 135–40); perhaps the first line was originally: ME.E AN.SAR.RA A.RA.ZU ‘I want to bring my prayer to the shining heaven’ (AN.ŠAR = AN+SAR = *napāḫu* ‘to shine’)(?).

The interpretation of these incipits was suggested to me by Th.J.H. Krispijn (Leiden).

l. 24, SAR = SÁḪAR = *šaḫarru* ‘porous’(?), cf. *AHw*, 1129a. *CAD*, Š/1, 80a does not translate *šaḫarru*.

l. 24–25, the ritual described here has received some attention, see II.6.1.

l. 24–26, rev. 1, these lines are duplicated by *Bagh. Mitt. Beih.* 2, no. 11, obv. fragment 3:

1′ […] ⸢x⸣ […]
2′ [… *a-na* LUGAL *tu-šad*]-*bab uš-ke*[*n*(?) …]
3′ [… *a-n*]*a* É ⸢GAL-*šú*⸣ SI.SÁ [uduSÍSKUR …]
4′ [… *ina*] TÚG.SÍG LUGAL PAP(?) *kul-lat* KI.ŠU!.[PEŠ$_{5}$ …]

---

l. 4′, LUGAL PAP *kul-lat*, or badly written LUGAL *ina kul-lat* as in the duplicate *TU* 45, rev. 1?

l. 25, *ta-kam*!-*mis-ma*, the copy looks more like *te*. See *RAcc.*, 56, n. 93.

l. 25, *a-na mi-ṣir* lúKÚR TAG$_{4}$-*šu* ‘send it off to the enemy’s border’, this phrase has been discussed by W.R. Mayer, *OrNS* 57 (1988), 150, contra *CAD*, E, 417–18, 1, a, 3′ (‘leave it at the enemy’s border’).

l. 26, we would expect ŠID-*nu* at the end of this line (see rev. 7 and 11), although the duplicate *Bagh. Mitt. Beih.* 2, no. 11, obv., fragment 3, 4′ does not have the verb (*ina*] TÚG.SÍG LUGAL PAP *kul-lat* KI.ŠU!.[PEŠ$_5$).

Rev.

l. 1, *an-nam*$^{a\text{-}am}$ DÙ.DÙ-*uš-ma* ḪUL *ana* LUGAL NU TE-*ḫi*, paralleled in rev. 13 and *Bagh. Mitt. Beih.* 2, no. 11, rev. fragment 2, 7′. For the orthography of *an-nam*$^{a\text{-}am}$ (cf. also rev. 13) see B. Lewis, *The Sargon Legend*, 1980, 14 with n. 11.

l. 3, AMA, or ARḪUŠ? The copy reads: KAL. See *RAcc.*, 57, n. 97.

l. 4, 5, these lines are duplicated by *Bagh. Mitt. Beih.* 2, no. 11, rev. fragment 1, 2′, 4′:

1′ […] ⸢x⸣: DIŠ ⸢x⸣ […]
2′ […*ana* ŠÀ] URU KU$_4$-*ma* IGI-*ir mi*[*m-ma* …]
3′ […] x x: DIŠ ŠAḪ *ana* É.GAL […]

4′ [… *a-na* DING]IR URU ^{d}INNIN URU [^{d}LAMMA …]

5′ […] ⸢x⸣ […]

l. 4, *ú-ma-mu* EDEN 'a wild animal', lit. 'an animal of the open country'.

l. 4, IGI-*ir mim-ma ú-šal-pit* 'is seen and defiles something', following *CAD*, L. 93a, c.

l. 6–13, these lines are duplicated by *Bagh. Mitt. Beih.* 2, no. 11, rev. fragment 2, 1′–7′:

1′ [… ^{uzu}] ⸢KA⸣.[NE *tu-ṭaḫ-ḫa* …]
2′ [… MÚ-*aḫ*] *taq-rib-tu*$_4$ GAR-*an* ÉR.ŠEM$_4$.ŠÀ.ḪUN.GÁ.MEŠ-*šú*-[*nu* …]

3′ [… KI GÌR^{II}] *pár*!-*kat*! KI SÙ A KÙ SÙ 3 GI.D[U$_8$.MEŠ …]
4′ [… BAL]-*qí* [^{uzu}ZAG.LU ^{uzu}ME].ḪÉ *u* ^{uzu}KA.NE *tu-ṭaḫ-ḫa u* KAŠ SAG GEŠ[TIN …]
5′ [… GAR-*an*] ÉR.ŠEM$_4$.ŠÀ.ḪUN.GÁ.MEŠ-⸢*šú-nu*⸣ [*ina*] TÚG.SÍG LUGAL ŠID-*nu* ⸢EGIR-*šú a-na* DINGIR EDEN⸣ ^{d}INNIN [EDEN …]
6′ [… ^{uz}]^{u}ZAG.LU ^{uzu}ME.ḪÉ *u* ^{uzu}KA.⸢NE *tu-ṭaḫ*⸣-*ḫa* ⸢KAŠ⸣ BAL-*qí* ÉR [GAR-*an*]

7′ [… *te-*]*ep-pu-uš-ma* ḪUL *a-na* LUGAL NU TE.ME

The duplicate *TU* 45, rev. 12 has additionally KAŠ SAG GEŠTIN GA BAL-*qí*, and ^{lú}MAŠ.MAŠ *u* ^{lú}GALA URU.BI *ú-kap-ru-*ʾ.

l. 8, KI SÙ A KÙ SÙ, although we have an exact parallel in l. 20 and *Bagh. Mitt. Beih.* 2, no. 11, rev. fragment 2, 3′, we must ask whether the first *tasallaḫ* (SÙ) is not a mistake for *tašabbiṭ* (SAR) 'you will sweep', which would make much more sense. The phrase *qaqqara tašabbiṭ mê ellūti tasallaḫ* (KI SAR A KÙ SÙ) is well-known, see my comments on obv. 6–7 above, and on *TU* 44, I, 8.

l. 14, 15, 16, these lines, containing several omina, are duplicated by *Bagh. Mitt. Beih.* 2, no. 11, rev. fragment 2, 13′, 14′, 15′a, 16′.

l. 14, *uk*[!]*-kil* stands for *uk-kul*, a stative D-stem of *ekēlu*.

l. 15, for TÙM-*ma*, see *CAD*, E, 72b.

l. 15, *tazzimtu* (I.^{d}UTU, see *MSL* XIII, 161, 23) rather than *i-ìl-tú* (*RAcc.*, 38).

l. 16, GIR UB is not clear to me.

l. 17, *ina* UD ŠE.GA(!?), the copy reads GAB, but perhaps the scribe erroneously wrote GA[!].ŠE for ŠE.GA. A similar phrase is attested in *TU* 46, obv. 2. Or should we read: *ūmu* (UD) *rēqu* (DU_8) 'a free day' (suggestion M. Stol)?

l. 17, ^{d}MAŠ.DÚB, cf. St. M. Maul, *Herzberuhigungsklagen*, 248, 19.

l. 23, *tak-per*[!]*-tu*$_4$ (the copy reads RIB), similar in *TU* 46, rev. 13. This reading was already suggested by F. Thureau-Dangin (*RAcc.*, 57, n. 105).

TU 46 (O.174)[43]

This is a building ritual text from Hellenistic Uruk, written by Anu-bēlšunu, son of Nidintu-Anu and dated 28-III-81 S.E. (13-VII-231 B.C.) This Anu-bēlšunu is perhaps the same person who wrote *TU* 45 and *Bagh. Mitt. Beih.* 2, no. 12, dated 112 S.E. (200/199 B.C.), and the grandfather of Anu-bēlšunu who is attested in *Bagh. Mitt. Beih.* 2, no. 5 and no. 89 (see the Introduction of these texts, above). The text is partially duplicated by *TU* 45, F.H. Weissbach, *Misc.*, no. 12 and *SpTU* 4, no. 141.

The text is discussed in II.6.

Obv.

1 [*e-nu-ma*] ⸢É⸣.GAR$_8$ É DINGIR *i-qa-pu a-na na-qa-rim-ma uš-šu-ši šá* É *šu-a-tu*
2 [*áš-ri-šu* ^{lú}Ḫ]AL *uš-šar-ma ina* ITI *šal-me ina* UD ŠE.GA *ina* GE$_6$ 3 GI.KU$_8$
3 [*ana* DINGI]R É ^{d}INNIN É *u* ⸢^{d}LAMMA É⸣ *tar-kás* ⸢^{udu}⸣SÍSKUR BAL-*qí* ^{uzu}ZAG
4 ^{uzu}ME.ḪÉ *u* ^{uzu}KA.NE *tu-*[*ṭaḫ*]*-ḫa* KAŠ GEŠTIN GA BAL-*qí ab-ru a-na* ^{d}IDIM
5 *u* ^{d}ASAL.LÚ.ḪI *tu-nam-mar* ^{udu}SÍSKUR *a-na* ^{d}*É-a u* ^{d}ASAL.LÚ.ḪI BAL-*qí*
6 KAŠ GEŠTIN GA BAL-*qí* ^{d}UTU.GIN$_7$ È.TA ÉR Ù.LI.LI EN.ZU ⟨SÁ⟩.MA[R.MA]R
7 ÉR.ŠEM$_4$.MA ŠÌR *ina še-rì ina* ÙR É DINGIR *šu-a-tu a-šar* [*ta-šab-biṭ*]
8 A.MEŠ KÙ SÙ-*aḫ* 3 GI.DU$_8$ *a-na* ^{d}*É-a* ^{d}UTU *u* ^{d}ASAL.⸢LÚ.ḪI⸣
9 GUB-*an* 3 ^{udu}SÍSKUR BAL-*qí* ŠE.NUMUN DÙ.A.BI DUB-*aq* A.MEŠ GUB-[*an*]
10 *ab-ru* MÚ-*aḫ* É.ZI GUL.GUL.LU.DÈ NÍ.BI.ŠÈ ÉR IM.Š[E$_8$.ŠE$_8$]
11 *ina ter-ṣi* É ŠÌR EGIR-*šú* DILMUN^{ki} NIGIN.NA ^{d}UTU LUGAL.À[M]
12 É.ŠÀ.AB.ḪUN.GÁ.TA *ina ḫal-ḫal-la-ti a-na* ^{d}IDIM ^{d}UTU *u* ^{d}ASAL.LÚ.[ḪI]
13 ŠÌR *i-kal-la* A.MEŠ ÍL-*ma* ^{túg} *šid-du tu-na-aḫ* ^{lú}ŠITIM *šá* [É]
14 *šu-a-tu* TÚG DADAG MU$_4$.MU$_4$-*aš* ḪAR AN.NA *ina* ŠU-*šú* GAR-*an ḫa-ṣi-in* A.G[AR$_5$]
15 ÍL-*ma* SIG$_4$ *maḫ-ri-ti i-de-ek-ku ina* É *pár-si* GAR-*an* 1-*en* GI.D[U$_8$]
16 *a-na* IGI SIG$_4$ *ana* DINGIR URU$_4$ *tar-kás* ^{udu}SÍSKUR BAL-*qí* ŠE.NUMUN DÙ.A.BI DUB-[*aq*]
17 K[AŠ GEŠTIN G]A BAL-*qí uš-ken a-di na-qa-ri u e-pe-ši-ka* A [...]
18 [...]x-*ma sír-qu* ^{lú}GALA *i-sar-raq* LÀL Ì.NUN.NA GA KAŠ GEŠTIN *u* Ì.GIŠ [DÙG.GA]
19 [*ina*] *muḫ-ḫi ú-naq-qu* ^{lú}GALA *e-nu-ma* ^{d}LX *ib-nu-ú* AN-*e ana* IGI SI[G$_4$ ŠID-*nu*]

---

20 [*n*]*é-pe-ši šá* ŠU ^{lú}GALA

---

21 [DI]RI.GA(?) *iš-tu* É *na-qa-ri u né-pe-ši i-te-né-ep-pu-š*[*ú*]
22 [*e-nu*]-*ma* É.GAR$_8$ É DINGIR *i-qa-pu a-na na-qa-rim-ma uš-šu-ši* ^{lú}ḪA[L]
23 [*ina* IT]I *šal-me ina u$_4$-me* ŠE.GA *ina* UGU TÚG.SÍG LUGAL {LUGAL} SILA$_4$ ÍL-*ma ki*[-*ma*]
24 [*ta-mit*] *ba-ru-ti e-nu-ma* É.GAR$_8$ É DINGIR *i-qa-pu* ŠI[D-*nu-ma*]
25 [*ki-a-am*] SILA$_4$ *an-na-a* ZAG *e-pu-uš šum-ma ana ṭa-ab-ti in-né-pu-u*[*š*]
26 [*ina* EGIR] *na-qa-ri u e-pe-ši an-nu-ú ana* LUGAL *u* KUR-*šú ana* SIG$_5$-*t*[*ì*]
27 [GAR-*an*] *a-di na-qa-ri u e-pe-ši mu-uḫ-ḫu-ru* ÉR.MEŠ *in-né-ep-pu-*[*šú*]
28 [*sír*]-*qu ma-aq-qa-a-tú u mi-nu-tu$_4$* ^{lú}GALA *ul i-kal-la*

---

43 Cf. *RAcc.*, 9, 40–45; A.J. Sachs, in: J.B. Pritchard, *ANET*^{2}, 340 f.

Rev.

1 *ṭup-pi ḫi-šiḫ-ti šá* ŠU^{II} ^{lú}GALA

---

2 *e-nu-ma* URU$_4$ É DINGIR ŠUB-*ú ina* ITI *šal-me ina u$_4$-me* ŠE.GA URU$_4$ É DINGIR BAD *e-ma* URU$_4$ É DINGIR

3 ŠUB-*ú ina* GE$_6$ 5 KEŠDA.MEŠ *a-na* ^{d}EN.ZU ^{d}AMAR.UTU ^{d}NIN.MAḪ ^{d}KULLA *u* ^{d}N[IN.ŠUB]UR

4 *tar-kás* ^{udu}SÍSKUR BAL-*qí* ŠE.NUMUN DÙ.A.BI DUB-*aq ab-ru* MÚ-*aḫ* KAŠ GEŠTIN GA

5 BAL-*qí* UD.DAM KI.MU.UŠ ÉR UMUN BÁRA.KÙ.GA ÉR.ŠEM$_4$.MA ŠÌR

6 EGIR-*šú* 3 KEŠDA *a-na* DINGIR É ^{d}INNIN É ^{d}LAMMA É *tar-kás ab-ru* MÚ-*aḫ*

7 A.MEŠ GUB-*an* ^{túg}*šid-du* GÍD.DA-*ad* É.ŠÀ.AB.ḪUN.GÁ.E.TA *ina tar-ṣi* É

8 *ina ḫal-ḫal-la-ti* ŠÌR EGIR-*šú ina še-rì* 3 KEŠDA *a-na* ^{d}LX ^{d}EN.LÍL *u* ^{d}[*É-a*]

9 *tar-kás* UMUN ŠE.ER.MA.AL.LA.ŠÈ AN.KI.A ÉR DILMUN^{ki} NIGIN.NA.À[M ÉR].ŠEM$_4$.MA ŠÌR

10 UD ^{d}LX ^{d}EN.LÍL.LÁ ^{d}EN.KI AN.KI.A MU.UN.DÍM.DÍM.E.NE ŠÌ[R …]

11 KEŠDA.MEŠ DUḪ-*ár-ma* URU$_4$ ŠUB-*di a-di* É DINGIR.BI *i-*⌜*qat-tu*⌝*-ú*

12 *mu-úḫ-*⟨*ḫu*⟩*-ru* ÉR.MEŠ *e-pe-šú u*[*l t*]*a-kal-la-*⌜*ma*⌝

13 ID URU$_4$ ŠUB-*ú tak-per-tu$_4$* KI.BI *tu-ḫa-ab*

---

14 *né-pe-ši šá* ŠU^{II} ^{lú}GALA

---

15 *e-nu-ma sip-*[*p*]*u ku-nu*

---

16 IM ^{I}*Ni-din-tu$_4$-*^{d}LX *qàt* ^{I}LX-UMUN-*šú-nu* DUMU.A.NI ^{lú}ŠÚ TUR UNUG^{ki}

17 ^{iti}SIG$_4$ UD.28.KAM MU.81.KAM ^{I}*Se-lu-ku* LUGAL

Obv.

1 [When] the wall of the temple buckles, to demolish and renovate that temple,

2 [the di]viner will release [the emplacement] of that temple and in an auspicious month, on a favourable day, during the night, you will arrange (l. 3) 3 offering tables

3 [for the go]d of the temple, the goddess of the temple and the protective spirit (*lamassu*) of the temple. You will make a sheep offering. You will bring (l. 4) shoulder,

4 *ḫimṣu*-omentum and roasted meat near. You will make a libation of beer, wine (and) milk. You will set fire to (l. 5) a brushwood pile for Ea

5 and Marduk. You will make a sheep offering for Ea and Marduk.

6 You will make a libation of beer, wine (and) milk. You will sing the *taqribtu*-lamentation 'Come out like the sun' (and) the *eršemakku*-lamentation (l. 7) 'O, wise En, planner'.

7 In the morning, on the roof of the temple, [you will sweep] (this) place,

8 you will sprinkle pure water. You will set up (l. 9) 3 offering tables in front of Ea, Šamaš and Marduk.

9 You will make 3 sheep offerings. You will scatter all (kinds of) barley seed. You will set up a water (basin).

10 You will kindle a brushwood pile. You will sing (l. 11) 'Because of the destruction of the old house, they spontaneously utter a *taqribtu*-lamentation',

11 in the direction of the temple. After this you will sing (l. 13) (the *eršemakku*-lamentations) 'Important one, who wanders abound', 'Utu is king'

12 (and) 'The heart of the temple will be calmed down' to the accompaniment of a *ḫalḫallatu*-drum for Ea, Šamaš and Marduk.

13 He will (then) stop (singing). You will lift up the water (basin) and loosen the curtains. The building-master of that (l. 14) temple
14 will put on a clean garment. He will place a tin bracelet on his wrist. He will lift up (l. 15) an axe (made) of lead
15 and he will remove the first brick. He will place (this) in a secluded temple. You will arrange (l. 16) 1 offering table
16 before the brick for the god of the foundation. You will make a sheep offering. You will scatt[er] all (kinds of) barley seed.
17 You will make a libation of be[er, wine (and) m]ilk. He will prostrate himself. While you are demolishing and (re)building, [...],
18 [...] and the lamentation priest will scatter a *serqu*-offering. They will make a libation of (l. 19) honey, ghee, milk, beer, wine and [good] oil
19 before (the brick). The lamentation priest [will recite] 'When Anu created Heaven' in front of the bric[k].

---

20 (This is) the ritual procedure of the lamentation priest.

---

21 [Supple]ment(?), after the demolishing of the temple, and the repeated performing(?) of the ritual procedure:
22 [Wh]en the wall of the temple buckles, to demolish and renovate it,
23 [in] an [auspic]ious month, on a favourable day, the divin[er] (l. 22) will lift up a lamb over the king's hem and in accor[dance with]
24 [the oracle answer] of divination he will reci[te] 'When the wall of the temple buckles' [and]
25 [thus] he will perform [the oracle question] (with/on) this lamb. If (this) is performe[d] with good (results),
26 [afterwards] this demolishing and renovating will be (l. 27) for the goo[d] of the king and his land.
27 During the demolishing and renovating *muḫḫuru*-offerings and *taqribtu*-lamentations will be performe[d].
28 The lamentation priest will not cease with [*ser*]*qu*-offerings, *maqqītu*-libations and recitations.

Rev.
1 (This is) the tablet (listing) the necessities for the use of the lamentation priest.

---

2 When the foundation is laid, in an auspicious month, on a favourable day, you will open up the (old) foundation of the temple. When you are laying (l. 3) the foundation of the temple,
3 you will arrange (l. 4) during the night 5 offering accoutrements for Sîn, Marduk, Ninmaḫ, Kulla and N[inšub]ur.
4 You will make a sheep offering. You will scatter all (kinds of) barley seed. You will kindle a brushwood pile. You will make a libation of (l. 5) beer, wine (and) milk.
5 You will sing the *taqribtu*-lamentation 'It touches the Earth like a storm' and the *eršemakku*-lamentation 'Lord of the Pure Dais'.
6 Next you will arrange 3 offering accoutrements for the god of the temple, the goddess of the temple (and) the protective spirit (*lamassu*) of the temple. You will kindle a brushwood pile.
7 You will set up a water (basin). You will draw the curtains shut. In the direction of the temple you will sing (l. 8) (the *eršemakku*-lamentation) 'The heart of the temple will be calmed down'

8 to the accompaniment of a *ḫalḫallatu*-drum. After this you will arrange (l. 9) 3 offering accoutrements for Anu, Enlil and [Ea].

9 You will sing the *taqribtu*-lamantation 'Lord, respected one of Heaven and Earth' (and) the *eršemakku*-lamentation 'Important one, who wanders abound'.

10 You will sin[g] 'When Anu, Enlil and Enki created Heaven and Earth'.[...]

11 You will clear away the offering accoutrements and lay the foundation of that temple. Until (the completion of) that temple comes to an end,

12 you will not stop performing the *muḫḫuru*-offerings (and) *taqribtu*-lamentations.

13 When(?) the foundation is laid, you will consecrate that emplacement with *takpertu*-purifications.

---

14 (This is) the ritual procedure of the lamentation priest.

(Catchline:)

15 When the doorframes are in place.

(Colophon:)

16 Tablet of Nidintu-Anu, (written by) the hand of Anu-bēlšunu, his son, the apprentice lamentation priest,

17 the (third) month Simānu, day 28, year 81, Seleucus being king.

Comments

Obv.

l. 2, '[the di]viner will release (i.e. deconsecrate) [the emplacement (i.e. the building plot)] of that temple', namely from the status of holiness, compare rev. 13, where the emplacement is consecrated. Cf. *CAD*, A/II, 459a and *AHw*, 1486a, 8, d ('freigeben'). Obv. 1–2 is paralleled in F.H. Weissbach, *Misc.*, no. 12, obv. 1–2. For *ašru* 'emplacement', see also W. Baumgartner, *ZA* 36 (1925), 30 ff. ('Baustelle').

l. 3 (see also rev. 6), 'the god of the temple, the goddess of the temple and the protective spirit (*lamassu*) of the temple' (DINGIR É ^{d}INNIN É *u* ^{d}LAMMA É) are anonymous protective spirits which have to be distinguished from the main gods of the temple, see K. van der Toorn, in: K.R. Veenhof (ed.), *Houses and Households in Ancient Mesopotamia*, 40e RAI Leiden 1993, Leiden, Istanbul, 1996, 70 f. The line is paralleled in *TU* 45, obv. 2.

l. 4–5, *ab-ru a-na* ^{d}IDIM *u* ^{d}ASAL.LÚ.ḪI *tu-nam-mar* ^{udu}SÍSKUR *a-na* ^{d}*É-a u* ^{d}ASAL.-LÚ.ḪI BAL-*qí*, also in the parallel F.H. Weissbach, *Misc.*, no. 12, obv. 3–4, but in the third person plural.

l. 6, instead of the lamentation 'Woe, who has destroyed (the temple)?' in *TU* 45, obv. 6, *TU* 46, obv. 6 has 'O, wise En, planner', cf. M.E. Cohen, *Eršemma*, 125–127.

l. 7, for [*ta-šab-biṭ*] see my comment on *TU* 45, obv. 6–7, and on *TU* 44, I, 8.

l. 11–20, these lines are duplicated by *Bagh. Mitt. Beih.* 2, no. 11, obv. fragment 1, 2′–8′. For a transliteration of this fragment see my comments on *TU* 45, obv. 11–14, 15, 16.

l. 13, for the 'building master', wr. lúŠITIM = *itinnu* (cf. F.H. Weissbach, *Misc.*, no. 12, obv. [14]; also attested in *BRM* 4, 6 (describing the eclipse of the moon ritual), obv. 30′), and not lúDÍM = *mubannû*, the 'arranger (of the offering table)', see III.4.3.

l. 15, *i-de-ek-ku*, a plural, although a singular is intended.

l. 15, SIG_4 *maḫ-ri-ti* 'the first brick', also in F.H. Weissbach, *Misc.*, no. 12, obv. 17. See W. Baumgartner, *ZA* 36 (1925), 247 with n. 3 ('Grundstein'); R. Borger, *Esarh.*, 5 ('erster Ziegel'); R.S. Ellis, *Foundation Deposits in Ancient Mesopotamia*, New Haven and London, 1968, 26 ff.

l. 17, the end of this line is duplicated by *Bagh. Mitt. Beih.* 2, no. 11, obv. fragment 1, 6′, but not clear to me.

l. 18, [...]x-*ma sír-qu*, the duplicate F.H. Weissbach, *Misc.*, no. 12, obv. 20 reads: [UGU] NÍG.NA *si-ir-qí*, but the copy does not allow this restoration here.

l. 18, Ì.GIŠ [DÙG.GA] '[good] oil', see F.H. Weissbach, *Misc.*, no. 12, obv. 20.

l. 19, *e-nu-ma* dLX *ib-nu-ú* AN-*e*, recited in full in F.H. Weissbach, *Misc.*, no. 12, obv. 24 ff. See my comments on these lines, below.

l. 21–28, see the parallel *SpTU* 4, no. 141, rev. 14–19.

l. 21, DI]RI.GA(?) 'supplement', this was suggested by F. Thureau-Dangin (*RAcc.*, 42), although the copy reads: [...] A GUD. The parallel *SpTU* 4, no. 141, rev. 14 cannot help, because the beginning of this line is damaged.

l. 21, *i-te-né-ep-pu-š*[*ú*] 'the repeatedly performing(?)' (see also the duplicate *SpTU* 4, no. 141, rev. 14), here perhaps as infinitive? See *AHw*, 227b.

l. 28, the parallel *SpTU* 4, no. 141, rev. 19 here includes: lúNAR *in-ḫa ul i-kal-la* 'the singer will (then) stop (singing) the *inḫu*-song'. See also F.H. Weissbach, *Misc.*, no. 12, obv. 5.

Rev.

l. 2–13, these lines are also translated in M.E. Cohen, *Lamentations*, 26–27.

l. 5 ff., among the lamentations mentioned here but not in *TU* 45 are the *taqribtu*s:

'It touches the Earth like a storm', also in the Uruk *mīs pî*-ritual text *Bagh. Mitt. Beih.* 2, no. 1 (+ //), 9, and in the Kislīmu ritual from Babylon BM 32206 +, IV, 158. Also mentioned in the Uruk cultic calendar text *TU* 48, rev. 3, see II.2.2;

'Lord, respected one of Heaven and Earth', in rev. 9; see also *Bagh. Mitt. Beih.* 2, no. 1 (+ //), 24; 25, and the Uruk New Year text *TU* 39, rev. 10.

and the eršemakku:

'Lord of the pure Dais', see also *Bagh. Mitt. Beih.* 2, no. 1 (+ //), 9.

l. 10, this bilingual hand-raising prayer (*šuillakku*) is recited in full in *Bagh. Mitt. Beih.* 2, no. 12, see W.R. Mayer, *OrNS* 47 (1978), 438–441.

l. 12, for *mu-úḫ-*⟨*ḫu*⟩*-ru*, see III.7.2.

l. 13, ID for UD = *enūma*? See *RAcc.*, 45: 'lorsque(?)'.

l. 16, for the scribe Anu-bēlšunu see my comments on *Bagh. Mitt. Beih.* 2, no. 5, rev. 34.

Bagh. Mitt. Beih. 2, no. 10 (W 20030/2)[44]

This building ritual text from Hellenistic Uruk is partially a duplicate of *TU* 45, *TU* 46 and F.H. Weissbach, *Misc.*, no. 12.

The text is discussed in II.6.

U.E. [*ina* INIM ^{d}LX *u An-t*]*u*$_4$ ⸢*liš-lim*⸣(?)

Obv.

1 [*e-nu-ma* É.GAR$_8$ É ^{d}LX *i-qa-pu a-na na-qa-rim-ma u*]*š-šu-ši* ⸢*šá*⸣ [É *šu-a-tu*]
2 [*ina*] ITI *šal-mu ina* [UD ŠE.GA] *ina* GE$_6$ 3 [GI.DU$_8$] ⸢*a-na* DINGIR⸣ [É]
3 [^{d}INNIN] É *u* ^{d}[LAMMA É *tar-kás* ^{udu}]⸢SÍSKUR⸣ BAL-*qí* ^{u}[^{zu}ZAG.LU]
4 ^{uzu}ME.ḪÉ *u* ^{uzu}[KA.NE *t*]*u-ṭaḫ-ḫa* KAŠ SAG GEŠTIN [GA]
5 BAL-*qí ab-ru a-na* ⸢^{d}*É*⸣*-a u* ^{d}ASAL.LÚ.ḪI *tu-na*[*m-mar*]
6 ^{udu}SÍSKUR *a-na* ^{d}*É-a u* ^{d}ASAL.LÚ.ḪI BAL-*qí* [KAŠ SAG]
7 GEŠTIN GA BAL-*qí* ^{d}UTU.GIN$_7$ È.TA UB LA Ú(?) ⸢ÉR⸣
8 Ù.BA MU.ḪUL ÉR.ŠEM$_4$.MA ŠÌR *ina še-rì ina* ÙR
9 É DINGIR.MEŠ *šu-a-tu a-šar ta-ši-biṭ* (sic) A KÙ.MEŠ *ta-sal-*⸢*làḫ*⸣
10 3 GI.DU$_8$.MEŠ *a-na* ^{d}*É-a* ^{d}UTU *u* ^{d}ASAL.LÚ.ḪI KEŠ[DA]
11 3 GADA *ina muḫ-ḫi* KI.TUŠ.MEŠ GAR-*an* NINDA.Ì.DÉ.ÀM ⸢LÀL⸣
12 Ì.NUN.NA ZÚ.LUM.MA ^{zì}EŠA Ì.GIŠ BÁR.GA GAR-*an* [3]
13 A.DA.GUR$_5$ KAŠ SAG GEŠTIN GA GUB-*an* NÍG.NA ^{šim}LI [GAR-*an*]
14 ŠE.NUMUN DÙ.A.BI DUB-*aq* 3 ^{udu}SÍSKUR BAL-*qí* [^{uzu}ZAG]
15 ⸢LU⸣ ^{uzu}ME.ḪÉ *u* ^{uzu}KA.NE *tu-ṭaḫ-ḫa* KAŠ SA[G GEŠTIN GA]
16 BAL-*qí* A.MEŠ GUB-*an* ⸢^{túg}*šid-du*⸣ GÍD.DA-*ad* É.Z[I GUL.GUL.LU.DÈ NÍ.BI.ŠÈ]
17 ÉR IM.ŠE$_8$.ŠE$_8$ ⸢*ina ter-ṣi*⸣ É ŠÌR [EGIR-*šú*]
18 DILMUN^{ki} NIGIN.NA ^{d}[UTU LUGAL].ÀM ÉR.[ŠEM$_4$.MA.MEŠ(?)]
19 *ina ḫal-ḫal-la-at a-na* ⸢^{d}⸣[*É-a* ^{d}UTU *u* ^{d}ASAL.LÚ.ḪI]
20 ŠÌR *i-kal-la* A.[MEŠ ÍL-*ma* ^{túg}*šid-du tu-na-ḫa*]

---

21 *né-pe-ši šá* ŠU^{II} [^{lú}GALA]

The reverse is not written.

U.E.

[By the command of Anu and Ant]u may (this work) be succesful(?).

Obv.

1 [When the wall of the temple of Anu buckles, to demolish and re]novate [that temple],
2 [you will arrange (l. 3) in] an auspicious month, on [a favourable day], in the night 3 [offering tables for the god of the temple],
3 [the goddess] of the temple and [the protective spirit (*lamassu*) of the temple]. You will make [sheep o]fferings. [Y]ou will bring (l. 4) s[houlder],
4 *ḫimṣu*-omentum and ro[asted meat] near. You will make a libation of (l. 5) first-quality beer, wine (and) [milk].
5 You will set fire to a brushwood pile for Ea and Marduk.

[44] Cf. W.R. Mayer, *Bagh. Mitt. Beih.* 2, p. 16.

6 You will make a sheep offering for Ea and Marduk. You will make a libation of (l. 7) [first-quality beer],
7 wine (and) milk. You will sing (l. 8) the *taqribtu*-lamentation 'Come out like the sun' …,
8 (and) the *eršemakku*-lamentation 'Woe, who has destroyed (the temple)?'. In the morning, on the roof
9 of that temple, you will sweep (this) place, you will sprinkle pure water.
10 You will arran[ge] 3 offering tables in front of Ea, Šamaš and Marduk.
11 You will place 3 linen (cloths) on the seats. You will place (l. 12) a *mirsu*-confection (made with) honey,
12 ghee, dates, *sasqû*-flour (and) pressed oil. You will set up (l. 13) [3]
13 *adakurru*-containers (with) first-quality beer, wine (and) milk. [You will place] a censer with juniper.
14 You will scatter all (kinds of) barley seed. You will make 3 sheep offerings. You will bring [shoul-]
15 der, *ḫimṣu*-omentum and roasted meat near. You will make a libation (l. 16) of fir[st-quality] beer, [wine (and) milk].
16 You will set up a water (basin). You will draw the curtains shut. You will sing (l. 17) ['Because of the destruction of] the [o]ld house,
17 they spontaneously utter a *taqribtu*-lamentation', in the direction of the temple. [After this]
18 you will sing (l. 20) the *er*[*šemakku*-lamentations] 'Important one, who wanders abound', (and) '[Utu] is [king]'
19 to the accompaniment of a *ḫalḫallatu*-drum for [Ea, Šamaš and Marduk].
20 He will (then) stop (singing). [You will lift up the] wat[er (basin) and loosen the curtains].

---

21 (This is) the ritual procedure of the lamentation priest.

Comments

Obv.

See the duplicates *TU* 45, obv. 1–15; *TU* 46, obv. 1–13. See also F.H. Weissbach, *Misc.*, no. 12, obv. 1–14.

l. 7, UB LA Ú(?), not attested in the duplicates *TU* 45, obv. 5, and *TU* 46, obv. 6. Since ÉR follows these three signs, apparently it belongs to the incipit.

l. 8, Ù.BA MU.ḪUL, the duplicate *TU* 45, obv. 6 reads: Ù.Ù.A.BA MU.ḪUL.

l. 8–9, *ina še-rì ina* ÙR É DINGIR.MEŠ *šu-a-tu a-šar ta-ši-biṭ* (= *tašabbiṭ*) A KÙ.MEŠ *ta-sal-*⸢*làḫ*⸣, this phrase is partly preserved in the duplicates *TU* 45, obv. 6–7 and *TU* 46, obv. 7–8. Similar in *TU* 44, I, 8 and written syllabically perhaps in *Bagh. Mitt. Beih.* 2, no. 14, 2′. However, the preceding status constructus *a-šar* is problematic. See also my comment on *TU* 44, I, 8 and *TU* 45, obv. 6–7.

l. 18, DILMUN^{ki} NIGIN.NA ^{d}[UTU LUGAL].ÀM ÉR.[ŠEM$_4$.MA.MEŠ(?)], the duplicates *TU* 45, obv. 13 and *TU* 46, obv. 11–12 include a third incipit (É.ŠÀ.AB.ḪUN.-GÁ.TA), but there does not seem to be enough space here.

F.H. Weissbach, *Misc.*, no.12 (BE 13987 = IM 11087, 11 + 11053, 20 + 11053, 325 + 11087, 59)[45]

This tablet from the Late Babylonian period contains a building ritual text from Babylon. The reverse was left unpublished by Weissbach. The text with the reverse was also published by J.J.A. van Dijk, *Sumer* 11 (1955), 110, no. 7, pl. X–XII, however without the lost fourth fragment IM 11087, 59. The latter was published by van Dijk in *TIM* 9, no. 77. Partial duplicates of the text are: *TU* 46, *Bagh. Mitt. Beih.* 2, nos. 10 and 11 and *SpTU* 4, no. 141.

The text is discussed in II.6.

Obv.

1 *e-nu-ma* É.GAR$_8$ É DINGIR *i-qa-a-ap a-na na-qá-rim-ma uš-šu-ši*
2 *ša* É *šu-a-tu áš-ri-šu* ^{lú}ḪAL *uš-šar-ma*
3 *ina* ITI *šal-me ina* UD ŠE.GA *ina* GE$_6$ *ab-ra ana* ^{d}*É-a u* ^{d}ASAL.LÚ.ḪI *ú-nam-ma-ru-ma*
4 $^{(udu)}$SÍSKUR *a-na* ^{d}*É-a u* ^{d}ASAL.LÚ.ḪI *i-naq-qu-ú* GALA ÉR GAR-*an*
5 ^{lú}NAR *in-ḫa in-ni-iḫ ina še-e-ri ina* ÙR É *šu-a-tu*
6 3 *ri-ik-si ana* ^{d}*É-a* ^{d}UTU *u* ^{d}ASAL.LÚ.ḪI *tar-k*[*ás*]
7 9 PAD NINDA ZÍZ.AN.NA ZÚ.LUM.MA ^{zì}EŠA *ta-sar-*[*raq-ma*]
8 NINDA.Ì.DÉ.ÀM LÀL Ì.NUN.NA *u* Ì.GIŠ BÁR.GA [GAR-*an*]
9 3 ^{dug}A.DA.GUR$_5$ GAR-*an* KAŠ SAG [GEŠTIN GA BAL-*qí*]
10 NÍG.NA ^{šim}LI GAR-*an* [ŠE.NUMUN DÙ.A.BI DUB-*aq*]
11 2 ^{udu}SÍSKUR BAL-*q*[*í* DILMUN^{ki} NIGIN.NA ^{d}UTU LUGAL.ÀM É.ŠÀ.AB.ḪUN.GÁ.TA]
12 GALA *ina ḫal-ḫal-la-*[*ti a-na* ^{d}*É-a*] ⸢^{d}UTU⸣ ^{d}ASAL.LÚ.ḪI *i-za-am-mur*
13 EGIR-*šú* É.ZI G[UL.GUL.LU.DÈ N]Í.BI.ŠÈ ÉR IM.ŠE$_8$.ŠE$_8$ *i-za-am-mur*
14 *i-kal-la* [^{lú}ŠITIM *š*]*á* É *šu-a-tu*
15 TÚG DADAG MU[$_4$.MU$_4$-*aš* ḪAR AN.N]A *ina* ŠU-*šú* GAR-*an*
16 ⸢*ḫa-ṣi*⸣-[*in* A.G]AR$_5$ ÍL-*ma*
17 [SIG$_4$ *maḫ-ri-t*]*ú i-de-ek-ki-ma*
18 [*ina muḫ-ḫi*] ⸢É⸣ *i-sa-ap-pid ù-ù'-i i-qab-bi-ma* SIG$_4$ *šu-a-tu*$_4$
19 [*ina* É] ⸢*pár*⸣*-si i-šak-ka-nu-ma*
20 [UGU] NÍG.NA *si-ir-qí* GALA *i-sar-raq*
21 [LÀL Ì].NUN.NA GA KAŠ GEŠTIN *u* Ì DÙG.GA
22 [*ina muḫ-ḫ*]*i ú-naq-qu-ú*
23 ⸢*ù*⸣ *e-nu-ma* ^{d}*A-nu ib-nu-ú* AN-*e ana* IGI SIG$_4$ ŠID-*nu*

---

24 *e-nu-ma* ^{d}*A-nu ib-nu-ú* AN-*e*
25 ^{d}NU.DÍM.MUD *ib-nu-ú* ABZU *šu-bat-su*
26 ^{d}*É-a ina* ABZU *ik-ru-ṣa ṭi-da-*[*am*]
27 *ib-ni* ^{d}SIG$_4$ *ana te-diš-ti* [É DINGIR.MEŠ]
28 *ib-ni* ^{giš}GI *u* ^{giš}TIR *ana ši-pir nab-ni-ti-*[*ki*]
29 *ib-ni* ^{d}NIN.ÍLDU (IGI.NAGAR.BU) ^{d}NIN.SIMUG *u* ^{d}A.RA.ZU *ana mu-šak-lil ši-pir na*[*b-ni-ti-ki*]
30 *ib-ni ša-di-i ù ta-ma-a-ti ana mim-ma* ŠUM ⸢TI(?)⸣ DU ⸢x⸣ [...]
31 *ib-ni* ^{d}GUŠKIN.BÀN.DA ^{d}NIN.Á.GAL ^{d}NIN.ZADIM *u* ^{d}NIN.KUR.RA *ana ep-še-ti-*[*ki*]
32 *ù ḫi-ṣib-šu-nu du-uš-šá-a ana nin-da-bi-ki ra-bu-ti* ⸢*šu*(?)⸣ [...]

---

45 Cf. P. Jensen, *KB* VI/2, 46–51; *RAcc.*, 44–47; E. Ebeling, in: H. Gressmann, *ATAT*^{2}, 129 f.; A.J. Sachs, in: J.B. Pritchard, *ANET*^{2}, 341 f.

33 *ib-ni* ^{d}AŠ.NA.AN ^{d}LA.ḪAR ^{d}ŠIM ^{d}NIN.GIZ.ZI.DA ^{d}NIN.MÚ ^{d}A.[...]
34 *a-na mu-deš-šu-ú sa-at-*[*tuk-ki*]
35 *ib-ni* ^{d}UMUN.MU.TA.ÀM.GU$_7$ ^{d}UMUN.MU.TA.ÀM.NAG *ana mu-kil nin-da-*[*bi-ki*]
36 *ib-ni* ^{d}KÙ.SÙ GA.ÙZ.MAḪ DINGIR.MEŠ GAL.MEŠ *ana mu-šak-lil par-ṣi-ki* [...]
37 [*i*]*b-ni* LUGAL *ana za-ni-nu* [É DINGIR.MEŠ(?)]
38 [*ib-n*]*i a-me-lu-ti ana i-pí-*⌜*i*(?)*-šu*(?)⌝ [...]
39 [...] *te-*ʾ ⌜x x⌝ [...] ⌜x⌝ [...] ⌜^{d}⌝*A-nù* ^{d}EN.LÍL ^{d}*É-a u* ^{d}[...]
40 [...] ⌜x⌝ [...] ⌜*ú*⌝*-šen-nu* ⌜SAG(?)⌝ [...]

Rev.

1′ [...] ⌜x⌝ [...]
2′ ^{d}GUŠKIN.BÀN.DA ^{d}NIN.SIMUG [...]
3′ ⌜DINGIR x x⌝ MA *ra-bu-ti* NU MA AN [...]
4′ ⌜GIŠ.ḪUR⌝.MEŠ *ṣi-ra-a-ti* [...]
5′ *ne-eb-ṭe-e* ⌜*šu*⌝*-qu-ru-*[*ti*...]
6′ *ina ip-ti u ne-me-*⌜*šá*(?) AN⌝ [...]
7′ *pu-ú* AN.ŠÁR ^{d}ŠA.[LA(?)...]
8′ [...]
9′ *ù la gam-*⌜*mu*(?)*-*x⌝ [...]
10′ *ina ḫi-ṭa a-na* [...]
11′ *a-a i-*⌜x⌝ [...]
12′ *ki-ma* ⌜x⌝ [...]
13′ [...]
14′ *i-*[...]
15′ AD [...]
16′ ⌜DÙ⌝ [...]
17′ ⌜x⌝ [...]

Obv.

1 When the wall of the temple buckles, to demolish and renovate it,
2 the diviner will release the emplacement of that temple and
3 in an auspicious month, on a favourable day, during the night, they will set fire to a brushwood pile for Ea and Marduk and
4 they will make a (sheep) offering for Ea and Marduk. The lamentation priest will perform a *taqribtu*-lamentation.
5 The singer will sing the *inḫu*-song. In the morning, on the roof of that temple,
6 You will arra[nge] 3 offering accoutrements for Ea, Šamaš and Marduk.
7 You will sca[tter] 9 pieces of emmer-bread, dates and *sasqû*-flour [and]
8 [you will place] a *mirsu*-confection (made with) honey, ghee and pressed oil.
9 You will place 3 *adakurru*-containers. [You will make a libation of] first-quality beer, [wine (and) milk].
10 You will place a censer (with) juniper. [You will scatter all (kinds of) barley seed].
11 You will mak[e] 2 sheep offerings. The lamentation priest will sing (l. 12) (the *eršemakku*-lamentations) ['Important one, who wanders abound', 'Utu is king' (and) 'The heart of the temple will be calmed down']
12 to the accompaniment of a *ḫalḫalla*[*tu*-drum for Ea], Šamaš (and) Marduk.
13 After this he will sing 'Because of the des[truction] of the old house, they spontaneously utter a *taqribtu*-lamentation'.
14 He will (then) stop (singing). [The building-master o]f that temple
15 will p[ut on] a clean garment. He will place a [ti]n [bracelet] on his wrist.

16 He will lift up an ax[e] (made) of [le]ad,
17 remove the [fir]st [brick] and
18 he will mourn [for] the temple, say 'woe!' and they will place (l. 19) that brick
19 [in a] secluded [room].
20 He will scatter a *serqu*-offering on a censer.
21 They will make a libation of (l. 22) [honey, g]hee, milk, beer, wine and good oil
22 [o]n (the brick)
23 and he will recite 'When Anu created Heaven' before the brick.

---

24 When Anu created Heaven,
25 (and) Nudimmud created the Subterranean Water, his dwelling,
26 Ea pinched off cla[y] in the Subterranean Water,
27 he created the brick god for the renovation [of the temple(s)],
28 he created reed thicket and forest for the making of [your] shape,
29 he created Ninildu, Ninsimug and Arazu to complete the making of [your] sh[ape],
30 he created mountains and seas for whatever … […],
31 he created Guškinbanda, Ninagal, Ninzadim and Ninkurra for [your] ritual acts,
32 and their abundant produce for your large cereal offerings … […],
33 he created Ašnan, Laḫar, Siriš, Ningizzida, Ninmu, A[…],
34 for making abundant [your] regul[ar offerings],
35 he created Umunmutamgu (and) Umunmutamnag for presenting [your] regula[r offerings],
36 he created Kusu, the *šangammāḫu*-exorcist of the great gods, for completing your rites,
37 [he c]reated the king for providing [the temple(s)(?)]
38 [he creat]ed mankind for doing(?) […]
39 […] … […] … […] Anu, Enlil, Ea and … […]
40 […] … […] they repeated(?) … […]

Rev.
1′ […] … […]
2′ Guškinbanda, Ninsimug […]
3′ the great … … […]
4′ exalted plans/decrees […]
5′ esteemed horizon(?) […]
6′ with tribute(?) and … […]
7′ word of Aššur, Ša[la(?)…]
8′ […]
9′ and not … […]
10′ in sin for […]
11′ May not … […]
12′ as soon as/like […]
13′ […]
14′ … […]
15′ … […]
16′ … […]
17′ … […]

Comments

Obv.

l. 2, for *uš-šar-ma* ‘release’, see my comment on *TU* 46, obv. 2.

l. 3–4, *ab-ra ana* ^{d}*É-a u* ^{d}ASAL.LÚ.ḪI *ú-nam-ma-ru-ma* $^{(udu)}$SÍSKUR *a-na* ^{d}*É-a u* ^{d}ASAL.LÚ.ḪI *i-naq-qu-ú*, the parallels *TU* 45, obv. 4–5, *TU* 46, obv. 4–5 and *Bagh. Mitt. Beih.* 2, no. 10, obv, 5–6 have the second person singular.

l. 4, GALA, although van Dijk’s copy reads UŠ.ŠU.

l. 5, É *šu-a-tu* lit. ‘that house’, the duplicate *TU* 46, obv. 7 has É DINGIR *šu-a-tu* ‘that temple’.

l. 7, ‘9’, as in *RAcc.*, 44, rather than ‘30’ (cf. F.H. Weissbach, *Misc.*, 32 and P. Jensen, *KB* VI/2, 48).

l. 11, this reconstruction was suggested by F. Thureau-Dangin (*RAcc.*, 44).

l. 14–38, these lines were also discussed by R. Labat, *Les religions du Proche-Orient asiatique*, Paris, 1970, 76–77.

l. 15–17, 22 f., these lines are also duplicated by *Bagh. Mitt. Beih.* 2, no. 11, obv. fragment 1, 4′ and 7′.

l. 17, [SIG$_4$ *maḫ-ri-t*]*ú i-de-ek-ki-ma*, see the parallel *TU* 46, obv. 15.

l. 24 ff., here the first lines of the prayer *Enūma Anu ibnû šamê* are presented. See also J.J.A. van Dijk, *TIM* 9, pl. LXI, no. 77, obverse. It is duplicated by *SpTU* 4, no. 141, obverse. These lines were also discussed by A. Heidel, *The Babylonian Genesis, the story of creation*^{2}, Chicago, 1951, 65–66; J. Bottéro, *Mythes et rites de Babylone*, Paris, 1985, 294–95.

The incipit *e-nu-ma* ^{d}*A-nu ib-nu-ú* AN-*e* is mentioned in *TU* 46, obv. 19. The incipit is also attested in the astronomical diaries from Babylon, A.J. Sachs–H. Hunger, *Diaries*, no. -270, B, rev. 15′–17′, see my comments in II.6.2. Another part of *Enūma Anu ibnû šamê* is probably attested in the unpublished Rm 101 (published here, see Plate IV), as the mention of several deities (Umunmutamgu and Umunmutamnag in line x + 11, Kulla in line x + 15) indicate, but the reading is difficult because the beginning of the lines are lost. The fragment does not belong to the Weissbach tablet, but, based on the script, was probably written in the Late Neo-Assyrian period (see for example the sign LI in line 3 and passim). The text on the reverse is completely lost.

l. 27, ‘the brick god’, i.e. Kulla. Cf. R.S. Ellis, *Foundation Deposits*, 18 ff.

l. 28, *nab-ni-ti-*[*ki*] ‘[your] shape’ (see also obv. 29: *na*[*b-ni-ti-ki*]), i.e. the shape of the first brick, as in obv. 32: *nin-da-bi-ki* and obv. 36: *par-ṣi-ki* (see *CAD*, K, 348a), rather than: *nab-ni-ti-*[*šú-nu*], cf. *RAcc.*, 46 and other editions. For this reason we also restored in obv. 31: *ep-še-ti-*[*ki*] and in obv. 34: *sa-at-*[*tuk-ki*]. Cf. *CAD*, N/I, 29a, b and Š/III, 78a. So, the lines 28 ff. are first of all concerned with the first brick, rather than with the temples.

l. 30, TI(?), more clear on the copy of van Dijk than of Weissbach.

l. 32, *ra-bu-ti* (especially clear in van Dijk's copy), as in the duplicate *SpTU* 4, no. 141, obv. 10?

Rev.

l. 1′ff., the transliteration presented here is based on *TIM* 9, pl. LXI, no. 77, reverse, which is better preserved than the rest of the reverse (cf. J.J.A. van Dijk, *Sumer* 11 [1955], pl. XII). Nevertheless the translation remains tentative.

l. 2′, ᵈNIN.SIMUG is also attested in obv. 29. Or should we read ᵈNIN.Á!.[GAL …], as in obv. 31, here also preceded by Guškinbanda?

g. The eclipse of the moon ritual

BRM 4, 6 (MLC 1872)[46] and BM 134701[47]

The Uruk text *BRM* 4, 6 describes the first part of a ritual which had to be performed during an eclipse of the moon. The last section of this text is duplicated by another Uruk text, BM 134701, which also contains the final part of the eclipse ritual.[48] For this reason the latter will be presented here again together with *BRM* 4, 6. Contents and script suggest strongly that both were written during the Hellenistic period. *BRM* 4, 6 is also partially duplicated by *CLBT*, pl. 1.

BRM 4, 6 and BM 134701 are discussed in II.7.

BRM 4, 6

Obv.

1′ [...] *ù* RA [...]

2′ [^{lú}GALA DÚR-*ab-ma*] *né-peš šá* ŠU^{II} ^{lú}GALA *šá* DAR(?) [...]

3′ [DÙ-*uš*(?)] ⸢*it-ta*(?)⸣-*ṣi rim-tú* TA *bi-it* ^{d}NIN.GAL *sin-niš-tu*$_4$ *ša* ⸢x⸣[...]

4′ [*sin-niš*(?)]-*tu*$_4$ *um-mu* ^{d}NIN.GAL *ina a-lu it-ta-ṣi*

5′ [^{lú}EN(?)]-*ka šá i-dul-lu-ma la i-ṣa-al-lal ana-ku*

6′ [*šá ina ma*]-*na-aḫ-ti-šú a-kal la i-kul ana-ku šá ina ma-na-aḫ-ti-šú me-e la iš-tu-ú ana-ku*

7′ [*ina* É-*i*]*a ba-aṣ it-taš-pak i-pi-ir it-ta-*⟨*at*⟩*-bak kab-tu šá di-im-ma-at da-ma-ma ul i-kal-lu*

8′ [*ina ṣir*]-*ḫi* URU-*šú ru-bu-ú ina qaq-qar na-pal-si-iḫ*$^{!}$ *me-ḫu-ú it-ba-am i-pi-ir pa-ni ik-tu-mu*

9′ [*u*$_4$-*m*]*u a-mat* ^{d}LX *u*$_4$-*mu a-mat* ^{d}EN.LÍL *u*$_4$-*mu ug-ga-at lìb-bi šá* ^{d}LX *ra-bi-i*

10′ [*Di*]*l-mun-nu-ú šá ina ṣu-ṣe-e e-lip-šú iṭ-bu-ú ana-ku*

11′ *šá lìb-bi i-šu-ú u e-mu-qu la i-šu-ú ana-ku*: *ú-a lìb-bi ú-a ka-bat-ta*

12′ *ma-kur-ru šá nin-da-bu-ú iz-bil ta-ni-iḫ iz-za-bil*

13′ *šá nin-da-bé-e nin-da-bé-e ul ú-še-rib*: *šá ni-qa-a ni-qa-a ul ú-še-rib*

14′ *an-na-a šá a-na* ^{d}XXX *ina* AN.GI$_6$ *iz-za-mi-ir*: *ina* KÁ É DINGIR.MEŠ *u* SILA DAGAL.LA *ga-rak-ku* ŠUB-*di*

15′ ^{giš}EREN ^{giš}ŠUR.MÌN ^{šim}GÍR GI DÙG.GA ^{giš}ŠINIG KUR.RA *u lu-te-e* ^{giš}MA.NU *ina muḫ-ḫi ga-rak-ku te-ṣe-en*

16′ *ki-ma* AN.GI$_6$ *ú-šá-ru-ú* ^{lú}KU$_4$-É GI.IZI.LÁ *i-qa-da-ma it-ti ga*$^{!}$[49]*-rak-ku ú-šá-aṣ-ba-at*

17′ ^{lú}GALA DÚR-*ab-ma né-peš šá* ŠU^{II} ^{lú}GALA *a-di* AN.GI$_6$ *ú-nam-mir* DÙ-*uš*

18′ *a-di* AN.GI$_6$ *ú-nam-mar* IZI *ina muḫ-ḫi ga-rak-ku la te-bel-*⟨*li*⟩

19′ *ki*$^{!}$[50]*-is-pi a-na* A.GÀR ŠUB.MEŠ *ta-kàs-sip*$_4$ *ki-is-pi a-na* ÍD.MEŠ *šá me-e la ub-bal* KI.MIN

20′ *ki*$^{!}$[51]*-is-pi a-na* ^{d}*A-nun-na-ki ta-kàs-sip*$_4$

[46] Cf. *BRM* 4, p. 12 ff.; *TuL*, no. 24, 91 ff.; W. Farber, *TUAT* II/2, 236 ff.

[47] This text is published by D. Brown and the present author in: BM 134701 = 1965–10–14,1 and the Hellenistic period eclipse ritual from Uruk, *RA* 91 (1997), 147–166.

[48] For the date of these text see I.2 and the above mentioned *RA* article by David Brown and the present author.

[49] Copy: *ta*.

[50] Copy: *di*.

[51] Copy: *di*.

21′ *a-di* AN.GI$_6$ *ú-nam-mar* UN.MEŠ KUR *ṣu-bat* SAG.DU-*šú-nu šá-aḫ*$^{!}$[52]*-ṭu ina lu-bar-ra-šú-nu* SAG.DU-*su-nu kat-mu*

22′ *me-sér ner-ti bar-tu*$_4$ *u* AN.GI$_6$ *a-a iṭ-ḫu-ú a-na* UNUG^{ki} É *re-eš* ÈŠ.GAL BÁRA.MAḪ É.AN.NA

23′ *ù* É.MEŠ DINGIR.MEŠ ^{d}TIR.AN.NA^{ki} *i-šá-as-su-ú a-na ṣi-ri-iḫ-ti ri-gim-šú-nu i-nam-du-ú*

24′ 7 ^{lú}ÉRIN-*ni* UN.MEŠ *ma-a-tú* ^{im}*ṭe*$^{!}$*-ru-ut* ÍD IGI.MEŠ-*šú-nu* ŠU^{II}.MEŠ-*šú-nu u* GÌR.MEŠ-*šú-nu pa-áš-šú*

25′ GÍR *ina kir-ri* XV-*šú-nu ta-al-lal*

26′ *me-sér ner-ti bar-tu*$_4$ *u* AN.GI$_6$ *a-a it-ḫu-ú a-na* UNUG^{ki} É *re-eš* ÈŠ.GAL BÁRA.MAḪ É.AN.NA

27′ *ù* É.MEŠ DINGIR.MEŠ ^{d}TIR.AN.NA^{ki} *i-šá-as-su-ú a-na ṣi-ri-iḫ-ti ri-gim-šú-nu i-nam-du-ú*

28′ *a-di* AN.GI$_6$ *i-zak-ku-ú i-šá-as-su-ú*: *ki-ma šá* ^{d}XXX AN.GI$_6$ *ú-nam-mar*

29′ IZI *ina muḫ-ḫi ga-rak-ku ina* KURUN (KAŠ.DIN).NAM *tu-kab-bat*

30′ *ina 2-i u*$_4$*-mu* ^{lú}ŠITIM *ga-rak-ku a-di ṭi-ik-me-en-šú* ÍL-*ši-ma a-na* ÍD ŠUB-*di*

Rev.

31′ *ina 2-i u*$_4$*-mu la-am* ^{d}UTU KUR-*ḫa* KÁ.MEŠ *š[á] tu-kan-nik*$_5$ BAD-*te* ^{giš}URÌ.GAL ZÌ.SUR.RA-*a*

32′ ^{túg}*ú-li-in* BABBAR-*ú u* GE$_6$ *tu-rab-ba a-na* ÍD ŠUB-*di tak-pe-ra-at* É.MEŠ DINGIR.MEŠ DÙ.A.BI

33′ *ù* É DUMU.NUN.NA É ^{d}XXX *tu-kap-par* ^{d}XXX MU$_4$.MU$_4$ ^{dug}A.GÚB.BA *uk-tan-nu*

34′ ZI ^{d}LX ^{d}EN.LÍL.L[Á].BI ḪÉ.PÀD.DA.EŠ: *niš* ^{d}*A-nù u* ^{d}EN.LÍL *tùm-mu-šú-nu-ti*

35′ 1-*en* ^{lú}MAŠ.MAŠ XV É *ù šá-nu-ú* GÙB É ÉN UD.UL.UL.A.MEŠ ŠID-*nu-ú*

36′ *ù šit-ti* ^{lú}MAŠ.MAŠ.MEŠ ÉN UDUG.ḪUL.MEŠ ŠID-*nu-ú zi-pa-de-e*.MEŠ *ú-ta-am-mu-ú-šú-nu-ti*

37′ *ina 2-i u*$_4$*-mu* ZÌ.SUR.RA-*a tak-pe-rat ù ga-rak-ku ana* ÍD ŠUB-*di*

38′ *šá-niš ina u*$_4$*-mu* AN.GI$_6$ ^{d}XXX ^{lú}SANGA.MEŠ *šá* É.MEŠ DINGIR.MEŠ TIR.AN.NA^{ki} *ina* KÁ É DINGIR.MEŠ-*šú-nu ga-rak-ku* ŠUB-*di-ú* (sic)

39′ *nu-ur ú-šá-aṣ-bat me-sér ner-ti bar-tu*$_4$ *u* AN.GI$_6$ *a-a it-ḫu-ú a-na* UNUG^{ki} É *re-eš* ÈŠ.GAL

40′ BÁRA.MAḪ É.AN.NA *ù* É.MEŠ DINGIR.MEŠ TIR.AN.NA^{ki} *i-šá-as-su-ú*

41′ *a-na ṣi-ri-iḫ-ti ri-gim-šú-nu i-nam-du-ú a-di* AN.GI$_6$ *i-zak-ku-ú i-šá-as-su-ú*

42′ *u*$_4$*-mu* AN.GI$_6$ ^{d}XXX *ḫal-ḫal-lat* ZABAR MEZE ZABAR LI.LI.ÌZ ZABAR TA É *am-mu-uš-mu* ÍL-*nim-ma*

43′ *it-ti* BÁRA.KI.BALAG GAR-*an ki-ma šá* AN.GI$_6$ ^{d}XXX TAB-*ú* ^{lú}GALA.MEŠ TÚG GADA MU$_4$.MU$_4$

44′ *ina lu-bar-šú-nu nu-uk-*⟨*ku*⟩*-su-tu* SAG.DU-*su* {*šú*}-*nu kát-mu ṣi-ri-iḫ-tú ni-is-sa-ti u bi-ki-ti*

45′ *a-na* ^{d}XXX *ina* AN.GI$_6$ *na-šu-ú* 3 ZÌ.DUB.DUB.BU *a-na mi-iḫ-rat* LI$^{!}$.LI$^{!}$.ÌZ *ina* ZÌ.SUR.RA-*a* ŠUB-*di*

46′ 1-*en ku-uk-ku-bu di-im-ti šá* ŠINIG *qu-ud-du-uš ù me-e ina* ZAG ZÌ.DUB.DUB.BU 3-*šú-nu*

---

[52] Copy: *gud*.

47′ *ina* ZÌ.SUR.RA-*a a-na kun-nu* ŠU^{II} *a-na* ^{lú}GALA.MEŠ *a-na mi-iḫ-rat* ^{d}XXX *ina* AN.GI$_6$ GUB-*an*

48′ *ki-i šal-šú* NÍGIN-*rat ši-kin* AN.GI$_6$ AM AMAŠ.NA GAR-*an* ME.ER.ME.ER ZI GU$_7^!$.E *a-na lìb-bi i-ru-bu*

49′ A ABZU.MU MU.UN.ḪUL.ÀM ÉR.ŠEM$_4$.MA: *ki-i* 2-*ta* ⸢ŠU^{II}⸣ NÍGIN-*rat ši-kin* AN.GI$_6$ AM AMAŠ.NA

50′ Ù^{ʾ}.Ú A.A ŠÀ.ZU GAR-*an ù* A ABZU.MU MU.UN.[ḪUL.ÀM ME.]ER.ME.ER ZI GU$_7^!$.E *ana* ŠÀ KU$_4$-*bu*

51′ *ki-i gam*$^!$-*mar-tu*$_4$ GAL^{sic}-⸢*tu*$_4$ *ši-kin* AN⸣.GI$_6$ AM.AM[AŠ.NA AN.NA E.LUM.MA] GAR-*an*

52′ Ù^{ʾ}.Ú ⸢A.A ŠÀ⸣.[ZU ME.ER.ME.ER ZI GU$_7$.E *a-na lìb-bi* KU$_4$-*bu ki-i gam-mar-tu*$_4$ GAL-*tu*$_4$ *ši-kin* AN.GI$_6$ AM A]MAŠ.NA

53′ AN.NA [E.LUM.MA GAR-*an* É.TÙR.GIN$_7$ NIGIN.NA.A Ù..Ú A.A ŠÀ.ZU ME.ER.ME.ER ZI GU$_7$.E *a-na lìb-bi* KU$_4$-*bu*]

54′ ⸢*ki-ma*⸣[AN.GI$_6$ *ut-ta-mi-ir* LI.LI.ÌZ ZABAR *i-šit-tam-ma*]

55′ [... ZÌ.DUB.DUB.BU *ù ku-uk-ku-bu di-im-tu*$_4$ *i-šit-tam-ma a-na* ÍD ŠUB-*di*]

BM 134701

Obv.

1′ ⸢*u*$_4$-*mu* AN.GI$_6$ ^{d}⸣XXX ⸢*ḫal-ḫal-lat* ZABAR MEZE ZABAR LI.LI.ÌZ ZABAR⸣ TA É *am-mu-uš-mu* [ÍL-*nim-ma*]

2′ *it-ti* BÁRA.KI BALAG *i-šak-kan ki-ma* AN.GI$_6$ ^{d}XXX TAB-*ú* ^{lú}GALA.MEŠ TÚG GADA MU$_4$.M[U$_4$]

3′ *ina lu-bar-ri-šú-nu-ti nu-uk-ku-su-tu* SAG.DU-*šú-nu kát-mu ṣi-ri-iḫ-tu*$_4$ *ni-is-sa-t*[*u*$_4$ *u bi-ki-ti*]

4′ *a-na* ^{d}XXX *ina* AN.GI$_6$ *na-šu-ú* 3 ZÌ.DUB.DUB.BU *ina mi-iḫ-rit* LI.LI.ÌZ *ina* Z[Ì.SUR.RA-*a* ŠUB-*di*]

5′ *ina* 1-*en ku-uk-ku-bu di-im-ti šá* ŠINIG *qu-ud-du-uš ù me-e ma-l*[*u-ú*]

6′ *ina* ZAG ZÌ.DUB.DUB.BU 3-*šú-nu ina* ZÌ.SUR.RA-*a a-na kun-nu* ŠU^{II} *ana* ^{lú}GALA.MEŠ *ana mi-i*[*ḫ-rit* ^{d}XXX *ina* AN.GI$_6$ GUB-*an*]

7′ *ki-i šal-šú* ⸢NÍGIN⸣-*rat ši-kin* AN.GI$_6$ AM.ME AMAŠ.AN.NA *iš-šak-kan* ME.ER.ME.ER ZI GU$_7$.[E *ana lìb-bi* KU$_4$-*bu*]

8′ A ABZU.MU MU.UN.ḪUL.ÀM ÉR.ŠEM$_4$.MA: *ki-i* 2-*ta* ŠU^{II} *ina*(?) NÍGIN-*rat ši-kin* AN.⸢GI$_6$⸣

9′ AM.ME.E AMAŠ.AN.NA Ù^{ʾ}.Ú A.A ŠÀ.ZU *iš-šak-kan*

10′ *ù* A ABZU.MU MU.UN.ḪUL.ÀM ÉR.ŠEM$_4$.MA ME.ER.ME.ER ZI GU$_7^!$.E *ana lìb-bi* [KU$_4$-*bu*]

11′ *ki-i gam-mar-tu*$_4$ GAL^{sic}-*tu*$_4$ *ši-kin* AN.GI$_6$ AM.ME.E AMAŠ.AN.NA AN.NA E.⸢LUM.MA⸣ [GAR-*an*/*iš-šak-kan*]

12′ Ù^{ʾ}.Ú A.A ŠÀ.ZU ME.ER.ME.ER ZI GU$_7$.E {x} *a-na lìb-bi* KU$_4$-[*bu*]

13′ *ki-i gam-mar-tu*$_4$ GAL-*tu*$_4$ *ši-kin* AN.GI$_6$ AM.ME.E AMAŠ.AN.NA AN.NA E.L[UM.MA GAR-*an*/*iš-šak-kan*]

14′ ⸢É⸣.TÙR. {x} GIN$_7$ NIGIN.NA.A Ù^{ʾ}.Ú A.A ŠÀ.ZU ME.ER.ME.ER ZI GU$_7$.E *ana lìb-bi* K[U$_4$-*bu*]

15′ ⸢*ki-ma*⸣ AN.GI$_6$ *ut-ta-mi-ir* LI.LI.ÌZ {x} ZABAR *i-šit-ta*[*m-ma*]

16′ [... ZÌ].DUB.DUB.BU *ù ku-uk-ku-bu di-im-tu*$_4$ *i-šit-tam-ma a-na* ÍD [ŠUB-*di*]

17′ [*ki-ma šá* AN.GI$_6$ ^{d}]XXX *ú-šá-ru-ú* LUGAL *til-le-e-šú me-lam-mu* LUGAL-*ú-tú ina* É.GAL *ina šub-tu*$_4$ *el*-[*lam-me*(?)...]

18′ […] x BU ^{giš}ŠÀ.GIŠIMMAR *ta-lam-mu ú-li-in-ni bur-ru-mu-tú šá šá-rat* ^{sal}ÁŠ.[GÀR]
19′ [*la pe-ti-ti šá-rat* ^{sal}SILA$_4$ *l*]*a pe-ti-ti* KÁ É MU.MEŠ *a-šar til-le-e* LUGAL *šá* ⸢IŠ⸣ […]
20′ […] É-*a-ni u* KÁ-*a-ni ta-lam-mi-i-ma* ZÌ *tap-pi-in* ZÌ *ši-*[*gu-šú* …]
21′ […]x É SÙ KÁ É *ta-kan-nak til-le-e la eb-bu-tu* LUGAL MU$_4$.MU$_4$ […]
22′ [… *ú-li-in-ni*] *bur-ru-mu-tu šá šá-rat* ^{sal}ÁŠ.GÀR *la pe-ti-ti šá-rat* ^{sal}SI[LA$_4$ *la pe-ti-ti*(?) …]
23′ […] KEŠDA-*as* $^{giš(!)}$*e-ri* ^{giš}TUKUL *dan-nu ṣi-rì šá* ^{d}LX […]
24′ [… AN].GI$_6$ ⸢*šá ina u*$_4$⸣-*mu* AN.GI$_6$ LUGAL ⸢x x x⸣ […]
25′ […]

Rev.
1′ […]
2′ […] ⸢*pa*⸣-*pa-ḫa ana* ⸢x A x⸣ […] ⸢x ú⸣ […]
3′ […]-*a-tú šá* ZÌ.DA *ú-*⸢*de-e*⸣ ⸢*u*/*ana*(?) *gi*⸣-*nu-ú* DÙ.A.BI [x] […]
4′ [… ZÌ *tap-p*]*i-in* ZÌ *ši-gu-šú* KÁ.MEŠ *te-e*[*ṣ-ṣir*(?)…]
5′ […] ⸢x⸣ IGI K[U(?)] LU *pa-ni* KISAL *šá* É *re-eš* ÈŠ.GAL BÁRA.MAḪ É.AN.NA *u* ⸢É⸣[.MEŠ DINGIR.MEŠ TIR.AN.NA^{ki} DÙ-*uš*]
6′ [… É *a-k*]*i-tu*$_4$ KI.MIN DÙ-*uš*: É *pi-riš-ti* KI.MIN DÙ-*uš*: UB.ŠU.UKKIN. [NA.KI KI.MIN DÙ-*uš*]
7′ [DÙ.A.BI(?)] É.MEŠ DINGIR.MEŠ ZÌ.SUR.RA-*a šá* ZÌ *tap*$^{!}$-*pi-in* ⸢NIGIN⸣ […]
8′ […KÁ.]TÚL *tu-kan-nak* KÁ.GAL.MEŠ UNUG^{ki} KI.MIN ⸢DÙ⸣[-*uš*]
9′ […] BAR *šá* UB 7 KI *su-uš-šú šá* DA 7 KI *la ta-kan-nak* ⸢x⸣ […]
10′ [… DUMU] *šip-ri* 7 MEŠ-*šú-nu šá ina* AN-*e rap-šu-tu ina šu-bat* ^{d}LX *šar-ri ra-biš* ⸢x⸣ […]
11′ […]*ṭè-e-me šu-a-*⸢*tu*$_4$ *a*⸣-*na bi-bil* ŠÀ ^{d}LX ^{d}EN.LÍL *u* ^{d}*É-a* ⸢x x⸣ […]
12′ [*ina ma*]-*ḫar* ^{d}ŠEŠ.KI-*ri* {x} ^{d}XXX *ez-*{x}*zi-iš il-ta-n*[*am-mu-u*…]
13′ [*e*]*ṭ-lu* ^{d}UTU ^{d}IM *qar-du a-na i-d*[*i-šú-nu ut-tir-ru*]
14′ ⸢^{d}⸣XXX *ina qé*$^{!}$-*reb* AN-*e ú-šá-d*[*i-ru* …]
15′ […] *ú*$^{!}$-*šá-dir* ^{d}*A-nù šar-ri a-bi* DINGIR.MEŠ GAL.MEŠ *šá ina ba-li-šú šip-ṭu la* [*ú-gam-mir*(?)…]
16′ $^{[l]ú(?)}$MAŠ.MAŠ-*ú-tu a-na muḫ-ḫi* DUMU.MEŠ *šip-ri šá* ^{d}*A-nù* ⸢x⸣ […]
17′ [*e*]-*la-šú-nu ina* AN-*e* DINGIR.MEŠ *mam-am ul* ⸢*in*⸣-*naṃ-ba* ^{d}*A-nù* ^{d}EN.LÍL *u* ^{d}*É-a im-*[*bu-šú-nu-ti*]
18′ $^{[d]}$XXX *ina* AN-*e ú-šá-di-ir-*ʾ ⸢*a-ga-šú iš-ḫu-ṭu*⸣ *ti-iq-ni-šú ú-paṭ-ṭi-ir-*[ʾ …]
19′ [*z*]*i-mu-šú uk-ki-il* […] x BAL RAD Ú […]
20′ [*m*]*u-ši u ur-ra a-*[*dir ina šu-bat be-lu-ti*]-*šú ul a-šib* ⸢x⸣ […]
21′ […] *šá ina u*$_4$-*mu* AN.GI$_6$ ⸢*šá*(?)⸣ ^{d}XXX ⸢x⸣ […] ⸢x GAB⸣ ŠUD […]
22′ […] ⸢^{d}⸣XXX […]

L.E.
IM ^{Id}LX-[…]
[…] ⸢$^{d(?)}$x⸣ […]

***BRM* 4, 6**

Obv.
1′ […] … […]
2′ The lamentation priest will sit and [perform (l. 3′)] the ritual procedure of the lamentation priest of … […]
3′ ‘The wild cow [has l]eft(?) the temple. Ningal, the woman … […].

4′ [the woma]n(?), the mother, Ningal, has left the city'.
5′ 'I am your [lord(?)], who wanders around in despair and cannot sleep.
6′ I am [one, who] did not eat bread [during] his [ha]rdship, I am one, who did not drink water during his hardship'.
7′ 'Sand is heaped up, earth piled up [in m]y [house]. O honored one, the moaner can not refrain from mourning.
8′ [In mourn]ing about his city the prince squats on the ground; a storm arose, covered the face with dust'.
9′ '[Sto]rm is the word of Anu, storm is the word of Enlil, storm is the wrath (in) the heart of the great Anu'.
10′ 'I am (like) a man from [Di]lmun, whose boat has sunk in the marshes'.
11′ 'I am one who does have a heart, but not strength'. 'Woe over my heart, woe over (my) mind!'
12′ 'The *makurru*-boat, which (until now) carried cereal offerings, (now also) has brought suffering.
13′ He who is responsible for the cereal offerings, did not make the cereal offerings enter, he who is responsible for the (meat) offerings, did not make the (meat) offerings enter'.
14′ This is what was sung for Sîn at the time of an eclipse. In the gates of the temples and on the main street you will lay down a *garakku*-brazier.
15′ You will heap cedar, cypress, myrtle, sweet reed, tamarisk of the mountains and twigs of the *ēru*-tree on the *garakku*-brazier.
16′ As soon as the eclipse begins, a temple enterer will kindle a torch and light the *garakku*-brazier.
17′ The lamentation priest will sit and perform the ritual procedure of the lamentation priest, until (the moon) has cleared up the eclipse (again).
18′ Until he clears up the eclipse, the fire on the *garakku*-brazier must not go out.
19′ You will make funerary offerings for the fields that lie fallow, you will make funerary offerings for the canals that bring no water,
20′ you will make funerary offerings for the Anunnaki.
21′ Until he clears up the eclipse, the people of the land will remain with their headdresses removed, (and) they will keep their heads covered with their *lubāru*-clothing.
22′ They will cry (l. 23′) 'May hardship, murder, rebellion and (the evil predicted by) the eclipse not reach Uruk, Rēš, Ešgal, Baramaḫ, Eanna
23′ and the (other) temples of Tiranna', calling loudly in lamentation.
24′ 7 soldiers, people of the land – their eyes, hands and feet are smeared with mud from the river –,
25′ you will hang a sword on their right shoulder.
26′ They will cry (l. 27′) 'May hardship, murder, rebellion and (the evil predicted by) the eclipse not reach Uruk, Rēš, Ešgal, Baramaḫ, Eanna
27′ and the (other) temples of Tiranna', calling loudly in lamentation.
28′ Until the eclipse becomes (totally) clear, they will cry (this). As soon as the moon clears up the eclipse,
29′ you will extinguish the fire on the *garakku*-brazier with *kurunnu*-beer.
30′ On the next day the building master will lift up the *garakku*-brazier including its ashes and throw (everything) into the river.

Rev.

31′ On the next day, before sunrise, you will open the gates which you have placed under seal. You will moisten (l. 32′) the reed *urigallu*-standard, the magic circle of flour,

32′ (and) a white and black cord (and) throw (it) into the river. You will purify (l. 33′) all the temples (with) *takpertu*-purifications

33′ and (especially) Edumununna, the temple of Sîn. (The statue of) Sîn will be robed. The holy water-basin will be set up.

34′ (You will say:) 'Verily, by the life of Anu and Enlil they are conjured'.

35′ One exorcist on the right side of the temple and a second on the left side of the temple will recite the incantation 'Storm of jubilating water'

36′ and the rest of the exorcists will recite the incantation 'Evil *utukku*-demons', they will conjure them with *zipadû*-incantation formulas.

37′ On the next day you will throw the magic circle of flour, the *takpertu*-purification necessaries and the *garakku*-brazier into the river.

38′ Alternatively: on the day of the eclipse of the moon the *šangû*-priests of the temples of Tiranna will lay down a *garakku*-brazier in the gate of their temple (and)

39′ light a fire. They will cry (l. 40′) 'May hardship, murder, rebellion and (the evil predicted by) the eclipse not reach Uruk, Rēš, Ešgal,

40′ Baramaḫ, Eanna and the temple of Tiranna',

41′ calling loudly in lamentation. Until the eclipse becomes (totally) clear they will cry (this).

42′ On the day of the eclipse of the moon they will carry the bronze *ḫalḫallatu*-drum, the bronze *manzû*-drum, (and) the bronze kettledrum back here from the storehouse(?) and

43′ place (them) next to(?) the 'Dais, place (of) the Harp'. As soon as the eclipse of the moon begins, the lamentation priests will put on a linen garment.

44′ With their torn *lubāru*-clothing their heads will remain covered.They 'raise' (l. 45′) lamentations, wailings and mourning

45′ for the eclipsed moon. You will pour 3 heaps of flour facing the kettledrum in the magic circle of flour.

46′ You will set up (l. 47′) 1 *kukkubbu*-jar (filled) with 'tears of the holy tamarisk' and water at the right side of the 3 aforementioned heaps of flour

47′ in the magic circle of flour, for the procedures of the lamentation priests, facing the eclipsed moon.

48′ When the extent of the eclipse is one-third of (the area of) the moon-disc, (the lamentation) 'The bull in his fold' will be performed. (The lamentation priests) will join in with 'A storm, which eats life'

49′ (and) the *eršemakku* is 'Woe, he is the one who has destroyed my Subterranean Water'. When (however) the extent of the eclipse is two-third of (the area of) the moon-disc, 'The bull in his fold' (and),

50′ 'Alas and woe! your heart' will be performed and (the lamentation priests) will join in with 'Woe, he is the one who has destroyed my Subterranean Water', (and) 'A storm, which eats life'.

51′ As soon as the extent of the eclipse is the 'small(!) completion', 'The bull in his fo[ld' (and) 'The honored one of Heaven'] will be performed.

52′ (The lamentation priests) [will join in with] 'Alas and woe! [your] heart' [(and) 'A storm, which eats life'. As soon as the extent of the eclipse is the 'large completion', 'The bull in his f]old' (and),

53′ '[The honored one] of Heaven' [will be performed. (The lamentation priests) will join in with 'The house is encircled like a cattle pen', 'Alas and woe! your heart' (and) 'A storm, which eats life'].

54′ As soon as [(the moon) has cleared up the elipse, he will … the bronze kettledrum and].

55′ [he will (also) … … the heaps of flour and the *kukkubbu*-jar (filled) with 'tears (of the holy tamarisk)', and throw it into the river].

BM 134701[53]

Obv.

17′ [As soon as the eclipse of the m]oon begins, [you(?) will make(?)] the king [wear(?) (l. 18?)] his *tillû*-uniform, the royal sheen, in the palace, in the dwelling wh[ose rites are pure(?) …]

18′ […] … which you will wrap in palm leaf. A multicolored cord from the hair of an [unmated] (l. 19′) k[id],

19′ [(and) the hair of an] unmated [lamb] [you will use to tie closed(?)] the gate of this temple, the place of the *tillû*-uniform of the king, of … […]

20′ […] inside and outside you will wrap and *tappinnu*-flour (and) *še*[*guššu*]-flour […]

21′ […] … you will sprinkle the temple, seal the gate of the temple. The king will be robed in an unclean *tillû*-uniform […]

22′ [… a m]ulticolored [cord] from the hair of an unmated kid, (and) the hair of an [unmated] la[mb]

23′ […] you will bind, a (stick of) *ēru*-wood, the strong (and) sublime weapon of Anu [you will take?]

24′ […the ec]lipse, which on the day of the eclipse the king … […]

25′ […]

Rev.

1′ […]

2′ […] the cella for … […] and […]

3′ […] … of flour, utensils and/for(?) all the regular offerings […]

4′ […with(?) *tapp*]*innu*-flour (and) *šeguššu*-flour you will d[raw(?)] outside […]

5′ [You will perform … which is] … before the courtyard of the Rēš-temple, the Ešgal-temple, the Baramaḫ, the Eanna-temple and the (other) tem[ples of Tiranna]

6′ […the *a*]*kītu*-temple you will perform ditto; the *bīt pirišti* you will perform ditto; the Ubšukkin[aku you will perform ditto]

7′ […] (With) a magic circle of *tappinnu*-flour you will surround [all(?)] the temples […]

8′ […] you will place the storeroom [gate] under seal. The great gates of Uruk you will perfor[m] ditto.

9′ […] … you will not seal the […]x (gate) of 7 corners and the *suššu* (gate) of 7 sides(?) […]

10′ [… the me]ssengers, these seven, which are in the wide sky, in the dwelling of Anu, the king, is great … […]

11′ […] that decision according to the wish of Anu, Enlil, and Ea … […]

12′ They (the seven evil gods) kept sur[rounding] fiercely [in fr]ont of the divine crescent, Sîn […]

13′ [Yo]ung Šamaš (and) heroic Adad [they brought] towa[rds them].

14′ They caused the eclipse of the moon in the sky.

15′ […] he caused the eclipse. Anu, the king, the father of the great gods, without whom judgement (was) not [passed].

16′ [The o]ffice of exorcist before the envoys of Anu … […]

[53] *BRM* 4, 6, rev. 42–55 is duplicated by BM 134701, obv. 1–16.

17′ [Be]sides them none of the gods in the sky were called upon. Anu, Enlil and Ea cal[led upon them].
18′ They caused the eclipse of the [m]oon in the sky, took off his crown, (and) [they] cleared away his equipment [...]
19′ His [appe]arance darkened [...] ... [...]
20′ [Ni]ght and day it was ec[lipsed], it did not dwell [in the dwelling of] his [rule] ... [...]
21′ [...] which/who on the day of the eclipse of(?) the moon ... [...] ... [...]
22′ [...] the moon [...]

L.E.
Tablet of Anu-[...]
[...] ... [...]

Comments

(see also the comments on this text made by D. Brown and the present author in: BM 134701 = 1965–10–14,1 and the Hellenistic period eclipse ritual from Uruk, *RA* 91 (1997), 147–166).

***BRM* 4, 6**

Obv.

l. 2–3, this line is similar to obv. 17.

l. 3–13, in these lines several Akkadian translations are given of lines from the Emesal-cult lyric, see II.7.1.

l. 3,⸢*it-ta*⸣-*ṣi*, as at the end of obv. 4?

l. 3, E. Ebeling in *TuL*, 92 restored for the end of this line: [Eturnunna].

l. 4, [*sin-niš*(?)]-*tu*$_4$, as suggested by E. Ebeling in *TuL*, 92.

l. 5–11, these lines are duplicate in *CLBT*, pl. 1, col. B, 1–14.

l. 5, [^{lú}EN]-*ka*, see *CLBT*, pl. 1, col. B, 1: *be-e*[*l-ka*(?)...], rather than [^{lú}ÌR]-*ka*, as suggested by E. Ebeling in *TuL*, 92, who did not use the duplicate *CLBT*, pl. 1.

l. 7, [*ina* É-*i*]*a ba-aṣ*, see see *CLBT*, pl. 1, col. B, 4.

l. 7, see for this line also J. Krecher, *Kultlyrik*, 144.

l. 7, *i-kal-lu* is a mistake for *i-kal-la*, as in the parallel *SBH*, p. 133, no. I(!), 66. Several deviations from traditional grammar can be found in this text: the subjunctive ending -*u* is missing in *iz-bil* (obv. 12); *iz-za-mi-ir* (obv. 14); *ú-nam-mar* (obv. 18, 21, 28, but cf. *i-zak-ku-ú* in obv. 28 and rev. 41); *tu-kan-nik*$_5$ (rev. 31) (preterite D-stem, rather than *tu-kan-nak*). A singular is intended in *ik-tu-mu* (obv. 8, see the duplicate *CLBT*, pl. 1, col. B, 9: *ik-tu-u*[*m*]); a plural is intended in *ub-bal* (obv. 19), *ú-šá-aṣ-bat* (rev. 39) and GAR-*an* (rev. 43, see the preceding plural verb with ventive ÍL-*nim-ma*). See also *na-pal-si-iḫ* (obv. 8, for *napalsuḫ*), ŠUB-*di-ú* (rev. 38) and *i-ru-bu* (rev. 48, for *ir-ru-bu*; cf. KU$_4$-*bu* in rev. 50, [52] and [53] // BM 134701, obv. [7], [10], 12 and 14).

l. 7, *CLBT*, pl. 1, col. B, 6 supplements: *šá i-dam-mu-um mar-ṣi-iš li-di-mu-mu* 'may the moaner moan bitterly'.

l. 8, [*ina ṣir*]-*ḫi*, see *CLBT*, pl. 1, col. B, 7′.

l. 8, *CLBT*, pl. 1, col. B, 8–9 then reads: *šá* dXXX *iq-bu-ú me-ḫu-ú* ZI-*am-ma i-pi-ir pa-ni ik-tu-u*[*m*] 'Of Sîn they said: a storm arose, covere[d] the face with dust'.

l. 10, *e-lip-šú*, see *CLBT*, pl. 1, col. B, 12′: gišMÁ-*šú*. This line is also discussed by R.C. Thompson, *AAA* 20 (1933), 101–2.

l. 11, 'one who does have a heart' i.e. courage.

l. 12, *CLBT*, pl. 1, col. B, 15 ff. different. Similar in J. Krecher, *Kultlyrik*, 57 and 70, IV, 12 (see also the comments on 187).

l. 12, 'The *makurru*-boat, which (until now) carried cereal offerings', probably an allusion to the boat-shaped moon-sickle.

l. 16–21, these lines were also discussed by T. Podella, *Ṣôm-Fasten*, Kevelaer, 1989, 48–49.

l. 16, 'light (a fire) with the *garakku*-brazier', see rev. 38–39. See also *TU* 41, rev. 15 (*nu-úr* TA GI.IZI.LÁ *i-qád-du-ú-ma*).

l. 17–21, these lines were also discussed by A. Tsukimoto, *Untersuchungen zur Totenpflege*, Kevelaer, 1985, 197–8.

l. 17, 'until he (the moon) has cleared up the eclipse', i.e. 'until the eclipse has come to an end'. See l. 28.

l. 22–23, 26–27, rev. 39–40, a generally used apotropaic formula. Cf. *CAD*, Š/II, 152a.

l. 24, *ummânu* 'soldiers' rather than 'craftsmen', because a sword is mentioned in l. 25.

l. 24, im*ṭe*! (copy: KI)-*ru-ut* ÍD, following *AHw*, 1388b.

l. 30, for lúŠITIM = *itinnu* 'building master', and not lúDÍM = *mubannû* (cf. *KAR* 132, III, 3 and 16) the 'arranger (of the offering table)', see III.4.3.

l. 30, *ṭi/di-ik-me-en-šú*, see *AHw*, *dikmēnu*, 169.

Rev.

l. 32, the white and black cord are probably already mentioned in the broken beginning of the text; a multicolored cord is also mentioned in BM 134701, obv. 18 and 22. See III.3.

l. 33, for Edumununna, the temple of Sîn, see A.R. George, *House Most High*, no. 214.

l. 33, for *uk-tan-nu* see my comment on *TU* 41, obv. 6.

l. 36, for the incantation 'Evil *utukku*-demons', see II.7.

l. 36, for the *zipadû*-incantation formula see R. Borger, in: *AOAT* 1, 1 ff.

l. 42 ff. is duplicated by BM 134701, obv. 1 ff.

l. 42, É *am-mu-uš-mu*, see *CAD*, A/II, 77a; it is only attested here, and in the duplicate BM 134701, obv. 1. Cf. W. Farber, *TUAT* II/2, 239: 'Instrumentenspeicher'. Or is it perhaps related to *amašpû* (*amašmû*), see *CAD*, A/II, 27–8?

l. 43, BÁRA.KI BALAG 'Dais, place (of) the Harp', cf. W. Farber, *TUAT* II/2, 239.

l. 43, TAB = *šurrû* 'to begin'. *šurrû* is a typical technical verb used in astronomical context. See the syllabic writing in obv. 16, and BM 134701, obv. 17: *ú-šá-ru-ú*.

l. 45, *na-šu-ú* 'raise', i.e. 'recite', as in *RAcc.*, 136, 282 and 283?

l. 46, '(filled) with "tears of the holy tamarisk" and water', the verb is attested in the duplicate BM 134701, obv. 5: *di-im-ti šá* ŠINIG *qu-ud-du-uš ù me-e ma-l*[*u-ú*].

l. 47, *a-na kun-nu* ŠU^{II}, usually refering to the procedures of the diviner, cf. *CAD*, K, 543b, 2. Here apparently the lamentation priests were associated with it.

l. 48 ff., several lamentations which are mentioned here are also attested elsewhere:

'The house is encircled like a cattle pen', in *BRM* 4, 6, rev. [53] and the duplicate BM 134701, obv. 14, also in the Uruk cultic calendar text *TU* 48, obv. 12, see II.2.2.

'The bull in his fold', in *BRM* 4, 6, rev. 48, 49, 51, 52, and the duplicate BM 134701, obv. 7, 9, 11, 13, also in the Uruk New Year text *TU* 39, rev. 15, and *TU* 48, obv. 13, rev. 5, see II.2.2.

'The honored one of Heaven', in *BRM* 4, 6, rev. [51] and [53] and the duplicate BM 134701, obv. 11 and 13, also in *TU* 39, rev. 10 and *TU* 48, rev. 6, see II.2.2.

l. 48, or for NÍGIN-*rat* perhaps *ḫap-rat*? See A. Livingstone, *Mystical*, 90.

l. 49, after ŠU^{II}, the duplicate BM 134701, obv. 8 perhaps reads *ina*.

l. 50, MU.UN.[ḪUL.ÀM ME.]ER.ME.ER ZI GU$_7$.E, the duplicate BM 134701, obv. 10 reads MU.UN.ḪUL.ÀM ÉR.ŠEM$_4$.MA ME.ER.ME.ER ZI GU$_7$.E, but there appears not to be enough space here.

l. 51, *ki-i gam-mar-tu*$_4$ GAL-*tu*$_4$, as is clear from the duplicate BM 134701, obv. 11, but probably a mistake for *gam-mar-tu*$_4$ TUR-*tu*$_4$ 'the small completion', because we also have *ki-i gam-mar-tu*$_4$ GAL-*tu*$_4$ in l. [52] // BM 134701, obv. 13. Cf. *CAD*, G, 24b. W. Farber, who used BM 134701, reads (*TUAT* II/2, 239) 'die kleine Vollständigkeit' in rev. 51 and 'die große Vollständigkeit' in rev. 52, although the writing GAL-*tu*$_4$ is very clear in BM 134701, obv. 11 and 13.

l. 54 and 55, the verb *i-šit-tam* (// BM 134701, obv. 15 and 16) remains unclear to me. Perhaps *šêtu* is intended? W. Farber, *TUAT* II/2, 239, translates 'räumt ... beiseite/ab', but note that he writes in italics, meaning the translation is uncertain.

BM 134701

Obv.

l. 17, [*ki-ma šá* AN.GI$_6$ ^{d}]XXX *ú-šá-ru-ú*, see *BRM* 4, 6, obv. 16 and rev. 43.

l. 18–19, and 22, see the parallel in *CT* 16. 21, 180 ff. The Akkadian translation reads: *ú-li-in-na bur-ru-um-ta šá-rat ú-ni-qí la pe-ti-ti šá-rat pu-ḫat-ti la pe-ti-ti ṭi-me-ma*.

l. 20, É-*a-ni u* KÁ-*a-ni* 'inside (*bītānû*) and outside (*bābānu*)'; probably also in rev. 4 (KÁ.MEŠ). Not: É.A.NI *u* KÁ.A.NI 'his temple and his gate'.

l. 21 (see also 17 and 19), *til-le-e la eb-bu-tu* LUGAL MU_4.MU_4, see the parallel in *TU* 42 +, obv. 16′; see also rev. 25′. For *tillû* see F.A.M. Wiggermann, *Mesopotamian Protective Spirits. The ritual texts*, Groningen, 1992, 53 f.

l. 23, $^{\text{giš(!)}}$*e-ri* '*ēru*-wood', also used in *BRM* 4, 6, obv. 15, written ^{giš}MA.NU.

For parallels of this line see *AHw*, 247a, *ēru* II, 2; *CAD*, E, 319b, sub 3′, a' and *CAD*, Ṣ, 211b (Suggestion A. Cavigneaux).

l. 24, LUGAL ⸢x x x⸣, or: *ina šat* ⸢*ur-ri*⸣ x [...]?

Rev.

l. 3, *ú-*⸢*de-e*⸣ ⸢*u*/*ana*(?), this is very uncertain.

l. 4, *te-e*[*ṣ-ṣir*, similar for example in *LKA* 108, 11, see the dictionaries sub *qēmu*, *šegušša* and *eṣēru*.

l. 6, for the *bīt pirišti*, a storage room for the ornaments and garments of the divine statues in the temple, also attested in the ritual W 18728 (A. Falkenstein, *UVB* 15 [1959], 40–44), see L.T. Doty, in: *Studies W. W. Hallo*, Bethesda, 1993, 87–89. See also II.3.1 and II.3.3.

l. 7, *tap*$^{!}$*-pi-in,* although the copy reads PA.

l. 11, *ṭè-e-me* 'that decision', suggestion A. Cavigneaux.

l. 12, see *CT* 16, 20, 73 f. and 21, 148 f.

l. 13, see *CT* 16, 20, 75 f. and 21, 150 f.

l. 14, see *CT* 16, 22, 238 f.

l. 15, For parallels of this line see *CAD*, B, 71–2, j (suggestion A. Cavigneaux).

l. 17, [*e*]*-la-šú-nu* ... ⸢*in*⸣*-nam-ba*, see *CT* 16, 22, 234 f.; ^{d}*A-nù* ... *im-*[*bu-šú-nu-ti*], see ib., 236 f.

l. 18, see *CT* 16, 22, 240 f. Cf. also *CAD*, Š/I, 93b with a citation of F. Rochberg-Halton.

l. 19, ⸢*zi*⸣*-mu-šú uk-ki-il*, similar in *ACh* Supp. 2 Adad 105b, II, 4.

l. 20, see *CT* 16, 20, 98 f.

CLBT, pl.1 (AB 249)[54]

This text, most likely from Uruk (see I.2), contains what appears to be a ritual (col. A), and furthermore some quotations from perhaps a lunar eclipse myth (similar to *CT* 16, pl. 19 ff.) together with commentary or explanatory remarks (col. B). From Col. A only the right edge is preserved, and the contents remain largely unclear. Col. B is partly duplicated by *BRM* 4, 6.

The text is discussed in II.7.

col. A.

1 […] ⸢^{d}AG⸣-A-PAP
2 […] ḪI *ik-la-*ʾ
3 […] ⸢x⸣ *ṭup-pi*
4 […] ⸢x⸣ *iš-ṭur*
5 […] DUB.MEŠ *an-na-a-tú*
6 [… *i*]*š-ṭur*
7 […]⸢*a*(?)⸣-*na ṣa-bit*(?)-*su*

---

8 […] É SÍSKUR
9 […] *a-na* LUGAL-*ú-tú*
10 […]⸢x⸣ *ú-gam-mir par-ṣi-šú*
11 […] KUR.MEŠ *šá* SAR.MEŠ
12 […]-*ú šil-lat*.MEŠ
13 […] SAR.MEŠ-ʾ
14 […] *ra-bu-ú šá* AN-*e*
15 […] *man-za-za šá-qu-ú*
16 […]⸢x⸣ SUḪ DU *šu-bat-su*
17 […]-*ri ra-mu-ú ina* SAG.DU-*šú a-si-im*
18 […] *si-mat* LUGAL-*ú-tú ta-mi-ḫi*
19 [… *l*]*u*$_4$(?) *a-na te-di-iq la-biš*
20 […^{mu}]^{l} ^{d}UR.GU.LA *ṣa-mi-du*
21 […] ^{mul} ^{d}MUŠ *ka-bi-is*
22 […]-*e šá* ^{I}U$_4$-^{d}LX SAR
23 […] *in-nam-mi-ir*
24 […]-*na an-né-e*
25 […] *šá* AN-*e*
26 [… *šu*]-*bat* GUŠKIN *ina* UGU *ki-gal-lu*$_4$
27 […] É *re-eš ina* É.NAM.EN.NA
28 […] KU *a-ši-ib*
29 […] *ul iš-ṭur*
30 […*šá* ^{I}]⸢U$_4$⸣-^{d}LX SAR
31 […] ⸢*šá*(?)⸣ É ^{d}LX *šú-nu*
32 […-*r*]*i*(?) É-*su*

---

[54] The text was discussed by Thompson in *CLBT*, 29–34. See also my discussion of *BRM* 4, 6 and BM 134701 in this Appendix, and the remarks made by D. Brown and the present author in the *RA* 91 (1997), 147 ff.

33 [...] ⸢x⸣ [...]

Col. B.

1 *be-⸢el⸣-k*[*a šá i-dul-lu-ma la i-ṣa-al-lal ana-ku*]
2 *šá ina ma-na-aḫ-ti-⸢šú a-kal la⸣* [*i-kul ana-ku*]
3 *šá ina ma-na-aḫ-ti-šú me-e la iš-tu-ú ⸢ana⸣-k*[*u*]
4 *ina* É-*ia ba-aṣ it-taš-pak i-pi-ir it-ta-*⟨*at*⟩*-b*[*ak*]
5 *kab-tu šá di-im-ma-at da-ma-ma ul i-kal-*lu_4
6 *šá i-dam-mu-um mar-ṣi-iš li-di-mu-mu*
7 *ina ṣir-ḫi* URU-*šú ru-bu-ú ina qaq-qar na-pal-s*[*i-iḫ*]
8 *šá* ^{d}XXX *iq-bu-ú me-ḫu-ú* ZI-*am-ma*
9 *i-pi-ir pa-ni ik-tu-u*[*m*]
10 u_4*-mu a-mat* ^{d}*A-nù* u_4*-mu a-mat* ^{d}EN.LÍ[L]
11 u_4*-mu ug-gat lìb-bi šá* ^{d}*A-nù ra-bi-⸢i⸣*
12 *Dil-mun-nu-ú šá ina ṣu-ṣe-e* ^{giš}MÁ-*šú iṭ-bu-⸢ú⸣* [*ana-ku*]
13 *šá lìb-bi i-šu-ú ù e-mu-qu la i-šu-ú* [*ana-ku*]
14 *ú-a lìb-bi ú-a ka-bat-*[*ta*]
15 ^{d}XXX *be-lu* ÚRI^{ki} *i-bak-*[*ki*]
16 *be-lu* DINGIR *nam-ra-ṣi-it ut-ta-bi* ⸢x⸣ [...]
17 *ki-ma šá an-na-a* ^{d}XXX *ana muḫ-ḫi ra-man-ni-šú i-*[*bak-ki*(?)]
18 *ina a-dan-nu šu-ú* ^{d}XXX *šá-niš* ^{d}AG *man-nu ana mu*[*ḫ-ḫi*]
19 ^{giš}GU.ZA *šá* ^{d}*A-nù a-na* LUGAL-*ú-tú ú-qa*[*r-rab*]
20 LÚ *šá* ^{iti}BAR.SAG.SAG SAR-*u i-qab-bu-ú šá* ^{d}X[XX]
21 *ul i-de šá an-na-a* ^{d}XXX *ana* UGU *ra-man-ni-*[*šú i-bak-ki*(?)]
22 *šá-niš* LÚ *šá i-qab-bu-ú šá-ma-ʾ* ^{d}AG KAM *ú-*[...]
23 *ina* ^{giš}GU.ZA ^{d}LX *ir-mu-ú a-na* L[UGAL-*ú-tú*(?)]
24 *a-na muḫ-ḫi šil-lat an-ni-*tu_4 *šá i-qab-bu-*[*ú*]
25 *ik-kaš-ši-du šá ina* ^{d}GIŠ.BAR *i-šak-kan-nu*
26 *ma-qa-lu-*[*tú*(?)]

---

27 ^{d}AMAR.UTU *a-ši-pu* ^{d}NIN.GÌRIM [...]
28 ^{d}ME.ME *a-zu-un-gal-lat* GAL-tu_4 *i-⸢x⸣*[...]
29 *šal-šú* ḪA.LA *šá* ^{d}AMAR.UTU *ina a-ši-*[*pu-ti*(?)]

col. A.

1 [...] Nabû-aḫ-uṣur
2 [...] ... he detained/stopped
3 [...] ... tablet
4 [...] ... he wrote
5 [...] these tablets
6 [... he] wrote
7 [...] for(?) his/its ...

---

8 [...] the (*akītu*-temple named) *Bīt ikribi*
9 [...] for kingship
10 [...] ... he brought his rites to an end
11 [...] the lands, which they wrote
12 [...] ... blasphemies

13 […] they wrote
14 […] the great […] of Heaven
15 […] exalted position
16 […] … his seat
17 […] … in/on his head will be proper(?).
18 […] he is holding(?) the insignia of kingship.
19 […] he is robed with fine attire.
20 […] the constellation Leo, who makes ready(?)
21 […] the constellation Hydra, who walkes about(?)
22 […] … which Ūma-Anu wrote
23 […] was seen
24 […] … this
25 […] of Heaven
26 [… the] golden [seat] on the platform
27 […] the Rēš-temple, in Enamenna
28 […] … is seated
29 […] he did not write
30 […which] Ūma-Anu wrote
31 […] they belong to the temple of Anu
32 […] … his temple

---

33 […] … […]

Col. B.

1 [I am] your lord(?), [who wanders around in despair and cannot sleep].
2 [I am] one, who did not [eat] bread during his hardship,
3 I a[m] one, who did not drink water during his hardship.
4 Sand is heaped up, earth piled [up] [in m]y [house].
5 'O honored one, the moaner can not refrain from mourning,
6 may the moaner moan bitterly'.
7 In mourning about his city the prince squat[s] on the ground.
8 Of Sîn they said: 'a storm arose,
9 covere[d] the face with dust.
10 Storm is the word of Anu, storm is the word of Enli[l],
11 storm is the wrath (in) the heart of the great Anu.
12 [I] am (like) a man from [Di]lmun, whose boat has sunk in the marshes.
13 [I] am one who does have a heart, but not strength.
14 Woe over my heart, woe over (my) mind!'
15 (Accordingly) Sîn, the lord of Ur, cries.
16 (Accordingly) the lord, the god who is brilliant at his rising, laments … […]
17 In this manner Sîn will c[ry(?)] over himself.
18 Who will lead Sîn or Nabû at the proper moment t[o]
19 the throne of Anu to be king?
20 'He, who wrote(?) the month Nisannu', they will say of S[în]
21 He does not know that this is Sîn, [crying(?)] about [him]self.
22 Or: he of whom they say: … of Nabû … […]
23 On the throne of Anu they have sat down to be k[ing(?)].
24 Because of this blasphemy which they utte[r],
25 they will be captured(?); he who places into the fire,

26 burnt offerin[gs(?)]

---

27 Marduk, the exorcist, Ningirim [...]
28 Gula, great chief woman physician ... [...]
29 One-third, the share of Marduk in the office of exor[cist(?)]

Comments

Col. A.

l. 9, 'for kingship', or, as in Col. B, l. 19 and 23: 'to be king'?

l. 11, SAR.MEŠ is probably *išṭurū*. See also col. A, 4, 6, 29 (*iš-ṭur*), 30 (SAR); B, 13 (SAR.MEŠ-'), 20 (SAR-*u*).

l. 12, *šil-lat*.MEŠ, see also col. B, l. 24.

l. 16, SUḪ DU not clear to me. Thompson transcribed *ipparkā* and apparently read GIB.

l. 18, *ta-mi-ḫi* perhaps a mistake for *ta-mi-iḫ*, a stative, as in l. 17 and 19?

l. 22 (see also l. 30), Ūma-Anu, i.e. Oannes, cf. W.G. Lambert, *JCS* 16 (1962), 74b. See also E. Weidner *AfO* 14 (1941–44), 181a and J.J.A. van Dijk, *UVB* 18 (1962), 48a.

l. 27, for the Enamenna-cella see A. Falkenstein, *Topographie*, 18–20 and A.R. George, *House Most High*, no. 837.

Col. B.

l. 1–14, these lines are duplicated by *BRM* 4, 6, obv. 5–11.

l. 6, note the unusual grammar: *šá i-dam-mu-um* (without the subjunctive ending -*u*) *mar-ṣi-iš li-di* (sic)-*mu-mu* (plural ending).

l. 20, itiBAR.SAG.SAG 'Nisannu', see *CAD*, 265b.

TEXT CONCORDANCE

According to publication[1]

According to museum/excavation numbers[2]

	publication
AB 249*	*CLBT*, 29 ff. and pl. 1[3]
AO 6451*	*TU* 38
AO 6459*	*TU* 39
AO 6460*	*TU* 41
AO 6461*	*TU* 43
AO 6465*	*TU* 40
AO 6467	*TU* 48[4]
AO 6472*	*TU* 45
AO 6479*	*TU* 44
AO 7439 + AO 8648 + AO 8649*	*TU* 42, S. Lackenbacher, *RA* 71 (1977), 39–50
AO 17626	J. Nougayrol, *RA* 41 (1947), 30–33[5]
AO 17662	J. Nougayrol, *RA* 41 (1947), 32–38
Ash. 1924.1792 + 1806 + 1818	*OECT* 11, 47 (W.G. Lambert)

[1] The numbers refer to the pages in the Appendix.
[2] The texts marked by an asterisk (*) are discussed in the Appendix.
[3] Col. B 1–14 // MLC 1872, obv. 5–11.
[4] Cf. R. Borger, *HKL* 1, 574; G.J.P. McEwan, *FAOS* 4, 164 and 172 f.; M.E. Cohen, *Eršemma*, 50; id., *Lamentations*, 27; H. Hunger, *AOAT* 2, 48, no. 115 (colophon).
[5] Partial duplicate of O.175 and W 20030/122.

BE 13987* (= IM 11087, 11 + 11053, 20 + 11053, 325 + 11087, 59)	F.H. Weissbach, *Misc.*, no. 12[6]
BM 32206 + 32237 + 34723	G. Çağirgan, W.G. Lambert, *JCS* 43–45 (1991–1993), 89–106[7]
BM 32485 + DT 109	See sub DT 15 +
BM 32516 // 41239 (81–4–28, 787)	A.R. George, *Studies W.G. Lambert*, no. 4,289 ff.[8]
BM 32654 + 38193 // DT 15 +, 69–79	G. Çağirgan, *Festivals* (unpub.), 7–9[9]
BM 32656	A.R. George, *Studies W.G. Lambert*, no. 2, 270 ff.
BM 34035 (Sp I 131)	J. Epping, J.N. Strassmaier, *ZA* 6 (1891), 228, 241–244[10]
BM 34643	*CT* 51, 94
BM 34679	*CT* 51, 101
BM 34689	*CT* 51, 95
BM 34768	*CT* 51, 99
BM 34796	*CT* 51, 100
BM 34804	*CT* 51, 97
BM 34817	*CT* 51, 96
BM 34829	*CT* 51, 104
BM 34878, rev. // BM 77236	*CT* 51, 92[11]
BM 35019 (Sp II, 546)	A.R. George, *BTT*, no. 45, 230, pl. 51
BM 35046 (Sp II 578)	A.R. George, *BTT*, no. 6, 94, pl. 21
BM 38293 (80–11–12, 175)	A.R. George, *BTT*, no. 40, 227, pl. 50
BM 41577	A.R. George, *Studies W.G. Lambert*, no. 1, 260 ff.
BM 46060 (SH 81–7–6, 507)	A.R. George, *BTT*, no. 43, 228, pl. 51
BM 47902 + 48320	B. Pongratz-Leisten, *ina šulmi īrub*, no. 9[12]
BM 50503	St.M. Maul, in: *Munuscula Mesopotamica. Festschrift für Johannes Renger*, Münster, 1999, 285 ff.
BM 54312	unpublished
BM 54901	unpublished
BM 54952	unpublished
BM 75144	A.R. George, *BTT*, no. 30, 208, pl. 8
BM 77433 (84–2–11, 173)	A.R. George, *BTT*, no. 38, 224, 226, pl. 50
BM 78076	A.R. George, *Studies W.G. Lambert*, no. 3, 280 ff.
BM 93046 (83–1–21, 1782)	A.R. George, *BTT*, no. 44, 229, pl. 51
BM 119282	B. Pongratz-Leisten, *ina šulmi īrub*, no. 6[13]
BM 134701*	D. Brown, M.J.H. Linssen, *RA* 91 (1997), 147–166. See also sub MLC 1872[14]

[6] Cf. unpublished Rm 101, see my copy, Plate IV.
[7] Cf. G. Çağirgan, *Festivals*, 86 ff. and 98 ff. See also S. Parpola, *LAS* II, 186–87.
[8] BM 41239 = T.G. Pinches, *Oriental Studies Haupt*, 217 f.; E. Unger, *Babylon*, 145; A.R. George, *BTT*, no. 57, 232, pl. 54; B. Pongratz-Leisten, *ina šulmi īrub*, no. 17.
[9] Only transliteration. The text will be published by W.G. Lambert.
[10] Cf. R. Borger, *HKL* 1, 519–20 and 2, 276. See J. Oelsner, *Materialien*, 227. The text was also discussed by A. Livingstone, *Mystical*, 61, 62, 73, 96, 163, 172, 255, 256, 259.
[11] = BM 34878; A.R. George, *BTT*, no. 9, 100, pl. 18, 19.
[12] Cf. G. Çağirgan, *Festivals*, 48 ff. See the new edition by W.G. Lambert in *RA* 91 (1997), 52–6.
[13] See the new edition by W.G. Lambert in *RA* 91 (1997), 74–8.
[14] BM 134701, which is partly a duplicate of *BRM* 4, 6 (MLC 1872), was published by D. Brown and the present author in *RA* 91 (1997), 147–166.

Bu 91–5–9, 104	H. Zimmern, *Neujahrsfest* I, 131, n. 1[15]
DT 15, DT 109 + BM 32485, DT 114, MNB 1848*	*RAcc.*, 127 ff.; BM 32485 published here[16]
IM 44150 // IM 76975 (W 22758/5) // K 2892 + 8397 // K 10062 // BM 38413 (80–11–12, 296)	A.R. George, *BTT*, no. 18, 145–62, and pl. 29–34[17]
K 2724 + 8207	S. Langdon, *AJSL* 42 (1925–26), 115 ff.[18]
K 3446 + 8830 + Sm 211, 1–6 (+) 10282	K. Watanabe, *ASJ* 13 (1991), 378–380[19]
K 3655	A.R. George, *BTT*, no. 42, 228, pl. 51
K 3753	E. Weidner, *GDBT*, 10 f., pl.11 f.[20]
K 4806 + K 9421*	IV R², 23, no. 1, K 9421 unpub.[21]
K 6060 + 10820	*BBR* 2, no. 56, K 10820 unpub.[22]
K 9876 + 19534	H. Zimmern, *Neujahrsfest* I, 136–143, no. 2[23], and S.A. Pallis, *Akîtu festival* pl. VIII–XI[24]
MLC 1872*	*BRM* 4, 6[25]
MLC 1873*	*BRM* 4, 7
MLC 1886 // 1859	*BRM* 4, 19 // 20[26]
MLC 2608	*BRM* 4, 25, see also sub VAT 398
O.174*	*TU* 46
O.175	*TU* 47[27]
Rm 101	published here[28]

15 Cf. B. Menzel, *Tempel*, no. 33.
16 See my copy, Plate I.
17 'The Nippur compendium'; see A.R. George, *BBT*, 146 for earlier editions.
18 Cf. R. Borger, *HKL* 1, 274 and 2, 170; G. van Driel, *Cult of Aššur*, 140 ff.; 152; B. Menzel, *Tempel*, no. 34 (new edition); M.E. Cohen, *Eršemma*. 50; id., *Lamentations*, 22 f.
19 Cf. also A.R. George, *BTT*, 275–6 (rev. 4–9, with Sm 211, 1–6), 280 (obv. 19-rev. 3), 288 (obv. 15–18), 394 (rev. 17); B. Pongratz-Leisten, *ina šulmi īrub*, no. 12. See now the new edition by W.G. Lambert in *RA* 91 (1997), 56–62.
20 Earlier published by J. Oppert, J. Ménant, *Doc. jur.*, 34 ff.; cf. R. Borger, *HKL* 1, 375 and 2, 215; G. Çağirgan, *Festivals*, 183 ff.; G.J.P. McEwan, *FAOS* 4, 174–178. See also J. Oelsner, *Materialien*, 173, n. 649.
21 Cf. R. Borger, *BiOr* 30 (1973), 176a. See my copy, Plate III.
22 See my copy, Plate II. The text is duplicated by VAT 8247 (*KAR* 50), obv. 17-rev. 9.
23 = *BSGW* 58.
24 Cf. P. Jensen, *KB* 6/II, 32 ff.; G. Çağirgan, *Festivals*, 40 ff. See now B. Pongratz-Leisten, *ina šulmi īrub*, no. 8 (K 9876 + 19534). Cf. also A.R. George, *BTT*, 333–34 (obv. 25).
25 The text is partly duplicate of BM 134701, see above.
26 Paralleled by *STT* 2, 300, compare Gurney's remark on p. 15. Cf. R. Borger, *HKL* 1, 57 and 2, 34. See also G.J.P. McEwan, *FAOS* 4, 166, n. 381.
27 Cf. F. Thureau-Dangin, *RA* 16 (1919), 145; A. Livingstone, *Mystical*, 187–204. Partial duplicate is: W 20030/122 (obv.// O.175, obv. 6–11(?); rev.// ib. rev.); for the lower half of the rev., cf. also AO 17626, 31. For l. 10 ff. cf. *TU* 44, III, 1–14; K 4806, I, 1–6; *CT* 24, pl. 4–5, 29–36 (series AN = Anum). It is probable but not certain that *TU* 47 comes from Uruk, cf. J. Oelsner, *Materialien*, 169, with n. 641 and n. 624.
28 Reference W.G. Lambert, cf. R. Borger, *HKL* 2, 320. See my copy, Plate IV. See also sub BE 13987.

Sp I 131	see sub BM 34035
VAT 398 // MLC 2608	*SBH* VII[29]
VAT 662 + 663	*SBH* VIII[30]
VAT 7815	E. Weidner, *GDBT*, 45–48, pl. 15 f.[31]
VAT 7816	E. Weidner, *GDBT*, 41–45, pl. 13 f.[32]
VAT 7849*	*KAR* 132
VAT 7897	*VS* 17, 58[33]
VAT 8022*	*KAR* 60
VAT 8247*	*KAR* 50[34]
VAT 14521	*LKU*, no. 48
VAT 14524	*LKU* no. 51[35]
VAT 17382 (+) 17350 // VAT 17306	*VS* 24, 108 (+) 109 // 110[36]
W 18728	A. Falkenstein, *UVB* 15, 40–44, pl. 29, 34[37]
W 18828	A. Falkenstein, *UVB* 15, 36–40, pl. 28a, 32–33[38]
W 20030/1	*Bagh. Mitt. Beih.* 2, no. 6[39]
W 20030/2*	*Bagh. Mitt. Beih.* 2, no. 10
W 20030/3 // W 20030/5 // W 20030/98	*Bagh. Mitt. Beih.* 2, no. 1–3
W 20030/4*	*Bagh. Mitt. Beih.* 2, no. 5
W 20030/6	*Bagh. Mitt. Beih.* 2, no. 12[40]
W 20030/15	*Bagh. Mitt. Beih.* 2, no. 11[41]
W 20030/19	*Bagh. Mitt. Beih.* 2, no. 14[42]
W 20030/20 (IM 65063)	*Bagh. Mitt. Beih.* 2, no. 97[43]
W 20030/81	*Bagh. Mitt. Beih.* 2, no. 13[44]
W 20030/83	*Bagh. Mitt. Beih.* 2, no. 9[45]
W 20030/89	*Bagh. Mitt. Beih.* 2, no.7[46]
W 20030/97	*Bagh. Mitt. Beih.* 2, no. 4

[29] Cf. R. Borger, *HKL* 1, 57; E. Weidner, *AfO* 16, (1952/53), 71 ff.; G. Çağirgan, *Festivals*, 189 ff.; G.J.P. McEwan, *FAOS* 4, 184; J. Oelsner, *Materialien*, 450, n. 772 and 469, n. 879.

[30] Cf. R. Borger, *HKL* 1, 425; G. Çağirgan, *Festivals*, 168 ff.; M.E. Cohen, *Cultic Calendars*, 449.

[31] The text is similar to VAT 7816.

[32] The text is similar to VAT 7815.

[33] Cf. R. Borger, *HKL* 2, 53, and W.R. Mayer, *OrNS* 58 (1989), 274; listed as a ritual by J. Oelsner, *Materialien*, 169.

[34] L. obv. 17-rev. 9 is duplicated by K 6060 (*BBR* 2, no. 56) + 10820, see my copy, Plate II.

[35] Cf. G. Furlani, *Riti*, 221–6.

[36] Cf. B. Pongratz-Leisten, *ina šulmi īrub*, nos. 10 and 11, 236–39.

[37] Cf. R. Borger, *HKL* 2, 64.

[38] Cf. R. Borger, *HKL* 1, 118.

[39] Discussed by W.R. Mayer in *OrNS* 47 (1978), 432–437.

[40] Discussed by W.R. Mayer in *OrNS* 47 (1978), 438–441.

[41] For obv. fragment 1, see my comments on *TU* 45, obv. 11–14, 15, 16; for obv. fragment 2, see my comments on *TU* 45, obv. 17–18; for obv. fragment 3, see my comments on *TU* 45, obv. 24–26, rev. 1; for rev. fragment 1, see my comments on *TU* 45, rev. 4, 5; for rev. fragment 2, see my comments on *TU* 45, rev. 6–13.

[42] See my comments on *TU* 44, I, 8.

[43] = A.R. George, *BTT*, no. 31, 208 ff., pl. 48.

[44] See my comments on *KAR* 132, II, 4–8.

[45] See my comments on K 4806, I, 17.

[46] For the obverse see my comments on *KAR* 60, rev. 10–15; for the reverse see my comments on K 4806, IV, 15–22.

W 20030/107	*Bagh. Mitt. Beih.* 2, no. 95[47]
W 20030/122	*Bagh. Mitt. Beih.* 2, no. 8[48]
W 20030/127	*Bagh. Mitt. Beih.* 2, no. 79
W 22282a	*SpTU* 1, no. 136
W 22293	*SpTU* 1, no. 5
W 22307/52	*SpTU* 1, no. 141
W 22307/70	*SpTU* 1, no. 142
W 22313	*SpTU* 1, no. 140
W 22317b	*SpTU* 1, no. 143
W 22667/0	*SpTU* 4, no. 125[49]
W 22704	*SpTU* 3, no. 104
W 22705/5	*SpTU* 4, no. 141
W 22712/2	*SpTU* 3, no. 61
W 22728/2	*SpTU* 3, no. 62
W 22758/5 (IM 76975)	see sub IM 44150
W 22760/0	*SpTU* 2, no. 27[50]
W 23006	*SpTU* 3, no. 63
82–3–23, 100	A.R. George, *BTT*, no. 41, 227–8, pl. 51
83–1–18, 464 +	W.G. Lambert, *Divine Love Lyrics*[51]
number unknown	G. Çağirgan, *Festivals* (unpub.), 1 (text a)
number unknown	T.G. Pinches, *Berens Coll.* no. 110

47 Cf. W.R. Mayer, *Bagh. Mitt. Beih.* 2, 20 and J. Oelsner, *Materialien*, 173.
48 Partial duplicate of O.175 and AO 17626. See my comments on *TU* 44, III, 1–14.
49 Part of the lamentation IMMAL GUDEDE, see M.E. Cohen, *Lamentations*, 604 ff.
50 See *SpTU* 2, 134 for duplicates and editions.
51 In: H. Goedicke and J.J.M. Roberts (eds.), *Unity and Diversity*, Baltimore, London, 1975, 98 ff. This text, based on Late Assyrian and Late Babylonian fragments (see ib., 99) is referred to here by the museum number of the first Late Assyrian fragment. For further unpublished texts see A.R. George, *Studies W.G. Lambert*, 259 ff.

SELECTIVE WORD INDICES

I. Sumerian, Akkadian and Greek words

II. Subject matter

III. Names

PLATES

BM 32485
6.7 × 4.2 × 2.7

Obv.

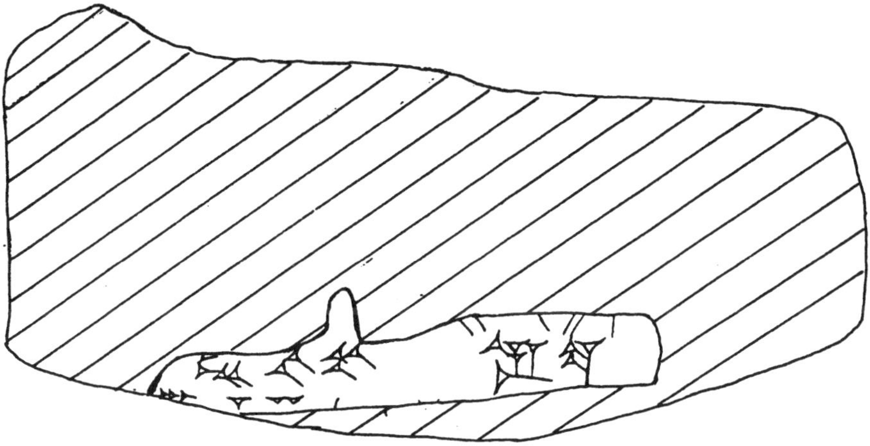

Rev.

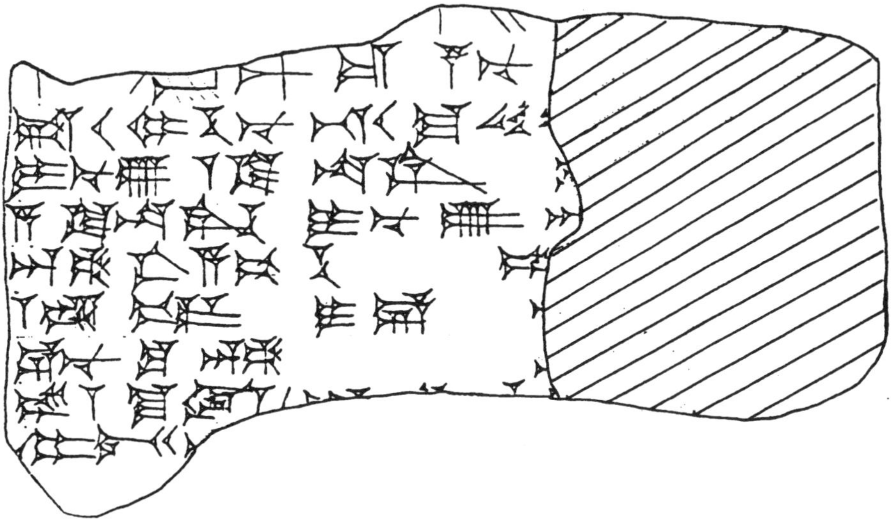

K 6060 + K 10820
7.0 × 7.3 × 1.7

Obv.

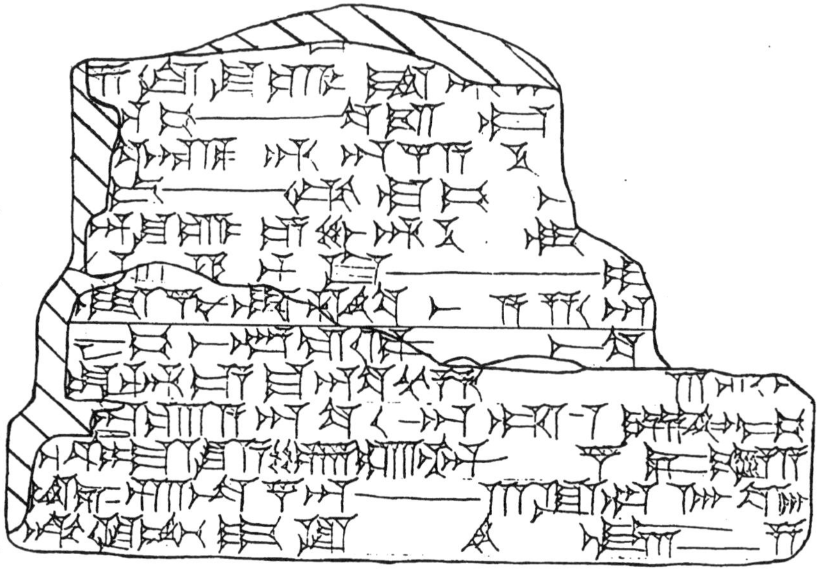

Rev.

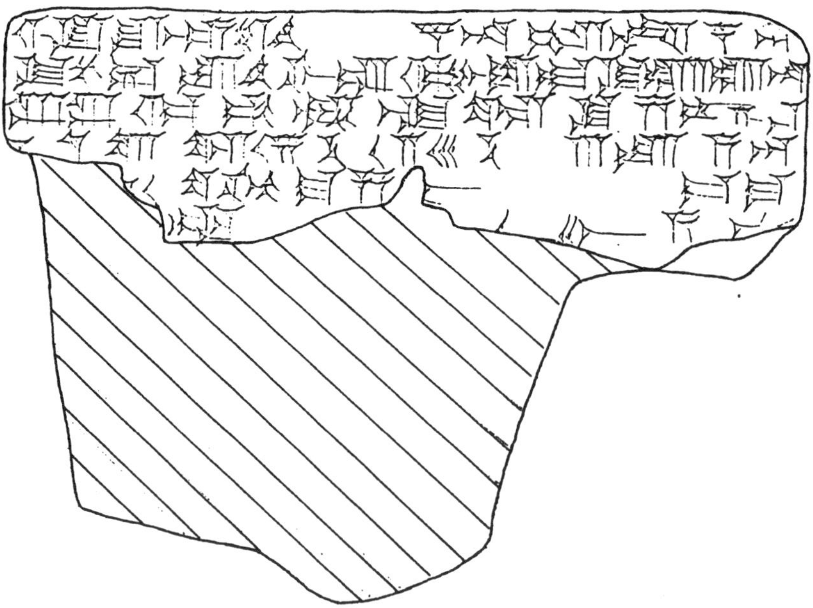

K 9421
5.1 × 3.8 × 1.7

Obv.

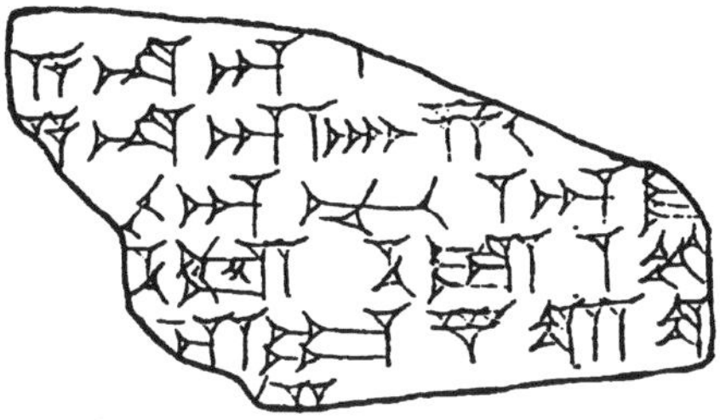

Rev.

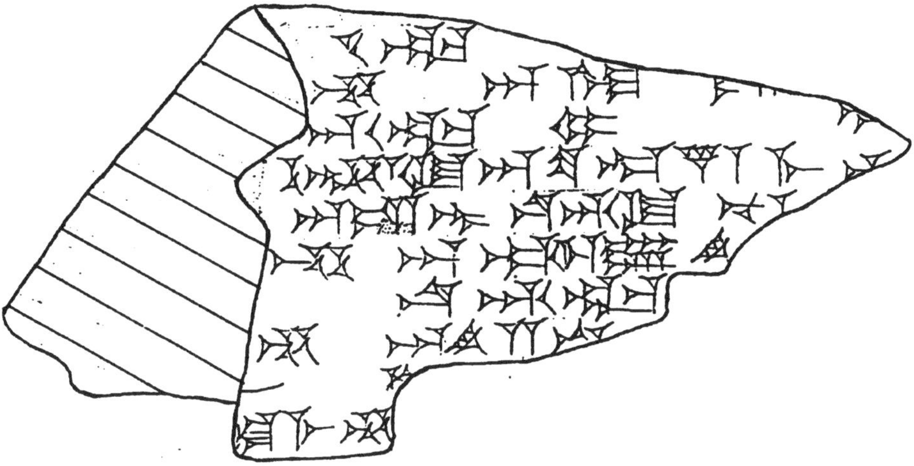

Rm 101
10.5 × 9.0 × 1.2

Obv.

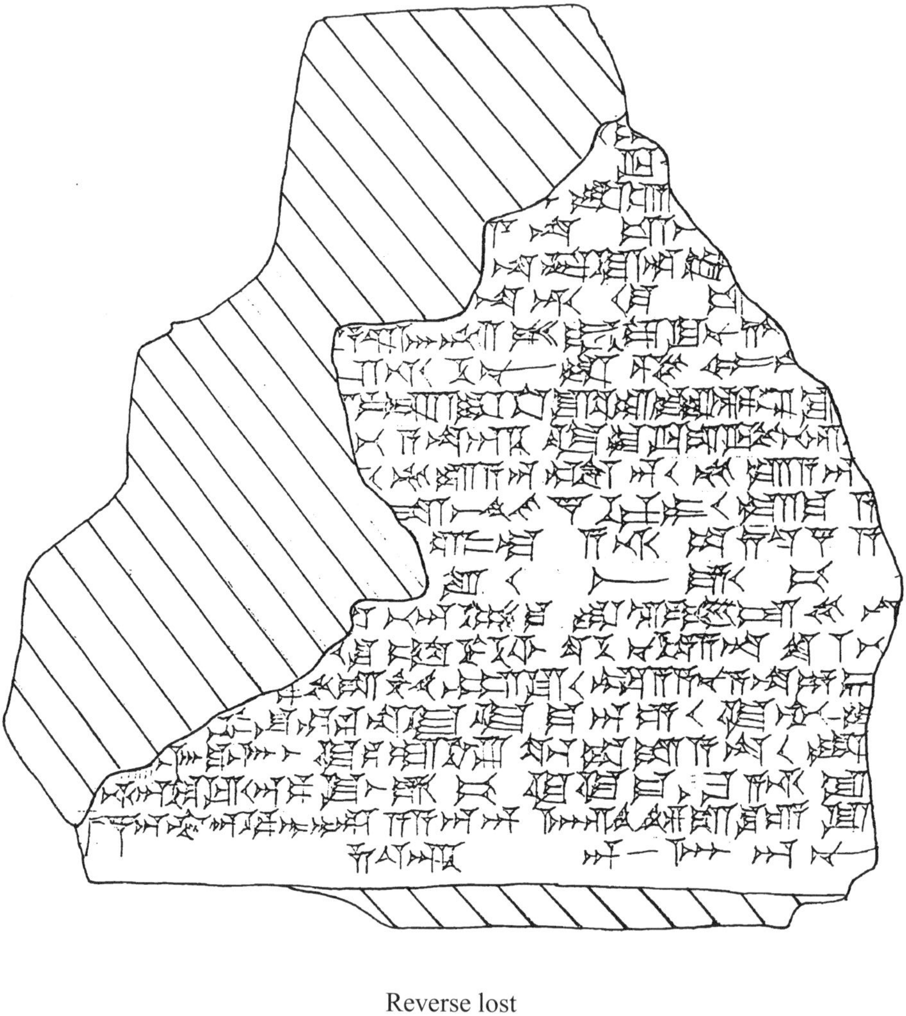

Reverse lost

SUMMARY

In this study we have examined whether the temple ritual texts, which were copied during the Hellenistic period from older original compositions, are a reliable source of information on the cult practices of Hellenistic Uruk and Babylon. Having surveyed the textual evidence we can conclude that there is enough evidence to suggest that the temple ritual texts indeed describe the cultic activities as they took place during the Hellenistic period.

The extensive descriptions of festivals, rituals and offerings in the temple ritual texts show how important the public cults were in Hellenistic times, at least until the first century B.C. Daily, monthly and annual ceremonies are well attested in ritual texts and cultic calendars. Many of the important temple rituals are extensively described, but other less well-known temple rituals are also attested. They clearly show how active the Babylonians were in matters of religion and cult during the Hellenistic period. The large corpus of cult songs (particularly from Babylon) underlines this. Admittedly, these literary texts are copies of older compositions, but the information of other, contemporary sources shows that the cults were still very important in the Hellenistic period.

The Babylonian cults practised in the temples of Uruk and Babylon in the Hellenistic period are not different from those attested in pre-Hellenistic times. All the evidence clearly shows that the Babylonians held on to their old Babylonian traditions. We found one possible exception to this rule. From Babylon we may have some references to a local ruler cult for the king and his family, a custom well-known to the Seleucid monarchies. Also, for Uruk we cannot exclude the possibility that certain texts contain references to a ruler cult practice, in which Seleucid kings were honoured as superhumans.